CW00969511

CAMDEN MISCELLANY

XXX

CAMDEN MISCELLANY
XXX

CAMDEN FOURTH SERIES

Volume 39

LONDON

OFFICES OF THE ROYAL HISTORICAL SOCIETY

UNIVERSITY COLLEGE LONDON, GOWER STREET, WC1E 6BT

1990

British Library Cataloguing in Publication Data

Camden miscellany XXX.—(Camden fourth
   series; v. 39).
   1. History—Periodicals
   I. Royal Historical Society   II. Series
ISBN 0-86193-122-x

Printed and bound in Great Britain by
Butler & Tanner Ltd, Frome and London

CONTENTS

I

THE HOSPITALLERS' WESTERN
ACCOUNTS, 1373/4 AND 1374/5[1]

Edited by Anthony Luttrell

1. This text was published in A. Luttrell, 'The Hospitallers' Accounts for 1373/4 and 1374/5: an Aragonese Text,' *Medievalia*, vii (1987), without my being able to see proofs or correct innumerable errors; the introduction is here expanded considerably and various amendments are made. A. Luttrell, 'Papauté et Hôpital: L'Enquête de 1373,' in A.-M. Legras, *L'Enquête pontificale de 1373 sur l'Ordre des Hospitaliers de Saint-Jean de Jérusalem*, i: *l'Enquête dans le prieuré de France* (Paris, 1987), 22–28, 35–37 *et passim*, contains preliminary information on the Hospital's finances.

INTRODUCTION

The military order of the Hospital of Saint John of Jerusalem had a Treasurer from the time of its early years in the mid-twelfth century; by 1268 he was employing two scribes at the Convent, the order's headquarters in Syria. A statute of 1283 provided for a monthly *computum* or audit to be held by the Master and a group of senior brethren. Fr Joseph Chauncey, who was Treasurer for some twenty-five years, was so competent that Edward I made him Treasurer of England in 1273.[2] At Rhodes during the fourteenth century the Treasury apparently kept no budget showing the overall state of the Hospital's finances, though by about 1478 there was a lengthy list of the incomes of the Western priories and commanderies, of receipts from Rhodes and Cyprus, and of the Convent's expenses in the East.[3] The dues or *responsiones* from the rich Commandery of Cyprus were received by the Treasurer at Rhodes and the Master issued a quittance for them.[4] The Master had separate incomes of his own, and by 1365 these were being managed by the Seneschal of his household; the Master gave a receipt for them.[5]

The bulk of the Convent's income came from the Western priories, the monies being collected and transferred to Rhodes by a Procurator-General in the West, alternatively known as Receiver-General in the West, who was based in Southern France. His accounts, usually presented in Latin, were normally inspected and approved by the Master and certain senior brethren at Rhodes, where a quittance was sealed; the document was sometimes copied into the Master's register.[6] The accounts for 1367/8 and 1368/9 were approved in Rhodes on 1 March 1371; they covered financial years which commenced on 26 March, the beginning of the Incarnation year, but they were complicated by the fact that priories owed their dues for a different year which ended on 24 June, the day of the Hospital's patron Saint John.

2. J. Riley-Smith, *The Knights of St. John in Jerusalem and Cyprus: c. 1050–1310* (London, 1967), 310–312; *Handbook of British Chronology*, ed. E. Fryde *et al.* (3rd ed: London, 1986), 104.

3. Paris, Bibliothèque Nationale, Ms. latin 13,824, fos. 75–96v, and London, British Library, Add. Ms. 17,319, fos. 20–38 (lacking the expenses); the date and contents await study. The archives of the Treasury at Rhodes do not survive.

4. The accounts for 1349/50 and 1350/1 are published in A. Luttrell, 'The Hospitallers in Cyprus: 1310–1378,' *Kypriakai Spondai*, 50 (1986), 178–179.

5. Valletta, National Library of Malta, Archives of the Order of St John, Cod. 319, fo. 265.

6. J. Nisbet, 'Treasury Records of the Knights of St. John in Rhodes,' *Melita Historica*, ii no. 2 (1957); Nisbet lists the accounts of Procurators-General in the West between 1364/5 and 1396/9, publishing those for 15 April 1364 to 26 May 1365. No other such accounts have been published.

The returns for 1369/70 were also quitted at Rhodes on 1 March 1371.[7] All these figures were presented by Fr Arnaud Bernard Ébrard, Commander of Bordeaux, who was already Procurator-General by 27 May 1362.[8] On 2 February 1372 the Master relieved him of his post, instructing him to hand over 15,000 florins to the Archbishop of Nicosia, who had deposited that sum in the Treasury at Rhodes, and 15,698 florins to the new Procurator-General, Fr Aimery de la Ribe, Commander of Raissac.[9]

In October 1374 Fr Aimery de la Ribe presented to the Master, then at Beaucaire, a detailed list of receipts and payments; this was in Latin and it mentioned that Ribe paid a notary to record Treasury business.[10] These accounts noted sums received from Ébrard, other monies which had been due for 1369/70 and 1370/1, and sums received by Ribe as recently as 23 December 1373; they referred to monies sent to Rhodes in 1372. The periods covered were not specified precisely though most of the transactions reported concerned the years 1371/2 and 1372/3. No total was given but the sums listed amounted to just over 37,955 florins. The parchment was written out in the form of a magistral bull approved, sealed and dated at Beaucaire on 18 October 1374, but it was not in fact sealed there, presumably because the approval of the brethren in the Convent at Rhodes was required. Not until 26 May 1376 at Rhodes, following an audit by the Master and certain associates who included the layman Giovanni Corsini, the Treasurer Fr Henri de Saint Trond, Fr Focauld de Conac and many others, was a quittance issued in a brief and separate new bull copied onto the foot of the original parchment; it had holes for two seals and was marked Cor.ta and Reg.ta, corrected and registered.[11] On 10 October 1374, just eight days before Ribe presented these accounts, the Master had appointed Fr Juan Fernández de Heredia as his lieutenant in the West and as generalis negotiorum gestor with powers over responsiones and other monies,[12] and it was he who presented the Western accounts for 1373/4 and 1374/5. Fr Aimery de la Ribe none the less remained procurator generalis in the West at least until September 1375.[13]

The parchment containing the Western accounts for the financial

7. Malta, Cod. 16, nos. 46, 48.

8. Malta, Cod. 16, no. 9; on Ébrard, see J. Delaville le Roulx, Les Hospitaliers à Rhodes jusqu'à la Mort de Philibert de Naillac: 1310–1421 (Paris, 1913), 144 n. 2.

9. Malta, Cod. 16, no. 50.

10. Item solui notario scriptori negociorum Thesauri mecum commoranti xxv flor' auri: Malta, Cod. 16, no. 53.

11. Malta, Cod. 16, no. 53: total calculated in Nisbet, 102. How this text was registered cannot be established as the register for 1376 is lost.

12. Malta, Cod. 23, no. 3.

13. Document dated at Rhodes on 30 September 1375: Malta, Cod. 23, no. 1.

years 1373/4 and 1374/5 was written out for, and in the native tongue of, the Aragonese Hospitaller Fr Juan Fernández de Heredia, who was *Castellán de Amposta* as the prior in Aragon was confusingly entitled. Aragonese was little used, or at least seldom written, outside Aragon. The most notable exception was the series of translations and compilations produced at Avignon between about 1370 and 1396 for Fernández de Heredia, who in 1377 became Master of the Hospital. His personal letters and the documents in the registers of his Hospitaller priories were often in Aragonese and there were evidently one or more scribes in his household at Avignon who wrote in that language. In 1374 Fernández de Heredia was the papal Captain-General of Avignon and the unofficial representative there of the Aragonese king, while he was also the Hospitallers' prior in both Aragon and Catalunya and the Lieutenant in the West of the Master of Rhodes; until about 1369 he also held the Provençal priory known as the Priory of Saint Gilles.[14] The Hospital made use of Fernández de Heredia's financial capabilities. In 1373 an assembly of Hospitallers at Avignon agreed, somewhat unrealistically, to raise large sums by imposing extraordinary taxes in order to finance a *passagium* against the Turks. There was to be a special taille and efforts were to be made to collect debts, arrears, mortuaries and other sums due. Fernández de Heredia was appointed to manage these incomes many of which were to be transferred to Avignon by the papal bankers, the Alberti Antichi of Florence.[15]

Though the accounts for 1373/4 and 1374/5 were in Aragonese, the opening passage of the parchment on to which they were copied in the form of a quittance to be validated by the Master and Convent was in Latin, as were its closing clauses. The eventual date when the quittance would be sealed could not be determined when the parchment was written out at Avignon, and when it reached Rhodes the leaden bull of the Master and Convent was attached to it; however, the dating clause was not added, nor were the phrases *Cor.ta*, or corrected, and *Reg.ta*, or registered. Possibly another copy, subsequently lost, was sent back to Fernández de Heredia as a receipt while the undated parchment was retained at Rhodes. In general, the annual accounts kept in the West recorded the *responsiones*, that is the ordinary dues collected by the priors from the commanders for transfer to Rhodes; any arrears or *arrerages* which happened to have been paid; the *spolia* or *despullya*, the personal effects and monies of deceased brethren; the mortuaries or *mortuoria*, apparently the wealth and

14. See A. Luttrell, *The Hospitallers in Cyprus, Rhodes, Greece and the West: 1291–1440* (London, 1978), and *idem, Latin Greece, the Hospitallers and the Crusades: 1291–1440* (London, 1982).

15. Luttrell (1982), XV 404–406; in Legras, 21–25, 35–37.

revenues of offices from the time of their incumbent's death until the day of the following chapter, that is of the financial year in which the incumbent died;[16] and the vacancies or *vagantes*, probably the income of such offices for the year following the financial year in which the incumbent died.[17] Certain commanderies which were set aside as magistral *camere* or *cambras* also paid their income to the Master, and these payments were in some cases handled by the Procurator-General in the West. In 1373/4 and 1374/5 the special taille fixed at one third of the *responsiones* was also being collected. All these incomes were channelled through the priories except that, for special historical reasons, five large Southern Italian commanderies paid their dues directly. Non-payments were often noted and were so frequent that no individual annual account represented a complete or nearly-complete record for a given financial year. Payments in various currencies were translated into florins current at Avignon.[18] Expenses in the West were for the securing and writing of bulls, for couriers, and for pensions and retaining fees paid to the Hospital's Cardinal Protectors and to a number of Hospitaller and papal officials at the *curia*. In 1373/4 and 1374/5 there were expenditures on repaying monies advanced by the Alberti Antichi, on the papal mission of Hospitallers and theologians sent to Constantinople, and on repayments in the West of loans made by Latin merchants at Rhodes.

16. According to a statute of 1367: Delaville, 162 n. 5. All brethren owed *spolia*, while only those holding office paid mortuaries; numerous entries in the accounts for 1378/88 (Malta, Cod. 48) showed confusions between an officer's personal effects and liabilities, and the possessions and incomes of his office. Thus the commander's silver or animals could be paid as mortuaries after the deduction of his funeral expenses.

17. The Master and Convent could at moments of crisis temporarily be granted the revenues of vacant priories or commanderies, as in 1344 and 1357: texts in M. Barbaro di San Giorgio, *Storia della Costituzione del Sovrano Militare Ordine di Malta* (Rome, 1927), 221–223. Nisbet, 96, without sources, and B. Waldstein–Wartenberg, *Rechtsgeschichte des Malteserordens* (Vienna, 1969), 114, citing the text of 1357 in Barbaro, 223, state that the vacancy was the income of the office in the financial year following that of the mortuary year, that is of the year in which the officer died; that is not, however, what the 1357 text stated. The accounts for 1373/4 and 1374/5 show that mortuaries were referred to a commander, vacancies to a commandery. These questions await clarification.

18. In 1372/5 a florin *de camera* was worth 28 sous of Avignon; a florin *currens*, 24 sous; a florin *de sententia*, 27½ sous; 6 florins *correntes* were worth 5 francs; etc. Except that in 1373/4 the accounts calculated the florin *de sententia* at 27⅔ sous, the equivalencies in the 1373/5 accounts coincided with those in the papal documents: K. Schäfer, *Die Ausgaben der apostolischen Kammer unter Johann XXII. nebst der Jahresbilanzen von 1316–1378* (Paderborn, 1911), 54*, 59*. Florins *correntes* were apparently equivalent to, or identical with, those of Provence current in Avignon: H. Rolland, *Monnaies des Comtes de Provence: XII–XIV Siècles* (Paris, 1956), 153–154, 164. Twelve *denarii* made one sou; one groat or *grossus*, a silver coin, was apparently worth 2 sous. Sums in the tables are given correct to the nearest florin; brackets indicate calculated or corrected sums; in the notes *grossi* are converted into sous.

6 CAMDEN MISCELLANY VOLUME XXXIX

These transactions were set down with a variety of ambiguities. The totals which could be derived from the accounts gave a very incomplete impression of the Hospital's overall incomes, and they did not include other revenues collected in Rhodes and Cyprus; furthermore, the Master had personal incomes which were separate from those of the Convent. The payments recorded in the West for the years from 1367 to 1373 averaged about 22,700 florins annually, and those between 1378 and 1399 about 38,500 florins annually; the years 1367/9 brought in 50,412 florins, 6 *grossi* and 4 *denari*, at 25,206 florins a year, and the year 1369/70 brought in 23,044 florins 3½ *grossi*.[19] The marginally higher figures for 1373/4 and 1374/5 reflected the extraordinary measures agreed in 1373 for the *passagium* against the Turks. The totals were somewhat uncertain, and the accounts often contained mistakes.[20] In 1365 there were complaints that one Procurator-General in the West had omitted 4,000 florins which were missing *in cartularijs rationum thesauri*,[21] while a remark on the obverse of the accounts for 1367/9 noted an error which was corrected in the accounts for 1369/70.[22] Where the sums in the surviving copy of the 1373/4 and 1374/5 accounts did not add up to the totals given, this was apparently because the figures were transferred incorrectly from the original accounts rather than because the totals had been added wrongly in the first place in the records kept at Avignon.

Anyone in the Treasury at Rhodes who attempted to analyse these accounts would have found careless copyings and other difficulties. Fluctuations in exchange rates and the costs of exchanging monies must have caused discrepancies. The text for audit in Rhodes copied totals from individual pages of an account book being kept in Southern France.[23] Errors in the parchment sent to Rhodes would have frustrated calculations there but that particular text was a receipt, not the original accounting record. Nine priories were listed as paying nothing in 1373/4, though some of these paid their arrears in 1374/5; Portugal had paid nothing for nine years. No total was given for 1373/4 but incomes seem to have amounted to 42,230 florins and expenditures to 35,263, leaving a considerable unaccounted difference which may eventually have reached Rhodes. Of the expenditures, over 5,000 florins went to the Constantinople mission; other expenses in the West amounted to more than 3,000 florins; and over 26,000

19. Based on details in Nisbet, 102–104.
20. Luttrell, in Legras, 36–37, notes some accounting anomalies in these years.
21. Malta, Cod. 319, fos. 3v–4.
22. Malta, Cod. 16, nos. 46, 48.
23. An extremely detailed account book for the Western incomes and expenditures from 1378 to 1389 is in Malta, Cods. 48 and 55. In 1371/3 Fr Aimery de la Ribe, Procurator-General in the West, paid 4½ florins *pro uno libro empto ad copiandum ibidem bullas vel alia negotia Thesauri*: Malta, Cod. 16, no. 53.

florins were paid to the Master, who was then in the West and must have expended part of this sum before reaching Rhodes. The incomes from Italy seem to have arrived in Avignon en bloc, as suggested by the unlikely equalities in the figures given; they may have been transferred by the Alberti who regularly moved monies for the Hospital.[24] The English Hospitallers, whose returns were listed as nil in the accounts for 1373/4 and 1374/5, may have preferred to send their monies by way of Venice rather than through France.[25]

The returns for 1374/5 were presented less carefully than those for 1373/4. They included special payments imposed on 25 September 1374 in order to raise 10,000 florins for the journey or *passage* to Rhodes of the newly-elected Master, Fr Robert de Juilly.[26] 46,830 florins were apparently recorded as having been received while sums totalling perhaps 6,111 florins were said still to be owing from Italy together with 500 florins due from the Archbishop of Rhodes; these would, if eventually paid, have produced a grand total of 53,441 florins. Expenditures amounted to 34,278 florins of expenses detailed and a further 17,765 paid to the Grand Commander of the Hospital; these would have totalled 52,043 florins, a sum not unlike that of the expected total incomes. These figures were subject to various cautions and reservations, but they did indicate the general order of magnitude of the Convent's Western incomes.

The accounting methods employed by the Hospitallers in Southern France were capable of dealing with the collection of monies from the priories, with the transfer of funds to the East, with repayments in the West of sums advanced to the Treasury at Rhodes, and with a variety of payments and pensions in the West. A religious order could certainly handle the necessary calculations. The Templars had operated quite complex banking procedures in the thirteenth century,[27] and the Cistercians were keeping accounts of their central receipts by 1290; by about 1340 they had something like an overall budget of their incomes and expenses.[28] The Hospital faced the complication of having to integrate two separate operations, the collection of a surplus in the West and the management of receipts and expenditures in the East; its survival at Rhodes was heavily dependent on the efficient functioning of its Western financial organisation.

24. Luttrell (1978), VII 180; VIII 322, 325.

25. Luttrell (1978), V 199; (1982), I 259.

26. Malta, Cod. 320, fos. 32–32v.

27. J. Piquet, *Des Banquiers au Moyen Âge: Les Templiers* (Paris, 1939).

28. P. King, *The Finances of the Cistercian Order in the Fourteenth Century* (Kalamazoo, 1985).

THE HOSPITALLERS' WESTERN INCOMES FOR 1373/4

Priory or Commandery	Responsiones	Taille	Arrears	Mortuaries	Spolia	Vacancies	Total
England	—	—	—	—	—	—	—
France	6,000	2,000	—	600	1,928	—	[10,528]
Aquitaine	2,670	—	—	—	—	—	[2,670]
Champagne	1,000	312	—	—	—	—	[1,312]
Auvergne	2,180	250	—	70	—	—	[2,500]
S. Gilles	3,919	1,000	530	1,939	—	—	[7,387]
Toulouse	1,646	246	305	301	—	—	[2,498]
Catalunya	2,742	1,711	950	—	—	—	5,403
Amposta	917	—	1,500	—	—	—	2,417
Navarre	500	231	—	—	—	—	731
Castile	—	—	—	—	—	—	—
Portugal	—	—	—	—	—	—	—
Lombardy	—	—	41	—	217	—	258
Pisa	922	288	—	—	—	—	1,210
Rome	—	288	—	—	—	—	288
Messina	—	—	—	—	—	—	—
Naples	692	346	—	—	—	—	1,038
Alife	—	—	—	—	—	—	—
Capua	692	231	—	39	—	—	963
S. Eufemia	—	—	—	—	—	—	—
Venosa	346	115	—	—	—	—	461
Monopoli	—	—	—	—	—	—	—
Barletta	—	—	—	—	—	—	—
Venice	922	288	—	—	—	—	1,210
Hungary	—	—	—	—	—	—	—
Alamania	1,012	344	—	—	—	—	1,356
Bohemia	—	—	—	—	—	—	—
	[26,160]	[7,650]	[3,326]	[2,949]	[2,145]	[—]	[42,230]

THE HOSPITALLERS' WESTERN INCOMES FOR 1374/5

Priory or Commandery	Responsiones	Taille	Arrears	Mortuaries	Spolia	Vacancies	Total
England	—	—	—	—	—	—	—
Ireland	—	—	—	—	—	—	—
France	6,250	1,250	—	1,042	—	1,317	9,859
Champagne	1,042	312	—	—	—	—	[1,354]
Aquitaine	1,250	—	—	—	—	—	[1,250]
Auvergne	2,000	500	—	—	—	—	[2,500]
S. Gilles	4,548	852	646	650	—	893	7,589
Toulouse	817	178	380	—	—	—	1,375
Catalunya	2,900	1,769*	—	—	—	—	[4,668]
Amposta	916	1,327*	—	—	—	—	2,243
Navarre	500	337*	—	—	—	30	867
Rome	922	288	—	—	—	—	[1,210]
Venosa	342	114	—	—	—	—	[456]
Pisa	922	288	—	—	—	—	[1,210]
Alamania	1,000	459	100	—	—	—	[1,559]
Bohemia	1,200	612*	2,008	—	—	—	[3,820]
Hungary	300	—	—	—	—	—	[300]
Venice	800	382	—	—	—	—	[1,182]

Barletta	2,000	1,024*	—	—	—	—	[3,024]
Monopoli	400	229*	553	—	—	—	[1,182]
Messina	—	1,182*	—	—	—	—	[1,182]
Lombardy	—	—	—	—	—	—	—
Castile	—	—	—	—	—	—	—
Portugal	—	—	—	—	—	—	—
	[28,109]	[11,193]*	[3,687]	[1,692]	[—]	[2,240]	[46,830]

SUMS SAID TO BE OWING FOR 1374/5

Priory or Commandery	Responsiones	Taille	Arrears	Mortuaries	Spolia	Vacancies	Total
Venosa	300**	51*	—	—	—	—	[351]**
S. Eufemia	600	255*	804	—	—	—	[1,659]
Naples	600	459*	—	—	—	—	[1,059]
Alife	500	229*	653	—	—	—	[1,382]
Capua	600	306*	—	500	—	—	[1,406]
Rome	—	127*	—	—	—	—	[127]
Pisa	—	127*	—	—	—	—	[127]
	[2,600]	[1,554]*	[1,457]	[500]	[—]	[—]	[6,611]***

* Includes sums paid or due for the Master's passage to Rhodes
** Incomplete sum
*** Total given by the ms. plus 500 florins owed by the Archbishop of Rhodes

THE HOSPITALLERS' WESTERN
ACCOUNTS, 1373/4 AND 1374/5

Valletta, National Library of Malta, Archives of the Order of St John, Cod. 16, no. 52: original parchment with seal.[1]

Nouerint Vniuersi, et singuli presentes inspecturj et auditurj. Quod Nos frater Robertus de Julliaco, dei gratia sacre domus hospitalis sancti Johannis Jerosolimitanj Magister humilis et pauperum Christi custos. Et Nos Conuentus Rodj domus eiusdem Confitemur et in uerbo ueritatis publice recognoscimus nos uidisse et recepisse computa et raciones per Religiosum in Christo nobis carissimum fratrem Johannem Ferdinandj de Heredia domus eiusdem Castellanum Emposte et priorem Cathalonie, ac locum nostrum tenentem in ultramarinis partibus generalem ad nos missa et missas videlicet de omnibus vniuersis et singulis pecunijs parcium ultramarinarum per eundem locum nostrum tenentem receptis datis solutis et assignatis ad nos et nostri Conuentus Thesaurum spectantibus, et alijs expensis missionibus et solucionibus per eum factis, scilicet de annjs dominj Millesimo, Trecentesimo Septuagesimo quarto, et Septuagesimo quinto prout infra sequitur. Primerament del Priorado d'Anglaterra por responsio del anyo suso escripto de lxxiiij nichil. Item por tallya nichil. Item por arrerages nichil. Item por mortuorum nichil. Item por vagantes nichil. Summa nichil. Item recebio de Francia los quales recebio el senyor maestro por responsion del priorado de Francia conptando v. francos por vj flor.', et tornan dellos a florines correntes que fazen por todos .vj.^{m} flor.' Item recebio por tallya del dito priorado, la qual tallya es ij^m. xxx flor.' de sentencia conptando los arazon de xxvij sol.' viij. drs.' por florin tornando los a florines correntes .ij.^{m} flor.'[2] Item por arrerages del dito anyo nichil. Item por mortuorum del anyo suso scripto conptando arazon de v. francos por vj flor.' et tornandolos a florines correntes vj^c flor.' Item por la despuylla de fray G. de Chaucony spitallero del Couent de Rodes,[3] el qual morio en Auinyo en lanyo suso scripto entre dineros et vaxella dargent .m. viiij^c xxviij

1. In the transcription *flor.', sol.', drs.'* and *gros.'* are left in those forms, while "7" is normally transcribed as *et*, *n̄y* as *ny*, *añyo* as *anyo, nich'* as *nichil*, and *s. de p.* as *summa de priorado* or *pagina* spelling and punctuation follow the original, but proper names are capitalised.

2. Ms. "*m*", but "*ij*", making 2,000 florins, is almost precisely the equivalent of 2,030 florins *de sentencia*; furthermore, on 29 August, 11 September and 11 October 1374 the Master gave Fernández de Heredia quittances for 6,000 florins of *responsiones* and 2,000 florins of taille from the Priory of France which the Master had received directly from the collector of that priory: Malta, Cod. 23, no. 4; Cod. 320, fos. 2, 11v, 44v–45.

3. Fr Guillaume de Chauconnin, the Hospitaller of Rhodes, who apparently died in Avignon in June or July 1374: Legras, 417.

flor.' Item por Vagantes nichil. Summa de priorado .ix^m v^c xxviij
flor.[4] Item recebio del priorado de Aquitania por responsion del dito
priorado del anyo suso scrito conptando v. francos por vj florines et
fagon flor.' correntes ij^m vj^c lxx flor.' Item por tallya nichil. Item por
arrerages nichil. Item por mortuor' nichil. Item por vagantes nichil.
Item recebio del priorado de Champanya por responsion del dito
priorado del anyo suso scripto mill.' flor.' Item por tallya del dito
priorado del dito anyo es assaber a razon de v. francs per vj flor.'
fazen de Correntes .iij^c xij. flor.' vj gros.' Summa de priorado .ij^m dC.
lxx flor.'[5] Arrerages, mortuor' et vagantes nichil. Item recebio, del
priorado de Aluernia por la responsion del dito priorado del anyo
suso scripto, ij^m Clxxx flor.' Item por tallya del dito priorado del dito
anyo .ij^c l. flor.' Item per mortuor' del dito anyo lxx flor.' Summa del
dito priorado. S(umma) de p(agina)[6] ij^m V^c x. flor.'[7] Item recebio del
priorado de sant Gilj por responsion del dito priorado del anyo suso
scripto .iij^m viiij^c xviij flor.', sol.' xvj. Item por tallya del dito priorado
del anyo suso scripto, M flor.' Item por arrerages V^c xxix flor.' sol.'
xvj. Item por mortuor' M. viiij^c xxxviij flor.' sol.' xv. Summa del
priorado .vij^m ij^c xcvj flor' xj gros.'[8] Item recebio del priorado de
Tholosa por responsion del dito priorado del anyo suso scripto .M. vj^c
xlv. flor.', xxij sol.' Item por talha .ij^c xlvj flor.' .ij. sol.' x. Item por
arrerages .iij^c iiij. flor.' xxvj sol.' Item por mortuor' iij^c flor.' xviij. sol.'
x. drs.' Summa del priorado .ij^m iiij^c xcvij. flor.' x. gross. Summa de
priorado .ix^m viiij^c xciij flor.' .x. gross.'[9] Item recebio del priorado de
Catalunya por la responsion del dito priorado del anyo suso scripto
.ij^m vij^c xlj flor.' .xiij sol.' ij dr.' Item por tallya del dito priorado, M
.vj^c ij. flor.' xviij sol.' iiij. Item daltra part por tallya del dito priorado,
C. viij. flor.' v. sol. xj. Item por arrerages viiij^c l. flor.' Summa del
priorado v^m[10] .iiij^c j. flor.' xxxvij sol.' v. dr.' correntes. Item recebio
dela Castellania d'Amposta[11] por responsion dela dita Castellania[12]
del anyo suso scripto es assaber xj^m torneses que fazen de flor.' correntes viiij^c xvj flor.' xvj. sol.' Item por tallya (nichil).[13] Item por
arrerages .m.d. flor.' Summa dela Castellania, ij^m iiij^c xvi. flor.' xvj

4. The correct total is 10,528 (not 9,528) florins.
5. The figures amount to 1,312 florins 12 sous (not 2,670 florins, which was the total for the previous entry for Aquitaine).
6. Total from the page in the account book being copied.
7. The figures amount to 2,500 (not 2,510) florins.
8. The figures amount to 7,385 florins 23 sous (not 7,396 florins 22 sous).
9. This entry of 9,893 florins 20 sous represents the combined totals for Saint Gilles and Toulouse.
10. Ms: v^c
11. *Castellania d'Amposta:* the Priory of Aragon.
12. Ms. repeats *dela dita Castellania*.
13. Ms. omits *nichil*.

sol.' correntes. Summa de priorado vij^m viij^c xix. flor.' iiij. gros.', v. drs.' correntes.[14] Item Recebio por responsion del priorado de Nauarra del anyo suso scripto V^c flor.' Item por tallya del dito priorado .ij^c xxx. flor.' xiij sol.' iiij. dr.' Summa del priorado vij^c xxx flor.' xiij sol.' .iiij. dr.' Item recebio dei priorado de Castella por responsion del dito priorado del anyo suso scripto nichil. Item por tallya del dito priorado nichil. Item por arrerages nichil. Item por mortuoris nichil. Item por vagantes nichil. Summa de priorado vij^c xxx flor.' xiij sol.' iiij dr.'[15] Item recebio del priorado de Portugal por responsion del dito priorado del anyo suso scripto nichil. Item por tallya nichil. Item por arrerages nichil. Item por mortuor' nichil. Item por Vagantes nichil. Item Recebio por arrerages del priorado de Lombardia xlj flor.' .ij. sol.' i ij. Item por la despulla de fray Milan Farina[16] .ij^c xvij flor.' viij sol.' iij. Summa del priorado. S(umma) de p(agina) .ij^c lviij flor.' x sol,' vij drs.' Item recebio por responsion del priorado de Pisa del anyo suso scrito .viiij^c xxij. flor.' .v. sol.' viij. Item por la talha del dito priorado .ij^c lxxxviij. flor.' sol.' iiij. dr.' viij. Summa del priorado .m.ij^c x. flor.' .x. sol.' iiij dr.' Item Recebio del priorado de Roma por la tallya del dito priorado del anyo suso scrito .ij^c lxxxviij. flor.' .iiij. sol.' Summa de priorado m.iiij^c xcviij. flor.' correntes .xv. sol.'[17] Item recebio del priorado de Messina por responsion del dito priorado del anyo suso scripto nichil. Item por tallya nichil. Item por arrerages nichil. Item por mortuor' nichil. Item por vagantes nichil. Item Recebio del priorado de Napols por responsion del dito priorado del anyo suso scripto vj^c xcj. flor.' sol.' xvj. Item por tallya del dito priorado .iij^c xlv. flor.' xx sol.' Summa del priorado. S(umma) de p(agina). m.xxxvj flor.' correntes .xxvj sol.'[18] Item Recebio por responsion del Scambi d'Alif[19] delanyo suso scripto nichil. Item por tallya nichil. Item por arrerages nichil. Item por mortuor' nichil. Item por vagantes nichil. Item Recebio del priorado de Capua por responsion del dito priorado del anyo suso scripto vj^c xcj flor.' xv. sol.' xj dr.' Item por tallya del dito priorado .ij^c xxx flor.' xiij sol.' iiij. dr.' Item por mortuoris xxxix flor.' xiij sol.' .x. dr.' Summa del priorado S(umma) de p(agina). viiij^c lx flor.' xliij sol.' j. dr.' correntes. Item Recebio del Priorado de Sancta Eufemia[20] por responsion del anyo suso scripto nichil. Item por tallya nichil. Item por arrerages nichil. Item por mortuoris nichil. Item por vagantes nichil. Item recebio del

14. 7,819 florins 8 sous 5 *drs.*' is the total for Catalunya and Amposta.

15. This entry for Castile, which paid nothing, results from adding Castile and Navarre.

16. Fr Milano Farina: unindentified.

17. 1,498 florins 15 sous is the total for Rome and Pisa.

18. *xxvj sol.*' should read *xxxvj sol.*'

19. *Scambi d'Alif:* the Commandery of Alife in the Kingdom of Naples.

20. Naples and Santa Eufemia were Commanderies, not priories.

priorado de Venosa[21] por la responsion del dito priorado del anyo
suso scripto .iiiͨ xlv. flor.' .xx. sol.' Item por tallya .C. xv. flor.' .vj.
sol.' .viij. Summa de priorado .iiijͨ lx. flor.' xxvij. sol.' viij drs.'
correntes. Primo Recebio del priorado de sant Esteue de Monopoly,[22]
por la responsion del dito priorado del anyo suso scripto, nichil. Item
por tallya nichil. Item por arrerages nichil. Item por mortuoris nichil.
Item por vagantes nichil. Item recebio del Priorado de Barleta por la
responsion del anyo suso scripto nichil. Item por tallya nichil. Item
por arrerages nichil. Item por mortuoris nichil. Item por vagantes
nichil.[23] Item recebio del priorado de Venecia por la responsion del
dito priorado del anyo suso scripto .viiijͨ xxij flor.' V° ss.' iiij. dr.' Item
por tallya del dito priorado .ijͨ lxxxviij. flor.' sol.' iiij. viij. dr.' Summa
del priorado.[24] Item recebio del priorado d'Ongria por la responsion
del dito priorado del anyo suso scripto nichil. Item por tallya nichil.
Item por arrerages nichil. Item por mortuoris nichil. Item por vagantes nichil. Summa de priorado .m.ijͨ x, flor' x. sol.'[25] Item Recebio
del priorado d'Alamanya por responsion del dito priorado del anyo
suso scripto .m. xj. flor.' xij sol.' Item por tallya .iijͨ xliiij flor.' vj. sol.'
Summa del priorado.[26] Item Recebio por responsion del dito priorado
de Boemia del anyo suso scripto nichil. Item por tallya nichil. Item
por arrerages nichil. Item por mortuoris nichil. Item por vagantes
nichil. Summa de priorado m.iijͨ lv. flor.' xviij sol.' Pagamentos fechos
enel anyo de lxx(i)v°.[27] Primerament fueron liurados por la companya
de los Albertes antigos mercaderos de Florença, a xx. dies de octobre
del anyo .m.ccc.lxxiiij. en Auinyo al senyor Maestro del Hospital, es
assaber en florines doro de Cambra .xijᵐ ijͨ l. Item en florines correntes
doro .xijᵐ ijͨ l. por las manes de Matheu de Vita dela dita companya
conptando el flor.' de Cambra a xxviij sol.', e lo flor.' corrent a xxiiij
sol.', fazen flor.' correns xxvjᵐ vͨ xlj flor.' xvj. sol.' correntes.[28] Item
pago la dita Companya al Cardenal de Mende, al Cardenal de
Thoroana, a monss. de Florença, a mons. de sant Eustati,[29] es assaber
a cascuno dellos por la pension del anyo de lxxiiij. iijͨ flor.' doro
correns a cascuno que fazen m.ijͨ flor.' correntes. Item pago la dita
companya a fray R. Asam procurador en cort de Roma porel el dito

21. Santa Trinità di Venosa in Puglia: a commandery, not a priory.
22. San Stefano Monopoli in Puglia: a commandery not a priory.
23. The whole entry for Barletta is repeated.
24. The missing total is 1,210 florins 10 sous.
25. This sum of 1,210 florins 10 sous is the total for Venice.
26. The total for *Alamania* is 1,355 florins 18 sous.
27. Ms: lxxv̊.
28. 26,541 florins 16 sous were paid to the Master.
29. The Hospital's cardinal Protectors were Guillaume de Chanac (*Mende*), Aycelin
de Montaigu (*Thoroana*), Pietro Corsini (*Florença*) and Pierre Flandrin (*S. Eustati*).

senyor Maestro[30] por la pension del anyo suso scripto, l. flor.' correntes. Item pago la dita companya e los quales fueron pagados enel palacio del papa, es assaber alos porteros dela primera puerta florins viij. Item a los dela .ij.ª porta flor.' xij. Item a los maceres[31] del papa flor.' xxv. Item a los maestres vxeros del papa flor.' l. et esto por pension del anyo de lxxiiij, que fazen en somma, xcv flor.' correntes. Item pago la dita Companya a miss' Alexandre Delantella,[32] et a miss. Francisco Bru,[33] et a miss. Jac(omo) Sona[34] por la pension del anyo de lxxiiij, es assaber a cascuno .l. flor.' correntes que fazen, Cl. flor' correntes. Item pago la dita companya a fray Pere Buxon[35] por la pension suya dela procuracion de la religion de lanyo de lxxiiij. iijᶜ flor.' correntes. Item pago la dita companya a maestro Feri Casinell procurador del senyor Maestro[36] por la pension del anyo lxxiiij. iijᶜ flor.' correntes. Item pago la dita companya a fray Aymeric dela Riba[37] por la pension del anyo lxxiiij. iiijᶜ flor.' correntes. Item pago la dita companya a miss. Ramon Bernat[38] por la pension del anyo suso scripto .l. flor.' correntes. Item pago la dita companya a Matheu Sobolinj[39] notario por scripturas xxv flor.' correntes.[40] Item fueron pagados a fray Thomas dela orden de los predicadores[41] por lo viage de Constantinoble .C. florins correntes. Item a el mismo por la dita razon, xlvj flor.' correntes xviij sol.' Item pago la dita companya a maestro Bartholomeu Cieras dela orden delos menores[42] por el viage de Costantinoble es assaber iijᶜ lxxx flor.' de sentencia conptando el flor.' a razon de xxvij. sol.' viij drs.' que fan flor.' correntes .iiijᶜ xxxviij flor.',

---

30. Fr Raymond Adizam, later styled *presbiter bacallarius in decretis*, who was here pensioned as the Master's procurator in the *curia*. He was possibly the earliest Hospitaller with legal qualifications to hold such a position: cf. Luttrell (1978), XVI 453. His pension was augmented on 20 October 1374: Malta, Cod. 320, fo. 50.

31. The *servientes armorum seu masserii*, the pope's sergeants-at-arms or noble guard: B. Guillemain, *La Cour pontificale d'Avignon, 1309–1376: Étude d'une Société* (Paris, 1962), 419–421.

32. Alessandro d'Antella, *advocatus* in the *curia*: ibid., 573 n. 69, 606–607.

33. Francesco Bruni, papal secretary: *ibid.*, 297–299, 568 n. 40, 571, 712.

34. Jacopo da Ceva, papal *advocatus* fiscal: *ibid.*, 607.

35. Fr Pierre Boysson, chaplain and *familiarius* of the Master, a procurator of the Hospital at the *curia* in 1370, and by 18 March 1379 Prior of the Convent at Rhodes: Delaville, 151, 164, 212, 214–215, 299; Luttrell (1978), XVI 453.

36. Ferry Cassinel, doctor in theology and professor of law, a kinsman of the new Master Fr Robert de Juilly, his procurator in the Priory of France, and in 1374 his procurator at the *curia*; Delaville, 197; Luttrell (1978), XVI 453.

37. Fr Aimery de la Ribe, Commander of Raissac, nominated Procurator-General in the West on or shortly before 2 February 1372: Delaville, 144 n. 2; *supra*, 3.

38. Ramon Bernat: unidentified.

39. Matteo Sobolini, notary: unidentified.

40. Pensions and 25 florins for *scripturas* amounted to 2,570 florins.

41. Tommaso de Bosolasco, OP: Luttrell (1982), XV 407 n. 68.

42. Bartolomeo Cherrazio, OFM: *ibid.*, XV 407 n. 68.

sol.' .j. dr.' .iiij. correntes. Item pago la dita companya a Maestro Thomas de Boço dela orden delos fraires predicadores por el viage de Costantinoble es assaber .iij.ᶜ lxxx flor.' de sentencia conptando el flor.' a razon de xxvij sol.' .viij. dr.' por flor.', que fan .iiij.ᶜ xxxviij flor.' sol.' .j. dr.' iiij correntes. Item pago la dita companya a fray Hesse d'Alamanya,[43] por la messageria de Costantinoble por paga de vj meses es assaber .iiij.ᶜ lxj. flor.' ij. sol.', viij correntes. Item pago dotra parte la dita companya al dito fray Hesse por la paga de .v. meses por la dita missageria es assaber, v.ᶜ xviij flor.', xviij sol.' correntes. Item pago la dita companya a fray Bertran Flota[44] por la paga de v. meses por la messageria de Costantinoble es assaber V.ᶜ xviij flor.' correntes xviij. sol.' Item pago dotra parte al dito fray Bertran Flota por paga de vj meses por la dita missageria es assaber .iiij.ᶜ lxj flor.' correntes .ij. sol.' viij dr.' Item pago la dita companya a los de suso nombrados por nolit dela galea en que andaron es assaber V.ᶜ lxxvj flor.' correntes sol.' ix. drs.' iiij. Item pago la dita companya a Johan Corsin[45] por su prouision dela missatgeria que fizo en Jenoua et en Venecia por los afferes dela missageria de Costantinoble es assaber flor.' .vij.ᶜ lxvij flor.' correntes. .xviij sol.' Item pago la dita companya a Michel de Rodulfo, et a Luys de Felipo Marin mercaderos de Jenoua, et a miss. Rafael Espindola[46] por cambio que fezieron alos missageros suso scripto, el qual cambio recebiron a Pera segunt que aparesce per vna scriptura seyellada con .iiij. seyellos delos ditos .iiij missatgeros et pagueren ne en flor.' correntes .M.Clij. flor.' correntes .xviij sol.' viij dr.'[47] Item posen en paga la dita companya los quales fezieron de messiones en los afferes dela religion es assaber por xviij processos apostolicals las quals fueron embiadas por los priorados dela religion et desto mostraren los jnstrumentes xxxviij flor.' Item por .j. correu, que embiaren en Anglaterra por afferes dela religion, vij flor.' .xij sol.' Item por correus que embiaron en Francia en Champanya, en Aluernia, en Aquitania por afferes dela religion xv flor.' Item por .j. correu que enbiaron en Portugal por los afferes dela religion xxx

43. Fr Hesso Schlegelholtz, Commander of Freibourg-im-Breisgau: Delaville, 185; Luttrell (1982), XV 407–408.

44. Fr Bertrand Flotte, Commander of Naples until December 1374 or a little later, who became Grand Commander of the Convent on 6 May 1375: Delaville, 150 n. 1; Luttrell (1982), XV 407–408.

45. Giovanni Corsini, brother of Cardinal Pietro Corsini, acted for the pope in crusading negotiations at this time: Luttrell (1982), XII 286; XV 400, 407, and A. Benvenuti Papi, 'Corsini, Giovanni,' Dizionario Biografico degli Italiani, xxix (Rome, 1983), 638–640.

46. Michele di Ridolfo, Luigi di Filippo Marino, Raffaele Spinola: Genoese.

47. The Constantinople mission expended 5,479 florins 12 sous plus 728 florins in the 1374/5 accounts, a total of 6,207 florins 12 sous; amend Luttrell (1982), XV 467 n. 68, which gives 6,677 florins. Pera was the Genoese suburb of Constantinople.

flor.' Item por .j. correu que embiaron en Pulha, et enel Regno[48] en
Jenoua, et en Venecia, en Pisa, et en Florença .x. flor.' Item por .j.
correu que embiaron en Alamanya et en Boemia xxx flor. Item por
scripturas et processos en pargamin los quales se fueron delantes delos
Cardenales .liiij. flor.' Item por bollas, et obliganças que fezieron en
la Assembleya que se tuuo en Auinyo .Cxcv. flor.' xij sol.' Item por
v. bollas las quales fueron por aferes dela religion .l. flor.' Item por
vna bolla de franquesa dela Religion la qual bola preso M(aestr)o
Ferri[49] C.xvj flor.' xvj sol.', Item por message que fizo .j° dela companya como ando a Marselha por afferes del Maestro.[50] Item que
fueron dados a Duran correu que ando al prior de Nauarra et de
Castella por requerir los xxv. flor.' Item por .j. correu que aporto
letras al valcho[51] .xx. sol.' Item por libros en que escriuron los comptos
dela religion xvj flor.' Item por messiones que fizo Matheu de Vita
como ando a Belcaire por aportar moneda al Maestro,[52] et por contar
con el .vij. flor.' los quales messiones totas fazen en summa .vjˢ j. flor.'
correntes .xij sol.' Item posen en dat.'[53] los quales pagoron por cambio
de los Mil ducados doro los quales fueron pagados alos (a)mbaxadores
que fueron en Costantinoble a razon de vij flor.' por cento et son en
Summa .lxx flor' correntes.[54] Reebudas fechas por parte del senyor
Castellan d'Amposta prior de Cathalunya, lugartenient del senyor
Maestro et Couent en todas las partidas daquamar delas monedas
delos priorados daquamar[55] segunt que se sieguen .. Primerament
Reebe del priorado d'Anglaterra por la responsion del dito priorado
del anyo suso scripto nichil. Item por tallya nichil. Item por arrerages
nichil. Item por mortuoris nichil. Item por Vagantes nichil. Item
Recebio del priorado de Yrlanda por responsion del dito priorado del
anyo suso scripto nichil. Item por tallya nichil. Item por arrerages
nichil. Item por mortuoris nichil. Item por vagantes nichil. Summa
de pagina nichil. Item recebio del priorado de Francia por responsion
del dito priorado a razon de cinco francos por vj flor.' et fazen de

48. *enel Regno*: to the Kingdom of Naples.

49. Ferry Cassinel: *supra*, note 36.

50. Amount omitted.

51. *valcho?*

52. Matteo de Vita of the Alberti Antichi was received by the Master as a *confrater*
of the Hospital at Beaucaire on 22 October 1374: Malta, Cod. 320, fo. 49v.

53. *en dat.*': in credit.

54. Couriers, bulls and 70 florins in exchange expenses *apparently* amounted to 671
florins 12 sous, making an apparent total of expenses for 1374/5 of 35,263 florins 4 sous.
A quittance issued by the Master on 11 October 1374 before he left Avignon showed
he had received 35,500 florins for the year: Malta, Cod. 23, no. 4. The version registered
in Cod. 320, fos. 44v–45, was full of errors with some figures being changed to match
those in Cod. 23, no. 4, but with others being left unaltered so that the totals no longer
added correctly. The 1374/5 accounts commence at this point.

55. Ms: *daquamas*.

florins correntes .vj ͫ ij.ᶜ l. florins correntes. Item recebio por la tallya del dito priorado de aquellos xij ͫ xl⁵⁶ flor.' de sentencia que fazen de sentencia por tallya comptando a razon xxvij sol.' .viij drs.' por florin, et ha paga de correntes .M.ij.ᶜ l. flor.' correntes. Item recebio por vagaciones del dito priorado comptando a razon de v. por vj .M.xl flor.' correntes gros.' viij. Item por vagacion dela baylia de Henaut .C.iiij flor.' correntes gros.' .ij. Item por vagacion dela baylia de Sant Baubure .C. xiiij flor.' correntes gros.' .vij. Item por vagacion dela baylia de Orliens xxxj flor.' correntes gros.' .iij. Item por la baylia que vago de Mont de Sisons xxvj flor.' sol.' .j.⁵⁷ Item por mortuoris fray G. de Huyllac⁵⁸ .M.xlj flor.' correntes viij gros.' Summa del priorado de Francia .jx ͫ viij.ᶜ lviiij flor.' iiij gros.' correntes, Item recebio del priorado de Champanya por la responsion del dito priorado del anyo suso scripto .M.xlj flor.' correntes gros.' viij. Item por la tallya del dito priorado .iij.ᶜ xij flor.' et medio correntes. Item arrerages nichil. Item mortuoris nichil. Item vagantes nichil. Item recebio del Priorado de Aquitania por responsion del dito priorado del anyo suso scripto .m.ij.ᶜ l. correntes. Item tallya nichil. Item arrerages nichil. Item mortuoris nichil. Item vagantes nichil. Item recebio del Priorado de Aluernia por responsion del dito priorado del anyo suso scripto .ij ͫ flor.' correntes, Item por la tallya del dito priorado V.ᶜ flor.' correntes. Item por arrerages nichil. Item por mortuoris nichil. Item por Vagantes nichil . . Item recebio del priorado de Sant Gili por responsion del dito priorado del anyo suso scripto .iiij ͫ v.ᶜ xlviij flor.' correntes. Item por la tallya viij.ᶜ .lij. flor.' gros.' iij. Item por arrerages delos anyos lxxiij. lxxiiij. V.ᶜ xxij. medio correntes. Items por arrerages delas tallyas delos anyos passados .C.xxiij. gros.' viij. Item por vagantes viij.ᶜ xciij. flor.' Item por mortuoris vj.ᶜ l. flor.' Summa del priorado de sant Gilj que ha pagado vij ͫ v.ᶜ lxxxviiij. flor.' gros.' v. correntes. Item Recebio del Priorado de Tholosa por responsion del dito priorado del anyo suso scripto .viij.ᶜ xvij. flor.' correntes, gros' .ij. ½. Item por la tallya del dito anyo .C.lxxviij. flor.' gros.' ij. Item por arrerages del anyo de lxxiiij .C.xxix flor.' gros' viij. Item pago mas por arrerages del anyo lxxiiij por las cambras del prior .ij.ᶜ l. flor.' gros.' viij correntes. Summa que ha pagado el priorado de Tholosa segunt damunt, M. iijᶜ lxxv flor.', gros' ij, drs.' xj correntes,⁵⁹ Item recebio del dito Priorado⁶⁰ por responsion

56. Ms: *aquellos xi^m xl*, perhaps for *Mii.ᶜxl*, but the arithmetic gives approximately 1,084 florins. After *aquellos* is a sign which is repeated in the margin, perhaps to indicate some doubt; the passage is evidently garbled.

57. Exceptionally, the accounts listed the vacancies of four French commanderies: Hainaut, Sainte Vaubourg, Orléans and Mont-de-Soissons.

58. Fr Guillaume de Huillac: unidentified.

59. The figure given amount to 1,296 florins 4 sous (not 1,375 florins 4 sous 11 *drs'*.).

60. ie. Priory of Catalunya.

del anyo suso scripto, ij^m viiij^c flor.' correntes, Item por la tallya del dito anyo, m.ij^c xxxiij flor.' xj sol.' drs.' iiij correntes, Item por el passage del senhor Maestre V^c xxxv. flor.' correntes .. Los delas Cambras de Cathalunya M(aestre)e Ferri lo ha preso del anyo lxxiiij.lxxv. Summa, que ha pagado Cathalunya .iiij^m vj^c lxviij flor.' xj sol.' drs.' iiij.[61] Item recebio dela Castellania d'Amposta por la responsion del anyo suso scripto viiij^c xvj flor.', gros.' iiij. correntes. Item ha pagado de tallya .V^c lxxvj flor.' gros.' iiij, drs.' xvj correntes. Item por el passage del senyor Maestre .ij^c l. flor.' correntes, Item por las cambras del senyor Maistre .V^c flor.' Summa que ha pagado lo Castellan d'Amposta entre todo .ij^m ij^c. xlij. flor.' correntes gros.' viiij drs.' .xvj. Item recebio del priorado de Nauarra por responsion del dito priorado del anyo suso scripto .v^c flor.' correntes Item por la tallya .ij^c xxxv flor.' gros.' .j. drs.' xvj. Item por el passage del senyor Maestre .C.ij. flor.' correntes. Item por vagantes .xxx. flor.' correntes. Summa que ha pagado el priorado de Nauarra segunt que desuso viij^c lxvij flor.' correntes gros.' .j. drs.' xvj. Item fazo Reebuda los quales recebiron la companya delos Albertes del priorado de Roma por la responsion del dito priorado del anyo de lxxv^o viiij^c xxij. flor.' correntes sol' v. dr' .iiij. Item que Reebiron la dita companya por tallya del dito priorado de Roma .ij^c lxxxviij flor.' correntes sol' .iiij dr' viij. Item faze reebuda los quales reebiron los ditos Albertes del priorado de Venosa por la responsion del dito priorado del anyo de lxxv .ij^c xlij flor.' correntes, gros' iiij $\frac{1}{2}$. Item por la tallya del dito priorado .C. xiiij flor.' correntes gros.' j$\frac{1}{2}$. Item faze reebuda los quales recebiron la dita companya delos Albertes por la responsion del priorado de Pisa del anyo lxxv. Viiij^c xxij flor.' correntes, sol.' v. dr.' iiij. Item por la tallya del dito priorado .ij^c lxxxviij flor.' correntes gros.' ij. dr' .viij. .. Las quantitas suso scriptas son stadas assignadas porell Castellan d'Amposta al grant Comandador.[62] Primo por la responsion de Alamanya .M. flor.' Item por la tallya iij^c vj. flor.' Item por arrerages .C. flor'. Item por el passage del senyor Maestro .Cliij flor.' Item por la responsion del priorado de Boemia del anyo de lxxiiij. M.ij^c flor.' Item dela tallya .iiij^c viij flor.' Item la responsion del anyo de lxxv. M.ij^c flor.' Item dela tallya .iiij^c viij flor.' Item de arrerages .iiij^c flor.' Item del passage del senyor M(aestr)e .ij^c iiij. flor.' Item la responsion del priorado de Vngria los quales ha recebidos el prior de Venecia .iij^c flor.' Item la responsion del priorado de Venesia viij^c flor.' Item por la tallya .ij^c lv. flor.' Item del passage del senyor M(aestr)e .C.xxvij flor.' $\frac{1}{2}$. Item del priorado de Barleta por la

61. Ferry Casinell, the Master's procurator, took the incomes of the magistral *camere* which are not in the accounts.

62. The Grand Commander of the Convent was Fr Bertrand Flotte nominated on 6 May 1375: Delaville, 150 n. 1; *supra*, note 44.

responsion que non de ha pagado ren de todo el tiempo que ha tuuido lo priorado, et el grant comendador ha firmado porell .ij.ᵐ flor.'⁶³ Item por la tallya del anyo de lxxiiij.lxxv. viijˢ xvj flor.' Item porel passage del senyor Maestro .ijˢ viij. flor.' Summa de pagina delas assignaciones fechas viiij.ᵐ viiiˢ lxxxv flor' .½.⁶⁴ Sant Esteue de Monopolj la responsion del anyo de lxxiiij .iiijˢ flor.' Item por la tallya .C.liij. flor.' Item por la responsion del anyo de lxxv .iiijˢ flor.' Item por la tallya .C.liij flor.' Item porel passage del senyor M(aestr)e lxxvj flor.' ½. Venosa ha pagado responsion et tallya a los Albertes, et deue porel passage de mons. lo m(aestr)e .lj. flor.' Item deue dela responsion .iij. flor.' Item deue .iij. flor'⁶⁵ .. Santa Eufemia deue de .ij. anyos responsion et tallya, et faze por .ij. anyos la responsion .vjˢ flor.' Item por tallya .ijˢ iiij flor.'⁶⁶ Item porel passage del senyor M(aestre) .lj. flor.' Napol de Responsion vjˢ flor.' Item de tallya .iijˢ vj. flor. Item porel passage del senyor M(aestre) .Cliij flor.' Los Escambis d'Alif deue dela responsion del anyo de lxxiiij .vˢ flor.' Item por tallya .Cliij. flor.' Item porel passage del senyor Maestro .lxxvj flor.' Item por la responsion del anyo de lxxv? Vˢ flor.' Item por la tallya .Cliij flor' .. Capua de responsion .vjˢ flor.' Item por tallya .ijˢ iiij. flor.' Item porel passage del senyor Maestre .C.ij. flor.' Roma ha pagado responsion, et tallya deue porel passage del senyor Maestre .C.xxvij flor.' ½. Pisa ha pagado responsion tallya alos Albertes, et deue solament porel passage del senyor M(aestre) .C.xxvij flor.' ½. Mescina no ha pagado res delos anyos de lxxiiij et lxxv, et por la tallia, et por lo passage del Maestre M.C lxxxij. flor.' ½. Lombardia no ha pagado res delos anyos de lxxv, lxxv mas esta hombre en sperança de auer ne alguna cosa. fray Richardo Caracho de Chichano tiene por mortuor' Vˢ flor.'⁶⁷ Item que son stados inprestados a larceuispo de Rodas lo quales deue pagar en Rodas .Vˢ flor.' Castiella non ha pagado res despues que esti prior⁶⁸

63. The Prior of Barletta at least between 25 November 1373 and about 30 October 1375 was Fr Raymond de Sabran: *Lettres Secrètes et Curiales du pape Grégoire XI(1370–1378) relatives à la France*, ed. L. Mirot—H. Jassemin (5 fascs., Paris, 1935–57), nos. 3137, 3779. The Grand Commander apparently pledged to pay the 2,000 florins.

64. The *pagina* contained the 9,885½ florins (to be corrected to 9,732½ florins) for *Alamania*, Bohemia, Hungary, Venice and Barletta, which had been assigned to the Grand Commander, who was probably charged to collect them in Italy; the monies from *Alamania* and Bohemia were normally sent to Venice.

65. Venosa had paid its dues (*supra*) and can scarcely have owed two sets of only three florins; the copyist must have erred, and 300 florins may well have been the sum owed.

66. This perhaps meant that Santa Eufemia owed 600 plus 204 florins each year for two years.

67. Fr Riccardo Caracciolo, Commander of Cicciano in the Priory of Capua: Delaville, 249.

68. Fr Lop Sánchez de Somoza, destituted in 1375 for his refusal to pay: *ibid.*, 195–196.

tiene el priorado. Portugal deue de ix anyos que non ha pagado res
.. Aquestos son los pagamientos et assignaciones fechas porel senyor
Castellan delas monedas de suso scriptas del anyo de lxxv. Primerament ha pagado dela moneda de Francia ala cambra de nuestro
senyor el papa porel deudo que mons. el Maestre deuie ala cambra
del papa .V ꝛ flor' de Cambra que ualen conptando v. francos por vj
flor', et ualen flor' correntes .V ꝛ viij꞉ xxxiij flor.' Esti pagamento fue
fecho porque la cambra fizo arestar las monedas de Francia entroque
se pagoron delos ditos V ꝛ flor' de Cambra. Item ha pagado ala
companya delos Albertes los quales fueron deuidos a ellos porel pre-
stamo que se fizo delos xxiiij ꝛ v꞉ flor' que priso mons. el Maestro por
(ir) al Couent, et por otras expensas fachas porels ditos Albertes .iij ꝛ
lxiiij flor.'⁶⁹ Item pago por mandamento de mons. lo M(aestre), et del
Couent segunt paresce por bulla de mons. el maestro, et del Couent,
la qual fue dada en Rodas los quales fueron pagados a algunos
mercaderos segunt aparesce por carta fecha por m(aestre) Antonj
not(ario),⁷⁰ florines de Cambra, iij ꝛ que ualen a flor' correntes .iij ꝛ
V꞉ flor.' Item por perdua de monedas .iij flor.' Item a pagado per
mandamiento de mons. lo m(aestre) et del Couent segunt paresce por
bulla de mons. el Maestro et Couent la qual fue dada en Rodas los
quales fueron pagados alos mercaderos segont paresce por carta
publica fecha por not(ario) flor' de Cambra .vj ꝛ vij꞉ lxxv. que fazen
flor' correntes vij ꝛ ix꞉ xv flor' gros' .x. Item pago alos freres menores
et predicadores que fueron en Costantinoble por mandamiento de
nuestro senyor el papa, ultra la somma que les fue pagada en lanyo
de lxxiiij vij꞉ xxviij flor.' Item pago alos officiales de nuestre senyor el
papa xcv. flor.' Item pago a mons. Anchelet⁷¹ segunt paresce por la
bulla de mons. el M(aestre) .V꞉ flor.' Item pago por la pension de iiij
Cardenals m.ij꞉ flor.' Item pago alos officiales de nuestre senyor el
papa xcv. flor.' Item pago a iij aduocados, et a miss. Frances Bru,⁷² a
cascu .l. flor', fazen .ij꞉ flor.' Item pago a M(aestr)e Matheo procurador delas contradichas⁷³ xxv. flor.' Item pago al procurador
general de Cort de Roma, iij꞉ flor.'⁷⁴ Item pago por bollas processos
correus andantes por diuersas partidas por los negocios dela religion

---

69. These 24,500 florins appeared above as 26,541 florins 26 sous, and the 3,064
florins of charges listed here probably included interest on money loaned; the 'ir' is
supplied.

70. *Antonio notario:* unidentified.

71. *Mons. Anchelet*, possibly the papal scribe Ancelin Martin: Guillemain, 342, 366.

72. Francesco Bruni, papal secretary.

73. Matheo, *advocatus* in the *audientia litterarum contradictarum*.

74. One of the Hospital's procurators, *magister* Matteo de Lucha, was confirmed as
procurator in the *curia* on 10 October 1374: Malta, Cod. 320, fo. 45. The total for
pensions was 1,795 florins.

clvj flor.' gros' .j. Item pago a Loys Tallaborch[75] por la pension a el assignada por mons. lo maestre .xxx. flor.'[76] Item que ha pagado manualment al grant comendador segunt aparesce por carta f(act)a conptando v. francos, por vj flor' et fazen flor' correntes vj ꝫ vjᶜ xxix flor.' Item pago al grant Comendador dotra parte por man de fray Aymeric dela Riba .m. vᶜ xcvij flor' gros' vj, drs' .iiij. Item pago al dito grant Comendador dotra part .ij ꝫ vᶜ flor.' Summa que son las pagas fechas del anyo de lxxv a florines xxxiiij ꝫ ijᶜ xxviij gros.'[77] Item las assignaciones fechas al grant comandador las quals son de suso scriptas .xvij ꝫ vijᶜ lxv. flor' .. [78] Que quidem computa et rationes, ut premittitur sic uisa et recepta ipsa tenore presencium ratificamus aprobamus et omologamus et dictum fratrem Johannem Ferdinandj de Heredia nostrum locumtenentem, ac omnia bona sua et arnesia presentia et futura quitamus liberamus et absoluimus per presentes.

[a leaden bull attached with string is inscribed:]
BVLLA MAGISTRI ET CONVENTVS/
HOSPITALIS IHERVSALEM

75. Lodovicus Tailleburgui, inhabitant of Avignon, was granted a life pension of 30 florins a year by the Master on 22 October 1374: Malta, Cod. 320, fo. 50v. He was a *campsor* or moneychanger: Cod. 16, no. 53.

76. Couriers, bulls and Tailleburgui's pension amounted to 186 florins 2 sous.

77. These expenses included 4 florins lost, 11,415 florins in repayments of monies advanced at Rhodes, and 728 florins to the two friars who went on the Constantinople mission; the total of sums as given was 34,277 florins 22 sous (not 34,228 florins).

78. These 17,765 florins do not seem to be 'written above' (*suso scriptas*) since the three sums listed as having been advanced to the Grand Commander amounted to 10,726 florins, and this entry remains somewhat inexplicable; the 17,765 florins probably represented a hypothetical balance between incomes and expenses, since 34,278 plus 17,765 amounts to 52,043 florins while incomes would apparently have amounted to 53,441 florins if monies said to be owing were added to those paid.

II
WILLIAM LATYMER'S CRONICKILLE OF ANNE BULLEYNE

Edited by Maria Dowling

CONTENTS

ACKNOWLEDGEMENTS

I am grateful to the Keeper of Western Manuscripts, the Bodleian Library, Oxford for permission to publish the text offered here, Bodleian MS Don. C. 42, fos 21–33. I wish to thank Mr J.A.S. Green, the County Archivist of Berkshire, for information about Trumble MS 5, and the staff of the following institutions for their assistance and cooperation: the Bodleian Library, Oxford; the British Library, Dr Williams's Library, Institute of Historical Research and Public Record Office, London; and the Bibliothèque Albert I, Brussels. Professor E.W. Ives has given valuable advice and constructive criticism, and Mr L.R. Gardiner offered much useful discussion of the nature of Tudor biography. I would like to thank Ms Catharine Davies and Ms Joy Shakespeare both for references and for suggestions. Thanks are due to Mr Stephen Baskerville, Miss Joan Henderson and Ms Susan Wabuda for enthusiastic discussion and kind encouragement.

ABBREVIATIONS

Alumni Cant.	*Alumni Cantabrigienses, Part One, from the Earliest Times to 1751* ed. John and J.A. Venn (4 vols., Cambridge, 1922–27)
Athenae Cant.	*Athenae Cantabrigienses, i, 1500–85* ed. Charles Henry and Thompson Cooper (Cambridge, 1858)
BL	British Library, London
CSP Dom.	*Calendar of State Papers, Domestic, 1547–80* ed. Robert Lemon (1856)
CSP For.	*Calendar of State Papers, Foreign, 1558–9* ed. Joseph Stevenson (1863)
Ellis, *Original Letters*	*Original Letters Illustrative of English History* ed. Sir Henry Ellis (3 ser., 11 vols., 1824, 1827, 1846)
Forrest, *Grisild the Second*	William Forrest, *History of Grisild the Second* ed. W.D. Macray (Roxburghe Club, 1875)
Foxe, *A & M*	John Foxe, *Acts and Monuments* ed. S.R. Cattley (8 vols., 1837)
Ives, *Anne Boleyn*	E.W. Ives, *Anne Boleyn* (Oxford, 1986)
L & P	*Lettters and Papers, Foreign and Domestic, of the reign of Henry VIII* ed. J.S. Brewer, J. Gairdner, R.H. Brodie (21 vols., 1862–1910)
Parker, *Correspondence*	*Correspondence of Matthew Parker* ed. John Bruce and Thomas Perowne (Parker Soc., Cambridge, 1853)
PRO	Public Record Office, London
Span. Cal.	*Calendar of State papers, Spanish* ed. G. Bergenroth, P. Gayangos, M.A.S. Hume (8 vols., 1862–1904)
Wyatt, *Anne Boleigne*	George Wyatt, *Extracts from the Life of the Virtuous, Christian and Renowned Queen Anne Boleigne* ed. R. Triphook (1817)

INTRODUCTION

The text

The manuscript presented here, which has scarcely been noticed by historians of the Tudor period, is Bodleian MS Don. C 42, fos. 21–33, 'A briefe treatise or cronickille of the moste vertuous ladye Anne Bulleyne late quene of England' by William Latymer.[1] It forms part of a miscellaneous volume of early modern letters and papers. It consists of twenty-six folio pages on paper, and is prefaced by a dedicatory epistle to Elizabeth I. Although this letter is carefully signed by Latymer in an italic hand different from that of the rest of the treatise, the manuscript would seem to be a working copy rather than one prepared for presentation to the queen; there are numerous interlineations and scorings-out, many of which confuse the grammatical sense of the text. Professor E.W. Ives has suggested to me that the manuscript might be a draft submitted to the authorities for approval, and has pointed out that a number of Elizabethan writers allude to the forthcoming production of an 'official' biography or biographies of Anne Boleyn.[2]

It cannot be known whether the treatise was presented to Elizabeth, though as Latymer received a great deal of preferment from her it seems a strong possibility. If there was a presentation copy it is not extant, as it would presumably be among the Royal manuscripts in the British Library. However, the importance of the treatise lies not in its possible effect on Elizabeth and her advisers, but rather in Latymer's portrayal of Anne Boleyn and his reasons for recording her life.

The author

There is a large amount of information about the life of William Latymer, who must not be confused with an older namesake, the classical scholar and friend of Erasmus. Born in 1498, he graduated MA of Cambridge in 1536 as a member of Corpus Christi, Matthew Parker's college. He may have owed his appointment as Anne's chap-

1. For notices of Latymer and his treatise, Charles C. Butterworth, *The English Primers* (Philadelphia, 1953), 54–5; David Knowles, *The Religious Orders in England* (3 vols., Cambridge, 1948, 1955, 1959), iii, 215–7; Allan G. Chester, *Hugh Latimer, Apostle to the English* (Philadelphia, 1954), 111; Mortimer Levine, 'The place of women in Tudor government,' in *Tudor Rule and Revolution: Essays for G.R. Elton from his American Friends* ed.Delloyd J. Guth and John W. McKenna (Cambridge, 1982); Arthur Slavin, 'Bishop Bonner and the Devil's Art', in the same collection. Slavin does not mention Latymer's connection with Anne Boleyn. E.W. Ives, *Anne Boleyn* (Oxford, 1986) makes extensive use of the 'cronickille'.

2. For example, Holinshed and Foxe, both quoted in Ives, *Anne Boleyn*, 63.

lain to Parker, who was in her service from March 1535. Certainly there is no evidence for Chester's supposition that he was a kinsman of Hugh Latimer.

William Latymer occurs twice in the records as chaplain to Anne Boleyn. First, early in 1536 Tristram Revell, a former Cambridge scholar who needed support for his studies, tried to present Anne with an English version of Lambertus' *Farrago Rerum Theologicarum.* He gave a copy to Cranmer's brother Edmund who passed it to the archbishop, but Cranmer turned it over for examination to Edmund and to Hugh Latimer. Meanwhile, Revell gave another copy to William Latymer to present to Anne. The book was dangerously radical and Anne's position was extremely insecure; therefore she 'would not trouble herself' about the work.

Secondly, in spring 1536 Latymer was sent to Flanders to buy books for his mistress. On his return he was apprehended by the authorities at Sandwich and was astounded to learn that Anne was in the Tower. He wisely proved cooperative, giving the mayor of Sandwich a list of books he had bought for Anne, some of which were sent to her silkwoman, Jane Wilkinson. The list, unfortunately, is not extant.

Anne Boleyn does not seem to have given him any ecclesiastical preferment, though early in 1536 he received the living of Stakpoll, St David's diocese, from the king. In July 1537 one William Latymer, clerk, was given licence to hold incompatible benefices of any annual value and to be non-resident. Indeed, for a reformer he was a notable pluralist. In October 1538 he became rector of Witnesham, Suffolk, on the presentation of Edward Latimer, who may have been a relation. In the same month Henry VIII made him master of the college of St Laurence Pountney, London in succession to Thomas Starkey. As master he held several college livings, including that of Little All Hallows in the city. He was also rector of Speldhurst, Kent from 1538.

Latymer was master of St Laurence Pountney until the dissolution of the college in 1547. During his tenure he was in conflict with his diocesan Bonner, ostensibly over ecclesiastical taxation, and he seems to have been involved in dubious deals over college land, lead from the roof and other property. Among other sins he was accused of failing to appoint curates in two of his benefices and to provide thirty sacks of coal for the poor as stipulated in the college charter: charges which would not have pleased the Anne Boleyn delineated in Latymer's 'cronickille'.

In 1547 he sat in convocation as one of the proctors for Norwich diocese, and voted in favour of clerical marriage. In 1549 he had his revenge on Bonner when he joined with Hooper to accuse the bishop of popery. Bonner for his part called Latymer a notorious heretic, sacramentary and holder of conventicles who preached heresy openly in London and the suburbs.

On Mary's accession Latymer lost all his preferments because he was a married priest. He was deprived by Bonner and lived in Norwich on the pension of £28 13s 4d he derived from St Laurence Pountney. On Elizabeth's accession he was restored to his living of St Mary Abchurch, London, and in April 1559 the queen presented him to the rectory of St George, Southwark. In 1560 he was made dean of Peterborough and a canon of Westminster; in documents he is occasionally styled archdeacon of Westminster. Resigning his two parishes in London and Southwark, he became Elizabeth's chaplain and clerk of her closet. As a member of convocation in 1563 he signed the Thirty-Nine Articles. In August 1564 he accompanied the queen to Cambridge and was created DD in her presence, and in 1565 he was one of the Lent preachers at court. He apparently held two livings in Suffolk, Kirkton and Shotley.

William Latymer died in August 1583 and was buried in Peterborough cathedral. His will, dated 29 July 25 Elizabeth, alludes to his wife Ellen and sons Edward and Joshua. It also displays a number of concerns which recall the Anne Boleyn of the 'cronickille'. First, he left money for preaching at Peterborough; ten shillings for his funeral sermon, and 6s 8d each for two sermons in the near future. Secondly, he showed charity to the poor, leaving £3 6s 8d in general alms and forty shillings 'to the poore whose howses were lately burned'. Finally, he required that all servants dismissed by his wife on his death should receive a quarter's wages.[3]

Latymer's purpose in writing the 'Cronickille'

Latymer's motives in composing his biography of Anne Boleyn are open to interpretation. The least creditable possibility is that he wrote for monetary gain or ecclesiastical promotion. Latymer had served Elizabeth's mother and been arrested at her fall, and had suffered under Mary for his Protestant faith. Possibly he felt that some compensation was due him, and it is notable that near the close of his

---

3. General summaries of Latymer's career are in *Athenae Cant.*, 481 and *Alumni Cant.*, iii, 50; see also Slavin, 'Bishop Bonner', 18–20. The documents connecting Latymer with Anne Boleyn are PRO, SP1/102, fo.125, confession of Tristram Revell, and SP1/103, fos 262–3, Mayor and Jurates of Sandwich to Henry VIII, 8 May 1536; calendared in *L & P*, x, nos 371, 827. Revell's book is *The summe of christianitie gatheryd out almoste of al placis of scripture, by that noble and famouse clerke, Francis Lambert of Avynyon* (Redman? London, 1536). Latymer's will is PRO, Prob. 11/66/27, fos 214–15. Additional notices of him are calendared in *L & P*, x, no.226 (28), xi (2), no.411 (39), xvi, no.333, xvii, no.73, xviii (1), no.101, xix (1), no.82, xx (1) no.2; and in *CSP Dom.*, Addenda, 471, 512, 525, 534, 539, 546, 554, 555. There are also miscellaneous papers in PRO, SP46/117, fos 99–114.

'cronickille' he expatiates on the reciprocal duties of servants and masters. Material considerations alone, however, are not sufficient to explain why he undertook the labour of composing the treatise. Two major aims are apparent in the work: to rehabilitiate Anne, and to advise Elizabeth by presenting her mother as an exemplar.

In the first instance Latymer, as an evangelical who had benefited from Anne's patronage, was anxious to rescue her memory from obliquy. Anne Boleyn had never been popular, but had been hated as an arrogant upstart, adulteress and heretic who had ousted the true and beloved queen, Katherine of Aragon. To the majority of the people of Henrician England she was, in the phrase of James Harrison of Leigh, 'Nan Bullen that hoore'.[4] She had died as a convicted criminal, and few had mourned her. Even her evangelical clients had had to be careful to dissociate themselves and the cause of the gospel from the disgraced favourite. Latymer had been absent from court circles since the 1530s and was probably unaware how far Anne's virtues were remembered. In addition, Elizabeth would have no memory of her mother, and Latymer may have wished to redeem Anne in her daughter's eyes.

Latymer's purpose of rehabilitating Anne is evident in his treatment of her life. Though he terms his work a 'chronicle' and begins precisely with the date of her acknowledgment as queen, the treatise is not a chronological account but a series of anecdotes. Thus Latymer can be selective in the material he presents, and the picture he draws is determinedly onesided. The Anne Boleyn who emerges from the 'cronickille' is devout, well-read in scripture, generous to the poor and a strict moral censor to her household people. She is never shown enjoying music, dancing, feasting or other courtly pleasures. Far from delighting in the poetry of gentlemen like Sir Thomas Wyatt and her brother George, Lord Rochford, she reproves her maids for wasting time on such licentious fripperies. In short, Latymer obliquely corrects the popular image of Anne as a frivolous, flirtatious hoyden, depicting instead a rather sombre figure of womanly rectitude.

In repairing Anne's reputation Latymer has another instrument besides careful selection of data. This is the subtle denigration of Katherine of Aragon, who had been immensely popular and admired even by those who worked for her divorce and deposition. It might be thought that after the traumatic events of Mary's reign few in England would regard Katherine in a favourable or sympathetic light. In fact, Protestant commentators, though sometimes regretting her popish superstition, continually stress her goodness.[5]

---

4. Ellis, *Original Letters*, 1 ser., ii, 42–5, earl of Derby and Sir Henry Farringdon to Henry VIII, 10 Aug. 1533 (*L & P*, vi, no.964).

5. Wyatt, *Anne Boleigne*, 7.

Katherine's post-Marian reputation is perhaps seen most clearly in the play *Henry VIII*, attributed to Shakespeare. Here Anne Boleyn is a minor and somewhat lifeless figure whose chief function is to be the mother of 'some blessing to this land'. Attention in the play focuses, not on Anne or the king, but on Katherine, depicting her dignity and the pathos of her predicament. Indeed, Dr Johnson commented that, in this play, 'the genius of Shakespeare comes in and goes out with Katherine'.[6]

While Katherine was held in some esteem by the Elizabethan public, Anne Boleyn was largely unknown to it. Thus denigration of the older woman could only add lustre to the younger. Katherine was particularly praised for her piety and charity to the poor, and though Latymer does not mention her by name once, his description of Anne's activities in these spheres silently invites a comparison of the two rivals.

Two incidents in particular are treated by Latymer to show Katherine in an unfavourable light because they concern her particular devotional interests. The story of the Maundy is used to display Anne's munificence and Katherine's meanness, but in fact the Maundy was a practice assiduously used by Katherine. In 1534 she was greatly distressed when the authorities tried to pressure her into acknowledging the divorce by refusing to allow her to hold the ceremony except as princess dowager. She was warned that if she kept the Maundy in the name of queen, 'not oonly she but also ... all suche pore people as shulde receyve her said Maundy shuld encurre to farre in daungier of ... lawes, and of high treason'. Chapuys reported to the emperor that Katherine had been forbidden to hold a Maundy and that the poor had been forbidden to approach her house. Most interestingly, he said that the reason for this was that Anne Boleyn had declared that her almsgiving was the true source of Katherine's popularity.[7]

Similarly, in Latymer's work Anne is shown reforming the pietistic practices of the nuns of Syon. This house was a Bridgettine double-monastery noted for its religious fervour and humanist learning. Katherine often visited it before the divorce, and Syon produced one martyr for papal supremacy, the scholar Richard Reynolds. The rest of the community only submitted to royal authority with reluctance and after a prolonged struggle. Indeed, Ives has shown that Anne's visit probably took place, and that it coincided with a concerted

---

6. Quoted in *The Life of King Henry VIII by William Shakespeare* ed. M.R. Ridley (London and New York, 1962), viii.

7. Ellis, *Original Letters*, 1 ser., ii, 27–8, Fitzwilliam to Cromwell; *Span. Cal.*, v (1), no.40, Chapuys to Charles V.

attempt to secure Syon's obedience.[8] By casting aspersions on the nuns Latymer derogates both Syon and its patron Katherine.

In view of these efforts it is ironic that Latymer's eulogy of Anne is almost identical to Catholic paeans of Katherine. One such work is William Forrest's *History of Grisild the Second*, written in Mary's reign and finished on 25 June 1558 but not published until 1875. It is a long poem in English which characterises Katherine as the patient Griselda of legend whose love and fidelity are repeatedly tested by her husband. Like Latymer's 'cronickille' of Anne Boleyn, Forrest's 'history' was written for the eye of the heroine's daughter.[9] However, there are two differences in the circumstances surrounding Forrest's work. First, whereas Elizabeth was an infant when her mother died, Mary was an adult, and so had her own memories of Katherine. Secondly, Forrest was not a servant or intimate of Katherine, and so his work is less personal than Latymer's record of Anne. Forrest's work is, of course, as selective in its material and biased in its presentation as is Latymer's. Indeed, he praises various aspects of Katherine's virtuous career in terms which are strikingly similar to those used by Latymer for Anne. He stresses her pious reading, charity to the poor (especially women in childbed), patronage of education and devotional life.

So similar are the two accounts that one is tempted to suspect that Latymer had seen Forrest's manuscript and had imitated it in order to depict Anne outshining Katherine in good deeds. At the same time, Anne's interest in religion and charity is well documented, and Latymer's veracity need not be doubted. Certainly, the two works do not present mere stereotypes of a virtuous queen. Ladies were not necessarily expected to be patrons of education, Margaret Beaufort's example notwithstanding. In addition, though women should be generally good to the poor, the systems of relief presented in both works are quite elaborate. Perhaps in reality Anne consciously imitated Katherine; perhaps in literature Latymer imitated Forrest.

The rescue of Anne Boleyn's memory from obloquy is linked with the other purpose of the 'cronickille', that of influencing Elizabeth towards a Protestant policy. Anne could be depicted, not as a disgraced harlot, but as a serious and godly proponent of reform. Latymer's treatise can thus be seen as an answer to Catholic gibes about the unsavoury beginnings of the English Reformation, rooted (as Catholics saw it) in the king's unlawful lust. Thus English Protestantism, espoused and forwarded by the pious Anne, had a respectable pedigree. Consequently the assertion of Anne's goodness is not

8. Ives, *Anne Boleyn* 309–10. For Anne's dealings with Syon, see note 30 to the text, below.

9. William Forrest, *History of Grisild the Second* ed. W.D. Macray (Roxburghe Club, 1875), 3.

meant simply to gratify Elizabeth personally, but to urge her to fulfil her mother's wishes for the English church. Certainly Protestants, having suffered persecution under Henry VIII and Mary, hoped for the building of the new Jerusalem under the auspices of the new queen. At the same time, they were painfully aware that vestiges of popery remained in the church. Elizabeth, Latymer implies, should eradicate these as her mother had begun to do. It is notable that, apart from occasional references to Anne as Henry's humble consort, raised up to glory like Esther and the Virgin Mary, Latymer describes Anne as a reigning monarch rather than a king's mere wife. He calls her a prince and speaks of her reign, acclaiming her as a specimen of that Platonic and Erasmian ideal, the philosopher-king.[10]

Latymer describes Anne's actions in four spheres: regulation of the court and remuneration of servants; protection and promotion of good Protestants; poor relief; and educational patronage. These are meant to suggest lines of policy to Elizabeth. Anne keeps a decorous, moral court and rewards her servants. She promotes good men in the church, compensates Protestants who (like Latymer himself?) have suffered in this world, and offers shelter to religious exiles. She throws down ungodly superstition by reforming the devotions of nuns and attacking relic-worship. She organises a massive programme of poor relief which is systematic, not haphazard and indiscriminate. She is herself generous to the universities and to students, and persuades the religious houses to provide exhibitions and benefices for scholars. (The monasteries had been dissolved in Elizabeth's childhood, but money was still badly needed for educational endowment.) Thus Anne Boleyn is made to serve as a model of a godly prince for her daughter. Indeed, Elizabeth as Anne's heir was duty-bound to complete her policy of reforming the church.

Latymer's veracity

Latymer's portrait of Anne Boleyn is unquestionably partial and subjective. Can his claims for her virtues and godliness be substantiated by independent documentary evidence? A letter of Sir Edward Baynton would seem at first sight to give the lie to Latymer's assertions about Anne, her court and Baynton himself. Writing in June 1533 to George Boleyn, who was absent on embassy in France, he warns him playfully:

> And as for passe tyme in the quenes chamber, [there] was never more. Yf any of you that bee now departed have any ladies that ye thought favoured you and somwhat wold moorne att parting of

10. 'Cronickille', fos 22, 23, 24, 24^v, 26, 26^v, 30^v, 32, 32^v, 33.

their servauntes, I can no whit perceyve the same by their daunsing
and passetyme they do use here, but that other take place, as ever
hath been the custume ... Thus I leve you with these fantasyes.[11]

These allusions to the game of courtly love show that Anne Boleyn's
household did not devote itself singlemindedly to piety or to abstinence
from more worldly pleasures. However, though Latymer's account is
purposely one-sided, there is abundant corroboration of his claims for
Anne in contemporary sources. Detailed references are given in the
notes to the text, and a broad summary is offered here.

In the first place, Anne was associated with a number of books of
an evangelical nature. She is credited with bringing two polemical
works to the king's attention during the divorce, Simon Fish's *Supplicacyon for the beggers* and William Tyndale's *Obedience of a christen man*.
Foxe says that a copy of the former book was sent to Anne, and that
her brother George advised her to show it to Henry. However, Foxe
has another version of the story which credits two merchants and a
royal footman with bringing the book to the king's notice. Ives prefers
the latter version, which can be substantiated from other sources, but
it is possible that Henry learned about Fish's work both from the
Boleyns and from the merchants. The story of Anne's dealings with
Tyndale is much more easily authenticated, as two independent
informants—Anne Gainesford and John Louthe—tell the tale with
slight variations of detail. Anne Boleyn also received the dedications
of two printed books, William Marshall's work on poor relief and
Tristram Revell's translation of Lambertus.[12]

Latymer says that Anne kept a bible open on a desk in her chamber;
it is known that she owned a copy of Tyndale's new testament of 1534.
His statement that she imported manuscript versions of scripture in
French is substantiated by the account of Rose Hickman, a merchant's
daughter, and a psalter in French which was sold in London in 1982
once belonged to Anne. The French books she owned (some of them
rediscovered or elucidated by Ives) offer one of the clearest indications
of her reformist position. Through her books Anne is linked with the
early proponents of reform in France. She owned a copy of Jacques
Lefèvre d'Etaples' French translation of the bible. A kinsman prepared
for her a manuscript volume of the epistles and gospels for the Sundays
in the year, with the texts in Lefèvre's French translation and English
versions of his commentaries on each. Similarly, she owned a manuscript volume of the book of Ecclesiastes, which had a French text

11. PRO, SP1/76, fo.195 (*L & P*, vi, no.613), Baynton to Rochford, 9 June 1533, Greenwich.
12. Foxe, *A & M*, iv, 657–8; Ives, *Anne Boleyn*, 163n; John Strype, *Ecclesiastical Memorials* (2 vols., 1820–40), i, 171–3; J.G. Nichols, *Narratives of the Days of the Reformation* (Camden Soc., 1859), 52–7; Wyatt, *Anne Boleigne*, 16–17.

and an English commentary. Finally, she received the dedication of a manuscript version of Clément Marot's *Sermon du bon pasteur et du maulvais* which has been altered from the published text to include references to Anne and Henry and to the French royal family.

If there are links between Anne Boleyn and French evangelical reformers, there is little to connect her with the more cautious humanist Erasmus. True, her father commissioned from Erasmus a commentary on pslam 23, a treatise on the apostles' creed and a book on preparing for death, but the scholar was under no illusions as to the motive behind this patronage. He told Sadoleto in May 1530 that since his book on matrimony—composed for queen Katherine before the divorce began—had provided many arguments for the indissolubility of the marriage tie, his production of a non-controversial work of piety for the Boleyns would seem to show his impartiality between the parties. Erasmus' cynicism seems justified by the publication of William Marshall's English translation of the work on the creed which was published after Anne's marriage. The treatise was given a propagandist twist by an addition to the preface which made Erasmus address Thomas Boleyn as 'father to the most gratious and vertuous quene Anne'; an embellishment he would never have countenanced.[13]

So Anne is ranked with the evangelical reformers of Lefèvre's type rather than with the more moderate Erasmus. Traditionally, she is pictured at the centre of a circle of brilliant gentlemen-poets who were devoted to the pursuit of courtly love and other frivolous matters. In fact, at least two of Anne's associates displayed evangelical piety as well as skill in composing love poetry. Sir Thomas Wyatt the elder, whose name has always been linked with Anne's in an amorous or scandalous context, shows in his religious verse a scriptural piety similar to her own.[14] Her brother George revealed in his speech from the scaffold a measure of concern with the fate of reformed religion as well as awareness of his own shortcomings as a sinner:

> Men do common and saye that I have bene a settar forth of the worde of God and one that hath favored the Ghospele of Christ; and bycause I would not that God's word shuld be slaundered by me, I say unto you all that yf I had followed God's worde in dede

13. *Opus Epistolarum Des. Erasmi Roterodami* ed. P.S. and H.M. Allen, H.W. Garrod (11 vols., Oxford, 1906–47), no.2315 to Sadoleto, May 1530. The works for Thomas Boleyn are *Enarratio triplex in Psalmum XXII* (Basle, 1530), *De praeparatione ad mortem* (Basle, 1534); and *Dilucida et pia Explanatio Symboli quod apostolorum dicitur* (Basle, 1533), trans. as *The Playne and godly expozytion of the commune crede* (1534).

14. Cf. *Thomas Wyatt, Collected Poems* ed. Joost Daalder (Oxford, 1975), 7, 90, 113–41.

as I dyd rede it and set it forth to my power, I had not come to
this.[15]

Latymer may be assumed to speak with authority on the subject of
Anne's chaplains, who included Hugh Latimer, Nicholas Shaxton,
Matthew Parker, John Skip and William Betts. It is noteworthy that
Anne took only evangelicals into her service. One incident which
Latymer does not record illustrates the chaplains' role in the disposal
of her patronage. In September 1535 John Cheke, fellow of St John's,
Cambridge and protégé of Dr Butts, asked Parker to intercede with
Anne for William Bill, a scholar of his college too poor to take up a
fellowship. Cheke praised Anne's generosity to students, saying that
it was known that it was sufficient for them to be recommended by
Parker, Skip or one of the other chaplains. His petition was successful,
and it is interesting that Bill was later Elizabeth's almoner and dean
of Westminster.[16]

Anne's concern for foreign refugees, which Latymer describes in
detail, is mentioned by Thomas Alwaye, an English evangelical pros-
ecuted by the bishops who petitioned her in 1530 or 1531. Though
there is no evidence to link her with Sturmius or with a Frenchwoman
named 'Marye', Nicolas Bourbon's *Nugae* of 1538 is replete with
allusions to Anne's mediation for him in France and generosity to him
in England.

Finally, a word must be said about Sir Edward Baynton and Dr
William Butts, and the part they played in the operations of patronage.
Both men were sponsors of the middle sort, more important for
connecting their clients with greater patrons than for the amount of
preferment at their own disposal. Both had Henry VIII's favour
before the rise of Anne Boleyn; Baynton was a Wiltshire magnate,
Butts a royal physician. Their achievement was to bring men like
Hugh Latimer to the king's attention, and to look after their interests
once they had gained Henry's notice. The success of the Protestant
Reformation depended to some extent on the survival and sustained
activity of such middlemen, so that despite the loss of major patrons
like Anne and Cromwell evangelical clergy could continue and
regroup under new patronage. Baynton was chamberlain to Anne's
four successors. Butts, the protector of Cambridge as well as of
reformed religion, lived until 1545. The religious importance of both
men is revealed by a letter of Hooper to Bullinger of January 1546
which numbers them among those courtiers who had been 'real

15. *Chronicle of Calais*, quoted in Edmond Bapst, *Deux Gentilshommes-Poetes de la Cour
de Henry VIII* (Paris, 1891), 27. Cf. the almost identical account in Bibliotheque
Nationale, Fonds Dupuy 373, fo.111ᵛ, quoted ibid., 137.

16. Parker, *Correspondence*, no.3. For Anne's chaplains see note 12 to the text, for her
patronage of education, notes 24–26.

favourers of the gospel, and promoted the glory of God to the utmost of their power'.[17]

Other early biographies and notices of Anne Boleyn

The sole surviving contemporary biography of Anne Boleyn is, curiously enough, the only early account of her which is free from religious bias; all the others are either Protestant eulogies or Catholic attacks on her morals. These early assessments of Anne will be examined here in order to estimate the value of Latymer's work and its place in historiography.

The earliest biography of Anne was finished in London on 2 June 1536. It was written in French verse by Lancelot de Carles, bishop of Riez. He was on embassy to England as secretary to the bishop of Tarbes, and he speaks from first-hand knowledge of Anne's early life in France, and of the events surrounding her fall. The work exists in several manuscripts; the one used here is in the Bibliothèque Albert I in Brussels. There is another in the British Library, London, while Crapelet printed a version taken from three manuscripts in Paris. The poem was first published at Lyons in 1545, and was edited by Georges Ascoli in *La Grande-Bretagne Devant L'Opinion Française* (1927).

The work contains a wealth of factual information. Carles states that Anne went to France in the train of Mary Tudor, Henry VIII's sister, and that on Mary's return to England she entered the service of queen Claude. He says that the birth of Elizabeth was very painful for Anne, that the child looked more like her father than her mother, and that the marchioness of Exeter—a great friend of Katherine of Aragon—became her godmother only reluctantly and out of fear of displeasing the king. He mentions Henry's accident of January 1536, news of which triggered Anne's miscarriage. He describes Edward Seymour's fraternal advice to Jane on how to deal with the king's advances. He gives an account of the fateful tournament at Greenwich on 1 May 1536, of Anne's dignified bearing at her trial, of Rochford's denial of the charge of incest, and of the scaffold speeches of brother and sister. As the record of an informed observer, Carles' work is invaluable.

It is also useful because its view of events is detached. Carles seeks to pass no judgment on Anne; rather, he depicts her as the victim of hubris and of the wheel of fortune. Anne, he says, was basically good and virtuous, but ambition turned her head; as the wheel revolved she reached the height of triumph, only to be flung down again. Like

17. *Original Letters Relative to the English Reformation* ed. Hastings Robinson (Parker Soc., Cambridge, 1846), 33ff. For Butts, the patronage system and its relation to the Reformation, Maria Dowling, 'Anne Boleyn and Reform,' *Journal of Ecclesiastical History* vol. 35 (1) (Jan. 1984). For Baynton, see note 7 to the text.

Baynton, and in contrast to Latymer, he shows her presiding over a
court of pleasure and love:

> Dances et jeux de divers appareil
> Chassis et bois de plaisir nonpareil
> Exercitoient seigneurs et damoiselles
> Plusiers tournois, sentreprenouent pour elles...

Carles speaks of Anne's indiscretion, but does not say directly that she
was guilty of adultery. However, she did enjoy the game of courtly
love, and played it dangerously:

> Et ce pendant la royne flousoit
> En son vouloir en tout accomplissoit
> Ayant loisir, moyen et liberte
> A son souhayt prendre sa volupte
> Elle pouuoit aller en toute part,
> En campaignie ou bien seulle a lescart
> Ou selle estoit par fortune saisie
> de quelque amour de personne choisie,
> Il loy estoit entierement permis.
> A son plaisir traitter ses amys
> Par le moyen de la grande licence
> Que luy donnoit la publicque defence
> Que nul nosat sur paine de martire
> Aucunement de la royne mesdire.[18]

Carles makes no mention of Anne's evangelical piety, but it must
be remembered that he was an outsider to her household. Many of
the books read there were illegal or dangerous in their theology;
Wolsey had hoped to convict Anne of heresy by confiscating her copy
of *The obedience of a christen man* and showing it to the king. Probably
much of the religious activity of her household was not known to those
outside the court.

Latymer's 'cronickille' is complemented to some extent by an
account of Anne's fall and death by the Scots reformer Alexander
Alesius. This occurs in a long letter to Elizabeth written at Leipzig in
1559.[19] Alesius resembles Latymer in being a witness of some of the
events he recounts and in composing his work after a lapse of years.
Unlike Latymer, Alesius never received preferment or employment
from Anne; thus, he claims objectivity for his statement.

---

18. Bibliothèque Albert I, MS 19378, 'Traictie pour feue dame Anne de Boulant,
Jadis Royne Dengleterre,' fos 3, 5–5ᵛ. First published as *Epistre contenant le proces criminel
faict a lencontre de la Royne Anne Boullant* (Lyons, 1545); reprinted in *Lettres de Henri VIII
a Anne Boleyn* ed. G.-A. Crapelet (Paris, 1835).

19. PRO, SP70/7, fos 1–11, Alesius to Elizabeth, 1 Sept. 1559 (*CSP For.*, no.1303).

Alesius congratulates Elizabeth on her accession and also hints at financial remuneration. His motives in writing, then, are not entirely free from self-interest, but nor, perhaps, were Latymer's. His account is also coloured by malice towards Cromwell, who had not fulfilled promises of patronage. It also has a supernatural element; Alesius had been inspired to write by a vision of Anne's severed neck which came to him on the morning of her execution. Despite all this, his statement is useful for what it says about Anne's evangelical reputation, and about the motives of those who destroyed her.

According to Alesius, Anne fell from favour because the king wanted a new wife and a male heir, but also because the enemies of reform were alarmed and outraged by her instigation of the sending of an embassy to the German Lutheran princes. Gardiner sent Wriothesley a letter from France reporting rumours that Anne was accused of adultery. Wriothesley passed this letter to Cromwell who, like himself and others, hated Anne because she threatened to tell the king that they were using reformed religion as a cloak for their own corrupt financial dealings. These enemies of Anne were appointed by Henry to investigate the matter. Her servants were bribed, and the facts that she danced with gentlemen of the king's privy chamber and informed her brother by letter that she was pregnant were taken as proofs of her guilt. Alesius himself saw Anne pleading with the king, the infant Elizabeth in her arms, at a window in Greenwich palace. He could not bring himself to attend her trial and execution, but he cites the evidence of eye-witnesses as to her silent fortitude at her trial and innocent and dignified bearing on the scaffold.

Alesius parallels Latymer in his description of Anne's religious activities. She promoted godly bishops, among them Cranmer and Hugh Latimer. He describes the grief of evangelicals at her death and their fears that a change in religion would result. He stresses Anne's significance in the history of reform: 'True religion in England had its commencement and its end with your mother.' Like Latymer, Alesius hoped that filial piety would incline Elizabeth to Protestant policies.

Naturally enough, Anne Boleyn was hated by religious conservatives as the direct cause of the breach with Rome. As the Reformation progressed she became the target of vicious Catholic polemic. The Carthusian martyrologist Maurice Chauncy made play with her surname, identifying her with Bellona, goddess of war because she brought religious strife to England.[20] Other writers like Nicholas

---

20. '*circa miseram mulierem Annam quandam cognomento Bolleynam (quam Bellonam, hoc est deam belli, non abs re nuncupare poterimus, gravissimi namque illius mox subsecuti ecclesiastici belli ipsa principium fuit et causa)*'. Maurice Chauncy, *The Passion and Martyrdom of the Holy English Carthusian Fathers* ed. G.W.S. Curtis (1935), 48, 49.

Sander and Nicholas Harpsfield concentrated less on her Lutheran leanings than on her immorality; not only was she the wanton who made the king dissolve his true marriage, but her own union with Henry was adulterous. Consequently her character and conduct were depicted in salacious and scabrous terms.[21] This genre of fantastic writing is typified by a manuscript account now deposited in the Berkshire Record Office. '*La Vie de Anne Boulein ou de Bouloigne mere de Elizabeth Royne Dangleterre*' is an attempt to discredit Elizabeth through Anne, and according to an endorsement was either written by Sander or used by him in his *Anglican Schism*.[22]

The tone of this account is prurient, its whole focus is on the sexual misdeeds of Anne, her mother and sister, and Henry VIII. Anne was the daughter of Thomas Boleyn's wife; her father was the king, who also seduced her sister Mary. Anne herself, besides being proud and arrogant, was lustful; at the age of thirteen she was willingly deflowered by her father's butler and one of his chaplains. Sent to France after this incident, she became a byword for immorality, numbering Francis I among her many lovers. On her return to England she captivated Henry, but kept him at a distance by pretending that she was saving her virginity for her future husband. This drove the king to divorce proceedings. So infatuated was he that he ignored Thomas Boleyn's warning that Anne was his own child, and Sir Thomas Wyatt's confession that she was his lover.

Sin does not go unpunished, however, and Anne paid the price for her disgusting way of life. The king grew tired of her, and when she saw him with his latest paramour on his knee she miscarried. Despairing of a son by Henry, she resorted to adultery, and thought the wicked deed would be better hidden if it were committed with her brother. In addition, her inordinate pride made her wish that the offspring of two Boleyns would inherit the throne. However, her lascivious nature made her also give herself to three gentlemen (Norris, Brereton and Weston) and to a mere musician, Marc. All six were executed for their hideous crimes.

This type of literature, which reduces her to a specimen of sexual depravity, grossly distorts Anne's character: the Imperial ambassador to Henry's court had called her 'la Messaline ou Agrippine angloyse'.[23] The lurid accounts of her misconduct are as partial and incomplete

21. Catholic views of Anne are in Nicholas Harpsfield, *Treatise on the Pretended Divorce between Henry VIII and Catharine of Aragon* ed. Nicholas Pocock (Camden Soc., 1878); Nicolas Sander, *Rise and Growth of the Anglican Schism* ed. and trans. David Lewis (1877); Henry Clifford, *Life of Jane Dormer, Duchess of Feria* ed. Joseph Stevenson (1887).

22. Trumble MS 5. I am grateful to Mr J.A.S. Green, County Archivist of Berkshire, for information about this manuscript, and to Ms Joanna Mattingley and Dr Thomas Cogswell for drawing my attention to it.

23. *Span. Cal.*, v (2), 120, Chapuys to Granvelle, 18 May 1536.

as the Protestant biographies, and both types of treatise ignore an important aspect of Anne's personality and career: her skill, nerve and ruthlessness as a politician.

The animadversions of Sander were answered by George Wyatt, who was anxious to clear the names of Anne and his grandfather, her alleged lover, and who was encouraged in his work by Matthew Parker. Wyatt covers much of the same ground as Latymer, speaking of Anne's piety, her chaplains, her interest in godly books, her patronage of education and her goodness to the poor. Like Latymer, Wyatt shows Anne as a beneficent influence on Henry VIII: 'Her mind brought him fourth the ritch treasurs of love of pietie, love of truith, love of learninge'.[24] Unlike Latymer, who avoids discussion of Anne's life before 1533 by tactfully commencing his account with her proclamation as queen, Wyatt is at pains to stress her chastity before marriage. Naturally she was never Henry's mistress. As for her alleged affair with Sir Thomas Wyatt, it was true that the poet greatly admired her, but as he was a married man and she a pure maid no scandal could touch their relationship. Wyatt could not speak from first-hand knowledge, but he was careful to draw on credible witnesses: a waiting-woman of Anne's who was undoubtedly Anne Gainesford; and an ancestor of his own, who was probably Margaret, lady Lee, sister of Sir Thomas Wyatt.

Latymer's and Wyatt's works are the only sympathetic accounts devoted exclusively to Anne, but she received honourable mention from other Protestant authors. Foxe, Burnet and Strype refer to her goodness and good works in their lengthy histories of the Reformation. Foxe wrote during Elizabeth's reign, Burnet and Strype much later. Yet within a few years of her death Anne was already being cited as a promoter of reformed religion. In 1541 Richard Hilles in a letter to Bullinger mourned the loss of those who had favoured the evangelical cause: 'And here I mean queen Anne, who was beheaded, together with her brother; also the lord Cromwell...'. A Protestant tract on communion written in Mary's reign has a papist taunting one of the godly with the disgraceful deaths of his leaders: 'Did not ... all the chiefe autors of your religion come to an ill ende? recken Anne Boleyne, Cromwel, the duke of Somerset, the duke of Northumberland, and the duke of Suffolke'.[25]

As might be expected, Anne figures in John Aylmer's defence of women rulers of 1559, *An Harborowe for faithfull and Trewe Subjectes*. This is a mild-mannered and reasonable answer to John Knox's *Monstrous*

24. Wyatt, *Anne Boleigne*, 16.

25. *Original Letters* (Parker Soc.), 203–4; Gracyouse Menewe (pseud.), *A confutacion of that popishe and antichristian doctrine* (1555?). I am grateful to Ms Joy Shakespeare for both these references.

Regiment. Aylmer agrees that women are weak, but argues that God often works through such people; David who slew Goliath, Judith who killed Holofernes, and Jeanne d'Arc who drove the English from Orleans.[26] Thus the English Reformation was precipitated, not by men, but by one woman:

> Was not quene Anne, the mother of this blessed woman [Elizabeth], the chief, first, and only cause of banyshing the beast of Rome, with all his beggerly baggage? Was there ever in Englande a greater feate wrought by any man then this was by a woman? I take not from kyng Henry the due praise of broching it, nor from that lambe of God king Edward, the finishing and perfighting of that was begon, though I give hir hir due commendacion. I know that that blessid martir of God Thomas Cranmer byshop of Canterbury, did much travaile in it, and furthered it: but if God had not gyven quene Anne favour in the sight of the kynge, as he gave to Hester in the sight of Nabucadnezar [sic]; Haman and his company, the cardinall, Wynchester, More, Roches[ter] and other wold sone have trised up Mardocheus with al the rest that leaned to that side. Wherfore though many deserved muche praise for the helping forwarde of it: yet the croppe and roote was the quene, which God had endewed with wisdome that she coulde, and gyven hir the minde that she would do it.

In a surprising passage Aylmer praises Katherine of Aragon as well as Anne and Elizabeth, and unequivocally links these last two as promoters of the Reformation:

> Who killed the Scottish king, when Henry .8. was in Fraunce? A woman, or at the least her army. Who brought in the light of Gods worde into Englande? A woman. Who lighteth now again the candle after it was put oute? A woman.

Thus for Aylmer Anne is not simply a good Protestant prince, as in Latymer's work, but the direct cause of the downfall of papal authority in England.

Anne Boleyn's rise to greatness and—more especially—her ignominious death created problems for Protestant panegyrists. John Bridges alludes to Anne in his *Supremacie of Christian Princes*, written against Sander and Stapleton and published in 1573. Far from passing over her fall (unlike other writers), he claims her death as a martyrdom which had furthered the Protestant cause:

---

26. Aylmer, *An Harborowe*, sigs. B ii', F iv, B v, l iii.

As for his [Henry's] firste true and lawfull wife [Anne], we maye saye indeede he had misfortune in hir too, that he so muche credited the sclanderous undermining papists, that never stinted to procure hir death, for the hatred of the gospel that she professed. And so at length most subtilly wrought it, and made hir a sweet sacrifice to God and a most holy martyr. No misfortune, but moste happie hap to hir, to sustaine so sclaunderous a death, in so innocent a cause; the misfortune was the king hir husbandes, to be so beguiled by such false papistes. And yet to us, this maryage was most fortunate, which God so blessed with such a fruit, as never the like did spring in Englande.[27]

Obviously, the Elizabethan accounts of Anne Boleyn should be treated with some reserve; Bridges' work was dedicated to the queen, and Aylmer's was a defence of her accession to and tenure of the throne. None the less, it is significant that they chose to speak openly of Anne as one who had favoured Protestantism when, given the circumstances of her death, it might have been more politic to pass her over in silence. After all Elizabeth, unlike Mary with Katherine of Aragon, made no attempt to reinstate or rehabilitate Anne, and indeed, seldom spoke of her at all.

The value of Latymer's account

Latymer's 'cronickille', then, has many shortcomings as a historical source for the reign of Henry VIII. It was written for the eye of Anne Boleyn's daughter, and probably in the hope of preferment and reward. It is a subjective study, and deliberately suppresses all material relating to Anne which is not consistent with Latymer's portrait of a pious and solemn reformer. The author's aims of rehabilitating Anne and advising Elizabeth lead him to wander somewhat from the truth on occasion. His anxiety not to offend persons still living nor to cast aspersions on the character of Henry VIII makes him disingenuous in passing over the events of the divorce and of Anne's fall. In addition, and probably through confusion of memory rather than deliberate distortion, he sometimes telescopes events in order to show Anne acting as a wise and Protestant prince.

All these are deserved criticisms, but they are outweighed by the immense importance of Latymer's treatise. It is an eyewitness account of Anne Boleyn by one who knew and served her, and though

27. Bridges, *Supremacie*, 852–3. I am grateful for this reference to Dr Peter Lake. Sander describes the tribulations of Katherine of Aragon as a sacrifice: 'Can any one be astonished that so saintly a woman was to be tried in a greater fire of tribulation, so that the fragrance of her goodness might be the more scattered over the Christian world?' *Anglican Schism*, 8. Cf. Clifford, *Jane Dormer*, 74.

undoubtedly subjective it thus speaks with more authority than, say, Wyatt's or Carles' biographies. It shows that Anne was regarded as a reformer by her own servants and associates, and that in both her private life and public policy she was a fervent and committed evangelical. Furthermore, much of what Latymer claims for Anne can be substantiated by independent evidence. There is ample documentation of the work of her chaplains and her promotion of evangelicals in the church; of her patronage of scholars; and of the activities of Baynton and Butts. Indeed, as a contribution to the Elizabethan version of the Henrician Reformation the treatise carries more weight than even Foxe's monumental work precisely because it was written by one who had first-hand knowledge of events and personalities.

Finally, Latymer's treatise is significant as one of several attempts to influence Elizabeth towards a Protestant policy. As Alesius' letter shows, it was by no means certain in 1559 that the young queen would commit herself to the Protestant cause. She had been circumspect about religion during the previous reigns. Moreover, she would have no memory of the mother whom Protestants regarded as the chief cause and promoter of the Reformation in England. Perhaps it was hoped that Latymer's work would have particular influence with Elizabeth because he could give her first-hand information about Anne's motives, actions and plans. Thus Anne Boleyn was rehabilitated by Latymer both to give a respectable ancestry to the Elizabethan church and to exhort her daughter to carry on the work of reformation which Anne had initiated.

EDITORIAL PROCEDURE

In editing the manuscript it has been thought necessary to make some alterations to Latymer's text. Punctuation has been modernised, and the modern usage of i and j, u and v, has been adopted. All standard abbreviations have been expanded, and capital letters have been standardised and kept to a minimum. Words or parts of words missing because of damage to the document have been restored and placed in square brackets. Because the interlineations and scorings-out often distort the meaning of Latymer's prose (where, for example, carets have been placed carelessly before the wrong word), words and phrases have been printed in the order which seems most correct grammatically. Where the sense is extremely confused, or where a significant or ambiguous alteration has been made, a footnote has been appended. Latymer's marginal headings, which add nothing to the text, have been omitted. In the Introduction and notes traditional spellings of the names of people and places have been used. However, Latymer's name is spelt throughout as he himself signed it. This is to avoid confusion with Hugh Latimer, who was also a chaplain of Anne Boleyn and who occurs frequently in the treatise and in the notes to the text.

WILLIAM LATYMER'S CHRONICKLLE
OF ANNE BULLEYNE

[*fo.21*] To the right highe, myghtye and moste excellente princesse Elizabeth, by the grace of God quene of Englande, Fraunce and Irelande, Defendor of the Faith, etc.

When I considered with my selve (moste mightie and moste excellente princesse, and my moste gracious sovereigne) the manyfolde gyftes of nature and vertuous qualiteis which sett forth and magnifie your royall name, I coulde not but remembre the excellente vertues, and princelye qualities wherewith your majesties dearest mother, the moste gracious ladye, quene Anne, was adornid and beautifyed in the tyme of his majesties noble regne. And that the same might not be utterly forgotton, but be commended to ymmortall memory, I have according to my bounden dutie gathered to gether in one litill volume, not only so many of them as I my selfe (being then one of hir highnes moste humble orators and ordinarie chappellaynes) did heare, see and certaynly know; but also of all suche as I coulde atteyne to the knowledge of, by the credible reporte of some being now in honour whoo did attende her highnes in dyverse kyndes of service, and of some whoo were then in like order of service as I was; and now moste obediently do presente the same unto your majestie, being compiled in this smale treatyse, rudely and playnly but symplie and truly (as the basenes of my low stile wolde permitt). I thought I coulde not accomplishe the duetie of an humble subjecte and of a faithfull and obediente servaunte bettre then yf I did exhibite the same to your highnes. [*fo.21v*] Wherein your majestie as in a myrror or glasse might beholde the moste godly and princely ornamentes of your moste gracious and naturall mother; not a litill to your highnes comforte, and to the aluringe of others by like example to embrace vertue, charite, equytee and godlynes; to acknowlege theire humblenes in the higheste estate, to advaunce goddes eternall glorie; to relyve the pour nedye, to suppresse wickidnes and vice; and fynally to mayntayne Christes true, pure and syncere religion, to the honour of your crowne, to the comforte of your moste humble subjectes, and to the enlarging of your realme. And now most humbly I crave of pardon for my boldnes and I do desire that this my simple labour and travell herin taken may be acciptid in good worthe, as the meaning of my endevour haith byne. And I acknowleging my moste bounden dutie shall ever mor wishe to your majestie longe lyfe and moste prosperous reigne.

> your majesties moste faithfull subjecte
> and obediente orator
> William Latymer.

[*fo.22*] A briefe treatise or cronickille of the moste vertuous ladye Anne Bulleyne late quene of Englande.

The moste gracious and vertuous ladie Anne Bulleyn, marques of Pembroke,[1] late wyef to the renowmed king Henrye of most famous memorye, the eight of that name, was proclaymed quene of Englande the xijth daye of Aprill in the yeare of Our Lorde God 1533 and the xxiiijthe yeare of his moste victorious reigne. On Whitsondaye following, being the laste daye of Maye, with greate tryumphe was solemplye and roially crowned at Westmynster, to the greate admiracion of the beholders, and worderfull comforte of the realme.[2]

Whoo in the begynning and verie entrie of her gracious reigne, callinge to remembraunce the princely estate whereunto yt had pleased God to advaunce her highnes, did not (as the moste parte of our age being raysed to the tippe of honour) forgett the loving kyndnes of almightie God, to whose only providence she did contynually attribute her royall estate; ne yet neglecte the honourable and moste faithfull affection of her sovereigne, whoo of an humble hand mayden chose her to be his wyef quene.[3] But in moste godly wyse and princely

1. Anne Boleyn was created marquess (nor marchioness) of Pembroke on 1 Sept. 1532; *L & P* v, nos. 1274, 1370 (1), (2), (3).

2. Anne was crowned on Sunday 1 June 1533; *L & P*, vi, nos. 563, 601. Accounts of the lavish ceremony which greeted her on her journey from the Tower to Westminster are in Edward Hall, *Chronicle* (1809), 798–803; *Miscellaneous Writings and Letters of Thomas Cranmer* ed. J.E. Cox (Parker Soc., Cambridge, 1846), 244–7. The Imperial ambassador Chapuys, on the other hand, was scornful about the cold reception Anne received and mentioned the popular indignation at her coronation; *L & P*, vi, no. 653, *Span. Cal.*, iv (2), no. 1081; cf. *L & P* vi, no. 585. In Sept. Chapuys reported that Elizabeth's christening 'has been like her mother's coronation, very cold and disagreeable both to the court and to the city'; *L & P* vi, no. 1125, *Span. Cal.*, iv (2), no. 1127. Obviously Chapuys was a partisan of queen Katherine, but even accounts favourable to Anne make no mention of demonstrations of pleasure or loyalty. Cf. *Calendar of State Papers, Venetian*, ed. Rawdon Brown *et al* (9 vols., 1864–97), iv, 418–19.

3. Anne's speech here echoes both the old testament queen Esther (Esther 2: 1–4, 17) and the *Magnificat* of the Virgin (Luke 1: 46–55). Cf. the suppositional letter from Anne to Henry VIII, printed in Gilbert Burnet, *History of the Reformation of the Church of England*, ed. Nicholas Pocock (7 vols., Oxford, 1865, iv, 291).

maner (esteming godlynes and integritie of lyfe to be the chefe and only ornamentes of a princesse) beganne ymediatly after her royall coronacion to converte her whole thought, ymaginaci[on] [*fo.22v*] and indevour to the godly order, rule and goverment of suche as was committed to attende her highnes in all her affayers. And therfor calling her councell and other officers in her highnes courte before her, entred in to talke with them to this effecte:

There is greate cause why I shoulde yelde moste heartie thankes to almighty God, for that it haith pleased hym of his bountifull clemencie and only goodnes to call me to this high and roiall estate. It standeth also with good reason that I shoulde moste humbly acknowlege my obedientt dutie to my soveraigne, whoo emongest all the reste of his ladies haith vowschesaved to accepte me as moste worthy to injoye his moste gracious personage. So nowe with this, to see my courte garnisshed with such grave and sage councellars, with such faythfull and experte officers (as you seme and are comendid to be) do replenish my hearte with passing joye. For to atteyne to high estate and glorious government from a meane degree is a mattre that may move wonderfull affections in a naturall persone, as I am; to beare also the titill and name of a prince may seme a glorious vaunte; to have the courte like wyse furnisshed with an innumerable multitude of servauntes increaseth in the beholders opynion a good successe. But to have the courte and the estate beautyfyed with the goodly garnishmentes of vertue, to performe the due office of a vertuous princes, and finally to rule and govern the multitude (whiche [*fo.23*] commonly refusethe to be maystred) is a praysworthye endevour. Truly the prince is bounde to kepe his awne persone pure and undefyled, his house and courte so well ruled that all that see it may have desyre to follow and do therafter, and all that heare therof may desire to see it. I dought not but as you are wyse, so you know my meaning. That is to saye, that as I have attayned unto this highe place nexte unto my sovereigne, so I might in all godlynes goodnes duely administre the same.[4] You are commended to be men of great honestye, modestye, wysedome and experience, such as wholy embrace vertue and utterly deteste and abhorre vice. Sethens therfor you are accompted to be menn of good name and fame, yt shalbe come you to declare the proof therof by your vertuous conversacion and governemente. Wherfor furste I do commende to your wysedoms all and singular my worldly affaires; nexte I do yelde wholy to your charge the governemente of my courte; lastelye you muste take upon youe the rule and over sight of my

4. The manuscript has been altered here by the author or his clerk and stands in the original thus: 'so I might in ~~the~~ all godlynes goodnes ~~so~~ ᵒᶠ ~~all godlynes~~ duely administre the same.' This is one of the rare passages where Anne speaks as a consort rather than a reigning prince.

inferiour officers and housholde servauntes. Wherin I requyre you (as you tendre our pleasure) to take esspeciall regarde, and to omitt nothing that may seeme to apperteinge to my honour; to employe your whole studyes to furder the same, so it be done without prejudice of any other persone; to ministre equytie and justice to all men, but in especially to tendre the pitifull cases and causes of the poore suters; and in my courte generally to use suche mediocritie that, neyther sparely pynchinge, nor prodigall consuming, may restrayne you from the golden meane of frugall expending. And yf any surplusage shall [*fo.23v*] be fownde at any tyme, let it be bestowid upon the poore, to whome I wyshe no reasonable distribucion to be denyed. My servauntes see that you governe in suche wyse that their quiet and godly lyvinge may be a spectacle to others, exhorte them to feare God, cause them dayly to heare the devine service. Suffer noo contencion emonges them, admitt noo brawling altercacions nor sedicious quarrels.[5] And above all other be very circumspecte that they frequente noo ynfamous places of resorte ne yet that they keape noo companye with evill, lewde and ungodly disposed brothels, that in all thinges they shew them selfes decent, civill and serviceable. And yf you shall fynde any persone of what estate or degree so ever he be, eyther wilfully reclayming at your wholesome councell, or negligently not admitting your godly and civill orders, or after twoo or three gentill admonicions obstinately persevering in unseemelie and licencious behavour, I commaunde you to correcte them presently to the example of others. Or yf they shalbe fownde voyde of grace, and with out hope of recovery, you shall banyshe and quitt expell them my courte, never to be admitted again within the precinctes of the same, to their utter shame, open shew of all the worlde, and to the fearefull terrour of all other their likes. For in this wyse you shall preserve my courte inviolate, and garde it from the obloquie of the envyous, and approve your selves to exceade in deedes the reporte of others wordes, to the greate contentacion of my mynde, and wonderfull commendacions of my honour. With this kynde of comendacion and of communicacion or the like her highnes did ende her exhortacion to her councellars and high officers; as it was very oftentymes [*fo.24*] reported by the lorde Borough, then lorde chamberlayne, Sir James Bulleyne, her majesties chauncelar, Sir Edwarde Baynton her vizchamberlayne, and Mr Udall hir secretary.[6]

5. Though strictly forbidden, brawling did take place at Henry VIII's court. The penalty was loss of a hand. Cf. Lacey Baldwin Smith, *Henry VIII: the Mask of Royalty* (1973), 280.
6. Biographies of Baynton, James Boleyn and Borough are in *The House of Commons, 1509–1558*, ed. S.T. Bindoff (1982). 'The lorde Borough' was Thomas, third baron Burgh or Borough of Gainsborough.

When her majestie hadd thus advertised her counseill and other her officers, the nexte daye ensuinge she commaunded her chappellayns to come before her presence, and used the like exhortacions to them as hereafter:

I have thought at this presente to cause you my chapellayns to be called before me that, as I have carefully chosyn you to be the lanterns and light of my courte, so you might be throughly advertised of my determinacion towchinge the same. Wherein, as you tender our pleasure, wee straightly charge you and every one of you to performe and accomplishe the good opynion I have conceived of you. You know the roiall estate of prynces, for the excellencie thereof doth farre passe and excell all other estates and degrees of lyfe, which dothe represente and outwardely shadow unto us the glorious and celestiall monarchee which God the governour of all thinges doth exercise in the firmamente. You knowe also that princes be the veray fontayns and well sprinnges of whome all other inferiour magistrates receive theire autoritee, of whome lawes have their force and might, of whome the whole bodye of the realme taketh example, whoo as in a theatre or open stage playe the chefe partes, to the admiracion of the inferior subjectes and multitude. And wee our selves are not altogether ignorante of the necessarye charge requyred in so high a personage; not founde wantones, not pampered pleasurs, not licencious libertie or tryfling ydilnes, but vertuous demeanour, godly conversacion, sobre communicacion and integritie of lyf. Regarde well therefore, [fo.24v] and forgett not that for the speciall truste I have reposed in you, I have chosen you the guydes and patterns of the good maners of my courte, by whose vertuous conversacion and syncire doctryn the same may the bettre be trayned, ordered and governed. And for that I am persuaded that of the good lyfe of the prince dependeth the good lyves of subjectes, and consequently their evill lyves the evil disposicion of the same; I requyre you, as you shall at any tyme herafter perceave me to declyne from the right path of sownde and pure doctryne, and yelde to any maner of sensualitie, to awayte some conveniente tyme wherin you may advertise me therof; the which I promise you to accepte in very thankfull parte, addressing my selfe wholy to reformacion and yelding good example to others, for the discharge of myne awne conscience. And as to rest of my courte, I straightly charge you vigilantly to wache their doinges, curiouslye to marke their procedinges, lyves and conversaciones; diligently to advertise them of their dutyes, esspecially towarde almightie God, to instruct them the waye to vertue and grace, to charge them to abandone and eschue all maner of vice; and a bove all thinges to embrase the wholesome doctryne and infallible knowlege of Cristes gospell, aswell in vertuous and undefiled conversacion as also in pure and syncerite understanding therof. Wherin you that be assigned to be their pastors in religion shall profytt very moche yf you yelde your lyves correspondent and agreable to your doctryne syncere preaching and that your pure conversacion may allure them to godlynes, and that they maye deme you by the example of your lyves, preaching and to be the very fountayns from whence the vertuous of all godlynes[7] streames do flowe. I assure you (my chappellayns) you shall profitt more in one daye with good examples then in a yeare with manye lessons; yet they are veray necessary. My servantes [*fo.25*] seing you to drawe to vertuous love will ensew the same; yf they see you studye, they will not be ydill; yf they see you peaceable, they will be at reste; yf they see you temperate, they will not be overcharged; yf they note shamefastnes in you, they will also be modeste; and surely yf you do contrary to godlynes, they will do the same. I will saye noo more, but that my whole care, desire and cheife peticione of God is that my courte may be nourterid by you in soche wyse as they may persever in the feare of God, delight in the true knowlege of his worde, ensewe the vertuous of our predecessors, embrase the quyet calme of their teachers, and fynally encrease in all vertue and godlynes. To the accomplishment wherof I proteste to God (in whose bosome I truste ones to reste) I will spare noo daye, noo hower, noo traville.

And concerninge myn ordynary and extraordynarie almes, the distributing wherof I have committed to you that be myne almners, and in your absence to you my chappelleynes, my pleasure is: that you all take esspeciall regarde in the choise of suche poore peopell as shalbe fownde moste nedye; not vagarante and lasie beggers, whoo in every place besides are releved abundantly, but poore nedie and impotente house holders over charged with children, not havinge any sustenance, comforte or relyve other wyse; and to such I commaunde mynne almes liberally. In like maner yf you assuridly perceive any poore men or women having cause of sute eyther to me or my counceill to be delayde from theire answere, whereby they suffre losse of tyme and goodes, to their greate hynderaunce, I commande you to open the mattre to my counseill and other officers to whome suche cases it shall apperteyne. And yet yf such poore suiters upon your significacion be deferred of their answers, then I charge you to make me [*fo.25v*]

---

7. The manuscript here has been greatly altered, and the original reads thus: 'wherein you that be assigned to be their pastors in religion: shall profytt very moche yf you yelde your lyves correspondent and agreable to your doctryne/syncere preaching and

that your pure conversacion. may allure them. to godlynes. and that they maye deme you by the example of your lyves. preaching and to be

the very fountayns from whence the vertuous $\genfrac{}{}{0pt}{}{\text{of all godlynes}}{\text{streames do flowe}}$'.

prevye therof, and I (quod she) shall with speade provide remedye
for the same. You have now hearde theffecte of your charge, you
know what I requyre to be perfourmed in your behalfe. Now yf
you faythfully applie your willing endevoures to further my wysshed
dessiars, you shall assure your selves of me to be a contynuall
patronesse to all your reasonable requestes. When hir majestie hadd
fynisshed her talk she dismissed[8] them, whoo according to her highnes
commaundemente, remembringe the carefull charge committed unto
them, they pratized from tyme to tyme and put in ure her graces
beheaste and commandement, noting therfore diligently the maners
of such as were in her highnes courte. And as tyme and occasion
served, they reprehended dyvers and sondrye persons aswell for their
horrible swearing as for their inordinate and dissolute talke, to gether
with their abhomynable incontynencye. And fynding certayne persons
incorrigible denownced their onhoneste demanour to the quenes
majestie, whoo either pryncely rebuked them or sharpely punisshed,
or els utterly exilide them her majesties courte for ever, having alwayes
an esspeciall regarde to the qualitie of the treaspace and consideracion
of the persone. This contynewall remembraunce and due perfourmaunce of her graces promisse made towching the reformacion
of her courte myght seeme a greate argumente to induce her chappellayns to execute her graces commaundemente to the correction of
others, but that the sequell of her princely courtesye dothe shewe the
same by farre more bettre proof; when as being advertized of her
fraile weaknes she wolde not only moste gratefully heare them, but
thankfully acknowlege their humble advertisementes, which by one
especiall token appeared.[9]

[*fo.26*] When on a tyme being in progresse at Woodstoke, one Mr
Jaskyne, sergiante of her majesties pantrye, was greviouslye sick at his
house in Essex, feling his maladye to increase sente for his wyefe to
come unto hym.[10] This Mrs Jaskyne attended the quenes highnes in
her prevy chambre, and being denyed licence to visitt her weake
husbande moved one of her chapellayns to solicite her cause to the

8. In the manuscript 'dismissed' has been crossed out and 'devisid' substituted. The
former makes more sense grammatically, but Latymer may have meant that the
almoners were appointed by Anne at this moment.

9. Cf. George Wyatt, *Anne Boleigne*, 18: 'She had procured to her chaplins, men of
great learning and of no les honest conversinge, whom she with hers heard much, and
privatly she heard them willingly and gladly to admonish her, and them herself
exhorted and encouraged so to do.' All Anne's more famous chaplains were Cambridge
men; Hugh Latimer, Nicholas Shaxton, Matthew Parker, John Skip, William Betts
and William Latymer himself.

10. There is no record of either of the Jaskynes being in Anne's service, but her
household is badly documented. The court was at Woodstock between 30 Aug. and
23 Sept. 1533 (*L & P*, vii, nos. 1099, 1128, 1168, 1180) and passed through it in July
1535 (*L & P*, viii, no. 989).

quenes majestie. Whoo, spyeing convenient tyme, when her highnes came to the chappell to devyne service, moste humbly opeind the gentilwomans requeste, and besought her majestie to have regarde to the juste peticion of the sick housbande, and to the dutyfull obedience to the wyef. Whoo, tendering their plighte (as pettye commith sone to a tender hate) not only graunted her licence to departe, to the comforte of her weake and sicke housbownde, but also most bountyfullye commaunded to be prepared for her sufficiente furniture of horse and other necessarys for her jorney, and tenne poundes in monye towarde the charge of her travaill. Now to intreate of this noble princesse royall magnificence towardes the poore it were not amysse to declare with how gladsome cheare her majestie releived their necessitie. It haith byne an aunciente custome tyme out of mynde that princes of this lande shoulde distribute on Mawndye Thursdaye to the releyfe of dyverse poore people a certayne some of monye; which custome conynuing to her graces reigne, she observed with noo lesse reverence then liberalitie. Forupon a certayne Mawndie Thursdaye, after she hadd moste humbly (humblye, I said, bicause kneeling on her knees she wasshed and kyssed the fett of symple poore women) embased her selfe to performe the ceremonyes of that daye, she commaunded to be put previlye into every poore womans purse one goerge noble, the which was vis viiid, over and besides the almes that wonted was to be given. [*fo.26v*] The mawndie being fynisshed, one of the poore women (whoo of like hadd byne partaker of the said almes in fore yeares, and was well acquaynted therwith) loking in to her purse fownde the said George noble. Wherat being somewhat dismaide and thinking in her conscience suche extraordynarye liberalitie apperteyned not to her, but to some others whome perhappes the quene her majestie might more tenderly be affeccioned unto, returnedd with all possible speade to the almner and opened the matter saing, Sir you have mistakyn, and given me a wronge purse. To whome the almner made this answere, yf any discompte be you muste impute the same to the quenes highnes, for she haith caused the reste to be used a like. Which mattre in after tyme beinge certyfied to her majestie, she praysing God that in her happy reigne was fownde so faythfull and undefiled conscience, she wysshed her almes hadd ben dobled to that poore woman in consideracion of her good conscience. Wherin she uttered her princelie nature, that where as God hadd indued her with greate riches, dignitie and estate, even so she wolde not spare thankefully to dedicate therof some porcion to his glorye. Which godly zeale seemed naturally eingraffed in her graces noble breaste, yelding contynually moste plentyfull and abundante fruitte. For whether she rested at her palace or accompanid the kinge his majestie in his progresse she wolde at all tymes expresse her care, her thought, her myndefull remembrance of the poore and indigente people. In so moche as yf significacion at any tyme were given of any progresse to be made by the kinge his majestie (for that she wolde not be unfurnisshed) she wolde geave in esspeciall commaudmente to her officers to buye a greate quantitie of [*fo.27*] canvas to be made into shortes and smockes and shetes to thuse of the poore. And to thende the ladyes and maydons of honoure attending her highnes might in the majestie of so vertuous a prince by like example learne like consideracion of the poore, she commaunded the said ladies and maydons of honour to make a greate nowmbre of the same shurtes, smokkes and shetes with their awne handes. Neyther coulde she staye here the course of her liberall and princely mynde of relieve of the poore, but added herunto the like quantitie of flannell which she caused likewyse to be made into pettycotes for poore men, wemen and children. And as the kinges highnes removed to any place she caused immidiatlye to be signified under the handes of the curates and twoo honeste men of every parishe by a good compase nexte aboughte the courte to her graces almners the nowmbre of all poor famylyes in every parishe and of every famylie the like nowmbre of persons of what age so ever they were, to every of whome was distributed by her graces commaundemente a shurte, smok or petticote, and xiid in monye, and to some more, according as here grace understod of their nede and necessitie. But yf any poore woman were presented to have traveled with childe lieing, yet not free from thoise paynefull bandes, she was rewarded with a payer of shetes and twoo shillinges in monye, such was the wonderfull affection of this vertuous quene to all nedee housholders.[11] Wherein she rayther semid to complayne the wante of habilitie (having sufficient) then lacke of forwarde will to supply the necessitie of the poore.

I cann not here omytt her graces wonderfull clemencie and munificence towardes such others whome the spiritt of God hadd indued with the knowlege of his ynfallible truethe, either fallen in decaye by the hande of God or at the leste not hable to yelde the fruitte of [*fo.27v*] suche excellente gyftes for wante of helpe, or that suffred persecucion by the crueltie and malice of the unlearned, leste happelye I might seeme to derogate some parte of her highnes praise and commendacion; I will therfore make the same evidente by one or twoo principall examples. I[t] happened that a certayne gentilman whose name was Mr Ive dwelling at Kington, a benifice some tyme of Mr Latymer (whoo afterwarde was bisshopp of Worcestre)[12] was visited

11. For Forrest's description of queen Katherine's similar activities, *Grisild the Second*, 46.

12. There is no other record of Mr Ive and his wife. Hugh Latimer's benefice was West Kington, in the king's gift. He was instituted rector on 14 Jan. 1531; *Alumni Cant.*,

by the hande of God in the losse of the moste parte of his cattell, almoste to his utter undoing. This gentilman was reported to be an earneste and zealous embraser of Goddes worde, and his wyefe also; to whome the enymyes of God reproched their distresse, for that they hadd forsaken (as they said) their Cathlick fayth and seemed to rejoyse at their losse and decaye. Mr Latymer, perceiving the malice of the ungodly, commended this gentilman and his wyefe in his lettres to the quene her highnes, comparing them to Priscilla and Aquila of whome mencion is made in the Actes of the Apostels,[13] and besought her majestie to tendre their afflicted case, and to considre of the worthynes of the said persons. The quenes grace received this letre at Sir Edwarde Bayntons house (which was in the circuite of the kinges progresse)[14] caused the gentilwoman his wyef to be called before her, and said as hereafter: I have redde Mr Latymers lettre in your behalfe. I conceive the contentes therof and am sory for your heavye chaunce. Yet sythyns yt hath pleased allmightie God to shew his pour in you, I advertise you to acknowlege his goodnes herin, whoo commonly useth to trye his electe (as the golde in the fornace)[15] by losse of goodes, sicknes or other adversities, that in theise transitorye vaniteis they shoulde professe their humble acknowleging of greater benifittes. Be you nothing dismayde herewith but procede in thoise your godly purposes and begynninges and lett [fo.28] not the rayling reproches of the enymyes of Goddes glorye daunte your undefiled conscience. God will preserve you and rayse you frendes of unaquaynted. I for my parte will put to my helping hande, and whiles God shall lende me lyfe, will not willingly suffer any such (as you are commended to mee to be) to perishe. And looe, have here (quod she) some what towardes your presente relyefe, and gave her a purse of gold with xxli in it. Yf this will not redresse your lacke, repaire to me an other tyme, and I will consider bettre of you. Suerly this was a wonderfull token of a princely mynde, worthy to be commended to her posteritie in letres of golde. Yet suche were the contynuall proofes of her constante affeccion towardes the poore gospellars, not tasted only in her own dominione, but moste abundantly powred out in foren realmes and strangers borne.[16]

i, 49. Here he was a neighbour of Baynton, and the two corresponded on religious matters; Latimer, *Sermons and Remains*, 322–51.

13. Aquila and Priscilla, a married couple, were companions of St Paul; Acts 18.

14. Henry VIII was on progress from Windsor to Bristol in Aug. and Sept. 1535, and stayed at Bromham-Baynton; *L & P*, viii, no. 989, ix, no. 186. Ives places this incident in late Aug. 1535 (*Anne Boleyn*, 327), but it may have occurred earlier; Latimer became bishop of Worcester in 1535, and Jane Seymour was in favour during this progress.

15. Zechariah 13:9; I Peter 1:7.

16. Anne's goodness to 'strangers and alyannes' is mentioned in a petition to her by

As for an example a gentilwoman of Fraunce named Mrs Marye fledd out of Fraunce into Englande for religion. Whome immediatly after her arryvall the quene her majestie sente for, and understanding the certeynte of the mattre enterteyned her so lovingly and honorably as she confessed that her troble hadd purchased her libertie, and that she gayned more by her banishment then she coulde have hoped for at home emongest her deare frendes and naturall countrye men of Fraunce.

In like maner one Mr doctor Buttes, receiving letres out of Fraunce from one Nicholas Borbonius, a lerned yong man and very zealous in the scriptures, declaring his impresonmente in his awne contrye for that he hadd uttered certayne t[a]lke in the derogacion of the bisshopp of Rome and his usurped autoritie, made his suyte to the quene hir majestie in his behalfe; did not only optayne by her graces meanes the kinges leters for his delyvery, but also after he was come into Englande his whole [*fo.28v*] maynetenaunce at the quenes only charges in the house of the said Mr Buttes.[17]

She procured the king his letres likewyse for that notable learned man Mr Sturmius, scolemaster in Parise, to the entente she wolde store this lande with the learned and true preachers of the worde of God. But before the delyvery of the lettres he hadde recovered Germanye, whether he was then fledd for religion.[18] She mayntayned also one Mr Beckynsall in the universiteis beyonde the seas, geaving hym towardes his exhibicion fortie poundes by yeare; whoo after-wardes answered the good expectacion conceaved of hym, to the greate comforte of his contrye.[19] But what do I sticke in theese smalle pointes, wheras an incredibile numbre of presidentes remaine of her graces liberalitie as well towardes the poore learned, as to all other that were knowen to be studious in the setting forthe of Godes glorye.

Thomas Alwaye, who was convicted of religious offences; BL, Sloane MS 1207. (Not calendared in *L & P*).

17. For Dr Butts see above, pp. 36–7. 'Borbonius' was the French poet Nicolas Bourbon of Vandœuvre. For confirmation of Latymer's statement, and Anne's employ-ment of him at court, Bourbon, *Nugae* (Lyons, 1538).

18. Sturmius planned to leave Paris after the affair of the placards of Oct. 1534, but was sheltered by Guillaume du Bellay and stayed until Dec. 1536. Charles Schmidt, *La Vie et les Travaux de Jean Sturm* (Strasbourg, 1855), 8–17, 32. Thus he had not 'recovered Germanye' before Anne's death, but possibly she sent him an invitation in 1534 which he declined.

19. This man is probably the 'Bekensall a scolar of Parys' who received £4 13s 4d from the king's privy purse in Feb. 1530. *Privy Purse Expences of Henry VIII* ed. Nicholas Harris Nicolas (1827), 23. John Bekynsaw studied at Paris with Thomas Wynter, Wolsey's bastard son. In June 1537 he announced his return to England 'by cause of uncertenty off my lyvyng and desperyre off any mo fryndes'; PRO, SP1/121, fos 58–9 (*L & P*, xii (2), no. 39). Cf. Maria Dowling, *Humanism in the Age of Henry VIII* (1986), 153, 159.

She favored good letters and learninge so muche that upon suche as she never sawe she emploied exhibicion moste largelie, as to bothe the universities, Cambridge and Oxforde, the too eyes of this realme, she sente greate sommes of monye to the maintenaunce of the poore scholers there; for the firste yeare of reigne she gave to eche universitie fortye poundes and everye yeare after to eche of the saide universities fore score poundes.[20] And because she was infourmed that the saide universities were charched with the paimentes to tentehes and sub-sidies she mad earneste peticion to the kinges majestatie in there behalf and obteyned pardon for the same.[21]

Likewise when her highnes was certifiede that all houses of religion of the yearlye valewe of too hundrethe poundes and under shoulde be suppressed, she commaunded that godlye preacher of Englande Mr Latimer to take some occasion in his nexte sermonde to be made befor the kinge to dissuade the uttere subversion of the said houses and to induce the kinges grace to the mynde to converte them to some better uses. Upon whose commaundimente Mr Latimer in his next sermonde alleaged for his [*fo.29*] purpose the perable of a certayne man that planted a vyniarde (*vide Luce vicessimo capite*)[22], wherein he framed this parte of the texte. That is to saye, when the owner of the vyniarde coulde not have his frutes in due season he gave not in charge by and by to distroye the vyneyarde but commaunded the same to be fearmed and letton to others, whoo shoulde by their industroye and hous-bandrye amende the negligence of the other fearmers. And therwith making his oracion to the kinges majestie besought hym it might please his grace of his goodnes to converte the abbeys and prioryes to places of studye and goode letres and to the contynuall releve of the poore. And from that tyme forwarde she advertized all other preachers of Goddes worde to be very curious how they shoulde mynistre occa-sione in anye of their sermons towching the subvertinge of any howses of religion, but rayther to make conynuall and earnest peticione for the staye of the same. The swete sownde wherof, after it came to the eares of the governers of the other religious houses, wonderfully revyved them, and gave them good hope yf mediacione were made to her grace their howses sholde not be suppressed. Wherupon they

20. There is no evidence of payments made by Anne to the universities, though she did support poor scholars there such as William Barker or Bercher; *The Nobility of Women by William Bercher* ed. R. Warwick Bond (Roxburghe Club, 1904), 33, 87. For Forrest's praise of Katherine, *Grisild the Second*, 48.

21. A letter from Cambridge university thanks Anne for persuading the king to remit and pardon their payment of first fruits and tenths; BL, Cotton MS Faust. C III fo. 456.

22. Luke 20:9–16. The manuscript is slightly damaged here and reads: 'ᵽ ᷓ luce vicessimo capite'. No sermon by Hugh Latimer on this text is extant, but he did preach before the king frequently. Cf. *L & P*, vii, nos. 29, 30, 32, 228.

suborned certayne of the graveste and sageste of their fraternitie to delyver in the name of the whole brotherod an humble supplicacion to the quenes majestie. Whoo, although tendering the spoile and decaye of such godly revenows, fownded at the furste to godly purposes, yet detesting their licencious lyf, spak unto them in this wyse:

I am sure and throughly perswaded that the godly disposed persons whoo furst erected your foundacions determyned their godly charge to be bestowed to his glorye and the relive of the learned. I know their will was that none shoulde injoye any benifitt of their charitie but such as shoulde be fownde pure of lyving and sownde and diligente professors of Goddes worde. But how negligently, nay reyther wilfully you for your parties have performed this good opinione and determinacion of your fownders all the worlde doth see. And I for my parte, yea in Goddes behalfe, [*fo.29v*] lamente to heare (lamente I saye) to see how obstinately you have departed from Goddes true religion, and forsaken your due obedience to your soveraigne, and moste cowardely yelded the same to the usurped poure of the bisshoppe of Rome, whoise detestable sleightes and frivelous ceremonyes you have taken to be the pillour of your fantasticall religioine, and like dissemblyng hypocrites have asscribed your erronious supersticions to the censure of the blynde pastouere. And like unprofitable drones (lurking in your hyves) do devour that which the lusty labouring bees have, and do travell for. Neyther will you taste your selves of the brede of lyfe, ne yet by your good willes permitt others to assaye therof. You keape your gates close from the preachers of Goddes worde, and yourselves sitt eyther ydell or skarse well occupied in your cloysters, cleane voyed of knowlege. Neyther will you employe anye parte of your benivolence to poure studentes in the universities, of whome their may be hope of profitting the congregacion of Christe and our native countrie. Wherfore know you for certeyne, that my opinion is the dissolucion of your houses to fall upon you for your juste demerites as a deservid plague from almightie God,[23] whoo abhorring your lewdenes derydeth your blynde ignoraunce. Untill such tyme as you shall cleanse and puryfye your corrupte lyf and insensible doctrine, God will not cease to sende his plagues upon you to your utter subversion. This oracion being ended the quene departed, and hadd striken such a dampe into their fearfull heades that they seemed wholy discomfited. But as men in extreame perell leve nothing unsought that may releve their daunted courages, so theise sely poore men, betwixte feare and hevynes halfe dismayde, beganne to recownte their harde adventure. And calling to remembraunce that theffecte of the quenes

---

23. Anne's denunciation of the religious echoes Matthew 23:13.

majesties talke did tende to the reliefe of the preachers of Goddes worde poore and nedye studentes in the universities, ons agayne humblyd their selves to her highnes, moste liberally offering to her grace large stipendes and exhibicions to be distrybuted yearely to preachers and scollars by the only [*fo.30*] assignemente of her majestie.[24] The quene being certifyed of their humble submission and offre, a ppoynted certeyne trustymen to take vewe of their offers made by the saide brotherodes, and to make true relacion as they shoulde fynde. And it was knowen for certen that one tyme by some was geoven one hundred pounds, by some more and some lesse, besides the advowsons of some of their beste benyfices, which likewyse they rendered moste francklye and freelye to be disposed at hir graces pleasure, from tyme to tyme as they sholde happen to be voyde. Wherin her highnes seemed to take greate pleasure, determyninge moste liberally and willingly to employe the same upon the syncere preachers of Goddes worde, whome she purposed for Goddes recuse to advaunce to such digniteis as might be come worthye membres of Christes church.[25] But this her godly enterprise and gracious endevour (although undertaken to the only glory of God) yet was cleane cutt of by the to lamentable and untymely death of this vertuous princesse, to the greate heavines and sorow of the godly and hynderance of the learned and good leters.

   Notwithstanding before it pleased God to call her out of this transitory lyfe she expressed throughly the wonderfull affectione she bare to the paynefull preachers and vigilante pastors of Goddes flocke, by her meanes and continuall mediacione the king his majestie for their prefermente. Emongest whome at her graces suyte the reverende fathers in Christe Mr Cranmere was advaunced to the arch bisshopricke of Canterburye, Mr Latymer Worcesture, Mr Shaxtone to the see of Sarum, Mr Goodruke the Isle of Elye, and Mr Skippe the busshoppricke of Hereforde, besides a nowmbre others that atteynid meaner dignities by her highnes only procuremente.[26] Whom as at any tyme she raysed to any ecclesiasticall dignitie, so wolde she

24. Mortimer Levine, commenting on this passage, questions 'whether or not the stipends and exhibitions were invented by Latimer to suggest something he wanted Elizabeth to do'; 'The place of women in Tudor government', in *Tudor Rule and Revolution: Essays for G.R. Elton from his American Friends* ed. Delloyd J. Guth and John W. McKenna (Cambridge, 1982), 122. In fact Anne assisted the studies of John Eldmer, monk of St Mary's, York; *Letters of Royal and Illustrious Ladies* ed. M.A.E. Wood (2 vols., 1846), ii, 191 (*L & P*, viii, no. 710).

25. For Anne's promotion of evangelicals in the church, John Strype, *Life and Acts of Matthew Parker* (2 vols., Oxford, 1821), i, 15–18 (Parker); Wood, *Letters of Ladies*, ii, 188 (Dr Edward Crome); BL, Cotton MS Cleop. E IV fo. 107 (William Barlow).

26. For Alesius' comments on the bishops Anne favoured, see above pp. 38–9. Cranmer was placed in Thomas Boleyn's household by the king in 1529, and possibly Anne's mediation did procure him the see of Canterbury; Foxe, *A & M*, vii, 6. For

likewyse geove them in esspeciall charge to take greate and advised care that they planted under them noo maner of persons, either for favour or for frendshipp, but suche as were knowne to be worthy the same, both for their integrytie of their lyf and for the synceritie and sowndnes [*fo.30v*] of their doctryne; leste by theire negligente admitting of the ignorante, Goddes worde, now begynnyng to florishe through her princely patronage, might be evill spoken of and suffer slawnder and reproche of the blynde and ensensate enyms of Criste not yet admitting the purite of the gospell, contrary to her greces expectacion.

It cann not be but that this realme was in moste fortunate estate when the prince hadd learning in suche price and was so carefull to rewarde it with honour. For as naturell moystre geveth strength and increase to all plantes, fruites and herbes, even so rewarde and large stipendes upholdeth the universities and norisseth in the same plentyfull store of grave, wyse and learned heades, whoo by the depe grownde of knowlege may dispose, order and correcte all unlawfull and ungodly lawes, and consequently establishe all godly and good in Goddes commone wealth. The notable philosopher Plato in his booke de re publica sheweth that the manyfest token of the prosperous commen wealth is where wysdome haith made the prince her[27] felow or companioune, and where he studieth wysedome that injoyeth governmente.[28] Then what shalbe said of this so rare a patronesse of learning, whoo omitted noo tyme that might be employed either to the furtheraunce of the purite of scriptures or to the extirping and abolisshinge of the blynde ignoraunce and abuses growen in this lande. Surely this may be said, that this our age is all wholye indebted unto hir highnes for the clearenes of our tyme. For she was the furste princesse that might justly vaunte the restitucion of the trewth and the over throwe of the pestyferous crepte in to the church of Criste, whoo hadd no lesse to supplante the one then to supplye the other. Which well appeared when, as being in progresse at Wynchecombe,

Latimer's early career, ibid., 454; William Gilpin, *Lives of Hugh Latimer and Bernard Gilpin* (1780), 32–5. For Shaxton's, Foxe *A & M*, iv, 650; John Venn, *Biographical History of Gonville and Caius College, volume 1* (Cambridge, 1897), 17, 19. When Shaxton and Latimer became bishops Anne lent them the money to pay their first fruits and tenths, debts which were outstanding at her death; *Sermons and Remains of Hugh Latimer*, 368–9; Allan G. Chester, *Hugh Latimer, Apostle to the English* (Philadelphia, 1954), 104, 230. Cf. *L & P*, ix, nos. 203, 252, 272–3, x, no. 1257 (ix), xi, no. 117. Thomas Goodrich, another Cambridge man, had been one of the divines consulted by convocation about the divorce. He became bishop of Ely on 19 April 1534. John Skip, Anne's chaplain, was frequently with her in the Tower. However, he did not become bishop of Hereford until 7 Nov. 1539.

27. In the manuscript 'his' was the original word here but 'her' has been written above it.

28. Plato, *Republic*, v, 473.

a place nexte adjoyning to an abbeye sometyme called the abbey of Hayles, wherein was a marvelous abominable pilgrymage to bloudd (surmised the bloudde of Criste); mistrusting that which afterwards she approved to be trew, sente thither certeyn of her chappellayns and others, straightly commaunding them [*fo.31*] truely and faythfully to vewe, searche and examyn by all possible meanes the trueth of this abomynable abuse. Whoo executing their charge percewed, partly by their industrye but esspicially by examinacion of certeyne that knew the coven therof, that it was nothing els but the bloode of some ducke, or as some saye, red waxe. Where upon hir highnes being throughly enformid never stayed, but made meanes to the king his majestie that this ydolatrous abuse might be taken awaye. And she optayned so that he caused the same ymediatly to be plucked downe, to the greate comforte of the ignorante and weake Cristians which other wyse must nedes have perisshed through the inordinate worshipping of what develishe invencione.[29]

Like wyse in the ende of that same progresse, her majestie lyeing then at Richemounde vowchsaved in her awne persone to visite the noones of Syon, whoo beinge at their commen prayer in theire close quyre (as their manner was) denyed her highnes entrye into the same and alleaged for their defence that it was not lawfull for anye maryed persone to entyre into their oratorye. The quene her highnes persisted earnest in her requeste and so at the laste with fayer and swete wordes haith optaynid free ingresse with her trayne, where she fownde them all prostrate and grovelinge with their faces downewarde to the grownde. Unto whome she made a brefe exhortacione, and in the same declared unto them the enormitie of their cloked libertye and wantone incontenence and, disswading them from their dissimuled holynes and ygnorante praying upon their Laten prymars, gave theme prayer bookes in Englishe to exercise them selves with all, that they might both understande what they did praye for, and therby be stired to more devocion; which they refusinge for a tyme (as profane) not to be admitted in their professione, at the laste received them not withstanding, moste humblye with faythfull promisse to performe her graces desire.[30]

29. Here Latymer confuses events; the blood of Hailes was not destroyed until 1538, when its authenticity was investigated by Hugh Latimer and others; *Sermons and Remains of Hugh Latimer*, 406–8; cf. ibid., 357–66. However the court was at Winchcombe in July and Aug. 1535. *L & P*, viii, nos. 1058, 1111, 1158, ix, nos. 4, 349, 488, x, no. 693. Perhaps Anne did institute some sort of inquiry which was remembered later. Indeed, Ives demonstrates both that a visit to Hailes by Henry and Anne was planned, and that she may have had the relic removed temporarily. *Anne Boleyn*, 308–9.

30. This story is meant to discredit both Syon and its former patron, Katherine of Aragon. For her visits to the house, *Vivis Opera Omnia* ed. Gregorius Majansius (8 vols., Valencia, 1782–90), vii, 208–11. For Syon's resistance to the divorce and royal

[*fo.30v*] And that her highnes might evydently declare that this godly indevour from a constante and fervente affeccion which she hadd to the setting forth of the lyvely worde of God, she saledome or never toke her repaste abrode with the kinge his majestie without some argument of scripture throughly debated. And in like maner the lorde chamberlayne and vizchamberlayne of her sidd[31] for the tyme being gave them selfes wholie in all their denars and suppers to the discussing of some one dought or other in scripture. Wherin the kinge his majestie to some tyme such pleasure that dyverse and sondry tymes he wolde not only here them but somtyme wolde argue and reason hym selfe. In so moche that of a tyme when Mr Latymer was there and dynid with my lorde chamberleyne, the kinges majestie with Sir James Bullen mayntayned argumente in a question of scripture agaynste the said Latymer and Doctor Shaxton; which ministred occasion afterwardes that the kinge his highnes wratte with the consente of Sir James B. dyverse epistelles, and received answer towchinge eyther of their opynions and judgementes in matters of controversye, wherof some were exstante of late yeares.[32]

And that her lades, maydons of honour and other gentilwomen shoulde use them selves according to their callinge, her grace wolde comonlye and generally wolde many tymes move them to modestye and chastertie; but in esspeciall to the maydons of honour, whome she wold call before her in the prevy chambre, and before the mother of the maydes wold geove them a longe charge of their behaviours. And they shoulde not consume the [time] in vayne toyes and poeticall fanses as in elder tyme they wonted were, she caused a deske in her chambre upon the which she commaunded an Englishe bible to be layed, wherunto every persone might have recurse to rede upon when they wolde, and gave streight commaundemente that all tryfels and wanton poeses shoulde be eschued upon her displeasure. After that there was a booke of prayers [*fo.32v*] whiche belonged to one of her maydes of honour called Mrs Mary Shelton presented unto her highnes where in ware written certeyne ydill poeses.[33] She wolde not

---

supremacy, C.J. Aungier, *History and Antiquities of Syon Monastery* (1840), passim. For the nuns' devotional books in English, *The Myrroure of oure Lady* (1530), and Richard Whitford, *A dayly exercyse and experyence of dethe*. See also Ives, *Anne Boleyn*, 309–10. The comment about Anne being married is ironic in view of Syon's loyalty to Katherine; either Latimer implies that they had accepted the Boleyn marriage, or the nuns themselves were being sardonic.

31. 'of her sidd' means her household; thus the debaters were Borough and Baynton.

32. This correspondence is no longer extant.

33. For prayer books allegedly given by Anne to her maids, Wyatt, *Anne Boleigne*, 18; BL, Stowe MS 956; *Archaeologia*, xliv (1), 259ff.. Cp. Ives, *Anne Boleyn*, 315–16. Mary (not Margaret or Madge) Shelton was probably the daughter of Princess Mary's governess who allegedly had an affair with Henry VIII in Feb. 1535; *L & P*, viii, no.

be satisfyed by any meanes before she understod certeynly to whome the booke perteyned. The matter was covered a whill by cause of the expresse thretyninges of her majestie, but nothing canne longe escape the percinge eyes of princes, esspecially in their awne pallacies, so that at the length the pensive gentilwoman (to whome the booke appertayned) was discovered. Wherupon the quene her majestie, calling her before her presence, wonderfull rebuked her that wold permitte suche wantone toyes in her book of prayers, which she termed a myrroure or glasse wherin she might learne to addresse her wandering thoughtes; and upon this occasione commaunded the mother of the maydons to have a more vigilante eye to her charge to thende that at all tymes and in the tyme of prayers esspecially they might comely and vertuously behave their selfes. Neyther did hir majestie disdayne in her awne persone sondry tymes to repayer to the commone deske where the said bible was placed, yeldinge herein example to others to the like indevour. And yet her highnes was very experte in the Frenche tounge, exercising her selfe contynually in reading the Frenche bible and other Frenche bookes of like effecte and conceivid greate pleasure in the same.[34] Wherfore her highnes charged her chapellayns to be furnisshed of all kynde of Frenche bookes that reverently treated of the wholye scriptures;[35] wonderfully lamenting her ignoraunce in the Laten tounge, for wante wherof she acknowlege her selfe marviously embased. Notwithstandinge, her majestie vowed to almighty God that yf it wolde please hym to prolonge her dayes to see the trayninge upp of hir younge and tender babe prince Elizabeth, she wolde endewe her with the knowlege of all tounges, as Hebrue, Greeke, Latyne, Italian, Spanishe, Frenche, in suche sorte that she might in after tyme be hable sufficiently to judge of all maters and embassages, and as occasion might serve [*fo.32v*] sufficiente knowlege to administre the estate. Which happelye sithens is allotted to your majestie, to the greate comforte, joye and desire of your moste obediente subjectes.[36]

I may not here forgett the loving kyndenes of this gracious prince

263. This would give a moral point to Latymer's story. Mary Shelton made several entries in the Devonshire Manuscript, a notable court poetry album, and was friendly with the poet earl of Surrey. I am grateful to Dr Helen Baron, who is working on the Devonshire MS, for information on this point.

34. A French treatise on letter-writing dedicated to Anne by one Loys de Brun at new year 1530 praises her love of scripture and other salutary works in French and mentions her reading the Pauline epistles during Lent. BL, Royal MS 20 B XVII. Other French books owned by Anne are BL, Harl. MS 6561 and Royal MS 16 E XIII. See also Ives, *Anne Boleyn*, 289–92, 317, 318.

35. For Anne's importation of scripture in French, BL, Add. MS 43, 827a, narrative of Rose Hickman; Ives, *Anne Boleyn*, 293–4.

36. Katherine of Aragon prepared her daughter Mary for rule by humanist education, and it seems probable that Anne would want to imitate her. Certainly she

towardes her trustye servauntes, whose necessities, siknesses and other adversityes she releved so abundantly that they all protested them selves more bownde to her highnes for her gracious benevolence then they might be hable in any kynde of service to acquitt. For some she rewarded with greate sommes of monye, some with offices, bay- lywickes and other places of charge wherento was annexed com- modittis; and to the same she wolde assuredly preferre her awne servauntes furste, whoo so ever made request to the contrarye. As evidently appeared when one of her majesties officers besought her grace to bestow a simple baylywik of smale value upon one of his awne servantes, whome her grace answered in this wyse: where it pleased allmightye God to call her to be ladye over manye, she thought it was to no other ende but that principally she was bounde to provide for suche as were in her awne housholde. And as she fownde her selfe naturally enclyned to pleasure all men to her poure, so yet she was resolved that of duetye her paynfull and aunciente servantes shoulde furste injoye such benifittes as were in her majestie to employe, for they (quod she) are true servauntes to yeld me their service, take payne to death, wherfore it is reason that sythens I injoye their service they may have some porcion of my lyving. Yf therfore there be none of myne awne servauntes that standeth in nede of that which you desire you shall injoye your request.[37]

[fo.33] A notable example and myrrour of princely courtesye, suche as declareth a princes noble mynde, whose tendre affeccion her ser- vauntes now proved to be greater towardes them then ever they durste have hoped or wysshed for.

But helas helas what avayleth theise godly and excellent giftes of nature and godly qualityes, when to some moste cruell Atropos with her sustres twoo have conspired to rashely to breake vertuous course eare halfe the race weer roone, and haith tripped her on the waye that wold have wone the goale yf lyfe might longer have last, and wolde have obteyned a highr place in the house of fame.[38] All Englande might be wayle the losse of suche a vertuous quene. But wee that did attende her majestie muste nedes justly lamente the soudaine departinge of so god a princes, the fame of whoise juste desertes (though corps do rest in clay) shall yet remayne as freshe in store as she were dayly in sight. And though our hertes might seeme for sorrow

committed Elizabeth to Parker's care shortly before her arrest. Parker, *Correspondence*, no. 46. For an account of Elizabeth's studies, which were very similar to Mary's, Roger Ascham, *Whole Works* ed. Giles (3 vols., Edinburgh, 1864–5), epistle no. 99.

37. For a humanist view of the reciprocal duties of masters and servants, Gilbertus Cognatus, *Of the Office of Servauntes* trans. Thomas Challoner (1534).

38. Atropos and her sisters were the Greek Fates or *Moirae*. Cf. Forrest, *Grisild the Second*, 125. Latymer's passage here is also reminiscent of II Timothy 4 and Hebrews 12:1.

to pynne and melte awaye, yet gladd some may wee be, that before she stepped from us she did leave such mirrours behinde, theirby our lyves to frame. And but that impe of her agayne noo age can tell, whose princely qualities by thankfull acknowlegement of theise statelye gyftes in your roiall persone all the world doo professe. And in her highnes behalfe wee hope your grace will contynew, and wee truste your highnes shall encrease to the whisshed desire of your moste deare and naturall mother, the glorye of God, and joyfull comforte of all your noble happy realme.

III
THE LETTERS OF RICHARD SCUDAMORE
TO SIR PHILIP HOBY,
SEPTEMBER 1549–MARCH 1555

Edited by Susan Brigden

ACKNOWLEDGEMENTS

Blair Worden first showed me these letters, and then became the most patient and perspicacious of editors. I am very grateful to him. Dr William Tighe might have edited these letters himself, for he discovered them too, but he ceded the edition to me. I am greatly indebted to him not only for this generosity, but also for his kindness in sending me information about Richard Scudamore.

ABBREVIATIONS

APC	*Acts of the Privy Council of England*, ed. J.R. Dasent, vols. i–ix (1890–1907)
BL	British Library
Chronicle of Queen Jane	*The Chronicle of Queen Jane, and of two years of Queen Mary*, ed. J.G. Nichols (Camden Society, xlviii, 1850)
CLRO	Corporation of London Record Office
CPR	*Calendar of Patent Rolls, Edward VI*, (1924–)
CSP, Domestic, 1601–1603	*Calendar of State Papers, Domestic Series, Elizabeth, 1601–1603; with Addenda, 1547–1565*, ed. M.A.E. Green (1870)
CSPF	*Calendar of State Papers, Foreign Series, of the Reign of Edward VI, 1547–1553*, ed. W.B. Turnbull (1861)
CSP, Scotland	*Calendar of State Papers, Relating to Scotland and Mary, Queen of Scots, 1547–1603*, ed. J. Bain (Edinburgh, 1898)
CSP Sp.	*Calendar of State Papers, Spanish*, ed. G.A. Bergenroth *et al.*, 13 vols. (1862–1964)
CSP Ven.	*Calendar of State Papers, Venetian*, ed. Rawdon Brown *et al.*, 9 vols. (1864–98)
DNB	*Dictionary of National Biography*, 63 vols. (1885–1900)
Edward VI, *Chronicle*	*The Chronicle and Political Papers of King Edward VI*, ed. W.K. Jordan (1966)
EHR	*English Historical Review*
'Eye-witness's account'	'An eye-witness's account of the *coup d'état* of October 1549', ed. A.J.A. Malkiewicz, *EHR* lxx (1955), pp. 600–9
Foxe, *Acts and Monuments*	John Foxe, *Acts and Monuments*, ed. S.R. Cattley and G. Townsend, 8 vols. (1837–41)
Hoak, *King's Council*	D.E. Hoak, *The King's Council in the reign of Edward VI* (Cambridge, 1976)
Jordan, *Edward VI: Young King*	W.K. Jordan, *Edward VI: the Young King: the Protectorship of the Duke of Somerset* (1968)
Jordan, *Edward VI: Threshold of Power*	W.K. Jordan, *Edward VI: the Threshold of Power: the Dominance of the Duke of Northumberland* (1970)
House of Commons, 1509–1558	*The House of Commons, 1509–1558*, ed. S.T. Bindoff, 3 vols. (1982)

House of Commons, 1558– 1603	The House of Commons, 1558–1603, ed. P.W. Hasler, 3 vols. (1981)
Journal	Journal of the Court of Common Council
L&P	Letters and papers, Foreign and Domestic, of the Reign of Henry VIII, ed. J.S. Brewer, J. Gairdner, and R.S. Brodie, 21 vols. (1862– 1932)
Narratives of the Reformation	Narratives of the Days of the Reformation, ed. J.G. Nichols (Camden Society, lxxvii, 1859)
NLS	National Library of Scotland
PCC	Prerogative Court of Canterbury Wills
PRO	Public Record Office
Register of Freemen	Register of Freemen of the City of London in the Reigns of Henry VIII and Edward VI, ed. C. Welch (1908)
SR	The Statutes of the realm, ed. A. Luders et al., 11 vols. (1810–28)
Stow, Annales	John Stow, The Annales, or generall chronicle of England ..., ed. E. Howes (1615)
Strype, Ecclesiastical Memorials	John Strype, Ecclesiastical Memorials, relating chiefly to religion, and the reformation of it ... under King Henry VIII, King Edward VI, and Queen Mary I, 3 vols. (Oxford, 1822)
Travels and Life	The Travels and Life of Sir Thomas Hoby, Knight, of Bisham Abbey, written by himself. 1547–1564, ed. E. Powell (Camden Society, Miscellany, x, 1902)
Trevelyan Papers	Trevelyan Papers, prior to A.D. 1558, ed. J. Payne Collier (Camden Society, lxvii, 1857)
Troubles connected with the Prayer Book	Troubles connected with the Prayer Book of 1549, ed. N. Pocock (Camden Society, new series, xxxvii, 1884)
TRP	Tudor Royal Proclamations, ed. P.L. Hughes and J.F. Larkin (1964–9)
Two London Chronicles	Two London Chronicles from the collections of John Stow, ed. C.L. Kingsford (Camden Society, miscellany, xii, 1910)
Tytler, England under Edward VI and Mary	P.F. Tytler, England under the Reigns of Edward VI and Mary, 2 vols. (1839)
VCH	The Victoria History of the Counties of England
Visitation of Worcester	The Visitation of the County of Worcester made in the year 1569, ed. W.P.W. Phillimore (1888)
Wriothesley, Chronicle	Charles Wriothesley, A Chronicle of England

during the Reigns of the Tudors, 1485–1559, ed.
W.D. Hamilton, 2 vols. (Camden Society,
new series, xi and xx, 1875–7)

Reference, unless otherwise stated, is to document numbers throughout. Place of publication, unless otherwise stated, is London throughout

EDITORIAL NOTE

The original spelling has been retained, except that, where appropriate, 'v' has become 'u'. Punctuation has been modernised. Abbreviations and contractions have been expanded throughout. Doubtful readings and missing passages are indicated in square brackets. All the letters are holograph, and all except no. 34 are from Richard Scudamore to Sir Philip Hoby.

INTRODUCTION

Between September 1549 and October 1550 Richard Scudamore wrote over 30 letters to Sir Philip Hoby, Gentleman Usher of Edward VI's Privy Chamber, who was serving as resident ambassador to the Imperial Court. Much of Scudamore's correspondence concerns the volatile politics of the Court and Council, with which Hoby was deeply concerned and in which he was personally implicated. All at Court was highly uncertain during this period. The return to power of the Duke of Somerset, which seemed imminent, and the likely reverse of the reformed religion, would be of the greatest consequence for Hoby, for in the *coup* of October 1549 which brought down the Protector he had, by traducing Somerset, joined the ascendant faction. But its victory seemed, as Scudamore wrote, to be evanescent, and if the Earl of Warwick were to be deposed by a Catholic faction Hoby could expect disfavour. He was known to be a committed Protestant.

As Hoby's financial agent, Scudamore dealt with his master's tangled finances: raising loans, and repaying (or not repaying) debts, and attempting to extract Hoby's own fees from a bankrupt government. He sent news of Hoby's family, of events in Parliament, of defeats in Scotland, of ambassadors' visits, and of grants of office and favour to Hoby's friends and rivals. But above all, Scudamore described intimately and immediately the changing fortunes of the leading courtiers and councillors. His letters provide a source for the politics of Edward's reign of almost unrivalled importance.

The manuscript

In the Advocates' Library of the National Library of Scotland is a volume containing 32 letters written by Richard Scudamore to Sir Philip Hoby between September 1549 and March 1555. This volume—Adv. MS 34.2.14—measures $12\frac{1}{2}'' \times 8''$ and contains 64 folios. The pages are watermarked with a gloved hand and flower. This volume, and another of letters addressed mainly to Sir Edward Hoby, c. 1550–1638—Adv. MS 34.2.15—are said to have belonged to Archibald Constable, the publisher, in the nineteenth century, but of their provenance there is no other evidence. Scudamore's letters were bound, in no particular order, in about 1820. Two other letters from Scudamore to Hoby, written during the same period, were purchased by the British Museum from Rodd on 10 February 1838 and added to a volume of 'Ancient letters of friendship, solicitation and business, chiefly addressed to the Scudamores of Holm Lacy': Additional MS 11042, fos. **53 and ***53. Within that volume there is also a letter from Richard Scudamore to his father, John Scudamore.

Richard Scudamore

Richard Scudamore entered the royal household in 1539 as one of the yeomen of the toils (tents).[1] He was the son of John Scudamore of Holm Lacy, Herefordshire, who was gentleman usher of the Chamber, and perhaps esquire of the body at Court, and J.P., sheriff, and M.P. for his county.[2] Through his receivership in the Court of Augmentations for Hereford and the neighbouring counties, John Scudamore shared in the dispersal of monastic lands at the Dissolution and strengthened his connections with leading local families and figures at Court.[3] He had found favour with Thomas Cromwell, 'a good master of myne'.[4] Richard Scudamore had three brothers. William, the eldest, was educated for a time at Oriel College, and Richard stayed with him in Oxford.[5] When William Scudamore moved to London to enter the Inns of Court it seems that Richard came with him. In July 1535 John Scudamore wrote in fury of a brawl between 'a lewde boy of myn' and one of Cromwell's servants in Lion's Inn: 'yff that unhapey boy come where y am, I schall sette hym ther as he schall see no sonne nor mone for oon yere'.[6] But William wrote to his father that Cromwell himself had summoned his errant brother, and warned him that 'he wold put hym as he shold cole hym self for the space of thys thre daye', but he had also, 'lyke a good master unto hym', promised him that he would pay for his fees.[7] This brother may well have been Richard. Richard Scudamore's education, though apparent in his letters, is obscure in the records.

Richard Scudamore served as yeoman of the toils for at least a decade; through the last years of Henry VIII's reign,[8] and still in the first years of Edward VI's,[9] apparently never finding promotion in

1. *L&P* xiv(2). 781, pp. 312, 313.
2. For his career, see *House of Commons, 1509–1558*.
3. Extensive correspondence to Scudamore is found in the files of Chancery Masters' exhibits, Duchess of Norfolk deeds: PRO, C 115/M 15–19. I am very grateful to Dr Tighe for providing these references. See also BL, Add. MS 11042.
4. PRO, SP 1/85, fo. 45ʳ (*L&P* vii. 951).
5. PRO, C115/M18/7475.
6. *ibid.* SP 1/85, fo. 45ʳ (*L&P* vii. 951). The editors date this letter 1534, but other evidence places the episode in July 1535.
7. BL, Add. MS 11042, fo. 55ʳ. This letter was written on 9 July from Furnivall's Inn. The reference in it to the plague dates it to 1535. William Skidmore was admitted to Lincoln's Inn in January 1538: *Records of the Honourable Society of Lincoln's Inn*, 2 vols. (1896), i. p. 50.
8. *L&P* xvi. 380, 745, 1489; pp. 181, 360, 701; xvii. 880, p. 476; xviii(1). 436, p. 264; xviii(2). 231, p. 126. His name appears among a list of 'yeomen, grooms and pages' in the Household drawn up in February 1547 for Henry VIII's funeral: PRO, LC 2/2, fo. 68ʳ (as Dr Tighe kindly told me).
9. PRO, E 101/426/5, fos. 13ᵛ, 105ʳ; E 101/427/6, fos. 15ᵛ, 72ᵛ (Treasurer of the Chamber's accounts, April–October 1548, October 1548–October 1549). Again, this information is owed to Dr Tighe.

the Court from this lowly position. But at some time, while still at Court, he entered the service of Sir Philip Hoby, Master of the Ordnance and English ambassador to the Imperial Court. Scudamore became Hoby's 'secretary' (as he called himself), instructed to write every week to his master with news, even if there seemed 'small occasyon'.[10] On 1 July 1553 the Privy Council issued a warrant for payment to Scudamore, as Hoby's 'servant', for bringing letters post from the Imperial Court and for returning with others.[11] Whether Scudamore still held a position at Court while in Hoby's service is uncertain, for his name disappears from the Court records just as his surviving letters to Hoby begin, but his familiarity with Court affairs and his access to councillors may suggest so.

The relationship between this master and this servant was close. Richard Scudamore's aunt Maud was Philip Hoby's sister.[12] John Scudamore and Hoby had long known each other; not only through this marriage, but also at Court and through Hoby's extensive acquisitions of monastic lands in the West.[13] But other connections, of faith and friendship, also bound Philip Hoby and Richard Scudamore. Hoby had been converted to evangelical religion, and so too had Scudamore. In 1543 Hoby and his wife had been accused of harbouring a sacramentarian heretic, and with them some of their friends in Henry VIII's Court, including Thomas Cawarden and his wife.[14] In the following year Cawarden was appointed Master of the Tents and of the Revels, and so became Scudamore's master.[15] In the precinct of the Black Friars Scudamore, Hoby and Cawarden were neighbours, for there the tents were stored and Hoby and Cawarden had their London houses.[16]

Scudamore's evangelical convictions resonate throughout his letters to Hoby. His valedictory references to the 'living Lord' marked him, ineluctably, as of the new faith. Only a reformer could have written so scornfully of Bishop Bonner's defiant affirmation of transubstantiation in September 1549, or could have referred so puritanically to 'Good Friday, as it is called'.[17] His many references to the 'quondam' bishops would have delighted Hoby, but Scudamore evidently shared his master's hopes for the removal of the conservative

---

10. See below, letters 19 and 21.

11. *CSP, Domestic, 1601–1603*, p. 425.

12. *Visitation of Worcester*, p. 16. Maud Hoby married Thomas Biggs, Scudamore's mother's brother.

13. See, for example, BL, Add. MS 11041, fo. 57ʳ (31 October 1539).

14. *APC* i, p. 97; *L&P* xviii (2). 241(6).

15. *House of Commons, 1509–1558* (Cawarden).

16. *Documents relating to the Revels at Court in the time of King Edward VI and Queen Mary*, ed. A. Feuillerat (Louvain, 1914); *House of Commons, 1509–1558* (Cawarden, Hoby).

17. See below, letters 1 and 20.

episcopate.[18] When John Scudamore wrote his will in 1571 he made no mention of Richard, alone of all his children. His was a testament of defiant Catholic piety, and it may have been that he was estranged from his son in part because of his evangelical faith.[19] When Richard Scudamore made his own will in 1576 he commended his soul, as a reformer would, to the 'ffree mercyes of my heavenly ffather of whome I doe assure myselfe to have ffree remission of all my synnes thoroughe the mediacon, deathe, passion and resurrection of . . . Christe', and he requested that he be buried without any 'vayne worldly pompe'. His goods, unspecified, he left to his 'kynnesman Richard Arnold'. His will was proved on 23 December 1586.[20]

Sir Philip Hoby

Philip Hoby was of ancient, if obscure, Welsh descent, the son of William Hoby of Leominster.[21] He was born c. 1505.[22] Hoby's education, like Scudamore's, is unattested. Later he would claim his ignorance of the civil law and of Latin,[23] the hallmarks of a conventional education, but his handwriting, his taste, his knowledge of languages proclaim an educated mind. He was the friend of Aretino and Titian, and of leading English humanists.[24] Hoby became one of that coterie of humanists who sought, and found, favour with Thomas Cromwell. He was already in contact with English humanists before he went as envoy to Spain and Portugal in 1535–6 for Cromwell.[25] He wrote to Thomas Starkey from Evora in April 1536, and at around the same time one of Cromwell's importunate suitors, returning from Spain, thanked Cromwell for his extraordinary kindness when, at Cranmer's table, he had declared his favour to him and to 'Philip and Morison, his dearest friends'.[26] Hoby and the humanist scholar Morison were always to remain closely associated. In 1535 Hoby had been described as Cromwell's servant, but by 1538 Cromwell wrote to him as 'my friend'.[27]

18. See below, letters 16, 17, 28, 34.

19. PRO, PCC, Prob. 11/53, fos. 314ʳ–315ʳ.

20. *ibid.* Prob. 11/69, fo. 520ʳ.

21. *Visitation of Worcester*, pp. 77–80.

22. For Hoby's life, see *DNB; House of Commons, 1509–1558*.

23. BL, Harl. MS 523, fo. 110ʳ. Harleian MS 523 is a contemporary volume of letters written and received by Hoby during Edward VI's reign.

24. S. Ticozzi, *Vite dei Pittori Vecelli di Cadore* (Milan, 1817), pp. 310–11; *APC* i, pp. 551–2.

25. For the mission, see *L&P* viii. 744; x. 208; xii(1) 254.

26. PRO, SP 1/103, fo. 162ʳ; SP 1/101, fo. 232ʳ ᵛ(*L&P* x. 719, 224). The suitor was William Swerder: G.R. Elton, *Reform and Renewal: Thomas Cromwell and the Common Weal* (Cambridge, 1973), pp. 22–3.

27. BL, Add. MS 5498, fo. 1ʳ. This volume contains papers, in a contemporary hand, relating to Hoby.

Early in 1538 Cromwell entrusted Hoby with a delicate mission: to visit possible consorts for a newly-widowed Henry VIII, to persuade them that it might 'please his Majesty to advance your Grace to the honour of Queen of England', and to invite them to have their portraits painted. Together, Hoby and Hans Holbein visited the Duchess of Milan and Marie of Guise.[28] On his return Hoby was appointed gentleman of the Privy Chamber.[29] Later that year Hoby was sent to the Emperor to explain Henry VIII's hopes for marriages between himself and the Duchess of Milan and between Princess Mary and the Infante of Portugal: a 'perdurable knot between their Majesties and posterities'.[30] There in Toledo Sir Thomas Wyatt was ambassador to the Imperial Court. The visit to Spain, and the time spent with Wyatt, left their mark upon Hoby. There he was confirmed in his resentment of the wealth and power of the clergy; and perhaps not least because of his likely allegiance to Wyatt in Wyatt's virulent quarrel with Edmund Bonner, future Bishop of London.[31] Notes Hoby made upon his return from Spain were significant for the future:

> ... to remember and aduertise my L. priuie seale of a redresse: ffirst to withdraw the Kinges councell more secrete together. And to auoide spirituall men therehens for diuers consideracons.
>
> And in short time to see prouision for the Comunaltie concerninge spirituall causes. And to remit them to such as will not deceiue God and the Kinge, wherby the people mai the more earnester cleaue unto it, and not to wauer as thei do.
>
> Concerning the bisshop of Rome, neuer better time to enflame malice against him then now. And in especiall with the potentates of Italie ... wherfor it were verie expedient for the Kinge to send some of his gentlemen abrode emong them ... wherby thei mai the better fall to the knowleag of Christes gospell and his abominable abuse.[32]

During this journey also Hoby's chronic failure to live within the diets he received for his journeys already became apparent. Cromwell

---

28. *ibid.* fos. 1ʳ–2ᵛ (*L&R* xiii(1). 380); *L&P* xiii(1). 507–8, 656; J. Rowlands, *Holbein: the Paintings of Hans Holbein the Younger* (Oxford, 1985), pp. 116–17. Hoby himself was drawn by Holbein: K.T. Parker, *The Drawings of Hans Holbein in the collection of his Majesty the King at Windsor Castle* (1945), no 50.

29. *L&P* xiii(2). 270, 585.

30. *L&P* xiii(2). 585; BL, Harl. MS 282, fo. 213ʳ (*L&P* xiii(2). 621); *L&P* xiii(2). 622, 914, 923–4, 941, 974, 1054, 1120, 1127.

31. G.F. Nott, *The Works of Henry Howard, Earl of Surrey, and of Sir Thomas Wyatt the Elder*, 2 vols. (1815), ii. pp. 277–308, especially p. 301; *L&P* xiii(2). 270; xvi. 641.

32. BL, Add. MS 5498, fo. 14ʳ ᵛ (*L&P* xiii(2). 974(2)).

rebuked the ever generous Wyatt for lending Hoby 200 ducats, even though Hoby had been granted liberal expenses.[33] Indeed he had: £250.[34]

Hoby was soon sent upon another diplomatic mission: to Cleves at the end of 1539 to prepare for the marriage of Anne of Cleves to Henry VIII. He was present at her reception at Calais and at London.[35] Not a fortunate association, as it turned out, but Hoby survived it, and his master's fall in the midsummer of 1540.[36] Around the king in his last years was a group of courtiers who had been Cromwell's men, placed in the royal household by Cromwell, or migrating there upon his fall. Among them was Hoby. They shared an evangelical faith close to their fallen patron's and far from Henry's own, and they were close companions: Hoby, Thomas Cawarden, Edmund Harman, Thomas Weldon, Thomas Sternhold, Richard Morison, Maurice Berkeley, Anthony Denny, Philip van Velde, George Ferrers.[37] Their names appear and reappear throughout Scudamore's letters. And Hoby by now had a wife who was not only a wealthy widow, but also 'much geaven to the Scryptures': Elizabeth, the daughter of Sir Walter Stonor.[38] Well aware how vulnerable their commitment to reform might make them, if ever their conservative enemies at Court moved against them, still these courtiers determined to profess the new faith. At Easter 1543 Bishop Gardiner found his chance to 'bend his bow against the head deer' at Court. Hoby was sent to the Fleet on 19 March on the charge of harbouring a sacramentary. 'For like causes' Cawarden, Sternhold, Harman, Weldon, and others, were troubled. Within days they, with Cawarden and Hoby's wives, were pardoned,[39] but they knew thereafter what risks they ran, and that their most dangerous enemy was Gardiner. Hoby did not forget this in 1550 when Scudamore speculated upon that bishop's release from prison.[40]

In 1543 Hoby joined the household of Queen Catherine Parr, where he was responsible for her 'foreign receipts'.[41] In the campaign against France in the following year Hoby had command of 201 men; 100

33. *L&P* xiv(1). 93.
34. *ibid.* xiii(2). 1280 (fos. 40ᵛ, 48ʳ).
35. *ibid.* xiv(2). 541, 572 (3 vii), 591, 781 (fo. 102ᵛ).
36. Hoby was examined by Convocation, which annulled the marriage: *L&P* xv. 860.
37. See M.L. Robertson, 'Thomas Cromwell's servants: the Ministerial Household in Early Tudor Government and Society' (University of California at Los Angeles, Ph.D. thesis, 1975), pp. 438ff; S. Brigden, *London and the Reformation* (Oxford, 1989), ch. viii. Hoby witnessed Philip van Velde's evangelical will: PRO, PCC, Prob. 11/36, fo. 7ʳ.
38. *L&P* xiii(1). 424, 586; see below, letter 7.
39. Foxe, *Acts and Monuments*, v, p. 486; *APC* i, pp. 97, 101; *L&P* xviii(2). 241(6).
40. See below, letters 11, 25, 26, 28.
41. *House of Commons, 1509–1558* (Hoby).

pikes and 101 demi-hakes.[42] There began then an important part of
his career when he became responsible for recruiting the foreign
mercenary troops which became so vital for strengthening England's
debilitated military forces.[43] For his services at the fall of Boulogne
Hoby was knighted in September 1544.[44] In the following May he
was appointed master of the ordnance northward, and commissioned
to take 40 carters and levy 100 footmen from his lands in Worcestershire against Scotland, under the Earl of Hertford's command. He
spent the autumn of 1545 in campaign against Scotland. There his
former expertise in surveying fortifications proved valuable.[45] When
in August 1546 an embassy came from France to London to treat for
peace, Hoby was in attendance.[46] He was favoured by Henry, so the
Imperial ambassador told Charles V later, because of his 'skill in
languages, and because he was in the habit of serving the King in the
entertainment of foreigners'.[47] When Henry VIII died, 'in token of
special love and favour', he bequeathed Hoby 200 marks (a sum
entered, invented, by Hoby's friend, William Paget). And, so Paget
remembered, the King had promised to appoint Hoby Master of the
Ordnance.[48]

Upon Edward's accession Hoby found favour still. On 26 March
1547 Hoby was granted the office of Master of the Ordnance for life.[49]
In February 1548 van der Delft wrote to the Emperor that 'Hoby is
much liked by the Protector as he takes the same view in religious
affairs as he does'.[50] Within months Hoby was sent in embassy to
the Emperor: his mission to secure permission to recruit Imperial
mercenaries.[51] And there in Germany Hoby observed and thought
upon ways to reform, which would be close to the Protector's hopes,
and his own. The 'ruine of Germanie', he wrote in January 1549, had
been due to the 'princely and lordely estate' of the Bishops. He warned
Somerset to take example and to 'appoint unto the good [English]
Busshoppes an honest and competent lyuyng, sufficient for their maintenaunce', and to sequestrate 'the rest of their worldly possessions and
dignities'. This would 'auoid the vaine glorie' that prevented them
from doing their duty, which was to 'preach the Gospell and word of

42. *L&P* xix(1). 273, 275.
43. *ibid.* xix(1). 583; xx(1). 59, 106, 345; xxi(1). 834; xxi(2). 399.
44. *ibid.* xix(1), 933, 947; xix(2). 334.
45. *APC* i, pp. 159, 167; *L&P* xx(1). 737, 1167, 1221, 1286; xx(2). 118, 187, 347,
359, 400, 432, 572.
46. *ibid.* xxi(1). 1384 (1, iii, 2).
47. *CSPSp.* ix, p. 254.
48. *L&P* xxi(2). 634(1); *APC* ii, p. 18.
49. *CPR, Edward VI, 1547–1548*, p. 101.
50. *CSPSp.* ix, p. 254.
51. *CSPF* pp. 20, 24–5.

Christe'. Their sequestered estates could then be spent on 'the defence of our country, and maintenaunce of honest poore gentilmen'.[52] The hopes for the deprivation of conservative bishops, that there will be 'more quondam Busshoppes shortely', recurs throughout Scudamore's letters. And from Germany too Hoby wrote for a preaching licence for Mr Harman to instruct the people of 'E', a town 'hitherto by blinde guides led out of the way', in the 'true religion'.[53] That Hoby's plans to sequestrate episcopal estates corresponded exactly with his own material interest; that he had already benefited greatly from the sale of monastic lands, and hoped for bishops' manors;[54] does not entirely vitiate the sincerity of his purpose. For Hoby, as he acted later upon commissions to try conservative bishops and embezzling prebends or to take chantry lands, an issue of principle was at stake.[55]

Through the summer of 1549, while England was threatened by military failure and bankruptcy and convulsed by rebellion, Sir William Paget and Hoby in Brussels and Bruges wrote of foreign affairs, and awaited news from home. And Somerset wrote anxiously and angrily to Hoby on 23 and 24 August and again on 1 September of the rebellions which threatened the realm doubly by allowing the French king the opportunity to attack.[56] Though Paget, Hoby's friend and associate, wrote repeatedly as a Cassandra to Somerset, offering advice and criticism, there was no evidence of adverse comment from Hoby. Indeed, the Earl of Warwick told van der Delft on 23 September: 'You must know that Ambassador Hoby is entirely devoted to the Protector, and his creature'.[57] But Hoby was receiving disturbing news of the turn of high politics at home, and was soon to show those quintessential skills of the diplomat which the Imperial ambassadors noted in him. Van der Delft wrote of Hoby that 'he is ... very cool and can dissemble well',[58] and Renard later warned the Emperor that 'the face and drawling tone of the said Hoby made me suspect that he might be the man to think one thing and say another'.[59]

52. BL, Harl. 523, fos. 19r–20v; Strype, *Ecclesiastical Memorials*, ii(1), pp. 138–9.

53. BL, Harl. MS 523, fo. 107v.

54. See *L&P* xiv(1). 651(21), 1321; xv. 436(48); xvi. 947(13), p. 721; xvii. 548, 556(30); xix(1). 610(90), p. 507; xx(1). 846(79), 1335(26); xxi(1). 1166(73), 1537(29); xxi(2). 332(7), p. 435; F.M. Heal, *Of Prelates and Princes: A Study of the Economic and Social Position of the Tudor Episcopate* (Cambridge, 1980), pp. 128–9, 142.

55. Edward VI, *Chronicle*, p. 82; BL, Add. MS 5498, fos. 39r–57r.

56. BL, Harl. MS 523, fos. 50r, 52r, 53v. The last is printed in F.W. Russell, *Kett's Rebellion in Norfolk* (1859), pp. 215–17.

57. *CSPSp.* ix, pp. 454–5.

58. *ibid.* ix, p. 254.

59. *ibid.* x, p. 329.

The Political Context of Scudamore's Letters

Scudamore's first surviving letters to Hoby were written early in September 1549, just as the threat from rebellion had passed, but as a revolution in Court politics began. Scudamore wrote on 5, 7 and 9 September of the capture of the rebels, the military reverses in Scotland, the falls of the Bishops of London and Norwich.[60] But it was other news which brought Hoby swiftly home. He returned 'to see his family', so Edward VI thought; 'for certain speciall affayres', according to another observer.[61] But reports of the deep divisions in the Council, and of the enmity between Warwick and the Protector, were reaching the Emperor by the end of September.[62] Self advancement, or self preservation at least, depended upon Hoby being at Court to defend his interests. Though Warwick warned van der Delft that Hoby was Somerset's 'creature', this was no longer so. Hoby wrote urgently to the Protector of 'mine unpossibilities to supporte anie longer so waightie a charge' as his embassy abroad, and besought his help 'to alleviate the same before my departing out of England'. For he had suffered 'great losse . . . in the exchange' in converting his diets, because of the fall in the exchange rate.[63] But, so van der Delft heard, Hoby was 'not particularly well received' by Somerset. Worse, the offices vacant by the death of Sir Anthony Denny on 10 September which Hoby had returned to claim, Somerset gave, not to Hoby, but to 'other of his henchmen'.[64]

Early in October a 'most daungerous conspiracye' formed against the Protector. On the 5th the king wrote to rally his subjects to his and his uncle's defence at Hampton Court.[65] On the following day the Lords of the Council, led by Warwick, with their retinues marshalled in London, proclaimed Somerset's 'falshoode and treason' and sought aid for the king's safety.[66] And Somerset and the king, with their depleted Court and Council, and the Lords in London waited to see which way Russell and Herbert with their troops in the West, and which way the City of London, would commit their support. Meanwhile Hoby rode to Hampton Court, where he was welcomed by the king and Somerset, for 'thei toke him to be faythefull and trustie and no partie'.[67] Accordingly, they entrusted him with vital letters for the Lords in London: from the king, expressing alarm that

60. See below, letters 1–3.
61. Edward VI, *Chronicle*, p. 18; 'Eye-witness's account', p. 607.
62. *CSPSp.* ix, pp. 445–6, 448, 450.
63. BL, Harl. MS 523, fo. 107ᵛ.
64. *CSPSp.* ix, p. 460.
65. *Troubles connected with the Prayer Book*, p. 76.
66. *ibid.* pp. 80–1; *APC* ii, pp. 330–2.
67. 'Eye-witness's account', p. 607.

they 'intend with cruelty to purge his [Somerset's] faults', and urging moderation; and a desperate plea from Paget, Cranmer and Sir Thomas Smith: 'Life is sweet, my Lords, and they say you seek his blood and his death . . . beseeching the living God to direct your hearts to the making of a quiet end of these terrible tumults'.[68]

On 8 October Hoby brought these letters to the Lords in London, and set out the following day for Windsor (where the Protector had moved with the king to be better defended) with their reply. But he 'fayned that he had loste the lordes lettres . . . and wolde not trust any body, but returned him selfe to seeke the lettres'; meanwhile sending one of his 'trustie seruauntes' to tell the Court that 'all was well'.[69] But this was a brilliant ruse, devised by the Lords 'to the end they might win time the better that they might do their feats'.[70] And that 'smoth messenger' delivered secretly through the Court at Windsor the printed articles which denounced the Protector, so subverting Somerset's seeming supporters.[71] On 9 October the City of London and Russell and Herbert declared for the Lords against the Protector.[72] By the time that Hoby returned the next morning to Windsor 'all the courte were conformable . . . to do what he wolde haue them do with a becke'. And, cool and dissembling, 'all the way he tolde them that all was well'.[73] In the Presence Chamber Hoby assured Somerset: 'My Lord, . . . be you not affraide. I will lose this, my necke . . . yf you haue any hurte'.[74] But immediately Somerset's treason was declared, and he was placed under guard.[75] Hoby's betrayal was the most complete of all Somerset's followers, and Somerset did not easily forget the 'lost' letter.[76]

Hoby did not remain at Court. A week after the *coup* the Council sent Hoby, with Sir Thomas Cheyne, in embassy to the Emperor to explain the 'alteracon', the fall of the Protector. More urgent still was the need for Imperial aid to defend Boulogne, and this they were to solicit.[77] The rumour at Court too was that they would propose a marriage between the king and 'one of the king of the Romans' daughters', for Hoby had taken Edward's portrait with him.[78] They

---

68. Tytler, *England in the reigns of Edward VI and Mary*, i, pp. 220–2, 223–7.
69. 'Eye-witness's account', pp. 607–8.
70. Tytler, *England in the Reigns of Edward VI and Mary*, i, p. 231.
71. 'Eye-witness's account', p. 608.
72. CLRO, Journal 16, fos. 37ʳ ᵛ; Tytler, *England in the reigns of Edward VI and Mary*, i, pp. 231–5.
73. 'Eye-witness's account', p. 608.
74. BL, Harl. MS. 353, fo. 77ʳ; Tytler, *England in the reigns of Edward VI and Mary*, i, pp. 238–40.
75. 'Eye-witness's account', pp. 608–9; *APC* ii, pp. 342–3.
76. See below, letter 26.
77. *APC* ii, pp. 346–7; *CSPF p. 47; Troubles connected with the Prayer Book*, pp. 113–18.
78. *CSPSp.* ix, p. 470.

arrived in Brussels on 6 November, and in several audiences with the Emperor achieved the first purpose of providing information, but failed in the second. Charles desired them to be 'all of one opinion' in religion; 'till then ... he could neither so earnestly nor so thoroughly assist his good brother as his desire was'.[79]

From 22 November 1549 Richard Scudamore began writing to Hoby again. Away from Court, Hoby's need for news was urgent, for he knew how swiftly reverses came in politics. The London Lords had protested that 'we had not a fewe of us dyned above twyes to gither', but 'immediatly' Somerset had suspected conspiracy.[80] He had been right. In the aftermath of the *coup* all was uncertain. Warwick and Wriothesley had together brought down the Protector, but their alliance was fraught and fragile.[81] Hoby feared another reversal of faction in Court and Council, and with it a reaction in religion. His own position was precarious. Warwick had suspected him before the *coup*, and now, after his cool betrayal of Somerset, no one could be without suspicion of him. His own faith and interest aligned him with religious reform, but many now awaited a 'subvercyon of religion', a return to political ascendancy of a Catholic faction led by Wriothesley and Arundel, or—at first most unlikely, but potentially most danger- ous of all for Hoby—by Somerset. This was the prospect as Scudamore wrote throughout the winter of 1549 and spring of 1550: 'besechyng God ... to kepe an unytye amongst or magistrates'.[82]

Scudamore reported to Hoby that on Christmas Day Hooper preached to the Duke of Somerset and 'thos other prysoners of his faccyon' in the Tower upon the penitential psalms of David, from which rulers should learn that God punished them for their sins, and urged them not to 'seke revengement'.[83] But Hoby was apprehensive that they would, and their release seemed imminent. Scudamore was sent to attempt to regain the Duke's favour to Hoby: first to his Duchess, and then to Miles Partridge.[84] Scudamore did not only report to Hoby, but also acted as his suitor and agent, as these letters show. Hoby had other sources of information than Scudamore through these months, but probably none so immediate, and none without political inwardness. By 11 January it seemed clear that the plans of the 'old sort', led by Wriothesley and Arundel, to overthrow Warwick and to remove him and Somerset, terminally, had been thwarted.

79. BL, Harl. MS 523, fos. 113ᵛ, 116ʳ; *CSPSp*. ix, pp. 478–9.
80. *Troubles connected with the Prayer Book*, p. 117.
81. For the best account of the political tergiversations, see Hoak, *King's Council*, pp. 55–61, 242–58.
82. See below, letter 4.
83. See below, letter 8.
84. See below, letters 12–13, 25–26.

Scudamore reported then the house arrest of the Earl of Arundel, Sir Thomas Arundel, of Rogers and Wriothesley, and the assault upon the locks of the Privy Chamber.[85] Hoby was sent this news too by the Council—lest 'untrue report ... of busie and light [persons]' reach him—but only a week later, and in anodyne form. The Council insisted that Wriothesley was not under arrest, 'but he may go at his pleasure ... ther him listeth'.[86] This report Scudamore himself confirmed on 18 January.[87] On 25 January Scudamore wrote of the imprisonment of Wriothesley, and of Sir Thomas Pope, and the rumours of Bishop Tunstall's arrest. (Hoby's office in the Tower gave Scudamore special access to such information). The same news also came to Paget from the Council on 1 February.[88] But Scudamore, unlike the Council, also told Hoby, if obscurely, the reason why: 'it was high time to take the byrdes, for they purposed to haue made a popys fflyght'.[89] Much of what Scudamore reported was rumour, but it was especially rumour that Hoby needed to know.

Hoby remained in embassy until the winter of 1550. His letters of revocation were sent in August, but his successor, Sir Richard Morison, did not arrive in Augsburg until 9 November.[90] Hoby's half brother, Thomas, had travelled from Siena to the Emperor's Court to meet him. Sir Philip and Thomas Hoby left Augsburg on 9 November and arrived at Court on Christmas day.[91] Upon Hoby's return from embassy Scudamore's letters ceased. For much of the rest of Edward's reign Hoby remained in England. He was admitted to the Council in the summer of 1551, and attended 56 of its meetings.[92] He was a member of the embassy which went to France that summer, ostensibly to invest Henri II with the Garter,[93] and he was sent to the regent of Flanders in February 1552 'upon pretense of ordering of quarrels of merchants', but really to repay and raise loans for the Crown on the Antwerp market.[94] It was not until April 1553 that he was sent as resident ambassador once more to the Imperial Court, this time to mediate a peace between Charles V and Henri II.[95] During all these absences no letter from Scudamore survives. In June

85. See below, letter 10.
86. BL, Harl. MS 523, fo. 56ʳ.
87. See below, letter 11.
88. BL, Cotton MS Caligula E iv, fo. 207ʳ.
89. See below, letter 12.
90. *APC* iii, p. 45; *CSPSp.* x, p. 167; see below, letters 25, 28–33.
91. *Travels and Life*, pp. 61–4.
92. Hoak, *King's Council*, pp. 70, 111.
93. Edward VI, *Chronicle*, p. 63; *Travels and Life*, pp. 66–70; *CSPF* p. 109.
94. Edward VI, *Chronicle*, pp. 109, 111, 113; *CSPSp.* x, pp. 476–81.
95. *CSPF* pp. 260, 261, 266, 268, 272, 277, 279; *CSPSp.* xi, pp. 21, 23, 32, 43, 66, 67, 81–2.

and July 1553, as Edward VI was dying, Scudamore himself was sent post to Hoby with news.[96]

Scudamore's last letter to Hoby in this collection was written when Hoby had left England for the last time. Hoby had been directed by Queen Jane on 12 July to remain resident with the Emperor, but he was recalled on 8 August by Queen Mary.[97] He could not, and did not, expect to find favour with the new queen, particularly since he had been commissioned in 1551 to examine her Catholic household.[98] Simon Renard believed that Hoby's mere presence in England threatened religious unity, and always suspected him of plotting. He wrote, hopefully but wrongly, in September 1553 that Hoby was in the Tower.[99] Yet Hoby ostensibly supported Mary's marriage to Philip of Spain, whom he knew, and was even appointed to conduct Philip into England.[100] That journey was prevented by Wyatt's rebellion, in which so many of Hoby's friends were implicated and Hoby's own part was later suspected, though never proven.[101] 'By long sute' to the queen and Council Hoby was given licence to take a cure in the baths of Italy.[102] Renard again believed that this was a cover for 'some new revolt'. He called Hoby 'one of the craftiest heretics in England', and suspected Paget's association with him.[103] Gardiner, Hoby's old adversary, was also alarmed by Mary's granting him licence for exile.[104]

Hoby, with his brother and other members of his family, left England at the end of May and travelled towards Italy. Thomas Hoby recorded their journey through Flanders, Cleves and the Empire, and their entertainments on the way.[105] They arrived at Padua on 23 August 1554, and there joined the most famous of England's Protestant exiles, favourites and luminaries of Edward VI's Court: Sir Thomas Wroth, Sir John Cheke, Sir Henry Neville, Sir Anthony Cooke, and others.[106] It was while at Padua that Hoby received Scudamore's last letter, warning him of the danger of open association with the religious exiles; 'much myslyked here at home, and ... ageynst yor promyes made to dyuers of yor ffrendes'. As he wrote on 2 March 1555, Scudamore was preparing to join Hoby in Italy. In August Hoby, 'Mr Skydmore' with him, left Italy for England, visiting the con-

96. CSP, Domestic, 1601–1603; Addenda, 1547–65, p. 425.
97. BL, Harl. MS 523, fo. 43ᵛ; MS Cotton Galba B xii, fo. 253ʳ; CSPSp. xi, p. 155.
98. Edward VI, Chronicle, p. 82; CSPSp. xi, p. 182.
99. ibid. xi, pp. 240, 257, 258.
100. ibid. xi, pp. 395–6, 416, 425, 427.
101. Travels and Life, p. 97; CSPSp. xii, pp. 269–70.
102. Travels and Life, p. 103. On 29 May Mary wrote to Charles V asking his favour for Hoby: CSPSp. xii, p. 265.
103. CSPSp. xii, pp. 214, 231, 239, 259.
104. ibid. xii, p. 267.
105. Travels and Life, pp. 103–21.
106. ibid. pp. 116–17.

gregation of English exiles at Frankfurt on the way. Early in November Blount, Scudamore and Thomas Hoby departed Antwerp for England, leaving Sir Philip behind.[107] Later that month Hoby had an audience, 'a long and gracious conversation', with Philip of Spain, who promised him that 'he might firmly rely on his favour'.[108] But for all his diplomatic conformity, Hoby was still, with accustomed doubleness, in contact with the queen's enemies. He and Edward Courtenay, whose proposed marriage to Princess Elizabeth Hoby was said to have planned, wrote to each other at the end of November, teasingly, ironically, of the death of Gardiner. 'You have, in him [Gardiner], lost a good schoolmaster [in religion]. But ... I doubt not you shall find such whose hot and burning charity will help to instruct you ...', wrote Courtenay.[109] In spite of the persecution, Hoby left for England in January 1556, bearing a message for the queen from her husband.[110]

Upon his arrival in England, Hoby withdrew to his estates at Evesham and Bisham. In April 1558 Hoby, dying, left Bisham for London to seek the aid of doctors, unavailingly.[111] He made his will on 1 May, with his friends William Cecil, William Sheldon, John Lovelace and Edward Warner as witnesses. Of his evangelical faith there is little sign in his will: he bequeathed his soul to 'the merciful handes of Allmightie God and unto my redemer and saviour', and a great basin 'graven with a storye of the newe testament' to his wife. Of his great gains through service to the Crown there is ample evidence. His will had a codicil, detailing bequests to his servants. There was nothing for Richard Scudamore.[112] Hoby died on Whitsunday, 29 May 1558. His brother's widow left this epitaph of him on the tomb at Bisham where he was buried with his brother:

> Two worthye Knightes, and Hobies both by name,
> Enclosed within this marble stone do rest.
> Philip, the fyrst, in Caesar's Court hathe fame
> Such as tofore fewe legates like possest,
> A diepe discoursing head, a noble brest,
> A Courtier passing and a curteis Knight,
> Zelous to God, whos gospel he profest
> When gretest stormes gan dym the sacred light,
> A happie man whom death hathe now redeemed
> From care to joye that cannot be esteemed.[113]

107. *ibid.* pp. 121–6.
108. *CSPVen.* vi(1). 288.
109. *CSPSp.* xii. pp. 266–7, 281; *CSPVen.* vi(1), 284–5.
110. *ibid.* 341.
111. *Travels and Life*, pp. 126–7.
112. PRO, PCC, Prob. 11/40, fos. 267ᵛ–70ʳ.
113. Printed in *Travels and Life*, p. xv.

THE LETTERS OF RICHARD
SCUDAMORE TO SIR PHILIP HOBY,
SEPTEMBER 1549–MARCH 1555

1 *5 September 1549 (Adv. MS. 34.2.14, fo. 35ʳ)*

It may please yow to be aduertesyd that upon Sonday last Master Pollydors[1] hors was presented to the kynges maiestye yn Saynt Jamys parke, who receaued the same very thankefully, and the sword and the daggar lyked the kyng very well. Mr Granado[2] toke much paynes for the delyuery of the same, howbeyt I was glad to moue my lord protectors grace myself on Setorday to knowe his pleasure theryn, who sayd that it shold be receauyd on the morowe. And I thynke ther shal be some thyng provyded for to gratyfye Mr Pollydor for his good wyll so that he shall haue no other cause but to judge his gyft well enployed. And to begyn they haue geaven yn rewarde to his maid xl crownes. The occurrauntes here are not greate but for matters of that syde of the seas wt the whiche I will not trowble yow, because I suppose ye are better aduertesyd of them then I am able to expresse it. My lord of Warrewyck remayneth as yett in Norffolke mynystreng iustyce upon dyvers of the ryngleders of the rebellyons, amongst whom ther goeth many preestes to wrake.[3] The Busshop of London preached at Pawlles crosse on Sonday last, and yn the latter knott of the sermon he began to perswade men to come to the communyon, but he fered that the lett therof was because he thought that men dyd not use the thyng wt as much honor and deverence as it was worthye, declaryng ffurther his conscience theryn that after consecracyon the very body of chryst that was borne of the vyrgyn mary (yef that weare a bodye) and the self same bodye that dyd hang on the crosse (yef that weare a bodye), for the which good sermon men doth much mervell that he is not commytted to the Towre.[4] It was told me this day that Captain Julyan ys taken prysoner yn Scottland and iiijˣˣof his men slayne, but I am not able to sey certenlye.[5] Other newes I haue not at this tyme

1. An Italian mercenary captain: *L&P* xx(1). 751(2).
2. Esquire of the Stable.
3. The Norfolk rebels had been routed at Dussindale on 27 August: Wriothesley, *Chronicle*, ii, p. 21.
4. Bonner had been ordered by the Council to preach: Foxe, *Acts and Monuments*, v, pp. 745–6. For an account of his sermon, see BL, M 485/52, vol. 198, fos. 34ʳ–46ʳ.
5. A captain of Spanish mercenary troops in Scotland. This defeat threatened the defence of Haddington, a vital garrison: *CSPSp.* ix, pp. 453–4.

to assertayne yow of but the kynges grace removeth upon tuysday next to Ruchemond. Mr Chamberlayne[6] was deceaued of that which I aduertesyd yow yn my last letters, for it was the Ryngrove that at that tyme here arryved who hath gentle enterteynment at the counselles handes.[7] Thus besechyng god to prospere yow yn all yor prosedynges do leaue to trouble yow eny more at this tyme. Wreten at the blake ffryers[8] the v day of september. The ffrenche ambassador[9] remayneth here as yett untyll some tydynges come from Mr Wootton.[10]
By yor most bounden seruaunt

Richard Scudamore

2 *7 September 1549. (Adv. MS. 34.2.14, fo. 15ʳ)*

It may please yow to be aduertesyd that I had wreten the letter heryenclosed to be brought unto yow by Mr Pollydors seruaunt, who entendyth as to morrowe to take shyppyng and to come by longe the seas, but for expedycyon and the oportunytye of the messinger thought it best to send it by this berer beyng dispatched in post. The occurrauntes here are not greate but contynuall punysshyng of rebellyons. And yesternyght Mr Audelay and Mr Constable[11] brought to the courte C[aptain] Keytt and a brother of his,[12] and after long examynacyon they weare both caryed on horseback by the conduccyon of the seyd gentlemen, with people suffycyent wondryng at them, to Nuegate this present day, and Keyte rode not lyke no stoute captain, for his sadell was but a shyp skynne. My lord of Warrwyck had dyuers gentlemen of his band slayne but manye more hurt, amongst whom I thynke Sir Andrewe fflammock to be one, upon a greate blowe with a clubbe upon his belly, hauyng on hym but a sherte of mayle, the which stroke was so surely stryken that it made hym voyde blude both wayes.[13] This present mornyng ffrancisco the post[14] with

6. Sir Thomas Chamberlain, ambassador to the regent of the Netherlands.

7. The Rhinegrave of the Palatinate, who had served the French king in Scotland, visited England, where he was 'well speeded'. *CSPSp.* ix, p. 455; *APC* ii, p. 325.

8. Hoby's London house, formerly the home of the attainted Countess of Salisbury: *L&P* xvi. 947(31); xvii. 881(18).

9. Odet de Selve, resident French ambassador.

10. Dr Nicholas Wotton, Dean of Canterbury and York, Privy Councillor, and resident English ambassador at the French Court.

11. Thomas Audley and Sir Marmaduke Constable: *APC* ii, pp. 323, 351.

12. Robert Kett, the leader of the Norfolk rebels, and his brother, William.

13. Sir Andrew Flammock of Warwickshire made his will on 6 September: 'An eyewitness's account', p. 603 n. 1.

14. Francisco Tomazo, an Italian courier, had returned to England on 6 September: *CSPF* p. 46.

a seruaunt of the ffrench ambassadors arrived at the courte and told me that Mr Wotton is come all redy to montruell and ther remayneth untyll the ffrenche ambassador shall come to Calleys, the which I suppose wylbe shortelye. And as for the ffrench kynges departure from Bolleyn, I shall not nede to trouble yow therwith because I dowpte not but ye haue better aduertyesment therof then I shalbe able to declare.[15] Ther are commyssyons directed furth to take up carte horse to goo northewarde. I thynke it be for nothyng elles but to vittayll Haddyngton, the which haue nede to be done with spede for it is seyd that they haue no greate store. Ther is great ffawlte leyd here to Sir Petro Negro for the takyng of Cap[tain] Julyan, but he is accused by Spanyardes who are Gamboais ffrendes.[16] This after none I moved Mr Controller[17] on yor behalf to be so good unto yow that some meanes may be had that yow myght receaue yor dyettes, who answeared me that he wold cause that to be don shortelye, so that I trust by the next letter ye shall be better satysffyed therof. My lady appoynted this nyght to be at Wresebury,[18] who is with all hur howsehold yn helth, thankes be therfore geaven to the lyvyng lord to whom I praye to prospere yow yn all yor affayres. Wreten at the blake ffryers the vij[th] day of September by yor most bounden seruaunt.

Richard Scudamore

3 *9 September 1549 (Adv. MS. 34.2.14, fo. 13[r])*

It may please yow to be aduertesyd that yesterday my lord Grey[19] arryved at the courte and brought with hym certeyn of the capytaynez of the traytours of the West contrey as Humfrey Arrundell, Wynslade and his sonne, Bery, Coffyn, Sergeant Harryes eldyst sonne, Wyes, Sergeant Harryes sonne yn lawe, ffortescue, Holmes, thes two last weare Sir Thomas Arrundelles men, and one other who was theyr clerk whos name I knowe nott.[20] And at theyr furst comyng theyr

15. Henri II of France had gone in person in August to command his army marshalled at Montreuil.

16. Julian, Negro, and Gamboa were captains of Spanish mercenaries serving in Scotland: *CSP, Scotland*, pp. 90. 140, 148.

17. Sir William Paget, Comptroller of the Household.

18. Wyrardisbury or Wraysbury manor in Buckinghamshire was the Hoby's home, let to them by Lady Hoby's father, Sir William Stonor: *VCH, Buckinghamshire*, iii, pp. 322, 323, 325.

19. William, Lord Grey of Wilton, who had been sent against the rebels of Buckinghamshire and Oxfordshire, and then against the Western rebels in July 1549: *Troubles connected with the Prayer Book*, pp. 25–9, 33.

20. The Council had ordered Lord Russell on 21 August to send the rebel leaders for trial: *Troubles connected with the Prayer Book*, pp. 63–4, 126. For Sir Thomas Arundel, an adherent of Warwick, see *House of Commons, 1509–1558*.

were brought to stand all togeather for that the kynges maiestye (standyng upon the leades) myght see them, and after theyr weare brought before the counsell and after examynacyon they weare conducted by my lord Greyes men ffurth and sett on horseback withoute saddelles, and so weare conveyd towardes London with the band of Albaneyses[21] attendyng upon them untyll they came to fflete bridge, from the which place they sent to the fflete yong Wynslade, Harryes, Wyes, ffortescue, and the clerck, and the resydue weare caryed throwgh London to the Towre. And this morning Bartevile,[22] the ffrenchman, was by the clerck of the check with vj of the garde brought to the Towre, and as the ffame goeth it was for that he thought to haue stolen awey and wold haue entysed Sir George Howard[23] to haue goon wyth hym, who I suppose was hys accuser. The newys was brought yesterday mornyng that yor ffrynd Mr Dynney was departed from this transytorye lyef, but thankes be therfore geaven to God he is yet alyve, trustyng that he shall escape this danger.[24] I had almost forgotton one traytor Sir Thomas Pomery, who remayneth at Hownslowe very syke or elles he had borne companye with the rest.[25] Mr William Grey[26] shewed unto me that the Busshop of Norwhich was indyted of treason for comfortyng of the traytors of Norffolk.[27] Other newys at this present I haue not worthye of aduertyesment savyng that ther arryved upon ffryday at nyght last vj[c] ffressh men at Bolleyn under the ledyng of my lord Thomas Grey, Sir John Norton, and Knevett. Capt Gavarr[28] and the ungaryan are appoynted to serve northwarde. Thus I beseche God to prospere yow yn all yor affayres. Wreten at the Blake ffryers the ix[th] day of September by yor most bounden seruaunt

Richard Scudamore

Thys yevenyng my lord of Warrewyck came to his howse yn Holborn[29]

21. German mercenaries: *CSPF* p. 32.

22. A reward of £125 had been paid to him in 1547: *Trevelyan Papers*, p. 197.

23. Howard's brother-in-law was Sir Thomas Arundel. For Howard, see *House of Commons, 1509–1558*.

24. Sir Anthony Denny, Chief Gentleman of the Privy Chamber, died the following day.

25. A leader of the Western rebellion.

26. William Grey of Reading.

27. William Rugge or Reppes was both opposed to the Prayer Book and deeply in debt. Ostensibly on the latter grounds he was compelled to resign his bishopric on 26 December, 1549. His family came from Norfolk, and his brother was mayor of Norwich: Heal, *Of Prelates and Princes*, pp. 134, 139, 170–1; *Visitation of Norfolk*, p. 229; *CPR, 1548–9*, pp. 67, 385; *1549–50*, p. 163.

28. Charles de Guevara was a Spanish mercenary captain: *CSPF* pp. 32, 34, 37, 38.

29. Ely Place had been ceded to Warwick by the Bishop of Ely.

beyng fetched yn by the pencyoners,[30] and ther came with hym Mr Lyttelton, who humblye comendyth hym unto yow, and he shewed me that the endytyng of the Busshop of Norwhich was very certeyn. I beyng desyrous to knowe somewhate of the Busshoppes behavyor, he declared unto me that upon Keyttes sendyng for the seyd Busshopp, eyther to come to the campe or elles to the towne of Norwhich, who immedyatly obeyd his commaundement and came to the seyd towne long before my lord of Warrwickes comyng thyther, wheare he remayned with owt my lord knowyng of it untyll the morrowe after the Battell. On which day the Busshopp sent his man to my lord with a present, my lord demaundyng of the messynger wheare his master the Busshopp was, who answeared my lord that he was yn the towne and declared further howe long his abode had ben ther. Whearupon my lord comaunded the [. . .] seruaunt to bryng unto the Busshop his present ageyn. And upon further serche made it was proued by ffyue of the Busshoppes seruauntes that Keytt had ben thryes yn the Busshoppes bedd chambor, they twoo alone, and also that the Busshopp had both vytayled the camp and ayded them with money.

4 *22 November 1549 (Adv. MS 34.2.14, fo. 27ʳ)*
It may please yow to be aduertesyd that upon Monday, after the openyng of the gattes at Calleys, I delyuered yor letters to my lord deputye[31] ther, ffurther desyryng his lordship to haue yow yn remembraunce towchyng that matter that ye brake unto hym at yor late beyng with hym. And my seyd lord answeared me that he was not fforgetful of yow but as oportunytye wold serve he wold haue yow yn remembraunce. My arryvall at London was upon Tuysday immedyatly upon Symons departure, and then delyuered the letter to the counsell at Westminster, and that day I delyuered yor letter to Mr Secretorye Petor and then to Mr Controller (who willed me to geave unto yow by my letters his harty comendacyons). And as consernyng the chase greyhounde that he shold haue of my lord of Huntyngton,[32] he can not help yow with the same for that he at his beyng at the Emperours courte promised hym to Monsieur Graunde Velle.[33] And the same evenyng I repayred to my lord of Warrwyckes to Ely place, who hath bene and yett is troubled with a rume yn the hedd that it caused his lordshyp to kepe his chambor. And to the delyuery of your letter I was brought to my lordes bedd chambor, to whom lyeng yn

30. Gentlemen Pensioners.
31. George Brooke, ninth Lord Cobham.
32. Francis Hastings, second Earl of Huntingdon, Lieutenant General at Boulogne.
33. Nicolas Perronet de Granvelle, Chancellor and chief adviser of Emperor Charles V.

his bedd I gave yor letters, and my lord very gentyllye axed of yor welfare and after the ouersyght of yor letters seyd that he wold gladly do for yow that pleasure that shold lye in hym to do, and as for yor matters yn the marches of Wales his lordshyp willed me to devyse what I thought good and he wold put his hand therunto. But the procedying theryn must staye untyll Symons retorne. And as well as my symplycytye wold suffre I gave unto my lord most umble thankes on yowre behalf, thynkyng it good also that it wold please yow to remembre hym with yor thankfull letters for the same, the which shalbe a good occasyon eftsones to repayre unto my seyd lord of Warrewyck. And on the morrowe I attendyd upon Mr Herbart[34] both with yor letter and also the patorns of the harnes, the which lyked hym very well and yn conclusyon determyned upon the ffasshyon the purporture wherof ye shall receaue with this letter, prayeng yow to cause it to be made with as much expedycyon as may be convenyentlye to serve both for a horseman and ffoteman, as by his letter ye may perceaue ffurther of his mynde. And as consernyng the dischardge of the statutes that yow so ernestlye gave yn commaundement, to soly-cyte it had bene fynysshed before this tyme yef ther had not bene some oversyght, for Symon and Starnhold had caused a byll to be made accordyng to the statute the which ye left behynde yow whereyn was conteyned litle aboue half the dett. And the same byll was delyuered to Master Honnynges,[35] who sett it so forward that it is sygned by the counsell, but for as much as it is not a dischardge of the hole and that my lord greate master[36] is very scrupulos to delyuer the other all though his bill doth specyfye of the hole somme, I haue had recourse to the clerk of the Staple and ther haue taken oute the effecte of both the seyd statutes and haue caused a newe byll to be made of the hole and delyuered the same to Mr Honnynges handes to proferr it to the counsell, trustyng that by my next letters ye shalbe ffully satisffyed theryn. And when ther shalbe a suffycyent dischardge had ffurth for the same I will at leysure sue to my lord greate master for thother statute. For such matters as passed here before my arryvall I referre them to Symons declaracyon. And sence my comyng as yett to my knowledge are fewe [occurrances], sauyng that yesterday one hosyer, callyng hym self at his beyng yn ffraunce Blaunche fflowre, was comytted to the Towre, and that Keytt shall shortely goo to Norfolke to execucyon. My lady my mastres is yn helth, thankes be therefore to God, but Mastres Anne[37] and dyuers others yn hur howse

34. Sir William Herbert, Master of the Horse.

35. William Honings, Clerk of the Privy Council.

36. William Paulet, Lord St John.

37. Lady Hoby's daughter by her second husband, Walter Welshe: *Visitation of Worcester*, p. 140.

be syck. Mr William Barryngton[38] is departed from this lyef. I haue stayed the iij yardes of newe cloth, as yor pleasure was, the which was ones packed to be sent unto yow. Others at this presentes I haue not to aduertyes yow of, but that Mr Phelpot[39] is not at the courte so that I can do nothyng for yor hors as yett. Thus besechyng God to prospere yow yn all yor affayres and kepe an unytye amongst or magistrates. Wreten at the Blake ffryers the xxij[th] daye of Nouember by yor most bounden seruaunt

Richard Scudamore

5 *27 November 1549 (Adv. MS. 34.2.14, fo. 17[r])*

It may please yow to be aduertesyd that this present afternoone, beyng the xxvij[th] day of Nouember, Perott,[40] my lord warden[41] is seruaunt, arryued at my lord of Warrwyckes (who kepith his howse for that he is troubled with a rume), wheare ther was assembled all the counsell except the Erle of Southampton, who lyeth syke at his howse yn London and, as some saye, verye wilde.[42] And after I had receauyd certeyn letters directed to the ambassadors of the Emperour and of Venyce the which I delyuered ymmedyatly. And yor letters to my lord of Warrwick I do deteyne accordyng unto yor pleasure. The dischardge for yor statutes is alredye sygned by the counsell and delyuered to be sygned by the kynges maiestye. My lord greate master entendyth to haue the kepyng of it for his discharge and will cancell the other statutes, but I will sue it furth under the greate seale and then it maketh no matter and yef my lorde greate master taketh his pleasure therwith, for it shalbe at all tymes redye to be exemplyed oute of the Chauncerye after it is once enrolled. My Honnynges hath shewyd hym self very gentle and ffryndly unto yow yn solycytyng of

38. Sir William Barentyne of Oxfordshire died that day. His son Francis was a Gentleman Pensioner: *House of Commons, 1509–1558*.

39. Groom of the Privy Chamber: *APC* ii, p. 389.

40. Sir John Perrot had been knighted on 17 November, perhaps as reward for support of Warwick against Somerset. He was also Sir Thomas Cheyne's son-in-law: *DNB; House of Commons, 1509–1558*.

41. Sir Thomas Cheyne, Lord Warden of the Cinque Ports, had been sent with Hoby by the Council on 22 October to tell the Emperor of the proceedings against the Protector, and to renew the request for the loan of troops in aid of Boulogne: *CSPF* p. 47; *CSPSp*. ix, pp. 478–9.

42. Thomas Wriothesley, first Earl of Southampton, had just lost a bitter struggle for primacy in Court and Council, or so it seemed. By 26 November all the councillors were attending upon Warwick at Ely Place, where all business was being carried out, and on that day Warwick appointed a reformer to the Council: *CSPSp*. ix, pp. 476–7; Hoak, *King's Council*, p. 253.

the same, wherfore, it may stand with yor pleasure to gratyfye hym with yor letters of thankes. My lord of Huntyngton maketh greate preparacyon to come shortlye ouer seas with a handsome band aswell as Englyssh men as of Almaynes. The sayeng is that Cortpennye[43] cometh to goo with hym with the most parte of the Almaynes that weare yn Scottland. Upon Sonday at nyght last past Sycell[44] and Walley[45] weare both comytted to the Towre, and sythens that tyme ffulmeston[46] and Kelwaye[47] are restrayned of theyr lybertyes. Yesterday ther was arrayngned at Westminster hall Arrundell, Wynslade, Bery, and Holmes, rebellyons of the West contrey, and the two Keyttes, who confessyng theyr ffawltes weare all condempned to be hanged, drawn and qwarteryd.

And withyn thes ij dayes ther was brought furth of the West contrey ij gentlemen beyng of the rebellyons ther, and pardoned, but theyr landes geaven awey, whos names is Bonfyld and Predaux,[48] for speakyng of sedycyous wordes myndyng to stere up a nue comocyon, but God I trust will shorten them from such theyr devyllesh purposes. I dyd send unto yow a letter of Sir William Herbartes with the patern of his harnes, but whether it be comen unto yor handes I knowe not. I haue spoken with Mr Phelpottes for yor horse, who shewyth me that he hath all redy wreten unto the contrey for hym but as yett he can here no answeare therof. My lord Cobham is not come to London.[49] Other occurrauntes I haue not at this tyme to trouble yow with, for Mr Broke[50] shewyd me that he had sygnyfyed unto yow of theyr procedyngs yn the Parlyament howse, synce which tyme nothyng hath passed but that the lower howse goeth abowtes to shue to haue the relyef for shypp and clothes to be remytted and yn the stede therof will graunt a subsydye,[51] the circumstaunce wheareof by my next

43. Conrad Pfening, a famous German mercenary captain, who had on occasion raised foreign troops for England.

44. William Cecil was one of Somerset's personal secretaries and Master of Requests in his household. He had been with Somerset at Windsor, and first placed in the custody of Richard, Lord Rich: *APC* ii, pp. 327, 343, 372.

45. Richard Whalley was another of Somerset's adherents who fell in the October *coup*: *House of Commons, 1509–1558*.

46. Richard Fulmerston, controller of Somerset's household and Marshal of the King's Bench, fell with Somerset in October: *House of Commons, 1509–1558*.

47. Richard Keilway was Surveyor General of the Court of Wards and another adherent of Somerset's who had fallen with him. On 26 November he entered into a bond to present himself weekly to the Council: *APC* ii, p. 362.

48. Humphrey Bonville of Ivybridge and John Prideaux of Tavistock: F. Rose-Troup, *The Western Rebellion of 1549* (1913), pp. 498, 500.

49. Lord Deputy of Calais.

50. Robert Broke, Recorder of the City of London. He was a neighbour of Hoby's in Carter Lane. *House of Commons, 1509–1558*.

51. 3 & 4 Edward VI c. 23; *SR* iv, pp. 122–5. Hoby was himself M.P. for Cardiff boroughs.

letters I trust to aduertyes yow. Mr Paston who hath hym commendyd
unto yow prayeth yow to remembre him with some hawkes either
ffleyng or sore hawkes.

It hath pleasyd God as upon Sonday last past to call yor seruaunt
Hugh Wynston unto his mercye. Thus I beseche God to prospere yow
yn all yor affayres. Wreten at the Blake ffryers the xxvij[th] day of
Nouember by yor most bounden seruaunt

Yor exchaunge was made in good tyme, for it is wors at this present
by vj[d] yn euery pownd then it was at that tyme.[52]

Richard Scudamore

6 *5 December 1549* (*BL. Add. MS 11042, fo. *53[r]*)

It may please yow to be advertesyd that upon ffryday at nyght[53] very
late I delyuered yor letter unto my lord of Warrewyck after the
departure from thens of all the kynges most honorable Counsell who
sate ther yn the Counsell, for that my lord of Warrewyck kepyth yett
his chamber. And after that my lord had perused yor long letter, seyd
unto me that he wold answeare yow yn certayn poyntes therof,
comaundyng me to attend upon his lordshyp on the morrowe, accor-
dynge unto whos appoyntment I wayted ther Setorday, Sonday, &
Mondaye, but by occasion that my lord was troubled with his disease
kept his bedd ij dayes. And on the monday[54] all the Counsell came
thether exept the Erle of Arrundell, the cause of whos absens I can
not lern. And the Erle of Sowthampton who abydeth styll syke yn his
howse.[55] And that nyght I, fearing lest my seyd lord of Warrwyck
shold iudge slacknes in me for not geavyng good attendaunce upon
him, found the meanes to come to his speche, puttyng hym yn remembraunce of his former pleasure, who seyd that he had not as yett
wreten but he wold shortlye, seyng ffurther thatt the kynges hyghnes
with all his most honorable Counsell had seen yowre hole discours.
And yor doyng theryn they much comendyd, allowyng both yor
dylygent servyce and also yor good intellygence. And my lord of
Warrewyck dyd geave unto yow a very good reporte, promysyng unto

52. The exchange rate in November 1549 was 20s 1d flemish; the rate in May had
been 20s. 6d.: J.D. Gould, *The Great Debasement: Currency and the Economy in Mid-Tudor
England* (Oxford, 1970), table ix.
53. 29 November.
54. 2 December.
55. The Earls of Southampton and Arundel were conspiring against Warwick to
win control of the Council and Court. Wriothesley had ceased to attend Council
meetings after 22 October: Hoak, *King's Council*, pp. 59–60, 246–51.

yow all such ffavor or pleasure as shall lye yn hym either for yor affayres abowte the Courte, the marches of Walys or elles wheare.[56]

Thearfore it may please yow to consyder his lordshyp with yor letters of thankes as ye shall haue occasyon to wryte unto hym. The dischardge of yor statute is sygned by the kynges maiestye and remayneth yn the custodye of my lord great master, but I ame promysed to haue it as to morrowe to sett it to the sygnet and privey seale, and afterwardes to the greate seale. And then I must bryng the greate seale to my lord greate master, whearfore I do entend to sue oute a duplycat, that is to haue it doble wreten to the greate seale and then to kepe the one. The ouer charge of the suyng furth of the same wilbe the more by ffoure nobles or ther abowtes. Ye shall ffurther understand that I haue receauyd CCxxiiij li for yor dyett money, more throwe the gentlenes of Mr Williams' clerk then of hym self,[57] the which money I wyll not delyuer oute before Symons retorne, at which tyme I trust yor pleasure shalbe knowen. I have put my lord lysle[58] yn remembraunce for the chase dogg that he promysed yow, who seyd that he merveled much thatt the dogg had not been sent unto hym before this, alledgyng further that yf it came not shortly that then he wold send a seruaunt of his owne for hym. And my lord of urmond[59] seyth that he fforgeateth yow not but that he will prouyde a hownd for yow as sone as he can. Vpon Setorday last ther was certeyn nues brought to the Counsell of a certeyn stere that was begon at newborye yn Berkeshyre, to the acquyetyng of the whych the capytayn of the garde wt all his men and lx of the garde weare appoynted to goo thetherwardes, but that appoyntment beyng alteryd Sir John Williams, Sir Thomas Carden,[60] and dyuers other gentlemen wear sent immedyatly awey for the redresse therof, but to whate ende it is come to I knowe not. But onles God doth extend his great mercy ouer us to kepe the Counsell yn an unytye and amytye, and to indue them with the grace to be very circumspect yn theyr doynges, the rage of the beastlye commons is such that it will (I feare) very shortly brast oute. Ther was sworn ynto the pryve Counsell vpon ffryday last the lord marqwess of Dorcett, and the Bushopp of Elye,[61] the which putteth all honest hartes yn good coumfort for the good hope that they haue of the perseueraunce of Goddes woord. Yett that notwith-

56. Warwick owed Hoby favour after his part in the October *coup*.
57. Sir John Williams, treasurer of the Court of Augmentations.
58. John Dudley, son of the Earl of Warwick.
59. Thomas Butler, Earl of Ormond.
60. Sir Thomas Cawarden, Hoby's Protestant friend, was Sheriff of Surrey.
61. Henry Grey, third Marquess of Dorset, and Thomas Goodrich, Bishop of Ely, rose to prominence at the height of the struggle between Warwick and Wriothesley for control of the Council. Protestants were admitted to counter the admission of Catholics. BL, Add. MS 48126, fos. 15[v]–16[r]; Hoak, *King's Council*, pp. 54–7, 245–6, 248–9.

stondyng ther be some wyse men yn a great perplexite of mynde theryn for that the brute goeth so openly of so ernest sute made for the [fo.* 53ᵛ] delyveraunce of the late duke of Norfolke, the which was almost brought to passe by the ernest suytt of my lady of Rychmond,[62] but by whom she receauyd ffyrst comfort theryn I knowe not. Many of the Counsell were perswaded that the late Duke was become as good a chrystyan as eny was yn england, but I am much affrayed that god hath not yett called hym. By the which perswasyon the most parte of the Counsell that favoreth goddes worde weare become almost his ffryndes, so much that his comyng furth was shortelye loked for, but I trust that God hath so reveled his cloked relygyon with much dissymulacyon that at this present the solycytors of his suytt are not yn so much comfort as they weare three dayes past, I trust this be the workyng of god for it can be judged non otherwyse, but the begynnyng of this suytt was pryvely procured by some of the old sort to the entent to make theyre part the stronger.[63] Ther was also a brute (and not amongst the meane sort) that master Courtney shold come at lybertye.[64] My lord Cobham arryved at London upon Setorday last, with whom I have ben twyse sence his comyng, puttyng his lordshyp yn remembraunce of yor request unto hym, who answeared that he wold wold withyn ffewe dayes take a tyme for it. Me semyth it shall not be so ernestlye performed as it was with wordes promysed. I have also spoken with Mr Arnold,[65] who promysed to paye unto my handes iiijˣˣ crownes or the value therof to the vse of his brother[66] as sone as his man cometh oute of Gloucester shyre, but when that wilbe he knoweth not the tyme certeyn. I can perceaue nothyng that they do yn the parliament howse but, as I by my last letters aduertesyd yow of, the remyssyon of a parte of the relyef, whos name is turned yn to a subsydye, and one payment more graunted than was before with the restoryng of the payment of ffee ffermes to the kyng ageyn immedyatly after the next payment payd.[67] This parlyament is called the styll parlyament. It is not misnamed for they do almost nothyng but

62. Thomas Howard, third Duke of Norfolk, had been attainted for treason on 27 January, 1547. His daughter was the widow of Henry VIII's son, Henry Fitzroy, Duke of Richmond.

63. Catholic councillors were attempting to win control in Council and, allegedly, to make Princess Mary Regent of England: BL, Add, MS 48126, fo. 15ᵛ; Hoak, *King's Council*, pp. 246–9.

64. Edward Courtenay, Earl of Devonshire, had been imprisoned in the Tower in November 1538 and attainted in 1539 for treason. He was released upon Mary's accession.

65. Nicholas Arnold of Gloucestershire, a Gentleman Pensioner. He was another of Hoby's Protestant friends, and Scudamore's cousin. *House of Commons, 1509–1558*.

66. Richard Arnold of Gloucestershire. Scudamore would be the principal beneficiary and executor of his will. *House of Commons, 1509–1558*.

67. 3 & 4 Edward VI, cc. 23, 18; *SR* iv, pp. 122–4, 118–19.

geave the lokyng ther one ouer thother. Upon Sonday last ther was
admytted ynto the ordre of the Garter the lord delaware, and Sir
William Harbart. And Mr Pagett is created lord pagett of
Beaudesert,[68] by the meanes whearof he is oute of his controllershypp,
ynto whose Roome is placed Sir Anthony Wyngfeld.[69] And Sir Thomas
Darcye appoynted vyce Chamberleyn and Capt. of the garde.[70] Ye
shall further perceaue that my lord of Warrewyck is nomynated to be
Marques of pembroke, and also shalbe lord Treasorer of England.
And the Erle of Arrundell shalbe lord greate Chamborleyn, and that
my lord pagett shalbe lord Chamberleyn.[71] The admyssyon of all the
seyd dygntyes stayeth, as it is seyd, of my lord of Warrwyckes comyng
to the Courte. I have solycyted Mr Chauncellor[72] for thallowance of
the reparacyons of Stanwell,[73] who declared unto me that he had yow
yn remembraunce but he requyred me to bere with hym theryn untyll
the parlyament be fynysshed. And then he wold take an order therof.
Mr Phelpott hath receauyd none answeare oute of the contrey as yett
consernyng yor hors, but he loketh daylye for the same. Mr Wroth
sayeth that he will burden yow with unkyndnes for that he hath
receauyd no letter from yow sence yor departyng.[74]

And wheare as I aduertesyd yow by my last letters of the comyttyng
of Sycell and Whalley to the Towre, ye shall perceaue that on the
morrow after theyr comyng to the Towre they had both the lybertye
of the Towre, and Sycell lyeth at Cornelys howse.[75] Mr Kelway is
ageyne at lybertye, but ffulmoston remayneth as yet yn sauffe kepyng
at my lord of Warrewyckes. And on ffryday last pynnock of Worcester
shyre was brought up, and that nyght he was comytted to the fllete
wheare he remayneth.[76] Thus haue I heapyd together such thynges
as I do knowe although it be not yn good ordre, but for as much as

68. Paget, who had been with Somerset at Windsor, was influential in attaining his peaceful submission. This was his reward. Tytler, *England under the reigns of Edward VI and Mary*, i, pp. 223–7, 239–43.
69. Wingfield had been aligned with the London Lords against the Protector, and had been sent to arrest him. *DNB*.
70. Darcy replaced Wingfield in these important Household posts: Hoak, *Kings Council*, pp. 82–3.
71. False rumours.
72. Sir Edward North, Chancellor of the Court of Augmentations.
73. Hoby had been made chief steward of the manor of Stanwell in Middlesex in 1545: *VCH, Middlesex*, iii, pp. 37, 46–7.
74. Sir Thomas Wroth was appointed one of the four Principal Gentlemen upon the reorganisation of the Privy Chamber at Somerset's fall. He was another of Hoby's Protestant friends. *APC* ii, pp. 344–5; *Travels and Life*, pp. 116, 117, 120.
75. Cecil was released from the Tower on 25 January upon a recognisance of 1,000 marks. John Cornelius was a gunfounder in the Tower. *APC* ii, p. 372; *House of Commons, 1509–1558* (John Cornelius).
76. William Pynnock of Hanley Castle, Worcestershire, was bound in recognisance for £100 on 18 December' *APC* ii, p. 367.

my ignoraunce is to yow well knowen I haue good hope that yow wyll take it yn good parte. Nowe hauyng none other thyng worthye of aduertyesment (but that yor rent of Yorke shyre is receauyd) do beseche the lord to prospere yow yn all yor procedynges. I have stayed the sendyng of this letter by the space of iiij or v dayes bycause my lord of Warrewycke told me upon monday last that a post shold be dispatched to come unto yow. Wreten at the Blake ffryers the vth day of december by yor most bounden seruaunt.

Yet may please yow that Mr fflemmyng[77] and John lymes hath declared unto me that a gonners Roome of xijd by the day is ffallen voyed by the deth of a gonner that was taken at Seynt Andrewes and lately dyed, the which Roome is stayed untyll yor pleasure be knowen theryn. For as much as John lymes hath ben a sutor unto yow yn that behalf, yn consyderacyon that his Roome is paynefull and hether to he hath had small recompence for his servyce, that it may stand with yor pleasure to directe yor letters to Mr lyeffetenant with spede declaryng yor pleasure yn that behalf, and yef I myght with yor ffavor comend eny man unto yow I do judge John Lyems both for his honestye and his dylgens to be worthye for the same.

Rychard Scudamore

7 *15 December 1549 (Adv. MS 34.2.14, fo. 31^r)*

It may please yow to be aduertesyd that upon Sonday towardes the evenyng my lord warden arryved at London and landed at the black ffryers, and ther toke his hors and rode yn post ynto Holborn to my lord of Warrewyckes, and from thens yn post to the courte.[78] I could not haue an occasyon to see hym because my ladye my mastres had sent for me, at whos commaundement I repayred to Wreyseburye, and before my retorne my lord warden was departed to hys howse yn Kent. Howbeit Mr Blount of the privey chambor[79] shewed me that my lord merveled greately that I had not come unto hym for that yow had declared unto his lordshyp that I had many suyttes of yors to solycyte. Wheareunto my lord beyng mynded (as he seyd) to putte his ffurderaunce. Whearefore at his retorne to the courte I will prove whether he will contynue yn the same mynd. The cause that my lady sent for me was to will me to ryde to Stonar ther to do my endeuor to qualyfye certeyn occasyons of unkyndenes conceauyd by Mr

77. Sir Frances Fleming was Lieutenant of the Ordnance.
78. Sir Thomas Cheyne returned from his mission to the Emperor while Hoby remained.
79. Sir Richard Blount of Mapledurham, Gentleman Usher of the Privy Chamber.

Stonar[80] and disclosed by his letters ageynst my ladye, accusyng hur
that it becomed hur not to goo abowt to sett hym to scole for he was
to olde to lerne at hur handes, and that she dyd not onlye disquyett
hym beyng hur father but also his hole howse. But after the wrytyng
of his letter unto my lady he sent one of his seruaunts to her prayeng
her to come to see hym this Chrystemas holydayes, wyllyng my
ladye yn any wyse she shold not haue yn rehersall any of his formar
accusacyons either with hym self or with any of his howsehold. My
ladye not beyng satysffyed hereyn but much disquyeted that her father
shold conceaue any displeasure ageynst hur undeservyng, fearyng lest
she clered not hur self yn thes thynges his displeasure shold encreas
hereafter, whearupon my lady willed me on hur behalf ffurst to desyre
hur ffather to stand so good ffather unto hur as at such tyme as she
accordyng unto hur bounden duetye shold come to vysyte hym that
it myght please hym to lycence hur to stand to hur declaracyon
towchyng the premysses, and yef that myght not be obteyned that
then it myght please hym to declare such gryeffes unto me as he had
conceauyd ageynst my lady. And when I had receauyd my hole
erraund I toke my journey and came to Master Stonars at such
tyme as he was at dynner accompanyed with his swete hart Mastres
Margaret. And after I had don unto Master Stonar my ladyes comendacyons, I began to move hym accordyng unto my ladyes commaundement to me geaven, but he wold in no manner wyse that eny
matter shold come eny more to rehersall, howbeit he was contented
to disclose his gryeff unto me whereyn he thought that he was disquyeted by my lady and so began to say that he was a man that had
leved long and thought that he knewe very well howe to ordre hym
self and that my lady was much geaven to the Scryptures[81] and that
she alwayes was arguyng and contendyng with hym yn the same, the
which thyng he cold in no wyse bere and specyallye at hur handes.
And an other matter he leyd to my ladyes chardge for that she shold
be offendyd with Sir Richard his prest for fetchyng home ageyne of
Margaret his woman. But after I had declared my ladyes excuses unto
hym hereyn he toke upon hym therewith to be well pleasyd and
satysffyed this quarell was pyked bycause my lady shold ffynde no
ffawlte with mastres Margaret, and yn conclusyon seyd that yef it
pleased my ladye to come unto hym to make merye and not to medle
with hym nor with eny of hys howseholde she shold be as welcome as

---

80. Sir Walter Stonor of Stonor, Oxfordshire, Lady Hoby's father. He had been
knighted on Flodden Field in 1513, and was Lieutenant of the Tower. He died in
August 1550. *APC* ii, pp. 43, 154. R.J. Stonor, *Stonor* (Newport, 1951).

81. Lady Hoby was as committed an evangelical as her husband. She had been
pardoned with him in 1543 for associating with a sacramentarian heretic. *L&P* xviii(2).
241(6).

euer she was, and so my lady hath determyned to kepe hur Chrystemas at hur ffathers. And Mr Stonar shewyd me further that he was a sykelye man (as at this present he is much troubled with the gowte), and for that he is alredye bound yn conscyence by his promys he neuer entendyth to marrye, and for asmuch as Margaret hath all redy receauyd a greate sclaunder by Rous his man (yett Master Stonar durst undertake ther was no harme don), to make amendes therof and to satisfye the world Rous and she shall marrye together. Yet, seyth Mr Stonar, I haue covenaunted with them both to remayne and to serue hym styll. Yef I shold declare unto yow the cyrcumstaunce of his communycacyon I shold be to tedyous. He taketh greate coumfort at yor last comunycacyon with hym and yn especyally with yor examples of my lord of Shrewysbury and the lord of Derbye. He wyll neuer forgeate them, but sheweth euery one that he taketh to be his frynd of them and that his sone Hoby was not ageynst his mariage. [fo. 31ᵛ] Mr Bygges,[82] Mr William, and Symon arryved upon Wenysday last at London, by whom I do perceaue that before theyre departure from yow ye had receauyd no letters from me sence my comyng ynto England, wheareat I do greatlye muse, for asmuch as I haue wekely wreten letters to yow and delyuered them to Mr Stacye,[83] who promysed me that they shold be delyuered, assuredlye trustyng that yn thys ye will conceaue no ffawlt yn me but that I haue done theryn and entend [...] for such thynges as I shall haue knowledge from tyme to tyme to satysfye yor expectacyons. And wheareas in my last letters I aduertesyd yow of an alteracyon of my lord of Warrewick to be Erle of Pembroke and to be lord treasorer, the ffame therof is at this present stylled. Whether it be that my lord contynueth as yett unrecouered or elles that he will not chaunge his old dygre I knowe not. The kynges lerned counsell hath ben many tymes with the lordes of the counsell: either it is for some greate matter to be had in the Parlyament or elles for matters consernyng prysoners beyng in the Towre, and it is the rather iudged to towche the prisoners, because manye of the counsell hath ben dyuers tymes this weke at the Towre with the Duke of Somersett. But howe so euer the world shall goo the prisoners are indifferent mery, and the most part of them hath ther wyffes comyng to them. And upon wenysday last my lady of Somersett went to my lord of Warrewickes and spake with my lady, but it was seyd that my lord wold not [...]. Upon wenysday last my ladye Elisabethes grace was mett by the most parte of the gentlemen of the courte, and so brought to Seynt Jamys wheare hur grace remayned untyll this present, on which day beyng accompanyed with a greate

82. Thomas Bigges was married to Magdalen, Hoby's sister, and was Richard Scudamore's uncle. *Visitation of Worcester*, p. 16.
83. Thomas Stacy, a City mercer, lent Hoby money. *Register of Freemen*, p. 109.

maynye of ladyes came to westminster and [...] to the closett, and after dyned with the kynges maiestye yn his chambor of presens and it was seyd that afterwardes dyuers great ladyes comyng from the courte by the duches of Somersett went yn and vysyted hur.[84] Court-peny is com to London with a great band of [...] to be transported ouer the seas, and as I suppose they with the resydue shall take journey with yn thes thre dayes. And it is seyd that Courtpenyes band shall mustre [...] the kyng as to morrowe. My lord Cobham hath don nothyng as yett yn yor matter for I spake [with] hym this daye but he speketh feyre wordes. The Erle of Worcester is deceassed and Sir William Herbart is placed yn all his places and offyces yn Wales.[85] My ladye of Ruchemond hath gotten lycence of the counsell that she may haue accesse to hir ffather, and to begyn sat with hym yesterday by the space of ij long howres. I pray to God it may be for the best. The gentlemen that accompanyed my lord warden doth so reporte yow so well that it [...] them to do it no better but how so euer it hapenyth they can not aforde one [...] by my lord warden. As for matters of Parlyament ther is as yett little or nothyng passyd, sauyng an ordre for punysshyng of rebellyons as yef ther be found eny com-panye of them under the nombre of xij that then ther shalbe a proclamacyon made yn the kynges name that they shall departe euery one home yn peaceable maner, and yef they faile so to do that then it shalbe lefull to put them to the sworde. And yef it happen that ther shalbe aboue the nombre of xij that then the rulers with the gentlemen ther to levey the power of the contrey and to subdue them by vyolence. And yef eny tenaunt or fermor shall refuse yn such case to goo with theyr londlordes ageynst any such rebellyons that then they shall forfett the ynterest of theyr seyd tenures. And yef [any] shalbe founde aboue the nombre of xij persons to breke up eny hedge or dyche that then it shalbe adiudged ffelonye.[86] I haue at this tyme non other thyng to aduertyes yow of save here by ij gentlemen whom they sey the be ambassadors from the Duke of Cleve. Besechyng God to prospere yow yn all yor proceadynges. Wreten at the black ffryers the xv day of December by yor most bounden seruaunt

Richard Scudamore

84. Van der Delft reported that she was 'received with great pomp and triumph, and is continually with the king'. *CSPSp.* ix, p. 489.

85. Herbert was rewarded for his support for Warwick during the *coup* of October 1549.

86. 3 & 4 Edward VI c. 5; *SR* iv, pp. 104–8.

8 *26 December 1549 (Adv. MS 34.2.14, fo. 21ʳ)*

It may please yow to be aduertesyd that accordyng as by my last letters I aduertesyd yow Mr Starnhold departed from London the xxjᵗʰ of December to Wreyseburye, and on the morrowe after, beyng Sondaye, the maryage was solemnysed, and on the Monday (after they had receauyd god chere at my ladyes handes) they departed towardes Hampshyre, beyng accompanyed with Mr Bygges, Mr Parker, Mr Wallwen, Edward Blount, Symon, Thomas Deryck, & certeyn other of my ladyes ffolkes.[87] And because I thought that the Parlyament shold haue bene proroged untyll after the holydayes, as yn very dede it is not, but contynueth styll, although of ccc persons and odd of the lowar howse ther remayneth at London not past a ffowre score.[88] I stayed the journey ynto Hampshyre and retorned that nyght to London, supposyng I shold haue had some occasyon for matters of Parlyament to haue sygnyfyed unto yow, but as yett I knowe none worthye of aduertyesment. And on the same day the Stuard Bulstrode and Charnelles arryved at London, and the Stuard had delyuered all yor letters before my comyng, and accordyng unto yor comaundement I repayred to Mr Herbart to knowe hys pleasure consernyng the harnes the which yow wrote unto hym of, whos answeare was furst that he gave unto yow his most hartye thankes for yor gentlenes theryn, and secondarelye he seyd that he wold send to Osemonde to take mesure of hym whereby ye shold perceaue whether that harnes be mete for hym or not, the which yef he accomplyssh ye shall perceaue by thys berer; yef not I trust to send it unto yow by my next letters. Symon hath delyuered to Mr Stacye cccˡⁱ and stayed the rest untyll yor ffee of thordynaunces and Master Arnoldes money may be receauyd. The somme that remayneth at Mr Scottes is abowtes lvˡⁱ besydes such money as ye appoynted to be delyuered oute. And the chardges of Mr Williams and his wyffes marryage amountyng aboue ffortye poundes, as it shall appere by Symons reconyng unto yow when he shall wryte unto yow his letters, and because I knowe no parte of yor pleasure theryn I toke no more upon me to do therwith then my comyssyon wold extend, so that I can not aduertyes yow of the partyclers therof. My lady of Ruchemond doth so dylygently folowe the suytte of the delyuerye of hur ffather so that ther be many aferde lest at length she shall obteynge, and to begyn she hath gotten hur fathers lodgeyng to be hanged with tapystree, hys wyndowes

87. Hoby's half sister Elizabeth was married to Parker; John Walwin and Edward Blount were of Worcestershire families. *Travels and Life*, facing p. xvi; *Visitation of Worcester*, pp. 17, 141.
88. Parliament was not prorogued until 1 February 1550. There were 379 seats in the Lower House. *House of Commons, 1509–1558*, appendices I, III.

glased, and also certeyn plate appoynted hym to be serued with. And on Christemas Eve ther was sent unto hym iij confessors, as the Busshop of Lyncoln, the Busshop of Rochester, and the Busshop of Seynt Davyes,[89] but whate absolucyon they gave hym or whate maner of man they perceauyd hym to be I knowe not. And as to the Duke of Somersett and thos other prysoners of his faccyon for the good coumfort that they are yn it appereth to be manyfest, for on Chrystmas daye the Duches of Somersett came unto hym to the Towre to his no litle coumfort, after whos comyng the Duke was sett at ffree prysoner and all the kynges seruauntes that attendyd upon hym weare imme-dyatlye discharged. And the same after none Mr Hopar preached yn the Towre before the Duke and thother prysoners, entreatyng upon a salme of kyng Dauyd, hauyng occasyon therby to speke ageynst gouernours that mysordred theyr vocacyons, perswadyng that God punysshed rulers for theyr synnes, exortyng such to take it pacyentlye and yn eny wyse not to go abowtes to seke revengement, sayeng that yef eny dyd procure or labor to revenge that then God wold punyssh thos with doble plages. And it is thought that upon Newe Yeres daye they shall haue theyr dischardge at the kynges handes for theyr Newe Yeres gyft. But whate a corrozye this wilbe to the Erle of Southampton who is contynually syck and thought to be yn a consumpsyon I referr that to the iudgement of doctor ffryor, his physyan,[90] (fo. 21^v) This present daye of Seynt Stephan ther passed yn the Comon howse a byll ageynst phantastical profycyers. After such sort that yef eny here after shall sett furth eny profecye either by w[orde] or yn wrytyng (not beyng auctorysed by the word of God) for the furst tyme the profecyer shall haue a yeres imprysonment and the ffyne of ten powndes, the second tyme to lose all his goodes, the thyrd tyme to lose his lyffe.[91] Also ther is byll sent from the lordes to the lower howse yn which is geaven auctorytye to all Busshoppes to haue powar to enquere of all matters towchyng the ecclecyastycall lawes yn as large and ample maner as they myght haue done at eny tyme with yn these .xx. yeres, the which byll (as it is thought) will not pas the Comon howse without advoydyng of manye inconvenyences that myght growe by the same.[92] Ther is a secrette t[old?] here of an yntreatye of a peace to be had betwyxt England and ffraunce, and yef it take pl[ace] my lord pryvey seale, my lord paget, and secretarye Wootton

---

89. Henry Holbeach, Nicholas Ridley and Robert Ferrar, all committed Protestants.
90. Wriothesley had plotted in the last part of December not only against Somerset's authority but also against his life: BL, Add. MS 48126, fo. 16^r; Hoak, *King's Council*, pp. 254–6.
91. 3 & 4 Edward VI c. 15; *SR* iv, pp. 114–15.
92. 3 & 4 Edward VI c. 11; *SR* iv, pp. 111–12.

shalbe comyssyoners for the k[ynges] maiestyes behalf.[93] Other newys at thys tyme I haue not worthy aduertysement but ye shall ... yn this pakett dyuers letters from whom ye shall perceaue by theyr contentes. Yeven as I was wrytyng this letter Mr Nicholas Arnold came and payd unto me for the money that his brother receauyd of yow the somme of twentye ffyve powndes syx shelynges and eight pence after the [rate] of vj^s iiij^d for euery crowne of the somme, prayeng yow to will his brother to play the parte of good husbond yn employeng of his money, for he shalbe sure of nomore then he hath alredy promised hym. This mornyng Mr Vaughan of the mynt,[94] Stephyns old master, is departed to the mercy of the lyvyng God who prospere yow yn all yor affayres. Yor sherte of mayle remayneth at ... whate yor pleasure shalbe to do with it I am desyrous to knowe. Yef the Emperours dep[arture] had not ben so sone after the holydayes the duke of Suffolk wold haue gotten leave to comen to haue kyssed the Emperours handes. Wreten at the blacke ffryers on Seynt [Stephans] daye beyng the xxvjth day of December by yor most bounden seruaunt

Richard Scudamore

9 *31 December 1549 (Adv. MS 34.2.14, fo. 7^r)*

It may please yow to be aduertesyd that I haue delyuered a sup-plycacyon on yor behalf to the kynges most honorable counsell for to dischardge the cth for the benevolens requyred yn the Excheker. Although the suytt wylbe somewhat tedyous, I dowpt not but it will take effecte, and the rather by the good ffurtheraunce of my lord warden, to whom for his good will and good wordes towardes yow ye are much bounden, for he told the counsell that this was not worthye to be named a suyte, desyryng them to bestowe upon yow iij or iiij thowsand powndes, sayeng further that yef they dyd not consyder yor chardges this journey wold utterlye undoo yow, whearfore yn the answearyng of his lordshyps letter, the which ye shall receaue yn this pakett, it may please yow to tendre unto hym yor most hartye thankes after such sort that he may perceaue that I haue sygnyfyed unto yow of his good mynd towardes yow, by the which meanes I may the boldlyer hereafter repayre unto his lordshyp yef occasyon shall serve. I haue bene with my lord Cobham, who shewed me that he had

93. The cessation of Boulogne was politically embarrassing for Warwick, but without Imperial aid and money it could no longer be defended. Jordan, *Edward VI: Threshold of Power*, pp. 118–20.

94. Stephen Vaughan, Under-treasurer of the Tower mint, was early an evangelical. W.C. Richardson, *Stephen Vaughan: Financial Agent of Henry VIII* (Baton Rouge, 1953).

wreten his letters unto yow withyn iiij dayes past. Newys of Parlyament matters ther is none sence the wrytyng of my last letters, sauyng ther is a byll for occupyeng of ffarmes exhibited to the lower howse. To what end it will come to I knowe not. The effecte wheareof is that no man shall occupie aboue iij ffarmes, and euery man that may dispend aboue the some of one hundreth powndes shall occupie but one ffarme, and that onlye for the mayntenaunce of his howse.[95] And I do ffurther perceaue that Mr Sherryngton shall haue restytucyon both of his landes and his goodes by acte of parlyament, payeng a certeyn some to the kyng, of the which the dett that is to yow remytted shalbe to hym deducted,[96] after which thyng brought to passe I dowpt not but that my lord great master will delyuer to yor use the other specyaltye. Mr Barkeley[97] came unto yor armorye and fetched from thens xx[ti] hackbuttes complete and xx pykes, and besydes he hath taken with hym ffyue of yor blacke anymattes. Notwithstandyng I declared unto hym that yor pleasure was that they shold be sent ynto Worcestershyre for the defence of yor howse ther, but none excuse wold serve but he wold haue had all .x. Then I told hym that weare not yors but yor mens. For all that he wold not otherwyse do but take ffyve of them, sayeng that yow had appoynted the hole armorye to be at his commaundement. Sir John Williams doth instantlye desyre yow to help hym with some armorer oute of thos partyes that can skele of makyng of harnessys, and he wyll geaue hym honest entertaynement, and yn this doyng ye shall do hym a greate pleasure. I ame constrayned to leave of wrytyng eny more at this tyme for that the dispatch of this messynger is so short. And wheare I by my last letters aduertesyd yow of takyng of a certeyn pryse with sugar, the vessell is comen with yn the Ryuer of Thamys and hath yn her aboue ccc[th] chestes of sugar. Thus I do alwayes pray to the lyvyng lord to prospere yow yn all yor affayres. Wreten at the blake ffryers the last day of december by yor most bounden seruaunt

Richard Scudamore

95. This bill did not pass.
96. 3 & 4 Edward VI c. 13. William Sharrington, Vice-treasurer of the Bristol mint, had been condemned in 1549 for coining testons below the legal weight. He had kept the surplus bullion for himself and used it for political purposes. Hoby had owed £1,000 to Sharrington, which upon Sharrington's attainder became due to the King. Edward pardoned Hoby the debt on 8 December 1549; another favour. *CPR, 1549–1551*, p. 114; Jordan, *Edward VI; The Young King*, pp. 373, 383–4.
97. Sir Maurice Berkeley, Gentleman of the Chamber.

10 *11 January 1550 (Adv. MS 34.2.14, fo. 23ʳ).*

It may please yow to be aduertesyd that I receauyd yor letter the xj day of Januarye beyng directed to me and to Symon, and wheare ye do mervell much why that the rest of the money was not delyuered to Mr Stacye, the consyderacyon therof was for that the somme of money remaynyng dyd not amount unto the somme of an hundreth poundes for bycause that the marchauntes doth not use to receaue and to kepe the ordre of Interest but upon hundrethes. But now, yor pleasure knowen, I wyll as to morrowe delyuer unto thandes of Mr Stacye the somme of ffoure score poundes (although ther shall growe no benefytt unto yow untyll it be made complete to the hundreth), the which somme doth ryse of the ffyftye and ffyue poundes left remaynyng behynd by Symon, and ffyve and twentye poundes of money payd unto my handes by Mr Nicholas Arnold. And as for your ffee of the ordynaunces can not as yett be receaued for that ther remayneth no money yn the handes of the tellers, nor is not lyke to be before the myddell of the next terme so that before that tyme ye can make none accompt of that somme. And immedyatly after my wrytyng of my last letters unto yow ther hapened a sodayne chaynge amongst the counsell, for the Erle of Southampton was comaunded sodenlye (lyeng before sycke yn the courte) to departe from thens and to repayre to his howse yn holborn and enyoyened ther to remayne and not to come abrode withoute the kynges and his counselles pleasure weare further knowen[98] and then the Erle of Arrundell was comaundyd to leave awey his staff and lykewyse to repayre to his howse that was lately the lord admyralles, and ther to kepe after the lyke sorte.[99] And Sir Thomas Arundell[100] and Mr Rogers of the pryvey chambor[101] weare lykewyse comaundyd to kepe theyr howse without ffurther lybertye. What is leyd to theyr chardge is not openlye knowen, but some imagyneth that they went abowt the subuercyon of relygyon, and wheare thear weare boltes on the doores of the kynges hyghnes

98. Warwick, having survived Wriothesley's assassination plot, now moved against his enemies. Wriothesley withdrew from Court before the order could reach him. *CSPSp.* x, p. 8; Hoak, *King's Council*, p. 59.

99. Arundel, Lord Chamberlain, was deprived of the office which gave him constant access to the King. St John revealed Arundel's conspiracy with Wriothesley, and Paget sought revenge for the Earl's opposition to him after the fall of Somerset. *CSPSp.* x, p. 8; BL, Add. MS 48126, fo. 15ᵛ.

100. Sir Thomas Arundel of Lanherne, receiver of the Duchy of Cornwall, had been a prime mover in the conspiracy to bring down the Protector. In the aftermath he had sought service with Princess Mary, and to make her Regent. *CSPSp.* ix, pp. 459, 467–70; Hoak, *King's Council*, pp. 245–6, 248.

101. Sir Edward Rogers was appointed one of the four Principal Gentlemen of the privy Chamber in the reorganisation after the fall of Somerset. He was soon reinstated after this disgrace: *House of Commons, 1509–1558.*

pryvy chambor the Erle of Arrundell caused dyvers of them to be taken awey.[102] What he ment therebye I knowe not, but his aunswer was theryn to Sir Andrew Dudley comyng to hym at the strykeng of the boltes that he wold not tarye at other mens pleasure to come to the kynges chambor.[103] I feare me lest ther me more trowble a bruyng, for this euenyng beyng of the xj[th] of this moneth my lord of Warrewick and my ladye hys wyeff weare caryed yn a lytter from hys howse yn holborn to Yorkes the sherryeff[104] and as yet my lorde came not at the courte, the which thyng maketh men to iudge that he dareth not to remayne yn his owne howse. And the same evenyng came to Yorkes my lorde marques of Northampton, the lorde pagett, and the master of the hors. More at thys tyme I can not sygnyfye unto yow at this present, but as occasyon shall serue I trust to accomplyssh yor expectacyon. My lord cobham is departed from hence furst ynto Kent to mustre more men to send ouer the Sea, and then repayreth hym self to Calleys. Thus besechyng god to prosper yow yn all yor affayres, wreten at the blake ffryers the xj th day of Januarye By yor most bounden seruaunt

Richard Scudamore

11 *18 January 1550 (Adv. MS 34.2.14, fo. 9′)*

It may please you to be aduertesyd that upon the xij day of Januarye I receauyd a pakett of letters from yow, wheare of suche as weare directed to me weare of the ij[de] of the same and the others weare delyuered immedyatlye. And as by my last letters I aduertesyd of the restraynt of lybertye of certeyn counsellors and others, they remayneth as yet after the same sort, sauyng that the Erle of Southampton seyth (although he had sodeyn warnyng to departe from the courte) that he was not commaunded to kepe his howse, and that he was ffurther assured that neyther the kyng nor his counsell had conceauyd any displeasure towardes hym, wyllyng his men so to report yef occasyon happened to be mynystred unto them. And upon sonday last[105] the

102. The Earl of Arundel and Sir Thomas Arundel were certainly Catholic, and hoped for the restoration of the old religion. Rogers was Protestant. Wriothesley, whatever his belief, found it politic to lead a Catholic faction.

103. Sir Andrew Dudley, Warwick's brother, had been promoted to become one of the four Principal Gentlemen and Keeper of the Palace of Westminster. His purpose was to guard the king, as here, perhaps, proved necessary. Edward VI, *Chronicle*, p. 19; *CSPSp.* x. p. 14.

104. Sir John Yorke was Under-treasurer of the Southwark mint and Sheriff of London. Warwick had stayed at his house during the October *coup* as York acted as intermediary between the City and the London Lords. *APC* ii, pp. 331–2; *CSPSp.* x, p. 13.

105. 13 January.

Erle of Arrundell was ffetched from his howse to the courte by the vice chamberleyn[106] to appere before my lorde greate master,[107] my lord marques of Northampton, the lord Wentworth, and M^{r}Secretorye Petor, commyssyoners appoynted for the examynacyon of the same persons, and after his beyng ther was retorned back ageyne to his howse. And on the same day Mr Thomas Carden was appoynted to goo to the towre to assyst the lyefetenaunt and to bryng with hym ffyftye of his seruauntes. And Mr Carden lyeth in yor offyce after whos comyng thether all the prysoners there were restrayned of theyr libertye, for before that tyme the Towre was used after suche sorte as though ther had bene no bondage yn yt att all, for euery one that desyred to come yn was suffred to speke with whom he lysted, but for advoydyng of such inconvenyences as by that sufferaunce might ensue, and for that the late duke of Norffolke and the Busshopp of Wynchester myght be brought ynto theyr prystynate estate, it was devysed (for that parcyallytye should not appere) that all the prisoners sholde bere the lyke fface of restraynte, but so used that the Duke of Somersett nor thothers of his faccyon weare nothyng dismayed therbye. And it is thought by some of the dukes ffrendes that he shall be at lybertye with yn thyes vj dayes.[108] And although the late Busshopp of Londons matter hath ben twyse hard before the kynges most honorable counsell yet it is not determyned,[109] but yn the meane whyle the knyght marshall,[110] perceauyng the seyd Busshopp neyther to be proffyttable nor benyfycyall to hym nor to eny of hys offycers, entred ynto comunycacyon with hym and after long talke they began both to heate with other, and wheare as the marshall before his ffume used the Busshopp by the name of Doctor Bonar, he forgate that name and called hym Coddeshedd and grossum caput, swearyng that he had nomore lernyng then his dogg onlesse it weare yn the popes decrees and lawes, but the stoute stobborn prelate, borrowyng nothyng at the marshalles handes, sett hym so uncurtoyslye that the marshall sware that yet it weare not for shame that he wolde fetche his ffyst ffrom hys eare, and the pacyent prelate boldely answearyd hym that yef he stroke hym hys ffyst shold not be long from hys, affyrmyng further by greate othes that yef the marshall shold haue spoken but half thos word unto hym yn chepesyde that then he wold haue cutt awey a pece of his fface. Therefore, yn recompence of his humbleness, the

106. Sir Thomas Darcy.

107. Paulet had been sent with Arundel and Southampton to the Tower in December to examine Somerset, and there he learnt of their plot. He warned Warwick. BL, Add. MS 48126, fo. 15^v.

108. Van der Delft reported likewise the freedom enjoyed by the prisoners and the rumours that the Duke and his adherents would be released. *CSPSp.* x, p. 7.

109. For Bonner's trial, see Brigden, *London and the Reformation*, pp. 449–51.

110. Sir Ralph Hopton.

knyght marshall comaunded hys offycers to take downe the hang-
gynges of the Busshoppes chambor and take a wey his bedd, plate and
other necessaryes such as he was serued with, and to suffre hym to
haue (9ᵛ) none onlesse he wolde send for some stuffe of hys owne, but
he, not myndyng that the offycers shold take any gayne by hym,
thought to take such lodgeyng as his man dyd, and one nyght laye yn
hys manes bedd, and thoffycers perceauyng that on the nexte daye
toke away that bedd so that sence that tyme both he and his man
haue leyn yn the strawe. Wheare upon he ffownd hym self moche
agreuyd and made a greate complaynte to the counsell upon the
marshall, and yesterdaye Mr Chaloner and Mr Armygyll Wade[111]
were sent to the Marshallsye to examyne the matter and to make
reporte on. To what it will come unto I know not. And wheare as
before this I have wreten unto yow that ther was a secrete talke of the
comyng ouer of certeyn counsellors it apperes now to be manyfest, for
the next weke thos three whos names I wrote unto yow doth appoynt
to be at Calleys.[112] More yn that can not I aduertyes yow of. I pray
god the effect may be honorable. I haue payd to Mr Stacye the iiijˣˣˡⁱ
accordyng to my last letter. And wheare yor pleasure was that I
shold make some meanes to provyde a Brace of masteves for Monsʳ.
Monfauconet,[113] ye shall understand that Mr Cheke hath promysed
to move the kynges maiestie for them, and when I shall [. . .] them I
with all convenyent spede shall send them on. Both Mr Cheke[114] and
Mr [. . .] hath promysed to wryte unto yow but I thynke it wilbe by
the next messynger not by this. Mr Barkeley wold gladlye wryte unto
yow, but he fferyth the dysclosyng of his letters, for he seyth that he
wrote a letter of late to Bulleyn and it was taken by the way, and
the same was layd to hys charge although the matter was of small
importaunce. Notwithstondyng I perswaded with hym the sure
delyuerye of my letters unto yow, so that he hath promysed to wryte
unto yow when he shall haue eny good newes worthye of wrytyng.
Secretorye Petor and Mr Mason accompanyeth thother ij in thys
jorney, as I thynke ye shall more amplyer perceaue by the counselles
letter to yow addressyd.[115] This day the byll con);ernyng the duke of
Somersett (theffecte wherof Mr Broke shewed me that he dyd aduertyes yow by his letter) was send from the [upper] to the lowyar howse,
and after it was redd ther it was concluded that xxiiij of that howse

111. Clerks of the Privy Council.
112. These were secret negotiations for peace with France and the cessation of
Boulogne.
113. Monsieur Monfauconet, Charles V's maître d'hôtel. *CSPF* p. 30.
114. John Cheke, tutor to Edward VI, with whom Hoby travelled in exile in Mary's
reign. *Travels and Life*, pp. 116, 117, 120.
115. Sir John Mason, Petre, Russell and Dr Wootton were sent to France to negotiate
peace. *CSPSp*. x, pp. 12–13.

shold repayre unto the Towre ther to examyne the duke upon such artycles as was comprysed yn the sayd byll more theryn hetherto is not passed.[116] Mr Granado desyreth yow to cause Senor Pollydor to be put in remembraunce for certeyn trees for the kynges sadelles, prayeng hym to help to prouyde them as sone as he mought. Mr Phelpott hath hard nothyng as yett consernyng yor hors. As to the rest of the effect of yor letter, I wyll accomplyssh to my power as tyme and oportunytye shall serue, as knoweth the lord who prospere yow yn all yor procedynges. My last letters I suppose wyll not come to yor handes before the receypt of thyes, but withyn two dayes after I dowpt not but ye shall receaue them.

Wreten at the blacke ffryers by yor most bounden seruaunt

Richard Scudamore

12 *25 January 1550 (Adv. MS 34.2.14, fo. 11ʳ)*

It may please yow to be aduertesyd that I receauyd by ffrancisco yor letters of the xix[th] of Januarye, with other letters upon thursdaye mornyng beyng the xxiij[th] day of the same. I delyuered my lord warden his letter, who receaued it verye thankefullye, but my lord great master was very loth to receaue his for I was constrayned to attempte hym thryees before he receuyd it. I suppose he fered lest it had ben for some suytte the which he is loth to trouble hym selffe with all, onlesse it be such that is to his owne contentacyon. And wheare ye by yor letter haue appoynted certeyn order for money aswell to be delyuered to Mr Stacye as also to paye certeyn dettes by yow owyng, I trust as tyme and occasyon shall serue therunto yor pleasure shalbe accomplysshed and the procedynges therof contynuallye ye shall haue aduertyesment. I haue not receauyd eny letter from Symon sence that I dyd wryte unto hym, and I thynke the cause is for that he entendyth to be shortelye at London: howbeit I mett with Mr Dytton of Glou-cestershyre who shewed me that he bargayned with Symon and others yor seruauntes for thole of yor last yeres woll at xxv[s] viij[d] euery towe, sauyng xx[s] to be abated yn thole some and all the money to be payd at Shrovetyde. More theryn I knowe not. And wheare I perceaue ffurther that ye weare yn doupt of whate money the iiij[xxli] last payd to Mr Stacye was, ye shall perceaue that it was of the ffyftye and ffyve pound remaynyng at Mr Crottes, and ffyve and twentye poundes of money receauyd of Mr Arnold. And as for yor ffees of thordynaunces they can not as yett be receauyd, for that the tellers hath no money

116. 3 & 4 Edward VI cc. 24, 31.

yn theyr handes, but withyn this sevenynghtes I haue good hope to
receaue it. And as for the dischardge of the c[thli] for the benyvolence
demaunded yn the Excheker remayneth yett yn my custodye under
the pryvey seale bycause the Speaker of the Parlyament[117] could haue
no leyser hetherto to sytt yn the Excheker for attendyng to the
Parlyament howse, the which Parliament it was iudged that this day
it shold haue ffynysshed, for the kynges maiestye was ones redye to
goo the parlyament howse, and dyuers of the lordes had sent for theyr
roobes, yett that notwithstandyng it is deferred untyll mondaye next
comyng, and the Actes therof I will send unto yow as sone as they
shalbe inprynted. My lord marques of Northampton hath alredye
declared unto Mr Doryngton[118] the kynges maiestyes pleasure for the
delyueraunce to yor use, as if his graces gyft, a brace of masteves, and
Mr Doryngton hath appoynted with me that withyn iiij dayes I shall
haue not onlye the brace of masteves geaven unto yow by the kyng
but also he wyll delyuer one masteffe to be sent unto yow of his owne
gyft, beyng verye sorye that it laye not yn hym to do unto yow a more
pleasure. I repayred to haue spoken with my ladye of Somersett, but
bycause she was and his somewhat acrased[119] I could not haue eny
oportunytye to speke with hur. And wheare I by a little paper of
remembraunce dyd sygnyfye unto yow of the deth of Gamboa and
Villa Cerga,[120] ye shall understand that Charles de Gavaro came yn
post oute of Skottland purposelye to kyll Gamboa, beyng
accompanyed with three of his soldyors whose names weare: Baltazar
de Gavaro, Michaell de Salmero and ffrancisco de ffallasco. And
Capt. Gavaro with his three companyons, beyng all ffour apparrelled
all in black ffryes coottes lyke englysshmen, hauyng intellygence of
Gamboas beyng att supper upon sonday at nyght last past withyn the
Cytye of London, they dyd lye in awayte for hym withoute Newgate
almost at Gamboas lodgeyng, and betwene eight and nyne of the
clocke the same nyght at his retorne toward his howse at the tornyng
of the strete besydes the kynges hedd withoute Newegate, they sett all
ffoure sodenlye upon hym geavyng vij or viij woundes with ffoynes
round abowtes his hart so that they weare sure that he was past
revengeyng, and Villa Cerga (fo. 11ᵛ) and others of Gamboas companye and seruauntes comyng to reskewe Gamboa, Villa Cerga was
slayne and one or twoo hurt.[121] Gavaro wold not confesse that Villa

117. John Baker, Speaker of the House of Commons, Chancellor of the Exchequer
and Under-treasurer, and Chancellor of first fruits and tenths.
118. Keeper of the King's mastiffs.
119. distracted, unbalanced.
120. Villa Cerga, an Italian mercenary captain, 'whom they esteem little'. *CSP
Scotland*, p. 90.
121. The story of the murder is told by other chroniclers: *Two London Chronicles*,
p. 20; Wriothesley, *Chronicle*, ii, pp. 31–2.

Cerga was kylled by hym or his companye, but leyd that to Englyssh-menes chardge, sayeng that whyles theyr beyng busye with Gamboa dyuers seruyng men comyng that wey seeyng affraye and the one partye beyng strangers and thother partye semyth to be Englyssh men bycause of their apparrell toke Gavaros parte, and he perceauyng (he seyd) the Englyssh men yn hand wyth the rest of the Spanyardes gate hym self and his companyons aweye so that by this meanes the ffurst brute of his deth upon monday mornyng was noysed to be don bye Englysshe man, but whate they shold be could not be knowen. Whearupon ther was greate serche made for the tryall [. . .], and assone as it was knowen that Gavaro was come to the towne it was suspected immedyatlye that it shold be he. And my lord Paget and the Master of the hors rode both ynto Holborn and at the sygne of the boll they ffound Gavaro hauyng a little skarr on the browe the nyght before and his three companyons, and brought those ffoure from thens to my lord at Warrewyckes to the Sheryeffes howse and ther beyng examyned, Gavaro confessyd that he had kylled Gamboa with his owne handes. They iiij weare sent that nyght to Newegate and on the morrowe they weare like wyse examyned, supposyng that ther weare more of theyr confederacye, but they wold confesse none, and on wenysdaye ther was a comyssyon appoynted for the deter-mynacyon of the same matter to the lord mayre of London and to the iudges who syttyng at the yeld hawle, before whom the iiij prisoners weare brought, upon whom was charged an enquest who indytted them all of wilfull murder of Gamboa. Whearupon they were arrayned, and Gavaro confessed that it was is onlye act, thynkyng therby to haue clered his companye, submyttyng hym self to Goddes mercy and the kynges, and the other iij pledyd not gyltye, and bycause it drew nere nyght they adiorned them ouer untyll the morrowe. And on thursday they weare brought ageyne to yeldhawle whear ther was sworen a iury upon lyeff and deth upon them iij; the one half of the iurye weare Englisshemen and thother half Strayngers, who ffound them gyltye of the deth and murder of Gamboa, so that iudgement was geaven upon them to dye, and on Gavaro by hys owne confessyon, so that upon ffryday beyng yesterday ther was a payr of gallowes sett up yn Smythfeld, and the prisoners beyng carryed ffrom Newegate thetherwardes (Gavaros hand cutt off by the way yn the place wheare the murder was comytted) weare hung and so they remayned this mornyng. Howbeit (prayse be therfore to God) they dyed very repen-tauntlye by the good perswasyon of Dowglas the Skott and ij mar-chauntes of theyr owne nacyon who rode yn the carte with the prisoners, for the which they deserued much comendacyon. And the same day Humfrey Arrundell and Holmes, rebelles of the West contrey, shold haue bene drawen to Tyborn and ther to be hung and quartered. The hardelles weare brought to the Towre hill and yet the prisoners did not die. The cause was when that they perceauyd that ther was no way but deth they dessyred to haue some respyte for the dischardge of theyr conscience, the which be both for the preseruacyon of the kynges maiestye and the sauffegarde of the [...] the realme, but whate is theyr confession I knowe not. And Wynslade and Bery shalbe both sent yn to the West countrey wheare they shall suffre accordyngly.[122](fo. 12ʳ) Ther was brought to London owte of Essex a rebell dwellyng abowtes Brayntre, a weuer by his occupacyon, who dyd conspyre that all the towneshypes ther abowtes shold haue bene assembled upon Wenysday next comyng yn a litle parke of my lord chauncellors,[123] and after theyr assemble ther they wold haue gon to my lord chauncellors howse and to haue spoyled it and then to haue sett it a ffyre. And at the same tyme ther shold haue rysen another companye yn the edge of Suffolk, who shold haue repayred ffurst to Mr Capelles[124] howse, and yef he shold refuse to do as they dyd then they wold kyll hym and spoyle his howse. And so from gentleman to gentleman, and both thes companyes to haue joyned together and to haue journeyed towardes London.[125] Whearupon immedyatlye after the Parlyament all gentlemen shalbe appoynted to repayre to theyr dwellynges. Syr John Arrundell is remoued from the fflete and brought to the Towre,[126] and this day ther was sett at lybertye Mr Walley, Mr Seycell, Mr Wolff, and Paladye:[127] a fayr begynnyng: it is trusted that more shall ffollowe shortelye. The Erle of Southampton is comandyd, and hath ben sence Thursday, to kepe his howse, and lykewyse Syr Thomas Pope.[128] And Sir Walter Butler, and some seye that the Master of the Rolles[129] hath the lyke. A shrewde nest. It was high time to take the byrdes for they purposed to haue made a popys fflyght, and it is seyd that more shalbe openlyer known withyn v or vj dayes. God shorten theyr evell purpos, for by the devysyon of the greate the madd rage of the idell comoners is much prouoked therbye to ffollowe

122. Arundel, Holmes, Wynslade and Bery were all executed at Tyburn on 27 January. Wriothesley, *Chronicle*, ii, p. 32.

123. Richard, Baron Rich.

124. Sir Henry Capel had lands at Rayne and Stebbing, Essex: *House of Commons, 1509–1558.*

125. Bell, a Suffolk man, was executed on 10 February for stirring insurrection in Suffolk and Essex. *Two London Chronicles*, p. 21.

126. Arundel had been committed to the Tower 'for conspiracies in the western parts'. Edward VI, *Chronicle*, p. 19.

127. Richard Whalley, William Cecil, Edward Wolf, and Richard Palady, who had been imprisoned with Somerset at his fall, were released upon taking up substantial bonds: *APC* ii, pp. 322, 372.

128. Master of woods in the Court of Augmentations. Wriothesley made him executor of his will, a mark of their close association. *Trevelyan Papers*, p. 214.

129. Cuthbert Tunstall, Bishop of Durham.

theyr naughye pretences, so that (or onlesse God shewe his mercy ouer us) this yere to come is lyke to be wors then eny was yett. I haue spoken with Mr Stacye, declaryng unto hym yor pleasure and request, to the which he answered that he neuer ment to paye yor money unto yow ageyne yn eny other place then wheare he dyd receaue the same, and when I had shewed unto hym that it was alweys yor mynde to haue receauyd yor money on that syde of the seas that yow are of: then he seyd that he wold ffurst comon with his brother Cosworth[130] before he could geave unto yow a determynate answeare yn that behalf, and as yett they haue not consulted together, but by my next letters (the which I entend to send unto yow by the Master of the hors secretorye who setteth to Antwarp wardes on wenysday next comyng) I will aduertyes yow of theyr determynate purpos theryn. And wheare before this I dyd yn a small paper sygnyfye unto yow that Mastres Jelyan had a suter for maryage and ther rested nothyng but yor pleasure to be knowen theryn: and I suppose bycause they hard not ffrom yow they thought the tyme very long, whearfore they haue concluded (as I am enformed) to be marryed on thursdaye next comyng and to shue for yor ffauor afterwardes. Thus hauyng nothyng elles at this present worthye of aduertyesment, do beseche God to prospere yow yn all yor affayres. Wreten at the Blacke ffryers the xxv[th] day of Januarye by yor most bounden seruaunt

Richard Scudamore

13 *30 January 1550 (Adv. MS 34.2.14, fo. 33ʳ)*

It may please yow to be aduertesyd that as by my last letters I sygnyfyed unto yow that accordyng unto yor comaundement I repayred unto Mr Stacye to knowe his full determynacyon for the usyng of such money as he shold receaue of yow. Who, after he had consulted with his brother Cosworth, dyd wryte a lettre unto yow, the which he shewed unto me before he sealed the same so that I shall not nede to trouble yow eny thyng with the discourse of his mynde theryn, for that Mr Stacye hath ffullye declared his hole determynacyon to do con3ernyng the usage of the seyd money. And even as Mr Stacye is desyrous shortlye to knowe yor pleasure therof, so it may please yow that Symon and I may perceaue the same to the ende wee may accomplysshe yor will. I haue dischardged yor suytt yn the excheker towchyng the benyvolence, the chardge whearof ffrom the ffurst

130. John Cosworth was one of a syndicate of London mercers who speculated heavily in monastic estates. He was receiver of the Duchy of Cornwall. *House of Commons, 1558–1603.*

drawyng of the byll to the ende amounteth to the somme of xl^s viij^d. I trust ye shall receaue yor iij masteves by the ffurst shypp or howe that shall passe ffrom hence towardes Antwarpe. The coke that yow sent to my lord warden arryved here the xxviijth day of Januarye, with whom I repayred ymmedyatlye to my lordes howse at the Blakeffryers, wheare my lord was a preparyng hym self to departe to his howse yn Shesey, and after I had presented the coke to hym the coke delyuered hym a letter from yow the which my lord perused, callyng me unto hym began to rendre unto yow his most hartye thankes, and shewed unto me that he perceauyd by yor letter that yow had delyuered unto the coke xx^s, whearupon he put his hand yn his poke and drewe owte x^s yn shelynges or ther abowtes offryng it unto me sayeng, take ye thys yn parte of the seyd some, and when I perceauyd that, I answeared my lord that I had no comyssion or comaundement to receaue eny money of his lordshyp, sayeng ffurther on yor behalf that yow weare very sorye that ye had not more occasyon to requyte his good will towardes yow, and then my lord eftsones gaue unto yow his louyng thankes, assuryng yow that ffrom tyme to tyme yn all thynges that lyeth yn hym to do unto yow eny pleasure ye may assertayne yor selfe therof, so that at his retorne I will prove what he will do ffor to fforder yow for the avauncement of yor exchaunge. My lady of Somersett kepeth as yet hur chambor so it is that yett I can not come to hur speche. Upon Monday last ther was drawen ffrom the Towre to Tyborne Humfrey Arrundell, Wynslade, Berye, and Holmes, and ther weare put to execucyon. Hunnynges[131] remayneth yn the kepyng of Mr Controller,[132] but what the matter is I knowe, but this berer can declare unto yow many thynges more then I am able to shewe unto yow.

fo. 33^v

Ther is a newe alteracyon of offycers amongst certeyn of the greate counsell, as the Erle of Wyllshyre and late lord greate master is nomynated to be lord hygh Treasourer of England,[133] and my lord of Warrewyck (to whom ye haue not wreten by a long space) shalbe lorde greate master and presydent of the counsell. And the lord marques of Northampton shalbe lord greate chamberleyn. And also ther goeth a certeyn talke that my lord Wentworthe is like to be lord chamberleyn. And as I was yn wrytyng of thys letter I receauyd letters ffrom Symons, the which ye shall receaue with others, by the which

131. William Honnings, clerk of the Privy Council, was accused of stealing the copy of the judges' opinions upon Gardiner's offences, and thereby suspected of complicity with Wriothesley and the conservative faction. BL, Cotton MS Caligula E iv, fo. 207^r; *APC* iii, p. 7; Hoak, *King's Council*, pp. 162–3, 271, 334.

132. Sir Anthony Wingfield.

133. St John had been created Earl of Wiltshire on 19 January. This appointment was further reward for his support of Warwick.

ye shall perceaue of his procedynges yn yor affayres yn the contrey. Other occurrauntes I haue not at this present, sauyng that my lord fferrers is sworen of the pryvey counsell, and this berer is able to declare unto yow many thynges more at large. The sayeng is that the Parlyament shall break up upon Setorday next comyng. Thus [I] ernestlye pray God to prospere yow yn all yor affayres. Wreten at the blake ffryers the xxx[th] day of Januarye by yor most bounden seuaunt

Richard Scudamore

14 *6 February 1550 (BL, Add. MS 11042, fo. *** 53[r])*

It may please yow to be aduertesyd that the same nyght after the wrytyng of my last letters unto yow Sir Thomas Arrundell was com-ytted to the Towre where he remayneth yn straytte kepying.[134] And as by the same letters I sygnyfyed unto yow of the alteracyon of dyuers offycers, ye shall understand that on Candellmas Day[135] the Marques of Northampton receauyd his staffe for thoffyce of the lord greate chamberleynship, the lord of Wilteshyre his staffe for hygh treau-sorershyp, and the same day the lord Wentwoorth was sent with a staffe ynto London to my lord of Warrewycke for the lord great Mastershyp. And the same verye day my lord fferrers was created vicount hereford. Thes be all that latelye hath alteryd theyr offyces or receauyd hygher dygntyes, savyng that the lord marquees dorsett is cheeff Justyce of all the kyngs fforrests, parks and chases on thyssyde Trent. I haue moved my lord of Wilteshyre for the delyuery of thother specyaltye remaynyng yn his hands, whos answeare was that I shold haue it assone as his lordshyp myght be at leysure, so that I trust withyn ffewe dayes to receaue the same. Also I was a suter to my lord and to the rest of the offycers of the Courte of Wardes for the discherdge of certeyn dettes dependyng ther upon yow for the wardeshyp of Herry Myle.[136] And my lord and thother haue ofered that I shall bryng thether the warraunt for the estallment of yor dettes exem-plyfyed under the kynges seale of his Courte of the Augmentacyons, and then yow shold eyther have yor specyaltyes or elles suffycyent acquytaunce yn that behalf. My lord seyd that he was sorye to put yow to the chardge of the exemplyfycacyon of the seyd warraunt, neuerthelesse he seyd that theyre Courte could not be dischardged

134. On 30 January Arundel was moved from confinement in his house to the Tower. *CSPSp.* x, p. 21.

135. 2 February.

136. In 1543 Hoby had been granted the wardship of Henry Mile, who would inherit lands in the Welsh marches. *L&P* xviii(2). 449(7).

with oute matter of record. I suppose the chardge therof will amounte
to xxx^s or five nobles. Also Mr Chauncellor promysed to dispatche
yow shortelye for the reparacyons of Stanwell. My lord lysle showed
me that he loketh for the chaste dogg withyn thes fewe a dayes. And
when the dogg cometh I knowe not howe he shalbe conveyed unto
yow, but yn the meane tyme he shalbe well kept. I have iij feyre yong
masteves for yow, the which I leaue in kepyng at parys garden[137]
untyll I may haue shyppyng for them. The parlyament ffynysshed
upon Setordaye last and was proroged untyll the xxjth day of Apryell
next comyng. The notes of thactes passed Richard Ansham hath sent
to Mr Ansham his brother yn his letter. And immedyatelye after that
the Statutes shalbe yn prynte I entend to saufe a boke to be conveyed
unto yow. My cosyn Nicholas Arnold hath wreten a letter to his
brother Richard, the which as yett is unsealed for that he is verye
desyrous that yowe shold ffurst perceaue the contentes therof, but
wyllynglye he wold not that his brother shold be pryvey to that.
Whearfore it may please yow to comaund it to be sealed before that
it shalbe delyvered unto hym, for his brother is of that opynyon that
he will better consyder yor exhortacyon then eny woordes that he can
send unto hym by letter. And my cosin Arnold prayeth yow to bere
with hym for that he answeareth not yor letter. The cause is, he seyth,
for that he will not trouble yow with his thankes in woordes, but that
he ernestlye remayneth yors at all tymes (both for yor goodnes to his
brother and yor gentlenes towardes hym) to do eny thyng that shall
lye yn his powar. [*fo.* *** *53*^{v}] I receauyd yor ij seuerall letters dyrected
to the Master of the hors, the which I delyvered ffurwith upon the
recept of them, by the answeare whearof ye shall ffully at large
perceaue his mynde. I stayed the sendyng of this letter by the space
of ij dayes because the ffame went of the daylye delyueraunce of the
duke of Somersett and I beyng desyrous to aduertyes yow of the
certentye therof. Ye shall understand that on this afternone the duke
of Somersett was conveyd by Mr Lyefftenant and the Knyght Marshall from the Towre by water to the iij Cranes, and ther landed. And
the duke toke his mule and rode to the Sherryeffs howse wheare all
the whole Counsell sate, and after his beyng with them a certeyn
space departed towardes the Crane, accompanying him the lord
Wentworth and the Master of the hors, wheare the duke toke his
barge and passed to Savoye wheare my lady hys wyff lyeth and hath
kept hur chambor of a long tyme.[138] Ther was none other delyuered
with hym as yett. Thus hauyng nothyng elles at this tyme worthye

137. Paris Garden was an old manor in Southwark, and Cuthbert Vaughan, Scudamore's cousin, was its keeper.
138. The Lieutenant of the Tower was ordered to bring Somerset 'without much
guard or business' to Sheriff York's house. *APC* ii, p. 384; *CSPSp*. x, p. 28.

advertyesment, sauyng I have receauyd yor fee of thordynaunce, do praye the lyving lord to prospere yow yn all yor affayres and to kepe the present Counsellors yn an unytye. Wretten at the black ffryers the vjth day of ffebruarye by yor most bounden seruaunt.

Richard Scudamore

15 *13 February 1550 (Adv. MS 34.2.14, fo. 19^r)*

It may please yow to be aduertesyd that upon Setorday last past my lady my mastres came to London to commen with Mr Weldon[139] for the maryage of Mrs Anne, but Master Weldon (as it semed) beyng so hole yn love could not bere with long tyme thought good to knytt up the knott, and Sondaye mornyng the maryage was solempnyzed at Chanon rowe, so that nowe ther resteth nothyng to be don theryn but the assuraunce of hur joyntor, the which stayeth upon yor pleasure to be declared for the payment of such money as Mr Weldon shall haue with hur, and Master Catelyns[140] opynyon is that ye do forsee the performans of yor bond theryn. Yow shall perceaue Mr Weldons mynd by his letter, the answeare wheareof he desyred to receaue as tyme shalbe therunto convenyent. I haue dischardged the dettes dependyng on yow yn the courte of the wardes and haue receauyd yor three oblygacyons, the chardge whearof amonted (as well to the officers of the courte of augmentacyons as also to the offycers of the courte of wardes) to ffortye and one shelynges and eight pence. I haue also payd to Mr Stacye syx score poundes receauyd yn partye of payment of yor wolles, so with that Mr Stacy hath receauyd the ffull somme of ffyve hundreth powndes. Ther remayneth in money abowtes ffortye poundes, the which shalbe enployed ffurthewith towardes the dischardge of such dettes as ye haue appoynted to be payd. I haue bene a contynuall sutor to my lord high treausorer for the delyuerye of yor other statute, whos answeare is that yow shall haue it but as yett he can haue no leysure to seke for it. My lord lysle lokith euery day for the chaste greyhound. And yor masteves stayeth for the comyng oute of the shyppes. The occurrauntes are yn this present verye small, lokyng for some answeare from or lordes of thother syde of the seas. My lord of Somersett is appoynted to lye at his howse at Syon untyll the kinges pleasure be further knowen.[141] Ther is none as

139. Thomas Weldon, first master of the Household. With Sir Philip and Lady Hoby he had been accused in 1543 of maintaining a sacramentarian, and now he married Lady Hoby's daughter. *L&P* xviii(2). 241(6); *House of Commons, 1509–1558*.

140. Richard Catlyn was Marshal of Lincoln's Inn, and much in demand as feoffee in landed settlements. *House of Commons, 1509–1558*.

141. *APC* ii, pp. 384–5; *CSPSp*. x, p. 28.

yet delyuered oute of the Towre but Sir Rauff Vane, whos delyuerance was upon suretyes.[142] Mr Lee is remoued from the fflete to the Towre, and Hunnynges is commytted to the Marshallcye. And as consernyng the others that remayneth yn theyr howses, I thynke they be almost fforgotten for I can here nobodye in a maner to speake of them.[143] The Emperours armorer after his arryvall here I brought hym to Baynardes Castell[144] to the Master of the hors, and after I had declared unto hym the cause of the armorers commyng he answeared that he could not haue any leysure to talke with hym thys weke, and seyd ffurther that he shold not nede to speake with hym at all for that he had fully wreten unto yow his wyll theryn. Ther is a greate contencyon betwyxt Mr Lyeftenaunt of thordynaunces and Master Anthonye[145] for the devysyng of a stayer to the nue howse of thordynaunces, for Mr fflemmyng wold haue it made with yn the howse and Mr Anthony wold haue it made of the outesyde of the howse, on whose parte is the master carpenter, sayeng elles it shold something deface the howse withyn. Yet this greate argument notwithstondyng Mr fflemming is most likelye to acheue to his purpose onlesse it be determyned other ways by yor letter, for the which Mr Anthonye is a ernest sutor unto yow for. Thus hauyng nothyng elles at this presentes (but that I haue sent unto yow here with a boke of the actes of the Parlyament, the which I haue gotten before eny weare presented to the kynges maiestye), do praye to the lyvyng lord to prospere yow yn all yor affayres. Wreten at the Blake ffryers the xiij[th] day of ffebruarye by yor most bounden seruaunt

Richard Scudamore

16 *23 February 1550 (Adv. MS 34.2.14, fo. 5[r])*

It may please yow to be aduertesyd that I haue receauyd yor letter of the ixth of ffebruarye. Accordyng to theffecte therof I repayred unto Mr Stacye and Mr Cosworth, & haue taken assuraunce of them for yor money by indenture and an oblygacyon for the perfourmaunce of the same. Also with long suytt (bycause my lord Treasurer could

142. A Gentleman Pensioner, and adherent of Somerset's arrested with him in October 1549. He was an old friend of Hoby's. *L&P* xviii(2). 190; BL, Cotton MS Titus B ii, fo. 67[r].

143. Perhaps a reference to the Earls of Arundel and Southampton.

144. Sir William Herbert was keeper of Baynard's Castle in London.

145. Anthony Anthony was clerk of the ordnance. A close observer of political events, he was the author of the chronicle of them. Bodleian Library, MS Ashmole 861.

not be at eny leysure) I haue receyued at his hande yor other statute, the which I haue cancellyd. Mr Chauncellor hath appoynted me to attend upon hym on monday for the allowaunce of your reparacyons of Stanwell. I wold it weare ones at appoynte. I can not as yett receaue yor dyettes, but I traveyle theryn by all the meanes that I can. And Mr Dytton hath hetherto payd no more of yor woll money so that of yor dettes ther is no more payd as yett but xxvj^{li} to Mr Huett and xiiij^{li} to Mr Lock,[146] but as sone as the money shall come unto my handes I will paye such money as by yor letter is appoynted. And xxj^{li} and odd money more to Mr Partrich for yor chaffron dyssh the which he called ernestly for, swearyng that very necessytye made hym to call upon it. My lord lysle loketh euery day and howre for the chase dogge, mervelyng much that he is not brought before this unto hym. My lord of Warrewick, lorde greate master, hath ben this sevennight at the courte allredy metely well amendyd.[147] Tochee and Karsyes, ffrenchemen, are both stollen awey; such neclygence remayneth alweys amongste englyssh men and such lybertye geauen to prysoners. They offred before this to redeme both the lord Bowes and Sir Thomas Palmar but they are discharged now with lasse.[148] And to amend the matter Bruthye cragg yn Skottland is lost by syege leyd unto it. And three assawltes was geauen to it, and at the iij^{de} assawlte with the losse of many men of bothe partyes, and all or men for the moste parte beyng slayne, they gate the fforte, sauyng the castell, the which Sir John Lutterell, capytayn, with a fewe that remayned lyuyng repayred unto for his sauffegarde. And perceauyd that he was not able long to defend the same yelded it by composycyon, by the meanes wheareof hys lyeff is saued and remayneth prysoner.[149] Syr ffraunces Bryan is dedd yn Ireland, and it is seyd he dyed easelye, syttyng at table leanyng on his elbowe, none perceauyng eny likelyhode of deth yn hym, seyd thes wordes: I praye yow lett me be buryed amongeste the good ffellowes of Waterford (whiche weare good drynkers) and upon thos wordes ymmedyatly dyed. God send all chrysten men better

146. William Huet and Sir William Locke were wealthy citizens of London, sheriffs for 1553 and 1548 respectively.

147. Warwick had been ill and away from Court, often staying at York's house. *CSPSp.* x, pp. 13, 21, 28, 43.

148. Sir Robert Bowes, warden of the Western march, and Palmer, in command of the forces against the French at Haddington, had been routed and captured in July 1548. *CSP Scotland*, p. 148; Edward VI, *Chronicle*, pp. 9–10; Jordan, *Edward VI: Young King*, pp. 285–6.

149. Broughty Crag commanded the mouth of the Tay. When it surrendered the garrison, their wives and children were slaughtered. A mythological portrait of Luttrell, its commander, survives. *APC* ii, p. 407; Wriothesley, *Chronicle*, ii. p. 31; Jordan, *Edward VI: Threshold of Power*, pp. 147–8; R. Strong, *The English Icon: Elizabeth and Jacobean Portraiture* (1969), pp. 9, 86, 342.

departure. [150]And Mr Balyngeham is discharged of the depuetyshyp of Irelonde. And Mr Sentleger is restored to that roome and departeth hereence shortelye.[151] Mr Stanhope, Mr Smyth, Mr Thynne, Mr ffyssher and Mr Graye are all delyuered the xxij day of ffebruarye payeng greate ffynes accordyng to euery of theyr abylytye to the uttermost, to the which at the ffurst they wold not agree unto, whearupon they weare shutt up yn close pryson and all lybertye taken ffrom them so that by this ffolye they weare lykelye to haue hyndred them selves and neuerthelesse brought them selfes to a greater chardge.[152] Sir Thomas Pope is sett at lybertye, and I suppose that the Erle of Arrundell shalbe shortelye dischardged, payeng a good ffyne to the kynges maiestyes.[153] He hath bene teryes before the counsell, and to begyn he is owte of offyce, and ynto that roome is all redy placed the lord Wentworth, to whome the kyng [. . .] (*fo. 5*ᵛ)

Doctor Bonar remaynyng yn the marshallsye ys depryued from the Bisshopryck of London,[154] and the landes therof is seased ynto the kynges handes for the Master of the kynges woodes sellyng the wooddes growyng of the land of the late Busshoppes. And it is openly spoken that there shalbe more quondam Busshoppes yn England shortlye. And as thynges shall happen I truste from tyme to tyme to aduertyse yow therof, but the occasyon whye I haue not sonar wryten unto yow at this present is for lacke of messynger, whearefore I was constrayned to stay my letters untyll the departure of the ordyarye whos journey begynneth not before the xxiiij[th] daye of ffebruarye. Ther is non certenly knowen as yett to supplye the place of Mr Harvell yn Venyce, but the brute goeth upon Petor Vane, yett Mr Morryson and Mr

---

150. For the notorious Bryan: humanist, soldier, diplomat, poet, and libertine, Henry VIII's 'vicarius Inferni', see D. Starkey, *The Reign of Henry VIII: Personalities and Politics* (1985), pp. 69–70, 112–13. Scudamore had long known Bryan, who had been Master of the Toils: *L&P* xvi. 745, p. 360; xviii(1), pp. 264–5.

151. Sir Edward Bellingham, Lord Deputy of Ireland, was replaced by Sir Anthony St Leger, who returned for a second tour of duty. St Leger had written an epitaph of Hoby's friend Wyatt. Edward VI, *Chronicle*, pp. 9, 40, 42; *L&P* xvi. 641.

152. Sir Michael Stanhope, chief Gentleman of the Privy Chamber and half-brother of the Duchess of Somerset, Sir Thomas Smith, secretary of State, Sir John Thynne, steward of Somerset's household, Thomas Fisher, Somerset's private secretary, and William Grey were all imprisoned at the Protector's fall and charged with complicity in his 'ill government'. Their release was secured upon their acknowledgement that they owed huge sums to the Crown and upon taking up substantial bonds. BL, Cotton MS Titus B ii, fo. 67ʳ; *APC* ii, pp. 309, 343–4, 398, 401; iii, p. 57; *CSPSp.* x, p. 44.

153. Edward reported that the fine was £12,000, of which £8,000 was remitted; van der Delft that the fine was £7,000. Edward VI, *Chronicle*, pp. 19, 51; *CSPSp.* x, p. 44.

154. Bonner was formally deprived by the Lord Chancellor and Council sitting in Star Chamber on 7 February. His resistance continued from prison. Wriothesley, *Chronicle*, ii, pp. 33–4; Brigden, *London and the Reformation*, pp. 447–55.

Richard Shelley hath both sued for the same.[155] The newys is here at the full of a newe Busshopp of Roome to be elected which before was called cardynall de Monte,[156] but whether it be so or not yow remayne yn the place of knoweledge. Thus hauyng nothyng elles worthye of aduertyesment, I praye to the lyvyng lord to prospere yowe yn all your affayres. Wreten at the blacke ffryers the xxiij day of ffebruarye by yor most bounden seruaunt

Richard Scudamore

17 *2 March, 1550 (Adv. MS 34.2.14, fo. 29ʳ)*

It may please yow to be aduertesyd that wheare as by my last letters I sygnyfyed unto yow that Master Chauncellor had appoynted me on Monday last to attend upon hym for the allowaunce of the reparacyons of Stanwell, accordyng unto whos appoynted tyme I attendyd, wheare I receauyd of hym thys answeare, that he had such busynes that he could not be at eny leysure for it, but he seyd he wold ffynd a tyme for it. But that tyme is not yet ffownd, for he is ryden furth of the Cytye, and at is retorne I will make hym (with ymportunacye) as werye of me as I am now of hym. And as towchyng yor dyettes, they be not yett receauyed for the meane therof is very skaunt, but I haue used this practyes that I haue declared unto Mr Treausorer and to his clerkes that yow do owe unto the kyng ccˡⁱ withyn the receyttt of Mr Sheldon,[157] and onlesse that I may haue allowaunce at theyr handes of so much the kyng can not be payd therof, and I haue promysed Mr Sheldon to paye unto hym the xxˡⁱ that yow do owe unto hym, by the meanes whearof he is the ernester yn helpyng me therto, so that I haue litle dowpt to obteyne this payment shortlye. I haue receauyd a letter from Symon sence his departure herence, wheareyn he declareth that he hath bene at Rowell[158] and ther he hath weyd yor wooll sold to Dutton. The weyght whearof is twoo hundreth ffyftye and nyne codd, the money whearof is after xxvˢ viijᵈ for euery codd, abatyng yn thole payment xxˢ three hundreth thurtye and one poundes seven shelynges and ffoure pence, wheareof is alredye

155. Edmund Harvel was succeeded as ambassador to Venice by Peter Vannes, a native of Lucca, and Latin secretary to Henry VIII and Edward VI. *Edward VI, Chronicle*, pp. 24, 31.

156. Julius III had been elected on 8 February.

157. William Sheldon was receiver of the Court of Augmentations for the counties of Herefordshire, Leicestershire, Northamptonshire, Rutland, Shropshire, Staffordshire, Warwickshire and Worcestershire.

158. The manor of Rowell, Gloucestershire, formerly belonging to Winchcombe Abbey. *CPR, 1547–8*, p. 225.

receauyd syx score poundes, as by other letters ye haue bene aduertesyd. And I do loke howrly to receaue the rest. And not undesyred
of dyuers yor credytors. I haue bene a sutor to dyuers of the counsell,
almost to all (except to my lord treausorer, to my lord greate master,
and to my lord greate chamberlayne,[159] to whom I entend to sue as
tyme shall geave place), desyryng them of theyr ffavorable goodnes
towardes yow ffor the greate losse susteyned by yow yn the exchaunge
of yor money, at whos handes I receauyd very ffavorable and ffryndly
wordes. Whearefore I doupt not yef ye wold wryte yor letter unto my
lordes of the counsell yn that behalf I mystrust not but they wyll haue
yow yn consyderacyon, and yn the meane space I wyll endeuor to do
theryn as tyme shall geave occasyon. Occurrauntes are fewe yn thes
partyes but such as come from or lordes of that syde of the seas, of the
which I do well knowe ye haue better intellygence of then I can
aduertyece yow of. The Busshopp late of Rochestor is made Busshopp
of London and Westminster, and the late Busshopp of Westminster is
made Busshop of Norwiche,[160] and the brute goeth that ther shalbe
more quondam Busshoppes shortly. Mr Rogers is att lybertye but not
of the pryvey chambor. The prechers this Lent hetherto before the
kynges maiestye are thes: on the Wenysdays Mr Hooper, on the
ffrydayes Mr Poynett, a chapeleyn of the Busshopp of Cantorburyes,
and on the ffurst Sonday Doctor Byll. And this present day Mr
Latymar, who seyd that he came to take his leave of the kynges
maiestye.[161] Mr Paston hath receauyd from yow as cast of hawkes as
ye shall perceaue by his letter. And although the gentlemen of the
pryvey chambor do not wryte unto yow they do all send unto yow
theyr comendacyons. And yeven at the latter ende of the sermon
William ap Thomas[162] came home, of whome I receauyd from yow a
letter with a byll of dett ynclosyed, the which I will send to Symon
by the furst. And then we will accomplyssh the effecte therof to or
powars. Thus I pray to the lyuyng lord to prospere yow yn all yor
affayres. Wreten at the Blake ffryers the ij day of March by your most
bounden seruaunt

Richard Scudamore

159. Marquess of Northampton.
160. Nicholas Ridley was translated from Rochester to London, and Thomas
Thirlby from Westminster to Norwich, upon the resignation of Reppes.
161. John Hooper, John Ponet, William Bill and Hugh Latimer, leading reformers.
Van der Delft reported to the Emperor that the king chose his own Court preachers.
CSPSp. x, p. 63.
162. William Thomas, author of *The Pilgrim* and *The historie of Italie* (dedicated to
Warwick, 20 September, 1549), had arrived home from Italy, whence he had fled to
escape gambling debts. He had old association with the Scudamores. *L&P* xv. 688;
House of Commons, 1509–1558.

18 *21 March, 1550 (Adv. MS 34.2.14, fo. 25ʳ)*

It may please yow to be aduertesyd that I receauyd certeyn letters directed to Master secretorye Wotton, the which I delyuered ymmedyatlye. And synce the wrytyng of my last letters unto yow I haue bene twyse a sutor unto the Master of the hors on yor behalf, prayeng hym to be a meane to help that yor dyetes myght be payd. At my ffurst comyng unto hym he willed me to spare hym for iij or iiij dayes, and so I dyd, and as yesterday I eftsones repayred unto hym, and then his answeare was that he wold procure some ordre that yow shold be payd therof. Yet that notwithstandyng I haue thought good to put yow ageyne yn remembraunce (as by my other letters I haue don) to wryte yor letters to my lordes of the counsell aswell for the receytt of yor dyettes as also for the recompence of the greate losse of the exchaunge. And yn the meane tyme I will endeuor my self to solycyte the recouerye therof, yef oportunytye shall geave place, the which I thynk wilbe very hard untyll therbe a conclusyon had betwyxt or comyssioners and the ffrenche.[163] Master Mason came ouer and is retorned.[164] I haue payd xxᵗⁱ markes to Mr Stonar for the rent of Wreysburye. Occurrauntes ther are none that I can lern, sauyng that ther be some lewde persons that casteth abrode sklaunderous bylles ageynst the counsellors, and ther are dyuers of the ffyne wytted yong men examyned and stayed therfore, as the two yonger Chaloners, Patent of the Costome howse, Calfeld who beyng yn the Counter was removed to the Towre, and one Tyndale an audytors clerck.[165] My lord of Warrewick lyeth at Grenewhich and is very yll troubled with his sykenes. The lyuyng lord send hym amendement, to whom I do praye to prospere yow yn all yor affayres. Wreten at the Blacke ffryers the xxjᵗʰ day of Marche by yor most bounden seruaunt

Richard Scudamore

19 *1 April 1550 (Adv. MS 34.2.14, fo. 57ʳ)*

Jhus

It may please yow to be aduertesyd that I haue receauyd of Mr

---

163. Warwick was desperately seeking peace with France. Four commissioners to conduct the negotiations were appointed in January: Russell, Paget, Petre and Sir John Mason. The discussions were at a critical point as Scudamore wrote. *CSPSp*, ix, p. 469; x, pp. 12–13, 62; Edward VI, *Chronicle*, p. 20; Jordan, *Edward VI: Threshold of Power*, pp. 118–21.

164. Sir John Mason was secretary to the French tongue, and master of the posts. *House of Commons, 1509–1558*.

165. Frances Chaloner and Ralph Calfilde were bound upon £40 and 100 marks respectively. *APC* ii, p. 425; iii. pp. 40, 45.

Arnold by thandes of his seruaunt the somme of twentye and ffyve
poundes syx shelynges and eight pence to thuse of his brother Richard,
but whether this somme will countervayle the ffull nombre of iiij^{xx}
crounes of the somme I knowe not because the exchaunge is so base
and so uncerteyne. My lady came to London upon ffryday last and
laye at Mr Weldons, whether Mr Jervyes dyd come and brought with
hym the indenture of covenauntes towchyng the money apperteynyng
unto my ladyes doughters, the which indenture berith date the xixth
of May yn the xxxvijth yere of the late kyng of ffamous memorye kyng
Henry the eight,[166] yn the which it apperith that ye had receauyd the
day of the makyng therof three hundreth and ten poundes. And after
the date of the seyd indenture to be charged yerelye with .lx^{li}. goyng
owte of the lordeshyp of Abberley and Grafton,[167] whearfore it apperith by the seyd indenture that at or ladye day last it is fful ffyve yeres
so that the money alredy receauyd, and also for this last half yere,
doth amount to three hundreth poundes, the which is by one half yere
lesse then by my other letters I dyd aduertyes yow of, but for the
teythyng of Bradweye I omytted one hole yere or at the lest an half
yere, for the gyft therof made by my ladye apperith to be the xxth day
of Julye yn the xxxjth yere of the reign of the late kyng Henrye the
eight,[168] so that it semeth that the profyttes of aleven yere shold be
due at Michellmas last. And yef it so be then is ther due to Mastres
Weldon for the tythe of Bradwey ffoure score and eight poundes after
viij^{li} euery yere. And then ther is due also to hur the iiijth parte of the
receypt of the syx hundreth and ten poundes of the proffyttes of
Aburley and Grafton, the iiijth of which somme is one hundreth
ffyftye & twoo poundes and ten shelynges, and joyne the proffyttes of
Bradwey to that and then the somme due to be payd withyn half a
yere after hur maryage (for asmuch as ther was not an half yeres
warnyng geaven before hur maryage) is twoo hyndreth and ffortye
poundes and ten shelynges. Mr Stacye shewed me a letter that he
receauyd from George Nedham[169] wheareyn it apperyd that ye willed
hym to aduertyes Mr Stacye and Mr Coseworth to prepare such
money as they haue alredy receauyd of yors to be repayd at the ende
of syx monethes at which tyme it apperyth by the seyd letter that ye
offer to delyuer them the ffull somme of one thowsand poundes, the
which maketh them much to merveyll whate ye do meane therbye

166. 1545.
167. The manor of Grafton Flyford, Worcestershire, had been granted for life to
Walter Welshe, of Abberley and Elmley Castle, Lady Hoby's second husband. The
manor was held by her for her lifetime. *L&P* v. 559(3); *VCH, Worcester*, iv, p. 87.
168. Broadway, Gloucestershire, formerly belonging to Evesham abbey; *CPR, 1549–
1551*, pp. 311–12.
169. A London mercer who had been apprenticed to Thomas Stacy. *Register of
Freemen*, p. 109.

both to requyre to receaue of them money and at the same tyme to delyuer unto them a more somme. And Mr Stacye seyth yef that he had knowen that he shold not haue had yor money untyll Chrystmas at the nerest he wold not haue medled with it at all. I receauyd a letter from Symon with a copye of the survey of Lenchwyck and Norton,[170] but Lenchewick yef it myght be obteyned by it self is aboue the yerely value of xxxj^{li} by the yere. The copye whearof I haue stayed to send unto yow at this present for that I suppose that ther shalbe no salez of eny of the kynges landes, sauyng of such rentes as the kynges maiestye hath oute of the halles of the craftes of London, for the which the hole bodye of the Cytye doth prepare to ffurnyssh the kyng with so much money as the purchase of the seyd rentes doth amounte unto, and for the repayment therof euery company selleth so much land belongyng to theyr halles as the rent goyng oute of the same to the kyng doth amount unto.[171] (fo. 57^v) And by Symons letter I do perceaue that by sendyng a byll of dett supposed to be due by the stuard it had made hym almost oute of his witt and put hym yn such a rage that yef he had had yor secretorye he wold haue serued hym as he serued the bill; that was to haue cast hym lykewyse ynto the ffyre for an example to make other to be ware howe they shall counterfett a byll yn eny mans name, affyrmyng ernestlye that he wold neuer subscrybe his name so lowe to eny letter hereafter but that this shold be a suffycyent lesson for hym duryng his lyeff. Mr Nicholas Throckmorton is admytted one of the gentlemen of the kynges pryvey chambor.[172] And George fferreys remayneth at my lord of War-rewickes at Grenewhich upon suspycyon to be a counsell with the makyng of the sklaunderous letters ageynst the counsell.[173] One Curtopp, a chapleyn of the kynges, preached at the court on Sonday last before the kynges maiestye, and yn his sermon he ffownd hym self agreued yn many thynges and cheyfflye yn the dispocyon of the kynges landes, sayeng that the rulars spared neyther abbay landes nor chaunterye landes, Busshoppes landes nor yett the landes of the auncyent croune. And even as they weare gredye of the kynges landes so they wold be of the kynges subiectes landes, belykenyng the rulars to a spunge, the propertye of whom is yef it come to eny lyker to suck

170. Hoby had been granted the manor of Norton cum Lenchwick in Worcestershire, formerly belonging to Evesham abbey. *CPR, 1549–1551*, pp. 311–12; *1550–3*, p. 19.

171. In March 1550 the City companies, which had lost rents from the chantry lands which they administered at the Dissolution of the chantries, purchased all the quitrents from the Crown at 20 years' purchase at a cost of £20,000. Wriothesley, *Chronicle*, ii. pp. 35–6; Brigden, *London and the Reformation*, pp. 389–90.

172. Another zealous Protestant, and a favourite of the king.

173. A poet, a chronicler, and a deviser of Court pastimes, he could have been an effective critic. Although he had survived Somerset's fall, he had earlier been described as a 'gentleman of my Lord Protector's'. *House of Commons, 1509–1558*.

contynually untyll it be ffull, and they yef the spunge weare taken and hardely wrested and wrynge, all the moysture shold be cleane taken awey and nothyng left but the very spunge it self. So he aduysed the kynges maiestye to take thos gredye spunges and to wrest oute all the moysture ageyne and to leave spunges as they weare at the ffurst. And also he seyd he perceauyd that ther was a peace, but he seyd it was yll to be lyked that the kyng shold lose hys conquest land yn obteynyng of it. Yn recompence of which sermon he was immedyatlye sent for by the counsell and from them sent ffurthwith to the fflete. The proclamacyon of which peace was made at London on Setorday, and at courte on Sondaye, of the which I wold haue sent yow rather aduertyesment yef I had not ben oute of doupt that yow had had intellygence therof before it was openlye knowen here. Yet notwith-stondyng I haue sent unto yow herewith a proclamacyon.[174] And Mr Dymockes[175] man dyd not only [...] me (but also Nicho the curror who shold haue come unto yow) with whom I could not speake with for his sodeyn departure. Ther is appoynted to goo ynto ffraunce as pledgges the Duke of Suffolk, the Erle of Ertford, the lord Straunge, the Lord Matrevers, the Lord Talbott, and the Lord ffitzwarren, who setteth fforeward betwene this and Ester, as it is openly seyd.[176] Other occurrauntes I haue not at this tyme worthye of aduertyesment saue that ffraunces[177] arryved here yesterday. Thus I praye to the lyuyng lord to prosper yow yn all yor affayres. Wreten at the Black ffryers the ffurst day of Apryell by yor most bounden seruaunt.

Richard Scudamore

20 6 April 1550 (Adv. MS 34.2.14, fo. 3')

It may please yow to be aduertesyd that on good ffryday, as it is called, Mr Ausham and Nicholas Charnelles arryved at London, of whom I receauyd a lettre dyrected unto Mr Stacye, the which I delyuered the same day. And after he had perceauyd yor request he toke a tyme to answeare thereunto untyll he had spoken with his brother Coseworth, with whom the same nyght and on the morrowe he dyd theron consult, and gave me this to answeare that yef they

174. The peace with France was proclaimed in London on 28 March, and in Court on 30th. There was great acclamation, despite the ignominious cessation of Boulogne, according to Wriothesley; but 'with no great rejoicing', according to van der Delft. *TRP* i, 354; Wriothesley, *Chronicle*, ii, pp. 34–5; *CSPSp*. x, pp. 54–5.

175. Edward Dymmock was one of the Council at Boulogne. *CSPF* p. 294.

176. The heirs of England's premier nobles were sent to France on 6 April as hostages for keeping the peace. Edward VI, *Chronicle*, pp. 22–3; *CSPSp*. x, p. 62.

177. Francisco Tomazo, the courier.

had knowen that ye wold haue requyred yor money yn so short a tyme they wold not haue receauyd eny at all, for the takyng of yor money dyd occasyon them to occupye more than they entended to haue don, so that the most parte of theyr substaunce remayneth yn other mens handes delyuered upon fformer bargaynes, and yn wares aswell at home as yn fforeygn contreys. And such money as they had lyeng by them they weare constrayned to disburs upon a purchase of Mr Coseworths howse with certeyn other howses belongyng to theyr hall for the accomplysshment of a somme of money the which the heddes of the Cytye weare appoynted to make provysyon for the kynges maiestye.[178] So that ffurthwith they can not repaye yor money onlesse it shold be to theyr greate losse either by takyng up of money or elles by sellyng theyr wares to much under theyr pryses at this tyme. And they suppose that shold be small benyfytt unto yow, yet neuerthelesse they will make such prouysyon that betwyxt whitsontyde and mydsomer yow shall haue yor ffull money withoute ffayle, the which tyme they sey is at hand and this they may do with oute theyr greate losse, and yef yn case hereafter ye shall haue occasyon to occupye asmuch they will bere as longe with yow, whos myndes also ye shall perceaue by theyr letter. And as tyme and occasyon shall take place yor pleasure and comaundement accordyng to instruccyons to be receauyd by Mr Ausham it shalbe ffullfylled yn all poyntes by the help of God. Mr Secretorye Wotton shewed me that ye had wreten to the lordes of the counsell yor letter prayeng them that some ordre may be taken for the better payment of yor dyettes. Mr Secretorye shewed me that assone as he myght ffynde a convenyent tyme he wold put the lordes yn remembraunce of yor request, whearfore I entend to morrowe to goo to Grenewhich wheare the court lyeth[179] ther to attend upon Mr Secretorye untyll that I may haue some coumfort for the receytt of yor dyettes. And the ffame goeth that the Duke of Somersett and the Erle of Arrundell shold both as to morrowe come to the courte.[180] Mr Blount and Sir George Howoord with one of euery offyce of the courte are goon with the syx yong lordes to attend upon them and as to morrowe they are appoynted to be at Caleys. Mr Mason goeth not ynto ffraunce yett this ffortenyght.[181] Thus

178. The Mercers' Company were bound to pay £3,935.3s.4d. for the recovery of their rents from chantry lands. Mercers' Company, Register of Writings, ii, fo. 114ᵛ.

179. The Court moved from Westminster to Greenwich on 5 April. Edward VI, *Chronicle*, p. 23.

180. Edward had reported on 31 March that Somerset 'came to Court'. On 8 April Somerset dined with the Council at Greenwich, and on 10th was restored to the board. On 21 February Arundel had been ordered to retire to his Sussex estates. Edward VI, *Chronicle*, pp. 23, 24; *CSPSp*. x, p. 62; *APC* ii, p. 398.

181. Mason was still at Court, but it was widely known that he would soon be appointed resident ambassador to France. *CSPSp*. x, p. 62.

hauyng nothyng elles worthy of aduertyesment, do pray the lyvyng
lord to prospere yow yn all yor affayres. Wreten at the blacke ffryers
on Eester day by yor most bounden seruaunt

                                                  Richard Scudamore

21 *26 April 1550 (Adv. MS 34.2.14, fo. 39ʳ)*

It may please yow to be aduertesyd that (although ther be none
occurrauntes worthye of aduertyesment) I haue thought good to wryte
at thyes presentes unto yow onlye for ffullfyllyng of yor comaundement, the whych is wekelye to wryte unto yow notwithstondyng
therbe small occasyon. As yett synce Symons departyng I haue
receauyd no money, but thys next weeke I trust to begynn, and as I
shall receaue so I will aduertyes yow therof. This present day my lord
Lysle with dyuers gentle men are rydden to meete the three pledges
that remayned at Calleys.[182] It is comonlye talked here that my lord
of Warrewyck shall goo lye thys somer yn the north partes, and my
lord pryvey seale to lye yn the west contrey, and that Sir William
Herbart shalbe presydent of Wales.[183] My lord of Somersett lyeth at
the court and all men seketh upon hym.[184] Other occurrauntes I haue
not worthye of aduertyesment, but that they begyn to ponyssh vyce
very ernestlye yn London, the lord be praysed therfore,[185] to whom I
praye to prospere yow yn all yowr affayres. Wreten at the Blacke
ffryers the xxvjᵗʰ day of Apryell by yor most bounden seruaunt

                                                  Richard Scudamore

22 *3 May 1550 (Adv. MS 34.2.14, fo. 41ʳ)*

It may please yow to be aduertesyd that synce the wrytyng of my last

182. The Marquis de Mayenne, Count d'Enghien and Montmorency, the French
pledges for the peace treaty, were met by Lisle, Rutland, Grey of Wilton, Bray and
the Gentlemen Pensioners. Edward VI, *Chronicle*, pp. 27–8.

183. On 8 April Warwick had been appointed Warden of the North, and Herbert
President of Wales. Russell had been sent to the West to keep order. In the event, so
great were fears of disorder in the South that summer that Warwick did not go North.
Edward VI, *Chronicle*, p. 24; *APC* iii, p. 6; Jordan, *Edward VI: Threshold of Power*, pp.
49, 59–62.

184. Van der Delft, too, reported that at Court it was expected that the Duke would
be restored to his former authority. *CSPSp*. x, pp. 62–3.

185. Protestants hoped that a reform in morals would follow reformation in religion.
For the assault on the capital's immorality, see also Wriothesley, *Chronicle*, ii. p. 36;
Two London Chronicles, p. 45.

letters I haue receauyd no money but the half yeres rent of louelles inne yn pater noster rowe. I was promysed to haue bene payd this last weeke your ffee of thordynaunce, but at the same present that I was appoynted to haue bene payd ther was a commaundement geauen that no man shold receaue eny money owte of the Receytt of the Excheker before that a certeyn somme be payd to the cofferer, so that I suppose it wilbe towardes the latter ende of the next weeke before that I shall receaue it. And as for yor dyettes, I am enforced to sue to my lordes of the counsell to procure some ordre for the payment thereof. Ther ys dependyng upon your hedd yn the Excheker xxvij^{li} xv^s for the contribucyon being graunted to the kyng that dedd is, and also ther remayneth yn the court of wardes one obligacyon of xx^{li} for the payment of xvj^{li} xiij^s iiij^d for parte of the money for the wardeshyp of herry myle and not estalled amongst other yor dettes, so that yef ye haue none acquytaunces for the payment of the aforeseyd sommes then ye must be chardged with them. Ther was taken yn Kent this last weke aboutes a xij persons who had conspyred to haue stered the people to haue rebelled, and theyr assemble shold haue begonne on may day last,[186] whearfore dyuers of the nobles and gentlemen shall shortlye repayre ynto the countrey to see that the people may be stayed from theyr devylles rages, and the nexte terme is alredye by proclamacyon putt ouer untyll mychelmas, savyng the ffurst retorne. Yesterday Johan of Kent was burned yn Smythfeld for hur pervers opynyon, who, ragyng and raylyng ageynst Scorye that preached before hur to confute hur opynyon, contynued yn hur obstynacye untyll hur deth.[187] The ffame goeth here that the Erle of Warrewicke shalbe made duke of Gloucestre,[188] and shalbe lord warden of the north partyes, but god weare more mercyfuller unto hym yef he weare restored to his helth, for at this present he is very syke and lyeth at Canbury. My lord markes of Northampton hath Sudeley geauen unto hym so that I trust ye shall haue a good neighbor of hym.[189] William Thomas is placed one of the clerckes of the counsell yn hunnynges place.[190] Other occurrauntes I haue not presentlye worthy of aduertysement, onlesse I shold troble yow with the ffressh maskes and costlye bankettes that the ffrenche lordes are used withall and that

---

186. Edward VI also reported this foiled insurrection, led by a priest. *Chronicle*, p. 28.

187. Joan Bocher died for denying the incarnation of Christ, all attempts to convert her having failed. Wriothesley, *Chronicle*, ii, pp. 37–8; Edward VI, *Chronicle*, p. 28.

188. Warwick was created not Duke of Gloucester but Duke of Northumberland on 11 October 1551, five days before Somerset's arrest. Edward VI, *Chronicle*, pp. 86–7.

189. Sudeley had been the home of the late Sir Thomas Seymour, Lord Admiral.

190. Thomas was appointed on 10 April. He became adviser and confidant of the king. Edward VI, *Chronicle*, pp. xx–xxi, 25.

lyke wyse they do use,[191] but the reporte therof I do deferr untill Mr
Bygges comyng unto yow, who is now at London and entendyth to
take his jorney towardes yow aboutes wenysday next comyng by the
suffraunce of the euer lyvyng lord, to whom I praye to prospere yow
in all yor affayres. Wreten at the blacke ffryers the iij[d] daye of maye
by yor most bounden seruaunt

Richard Scudamore

23 *7 May 1550 (Adv. MS 34.2.14, fo. 53[r])*

It may please yow to be aduertesyd that for asmuch as ther remayned
none of the kynges revenues yn Sir John Williams handes so that I
could not receaue eny parte of yor dyettes, whearfore I was enforced
to make a nue sute to the lordes of the counsell, and yn especyall to
my lord pagett, to my lord warden, and to the master of the hors,
who very gentlye promysed theyr ffurderaunce. My suytt was to haue
a warraunt to be payd of the Salez, and the master of the hors
comaunded me to make a warraunt for the same and he wold geate
it sygned ffurthwith. I prouyded a warraunt and the master of the
hors gat it sygned ymmedyatlye, the which I brought to Sir John
Williams, by vertue whearof I receauyd yesternyght one hundreth
poundes yn partye of payment of yor dyettes with promys for the rest
assone as money shold be payd to his handes. Whearefore yef it may
please yow to rendre thankes unto the master of the hors by yor letters
then he shall perceaue that I haue aduertesyd yow of his gentle
ffurtheraunce towardes yow, and hereafter I may the boldlyer repayre
unto hym yef the lyke occasyon shall happen. And as for the ffee of
the ordynaunces (although therbe a restraynte for payment to be
made to eny man), Mr Baker hath promysed that ye shalbe payd
sometyme this terme. I haue spoken with the Erle of Rutland for yor
harnes, who, very gentlye ffurst rendryng unto you his most hartye
thankes, seyd that he had caused yor harnes to be made cleane, and
loked shortlye for it at London, and assone as it shall come up I shall
haue it delyuered unto me. The occurrauntes here are fewe. My lord
Clynton is made lord admyrall and all redy sworn of the counsell.[192]
Yesterday ther came to the court ij ambassadors oute of Skottland;
the one a ffrench man called Monsieur Morrett and the other a Skott

191. The French hostages were entertained at Court 'with much music at dinner',
so Edward reported: *Chronicle*, p. 28.
192. As a reward for his captaincy of Boulogne. Edward VI, *Chronicle*, p. 29; Hoak,
King's Council, pp. 61–2

called Mr Askyem,[193] and as they weare enterteyned by the counsell ther came to the court all or yong lordes that wheare sent pledges ynto ffraunce. And ther is comyng the ffrench ambassadors[194] by long seas with .v. galleys, for the conduccyon whearof a long the ryuer ther is alredy sent down Mr Broke and Mr Tyrell with ij pynneshes,[195] and dyuers masters of shyppes with them. And the iij last pladges of the ffrenchmen are departed herence, two of them ynto ffraunce, and the Skottysshe qweenes brother is gon to see his suster ynto Skottland.[196] Mr vanne prepareth him self yn aredynes to goo to Venyce. Other newys I haue not at this tyme worthye aduertyesment, but I continually praye to the lyvyng lord to prosper yow yn all yor affayres. Wreten at the Blacke ffryer the vij[th] day of Maye by yor most bounden seruaunt

Richard Scudamore

I haue receauyd synce the date aforeseyd as parcell of yor dyettes xl[li], and ther hath bene taken of late yn Hampshyre certen sorcerers who went aboutttes to practyes to consume certeyn of the cheyfyest rulers, and the sayng is that they thought to do the lyke to the kynges maiestye, but God the preseruer of all thynges I trust will so defend his highnes from all perell.[197] I haue sent unto yow yn this pakett the Busshopp of Londons iniunccyons with certeyn articles that the Busshop doth presently mynystre yn his vicytacyon.[198] Symon arryved here the xth day of thys moneth. Wreten the xij[th] day of the same. Yor bedstede is almost redye.

R.S.

24 _1 June 1550 (Adv. MS 34.2.14, fo. 51ʳ)_

It may please yow to be aduertesyd that my ladye came to London

193. Charles de Soliers, Seigneur de Morette, envoy extraordinary to England, and Thomas, Master of Erskine. Edward VI, _Chronicle,_ p. 29; _CSPF_ p. 49

194. Gaspard de Coligny, Seigneur de Chatillon, Andre Guillart, Seigneur de Mortier, Guillaume Bochetel, Seigneur de Sassy, François de Coligny, Seigneur d'Andelot, and Jean Pot de Rhodes, Seigneur de Chemault. Edward VI, _Chronicle,_ pp. 29, 31–2; Wriothesley, _Chronicle,_ ii, p. 39.

195. Pinnaces.

196. François de Lorraine, Marquis de Mayenne, had gone to comfort the Queen of Scotland at the death of their father, the Duke of Guise. Edward VI, _Chronicle,_ p. 29.

197. _APC_ iii, p. 32.

198. For Ridley's visitation articles, see W.H. Frere and W.M. Kennedy (eds.), _Visitation Articles and Injunctions of the Period of the Reformation,_ 3 vols. (Alcuin Club, xiv, xv, xvi, 1910), ii, pp. 230–45; Wriothesley, _Chronicle,_ ii, pp. 38, 41.

upon Tuysday last, and after hur ladyeshypp had bene with Mr
Jerveys (and as I suppose to knowe his advyse for thuse of the chylderns
money) I desyred to knowe hur pleasure of a day certeyn upon the
which I shold paye unto hur handes all such money as ye had alredye
receauyd of theyrs, to the which she answeared that she merveleyd
much whate shold move yow upon the sodeyn to repaye all such
money as ye had receauyd, ffearyng lest ye had conceauyd some
displeasure ageynst hur or some of hur chyldern, and further for that
she judgeth that this payment shold be burdenous unto yow she wold,
yef it myght stand with yor pleasure, that it shold remayn yn yor
handes. And then I declared unto hur ladyeshyp that yow dyd it but
for the advauncement of hur chyldern; and that the money shold be
alweys yn a redynes so that the lack therof shold be no hynderaunce
to theyr preferment. Then my ladye answeared, well yef there be non
other remedye but that yor master will dischardge his handes of the
seyd money then I must travayle to seke some ffrendes for the kepyng
of the seyd money, and she seyd that she wold send up for Richard
Sheldon and Thomas Taylor bycause they weare profectors of the
reconyng. And yef yor pleasure weare not yn the meane tyme alteryd
that then my lady wold appoynt a tyme certeyn for the receytt of the
money and then ther resteth thassuraunces of such money as hereafter
is to be receauyd to the chylderns use. To the which I answeared on
yor behalf that lett theyr lerned counsell devyse eny reasonable wey
that yow wold stand to it. And bycause ther is no tyme certeyn
appoynted for the payment of the seyd money I wyll forsee the
dischardge of yor bound therfore. I haue concluded with Mr Weldon
for to paye unto hym all such money as is due to Mastres Weldon
some tyme thys weke so that Mr Welden hath alredy appoynted
Wenysday next comyng to be the day of reconyng, after which tyme
I wyll sygnyfye unto yow of or procedynges as occasyon serveth. On
Tuysday next[199] my lord Lysley shalbe maryed at Shene wheare ther
is greate preparacyon made for the same; howbeit my lord of
Warrewick will not be ther at the same tyme but is alredye remoued
to hatfeld and well amendyd, therfor God be praysed.[200] My lord
Cobham was sworen on ffrydaye last of the pryvey counsell.[201] And the
ffrenchmen departed hence yesterday, and bycause theyr procedynges
here hath bene secrete to me I haue desyred Mr William Thomas,
one of the clerckes of the counsell, to wryte unto yow by whom

199. 3 June.
200. Van der Delft had reported in early January plans for the marriage of Lisle to
Anne, the daughter of Somerset. One story was that Warwick absented himself from
the marriage, because he 'suspected he should have been betrayed there'. *CSPSp.* x.,
pp. 8, 43; BL, Add. MS 48023, fo. 350ʳ; Edward VI, *Chronicle*, pp. 32–3.
201. Cobham was sworn on 23 May. *APC* iii, p. 36; Hoak, *King's Council*, p. 62.

(yef he kepe promys) ye shall perceaue partly of theyr doynges. Mr Secretory Wotton shewed this present daye that he thought shortlye to send letters unto yow but howe sone he knewe not. The court remoueth (as it is seyd) upon ffryday next comyng to Grenewhich and so ffurther yn Kent.[202] Other occurauntes I haue not at thys tyme worthye of aduertyesment, but I contynually pray to the lyuyng lord to prospere yow yn all yor affayres. I will not trouble yow with the ffayned tales that is used of the Emperour and of his greate power of men as well by land as by sees, the which thyng is not newly invented but it hath a long space contynued and yn especyall amongst the papystycall sort.[203] Wreten at the Blacke ffryers the ffurst day of June by yor most bounden seruaunt

Richard Scudamore

The exchaunge is yett but xix[s] viii[d],
the which causeth me to staye hopyng
to haue it to come to money for money.[204]

25 *11 June 1550 (Adv. MS 34.2.14, fo. 37[r])*

It may please yow to be aduertesyd that I haue ben a sutor on yor behalf to my lord marques[205] and to the master of the hors (but it was before that Syr Christoper Dyas had delyuered yor letters unto them), who promysed that they wold haue yow yn remembraunce. And the same day, beyng on Sondaye last,[206] Mr Harbart brake with the counsell towchyng yor suyttes upon my woordes, and bycause yor letters weare not delyuered I was very loth to trouble them eny more at that tyme. And the same after none my lord of Somersett with the most parte of the counsell and the gentle men of the courte came to Monsieur Vydame to a bankett (and such a one as the reporte goeth that the better hath bene seldome seene).[207] And on the morrowe,

202. For the 'gests', the progress of the Court that summer, see Edward VI, *Chronicle*, p. 33.

203. Imperial aid had always seemed one of the best hopes for the restoration of Catholicism. Charles V, however, had refused to intervene, so far. *CSPSp.* ix, pp. 460–1; Jordan, *Edward VI: Threshold of Power*, pp. 134–8.

204. The exchange rate in May 1550 was 20s. $\frac{1}{2}$d. flemish. Sterling fell during June: it has been calculated to have been 19s. $5\frac{1}{2}$d. to the £ sterling. Gould, *Great Debasement*, table ix.

205. Northampton, Great Chamberlain.

206. 8 June.

207. François de Vendôme, Vidame of Chartres, who, remarkably, led Edward to play. Edward VI, *Chronicle*, pp. 22, 33–4; *CSPSp.* x, pp. 97, 109–10.

beyng Monday, Syr Christopher Dyas delyuered yor letters at London
to my lord marques and to the master of the hors, on which day my
lord of Somersett with the most parte of the counsell dyned at the
Towre. And ther they vyewed both the treausorye and the mynt.[208]
And the Busshopp of Wynchester was brought before them, who came
to them with a stoute corage, but at his retorne his stoutenes was
much delayed, and ther be dyuers that haue good hope that he shalbe
a quondam.[209] And that evenyng all the counsell went downe to the
courte, and on the morrowe the counsell sate verye erlye, and they
answeared that they wold here no sutes for that day. Yett I thought
good to speke with the master of the hors, desyryng hym to haue yow
yn remembraunce yf accasyon serued, and then he answeared as he
dyd before that he had begon yor suyt upon Sonday last and as tyme
shold serve he wold procede therwith, and my lord Cobham standyng
by Mr Herbart, seyd unto hym, my lord you weare by when that I
moved the counsell for Mr Hobye, and then my lord Cobham seyd
that yow must forbere a whyles the recompence of the losses of the
exchaunge, and as for yor comyng home ther is a good ordre entryng
yn for it.[210] More theryn at thys tyme I can not declare unto yow, but
as I shall hereafter lerne I will sygnyfye unto yow. My lord Pagett
cometh this present day to the courte, and after that Syr Christopher
Dyas haue delyuered yor letters unto hym I will travayll to knowe
whate he will do yn youre suyttes. Wheare as the kynges maiestye had
thought to haue taken his progresse ynto Kent it is now otherwyse
altered, and on the morrowe after mydsomer day his grace is
appoynted to remove from Grenewhich to London, and from thens
to Hampton courte, and from thens to Wyndsore wheare his graces
lengst abode shalbe for this somer, and from thens to Oteland, and
from thens to Guylford, and from thens to Okyn, and from thens to
Ruchmond, and so ye jestes doth ffynyssh.[211] And after mydsomer the
most part of the counsell departeth ffrom the courte euery one to his
parte appoyneted, and the most parte of the soldyors of Bolleyn shall
attend upon the kynges maiestye thys progresse, and the rest shall goo

208. For the close supervision of the mint in this period of fiscal crisis, see C.E.
Challis, *The Tudor Coinage* (Manchester, 1978), pp. 103–4.

209. Somerset's return to the Council brought at attempt at reconciliation with
Gardiner. In return for his acceptance of the Prayer Book it was decided that he would
be offered pardon. Somerset, Northampton, Wiltshire, Bedford and Petre visited
Gardiner 'to know', as Edward put it, 'to what he would stick'. *APC* iii, p. 43; Edward
VI, *Chronicle*, p. 34.

210. On the same day a Council order was made that Hoby be recalled, at his
request, and Sir Richard Morison be sent at Michaelmas. *APC* iii, p. 45.

211. The alteration in plan may have been due to the Council's perennial fear of
popular disorder in Kent, and the reality of disturbance there that summer. *CSPSp.* x,
pp. 109, 116.

with my lord pryvey seale ynto the west countrey.[212] I do lack to furder yor suyttes my lord warden who is at home at his howse.[213] And mr Secretorye Wootton hath taken his leave and is alredy goon to Cantorburye. I haue spoken with Sir Myles Partriche,[214] who hath promysed unto me assone as oportunytye shall serve to knowe an answeare towchyng theffecte of yor letter. Ye shall understand that the counsell hath accomplysshed parte of yor request although they haue not accomplysshed the full, as by the counselles letters I doubt not but ye shall perceaue more at large. Other newys at this tyme I haue not worthye of aduertyesment, but I pray to the lyuyng lord to prospere yow yn all yor affayres. Wreten at the black ffryers the xj[th] day of June by yor most bounden seruaunt

Richard Scudamore

26 *15 June 1550 (Adv. MS 34.2.14, fo. 55ʳ)*

It may please yow to be aduertesyd that I receauyd yor letters of the ix[th] of June with dyuers other letters, the which I haue delyuered accordyngly, and Mr Darcye[215] shewed me that ye had desyred hym to furder me yn such yor sutes as I shold haue to the lordes of the counsell, the which to do he seyd he wold wyllynglye do, commaundyng me when that I had nede of his help I shold repayre unto hym. I moved Sir Myles Partriche as yor pleasure was, who promysed to do assone as occasyon shold serue. And he fyndyng a tyme convenyent brake with my lord[216] consernyng yow, who beyng yncensed by dyuers that be abowtes hym had conceauyd unkyndenes towardes yow; howbeit Mr Partriche hath used the matter so ffryndlye, ne ffryndlye yn dede as he witnessith of hym self, so that my lord is reconsyled to stand yor good lord, as I suppose by his letter ye shall perceaue. Mr Partrich thought it good to remembre yow yef ther shold be eny occurrauntes yn thos partyes worthy of aduertysement that ye sometyme remember my lord with yor pryvate letter.[217] My

212. On 15 May orders were given for the horsemen of Boulogne and men of arms to be paid and be under Northampton's command, and for the guard of Boulogne to be under Clinton's command. Edward VI, *Chronicle*, p. 30.

213. Cheyne was keeping order in Kent. *CSPSp*. x, p. 116.

214. Partridge was an adherent of Somerset's.

215. Sir Thomas Darcy, Lord Chamberlain.

216. Hoby, aware of Somerset's reviving ascendency at Court and in Council, sought, through the mediation of Partridge, to return to favour.

217. One of the charges against Somerset at his fall in 1549 had been that he tried to conduct foreign policy secretly, without consulting the Council. Foxe, *Acts and Monuments*, vi, p. 290.

lord is appoynted to lye the most parte of this sommer at Readyng, for my lord hath the chardge of Barkshyre, Hampshyre, Wiltshyre, and Somersettshyre.[218] The greatest matter that I can lerne of whearof they haue imagyned ageynst yow was but consernyng the letter that yow forgotton at home at yor goyng to Wyndesore.[219] Mr Warden sayeth (although he can not accomplyssh yor desyre for eny parte of the cloystre bycause it is promysed to my lord of Somersett) yett ye shall not be unprouyded yef ye wold buyld a greater howse then ye entend to do. Mr Pykeryng is not yett arryved here, but assone as he cometh I will remembre to solycyte hym for such answeare as he shall receaue.[220] I had prepared .l. crownes of the somme to be sent ynto ffraunce, but by yor last letter yor pleasure is that I shall take order for the payment of such money as Mr Barnardyne shall aduertyes me of for the necessary ffyndyng of thos that be ther, by the reason whearof I haue stayed the sendyng of the seyd money untyll I knowe yor ffurther pleasure. And as for the dischardgyng of yor dettes, I do stay as yett for that I haue not receauyd yor dyettes and also for that my ladye hath not determyned upon the receytt of hur doughters money. My ladye taryeth on the comyng up of Mr Sheldon and Thomas Taylor for to be asserteynd of the reconyng, but this weeke comyng I entend to pay Mr Weldon such money as is due unto hym at this presentes accordyng unto yor indenture, and when so euer my ladyes pleasure shalbe to haue the resydue the money is yn a redynes for the same purpose. I haue receauyd of Mr Dutton iiij$^{xx li}$, and so remayneth yn his handes xxxj^{li} vij^{s} viij^{d}. Also I haue receauyd ffentons rent. Ther is remytted ouer cc^{li} as it may appere by ij bylles hereyn-closyd, the one somewhate wors then the other by the reason of covetyng to haue had more wee weare enforced sekyng a sure manner to take the losse. I haue sent the ij ffyrst bylles to Mr Gylpyn and he to ffollowe yor ordre. The exchaunge is lyke to be yett wors, for the merchauntes seyth that theyr clothers lyeth on theyr handes, and yn very dede they do scarsly demaund for eny at Blackwellhall. The counsell weare yesternyght at the Towre, and the Busshopp of Wyn-chester was before them, and it is thought that he shalbe delyuered shortly, but how I knowe not.[221] In all other thinges not specyfyed here I wyll ffollow yor ordre by the help of the lyuyng lord, to whom

218. Edward VI, *Chronicle*, pp. 41, 42.
219. See above, pp. 81–2.
220. Gentleman of the Chamber; another reformer at Court.
221. Somerset with five other councillors went to elicit Gardiner's response to the Prayer Book, which was: 'although I would not have made it so myself, yet I find such things in it as satisfy my conscience'. Edward VI, *Chronicle*, pp. 35–6; Foxe, *Acts and Monuments*, vi, pp. 113–15; *CSPSp.* x, p. 109.

I pray to prospere yow yn all yor affayres. Wreten at the blacke ffryers the xv[th] day of June by yor most bounden seruaunt

Richard Scudamore

Mr Chamberleyn entendyth to take his journey towardes the Regent withyn iiij or v dayes.[222]

27 *21 June 1550 (Adv. MS 34.2.14, fo. 45[r])*

It may please yow to be aduertesyd that I receauyd from yow a letter the which was directed to the lordes of the counsell. I delyuered the same on Thursday last at the courte, on which day the lord admyrall made a bankett unto the kynges maiestye at Detford wheare ther was a greate tryhumphe upon the water betwene certeyn pynnesshes that gave an assaulte to a fforte that was made upon the water, the whych pastyme pleasyd the kynges hyghnes very well.[223] Other occurrauntes I haue not to aduertyes yow of, sauyng wheare that the Busshopp of Wynchesters delyuerye hath bene by his ffrendes so ernestlye loked for, yet he remayneth yn the Towre hauyng more lybertye then he had before. He is suffred to walke yn the gallerye and sometyme yn the garden. Yef he do come oute it is thought to be by my lord of Somersettes meanes, and then I thynk it will cost hym ij of his best lordshyppes, that is ffernham and Caunden.[224] Yong Sir John Gressham hath ben comytted this sevenyght, and as I can perceaue upon a suspycyon for that he caused certeyn powder of dyamountes to be bought for hym at Antwarp, but he entended to do with them I knowe nott.[225] I haue receauyd yor dyettes due untyll the vth day of August next comyng, and I haue payd to my lord Thomas Howord xx[li] due unto hym for Cheppyng Norton, and I haue lykewyse payd Mr Locke and Mr Trott, and wheare I aduertesyd yow by my last letters (with the which I dyd send unto yow ij bylles of exchaunge for cc[li]) that I wold haue payd unto Mr Weldon such money as was due unto hym sometyme thys weke, he hath deferred untyll this next

222. Sir Thomas Chamberlain was appointed English ambassador to Brussels. *CSPSp.* x, p. 117.

223. So it did. Edward VI, *Chronicle*, pp. 36–7.

224. Gardiner's pardon and release were blocked by Warwick, who distrusted Gardiner's apparent conformity. Gardiner had expected to be freed upon the Protector's fall, but found instead a Council more reformed than before. Somerset, who seems to have assumed leadership of the conservatives upon the fall of Wriothesley, was now his principal ally. Stow, *Annales*, p. 600; *Letters of Stephen Gardiner*, ed. J.D. Muller (Cambridge, 1933), pp. 440–1; Jordan, *Edward VI: Threshold of Power*, pp. 241–3.

225. The brother of Sir Thomas Gresham, the king's financial agent in Antwerp. On 20 June he was bound in a recognisance of 500 marks. *APC* iii, p. 51.

weeke for that my ladye hath appoynted to be then at London, but to whate ende hur ladyesshypp will growe unto I am not as yett asserteyned, but I iudge the staye wilbe for the lacke of assuraunces of the money that is to be receauyd as by my letters heretofore I haue sygnyfyed unto yow. And I may perceaue my ladyes determynate pleasure then I will procede with the payment of the rest of yor dettes assone as opportunytye shall serue. Thus I contynually pray to the lyvyng lord to prospere yow yn all yor affayres. I haue receauyd a letter for yow from my lord warden who lyeth yn Kent. Wreten at the Blacke ffryers the xxj^th day of June by yor most bounden seruaunt

Richard Scudamore

I haue sent unto yow herewith the copye of yor ij warrauntes for the payment of yor dyettes, the which I haue long sued for.
Yor bedestede is amost redye and axeth vj^li xiiij^s iiij^d for the makyng of it.

28 *12 July 1550 (Adv. MS 34.2.14, fo. 1^r)*

It may please yow to be aduertesyd that sence the wrytyng of my last letters I haue wreten to Symon for to make sale of yor wooll as spedylye as he can and also to sett ordre for the levyeng of yor rentes as shortly after Michelmas as may be possyble, and to thende that he may the better understand yor pleasure I haue sent unto hym yor letter to me dyrected. I haue travaylled by all the meanes I could for to knowe the certeyn tyme of Syr Richard Morryeson comyng for yow (on Sonday last he receauyd the ordre of knyghthode), but as yett I can not lerne, but supposyng that it wilbe aboutes the latter ende of August[226] for this present daye Mr Morryeson was before the counsell aboutes the same matter. I lacked my lord pagett at the courte, who is presently at Drayton, by whom I shold haue had some intellygence therof. And I moved Mr Morryeson for the same, who answeared that he traveyled for the certeyn knowledge therof and as yet it is not appoynted, but he thynketh it shalbe aboutes the tyme before specyfyed, and by my next letters I trust I shalbe able to aduertyes unto yow very nere the certentye therof. Mr pykeryng arryved at London yesternyght and this day came to the courte at Westminster wheare he had good oportunytye with my lord of Warrewyck, at which tyme he moved my lord for such matters as yow desyred hym, to the which my lord answeared affyrmyng ernestlye

226. Sir Richard Morison was given instructions for his embassy to the Emperor on 18 August. *CSPF* p. 52; *CSPSp.* x. pp. 167, 169, 176–7, 187.

that yor request shold be ffullfylled. And wheare that yn my last letters I wrote unto yow of the kyng remouyng on ffrydaye last, it is defferred untyll ffrydaye next, and whether it wilbe at that tyme I suppose it be uncerteyn. This weeke that cometh yor lyueryes wilbe yn a redynes. Other occurauntes I haue not, sauyng that on Tuysday last that the Lord High Treausorer, my lord of Warrewicke, the Master of the hors, and Mr Secretory Petor weare with the Busshopp of Wynchester,[227] after whos departure from hym the Busshopp was verye jocund untyll thursday, on which daye the Master of the hors and Secretorye Petor came unto the Busshopp, and amongest theyr communycacyon one ouer herd Mr Secretorye sey to the Busshopp that he mervelyd much that the Busshopp wold stycke at that that all they (meanyng the counsell) had agreed unto. But synce that tyme the Bussopp hath had grubbes yn his belly and his soden joye is turned to pensyvenes. And it is thought that the counsell will once more goo to hym and then to be at appoynte with hym one way or other.[228] Yef I shold wryte unto yow all the commendacyons of yor ffrendes and of theyr reioysynges of yor comyng home I shold be to tedyous unto yow, therfore I do rest to trouble yow therwith, and do praye to the Almyghtye Lord to prospere yow yn all yor affayres. Wreten at the blacke ffryers the xij[th] daye of Julye by yor moste bounden seruaunt

Richard Scudamore

29 *31 July 1550 (Adv. MS 34.2.14, fo. 47ʳ)*

It may please yow to be aduertesyd that the xxviij[th] day of Julye I receauyd yor letters of the xv[th] of the same. I delyuered the Emperours ambassadors letter immedyatlye and afterwardes I rode to Wyndesore to delyuer the letter to the lordes of the counsell, the which I delyuered to Mr Secretorye Wootton. And of the counsell ther was nomore at that present at the courte but the lord high Treausourer, my lord marques of Northampton, Mr Controller and Mr Secretorye, whearupon Mr Secretorye willed me to repayre thether ageyne on Setorday, at which tyme he thought there wold be a greater nombre of the

227. At the end of June formal articles of subscription had been drawn up, which rehearsed Gardiner's contumacy and his 'notorious and apparent contempt', and these articles this committee, which excluded Somerset, presented to him on 8 July. Edward VI, *Chronicle*, p. 39; Jordan, *Edward VI: Threshold of Power*, p. 243.

228. On 10 July Pembroke and Petre visited Gardiner to tell him that the King 'marvelled that he would not put his hand to the confession'. Warwick now insisted upon the drafting of a new submission, more degrading than the last. Edward VI, *Chronicle*, p. 39; Jordan, *Edward VI: Threshold of Power*, pp. 243–4; J.D. Muller, *Stephen Gardiner and the Tudor Reaction* (Cambridge, 1926), pp. 195–203.

lordes of the counsell, and then I shold knowe by hym whether they wold send eny letters unto yow. And as for my lord of Somersett he is presentlye at Redyng, whos letter I haue sent unto Mr Sycell by a gentleman of my lordes.[229] My lord of Warrewick lyeth as yett at Seynte Jamys, and I suppose he wilbe at the courte upon Setordaye. My lord Pagett lyeth at Drayeton to whom I delyuered lykewyse yor letter. And yn my retorne from Wyndesore I came by Mr Ausham by whom I do perceaue that ye haue wreten that I haue made unto yow a declaracyon but of a thousand pound, but I suppose I made unto yow a ffull declaracyon howe much money was receauyd and whate whas payd therof and whate remayned and yn whos handes, but for yor ffurther contentacyon I haue made a brevyate aswell of the receyttes sence Symons reconyng with yow, as also of the paymentes, and lykewyse whate money remayneth yn my handes, and yn others, and whate of yor dettes are as yett unpayd, the which remembraunce ye shall receaue hereynclosed, the which I haue drawen as playnelye as I could devyse it, to the ende that ye may perceaue the reconyng at the ffull. Mr Morryeson is ryden ynto Lyncolnshyre so that I can not aduertyes yow eny thyng of his mynde consernyng Stephyn, but at his retorn I will repayre unto hym to knowe his pleasure theryn. And I can not lerne the certeyn tyme of his journey towardes yow, but it is thought that it wilbe abouttes the latter ende of August, and to begynne he hath alredy obteyned ffyve hundreth markes by the wey of rewarde towardes the ffurnyture of his jorney. And his retorne will not be (as I can lerne by Weston his man) this ffortenyght, and then he thynketh his master will not tarrye aboue one weke or nere there aboutes. The occurrauntes here is chefeleye of the Emperours shyppes that hath houered on the coostes of England, but now it is understanded at large whate theyr pretence was, howbeit it is so prouyded for that theyr purpos is lyke to take none effecte. Skyperios lyeng so long upon the seas cometh to small purpos, God be thanked therfore, and now the matter is so apparant and such watche leyde that I thynke it lyeth not yn the partyes to bryng theyre purpos to passe yet.[230] The remouyng was from White hall yn Essex to Malden, wheare theare is crycke that cometh from the seas verye apt for the purpos, yef knowledge had not ben had yn

229. On 26 July Somerset had gone to keep order on Oxfordshire, Sussex, Wiltshire and Hampshire. Edward VI, *Chronicle*, p. 41.

230. A plan had been conceived to carry Princess Mary away from England to the Regent in the Netherlands. In March Mary, desperate because she feared that the Council would prevent her from hearing Mass, had sought Imperial aid. A fleet, commanded by Corneille Scepperus (M. d'Eecke) waited off the Essex coast to rescue her. But the plan was thwarted because rumours leaked out. *CSPSp.* x. pp. 47–8, 94–7, 121–37, 146; Edward VI, *Chronicle*, pp. 40, 44; Jordan, *Edward VI: Threshold of Power*, pp. 256–8.

tyme, but now the kynges galleys with certeyn shyppes lyeth betwyxt the fflemmynges and the shore so that they shalbe dystryved yef they happen to approche nere the costes, and on the land syde there lyeth ij or three of the baundes of the souldyors that came from Bulloynge, besydes my lord chauncellor, Mr Secretorye Petor, and Sir John Gattes[231] dylygence theryn, who hath ben (as it is seyd) and examyned the partye, and the brute goeth that the partye shall come to the courte or very nere ther aboute. And yesternyght God hath called to his mercye the Erle of Southampton, for the which I geave to God most high thankes,[232] to whom I do pray to prospere yow yn all yor affayres. Wreten at the blacke ffryers the last day of June[233] by yor most bounden seruaunt

Richard Scudamore

30 *26 August 1549* (*Adv. MS 34.2.14, fo. 61ʳ*)

It may please yow to be aduertesyd that this present day I receauyd yor letters of the xiijᵗʰ day of August with a pakett to the lordes of the counsell, the which as to morrowe I entend (God willyng) to delyuer my self at the courte, the which wilbe at Otland. On the which day Mr Morryesson hath appoynted to ryde thether yef the sykenes of the ffover be not a lett unto hym, the which hath grudged the iiij or ffyve dayes. And then he thynketh to be dispatched verye shortlye after his comyng thether, and when that I shall understand the certeyne tyme of the begynnyng of his journey I will aduertyes yow by the ffurst.[234] And as for the receytt of yor dyettes, as yet ther can be none had for lack of money, although I haue obteyned a letter from the lordes of the counsell to be payd of the ffurst money that shall come to Mr Williams handes. I do loke euery day to receaue some money ffrom Symons, the which shold not come before that there be nede to occupye it, for I haue receauyd advertyesment from Mr Dansell[235]

---

231. Gates, Sheriff of Essex, was sent on 13 July to prevent Mary's escape. Edward VI, *Chronicle*, p. 40.

232. Wriothesley died on 30 July after long illness and despair. Some suspected suicide. 'He killed himself with sorrowe in so much as he said he wold not live in such misery if he might'. BL, Add. MS 48126, fo. 16ᵛ; *CSPSp.* x, pp. 44, 47; Wriothesley, *Chronicle*, ii, p. 41.

233. Scudamore meant July.

234. Hoby was in Augsburg, anxiously awaiting Morison's arrival to take over the embassy. His brother, Thomas Hoby, had joined him from Italy on 5 August. *Travels and Life*, p. 62.

235. Court Master to the English merchants at Antwerp and financial agent to the Crown.

that yow shold chardge hym with eight hundreth and ffourtye dallers, accomptyng it yn fflemysh money ccx^{li}, the which he estemyth to be of sterlyng ccxxx^{li}. And by yor letter and lykewyse by Mr Gylpynges ther apperith to be but cc^{li} the payment wheareof prouvysyon must be made ffurthwith. And yef money can not be receauyd the soner, I shall ffynd the meanes, yef I can, to borrowe cc^{li} for a ffortenyght for the satysffyeng of Mr Dansell, for I knowe he will make more to do then he nedeth yef he be not therof shortlye payd. Yef ye could ffynd the meanes to take up a certeyne somme of money for a yere at viij^{li} the hundred ye shold not lose so much yn the repayment therof as ye shall presently yn the exchaunge, for at the ffurst ther wilbe ffyve poundes lost, for wee shall scarse haue xix^{s} for xx^{s},[236] and yor money may be so delyuered ouer by exchaunge for syx monethes or more as occasyon shall serve, and by that meanes ye shall not lose so much as ye shall do presentlye, and yn the meane tyme ye shall ffurnyssh yor present nede. I haue thought good to put yow yn remembraunce hereof bycause ye may do theryn that shall seme unto yow best. Occurrauntes here are small save that Mr Wadham of the pryvey chambour, Mr Geoffrey Gattes, surveyor of the woods, and Mr Locke, Alderman of London, are departed oute of this lyeff. And as for ffyne geldynges and ffeyre dogges, the ffrenche men hath left ffewe yn England. Thus I do pray to the lyuyng lord to prospere yow yn all yor affayres. Wreten at the black ffryers the xxvjth day of August by yor most bounden seruaunt

Richard Scudamore

31　*29 August 1550* (*Adv. MS 34.2.14, fo. 43^r*)

It may please yow to be aduertesyd that I rode to the court for the delyuery of yor letters, the answeare whearunto ye shall receaue yn this pakett. Mr Morryesson hath not as yett bene at the courte, nor is not ffully recouered of his disease but somewhate on the mendyng hand, and he trusteth yn God that he shalbe able to take his journey to the courte aboutes monday or tuysday, and then hopeth withyn x or xij dayes to begynne his journey towardes yow.[237] Mr Pykeryng shold haue bene placed yn Mr Wadhams roome, but he hath ffound the meanes to haue dispatched hym self therof, bycause he seyth that he can abyde to take the paynes yn that place.[238] My lord of Warrewick

236. Gould, *The Great Debasement*, table ix.

237. Morison did not leave for Augsburg until about 18 September. *CSPSp*. x. pp. 167, 169, 173–4, 176.

238. Sir William Pickering preferred embassy abroad to service at Court. *CSPSp*, x, p. 218; *House of Commons, 1509–1558*.

was his ernest procurer for the placyng of hym ther. Occurrauntes I haue none worthye of aduertyesment. Mr Mason as I understand hath made a mocyon for his revocacyon, by the reason that he nor his howsehold can haue theyr helth yn ffraunce, and some thynkes his suytt shall take effecte.[239] Thus I praye to the lyuyng lord to prospere yow yn all yor affayres. Wreten at the black ffryers the xxix[th] day of August by yor most bounden seruant

Richard Scudamore

32 *15 September 1550* (*Adv. MS 34.2.14, fo. 49ʳ*)

It may please yow to be aduertesyd that I haue receauyd from yow sence the wrytyng of my last letters ij packettes, the which weare delyuered accordynglye, as by thansweare of yor last letters ye may perceaue. The which letters I haue thought good to send unto yow before my comyng because or jorney wilbe long. And as to morrowe Mr Morryeson sendyth his trayne and horses from London towardes Douer and he will make as much spede after as he convenyentlye may. His jorney wilbe at the least an hole moneth. I trust ye do understand before thys tyme of the ffullfyllyng of your comaundement for the sendyng of ccc[thli] fflemyng unto yow before yor comyng from Auxburgh. I haue alredye delyuered unto Mr Stacye ffyve hundreth poundes, wheareof ccciiij[xx]xij[li] xiiij[s] was for yor cottyswold wooll, and the rest of yor revenues, and yor wooll of Evysham is sold at xxvj[s] the codd, the money to be receauyd a weeke after Michelmas. Occurrauntes ther are none save that Sir Herry Gattes is placed yn Mr Wadhams place yn the pryvey chambor.[240] And at Mr Morryessons comyng to Andwarp I trust I shalbe able to aduertyes yow very nere the tyme that he shall arryve at Auxburgh, and yn the meane tyme I will pray to the lyuyng lord to prospere yow yn all yor affayres. Wreten at the black ffryers the xv[th] day of September by yor most bounden seruant

Richard Scudamore

33 *3 October 1550* (*Adv. MS 34.2.14, fo. 63ʳ*)

It may please yow to be aduertesyd that my lord ambassador arryved

---

239. By November Mason was begging for recall, wishing to die 'amongst Christian men'. Letters of revocation came in February 1551. *CSPF* pp. 60, 76, 77, 150.

240. Brother of Sir John Gates, Principal Gentleman of the Privy Chamber and right-hand man to Warwick.

at Antwarp the ffurst of October,[241] wheare he abydeth iij dayes, and ffrom thens he goeth to Brusselles, and he myndeth to make but small journeys, and also he determyneth to come by Argentyne[242] and Basyll, onlesse that yow by yor letters metyng hym at Spyres can alter his mynde. His trayne is xxx horses and he thynketh to be at Auxpurgh aboutes the latter ende of this moneth. Mr Nedeham shewed me that he thought that yow had receauyd yor money before this. And as for occurrauntes I haue none but that yor horses be sauffe at Calleys. Thus hauying nothyng elles at thys tyme do praye to the lyuyng lord to prospere yow yn all yor affayres. Wreten at Antwarp the iij^{de} day of October by yor most bounden seruant

Richard Scudamore

34 *Richard Scudamore to his father John Scudamore, 18 October 1551 (BL, Add. MS 11042, fo. 53^r)*

May it please yow to be aduertesyd that I haue receauyd yor letters, the ffyrst by my cosyn Wessheborne[243] and the last by Johnes my systers seruaunt, by the whych letters pleased yow and my mother to bestowe yor blessynges upon me. Prayeng yow to contynue the same and I wyll, accordyng to my duetye, beseche God for the preseruacyon of yor helthes. I receauyd of Johnes from yow ffortye shelyngs, for the which I do rendre unto yow my most umble thankes. I must be so bold to desyre ffauor of yow to bere with me for that I wryte no largyer unto yow, for that my hedd is so lyght that I can not abyde to wryte for this nite was don with the swett of the browse. Syr, I haue sent unto yow a letter hereyn closed a letter by the which ye may perceaue how much is done yn my systers matter. I wold it lay yn me to do hur pleasure, but she shalbe sure to haue my travayle as power shall extend. My cosyn Cutbert Vaughan[244] hath wreten a letter unto my master, the which is not as yett come to his handes, and whether it consernyth any thyng to that matter I knowe not, but yef it do I doubt not but that I shall haue the letter sent unto me assone as my master hath sene it, and then I will signyfye unto yow the effect therof. Thus desyryng my duetye to consydered to my mother & grandmother

241. Sir Richard Morison. He arrived in Augsburg on 9 November, and Hoby left the same day. *CSPSp.* x, pp. 176, 187; *Travels and Life,* p. 63.
242. Strasburg.
243. John Washbourne of Worcestershire. *Visitation of Worcester,* p. 142.
244. Master of Edward VI's bears, bulls and dogs, and keeper of Paris garden. *Chronicle of Queen Jane,* pp. 49. 53. 59, 64, 75.

and other my ffryndes, do comytt yow to the gouernaunce of the lyuyng lord. I thynke that on Setorday next the Busshoppe of Dure-sham shalbe depryued of his busshopprick for conceyllyng of a letter wheare yn was procurement of a rebellyon.[245] Wreten yn ffletestret the xviij[th] day of october, by yore sonne lyuyng yn hope for helth.

ther was a proclamacyon made
yn London that euery man shold haue
yn a redynes greate horses accordyng
to the statute

Richard Scudamore

yef it shall please to send ageyn the
letter hereyn closed lest that my master shalbe
absent when thoffyce shalbe retorned.

35 *2 March 1555 (Adv. MS 34.2.14, fo. 59ʳ)*

May it please yow to be aduertesyd that this present day I receauyd yor letter of the vth of ffebruarye wheareyn ye say that ye can not understand my meanyng consernyng the byll of exchaunge that I send by my letter that I had sent unto yow by my other letter next before that, merveylyng much that that letter came not unto yor handes. The effecte of that that was wreten yn that (the which I called a byll of exchaunge) was that yor kepyng of companye with thos yor countrey men was much myslyked here at home, and ffurther that it was ageynst yor promyes made to dyuers of yor ffrendes.[246] Thus much I wrote yn a litle paper enclosed yn my letter dated yn december. And as towchyng yor woolles (beyng only of yor owne store), I trust ye are aduertised the hole circumstaunce therof by seuerall letters before this. And wheare yor pleasure was that I shold repayre unto my lord Pagett for certeyn causes, it is so that my lord Pagett is

245. Cuthbert Tunstall had been under house arrest at Coldharbour in Thames Street since August 1550. His persistent opposition to Edwardian religious changes and his suspected allegiance to Somerset (who had just been arrested on 16 October) were more likely reasons for his fall than the supposed concealment of a letter. In September Hoby had been appointed to examine Tunstall and other conservative bishops. Edward VI, *Chronicle*, p. 82; *APC* iii. p. 381; C. Sturge, *Cuthbert Tunstal* (1938), pp. 284–97.

246. Hoby had been granted licence to travel to the Continent to visit the spas for his health. He had left, with his brother, on 5 June 1554 and was probably in Padua as Scudamore wrote. On the journey the Hobies were in contact with the leading Protestant exiles, in Padua, Frankfurt and Wesel, an association which threatened their estates and their families at home. *CSPSp.* xii, pp. 214, 231, 265, 267; *Travels and Life*, pp. 97, 103, 116–17, 123, 124.

presentlye at Drayton, and when he is at the courte medleth litle
or nothyng at all. Symon dyd send unto yow his accompt before
Christemas, merveylyng that it came not unto yor handes, and as yet
he is not come oute of Worcestershire, howbeit I haue loked for hym
euery day this iij wekes. And as for my accompt, I meane to bryng a
remembraunce of it with me, entendyng, God willyng, to begynne
my jorney towardes yow on Wenysday next, yn the companye of
Jerome Palmer and Thomas Litle, gentlemen of my lord Pagettes.[247]
Occurrauntes here are fewe. The sayeng is the qwene entendeth to
take hur chambor at Wyndezore wheare they make newe lodgeyng,[248]
for the ffurnyture whearof they haue taken certeyn of yor tymbre at
Bissham. They had taken awey .xiiij. lodes before that I understode
thereof, and upon aduertiesment had therof I repayred to Bradshawe
the surveior, who declared unto me that of very necessytie he was
enforced so to do, consyderyng the tyme of the yere and the hastynes
of the buyldyng, and promysed bothe that ther shold be nomore taken
then of nede he must be constrayned, and ffurther to restore asmuch
ageyne of the lyke leyngth and breadthe as he shall take awey. There
be xx^{ti} of the qwenes shyppes arygkyng; whether it be to carye the
kyng ouer or elles to kepe the seas I do not well understand.[249] The
kyng of Denmarke hath wreten for Mr Couerdale to the qwene, at
whos sute he hath a passeporte to departe the realme.[250] Bradford and
the other eight prisoners are yet lyuyng, and whate shalbe come of
them God knoweth.[251] Ther be dyuers of thos that hath bene relygyous
hath gotten such garmentes as theyr professyon requyred, but upon
that they weare long gownes and typettes. Thus hauyng nothyng elles
at this to aduerties yow of, do pray to the lyuyng lord to prospere yow
yn all yor affayres. Wreten at the black friers the ij^{de} day of Marche
.1554. by yor most bounden seruant

Richard Scudamore

247. Hoby and Paget had been closely associated before Hoby's departure, a friendship which Renard, the Imperial ambassador, feared threatened conspiracy. *CSPSp.*
xii, pp. 231, 239, 259.
248. The queen who was, so she thought, expecting a child left for Windsor and her
confinement on 20 March. *CSPSp.* xiii, p. 146.
249. Philip of Spain was planning to leave England for Flanders, and there were
rumours of his departure. *CSPSp.* xiii, pp. 143, 150, 249.
250. Miles Coverdale, translator of the Bible and Edwardian Bishop of Exeter, was
granted a passport for exile on 19 February. *APC,* v. p. 97.
251. John Rogers, the first of the Marian martyrs, died on 4 February. His fellow
prisoners, including John Bradford, awaited their fate. *CSPSp.* xiii, p. 138.

IV
THE UNDERGRADUATE ACCOUNT BOOK OF JOHN AND RICHARD NEWDIGATE, 1618–1621

Edited by Vivienne Larminie

CONTENTS

INTRODUCTION

The Oxford and Temple Book is one of a series of account books kept for and by the Newdigates of Arbury Hall, between Coventry and Nuneaton in Warwickshire, from 1608 to 1642, and now surviving among the family papers deposited at Warwickshire Record Office. All the accounts detail receipts from rents and farming, interest and borrowing, and expenditure on estate, household and personal items, but that kept between 1618 and 1621, printed here, also records the expenses of two brothers at university and the inns of court, of two family marriages and related settlements and of wardship and suing for livery of estates.[1]

The Warwickshire Newdigates sprang from the cadet branch of a family prominent in Surrey in the fourteenth century, which had settled at Harefield, Middlesex, around 1400. During the late fifteenth and sixteenth centuries the family produced a succession of notable lawyers, prominent at Lincoln's Inn, in Parliament and in posts in government, and its fortunes were 'materially advanced'.[2] With the accession as head of the family of a scholar, John Newdigate (1541–1592), this tide of prosperity ebbed. In 1585, apparently as an act of retrenchment, he exchanged most of his Middlesex estates for those of Sir Edmund Anderson at Arbury. This move failed to arrest his financial decline, and John Newdigate died intestate in the Fleet Prison.[3]

Newdigate's tangled and probably fraudulent provision for his widow and for his children by two marriages led to considerable bitterness and to expensive litigation among his descendants. The eldest son, John II of Arbury (1571–1610), was dependent for financial survival on his father-in-law, Sir Edward Fitton (d. 1606) of Gawsworth, Cheshire. After education, at Fitton's expense, at Brasenose College, Oxford, he lived at Arbury, taking an informed interest in his estates and in his duties as a justice of the peace, and devoting

1. Warwickshire Record Office, CR 136, B602. The text is reproduced by kind permission of Lord Daventry.

2. J.G. Nichols, 'The Origin and Early History of the Family of Newdegate', *Surrey Archaeological Collections*, vi (1874), 227–67; *Lincoln's Inn Admissions* (2 vols., 1896), i. 79, 160–3, 176, 183, 261–347; P.W. Hasler ed., *The House of Commons 1558–1603* (3 vols., 1981), iii, 125–9.

3. W. Sterry ed., *Eton College Register 1441–1698*; C.H. Cooper ed., *Athenae Cantabrigienses* (2 vols., 1858–1861), ii, 12; *Dictionary of National Biography*. The background to his move to Warwickshire is detailed in V.M. Larminie, *The Godly Magistrate: The Private Philosophy and Public Life of Sir John Newdigate, 1571–1610*, Dugdale Society, Occasional Paper 28 (Oxford, 1982), 3–4.

considerable time to painstaking annotation of a wide range of standard classical and devotional authors. He was knighted in 1603.[4]

In spite of, or perhaps because of, lawsuits to recover his inheritance, farming experiments and investment in coal and in ironworks, Sir John died in 1610 having failed to put the Newdigate finances on a stable footing. Almost two-thirds of his estate passed to his widow Anne, Lady Newdigate, in jointure, and the remainder was overburdened with debts and provisions for younger children.[5] The elder son, John III (1600–42), was a minor. Within a few months his mother succeeded in gaining the wardship and custody of her son from the Crown but, as *The Oxford and Temple Book* shows, expenses incurred in the Court of Wards were still regular and considerable.[6]

Between 1610 and 1618 John III, his brother Richard (1602–78) and sisters Mary (1598–1643), Lettice (1604–25) and Anne (1607–37) were under the joint supervision of Sir John's executors, his widow and his former steward, William Whitehall. Whitehall (d.1637), a younger son from a minor Staffordshire gentry family, who may have acted as an attendant on Sir John at Brasenose, had become his leading local tenant and chief assistant in the running of his estates.[7] On Lady Newdigate's death in July 1618, three months before this account book begins, Whitehall assumed the sole guardianship of all five Newdigate children.[8]

John and Richard Newdigate's entry to the university later that year was in accordance with their mother's wish, expressed in her will, first drafted in 1609,[9] Their early education had been undertaken by Henry Simpson, a graduate of Magdalen College, Oxford, who remained with the family for about ten years (c.1607–July 1617) and gained his M.A. while in their employ (1609).[10] Before going up to

4. Larminie, *Godly Magistrate, passim*, and 'Marriage and the Family: The Example of the Seventeenth Century Newdigates', *Midland History*, ix (1984), 4–5.

5. *ibid.*

6. WRO, CR 136, B311.

7. William Whitehall of Staffordshire, 'pleb.', was admitted to Brasenose in Feb. 1588, the month after Newdigate: *Brasenose College Register* (Oxford Historical Society lv, 1910), 73. He was entered on the register of the university 23 Feb. 1588 with William Newdigate of 'Middl. arm.', probably a mistake for John: A. Clark ed., *Register of the University of Oxford*, ii (OHS x–xii, 1887–8), pt ii, 162. Later he was described as a gentleman (e.g. WRO, CR 136, C371 & C2230) and by Lady Newdigate as 'my now servant' (WRO, CR 136, C1915). For the Whitehall family see: *Collections for a History of Staffordshire*, v (William Salt Archaeological Society, 1884–5), ii, 305–7; J. Foster ed., *Alumni Oxonienses 1500–1714* (4 vols, 1891–2), iv.

8. A trustee of Sir John's estates since 1603, he was named as a co-guardian with Lady Newdigate of the children, but seems not to have exercised this function in practice until after her death: WRO, CR 136, B311, B1025–6, B1270, B1320d, C1915.

9. WRO, CR 136, C1915.

10. *Alumni Oxon.*, iv; WRO, CR136 B312 (letter of recommendation) and B593–600 (account books recording salary).

Oxford Richard Newdigate also spent a year at a school in Coventry (September 1617–October 1618).[11]

There is no direct evidence of how Lady Newdigate or Whitehall came to choose Trinity College. It was popular with other Midland gentry such as the Hampdens, Chamberlaines and Dormers, to whom the Newdigates were distantly related, but Whitehall's contacts in and around the college may have counted for more. Among the many people appearing in the account book with whom Whitehall claimed kinship through the marriages of his neices and nephews were the Hollinses of Staffordshire and of Swerford, Oxfordshire. John Hollins, M.A., taught at Trinity while the Newdigates were there and William Hollins, B.D., a graduate of Trinity and at this time Rector of Swerford, offered hospitality on journeys home.[12] The college was, furthermore, experiencing considerable financial prosperity and physical expansion under its energetic and eccentric president, Ralph Kettell, elected in 1599.[13] The Newdigate brothers' tutor was the vice-president, Robert Skinner, M.A., a man with a reputation for 'good parts and proficiencyes' who later became successively Bishop of Bristol, Oxford and Worcester.[14] Concurrently with the Newdigates his pupils included William Chillingworth (admitted 1619) and Edward Shalcrosse, a relatively humble Cheshire gentleman who was apparently in the Newdigates' charge. A fellow member of the college who became a life-long friend was Gilbert Sheldon, the future archbishop, although he appears only briefly in *The Oxford and Temple Book*.[15]

In July 1620 the names of John and Richard Newdigate were entered in the pension book of Gray's Inn, but when they went up to London in December 1620 only Richard took up his place there. He was called to the Bar in June 1628, elected to the Bench in 1649 and

11. WRO, CR136, B600.

12. H.E.D. Blakiston, *Trinity College* (Oxford College Histories, 1898), 83; *Alumni Oxon.*, ii; *Coll. Hist. Staffs.*, v, part ii, 305–7; Oxfordshire Record Office, MS Wills Oxon., 132/1/10 William Hollins (1634); Trinity College Archives, 'Computi Bursariorum, 1600–1631', n.p. (I am grateful to the President and follows of the college for allowing me to consult this source and to the archivist, Mrs Clare Hands, for her assistance.)

13. Blakiston, *Trinity College*, 100–27.

14. *Alumni Oxon.*, iv; Bodleian Library, MS Ballard 46, fo. 85; A. Wood, *Athenae Oxon.* (3rd edn., ed. P. Bliss, 4 vols., 1813–20), iv, 842; A.M. Skinner, *Memorials of Robert Skinner* (1866). He was also paid for lectures 1618–20: Trinity MS, 'Computi Busariorum'.

15. Gilbert Sheldon (1598–1674) matriculated from Trinity in 1614, proceeded B.A. in 1617, M.A. May or June 1620: *DNB*; *Alumni Oxon.*, iv. His letters (1621–6) to John Newdigate and (1650–66) to Richard, and his long-standing relationship with the family is discussed in V.M. Larminie, 'The Lifestyle and Attitudes of the 17th Century Gentleman, with Special Reference to the Newdigates of Arbury Hall, Warwickshire' (unpublished Ph.D. thesis, University of Birmingham, 1980), 321–7.

became a serjeant at law in 1654. A very successful and lucrative career as a lawyer was crowned when he became, briefly, Lord Chief Justice in 1660 and a baronet in 1677. He was able to bequeath to his eldest son a yearly income of between £3,000 and £4,000, and he transformed the family fortunes, to which he had succeeded in 1642.[16]

John Newdigate took up residence at the Inner Temple, sharing chambers with Edward Holt, son of Sir Thomas Holt of Aston, Warwickshire. He gained a special admittance in January 1621 at the request of Paul Ambrose Croke (exploiting kinship and professional ties), but stayed only six months. In June he married Susanna Luls, daughter of a Dutch merchant and jeweller. Shortly afterwards he retired to his estates in Warwickshire, where he was an energetic farmer and breeder of race-horses. He represented Liverpool in the 1628 Parliament and was a J.P. from 1630.[17]

The Oxford and Temple Account

The account book ($15\frac{1}{2}'' \times 6''$) is divided into two sections. Part I (15 folios) covers the period 15 October 1618 to September 1620 when the Newdigate brothers were at Trinity College. Part II (18 folios, labelled 'Surrey and Temple') was begun on 18 November 1620, as John Newdigate left Surrey for the Temple, and closed in November 1621. The two accounts were bound together in reverse order, probably not long after 1621, and indeed form a natural unit since some entries, such as retrospective bills, overlap both periods.[18]

The accountant was ostensibly William Whitehall. As administrator of the Newdigate estates he was not continuously present either in Oxford or at the Temple. Thus his business trips to London, usually to conduct litigation, to Newdigate estates in Warwickshire and Middlesex, and to Newdigate relatives in Cheshire, Staffordshire, Northamptonshire and Surrey are also entered in the accounts. In his absence separate accounts were kept by Peter Olyff, who seems to have discharged the duties of a valet, or by the brothers themselves. Richard Newdigate in particular was left on his own at Oxford, for instance during the long vacation of 1620, and at Gray's Inn, and recorded his expenses. Such bills were subsequently entered in the

16. R.J. Fletcher ed., *The Pension Book of Gray's Inn 1521–1889* (1901); E. Foss, *A Biographical Dictionary of the Judges of England* (1870), 479; J. Campbell, *The Lives of the Chief Justices* (1849), 443–6. Richard's career is discussed in Larminie, 'Marriage and the Family', 7–8.

17. *Students Admitted to the Inner Temple 1571–1625* (1868), 150; F.A. Inderwick ed., *A Calendar of Inner Temple Records* (2 vols., 1896), 123; R.C. Johnson, M.F. Keeler, M.J. Cole and W.B. Bidwell eds., *Commons Debates 1628* (4 vols., Yale, 1977–8), i, 20–7, 59; S.C. Ratcliff and H.C. Johnson eds., *Quarter Sessions Order Book: Easter 1625 to Trinity 1637* (Warwick County Records i, 1935), pp. xxii, 154, 234.

18. WRO, CR 136, B602.

main account, together with bills from tradesmen like Whitehall's kinsman Thomas Rode, citizen and skinner, from the 'chamber-keeper' at the Inner Temple and from other Newdigate servants. These entries were usually made out of chronological order, owing to delay in reaching the accountant, and this gave rise to some mistakes and discrepancies. Some of these were recognised and visibly corrected by Whitehall, but the possibility remains of omission, inaccuracy or even deliberate falsification on the part of the account's contributors. The same might be said, however, of almost any account book before the adoption of double-entry book-keeping.

At Oxford the account book details purchases of books and station-ery, furnishings, fuel and candles for chambers, and payments of university, college and tutorial dues, in addition to spending on cloth-ing and on recreational activities. It also contains the living and educational expenses of the Newdigate sisters, lodging for much of the time in Daventry. The London-based account contains parallel, but less complete entries of such items, together with the expenses of Lettice Newdigate at boarding school and of general household and estate business. The costs incurred through litigation, through escap-ing from wardship and through settlements also figure prominently in the latter account. The differing slant of the two accounts is symptomatic partly of the less isolated circumstances of the inns as compared with the universities, partly of John Newdigate's privileged status at the Inner Temple and partly of the fact that Richard New-digate was living independently at Gray's Inn. Indications of the latter's expenses are, for this reason, rather sparse.

During vacations and, it is worth noting, also during terms, visits to relatives and friends are outlined, illustrating the 'social education' of, and the strength of family ties among, contemporary gentry. Sir Edward Fitton, first baronet (1572–1619), brother of Lady Newdig-ate, was a frequent host at his home at Gawsworth, Cheshire, and his eldest son Edward (1604–34) joined his cousins at Trinity in 1619. Sir Edward's younger sister Mary (1578–1647) and her second husband John Lougher (d.1636), a former M.P. for Pembroke, entertained the Newdigates at Perton, Staffordshire, and visited them in Oxford and London.[19] In spite of the bitterness that had existed between Sir John Newdigate and his stepbrother, Henry Newdigate (1581–1629) of Ashted, Surrey, had been reconciled to his nephews and neices, and visits were exchanged.

Throughout the period covered by the account book, the New-

19. For the Fitton family see: J.P. Earwaker, *East Cheshire: Past and Present* (2 vols., 1887–80), *passim*; B.E. Harris ed., *VCH Cheshire* (Oxford, 1979), ii, 102; *DNB*; A.E. Newdigate-Newdegate, *Gossip From a Muniment Room* (1897), *passim*; Larminie, *Godly Magistrate*, 5 and 'Marriage and the Family', 5.

digates' main patron of good social standing was John, later Sir John, Tonstal of Edgcombe, Surrey. A gentleman of the bedchamber to the Queen, he had been one of Lady Newdigate's contacts at Court, and may also have been Lettice or Anne's godfather. His wife Penelope Leveson was a distant relative of Lady Newdigate.[20] Other friends of their mother also took an interest in the children, notably Lettice, wife of William, Lord Paget of Beaudesert, and Elizabeth, Lady Grey.[21]

The young Newdigates did not move exclusively in high-ranking circles, however. In addition to contact with their peers—young Holts, Skeffingtons, Gresleys, Listers, Knightleys and Chesters—they kept company with Whitehall's mercantile and clerical kin and with their tenants.

The Newdigates and the education of the gentleman

The childhood and adolescence of the Newdigate siblings was spent in a period once seen as revolutionary in the history of education in England. Works on educational theory were streaming steadily from the presses, grammar and private school foundations were mush-rooming, the influx of gentry into the universities and inns of court was at its height and, it was argued, the general level of literacy in England had reached its pre-industrial zenith. Yet these signs of activity, seemingly so impressive, have provoked considerable contro-versy among historians over the past twenty years. More detailed research has served to modify the picture of unprecedented expansion and a host of questions have arisen as to its nature and significance.[22] The volume of contemporary complaint against the wave of well-born idlers among students, for instance, and the dissatisfaction with their experiences expressed by more dedicated and articulate under-graduates like D'Ewes, Hutchinson and Evelyn have prompted enquiry as to the motives impelling gentlemen to dispatch their sons to institutions of higher learning in such great numbers. How high was the quality of the curriculum offered? Having been originally designed for clerical scholars of poor or moderate means, or (in the

20. *The Visitations of the County of Surrey ... 1530, 1572 and 1623*, ed. W.B. Bannerman (Harleian Soc. xliii, 1899), 188–9; WRO, CR 136, B510–1 (his letters to Lady New-digate).

21. WRO, CR 136, B826b, C1913, C1915 (Paget) and CR 136, B173–4 (Grey).

22. See e.g.: W.T. Costello, *The Scholastic Curriculum of Early 17th Century Cambridge* (Harvard, 1958); M.H. Curtis, *Oxford and Cambridge in Transition 1558–1642* (Oxford, 1959); L. Stone, 'The Education Revolution in England, 1540–1640', *Past and Present*, 28 (1964), 41–80; K. Charlton, *Education in Renaissance England* (1965); W. Prest, *The Inns of Court Under Elizabeth I and the Early Stuarts* (1972). These and more recent views are discussed in J. Looney, 'Undergraduate Education at Early Stuart Cambridge', *History of Education*, xi (1981), 9–19; R. O'Day, *Education and Society 1500–1800* (1982).

case of the inns) for 'apprentices' in a modest profession, how relevant was it to gentlemen amateurs? How relevant was it, for that matter, to post-Renaissance scholars, to future parish clergy or to lawyers faced with an ever more complicated system of common law? What was the standard of discipline and devotion to study among all groups of students? At a more mundane level, what were the costs of higher education and, to pose an almost impossible question, did those who courted it so eagerly receive value for money?

Initially much of the debate among historians was conducted on the basis of evidence drawn from official, especially disciplinary, injunctions of the universities, colleges and inns, and from the experiences of a handful of well-known students who were sufficiently articulate to record their memoirs. With the former there is only the repetition of orders on curriculum or behaviour to hint at the effectiveness, or otherwise, of the authorities' efforts. With the latter there is the suspicion that the articulate may have been the untypical. As more recent work has recognised, more evidence of individual experience in higher education is clearly needed, and from a wide range of sources.[23] Account books like the Newdigates' are one such source, providing as they do evidence not only of costs but also, through them, of wider issues.

The Oxford account shows certain clear patterns of attendance and study. Although, on the evidence of their mother's will, university was for John and Richard Newdigate only a stage on the way to the inns of court, and possibly regarded as a mere formality, the brothers did spend some considerable time in Oxford, especially in their first year when they remained continuously in residence except for a month's break at Christmas and at Easter. In the second year they spent longer periods away, and John did not go to Oxford at all in the Trinity term of 1619–20. Richard, on the other hand, spent the entire long vacation of 1620 at college even though, as he informed his brother, 'company is small and good company exceeding scarce'.[24] He also bought a promising selection of books over the summer and, indeed, the Newdigates' book-buying habits as a whole suggest that their intellectual intentions should not be dismissed lightly. The purchase, immediately upon arrival in Oxford, of works by Horace, Juvenal, Pliny and Ovid as well as of the *Articles of Religion*, looks like a serious attempt to prepare for matriculation. Later entries in the account refer to authors, such as Quintillian, Livy, Seneca and Tacitus, who were recommended by contemporary tutors for well-advanced students, in addition to authors of more general interest such as

23. e.g. J. McConica ed., *The History of the University of Oxford III: The Collegiate University* (Oxford, 1986), *passim*.
24. WRO, CR 136, B338a (letter to John in London, 21 Aug. 1620).

Mercator, Ortelius, Camden, Daniel or Jewel. The account book clearly cannot reveal whether the Newdigates managed to master this impressive list, but it does indicate that Richard at least had made sufficient progress to participate in disputations in the Schools by the Hilary term of 1620.

Evidence of tutorial contact is almost non-existent. The fact that Robert Skinner appears rarely except in connection with the payment of his quarterly fees suggests that tutors did not invariably supervise their students' day-to-day expenditure and activities. Indeed, the Newdigates themselves, in their relationship with their fellow student Edward Shalcrosse, came somewhat nearer to exercising pastoral oversight.[25] The brothers themselves, especially during Whitehall's frequent absences from Oxford, seem to have enjoyed a very considerable degree of independence. This in turn makes evidence of their application to their studies the more remarkable.

Patterns of attendance and study at the inns of court, as suggested earlier, are less clear-cut. Of Richard Newdigate, the professional student, it can only be observed that he had some financial independence, that he had no obvious supervisor and that, by eschewing many of his brother's social activities, he avoided one potentially major distraction from work. His recorded book purchases were scanty, but Plowden was a formidable beginning.[26] In contrast his brother John, the 'gentleman amateur', by virtue of his special admittance to the Inner Temple was excused attendance at such aspects of the complete barrister programme as the vacation learning exercises. During term-time, apparently, he was usually resident in his chambers, but there is no entry in the Temple account indicative of an attempt to study law. Nor, perhaps more surprisingly, is there evidence of a sampling of the rich variety of educational activities available elsewhere in the metropolis. There is no mention of swimming, dancing, fencing, sciences, languages or even attendance at sermons. Instead the account book lists a constant stream of undemanding activities: river trips to the Old Swan, London Bridge, Lambeth and to Deptford to see his sister at school; regular dining out with relatives and friends; entertaining with Edward Holt in their chamber; seven visits to the theatre and two to the races.

Why then had it been thought worthwhile for John Newdigate to go to the inns of court at all? Several clear answers emerge from the account book. First, residence at the Temple, as also at university, provided the opportunity to pursue the acquaintance of gentlemen of a similar age. In John Newdigate's case one, Edward Holt, was

25. *Cf.* O'Day, *Education and Society*, 113; *Hist. Univ. Oxon.* III, 695.
26. *Cf.* L.A. Knafla, 'The Law Studies of an Elizabethan Student', *Huntington Library Quarterly*, xxxii (1969), 221–40.

a future neighbour in North Warwickshire and another, Richard Skeffington, later became his brother-in-law. Secondly, for a gentleman whose estates were encumbered, the Temple was a convenient base from which to look for a rich wife among the daughters of city merchants. Above all, however, it was a place where, in conditions of wardship in particular and litigation in general, the gentleman could supervise lawsuits, maintain close contact with his existing lawyers and through personal introduction acquire new ones. During his months there, John Newdigate paid for the services not only of members of the Croke family, with whom the Newdigates had had links for many years, but also of a wide range of other lawyers with whom they apparently had no previous connection. The pursuit of 'connection' indeed might be advanced as the keynote of John Newdigate's stay at the Inner Temple.

Such unquantifiable benefits as these ultimately make the question of value for money in higher education irrelevant. *The Oxford and Temple Book* shows that its costs could be heavy. Not only had a chamber to be rented, it had also to be furnished, equipped, heated and lit. In addition to official dues there were extra payments for food and services. The stabling of horses was a considerable further expense, as were the costs of travelling. Yet, while the quality of teaching and supervision offered in return may not have justified the financial outlay—and even here the Newdigate account indicates that the consequences of deficiencies in the system may have been exaggerated—higher education in its broadest sense brought incalculable social advantages.

EDITORIAL PRACTICE

In preparing *The Oxford and Temple Book* for publication I have generally followed guidelines in R.F. Hunnisett, *Editing Records for Publication* (British Records Association, 1977). The text of the account book has been reproduced in its entirety, with the exception of some marginal figures which seem to add little to the sense of the items. Chief among these are occasional numbers set against items in the right-hand margin, i.e. to the right of the columns of figures, which presumably relate to the original bills. Since these bills no longer survive, there seems little point in adding to problems of layout by reproducing the references. Modern punctuation has been introduced sparingly, in the interests of clarity. Original spelling has been retained except for u and v and y, i and j. Abbreviations the sense of which is in no doubt have been expanded silently; those over which there is uncertainty have been placed in square brackets, also used generally for editorial intervention. Round brackets are those employed by the accountant himself; angle brackets denote marginal dates, later additions and interlineations entered by him.

THE OXFORD AND TEMPLE BOOK

PART I: OXFORD

[*fo.1*]

folium 1   October the xv th 1618

Imprimis to Butler Roger Gee's[1] man for making packs to Oxford	o	o	6
<October 16>			
Item geven at Daiventrie[2] at Mr Newdigate his comming up to the 3 maides		2	6
Item to Ned for tending Mr Newdigate his horse	o	1	o
Item to Jo Boole wyping bootes		o	4
Item horsmeat by Sam at Sheaffe[3] 4 horse one night		4	4
Item ostlers there	o	o	4
Item Brackley beare & cakes	o	o	6
Item horsmeat at Oxford Reandeares[4] horses 1 night	o	10	8
Item ostlers	o	o	4
Item supper & breakfast there		12	6
Item to Sam for[5] doson of lut stringes	o	4	o
Item to the chamberlaine at Reandeare	o	o	4
Item yard quarter of <blacke> cloth that was wanting to make there gownes & hudes at xii*s.* the yard		15	7
Item bentes & buckerom	o	o	10
Item vi*oz.* dimi[6] of ryben at viii*d.*		4	4
Item silke for booth gownes	o	o	4
Item drawing the sleves	o	o	8
Item making 2 gownes	o	6	3
<October 17>			
Item Peter's dinner	o	o	3
Item vi bedstaves	o	o	9

1. Gee was a Newdigate tenant in Griffe and Chilvers Coton, Warwickshire: WRO, CR 136, A20 and B595–600 (account books).
   2. Where the Newdigate sisters were staying with Thomas Salter: see below.
   3. The Wheatsheaf Inn in Sheaf Street, built c.1610, was at the junction of roads to London, Oxford, Northampton and Coventry: N. Pevsner, *The Buildings of England: Northamptonshire* (1973), 175; A. Mee, *The King's England: Northamptonshire* (1975), 105.
   4. This inn, in the parish of St Mary Magdalen, appcars in H.E. Salter's list of inns and signs, *Oxford City Properties* (OHS, 1926), 413–5, but is not mentioned in his *Survey of Oxford*, ed. W.A. Pantin (OHS, xiv and xx, 1960 and 1969).
   5. Figure blotted out.
   6. Dimidium i.e. half.

Item a pound candles	0	0	4
Item a jugge ix*d*. nailes i*d*.	0	0	10
Item 4 doson of blacke silke button		1	4
Item a woman making cleane the chambers &			
stayres	0	0	2
Item iii strike of beanes at ii*s*.[7]	0	6	0
Item a paire of gloves [for] Mr Richard		1	0
Item lutte stringes for Mr Newdigate	0	1	6
Item a chamber pott, 2 candlestkes, a standish &			
tinderboxe	0	5	3
Item setting up a bed & cording it			6
Item[8] for entring thyre names (viz Mr Newdigate			
& Mr Richard) to the manciple, butler and			
cooke[9] eych vii*s*. vi*d*.	1	2	6
Item the butler's boye	0	1	6
Item the under cooke	0	4	0
Item to him that devides the commons	0	2	6
Item to the scullery boye	0	1	0
< October 18 >			
Item i*li*. suger i*oz*. nutmeges		1	10
Item ynke & glas iii*d*. paper iiii*d*.	0	0	7
	5	17	12
folium 1		4	14

[*fo.iv*.]

October the 20 1618

Item a pewter bason	0	1	10
Item a paire of bellowes & fyer shovell		2	0
Item bysomes i*d*. brimston i*ob*.		0	1*ob*.
Item Horrus, Juvinall & Percius[10] (Mr New-			
digate)	0	3	0

7. Smudged.
8. Marginal note '13–13/0', i.e. disbursed on 13 Oct.?
9. Following word crossed out. An account of college servants is given by C.J. Hammer Jr in *Hist. Univ. Oxon.*, iii, 77.
10. *Q. Horatii Flacci poemata omnia doctissimus scholiis illustrata.* (*Iunii Iuvenalis satyrae. Auli Persii satyrae.*) (1574), or a later edition: A.W. Pollard and G.R. Redgrave, *A Short Title Catalogue of Books Printed in England, Scotland and Ireland ... 1475–1640*, 2nd edn., revised by W.A. Jackson, F.S. Ferguson and K.F. Pantzer, (3 vols., 1976–1986), no. 13784–13795.5. I am indebted to Mr Paul Morgan for his help in identifying this, and subsequent, book purchases.

Item Plinnies Epistles[11] (Mr Newdigate)	o	2	o
Item 2 paper bookes (eyche one)	o	o	8
Item Juvinall & Percius (Mr Richard)	o	1	10
Item Plinies Epistles (Mr Richard)	o	2	o
Item a hachet xvi*d*.	o	1	4
Item 2 bookes of Articles of Religion[12]	o	o	8
Item 2 loades of wood cutt and carrying into the seler	1	6	o
To the bowsers [blank] for the cawsion[13] (to be received when they goe awaye wherof for Mr John five pounds)	8	o	o
Item geven to the Schowles[14]	1	o	o
Item Ovides Meamorfasis[15] for Mr Richard	o	o	6
Item Texters Epithetes[16] for him		o	4
Item by Mr Newdigate[17] to him that teacheth upon the lute		2	o
Item to him that brought letters from Mr Salter[18]		2	o
Item for a viall sticke	o	2	o
Item Centum Fabula[19]	o	o	6

11. Possibly an edition of *C. Plinii Secundi Epistolae, cum Annotationib. Joh. Mariae Catanei* (Geneva; Venice, 1519; Paris, 1533), recommended by Oxford tutors in the mid 17th century: A. de Jordy and H. F. Fletcher eds., *A Library for Younger Schollers* (University of Illinois Press, Urbana, 1961), 10, 127.

12. *Articles whereupon it was agreed by the archbishops and bishops ... 1562*, of which there were many editions: e.g. *STC* 10048 (1612), 10049 (1616). They were probably bought as part of preparation for matriculation: C.E. Mallet, *A History of the University of Oxford* (3 vols., 1924), ii, 121–2.

13. A refundable contribution to the common purse. Among receipts noted in 1618 by the bursars, Richard Brooke and Laurence Alcocke, were Johanne Nudigat (£5) – the highest rate – and Richardo Nudigat (£3): Trinity MS, 'Liber Trin. Coll. Oxon.'. This source records the refund of £8 in 1619; it was entered in the Newdigate account in Nov. 1620, see part ii, fo. 12.

14. A registration fee, giving entrance to lectures? The brothers were not entered on the register of the university until 6 Nov. 1618: A. Clark ed., *Registratum Universitatis Oxon.* II (OHS, x–xii, 1887–8), part ii, 372. For fees see G.E. Aylmer in McConica, *Hist. Univ. Oxon.*, iii, 555.

15. P. Ovidius Naso, *Metamorphosis*, many editions, but possibly *STC* 18952.3 (1612) or 18952.4 (1617).

16. Probably an edition of *Epithetorum Joann. Ravisii Textoris epitome, ex Hadr. Junii medici recognitione. Accesserunt Synonyma poetica, locupletoria* (1579), *STC* 20762.5, or possibly the school text edition of 1617, *STC* 20763.7.

17. The following indented items were all bought by John Newdigate according to marginal bracket and note.

18. The Newdigate sisters' host at Daventry.

19. This might be either an edition of Aesop (whose fables in Greek and Latin were, however, purchased later, fo. 8v.) e.g. *STC* 169–72.4, or even G. Gascoyne, *A hundreth sundrie flowres, bounde up in one small posie* (1573), *STC* 11635 or (1575), *STC* 11643a.

Item to the sextan at Christ Church (Mr New-digate)		1	0
Item a landresse table for clothes	0	0	4
Item lute stringes ii*d*. Rex Platonicus[20] vi*d*.			8
Item to the barber	0	1	0
<October 22>			
Item Daintrie going downe about the business betweene Mrs Mary[21] & to Ed dressing my horse	0	0	4
Item at Coventrie for the like (& setting him up)	0	0	1
Item at Plantes ale for my horse ii*d*. self i*d*.		0	3
Item Pearton[22] Motorshed dressing my ho[23] horse 2 nights	0	0	6
Item 2 maides & Janes eych vi*d*.	0	1	6
Item to Kitt ryding twyse to Mr Peter Gifforde[24]		0	6
Item to the boye dressing my horse when I came to Pearton	0	0	3
Item Daintre backe Ed for the like		0	4
Item John Poole for the like, Ed being gonne to Erdbury[25]	0	0	3
November the first 1618			
Item for the stoned horse at Roebucke[26] a weeke before I went downe		5	2
Item to the ostlers there dressing		0	4
Item the roeve[27] for making cleane your bootes and Mr Richardes		0	4
Item by Peter[28] a littell jugge	0	0	6
Item 2 thrimnes ii*d*. a helve for the hatchet ii*d*.		0	4
Item iii*li*. candles xii*d*.	0	1	0

20. Sir Isaac Wake, *Rex Platonicus: sive, de...Jacobi regis, ad academiam Oxoniensem, adventu, narratio*, most likely the 3rd edn. (Oxford, 1615), *STC* 24940. For James I's visit to Oxford in 1607, which is described here, see Mallet, *Hist. Univ. Oxon.* ii, 230–33.

21. Possibly related to her marriage negotiations: see below.

22. Home of the Newdigates' aunt, Mary Fitton, and her husband John Lougher: see *Introduction*.

23. Word crossed out.

24. The Newdigates had a long-running lawsuit with the Gifforde family over the purchase of land near Arbury: see below fos. 3, 19v. and WRO, CR 136, B159–162. The Giffords had some rights in the local manors of Griffe and Chilvers Coton at this period: L.F. Salzman ed., *VCH Warwickshire* iv (Oxford, 1947), 175–6.

25. Arbury Hall was on the site of the dissolved Erdbury Priory, and was often referred to by the old name: see also *VCH Warws.*, iv, 175.

26. The inn in Market Street, Oxford: Salter, *Survey of Oxford*, i, 15–16.

27. Apparently intended here in the sense of 'steward'.

28. The following indented items were all bought by Peter Olyffe, the Newdigate brothers' manservant, according to a marginal note and bracket.

Item to him that came with a letter from Daintrie his dinner	0	0	6
Item aples vi*d*. a hing & nayles iii*d*.		0	9
Item carrying lettres to London	0	0	2
Item a lantherne	0	1	6
Item a paire of cripers	0	1	4
Item the kitchen boy making cleane bootes			4
Item 2 paire of showes [for] Mr Newdigate	0	5	2
	12	13	8

[*fo.2*]

Item a paire of showes for Mr Richard	0	2	6
Item soling a paire for him	0	0	11
Item aples i*d*. licorise i*d*.	0	0	2
Item joyce of licorice vi*d*. licorice vi*d*	0	1	0
Item salett oyle viii*d*. honie xvi*d*. for Peter		2	0
Item by Peter[29] a paire of tonges	0	1	4
Item a come brush ii*d*. 3*li*. of candles xiiii*d*.		1	4
Item aples xix*d*. 1 ell of cloth for rubbers xvi*d*.		2	11
Item a loode of wood xiiii*s*. cutting viii*d*.	0	14	8
Item mylke iii*d*. peper ii*d*. ale ii*d*. letter i*d*.	0	0	8
Item a paire of showes [for] Mr Newdigate	0	2	6
Item bisketbread i*li*. xx*d*. Item more iiii*d*.	0	1	11
Item bringing 2 cheeses[30] to the colledg & carrying a lettre downe		0	6
Item mending Mr Newdigate his showes	0	0	6
Item v feldifares v*d*. geven Ales[31] xii*d*.		1	3
Item to the joyner for 2 bordes for 2 windowes[32]		1	8
Item at Cowley dinner for 4 <with yourself>	0	0	10
Item ii*li*. candles x*d*. a gunne steecke ii*d*.		1	0
Item to Ales for alle	0	0	2
Item malt for mashes viii*d*. a hooke for canobie i*d*.			9
Item horsmeate at my going to London: Roebucke		4	6

29. The following indented items were also bought by Peter according to marginal note.

30. Cheeses were produced in large quantities on the Arbury estate and often despatched long distances: Larminie, 'Lifestyle and Attitudes', 60, 64; J. Thirsk ed., *Agrarian History of England and Wales*, iv (1967), 94.

31. A maidservant responsible for the brothers' chambers: see below.

32. Windows were rarely glazed and the chambers likely to be damp and cold: J. Neuman and J. McConica in McConica, *Hist. Univ. Oxon.*, iii, 628, 646.

Item a poeticall dictionary[33] for Mr Richard	o	6	o
Item to the barber < Mr Richard >	o	o	6
Item a queare of paper by Mr Richard	o	o	4
Item to my cosen Rode[34] for 24 yards of East India spoted cloth at xx*d.* for curtains, valans, canabie, carpet and quissions	2	o	o
Item 2 ell corse cloth to line quissions	o	1	2
Item 2 ell canvas to packe all in	o	3	. . .
Item of Thomas Chapman[35] 39 *oz* of fine mocado fring at v*d.*	o	16	3
Item i*oz.* more for tufting the quissions	o	o	4
Item the appoulsterer buckeron to line the canapie & valans	o	3	6
Item ringes & tape for the cortens & canopie & hope & rod for itt	o	3	o
Item making the canopie, corten & vallans		7	o
Item 6 lether bottons for the quitions		4	o
Item flockes to fill them	o	2	8
Item making them	o	1	6
Item a close stoole with a strong pan		9	o
Item sending a lettre to London by the carryer November the xxixth	o	o	1
	5	1	7
	5	13	

follium 2

[*fo.2v.*]
< Mychellmas rent 1618 >[36]
Item received by Mr Newdigate & delivered to

33. Probably C. Stephanus (Charles Estienne), *Dictionarium historicum et poeticum* (1561 etc.), a copy of which was bought later for the same price: see part ii, fo. 18v.

34. The following indented items, according to marginal bracket, were bought by Rode. Thomas Rode (d.1634), citizen and skinner, of 'the sign of the crown near St Martin's steps', had married a niece of William Whitehall, and was prominent in a network of Whitehall's Staffs., Oxon. and London kin which supplied the Newdigates with goods and services in the early 17th century: WRO CR 136, B338a, B521–5, B565, B1032, B595–630 (account books); Public Record Office, PROB 11/165 fo. 18 (Rode's will); *Coll. for a Hist. of Staffs.*, V, ii, 249–50, 305–7.

35. Among the 'friends' who were recipients of mourning rings in Rode's will: PRO, PROB 11/165 fo. 18.

36. Marginal note, preceded by an entry subsequently struck through: 'Received < alow this xxiis. > of Sir Henry Sutton £1 2s.; < paid in goulde > Item of my cosen Whithall £4.' Rents on this page are from Middlesex estates only.

(neice)[37] of William Kelly in part for his rent dewe at Mychellmas last	11	0	0
Item from Winkfeilde	22	0	0
Item by my cosen Rode of William Kelley	19	0	0
Item of John Andero for a half yeare then ending	25	0	0
Item of the Countes of Derbie[38]	22	0	0
Item for the slype of meadowe <Webbe>		15	0
Item of Tyler his rent	3	6	8
Item Webbe for the spring	1	1	8
Item of Thomas Baldwin for the like	1	1	8
Item of Thomas Baldwen for his rent	25	3	4
Item of Tooke for a half year's exhibition[39]	1	10	0
	132	5	8

Aprill the xxth 1619: Received at Brack-enborough for a half yeares rent then dewe Imprimis of Mr Lovelas for the Lady Darbie <wherof for the slype xxs. (more) then before vs. which was but xvs.	23	0	0
Item of Mr Thomas Baldwen	26	5	0
Item of John Anderowe	25	0	0
Item of Thomas Winkfeild in part	22	0	0
Item of William Kelley in part	30	0	0
Item of Mychell Webbe for his half spring	1	1	8
Item of Taylor	3	6	8
Item of Malkin	0	6	8
<131–0–0>			
Item of Mr Tooke for half year exhibition	1	10	0
	132	10	0

37. ?Margaret Henshawe, Whitehall's neice, a servant at Arbury: WRO, CR 136, B519 and B526 (letters from Whitehall).

38. Alice Stanley, wife of Lord Chancellor Thomas Egerton, who lived at Harefield Place, the Newdigates' former Middlesex seat, from where she extended hospitality to the Newdigates and others: WRO, CR 136, B595–601 (account books); F.R. Fogle, 'Such a Rural Queen': The Countess Dowager of Derby as Patron', in F.R. Fogle and L.A. Knafla, *Patronage in Late Renaissance England* (Univ. of California, Los Angeles, 1983), 3–29.

39. James Tooke, feodary of London and Middlesex (member of a Hertfordshire office-holding family), was in receipt of rent due to the king from John Newdigate's land in the county during his minority. The exhibition was money allowed to the ward for maintenance. See H.E. Bell, *An Introduction to the History and Records of the Court of Wards and Liveries* (Cambridge, 1958), 25; J. Hurstfield, *The Queen's Wards: Wardship and Marriage under Elizabeth I* (1958), 85.

October the xiiiith 1619: Received of
Brackenborowes rent dew for a half yeare ending at
Mychellmas last 1619

Imprimis of the Countes of Darbie	23	0	0
Item of Mr Thomas Baldwen	26	5	0
Item of John Androwe	25	0	0
Item of Winkfeilde in part	22	0	0
Item of Kelley in part	30	0	0
Item of Tyler	3	6	8
Item of Malkin	0	6	8
Item of Mr Webber for his part spring	1	1	8
Item James Tooke for half yeare exhibition	1	10	0
	132	10	0

< Winkfeild[40] paying more then before xxci*s*.
viii*d*.

Item our Lady [Day] rents 1619 for Bracken-	133	16	8
borough which is set downe by me at length in	132	5	0
the mydle of this booke, Thomas Winkfeild	132	10	0
paying xxvi*s*. viii*d*. half year more then before	132	10	0
with Mr Richard	539	1	8

Item a half yeares exhibition dew at our Lady
[Day] 1619 is set with my uppermost some
being the Kinges rent >

[*fo.3*]
November

Imprimis going to London my super at Uxbridge with Baldwen and Winkfeild[41] ii*s*. vi*d*. breake-[fast] vi*d*.		3	0
Item horsmeat theare	0	10	0
Item Hampton Cowrt setting up my hors	0	0	6
Item to Auditor Gofton Nuneaton rent dewe at Michellmas last for the parsonage[42]	5	10	0

40. As Whitehall makes clear, these lines were inserted later.
41. Brackenborough tenants: see previous page.
42. Sir Francis Gofton (d.1628), auditor of the Imprests: G.E. Aylmer, *The King's
Servants: the Civil Service of Charles I* (1974), 78. Nuneaton Rectory was part of Anne,
Lady Newdigate's dowry and jointure, now reverting to John Newdigate and hence
occasioning the business in the Court of Wards described below: WRO, CR 136, C670a
and C1054–9.

Item to him for his harryote dewe upon the death of my Lady[43]	6	1	0
Item the atorney of the Cowrt of Wards perusing the sedule[44]	1	0	0
< Item his man >[45]	0	2	0
Item the feodary of Middlesex the King's rent with the xxi*d.* for ingrossing the acompt	2	15	6*ob.*
Item for his acquittance	0	0	5*ob.*
Item poundage for the exhibition	0	0	6
Item my super with Mr Henry Newdigate[46]	0	1	0
Item to Mr Randle[47] the King's rent for War-wickshire with his acquittans	1	8	6
Item to same more for lute strings	0	1	2
Item to Mr Edward Fyton[48] for consideration of 150*li.* half yeare	1	10	0
Item to Mr Attorney perusing the decrie & his hande to itt[49]	1	13	0
Item his man for drawing it twyse		16	0
Item transcripting the offis for Coton parsonage into the Petibage[50]	1	6	6

43. The herriot due on the death of Lady Newdigate, July 1618: see *Introduction*.

44. James Ley (d.1629), attorney from 1608 and author of a tract on the court and a collection of the cases heard before it. He was created baronet July 1619 and thereafter became Chief Justice of King's Bench, Lord Treasurer, Lord Ley (1626), Earl of Marlborough, Speaker of the Lords and President of the Council: *D.N.B.*; Aylmer, *King's Servants*, 39, 61, 88–9, 320; Bell, *Court of Wards*, 24, 68, 89. A 1623 commission of inquiry into fees found that the attorney was due 10*s.* for signing schedules (i.e. inventories of wards' property): Bell, 194.

45. This is in accordance with the official rate: Bell, 194.

46. Henry Newdigate (1581–1629) of Ashted, Surrey, step-brother of Sir John Newdigate: see J.G. Nichols, 'The Family Newdegate', 239–40 and *Introduction*.

47. ?Richard Randall of Stoke in Coventry, town clerk and coroner of the city 1614–36: W.B. Stephens ed., *VCH Warws.*, viii, (1969), 267. Two better known Warws. feodaries, Humphrey Colles of Hampton in Arden and Edward Chamberlain of Astley Castle, also appear in the account book. For them see: Bell, *Court of Wards*, 40; P. Styles, *Sir Simon Archer: A Lover of Antiquities and of the Lovers Thereof* (Dugdale Society, Occasional Paper 6, 1946), 24.

48. Cousin of Lady Newdigate and 'servant to the Lord Carewe' mentioned in her will: WRO, CR 136, C1915. Her brother of the same name had been created baronet Oct. 1617: J. Burke, *Extinct and Dormant Baronetcies of England, Ireland and Scotland* (2nd edn., 1844), 198.

49. The official fee for signing decrees was 20*s.*: Bell, *Court of Wards*, 193. The clerk's fee for 'penning' (cf. below) was normally 2*s.*.

50. Chilvers Coton, Warws., in Newdigate hands since 1610 and until 1618 part of Lady Newdigate's jointure: WRO, CR 136, C1045. The escheator's inquisition, taken after her death, was returned to Chancery, where it passed to the clerks of the Petty Bag, who transcribed it into the Court of Wards: see Bell, *Court of Wards*, 74–5.

Item Mr Audley[51] for ingrossing the decrie & his hande	I	3	4
Item inrowling the decrie Co(mptroller's) offis[52]	I	6	8
Item inrowling the sedule there	0	5	0
Item a copie of the Exchequer order[53]	0	2	0
Item for Mr West there to keepe Mr Gifford's commission for per(using) of the file[54]	0	11	0
Item to his man Francis for the same	0	1	0
Item Margaret[55] for 3*oz* of gould for Mistress Mary[56]		17	0
Item a paire of gloves for Mistress Lettis to gyve to Mr Wormehall[57]	0	3	4
Item 2 paire of blacke pricksen for yourself		2	0
Item 2 paire [for] Mistress Marie whit by Ashton[58]		1	10
Item a glasse for Mistress Anne[59]	0	5	0
Item eych of the gentlewomen a [pair] pantables*		2	0
Item diner with Mr Coles & Mr Robins[60] <having (writt) for you & would take noe monie>	0	3	8
Item 4 queare paper, 1*oz*. waxe	0	1	4
Nicke Beale[61] your blacke felt hat & band	0	13	0
Item a hat & band for Mr Richard	0	10	0

51. Hugh Audley of the Inner Temple (d.1662), private moneylender and from June 1618 clerk, with Richard Chamberlain of Shirburn, Oxon., of the Court of Wards: *D.N.B.*; Aylmer, *Civil Service of Charles I*, 90, 384; Bell, *Court of Wards*, 28–9, 35, 38 etc. He was here officially entering the decree.

52. According to the accountant's normal usage the abbreviation should be thus expanded, but the meaning is unclear: *cf.* Bell, *Court of Wards*, 190–205.

53. Presumably emanating from the escheator: *cf. ibid.*, 72.

54. William West, author of a precedent book, *Symboleography*: Bell, *Court of Wards*, 90–1. For Gifford see above fo. iv.

55. Probably Whitehall's niece, Margaret Henshawe: see above, fo. 2v.

56. Mary Newdigate (1598–1643), eldest sister of John and Richard, married in Jan. 1620: it seems possible that the gold had some connection with courtship.

57. Lettice Newdigate (1604–25), the second sister; an Edward Wormall wrote from Austin Friars to 'his friend' John Newdigate at Trinity college in June 1619: WRO, CR136, B533.

58. George Ashton, mercer: see below, and WRO, CR136, B1037 (bill 1619) and B565 (T. Rode to W. Whitehall, 1624).

59. Anne Newdigate (1607–37), third and youngest sister.

60. Probably William Coles of Herts., 'pleb.', who matriculated at Trinity, May 1619, and was of Gray's Inn 1621; there was no Robins at Trinity, but George Roberts of Oxfordshire, 'pleb.', matriculated from there also May 1619: *Reg. Univ. Oxon.*, II, part ii, 375.

61. According to a marginal note and bracket, the following indented items were purchased from Mr Beale. Nick or Mr Beale occur elsewhere in the account as suppliers of hats. Richard Beale, merchant, of Dowegate ward, was recorded in the 1634

Item a paire of gaters & scarf to hang your sord in	1	4	0
Item dying a paire of silke stockings	0	2	...
Item dying & lynig your whit bever		4	6
Item dying & lynig your felt		3	0
Item a box to cary the hats downe		0	6
	36	14	0

folium 3

[*fo.3v.*]

Item by my cosen Richard Whitehall[62] in Easter tearm 1618			
Imprimis a barell of gunpowther and for drenching 3 horses	0	15	4
Item in Midsomer tearme for 3 quarters of a yarde of crimson velvet of Mr (Parnels)	0	18	6
Item x*oz* of conserve of roses to Erdbury		2	8
Item 3 doson of riben poynts	0	7	0
Item a gyrdle & hangers (gredeline & silver)	1	5	0
George Ashton : 44 yard [of] tamet at ii*s*. ii*d*.	4	15	4
Item Normandie canvas ii*yd*. at xvii*d*.	0	2	x*d*.
Item ell broade searg viii*yd*. at ii*s*. iiii*d*.	0	18	8
Item whale bone 3 quarters	0	1	0
Item whit jame iii yard dimi. at x*d*.	0	2	11
Item a saten coller < Mr Richard >	0	3	4
Item < for him > a paire of blacke worsteed hose		6	8
Item a paire of silke garters [for] Mr Richard		3	10
Item a paire of silke garters [for] Mistress Mary		2	6
Item blacke buckerom iii yards at xiii		3	0
Item blacke taffatie quarter dimi.		4	6
Item by Mr Newdigate at the offering Mr Pr(esident)[63] (maide)		2	6
Item to the Lord Chancellor his assayes[64]	0	0	10

visitations: *The Visitation of London 1633, 1634 and 1635*, ed. J.J. Howard and J.L. Chester (Harleian Society xc, 1880), 57.

62. According to marginal note the indented items form one bill, from either Richard Whitehall of Ouldbury, Warws. (PRO, PROB 11/183, fo. 94), or perhaps more likely, William's nephew Richard, brother-in-law of Thomas Rode, who is mentioned in the wills of both (PROB 11/165, fo. 18; PROB 11/173, fo. 23).

63. Ralph Kettell, President of Trinity College: see *Introduction*.

64. This could be the edition of Francis Bacon, *Essayes. Religious meditations.* (1597) at Arbury Hall, *STC* 1137.5, or a later enlarged edition, e.g. of 1620, *STC* 1144.

Item to the beadles when they were mat(ricu- lated)[65]	10	0
Item to the Lankisher man which brought Mr Newdigate a box of marmalat from Daintrie	1	6
Item the pitture of David[66]	0	4	0
Item the Tryumpes of Nassawe[67]	0	3	0
Item Purchas his Pilgramage[68]	0	7	0
Item aples i strike	0	1	0
Item 1*yd*. iii quarter of riben xiiii*d*. broone thred ii*d*.	1	4
Item ii *oz* of joyce of lycorice smale	1	4
Item 4 dosen blacke silke buttons for [the] gen- tlewomen	1	0
Item 2 doson for the gent(lemen) theire dublets	0	6
Item my horse a iii weeke to Anthonie at London	1	0	0
Item carrying canopie, cortens, quissions, carpett & close stoole from London to Oxforde	0	5	4
Item yard dimi. riben for Mr Richard	0	9
Item diner with Mr Salter and cosen Holl(ins)[69]	1	0
Item geven at my cosen's to 2 children <lying there a 3 weekes>	11	0
Item to his man & maides	5	0
Item my horse at Harts Horne in Smythfeild the night before I came forth of London	0	1	4
Item for frosting that morning	0	0	2

65. 6 Nov. 1618: *Reg. Univ. Oxon.*, II, part ii, 372. As Aylmer concludes (in McConica ed., *Hist. Univ. Oxon.* iii, 552–3), bedells and others were making money from their offices: the brothers, as sons of a knight, should have paid 3*s*. 4*d*. each, unless John was being charged in his own right as an esquire.

66. Probably a painting or engraving. David was a popular subject for later illustrations, e.g. see M. Corbett and M. Norton eds., *Engraving in England in the 16th and 17th Centuries* iii: *The Reign of Charles I* (Cambridge, 1964), *passim*. Unfortunately there is no subject index to its companion vol., ii: *The Reign of James I*, ed. A.M. Hind (Cambridge, 1955).

67. Probably a book: J.J. Orlers and H. de Haestans, *The Triumphs of Nassau* [i.e. Maurice, Prince of Orange], trans. W. Shute (1613), *STC* 17676. The House of Orange was also a popular subject for engravings: *Engraving in England*, ii and iii.

68. S. Purchas, *Purchas his Pilgrimage. Or the relations of the world and the religions observed in all ages* (1613), *STC* 20505, or a later edition.

69. Thomas Salter, a former bailiff of Daventry and the Newdigate sisters' host, enjoyed a close relationship with the Newdigates in the 1610s and 1620s: 'I presume', he wrote to John Newdigate in March 1622/3, 'you are persuaded that I, both truly, and unfeignedly, owe you much love, service and respect, therefore I am bold the more to express myself' (WRO, CR 136, B457). His wife Nan was a beneficiary under Lady Newdigate's will: WRO, CR136, C1915. Which 'cosen' is referred to here is not clear. The three most likely are Francis Hollenshed, another former bailiff of Daventry, Edward Hollins of Swerford and his brother William. Hollenshed: see WRO, CR 136, B1031 (Rode to Whitehall), B1022 (letter and bill, 1607). Hollins: see *Introduction*.

Item my self and horsse [High] Wickam		2	10
Item boye walking my horse from Taylor's to Baldwin's < I going on foote to see Brackenborough howse >	0	0	2
Item a pecke of malt : Roebuck < for my hors being sicke >		0	8
Item vi snipes < for Mr Newdigate >	0	1	4
	14	15	8
	8	11	12

[*fo.4*]

December the viiith 1618

Item a paire of showes for Mr Richard	0	2	8
Item mending lanthern ii*d*. threid *d*. letter i*d*.		0	4
Item a yard dimi. riben for Mr Newdigate's showes < tong >		0	4
Item soling Mr Richard his showes	0	1	0
Item to my cosen Parson's[70] clarke ringing a pigg		0	6
Item bringing 4*li*. gunpowther from London		0	3
Item 3 paire of gloves for one gentlewomen to gyve Mistress Salter	0	4	6
Item the carrier of Coventrie a letter Mr Richard	0	0	2
Item a dixonary for Mr Richard bought by my cosen Parson	0	8	8
Item a doson turned pinnes & setting them up & glewing pistall & glas	0	1	0
Item bringing a turkie & 2 capons from my cosen James Whithall[71]	0	2	0
Item a paire of gloves sent his wife[72] by Mr Newdigat	0	1	0
17 [December] Item a lettre from Coventrie (to Mr Richard)	0	0	2
Item to landresse for you v*s*. Mr Richard & Peter vi*s*.		11	0

70. Since, as far as is known, Whitehall had no cousin called Parsons, this looks like an early use of the title for a clergyman, in this case probably William Hollins B.D., of Swerford.

71. James Whitehall (c.1580–1645), M.A., nephew of the accountant and a trustee of the Newdigate estates, graduate of Christ Church and rector-elect of Checkley, Staffs.: WRO, CR136, C2230–3; H.S. Grazebrook ed., 'Visitations of Staffordshire', *Coll. for a Hist. of Staffs.*, V, ii, 305–7, and W. N. Landor, 'Staffordshire Incumbents and Parochial Records', *ibid.*, (unnumbered, 1915), 58–9; O'Day, *Education and Society*, 32.

72. Elizabeth, daughter of John Hollins of Swerford: Landor, *Staffs. Incumbents*, 59.

Item to Jo Muchell caling to prayers		1	o
Item a knife for Mistress Tonstall[73]	o	6	o
Item to Mr Skinner[74] for a quarter ending at St Thomas daye[75]	2	4	o
Item to him which teacheth you upon the lute		6	8
Item for Mr Richard's deske[76]	o	5	o
Item a knife for Mr Tonstale[77]	o	5	o
Item ii*li*. gunpowther	o	3	o
Item 3 knyves for the 3 gentlewomen	o	3	4
Item a penknife & the cutler's box	o	1	o
Item a knyfe for Mr Newdigate		2	6
Item[78] lute strings	o	o	6
Item to Mr Richard for a horse to Daintrie		2	6
Item eggs the morning we went to [the Court of] Wards, Mr Tonstale iiii*d*. to Ales for fetching & boyling ii*d*.		o	6
Item geven to Mr Richard at our going	o	5	6
Item to Mr President for a quarter's rent of our chambers ending at Christmas	1	2	o
Item for horsmeate at Roebucke	1	2	o
Item[79] to the ostler there then	o	o	6
Item supper at [High] Wickam going to Mr Tonstalle		5	4
Item horsemeate & ostler there	o	3	2
Item the cooke there	o	o	2
Item our supper at the Greyhounde, a shoulder of mutton	o	3	o
Item a rabett xii*d*. bread & beare x*d*.	o	1	10
Item breakefast ii*s*. fyer ix*d*.	o	2	9

---

73. Penelope Tonstall or Tunstal, daughter of Walter Leveson of Lilleshall, Salop, and wife of John Tonstall of Edgcombe, Surrey: see *Introduction* and W.H. Hart and J.J. Howard eds., 'Genealogical and Heraldic Memoranda relating to the county of Surrey', *Surrey Archaeological Collections*, ii (1858), 16.

74. Robert Skinner, Vice-President of Trinity, tutor to the Newdigate brothers: see *Introduction*. The payment seems slightly high: McConica (*Hist. Univ. Oxon.*, iii, 694) suggests fees of up to £1 per quarter, although O'Day suggests £5 per year (*Education and Society*, 116).

75. i.e. 29 Dec.

76. Probably for the lockable timber-framed study provided for each occupant of a communal bedroom: see J. Newman, 'The Physical Setting', in McConica, *Hist. Univ. Oxon.*, iii, 628.

77. John Tonstall of Edgcombe, Gentlemen of the Bedchamber to Queen Anne: see *Introduction*, above fn. 73 and *CSPD 1611–18*, 189, 195; *CSPD 1629–31*, 331, 513.

78. Crossed out, 'to the swarver'.

79. Crossed out, 'To Ales for eges at breakfast iiii*d*., forgot & not set downe'.

Item horsmeat there that night[80]		3	10
Item ostler iii*d*. removing 4 showes iiii*d*.		0	7
Item to the Oxford carrier for a boxe with ruffes in (by William Plumley)[81]	0	0	6
Item to him < William Plumley > for v*li*. candles Oxford	0	2	0
Item a pecke of barley by him	0	0	4
Item a letter to London by him i*d*. mending stocking i*d*.			2
Item vi*oz*. of joyce of licoryce at London		4	0
folium 4	5	12	…
		12	

[*fo.4v.*]

December 1618

Item your going by water to Lambeth	0	0	6
Item to Mr Bates his boye helping with hors thyther		0	6
Item at Cashoulton[82] oates bought at Croydon		4	6
Item for our horses att ines there	0	4	3
Item to him that dressed our horse a weeke	0	2	6
Item geven Thomas & Griffen eyther ii*s*. vi*d*. you ryding in the cowtch from Lambeth & Griffen carrying a box from Smythfeild thyther		5	0
Item the 2 maides & boye of the kitchen		5	0
Item Thomas Blackman ii*s*. showing there vi*d*.		2	6
Item Bores Head White Chapell < ostler & beare > eyther ii*d*.		0	4
Item by Henry Thornton[83] for wyne at supper with my cosen Thickens[84]	0	1	6
< 30th >			
Item horsmeat at Crowne Whitechapel		4	4

80. Crossed out, '& ostler'.

81. William Plumley was butler and assistant steward at Arbury: WRO, CR 136, B595–612 (account books).

82. i.e. Carshalton, Surrey.

83. Mr Henry Thornton was among friends mentioned in Thomas Rode's will: PRO, PROB 11/165, fo. 18. This may have been another Daventry connection: Thomas Thornton, esq., of Newnham, was Recorder of the Town around this period (Baker, *History and Antiquities of Northants.*, i, 322).

84. Ralph Thickens or Thickness, baker, of Whitechapel, had married a niece of William Whitehall. He and his family were remembered in the wills of Whitehall, Thomas Rode and Edward Hollins: PRO, PROB 11/173, fo. 23 and 11/165, fo. 18; J.H. Morrison ed., *P.C.C. Register Scrope 1630* (1934), 28. See also *Alumni Oxon*, iv.

Item breakefast, fyer & chamberlaine	o	3	6
<January the 1>			
Item St Albans, Saresons Head diner		3	o
Item our horses there	o	o	9
Item supper at Dunstable with Sir George Belgrave[85] & others	o	6	o
Item washing your drawes & stockings	o	o	2
Item breakefast ii*s*. ix*d*. fyere xxiii*d*.	o	4	8
Item chamberlaines	o	o	4
Item diner Stoni Stratford with the same compenie		3	o
Item horsmeate there	o	o	10
<3 [January]>			
Item geven at Mr Salter's, 3 maides	o	3	o
Item Jo Poole & Powell tending hors		1	6
Item spentt by me in going[86] to Gawsworth[87] & commying backe which was to smale purposse therefore not set downe <going up to Oxford from Erdbury>			
<11th>			
Item removing your horse, Daintrie	o	o	4
Item geven Powell & Poole dressing horses		o	10
<13th>			
Item at Brackley <spent> comming to Oxford by you & <Daintrie>		o	4
Item by William Plumley for provander going downe		1	11
Item by him oweing for showing at Daintrie		2	1
<Peter> Item a pint of wine & a cake at Rugbie when you came up with Bon:fa[88]		o	8
Item 4 yards of caddis to bind your drawers			4
Item to Mr Brookes, bursar, in discharge of all commons, batles & other dewes for the last quarter ending the Frydaye before St Thomas day, witness Mr Skinner[89]	9	8	9

85. George Belgrave of Belgrave, Leics. and of Lincs., kt: Shaw, *Knights of England*, ii, 122. His son John matriculated from Trinity college in Oct. 1619 (*Alumni Oxon.*, i) and paid 40*s*. caution money (Trinity MS, 'Liber Trin. Coll. Oxon.', 1619).

86. Crossed out, 'and'.

87. The Cheshire estate of John Newdigate's maternal uncle, Sir Edward Fitton: see *Introduction*.

88. ?'Boniface'. It has not proved possible to identify this person from among Newdigate friends and relatives; it remains possible that it could have been a horse.

89. Skinner witnessed this transaction in his capacity as the Newdigates' financial guarantor: McConica, *Hist. Univ. Oxon.*, iii, 693.

[Item] 2 *li.* candles	o	o	10
Item horsmeat at Roebucke, 3 horses comming up after Christmas	o	4	6
Item a peare of showes for Mr Richard		2	2
Item[90] by him to a gathering for repair of <a church>		o	1
Item to Thomas, Mr Wedgwood's[91] man, for dressing his horse	o	o	6
Item fyshookes and lynes	o	1	6
	13	2	9
		4	14

[*fo.5*]

Item by Peter[92] for the gentlewomen for the making up of there gowne i*oz* silke	o	2	4
Item iii quarters blacke & browne threed	o	1	9
Item a quarter more at Daventrie	o	o	8
Item claspes & kepers for theire gownes		o	6
Item i *yd.* fustian russett	o	o	11
Item i *yd.* bayes for the sleeves	o	2	...
Item inkle to bind the bodies	o	o	4
Item iii *yd.* quarter of tamett at ii*s.* ii*d.*	o	7	o
Item a quarter of searg to mend Mistress Anne's gowne			6

January

Item by Mr Richard a kye for the garrat door	o	o	4
Item dressing his hatt vi*d.* inke & nayles ii*d.*	o	o	8
Item lost <by him> at cardes v*s.* geven at the communion vi*d.*		5	6
Item to a wassell in Christmas <by Mr Richard>	o	o	6
Item for a book Lucan[93]	o	2	o
Item Pertius in Englishe[94]	o	o	6

90. Preceding line crossed out, 'by him at Morton Pinkanie, alle & cakes'.

91. Wedgwoods of Haracles, Leek, Staffordshire, had several marriage connections with the Whitehalls at this period: *Coll. for a Hist. of Staffs.*, V, ii, 304; D. Pennington and I. Roots eds., *The Committee At Stafford 1643–5* (Staffs. Record Society 5th ser. ii, 1957), 356.

92. The following indented items were bought by Peter according to marginal note and bracket.

93. Probably M.A. Lucanus, *Pharsalia sive, de bello civile ... adjectis notis T. Farnaby* (1618), *STC* 16883.

94. A. Persius Flaccus, *His satires trans. into Eng. [verse] by B. Holyday* (1616), *STC* 19777.5–19778.5.

Item Matius Logicke[95]	0 7 0	
Item[96] dimi. quarter of taffatie, Mr New-		
digate's dublet		1 6
Item browne thred	0 0 8	
Item suger iiii*d*. for Mr Newdigate	0 0 4	
Item a paire of showes for Mr Richard	0 2 8	
Item candles iiii*li*. at v*d*.	0 1 3	
Item shott iiii*d*. beare at Cowley ii*d*.	0 0 5	
Item a candlesteeke & extinguisher	0 0 6	
Item a juge iiii*d*. gloves xii*d*.	0 1 4	
Item dying a hatt	0 0 6	
Item Martiall & Ovid[97] for Mr Richard	0 1 8	
Item a paire of golloshes for Mr Newdigate	0 1 8	
Item Lucan[98] ii*s*. Smyth & Brearewood[99] ii*s*. viii*d*.	4 8	
Item Romane Emperowres[100]	0 2 6	
Item orringes iiii*d*. toothpicke i*d*.	0 0 5	
Item showes & 'galoshes for Mr Newdigate	0 4 5	
Item to Mr Charles[101] for his viall, whereof iii*s*. is		
oweing by him to Mr Newdigate	0 11 0	
Item to Doctor Clayton[102] for his opinion & cast		
<water>	3 4	
Item for a woodcocke	0 2 ...	
Item a doson of lemons	0 1 6	
Item 2 pulletts	0 1 4	
Item the smyth, a locke for the chamber dore	2 7	
Item to him for a kye for your cabenets	0 0 8	
Item to Doctor Clayton more	0 11 0	

95. D. Masius, *Commentarii in Porphyrium et logicam Aristotelis* (Cologne, 1618): De Jordy and Fletcher, *Library for Younger Scholars*, 1, 20.

96. The following indented items were bought by Peter according to note.

97. M.V. Martialis, *Epigrammaticon libri: ed. T Farnaby* (1615), *STC* 17492. Ovid: see above, note 15.

98. See above, note 93.

99. S. Smith, *Aditus ad logicam* (1613 etc.), *STC* 22825–22829. An edition of this book was published in Oxford in 1618: F. Madan, *The Early Oxford Press* (Oxford, 1895), 110. Edward Brerewood, *Elementa logicae* (1614 etc.), *STC* 3612–3614.5, was often found bound with it. I am indebted to Mr Paul Morgan for this information.

100. A number of possibilities: J. Ursinus, *The Romane conclave. Wherein by way of history, exemplified upon the lives of the Romane emperors, the usurpations of the jesuited statists, are truely reported* [By I. Gentillet] (1609), *STC* 24526; C.T. Suetonius, *The historie of twelve ceasars* (1605), *STC* 23422–23424; T. Godwin, *Romanae historiae anthologia, an English exposition of the Romane antiquities* (Oxford, 1614), *STC* 11956–7 – definitely bought by the Newdigates later, see fo. 9v.

101. Thomas Charles, a dancing master employed by the Newdigates at regular intervals after Lady Day 1610: WRO, CR 136, B595–600.

102. Thomas Clayton, Regius Professor of Medicine: D. Macleane, *Pembroke College* (Univ. of Oxford College Histories, 1900), chapter ix.

Item i*li*. of preynes[103]	0	0	2
Item 4 snipes xii*d*. half a doson larks vi*d*.	0	1	6
Item barber for Mr Richard, trymming	0	0	6
Item the apoticary for almon mylke	0	2	6
Item a vomet x*d*. a jenelepe xviii*d*.	0	2	4
Item 2 plasters of turpen(tine) & olibanum	0	0	6
Item a loade of wood	0	14	0
Item carrying	0	0	11
Item for cutting to Anthonie	0	0	8
folium 5	5	11	11

[*fo.5v.*]

Item laid forth by Peter [104]: a loade of woode	0	12	8
Item a pirle for Mr Hatley's[105] bowe	0	0	4
Item scowring bason & chamber pott	0	0	2
Item for resen & brimstone	0	0	1
Item white threed	0	0	2
Item iii*li*. of candles xv*d*. lace for wrap iii*d*.		1	6
Item Ales for milke	0	0	9
Item 2 urinals vi*d*. to Mr Newdigate by Peter ii*d*.	0	0	8
Item iii quarter of a pounde of almons	0	1	1
Item dimi. pint of plantan water		0	4
Item 1 quarter of a pound suger	0	0	4
Item a glasse iii*d*. 3 doson buttons ix*d*.		1	0
Item lemons, 1 doson xii*d*. mend(ing) gallo(shes) iii*d*.		1	3
Item for a pigg ii*s*. carrying a lettre [to] London i*d*.		2	1
Item for Mr Richard's showes	0	0	4
<March 6>			
Item more to Ales for ale & mylke	0	1	6
Item i *li*. of candles	0	0	5
Item oyle for your bootes & Mr Richard's	0	0	2
Item a pint of almon mylke more	0	1	0
Item half a doson larkes	0	0	6
Item iii woodcocks at vii*d*.	0	1	0

103. Prunes?
104. The following indented items were bought by Peter according to marginal bracket and note.
105. William Hatley of Beds., 'arm.', matriculated from Trinity 1615 aged 18, B.A. 1619, M.A. 1622: *Alumni Oxon.*, ii, 672.

Item to the apoticary: muns christe losinges & pleasters for wrists	0	4	0
Item 2 *li*. candles	0	0	10
Item to Ales for ale & Mylke	0	0	10
Item geven her	0	0	8
Item geven Stephan the cooke	0	2	0
<6 [March]>			
Item horsmeate at King's Armes[106]: 1 hors xiii nights & 2 more v nights at vi*d*. the daye & night haye			
Item provander iii strikes at ii*s*. viii*d*.	0	8	0
Item mending Mr Newdigate's peece[107] by Peter		0	4
Item March the xii comming from Oxford:			
Item S[t]onie Midleton a posset for Mr Newdigate & cake for Mr Richard	0	0	4
Item Morton Pinkanie posset, ale & ca(ke)		0	8
Item Brackley the howse by Peter	0	10	0
Item 4 horses there 1 night	0	4	0
Item Daintrie 4 horses 2 nights, 2 hors vi nights & 4 hors 3 nights for haye	0	5	2
Item provander for them	0	6	2
Item geven Fowle-face for carrying Mr Richard his hors to Oxforde backe		2	2
Item 1 showe & 2 removes, stoned hors	0	0	6
Item to Mr Newdigate at Daintrie xxii*s*.	–	–	–
Item to Gilbert's[108] boye bringing a horse for Mr Richard to Daintrie	0	0	9
Item geven Isbell & Besse at your comming		2	0
Item Jo Poole & Fowl-face dressing hors & wyping bootes	0	0	10
Item 1 ell lace [for] Mr Newdigate's cufts by Peter	0	0	8
Item at [Nun]eaton by him: i*li*. corans vi*d*. suger dimi. *li*. viii*d*. candles iiii*li*. x*d*. nutmegs iiii*d*.		2	3
	4	11	9
		14	

---

106. The inn in Holywell, Oxford, opened in 1607. Situated close to Trinity it was also the most popular place for plays in the city: A. Crossley ed., *VCH Oxfordshire*, iv, (Oxford, 1979), 438.

107. Probably a fowling- or birding-piece, a gun which, as a student, Newdigate was officially forbidden to possess (*ibid.*, 428), but discipline was evidently not easily enforced: McConica, *Hist. Univ. Oxon.*, iii, 653–6.

108. If Richard was bound for Oxford, 'Gilbert' may be Gilbert Sheldon; if not, the name does not fit any Arbury friend or servant.

[*fo.6*]

January 1618[109]: This bill following I had writt in a paper & forgott to set it in his wright place

	£	s	d
Item commyng downe from you (after Christmas) at Oxford your hors at Mr Hilton's[110] i night	0	1	4
Item to Jo Browne at Erdbury for drenching bald gelding & an other	0	2	0
Item going & commyng to Oxford to see Mr Newdigate & Mr Richard	0	2	0
Item (at) Staynes walk my hors vi*s*.			
Item at Daintrie fetching Mistress Mary & Mistress Lettice from thence to go to Gawsworth, haye ii*s*. vi*d*. provander xvi*d*.	0	3	10
Item geven the 3 maides there at our gentlewoomen's coming downe	0	3	0
Item staying 2 nights at Daintrie to Ed & Poole fetching haye, provander and for dressing our hors	0	1	4
Item to Mr Charles for 3 dayes	0	5	0
Item Williamson carrying a boxe with bands & other things to Gawsworth	0	1	6
Item going to Gawsworth—Mistress Mary, Mistress Lettice, my self, William Plumley, Francis Cooke[111] at Lytchfeild beare		0	2
Item Heaward[112] supper & breakfast	0	6	0
Item horses there	0	6	4
Item Caster cakes & beare vi*d*. hors xii*d*.	0	1	6
Item Gawsworth dressing hors first night		0	6
Item to one dressing them all weeke	0	1	0
Item geven c(ooke), b(utler) and chamb(erlain)[113]	0	3	0
Item George Cooke & Ouldham	0	1	0
Item to Tom and the kytchen boye	0	0	6

---

109. The accountant has drawn a line down the middle of the previous 12 entries on this page (headed 'April 1st 1619') and reproduced them exactly on fo. 7.

110. Probably one of the Daventry family who had supplied the town with bailiffs: Baker, *Hist. and Antiquities of Northants.*, 321.

111. Francis Fayrefax or Cooke, a servant at Arbury between 1610 and 1630: WRO, CR136, B595–620.

112. ?Haywood Green, Staffs..

113. Usage elsewhere suggests that the abbreviation should be rendered thus.

Item Barton ale for your hors commyng from Sharpclif[114]	o	o	2
Item commyng up to Oxford when you had your agewe,[115] my hors Daintrie	o	I	o
	2	I	2

folium 6   4

[*fo.6v.*]

Receiptes[116]: Brackenborowes rents at our Lady Day 1620

Imprimis Aprill the xiith 1620 of the Lady Derbie her half yeares rent then dewe	23	o	o
Item of John Androwe for a half yeare ending at our Lady [Day] 1620	25	o	o
Item of Mr Baldwen	26	5	o
Item of Kelley	30	o	o
Item of Tyller	3	6	8
Item of Malkin	o	6	8
Item of Webber for his part of the spring	I	I	8
Item of Thomas Winkfeild <paying more then before xxvi*s*. viii*d*.>	23	6	8
	132	6	8
Item of Tooke for a half yeares exhibition ending at our Lady Day 1620	I	10	o
	133	16	8

[*fo.7*]

<March 29 1619>

Item going into Cheshire: Mr Newdigate, Mr Richard, Tom Salter, Peter & my self			
Imprimis at Lytchfeilde beare & cake	o	o	4
Item at Stoane[117] the howse, super & breakefast		I2	o
Item chamberlaines vi*d*. [the] pore iii*d*.	o	o	9
Item the old woman that made & warmed your bed iii*d*.		o	3

114. A Whitehall family home in the parish of Ipstones, near Leek, Staffs.: Pennington and Roots, *Committee at Stafford*, 356; N. Pevsner, *The Buildings of England: Staffordshire* (1974), 157.

115. Jan. or Feb. 1619 at Oxford: see fo. 5.

116. These rents are entered at the bottom of the page, upside down. The remainder of the page has been left blank.

117. Stone, Staffs..

Item horsmeate & ostlers for v hors		o	6	2
Item the smyth for showing there		o	1	o
Item the sadler mending Mr Richard's sadle		o	o	4
Item at Talke-of-the-Hill beare & cake			o	4
Item Knutsford supper and dyner		o	7	o
Item 2 maides by Mr Newdigate's apoyntment		o	o	6
Item a pint white wine & suger		o	o	5
Item horsmeat & ostler for v hors		o	5	o
Item geven a pore woman there		o	o	1
Item Hollen ferry[118], the feryman iiii*d*. ale ii*d*.		o	6	

Aprill the 3 1619[119]

Item geven at Holcroft[120] to the 2 butlers		2	o	
Item the cowtchman dressing our hors <being v> 2 dayes & nights and helping them to provander		2	...	
Item the cooke & chamberlaine eyther xii*d*.		o	2	o
Item a showe for Mr Richard's mare at Congleton		o	3	
Item Jo Shawes, Mr Richard, Tomm Salter, Peter & my self		3	o	
Item our 4 horses there & ostler <being with Mr Lowgher[121]>		o	4	3
Item geven Tomm Draper dressing our hors Gawsworth		4		
Item our dyner at Lichfeild & breakfast		2	3	
Item horses there then		1	o	
Item Daintrie going to Oxford (with Mr Richard), 2 horses 2 dayes & 2 nights, haye, provander & dressing		3	6	
Item geven 2 maides there		1	o	
Item geven at Swarforde[122] for our hors & selves		o	1	9
Item Kings Armes 2 hors[123]				
Item to Mr President for our chamber & other rowmes[124] the quarter ending March the xxvth		1	2	o

118. ?Hollinfare, just over the Mersey from Cheshire into Lancashire.

119. The date is repeated in the margin.

120. Probably at the home of the Newdigates' grandmother Alice Holcroft, Lady Fitton (d.1627): Earwaker, *East Cheshire*, ii, 565–6.

121. John Lougher (d.1636), second husband of the Newdigates' aunt Mary Fitton, M.P. for Pembroke 1601 and Sheriff of the county 1626–7: Hasler, *The House of Commons 1558–1603*, ii, 489.

122. Swerford, Oxon., the home of Whitchall's kinsmen the Hollinses.

123. The accountant has subsequently deleted the remainder of the entry: '2 hors 1 night keping, & myne 1 night downe'.

124. The Newdigates' accommodation cannot have been as cramped as that of some of their contemporaries: *cf.* Newman in McConica, *Hist. Univ. Oxon.*, iii, 628.

Item the Vice Presidend for reading to Mr Newdigate & his brother the quarter then ending	2	4	0
Item to Mr Brookes, burser, for a quarter then ending: Mr Newdigate's batles	5	17	9
Item his commons in that tyme	0	13	...
Item for gawdies iiii*d*. cooles iii*s*. iiii*d*.	0	3	8
Item Saterdaye supers xii*d*. the cooke iiii*d*.		1	4
Item for Mr Richard that quarter to Mr Brookes	3	15	0
Item to the landress for you, Mr Richard & Peter	0	11	0
<vi*s*.>Item to Gilbert's boye fetching Mr Richard's hors from Oxford	0	...	...
Item <2>[125] hors <Mr Richard's & myne> at Kings Arms <one night>		2	2
Item Uxbridg Wensdaye night and Thorsdaye, Mr Baldwen, Winkfeild & Kelley[126] the howse		6	6
Item horsmeat att Mr Webbes <& ostler>	0	1	2
Item <lying> at Mr Baldwen's <one night, to his> 2 men & 2 maids xii*d*.		1	0
Item geven his 2 boyes	0	1	0
Item to my cosen Rode for iii ell hollande at iiii*s*. the elne for Mr Newdigate a sherte	0	12	0
	18	10	3
folium 7		7	9

[*fo.7v.*]

Aprill 1619

Item paid Mr Fauncis Gofton [Nun]eaton rent	5	10	0
Item to Mr Fytton half yeares consideration	7	10	0
Item the King's rent for Mr Newdigat's land in Warwickshire to Mr Richard Randull, feodary	1	7	10
Item to him for Coton parsonage	3	6	8
Item to him for <2> acquitances & ingrosing the accompt	0	2	0
Item to Mr James Tooke, feodary, for lande in Middlesex	2	14	6
Item to him for his acquittance vi*d*. ingrossing xii*d*. poundage viii*ob*.	2	2	0
Item my self & hors from Frydaye till Tewsdaye morning, Mr (Tonstal) causing mee staye 2 dayes	0	7	6

125. Whitehall has here erased 'my' and obliterated his original entry after 'Armes'.
126. All Brackenborough tenants, as is Webb in the next entry: see fo. 2v.

Item vi yardes dimi. of grogerom for Mr Rich-			
ard's hosse & dublett at viis. xd.	2	10	11
Item 2 yards quarter Duch jayne for Mr Rich-			
ard's dublett at xiiiid.	0	3	0
Item i yd. Duch bayes for the same	0	1	4
Item i ell canvas for (scrait) lynige	0	1	4
Item ix doson of buttons at iiid. the doson	0	2	3
Item bayes for lynig his hosse iiyd. dimi. at xii		2	6
Item rybben for the knees iiioz quarter at iiiid.	0	1	1
Item vi els of lockeram at iis. iiiid. for Mr Richard	0	14	0
Item i ell cambricke left with Mary Dudley[127] for			
a band for Mr Newdigat	0	6	6
Item ii yd. quarter dimi. blacke & white tufted			
canvas [for] a wastcoot for Mistress Anne	0	4	9
Item for a sadle cloth of blacke valure bought by			
my cosen Rode	1	18	0
Item silke for Mr Richard's dublett	0	1	0
Item <for Mr Newdigate> fyne lockeram at iis.			
ixd.ob. xii ell dimi.	1	14	11ob.
Item my[128] hors att Kinges Arms coming backe			
from London <with iid. to the ostler>	0	1	4
Item <Brackley> my self & hors, breakefast &			
diner	0	1	0
Item Kidney[129] for Mr Richard's things & locker			
from London iis. for my self xiid.	0	2	0
Item for iii showes and iii removes	0	1	1
Item my self & hors at [High] Wickam <1			
night> comming down		2	6
Item at Daintrie comming from Oxford then hors		1	0

Maye the iiii 1619

Item Tom Morton[130], Peter & my self going to			
Gawsworth[131] for you & your sisters, at (Uttox-			
eter)		0	6

127. Mary Dudley, described as 'Mistress Anne's maid', was at Daventry with the Newdigate sisters, 1618–19: WRO, CR136, B601.

128. The next word has been blotted out.

129. A carrier employed regularly to transport goods between London and Coventry. One of his name had been patronised by the Newdigate family since the early years of the century: E.G. Grant, *A Warwickshire Colliery in the 17th Century* (Dugdale Society, Occasional Paper 26, 1979), 60; WRO, CR 136, B595–601. The accountant has presumably made a mistake in this entry, or in the total.

130. A long-standing tenant, and later steward, of the Newdigate family: WRO, CR 136, B602–30 (account books), C887 (lease, 1649).

131. John Newdigate's uncle, Edward Fitton, 1st Bt., died there 10 May: Earwaker, *East Cheshire*, ii, 566.

Item at Lockwood hors vi*d*. maide vi*d*.	0	1	0
Item geven at Gawsworth, cooke[132]		2	0
Item to the butler	0	2	0
Item to the chamberlaine gone to Chester	<your appointment>		
Item G. Cooke, Ouldham & Frances Brookes[133]	0	3	0
Item removing your hors there	0	0	4
Item at Talke for horsmeat by Tom Morton, your ante Lowgher[134] paying for you & the rest		4	6
Item a posset & beare by him for you & the others	0	1	2
Item Stafford dyner, you paying for your antt & all her compenie	0	11	0
Item horsmeate theare	0	1	0
Item geven the pore by Tom Morton by your apoynment			2
Item to Tom Morton spent going to Pearton		0	6
Item to him which he laid forth the last yeare for vi removes vi, for paper ii*d*.		0	8
Item to Auwen dressing your horses and getting the meate when you stayed at Gawsworth	0	3	0
	31	2	0*ob.*
	9	11	1

[*fo.8*]

Maye the xiith 1619

Item at Pearton for ii strike of oates	0	2	6
Item to Crofts fetching them 2 myles of	0	0	3
Item geven you for him at your coming	0	0	4
Item Mottershed dressing your horses		1	6
Item to Kitt for helping him	0	0	6
Item Joane Shawe, butler & washing	0	2	0
Item cooke & chamberlaines there	0	2	0
Item at Hampton with Mistress Levison, wyne & fyshe[135]		1	0
Item going to Oxford with you, Tom Morton, Peter & my self Daintrie, showing	0	2	0
Item our 4 horses there i night	0	2	0
Item to Ed for dressing, byeing haye & provander		1	0

132. Followed by 'butler & chamberlain', crossed out.
133. Laundress to the Newdigates, 1610–20: WRO, CR 136, B595–601.
134. Mary (Fitton) Lougher, sister of Lady Newdigate.
135. This line looks to have been squeezed in at a later date. The Staffs. and Salop family of Leveson were related to the Newdigates through the Fittons, and the kinship tie was actively pursued: Larminie, 'Marriage and the Family', 12–14.

Item geven Bes & Isbell there	o	2	o
Item Brackley diner	o	3	6
Item horsmeat there	o	o	10
Item to Peter upon his bill[136] for 2*yd*. ryben	o	2	o
Item i *yd*. whit cotton for styffeing	o	o	8
Item for whale bonne vi*d*. hookes iiii	o	o	10
Item blacke & browne thred	o	1	4
Item whit threid for Mistress Annes wastcoote			2
Item oringes & lemons	o	1	3
Item for washing Peter's clothes	o	o	3
Item[137] 2 yards iii quarter of Turkie grogeron at v*s*. viii*d*. the yard, which is more then it commeth to	o	15	8
Item for iii quarter of taffatie at x*s*. the yard more also by vi*d*.	o	8	o
Item i*oz* of silke	o	2	6
Item for xii doson of buttons	o	3	o
Item at Plants commying from Pearton, Peter		o	6
Item Oxford horsmeate at Kinges Armes for 4 horses 2 nightes iiii*s*. ostlers iiii*d*.	o	4	4
Item at Daintrie 4 hors one night <commying backe>	o	2	4
Item Mr (Chab) cowtchman for carying Mistress Mary & Mistress Lettice to the church & bringing them home affer supper	o	2	o
Item going to Daintrie with them 4 hors i night & one ii nights after	o	3	6
June the vth	o	3	6
Item going to see gentlemen & gentlewomen my hors 2 nights at Daintrie	o	1	o
Item at Oxforde 2 nights xiiii*d*. <beare iiii*d*.>	o	1	2
Item showing 2 removes ii*d*. to Ed iiii*d*. Jo Poole ii*d*.	o	o	8
Item geven Isbell	o	o	6
Item going to Gawsworth & backe geven & spent <x*s*.>	[*blank*]		
Item commying to Oxford with Sir Ed(ward)[138], my hors Daintrie	o	1	o
Item 2 nights at Oxforde	o	1	2

136. The following indent items are bracketed as Peter's bill.

137. The following word has been blotted out.

138. Probably Sir Edward Fitton, 2nd Bt. (d.1649), the Newdigates' cousin. He matriculated from Trinity Oct. 1619, aged 16, and paid the maximum £5 caution money: Clark, *Reg. Univ. Oxon.*, II, part ii, 377; Trinity MS, 'Liber Trin. Coll. Oxon.'.

Item Daintrie toow nights commying downe	o	I	o
Item spente up & downe	*[blank]*	

< 2 July >

Item to President for Mr Newdigats lodgings for a quarter ending the xviiith of June	I	2	o
Item the Vice President for Mr Newdigate & his brother	2	4	...
Item Mr Newdigate's battles & commons with other dewes	2	17	6
Item Mr Richard's batles & comons[139]	3	8	8

< 12 [July] >

Item going to fetch Mr Newdigate & Mr Richard from Oxford, my self, Tom Morton & 5 hors, baite at Banbury	o	I	11

< 13 [July] >

Item horsmeate at Oxforde	o	3	6
Item to the ostler at Brackley by Thomas Morton	o	o	4
Item horsmeate at Daintrie iiis. vid. Ed for then vid.		4	o
Item geven 2 maides iis. Jo Pole wyping boots iid.		2	2
Item at Coventrie beare iiiid. ostlers iiiid. by Thomas Morton senior[140]	o	o	8

folium 8	14	I	o

[*fo.8v.*]

Item to Peter upon his bill[141] to the landress for washing the quarter ending at mydsomer last		7	6
Item for 2 mapstaves xviiid. a paire of cumpasses iiiid.		I	10
Item 2 *li.* of cheryes vid. mending Mr Newdigate's boots iiid.		o	9
Item carrying 2 hatts for him & Mr Richard from London		I	o
Item a doson & halfe of poynts for Mr Richard		3	9
Item dressing Mr Bewdigate's sorde	o	I	o
Item setting buckles of Mr Richard's gyrdle	o	o	6
Item i *yd.* ryben vid. iyd. fring ixd.	o	I	3
Item quarter *oz.* soing silke viid. a paper booke xd.	o	I	5

139. As is evident from the account, Richard had spent more time in Oxford.
140. Tenant in Griffe, Warws., and probably a cousin of his namesake (fn. 130): WRO, CR 136, C872 (lease, 1627).
141. The following indented items were bought by Peter according to note.

	£	s	d
Item wax i*d*. carrying lettre i*d*. shoting glove vi*d*.		o	8
Item (pindrise) i*d*. oyle of (turmen) ii*d*. bysomes i*d*. ale i*d*.	o	o	5
Item cording your bed ii*d*. inke ii*d*. paper iiii*d*.	o	o	8
Item[142] Tacitus xx*d*.[143] S. Daniel's Histories vi*s*.[144]	o	7	8
Item Kyckerman's Logicke[145] for Mr Newdigate & Mr Richard at ii*s*. a peece	o	4	o
Item strawberies iiii*d*. 4 arowes xv*d*.	o	1	7
Item lost at booles xix*d*.[146] shooting iii*d*.	o	1	18[147]
Item strawberies v*d*. by water twyse Mr Newdigate & Mr Richard x*d*.	o	1	3
Item Mercator xii*s*.[148] Esop's Fables Greek & Laten xii*d*.[149]		13	o
Item dimi. yard popas ii*s*. dimi.*yd*. fustian vi*d*.	o	2	6
Item to a boote man going a fyshing	o	1	6
Item 3 pyes vi*d*. (for) blocking my hatt iiii*d*.	o	o	10
Item i *yd*. fustian xvi*d*. dimi. *oz*. silke xiiii*d*.	o	2	6
Item quarter of thred viii*d*. saten & horne for my braster vi*d*.		1	2
Item i quarter of suger iiii*d*. a lettre carrying ii*d*.	o	o	6
Item buckling my girdle ii*d*. i*li*. of candles iiii*d*.	o	o	6
Item straberyes with Mr Gresley & [Mr] Lister vi*d*.[150]		o	6

142. The following indented items are bracketed in the margin as Mr Newdigate and Mr Richard's bill.

143. Perhaps *The ende of Nero and beginning of Galba. Fower bookes of the Histories of Cornelius Tacitus. The Life of Agricola [trans. and ed. H. Savile]* (Oxford, 1591); for alternatives see: *STC* 23642–6; De Jordy and Fletcher, *Library for Younger Schollers*, 6, 141.

144. S. Daniel, either (i) *The Collection of the historie of England* (1618), *STC* 6248, or (ii) *Civile Wars* (1609), *STC* 6245, or (iii) *First part of the historie of England* (1612), *STC* 6246.

145. B. Keckermann, *Gymnasius Logicum* (1606), *STC*, 14895 – solidly Aristotelian: see Costello, *The Scholastic Curriculum*, 44–5.

146. Betting by undergraduates on sporting activities was forbidden at Trinity: McConica, *Hist. Univ. Oxon*, iii, 651.

147. There seems no adequate explanation for this error.

148. Possibly *Ptolomaei Geographia Grae-Lat: Per G. Mercatorem & P. Montanum* (Amsterdam, 1605), recommended as a geography text book c.1655: De Jordy and Fletcher, *Library for Younger Schollers*, 7, 130. The high cost may indicate that the purchase was an atlas.

149. Aesop, *Fabulae* (1614), *STC*, 173.2 or (1618), 172.4.

150. Thomas Gresley (d.1642), son of George, 1st Bt., of Drakelowe, Derbys., was admitted as a reader to the Bodleian 19 Nov. 1619, with John Newdigate, as a member of Trinity, and had paid caution money there in 1618: Trinity MS, 'Liber Trin. Coll. Oxon.'; Clark, *Reg. Univ. Oxon.*, II, part i, 280; F. Madan comp., *The Gresleys of Drakelowe* (Coll. for a History of Staffs. 2nd ser. i, 1899), 89–90. Like the Newdigates he maintained contact with Gilbert Sheldon after leaving Trinity: G. Wrottesley, 'An

Item one Ed(ward) shilling laid up xii*d*.[151] Aristotle well x*d*.[152]	1	10
Item Fabulous Fundation of the Poopedome[153]	0	6
Item The Maides Tragedie xii*d*.[154] a mappe iiii*s*. vi*d*.	5	6
Item Plinies Naturall Historie in Latten[155]	6	0
Item Urbium Theatrum[156]	0 2	0
Item diner at Brackley commying dowe	0 2	6
Item a playe booke vi*d*. fydlers Daintrie xii*d*.	1	6
Item laid forth which I forgotte to sett downe in my last reconinge	0 11	0
Item to Nicke the apoticary for manus christie[157] & an ellectuary	0 2	6
Item William focet xii*d*. William Wall mending (drum) xii*d*.	0 2	0
Item greene ginger vi*d*. 2 (drum) heades iiii*s*.	0 4	6
Item to William Plumley at Gawsworth to byue a shurt	4	0
Item xvi yards of lace at iiii*d*. for a ruffe	5	4
Item 2 gatherings at Gawsworth	0 1	0
Item geven Ouldham xii*d*. lost at horsrace v*s*. vi*d*.	6	6
Item 1 pair of gloves for my brother xi*d*. inkle i*d*.	1	0
Item a paire of booles (to) ii*s*. vi*d*. lost at bowles ix*d*.	3	3
Item at the communion vi*d*. barber xii*d*.	0 1	6
Item a booe & case iiii*s*. 4 arrowes viii*d*.	0 4	8
Item Camden's Britania ii*s*. vi*d*.[158] 3 Ed(ward) shillings iii*s*.	5	6

Account of the Family of Okeover ...', *Coll. Hist. Staffs.*, 2nd ser. vii, 1904, 106–7. Martin Lister (d.1670), later of Radclive, Bucks., and Thorpe Ernald, Leics., Kt., M.P. for Brackley 1640, who matriculated from Trinity 15 Oct. 1619, aged 17: *Alumni Oxon.*, iii; Clark, *Reg. Univ. Oxon.*, II, part ii, 377; T.D. Whitaker, *The History and Antiquities of the Deanery of Craven* (republished, 2 vols., Manchester and Skipton, 1973), i, 122.

151. Perhaps this, as an example of a debased coin, was a curiosity.
152. A well outside the city, at the entrance to Port Meadow: *VCH Oxon*, iv, 261.
153. R. Bernard, *The fabulous foundation of the popedom* (Oxford, 1619), *STC* 1938, and see also Madan, *Early Oxford Press*, 111.
154. F. Beaumont and J. Fletcher, *The Maides Tragedie* (1619), *STC* 1676–7.
155. Translations were also available, e.g. C. Plinius Secundus, *The [xylographic] historie of the world*, trans. P. Holland (1601), *STC* 20029, 20029.5.
156. Probably A. Romanus, *Theatrum urbium* (Frankfort, 1595), but possibly A. Ortelius, *Theatrum orbis terrarum. The theatre of the whole world*, trans. W. B[ledwell?] (1606), *STC* 18855. Both were geography textbooks: De Jordy and Fletcher *Library for Younger Schollers*, 6, 7, 123, 132; Ker in McConica, *Hist. Univ. Oxon.*, iii, 512.
157. See also above, fo. 5v.
158. Considering that this book was later acquired in Latin (see fo. 10v.), this may be a translation, e.g. that of 1610, *STC* 4510.

Item att cardes		5	o
	6	18	4
	6	19	

[*fo.9*]

July the xxth 1619

Item at Rugbie going to Daintrie for the gentlewomen, yourself, Mr Richard, Ned, Henry & Peter	o	o	8
Item Daintrie hors 7: provander, gras & haye, your mare lying in, & to Ed for dressing hors	o	4	o
Item for Mr Charles' horse one night at Sheafe		[*blank*]	
Item Jo Poole wyping boots	o	o	3
Item geven the 2 maides	o	2	o
Item showing at Daintrie then	o	o	8
Item to Mr Cham(berlaine)[159] his man Smyth fytcheing the blacke mare, wanting a showe	o	o	6
Item to Mistress Mary for her god daughter Walker[160]		o	6
Item Homes his boye bringing iii partrich [from] Ellinor Gee[161]		o	2
Item going toward Sir Charles Gerrard's[162] with you, myself, Ned, Henry & Peter by him at Plants		o	6
Item Colsell[163] the commission for tythes, walking my hors		o	1
Item Blecksich[164] ale	o	o	3
Item Pearton geve cook, butler, chamberlain & horskeeper	o	4	o
Item oates i strike xxd. Tomme iiiid.	o	2	o
Item to Tom more for showes	o	1	o
Item at Stafford beare & cakes	o	o	10
Item at Lockwood geven	o	2	3
Item at Leek with your hostis[165]	o	2	4

159. Probably Richard Chamberlain of Astley Castle, near Arbury: see below, fo. 11.

160. The Walkers were Newdigate tenants: WRO, CR 136, B595–602.

161. Henry Homes and Ellinor Gee were both Newdigate tenants in Chilvers Coton: *ibid.*

162. Kt., of Halsall, Lancs., married (1612) Penelope, daughter of Edward Fitton, 1st Bt.: Earwaker, *East Cheshire*, ii, 566.

163. Coleshill, North Warws.

164. ?Bloxwich, Staffs.

165. Probably the Wedgwoods: see above, fo. 4v.

Item geven at Gawsworth cook, butler & chamberlain	o	3	o
Item at Witch[166] with Sir Ed(ward) & Mistress Brerton[167]	o	1	8
Item geven at Aldforde by your apoyntment	o	4	o
Item provander there by Petter	o	o	10
Item at Chester with Mistress Brerton wyne[168]	o	1	o
Item Tom going before to Holcroft	o	o	6
Item at Warrington with Sir Ed(ward) & Mistress Brerton	o	5	o
Item at Wiggon the howse super & breakfast	o	6	o
Item to the chamber iiid. hors & ostler iiis. iiiid.		3	7
Item for soling your boots by Petter	o	2	o
Item showing white mare Peter	o	o	3
Item to Tomm by him	o	o	5
Item one showe & 2 removes [for] your mare	o	o	6
Item ale going to Ashton for (N mosse) & 3 boyes		o	6
Item showing at Ashton	o	1	o
Item geven at Mr Myderton's cook, butler & chamberlain	o	6	o
Item to him that geve provander there	o	1	o
Item mending sadles there	o	o	3
Item geve Ashton cook, butler, chamberlain & hors keper	o	8	o
Item washing and starching there	o	1	o
Item sterrup xviiid. 2 snafles iiis. webb iis.	o	6	6
Item Preston fidles	o	1	o
Item the howse super & diner for v	o	5	o
Item beare & cakes ixd. chamberlaine iiid.		1	o
Item 2 possets for Peter iiiid. suger iid.	o	o	6
Item hors 4, grasse & haye	o	1	4
Item iii (pound) dimi. oates xxid. ostler iid.	o	1	11
Item Holcroft geven cook, butler, chamberlain vis. (merso & sta[169]) iis.		8	o
Item Gawsworth cook, butler, chamberlain iiis. Ouldham xii[d.] washing xii[d.]	o	5	o
Item smyth vid. Castle ale & cakes xd.	o	1	4
Item pore man cast id. 3 paire gloves Cong(leton) iiis.		3	1

---

166. Perhaps Middlewich, lying almost on a straight line between Gawsworth and Aldford, but Nantwich is also possible.

167. Probably Edward Fitton, 2nd Bt., and his aunt Anne, wife of John Brereton of Brereton: Earwaker, *East Cheshire*, ii, 566.

168. This entry looks as though it was inserted at a later date.

169. Reading uncertain.

Item Utoxsater howse vii*s*. iiii*d*. horsmeate for v, one being my Lady Fytton's[170] iiii*s*. vi*d*.	o	11	10
Item helping Tom order with a botte iii*d*. gyde iii*d*.	o	o	6
folium 09[171]	5	14	6
	5	13	

[*fo.9v.*]

Item to you in part for linstye wolsey, Tomm	o	5	o
Item Northampton baite going to Chichley	o	2	o
Item hors x*d*. to a pore man by your apoyntment ii*d*.		1	o
Item geven the chamberlain setting us the way	o	o	4
Item at Mr Chester's[172]		[*blank*]	
Item Tomme commying from thence	o	o	6
Item to you for Besse Walker's < childes > cristenige[173]	o	5	6
Item to Mistress Letis for the child ii*s*. midwife i*s*.	o	3	o
Item to Mr Skinner < at Erdbury > for a quarter ending at Mychelmas < 1619 >	2	4	o
Item to Mr Newdigate for a bande by Mr Chester his man	o	6	o
Item to Bes Greene[174] for 2 fatt capons [for] Lady Fyton		3	o
Item for eges then xii[*d*.] cheakens viii*d*.	o	1	8
Item iii ell lockeram [for] Mistress Mary at ii*s*. ix*d*. *ob*.	o	8	4
Item[175] by Mr Richard for a paire of gloves for him self		1	2
Item Lucius Florus xviii*d*.[176] dressing his hatt vi*d*.	o	2	o
Item turnig his gowne sleeves vi*d*. pyes for breakfast xii*d*.	o	1	6

170. Either John Newdigate's grandmother, Alice Holcroft, or his aunt, Anne Barret: Earwaker, *East Cheshire*, ii, 566.

171. Preceded by an erased figure.

172. Probably Anthony, 2nd Bt., son of Anthony, Kt. and 1st Bt. (d. 1635). The Chesters of Chicheley, Bucks., were related to John Newdigate through his grandmother Martha Cave: G. Lipscomb, *The History and Antiquities of the County of Buckingham* (4 vols., 1847), iv, 94–8; W. Page ed., *VCH Bucks.*, iv (1927), 312–3.

173. Mary Newdigate was her godmother: see fo. 8v.

174. A John Greene was 'bailiff of husbandry' on the Arbury estate in the 1610s and 1620s: WRO, CR 136, B595 etc.

175. The following indented items were bought by Richard Newdigate according to marginal bracket and note.

176. L.A. Florus, *The Roman histories* (trans. 1619), *STC* 11103.

Item Theophrastus Carectors[177]	o	2	8
Item with his tewtor at Medley[178]	o	o	6
Item to the communion at Whitsontide	o	o	4
Item to the barber at Oxford for trimming him	o	o	6
Item a paper booke vii*d*.[179] to one bringing his garters and stockings from London <vi*d*.>	o	1	1
Item a paire of showes ii*s*. viii*d*. wryting tables viii*d*.	o	3	4
Item my brother & I by water & play (Mr Richard) xx*d*.	o	1	8
Item Livy in 2 volumes v*s*. vi*d*.[180] Godwin's Antiquities ii*s*.[181]	o	7	6
Item Lamdin upon Plautus vi*s*.[182] at Erdbury barbing vi*d*.	o	6	6
Item candles v*d*. inke ii*d*. an howerglas iiii*d*.	o	o	11
Item Salustius iiii*d*.[183] Case his Ethickes xviii*d*.[184]	o	1	10
Item 2 paper bookes viii*d*. a paire of showes ii*s*. viii*d*.	o	3	4
Item Sanderson & Bartho(lemew) Logicke xxii*s*.[185] string (ston) viii*d*.		2	6

177. Possibly I. Casaubon, *Theophrasti Characteres ethici* (1592).

178. A popular eating place, across Port Meadow: *VCH Oxon.*, iv 269.

179. There exist in the youthful hand of Richard Newdigate, two notebooks, one containing the date 1620, the other undated but probably also assignable to this period: WRO, CR 136, A18 and B3468. Contents include (i) Latin syllogisms, extracts from *Euphormes*, a chronological problem from the Old Testament, the dying words of Henry Cuffe (formerly of Trinity, exec. 1601?) and (ii) satirical verse and notes on the use of the perspective glass from M.A. de Dominis, *De radiis visus et lucis in vitris perspectivis et iride tractatus* (Venice, 1611).

180. T. Livius: given that there are two volumes, this looks like a continental edition of his *Romanae historiae* – cf. *STC* 16611.5–16613; de Jordy and Fletcher, *Library for Younger Schollers*, 116.

181. T. Godwin, *Romanae historiae anthologia, an English exposition of the Romane antiquities* (Oxford, 1614), *STC* 11956–7.

182. Probably one of Dionysius Lambinus' editions of T.M. Plautus, the poet recommended in De Jordy and Fletcher, *Library for Younger Schollers*, 8, 127, which cites a Geneva edition of 1622.

183. There were several Latin and English editions of C. Sallustius Crispus' history, *Coniuratio Catalinae, et, Bellum Jugurthinum*, *STC* 21622.2–21627. The low cost may indicate that this was bought second-hand.

184. J. Case, *Speculum moralium quaestorum in universam ethicen Aristotelis* (Oxford, 1585 etc.), *STC* 4759–4760. See also De Jordy and Fletcher, *Library for Younger Schollers*, 2, and McConica, *Hist. Univ. Oxon.*, iii, 714.

185. R. Sanderson, *Logicae artis compendium. In quo universae artis synopsis, breviter proponitur* (Oxford, Jos. Barnesius, 1615), *STC* 21701, or a later edition. See also Madan, *Early Oxford Press*, 104, 110.

Item more candles & a bisom xi*d*. Suetonius xvi*d*.[186]	o	2	3
Item a letre to London i*d*.[187] carriag from thence vi*d*.	o	o	7
Item Senica his Workes[188] by Mr Richard	o	4	6
Mr Richard his bill	**6**	**5**	**o**

4   11

By Peter[189]			
Item at Banbery his hors xii*d*. mending his sadle ix*d*.	o	1	9
Item for his self that night supper & breakfast	o	1	2
Item horsmeat at Oxford xii*d*. carrying 3 letters iii*d*.	o	1	3
Item a paire of showes for Mr Richard ii*s*. viii*d*. a bisom *ob*.		2	8*ob*.
Item iiil*i*. of candles xvi*d*.*ob*.	o	1	4*ob*.
Item i *oz*. soeing silke ii*s*. viii*d*. dimi. *oz*. stiching silke xx*d*.		4	4
Item 5 doson silver & silke buttons	o	2	11
Item dimi. ele of poledavis viii*d*. one quarter <dimi.> threde xi*d*.[190]		1	6
Item hookes & eyes iiii*d*. whalebone & pastbord vi*d*.	o	o	10
Item 3 doson heare buttons for Mr Richard	o	o	6
Item a coller for him	o	2	4
Item dimi. yard taffatie [for] Mr Newdigate	o	5	10
Item half yard of searg xii*d*. i *li*. of shott ii*d*.*ob*.		1	2*ob*.
Item carrying the velvet for a cape from London	o	o	2
Item i *li*. candles v*d*.*ob*. dimi. yard of fustian vii*d*.	o	1	o*ob*.
Item grinding his sheares ii*d*.	o	o	2
Item stuffe to line boothose toppes	o	...	4

186. P. Holland's translation of C. Suetonius Tranquillus, *The historie of twelve caesars* (1606), *STC* 23422–4, was a fine illustrated edition costing more than 1*s*. 4*d*., and thus this looks like a continental edition.

187. During the 'solitary, dull long vacation' Richard wrote from Trinity to his brother in London. Since 'good company [was] exceeding scarce', he should have had plenty of opportunity to read the books he had bought: WRO, CR 136, B338a. Staying up through the summer was evidently a Trinity tradition: O'Day, *Education and Society*, 113.

188. L.A. Seneca, *The workes of Lucius Annaeus Seneca, both morall and naturall* (1614), *STC* 22213.

189. The following indented items were all bought by Peter, according to marginal note.

190. Both 'xi' and the figure in the pence column have been blotted.

	o	i	3
Item half *oz*. of silke	o	i	3
Item binding 2 bookes	o	o	8
Item by Mr Richard going a fishing ii*s*. to the communion ii*d*.	o	2	2
Item by him to Mr Newdigate (of cosen W(hite hall)[191] his iii*li*.	o	7	o

	2	o	6
Some of this side is –8 –5 –6 and	6	5	is
	8	5	6

[*fo.10*]

October 1619

Imprimis to my cosen Rode upon his bill for things sent downe by him[192]: a bever hat for Mr Newdigate	i	12	o
Item i *yd*. iii quarters blacke velvett	2	o	o
Item 4 doson dimi. of saten lace	i	10	o
Item a hatt for Sir C(harles) G(erard)[193]	o	9	6
Item 6 yards dimi. of paragon at viii*s*.	2	12	o
Item for vi*yd*. of russett bayes	o	14	6
Item xxi ells dimi. of holland < for the gentlewomen > at ii*s*. vi*d*.	2	13	9
Item 3 doson of buttons & loopes	o	10	o
Item an imbrodered gyrdle	o	03	6
Item a boxe for Sir C(harles') hatt	o	o	6
Item an ell canvas to packe the things	o	i	i
Item ii ells holland [for] Mistress Anne, quisions	o	7	4
Item i cambricke [for the] gentlewomen	o	5	6
Item a paire of worsted stockings for Mr Richard by my cosen Rode	o	6	8
Item a paire of taffatie garters	o	8	o
Item a hatt for Mr Richard	o	10	o
Item Simachas Epistles[194] for him	o	4	o
Item 3 duble bands & cufts for him	o	10	o
Item a box for the bands & cufts	o	o	4
Item paid Mr Edward Fyton for a half yeares consieracon of 150*li*.	7	10	o

191. Since the expenses appear to have been incurred at Oxford, it seems likely that this is either James Whitehall of Christ Church or Robert Whitehall, Vicar of St Mary Magdalen.

192. According to a note further down the page, the following items were all purchased by Rode.

193. See above, note 162.

194. ?Q.A. Symmachus, *Epistolae*.

< 22 –8 –8
my cosen Rode >

October 12th going to Oxforde: Sir Edward
[Fitton][195], Mr Newdigate, Richard Ware, 2
men & myself

Item at Sowtham diner	0	1	6
Item ostler walking horses there	0	0	3
Item Banbury super & breakfast	0	10	6
Item to the President for chambers	1	2	0
< the quarter ending at Mychellmas 1619 >			
Item Oxford 4 hors: haye ii*s.* provander iii*s.* iiii*d.*	0	5	4
Item ostler for 7 hors	0	0	4
Item at Straitford upon Haven coming downe			
my hors and self	0	4	0
< 2 –7–11 >			
Item at Straitford going up to London	0	5	6
Item Oxford my hors 2 nights, haye	0	1	0
Item provander, 2 pecks dimi. at vii*d.*	0	1	8
Item removing 4 showes iiii*d.* ostler ii*d.*	0	0	6
Item beare at [High] Wickam	0	0	2
Item Uxridig my hors & self	0	3	6
Item supper the first night London	0	1	0
Item Oxford carryer carring a box < with wry-			
tings in >	0	1	0
Item supper there (Sundaie) night	0	1	0
Item diner & super with Baldwen Fryday	0	2	0
Item to Mr Briscowe of Lincoln's Inne[196] for his			
opinion	0	11	0
Item 3 paire of showes [for the] gentlewomen	0	7	0
Item a letre by Kidney	0	0	1
folium 10	26	12	0

< 22 –8 8   10   9
   1   7 11

   1–15 –5

25–12 –0 >

---

195. Sir Edward matriculated 15 Oct.: Clark, *Reg. Univ. Oxon.*, II, part ii, 377.
196. Probably John Briscoe of Herts., admitted 1594 and Reader 1622/3: *The Records
of the Honorable Society of Lincoln's Inn: Admissions 1420–1799* (1896).

[*fo.10v.*]

Item an imbrathered gyrdle for Mr Richard	0	3	0
Item a paire of stockings for him	0	6	0
Item a saten hatbande	0	1	6
Item a paire of gantlet gloves	0	0	10
Item for Mr Newdigate to gyve to the college a saltt iii*li*. x*s*. vi*d*., settings ar(gent) & ingra(ving) xviii*d*.[197]	3	12	0
Item a paire of silke stockins	1	13	0
Item a paire of worsted for him	0	9	0
Item Camden's Britania in Latten[198]	1	0	0
Item juice of licorice v*oz*., whereof 2*oz*. was paid for before at viii*d*.	0	2	0
Item x yards lace to edg garters	0	2	8
Item paper xx queares, whereof half to Oxford, the other for Erdbury	0	4	6
Item lute strings for Mr Newdigate & sisters		5	0
Item dying Mr Newdigate his silke stockings for Mistress Lettis	0	1	4
Item by Mr Richard[199] a loade of woode	0	12	8
Item to the landres for Mr Richard till Mychellmas		3	0
Item delivered to my brother <by Mr Richard>	1	4	0
Item for Senica his Tragedies[200]		0	6
Item Petronius vi*d*.[201] candles ii*s*.	0	2	6
Item a paper booke	0	1	...
Item binding 2 books for Mr Newdigate & Mr Richard		0	9
Item Laborels Logicke[202]	0	4	0

197. Under the presidency of Ralph Kettell, every commoner at Trinity was expected to contribute 20s. towards the plate fund. This sum was, however, excused those wealthier students who gave a piece of plate engraved with their name and arms: Blakiston, *Trinity College*, 106.
198. W. Camden, *Britannia sive florentissimonium Legnorum, Angliae, Scotiae, Hiberniae chorographia descriptio* (1586 etc.), *STC* 4503–4508.
199. According to bracket, the following indented items were bought by Richard Newdigate.
200. L.A. Seneca, *Seneca his tenne tragedies* (1581 etc.), *STC* 22221.
201. A continental edition: see R.H. MacDonald ed., *The Library of Drummond of Hawthornden*, 108 and no. 564.
202. ?Jacobus Zabarell, *Opera logica cum praefatione. Jo. Lud. Hawenreuten* (Cologne, 1597): De Jordy and Fletcher, *Library for Younger Schollers*, 1, 149; Ker in McConica, *Hist. Univ. Oxon.*, ii, 508.

Item David's Captreus[203]	0	0	10
Item 2 letters to London	0	0	2
Item Quintillian[204]	0	4	0
Item going a burding with my brother		0	7
<Received by Mr Richard ii*li*. Disbursed ii*li*. xiiii*s*. Remaining with him vi*s*. >[205]			
Item to Mr Randle for the rent to Coton parsonag, half ending at Mychellmas	3	6	8
<Mychellmas 1619>			
Item for Erdbury land	1	7	10
Item for 2 acquittances	0	1	8
Item to Mr Tooke for Middlesex rent	2	14	8
Item for ingrosing the acommpts	0	1	0
Item poundage vi*d*. acquittance vi*d*.		1	0
Item to Mr Rawlens in part for proving my Ladies will[206]	1	10	0
Item to Mr William Wright counsceler[207]		10	0
Item a paire of French bodies [for] Mistresses Lettice & Anne		9	0
Item a quarter of stuffe [for] Letis' quissions	0	2	8
Item vi*oz*. blacke Naples silke	0	12	0
Item half firken of soope	0	8	0
Item xii*li*. whit starch iii*s*. blewe vi*d*.	0	3	6
Item a drying pott	0	1	8
Item pines for [the] gentlewomen	0	2	3
Item my diner 2 dayes where my hors stoode		1	3
Item at Wiyte Hors, Holborne my hors	0	11	0
Item at [High] Wickam my hors & self	0	3	5
Item at my cosen Rode's geve 2 cheldron		10	0
Item 2 maids ii*s*. 2 men ii*s*. the boye vi*d*.		4	6
Item my cosen Parson's[208] man for my hors i night	0	0	4

203. It has not proved possible to identify this either among lists of books or of pictures.

204. Unspecified editions of Quintillian were recommended among 'oratores such as ... will well become your library': De Jordy and Fletcher, *Library for Younger Schollers*, 7, and see also McConica, *Hist. Univ. Oxon.*, iii, 702.

205. Rendered as an extensive marginal note.

206. Three lawyers of this name may have been currently at the Inner Temple: W.H. Cooke ed., *Students Admitted to the Inner Temple, 1571–1625* (1877). The will was proved in 1619: PRO, PROB 11 (106 Parker).

207. Probably William Wright of Tratforde, Northampton, barrister 1595 and Bencher 1611: *Master of the Bench of the Honorable Society of the Inner Temple* (1883, not published), 25.

208. From the context this is almost certainly William Hollins B.D. of Swerford: see above, fo. 4.

Item at Swarvard by hors & self on night	1	3
	23 18	6
	10 13	

[*fo.11*]

Mychellmas 1619

Imprimis for Mr Newdigat's comons paid Mr Brooke for a quarter ending at Michaellmas	3	17	4
Item for Mr Richard a quarter then ending	3	13	9
<7–10–10>			
Item x*yd*. dimi. silver & silke lace for your cloake by Peter[209] Item for dressing your cloake	0	2	0
Item[210] carrying a lettre to London	0	0	1
Item dimi. pound of candles	0	0	2*ob*.
Item to the landresse for a quarter	0	12	0
Item to Jo Mychell	0	0	6
Item carrying your satten & other things	0	0	8
Item for Mr Richard his dublett, i ell canvas	0	1	6
Item dimi. ell poledavis viii*d*. i*yd*. cotton viii*d*.	0	1	4
Item whale bonne iiii*d*. pastbord i*d*. thred iiii*d*.	0	0	8
<December the 6>			
Item going to Oxford, frosting at Long (F...)[211]	0	0	1
Item Warwicke a coller for your horse	0	1	6
Item raine & headstale for Mr Richard	0	1	6
Item Straitford my supper, breakfast & hors	0	5	0
Item frosting iiii*d*. Shepston [upon Stour] spent iii*d*.	0	0	7
Item Oxford my hors 2 nights	0	2	4
Item ostler ii*d*. frosting ii*d*.	0	0	4
Item Daintrie my hors <& Edward> xx*d*. maides xii*d*.	0	2	8
Item frosting there	0	0	2
<December>			
Item vampoting Mr Richard's bootes by him there	0	3	0
Item neats foot oyle for them & my brother's[212]	0	0	2
Item to Mr Newdigate by Mr Richard [at] Oxforde	0	0	10

209. The following indented items were bought by Peter according to marginal note and bracket.

210. Followed by 'di.' [i.e. dimi.] erased.

211. Long Itchington, Warws., lies near the route, but this does not appear to be what is meant.

212. Mr Newdigate is probably meant.

Item lost at cardes by Mr Richard <at Astley[213]>	o	1	6
Item to the fewellors there	o	o	6
January the 4 1619			
Item at Hampton (by Peter[214]) supper & breakfast at the Cocke	o	11	o
Item horsmeate there by him, & ostler	o	o	6
Item to the offysers at Mr Lowgher's by Peter	o	8	6
Item to Mr Newdigate there	o	15	o
Item a paire of showes for Tomme	o	2	o
Item to Mr Tong's man bringing a bottell of sacke from his mistress	o	o	6
Item to the Frenchman to stop his bawling	o	8	o
December xxviiith			
Item geven at Astley cook, butler & chamberlain	o	6	o
Item to Mr Newdigat there	o	10	o
January the viii geven at Astley to the cooke, butler & chamberlaine	o	3	o
Item to Dalton & Grundie by Mr Newdigate's apoyntment		2	o
Item to Mr Newdigate at tables there	o	2	o
Item to him that found your cloake	o	9	o
Item to Mr Newdigate at tables with R. Holl.[215]	o	5	o
Item more at cardes at Granborow[216]	o	5	o
Item geven in the howse staying there 2 nights, cooke, butler, chamberlain & stable	o	6	...
Item for wyping bootes < Mr Higenson with us >	o	o	4
folium 11	16	1	6ob.
9			

[*fo.11v.*]

Item Daintrie haye & ostler, litell Tomm fynding provander	o	3	o

213. Home of the Newdigates' near neighbours, the Chamberlains, with whom they were staying over Christmas and New Year: *VCH Warws.*, iv, 211.

214. The following indented items were bought by Peter according to marginal note and bracket.

215. It is impossible to expand this abbreviation with certainty since members of the Hollins, Hollinshed and Holland families were all numbered in the Newdigate circle.

216. Grandborough, Warws., home of Mary Newdigate's prospective husband, Edmund Bolton (b. 1595), grandson of Edmund Knightley, esq.: WRO, DR 111/1 (Grandborough parish register); O. Barron ed., *Northamptonshire Families* (VCH Genealogical Vol., 1906), 183–4.

Item 2 maides, Edward & Jo Poole	0	3	3
Item geven George Smyth's maid bringing a cake	0	0	3
Item 2 nights at Astle with ould Mr Bolton[217] geven there	0	3	...
Item to Mistress Marie then	0	10	0
Item to Mr Newdigate going to Astley in the holloe way neare the pinfoulde	0	5	0
Item geve Georg at Astley setting hors	0	0	6
Item a loyne of veale when your brother Bolton was heare	0	1	0
Item geven at Astley when your brother Bolton & your sister went thence[218], cook, butler & chamberlain	0	3	0
Item Sara for washing and making the gentlewomen's fyers & Georg setting hors	0	2	0
Item geven at Granberow in the howse when you brought your sister home	0	12	0
Item to the fidler there by you	0	1	0
Item to Mistress Lettis vs. Mistress Anne iis. vid.	0	7	6
Item by Mr Richard for Mr Newdigate his commons & batles the quarter ending at St Thomas daye 1619	6	9	9ob.
Item for Mr Richard's that quarter	4	13	10ob.
Item to Mr President for chambers, studies & [blank]	1	2	0
Item to theire tutor	2	4	0
Item[219] by Mr Richard to Mr Newdigate at Pearton	0	0	6
Item a remove of his mare id. the barber vid.	0	0	7
Item <Richard> to Thomas, Mr Wedgwood's man, by him	0	0	6
<February xxviii 1619>			
Item to Mistress Anne, which she gave to Mistress Sugborowe's[220] maide bringing her fysicke	0	5	0

217. Probably Laurence Bolton of Grandborough, Edmund's father: *ibid*.

218. Edmund Bolton and Mary Newdigate were married, probably at Astley, 2 Feb. 1620: WRO, CR 136, C2724 (settlement). The first indenture of settlement is dated as late as 20 June 1620; payment of the dowry was also postponed until the summer: see below, fo. 13.

219. The preceding 4 entries have been crossed out. They duplicate entries under Dec. 1619 (fo. 11) beginning 'vampoting Mr Richard's bootes'.

220. Neighbours of the Boltons and Knightleys, the Shuckburghs had land in Shuckborough and Napton, Warws., and Farthington and Farthinghoe, Northants, and married into a number of families with whom the Newdigates also had connections – Skeffington, Holt, Sneyd: see Baker, *Hist. and Antiquities of Northants.*, i, 371–3; W.

<28 [February]>
Item geven at Granborow, cook, butler,
   chamberlain & stable   0   4   ...
<29 [February]>
Item at Brackley the howse by Mr Newdigate
   <with 2 Mr Books>   0   6   0
Item horse there, 3 one night iiii*s*. ostler iii*d*.   0   4   3
<March 1>
Item Bister diner: Mr Newdigate, my self, Peter
   & boye   0   1   6
<2 [March]>
Item 2 suppers & breakfasts by Mr Newdigate,
   & Wensday   0   14   6
Item horsmeat & ostler those 2 nights   0   8   8
Item a juge of beare at race[221] for Mr Newdigate   0   0   3
<3 [March]>
Item Thorsday night supper & breakfast with Mr
   Vines,[222] you paing for all   0   8   3
Item horses iiii*s*. ostler iiii*d*.   0   4   4
Item Banbery the howse ix*s*. vi*d*. hors iiii*s*.   0   13   6
Item Southam diner xviii*d*. walking hors iii*d*.   0   1   9
Item to Tomme by Mr Newdigate vi*d*. Mr
   Moyles[223] man vi*d*.   1   0
Item geven at Mr Higenson's, the maides   0   2   0
Item to Mistress Lettis there   0   1   0
Item vi yards of lace for Mistress Anne at iii*d*.   0   1   6

                            21   1   7/0
                            8   10

[*fo.12*]
                March the xxiii 1619
Item[224] horsmeat at Cocke (standing by bottle)
   Peter   0   5   0

Dugdale, *The Antiquities of Warwickshire* (1730, republished in 2 vols., Manchester), i, 309.
  221. Probably a horse-race, John Newdigate's favourite recreation, judging by letters from Gilbert Sheldon (WRO, CR 136, B475 and B481) and account books (e.g. B608, entries for 6 Dec. 1624, 6 Mar. 1625, 27 Mar. 1625).
  222. Richard Vines, later schoolmaster at Hinckley, Rector of Weddington and Caldecot, and lecturer at Nuneaton: *DNB*; *VCH Warws.*, iv, 179.
  223. Henry and Robert Mayle were contemporaries of the Newdigates at Trinity, but there is nothing to connect them with the S.E. Warws./N. Oxon. area; William Moyle, created M.A. Nov. 1620, was probably from Oxon.: Trinity MS, 'Liber Trin. Coll. Oxon.'; *Alumni Oxon.*, ii.
  224. The first entry has been crossed out: 'to Mr Lowgher for consideracon over and above the x*li*. at London November last 4 –0 –0'.

Item by Tomm at Laverne, provander & ostler	o	6	9
Item cook, butler, chamberlain iii*s*. washing vi*d*. wyping boots ii*d*.		3	8
Item comming backe Thorsday night, hors by Tomm	o	2	6
Item the yong greae mare at Crowne one night	o	1	4
Aprill the 17 going toward Oxford Mr Newdigate, my self, Plumley & the boye/1620			
Imprimis at Daintrie Ned setting up hors & geving them meate		o	8
Item geven at Grandberow lying there 2 nights, cook, butler, chamberlain & stable		4	o
Item geven Mistress Anne then	o	2	o
Item for Mr Richard's batles quarter ending Lady Day	2	2	9
Item to the President for the chambers that quarter	1	2	o
Item horsmeat at Kinges Armes, 5 one night & myne one night more, haye at viii*d*. provander at viii*d*. ostler iii*d*.	o	8	3
Item lying at Mr Baldwen's, geven his 3 children	o	1	6
Item to his man & 2 maides	o	1	6
Item joyce of licorise io*z*.	o	o	8
Item my hors Holborne one night … ostler & c …[225]		1	6
Item St Albons my self & hors, Saresons Head	o	2	2
Item baite at Toster, Blannes	o	o	10
Item to the bursers (by Mr Richard) for Mr Newdigate his battles & comons for somme smale tyme before his comming downe at Christmas after that quarter ending at St Thomas daye 1619 & this ending at our Lady Day 1620[226]	o	17	6
Item to Mr Skinner for a quarter ending at our Lady [Day] 1620, for Mr Richard only, Mr Newdigate being that quarter in the country	1	2	o
Item laid forth by Mr Richard[227], a paire of showes	o	2	8

225. Both sums have been erased.
226. As is evident from the entries for the previous 3 months, in this quarter John had been away visiting in Warws., Northants and Staffs.
227. The following indented items were bought by Richard Newdigate, according to marginal bracket.

Item for lynig a paire of stockings by him	o	o	2
Item a commbe vi*d.* a pie ii*d.*	o	o	8
Item inke ii*d.* Hic Meinlier et Haec Mulier vi*d.*[228]	o	o	8
Item a paire of batledores vi*d.* a kye for the chamber vi*d.*	o	1	o
Item when Mr Richard answered: to the beadle[229]	o	1	o
Item wyne then in the Scholes	o	5	o
Item Aulius Gelli et Noctes Attice[230]		[*blank*]	
Item 2 pies iiii*d.* a letter to London i*d.*	o	o	5
Item K [*blank*]			
Item hard wax iii*d.* to the landress	o	2	3
Item Markames Booke of Horsmanship[231]	o	o	10
Item another paire of showes	o	2	8
Item [*blank*] baites & going a fishing	o	1	4
Item a pie ii*d.* mending my showes ii*d.*	o	o	4
Item dressing my hatt; i*li.* candles v*d.*	o	o	11
Item Laborels Phisicke[232]	o	2	6
Item exameninge morning[233]	o	2	2
Item to the communion ii*d.* barber vi*d.*	o	o	8
Item Juelles Apoligie[234] & [*blank*]	o	1	4
Item a picke hooke for my brother Bolton: by Mr Richard	o	o	3

228. *Hic mulier; or, The Man-woman: being a medicine to cure the staggers in the masculine-feminine of our times* (1620), *STC* 13374–13375.5, a pamphlet attacking the fashions currently adopted by some women. Extracts are printed and discussed in K. Usher Henderson and B.F. McManus, *Half Humankind: Contexts and Texts of the Controversy about Women in England, 1540–1640* (Urbana and Chicago, 1985), esp. 264–276.

229. Payment to the faculty beadle was for summoning to participate in disputations. The fact that Richard was actively involved in his second year rather than, according to normal practice, in his third, suggests that he had made substantial progress with his studies since coming to Oxford: Fletcher in McConica, *Hist. Univ. Oxon.*, iii, 165–8; O'Day, *Education and Society*, 111. Formal exercises and celebrations surrounding them could constitute a considerable expense: J.M. Fletcher and C.A. Upton, 'Expenses at admission and determination in 15th century Oxford: New evidence', *EHR*, c (1985), 331–6.

230. Aulus Gellius, *Attic Nights* was read by Simonds D'Ewes when he was studying ethics and moral philosophy with Richard Holdsworth at Cambridge at the same period: O'Day, *Education and Society*, 114. See also: Ker in McConica, *Hist. Univ. Oxon*, iii, 510; MacDonald, *Library of Drummond of Hawthornden*, 120 and no.499.

231. G. Markham, *Cavelrice or the English horseman* (1607 etc.), *STC* 17334–5, although other works by this author also deal with horsemanship.

232. ?A work by J. Zabarella: *cf.* Ker in McConica, *Hist. Univ. Oxon*, iii, 508.

233. Possibly an examination taken within the college: *ibid.*, 65.

234. J. Jewel, *Apologia Ecclesiae Anglicanae* (1562 etc.), *STC* 14581–6 or translation (1564 etc.), *STC* 14590–2.

Item by my cosen Rode November xvith 1619 to Mr Rawlens for my Lady's will[235] over and above the xxx*s*. which I gave him in parte[236]	2	10	2
Item 2 yards 3 quarters of carsie for Mr Newdigat	0	17	6
Item 2 yards dimi. of saten for him	1	15	2
Item ii*yd*. dimi. bayes	0	3	6
Item i ell canvis xviii*d*. v *yd*. dimi. whit homes vi*s*. v*d*.	0	7	11
Item December iiiith (asholer) velvett <dying>	0	4	2
Item dying a paire of stockinges	0	0	4
Item 2 books for Mr Richard by my cosen Rode	0	5	4
Item 9 ell dawlis for 3 shirts for him	1	2	6
Item a sadle covered with whit cotten with a cotten cloth & all furniture to ytt	0	14	0
[*fo.*] 12	16	14	2
	8	19	

[*fo.12v.*]

Maye 1620

Item paid Mr Edward Fytton (by my cosen Rode) for consideracon of 150*li*., half yeare then endinge	7	10	0
Item for 2 paire of Spanish lether showes for Mistress Lettice & Mistress Anne	0	4	7
Item one ell cambricke for Mr Newdigate	0	6	0
Item 2*yd*. pagon for Mr[237] Richarde	0	9	4
Item a paper book for Mistress Lettis of Hollande	0	2	8
Item to Tom Hammond carrying Lettis in his cowtch to the Lady Pagett[238] at Westmester	0	1	0
Item ryben for Mistress Letis	0	1	6
Item yarde 3 quarter pagon for Mr Newdigate	0	8	0
Item iii quarters of taffatie to lyne theire dublets	0	9	0
Item iii doson silver & silke buttons ii*s*. viii*d*. silke iii quarter of an *oz*. ii*s*. silke & silver lace iiii*oz*. quarter xii*s*. iiii*d*.	0	17	0

235. Following word crossed out.
236. See fo. 10v.
237. Followed by 'Newdigate', crossed out.
238. Lettice, wife of William, 4th Baron Paget of Beaudesert, Staffs., and daughter of Henry Knollys of Kingsbury, Warws.. Related to John Newdigate through their Cave ancestors, she had been a close friend and legatee of his parents and was possibly godmother to Lettice Newdigate: WRO, CR 136, B421, C1913–5; *VCH Warws.*, iv, 105, 166; S. Shaw, *The History and Antiquities of Staffordshire* (2 vols., 1798–1801), i, 216, 220.

Item v yards white jeane for lyniges	o	4	7
Item 2 ell canvis	o	I	I I
Item lace buttoms & silke for Mr Richard	o	8	o
Item a handle for his sorde	o	4	o
Item io*z*. lacoryse for Mr Newdigate <perfumed>	o	I	o
Item ii *yd*. tamett to sleeve Mistress Lettis' & Mistress Anne's gownes	o	4	o
Item a paire of stockings for Mr Richard	o	8	o
Item a paire for Mistress Anne	o	5	6
Item xvi yards of stuffe dimi. for Mistress Letis to make her a gowne	6	3	o
Item taffatie iii quarter of the elne	o	10	o
Item silke & silver lace v doson iii quarter at iiii*s*. iiii*d*.	I	4	6
Item to Lettis to paye for making it up and other things she should want	5	o	o
Item 2 doson ryben poynts for Mr Richard		[*blank*]	
Item a booke for Mistress Anne <lute booke>	o	I	8
Item lute stringes for her	o	2	o
Item to Mr Vines the fie for Mr Sheldon's buck[239]		I I	o
Item to Thomas Hammond carrying Lettis in his lady's cowtche to Sir John Tonstale and his ladie at Charing Crosse, & the daye after meeting them with her in St (James's)	o	I	o
Item my self & graye mare to London being forth a three weeks iii*li*. <& above>	I	10	o
Item to Mr Thomas Crewe[240] having his opinion upon the books, Sir Francis Gofton cleaming a harryot after the death of your uncle[241]—also for the stray beasts and other thinges	I	2	o
Item to Mr Randle for a yeares rent of Coton parsonage to the king, the half <yeare> my Lady dying in not being paid for till now	6	13	4
Item to him for Warwickshire lande	I	7	10

239. Probably Gilbert Sheldon. The entry here may relate to his gaining his M.A. in May or June 1620.

240. Thomas Crewe (1565–1634), of Gray's Inn and Stene, Northants.. His services had been retained by the Newdigates for some time, and ties between the two families subsequently deepened through personal friendship and godparenthood: *DNB*; WRO, CR 136, B53, B522 and B828; Larminie, 'Lifestyle and Attitudes', 170, 227, 421.

241. This may have arisen from the fact that Edward Fitton, 1st Bt. (d.1619), had been named with his sister in deeds relating to her dower property, Nuneaton Rectory: WRO, CR 136, C670a and C1054–9. See also above, fo. 3.

Item for 3 acquittances for those 3 half yeares rents	0	2	0
Item to Mr Tooke for Middlesex rentt	2	14	8
Item for ingrosing the acommpt	0	1	0
Item poundage for exhibition & acquittance	0	1	0
Item geven Mistress Anne, which she had laid forth at Granborowe, as I came downe	0	5	0
	39	17	1
	9	7	

[*fo.13*]

June the xvith 1620[242], going to London about your sister's business with Mr Bolton

Imprimis to Mr Bolton in part of your sister's portion[243]	500	…	…
Imprimis Daintrie going toward London my self & hors (Chester)	0	2	6
Item Brackley baite with Mr Savage	0	1	0
Item Oxforde my hors one night	0	1	4
Item Thorsdaye before midsomer diner at Whit Horse, Holborne <June 23rd>	0	1	0
Item to Mr Wright perusing & mending the books by Mr Bolton to your sister	0	11	0
Item to his man for wryting that which he added to the books	0	2	0
Item to Mr Georg Crowke[244] for his opinion upon the books	1	2	0
Item Fryday by water with Lettis to my Lady			

242. The preceding 5 entries, headed 'July the xiith 1620 to Oxford', have been crossed out. They correspond almost exactly with the first 4 and the 6th entry on fo. 13v., except that the hostelry at Daventry is specified to be Hilton's, and the Daventry maids are given 1s. instead of Isbell's 6d.

243. According to the terms of her father's will, the full dowry was £1,000; this instalment was probably paid on the day the first indentures of settlement were signed, WRO, CR 136, C2724. The parties and witnesses on this occasion were Laurence and Anne Bolton (the bridegroom's parents), Edmund Bolton, Thomas Ratton of Grandborough, Sir Seymour Knightley of Norton, John and Richard Newdigate, and William Whitehall.

244. George Croke (c.1560–1642) of the Inner Temple, law reporter and later justice of King's Bench: *DNB*. Related to the Newdigates through the Cave family, he and his brothers gave them legal advice on several occasions, and obtained John Newdigate's special admittance to the Temple: e.g. WRO, CR 136, B518; below, part ii.

Pagett & Lady Graye[245]	o	o	6
Item to Robert Higenson[246] <alowed back in payment> for a scarf [for] Mr Newdigate		12	o
Item for entring your name & brother's in the stewar's booke at Graies Inne[247]	o	5	6
Item Nic Beale for Mr Richard's hat & bande	o	16	6
Item a dressing for Mistress Anne	o	1	8
Item to Mr Goodman for the dedimus to take the fine at Mr Bolton's[248]	o	13	4
Item to Mr Holbache for the copie of the avowrie versus Swane[249]	o	4	o
Item for making bonds & covenant bonds for the monie I tooke upp	o	2	2
Item 2 doson ryben poynts for Mr Newdigate by my cosen Rode	o	6	6
Item iyd. holland [for] Mr Richard for hand-carchiefs	o	3	o
Item iyd. holland for boothose for him	o	2	6
Item by water with Mistress Lettis to Detford[250] July the threird 1620, the 3rd 1620 and for carring her trunke	o	3	6

July 1620

<3 [July]>

Item to Mistress Ginner[251] with Mistress Lettis	1	2	o
Item to Henry Thornton for packing & carrying things to Bosworth	o	o	6
Item my nag at Whit Hors xiii nights	o	11	8
Item chamberlaine & Ostler Whit Hors	o	1	o

245. Probably Elizabeth, widow of Sir John Grey (of Groby), and daughter of Edward Neville, Lord Abergavenny. Although she remarried (1614) John Bingley, she retained her previous style in her frequent communications with the Newdigates. She was godmother to Mary. *DNB*; WRO, CR 136, 166–181 (letters to Anne and to John).

246. A draper or haberdasher regularly patronised by the Newdigates, e.g. see above, fo. 11v. and below, part ii, fos. 6v., 8v.

247. John and Richard were formally admitted 3 July 1620: J. Foster ed., *Register of Admissions to Gray's Inn 1521–1889* (1889), 160.

248. Several Goodman's were currently members of the Inner Temple or Gray's Inn: *ibid.*; Cooke, *Students admitted to the Inner Temple*. A *dedimus postestatem* was an enabling writ giving power of attorney: W. Rastell, *Les termes de la Ley* (1624), 126; E. Jowitt ed., *The Dictionary of English Law* (2 vols., 1959), i, 591.

249. Probably Roger Holbeck of Westhall, Suffolk, admitted to the Inner Temple 1596, called to the bar 1606 (*ibid.*), although it could have been one of the Holbechs of Fllongley, near Arbury (*VCH Warws.*, iv, 72). Avowry: see *The Dictionary of English Law*, i, 189.

250. A fashionable place for the new ladies' academies: D. Gardiner, *English Girlhood at School* (1929), 209. Lettice was to stay there a year: see below, part ii.

251. Lettice's schoolmistress or hostess at Deptford.

Item Oxford my nage 2 nights & parson's man one[252]		3	0
Item to Mr President for chambers, quarter ending at midsomer 1620 xxii*s.* Mr Skinner ii*li.* iiii*s.*	3	6	0
Item Mr Newdigate commons & batles that quarter	5	8	0
Item Mr Richard commons & batles then ending	4	16	3

	521	0	3
follium 13: summa 521 –0 –5	7	6	

[*fo.13v.*]

July the xiith 1620, comming up to you at Oxford with my hors

Imprimis at Granborowe to Mistress Anne, havig laid forth most of it for things she wanted		10	0
Item 4 hors at Hilton's & the ostler	0	4	10
Item geven at Mr Salter's to Isbell	0	0	6
Item a scabbord & dressing your sorde	0	3	0
Item horsmeat at Oxford, Chester with you vii dayes & nights and 4 one night at viii*d.* haye & viii*d.* provander & ostler	0	14	0
Item a paire of spurres for Mr Richard	0	2	0
Item to Mr Richard to paye for his boots & <other things>	0	11	0
Item horsmeat at Wickham	0	5	0
Item super & breakfast there by Petter	0	7	4
Item Blacke Swanne, Holborne, supper & breakfast	0	8	6
Item horsmeat there	0	6	8
Item ostler & bringing our horses to Burgeses in Flyt Street	0	0	6
Item to my cosen Rode for a doson napkins for Mistress Lettis going to Detford	0	9	6
Item holland for socks for her	0	1	6
Item making 4 paire of socks for her	0	0	4
Item 2 paire of linnen stocking for Tomm	0	1	8
Item to Burges for a paire of boots <Mr Newdigate>	0	10	0
Item to Roceter teaching Mistress Letis upon lewte		15	0

252. The parson was probably either Robert Whitehall or William Hollins: see above.

Item mending Mistress Bolton's watch	o	5	o
Item seeing Mistress Lettis, walking hors	o	o	2
Item 2 yards dimitie [for] Mistress Anne	o	4	4
Item commyng to London, Mr Rawle[253] with you, supper & diner Whit Hors, Fleet Streete	o	14	6
Item horsmeat viiis. showing iiiid.	o	8	4
Item chamberlaine & ostler	o	1	o
Item at Lambeth by water	o	1	o
Item to Mary washing at Ashteed[254]	o	1	o
Item a paire of pumpes for Tomme	o	1	4
Item[255] by Peter 2yd. dimi. of silke grogerom at xiiis. the yard	1	12	6
Item ell quarter dimi. quarter of taffatie at xiiis.	o	14	6
Item 1oz. licoryse viiid. washing Tom's clothes iiiid.		o	11
Item to the offisers at Casholton by Peter	o	5	6
Item by him at Mr Newdigat's[256]	o	6	o
Item a paire of boothose	o	4	6
Item hemmyng Mr Richard his bootes	o	o	3
Item a cloake bag vs. vid. 1yd. riben iid.	o	5	8
Item Beckansfyld beare	o	o	5
Item Wickham the howse	o	5	10
Item chamberlaine	o	o	6
Item horsmeat, ostler & nayling	o	5	6
Item mending a sadle vid. mending (my) boots id.	o	o	7
Item Oxford diner iiiis. iiiid. hors then iis.	o	6	4
Item Brackley xiis. hors & ostler vis.	o	18	o
	12	19	6
		14	

[fo.14]

Item[257] Midleton Stonie for ale by Peter	o	o	3
Item showing at Ashteet by him	o	2	5
Item to Draper by my master his apoyntment	o	o	6

253. Probably Rawleigh Newdigate of London, cousin and trustee of Sir John Newdigate and legatee and 'brother' of Lady Newdigate: WRO, CR 136, C828a and C1915. There is no mention of him either in the acrimonious property wrangles between Sir John and Henry Newdigate or in family pedigrees, and neither his will nor his place of residence have come to light.

254. Home of Henry Newdigate: see above, fo. 3.

255. The following indented items were bought by Peter according to marginal bracket.

256. i.e. Mr Henry Newdigate.

These indented items are a continuation of Peter's bill on the previous page.

Item drinke for Tomm commyng from London		I
Item to you by Petter at [*blank*]	I	o	o
Item carying a hatt & bands from London		o	8
Item carying 2 hatbands backe	o	o	4
Item 2 yards ryben [for] Mr Newdigate his hose	o	I	o
Item dimi. queare paper	o	o	2
Item silvering gyrdle buckles	o	o	4
Item mending lute iiii*d.* carrying a letter i*d.*		o	5
Item to Mr Newdigat	o	o	8
Item binding 2 bookes	o	I	6
Item i*yd.* riben [for] Mr Richard's hosse	o	I	2
Item a paire of pantafles [for] Mr Richard	o	2	4
Item mending my master's showes	o	o	2
Item 1 pottle clarett, 1 quart sacke when Sir Henry Willoughby[258] suped with you	o	2	4
Item ii*li.* cheryes iiii*d.* candles ii*d.*	o	o	6
Item 2 paire of boote hosse	o	5	o
Item 2*yd.* riben [for] Mr Newdigate's scarffe	o	I	o
Item to Petter for the half year ending at our Lady's Daye 1620 which he said was behind of his wages		10	o
Item geven Galing for the lute	o	7	o
Item geve at Granborowe commong downe from Oxforde	o	4	o
Item at Mr Lowgher's	o	2	o
Item[259] by Peter going up with Mistress Anne, diner at Stockenchurch	o	2	3
Item ale at Beckansfeild	o	o	3
Item ale at Wickham	o	o	4
Item 4 paire of gloves for you	o	7	o
Item a band for Tomm	o	I	o
Item lut stringes	o	I	o
Item when Peter went to London for the lute, horsmeat that night		I	4
Item to the ostler	o	o	2
Item his supper that night	o	o	6
Item to the sadler's boye bringing snafles to you at Ashteed	o	o	4
Item a quart of wine Rick(mansworth) with Kelly	o	I	o
Item a remove at Dunstable	o	o	I
Item to a poore Cheshire man	o	o	2

258. Of Risley, Warws., Bt., husband of Elizabeth Knollys, sister of Lady Paget: *VCH Warws.*, iv, 105, 166; Dugdale, *History and Antquities of Warws.*, 870, 1060.
259. The following items were bought by Peter according to marginal note.

Item to Tomm at Perton	0	1	0
Item to the officers at Perton	0	4	0
Item peares commying from Perton	0	0	3
Item setting up the horses at Coventrie, you at the ordinarie	0	0	2
Item fine dowlis or lockerom at ii*s*. ix*d.ob*. xii ell for 3 sherts & boothose	1	7	11
	5	12	7
	3	9	

[*fo.14v.*]

August the xiiiith 1620

Item to Mr Bolton for Mistress Ann's table[260]	6	0	0
Item to Mr Goodman for the indentures consernig your sister Mary	2	10	0
Item geven mottle[261] & 2 maides	0	3	0
Item to Mary Dudley for making your ba...	0	1	0
Item bait at Dedington iii*s*. walking hors ii*d*.	0	3	2
Item Oxford supper & mornig	0	6	0
Item hors vi*s*. the ostler vi*d*.	0	6	6
Item sadler x*d*. a pore man i*d*.	0	0	11
Item baite at Stokenchurch	0	2	3
Item horsmeate there	0	1	6
Item beare at Wickham iiii*d*. Beckhansfeild iii*d*.	0	0	7
Item left with Mr Richard at Oxford	0	10	0
Item Uxbrig the howse (Webbes) by William Plumley	0	11	11
Item chamberlains vi*d*. maide iiii*d*.	0	0	10
Item horsmeat v*s*. iiii*d*. ostler v*d*. pillion i*d*.	0	5	10
Item ostler for Rodes iii*d*.	0	0	3
Item Kingston [upon Thames] wine & beare xviii*d*. ostler ii*d*.	0	1	8
Item a girdler by Peter xiii*s*. vi*d*. spurlethers iiii*d*.	0	13	9
Item Peter's hors at London vi*d*. feryman by him iii*d*.	0	0	9
Item a remove at Casholton i*d*. Epsom 5 removes v*d*.	0	0	6
Item to Tom to byue him pumpes	0	1	6
Item a paten showe [for] graye mare	0	0	10
Item Tom showing gray mare iiii*d*. geven Ashteed	0	4	6

260. Apparently considered too young at twelve to be sent away to school with Lettice, Anne seems to have lived with Mary after her marriage.
261. i.e. a fool?

Item to the farryer, Croydon [for] gray mare	o	2	6
Item the charges of measuring the land at Brackenborowes with the plot thereof	2	18	10
Item to Tomm Draper to fetch things at Letherheade	o	1	o
Item treakle for Mistress Lettis vi*d*. carrying a letter to Ginner xii*d*.	o	1	6
Item left with Mistress Anne v*s*. geven Wat, Mr Newdigate's man, ii*s*.	o	7	o
Item Harfeild beare [for] Tomm ii*d*. Sheule Inne vi*d*. Toster ii*d*.[262]	o	o	10
Item Dunchurch supper vi*s*. vi*d*. maide iiii*d*.	o	6	10
Item horsmeat & ostler	o	5	8
Item geven at Hopes Harboure by William Plumley	o	4	o
Item a showe for bald gelding iiii*d*. sorrell iiii*d*.	o	o	8
Item geven at Pearton with your sister Bolton by William Plumley	o	4	o
Item setting on a show, graye hors i*d*. Jackson for fruit sent from [Nun]Eaton xvi*d*. Merryes boy[263] for bringing (cheryes) vi*d*.	o	1	11
Item September 2: geven at Granborowe	o	3	6
Item to the teler for mending Mistress Ann's clothes	o	2	6
Item geven you to pay William Hill for raines & hed(stales)	o	3	o
Item going with you to Mr Lowgher's October 27 at Plants vi*d*. oweing by Tom there vi*d*.	o	1	o
Item geven at Pearton : (James), 2 maids & Mottershed	o	4	o
Item Kit helping about hors iiii*d*. wyping boots iii*d*.	o	o	7
Item 2 collers by Petter at Hampton	o	2	4
	17	18	11
	7	17	

[*fo.15*]
Received of Mr Shalcrosse to be disbursed for his

262. i.e. Towcester, Northants.

263. Whitehall acknowledged in his will 'the great pains and care taken in my business' by his servant, Richard Merrie: PRO, PROB 11/173, fo. 23.

sonne Edward at Trinitie Colledg in Oxforde 1619[264]

	£	s	d
Imprimis received at his going up	5	0	0
Item more of Mr Shalcrosse September 1619 the some of	6	...	...
Item June the xiith 1620 by my brother	6	...	...
Item received by Mr Richard Maye 1619	3	0	0
Item more by him March xiiii 1619	6	0	0
<6 –0 –0>			
For books, a trunke & divers other things bought by Mr Richard for him	1	4	10
Whereof the bursers for his cawsion monie which he is to have when he leaveth the howse[265]	2	0	0
Item geven to the Scholes[266]	0	2	6
Item to the bursers for his batles & comons till Fryday before Midsomer the quarter then ending	2	13	4
Item to his teutor for that tyme[267]	0	11	0
Item to the President [for] chamber & studie[268]		3	4
Item left with Ned Shalcrosse for his use till Mychellmas, coming downe at Acte[269]	2	4	0
Item to them then for plate monie[270]	0	13	4
Item to Ned October the xiiii	0	11	0
Item more at my commying from London November the viiith 1619	0	10	0
Item sent him up by Peter Ollif November the xxiith 1619	0	10	0
<2 –5 –4>			
Item to Vice President quarter ending at Mychellmas for reading to him	0	11	0

264. Edward Shalcrosse of Cheshire, gent., matriculated from Trinity 15 Oct. 1619, aged 17. His connection with the Newdigates is obscure, but he may have been a member of the family of Shalcrosse, Derbys., who had ties with the Wedgwoods of Leek: *Alumni Oxon.*, iv; W.H. Shawcrosse, 'The Owners of Shallcross', *Journal of the Derbyshire Archaeological and Natural History Society*, xxviii (1906), esp. 90, 99, 105.

265. Entered up in college accounts in 1619–20, this was returned during 1620–21: Trinity MS, 'Liber Trin. Coll. Oxon.'

266. One eighth of the sum given by the Newdigates the previous autumn: see above, fo. iv.

267. A student of Skinner's like the Newdigates (see below), but paying half the rate (*cf.* fo. 4).

268. *Cf.* payment for the Newdigates and their servants of £1 2s.

269. i.e. the Monday following 7 July, when M.A.s were formally taken: Fletcher in McConica, *Hist. Univ. Oxon.*, iii, 197.

270. Only 2/3 of the statutory amount (*cf.* fo. 10v. above), another indication of Shalcrosse's inferior social status.

Item to Mr President for his chamber	o	3	4
Item for his comons & batles the quarter ending at St Thomas daye 1619	3	13	11*ob.*
Item to Mr President for his chamber	o	3	4
Item to Mr Skinner his tutor	o	11	o
Item to his landres by Mr Richard whereof vi*d.* was for the quarter before	o	3	6
Item to him by Mr Richard in March 1619		10	o
Item to the landres for the quarter ending at our Lady [Day] 1620		3	o
Item Ned Shalcrosse commons & batles the quarter ending at our Lady Daye 1620	3	8	7
Item to the President for his chamber	o	3	4
Item Mr Skinner his teutor	o	11	o
Item geve to Ned by me then	o	10	o

July 1620

Item for his comons, batles & other dewes to the bursers the quarter ending at Mydsomer last	3	8	9
Item to the President for chambers & studie	o	3	4
Item to his teutor Mr Skinner	o	11	o
Item left with him for necessaries till Mychallmas	1	o	o

< 5 –2 –o*ob.* >		17	10*ob.*

PART II: INNER TEMPLE

[*fo.1*]

Disbursed: November the xiiiith 1620, from Erdbury to Surrey

	£	s	d
Imprimis at Mr Bolton's[1] to Sim walking and setting up horsses			6
Item vi hors at Mr Hilton's[2] one nighte		8	—
Item paid for Mr Higenson's[3] by Tome		1	4
Item at Mr Salter's[4] to Metle & Besse		2	—
Item to Ed vi*d*. Jo Pole wyping bootes iii*d*.			9
Item to the Presidente[5] for your chamber a quarter	01	2	—
Item to Mr Skinner your tewtor	02	4	—
Item Mr Newdigate commons & batles	2	19	1
Item for Mr Richard, quarter ending at Mychellmas	03	1	6
Item Mr Richard from Mychellmas to the 17th November	2	7	7
Item Brackley wine, beare & cakes by William Plumley[6]	0	1	6
Item Oxford supper & breakfast by him	0	17	3
Item to the maid vi*d*. hors & ostler viii*s*. x*d*.	0	9	4
Item wyping boots ii*d*. a show gray nage <iiii*d*.>	0	0	6
<18 [November]>			
Item at Wickham supper & breakfast	0	18	0
Item hors, ostler mending male (pillion) & chamberlain		8	—
Item musicke there by William Plumley	0	2	—
Item a tasker dressing[7] your horses the first night Ashteed[8]			3
Item going to London: Lambeth ferry by you, Peter[9] & my self sacke & cake		1	2
Item supper Lambeth vi*s*. chamberlain iiii*d*. by water to London vi*d*.		6	10

1. At Grandborough: see part i, fn. 216.
2. At Daventry: see i, fn. 110.
3. Much patronised Daventry glovers: see i, fos. 11v., 13 and below.
4. See i, fn. 69.
5. To President Ralph Kettell of Trinity College for the quarter ending at Michaelmas 1620.
6. Butler to the Newdigates: see i, fn. 81.
7. Repeated.
8. Home of Henry Newdigate: see i, fn. 254.
9. Peter Olyff, John Newdigate's manservant.

Item			
Item iii hors one night iiis. ostler iiid.	0	3	3
Item a show [for] Mr Newdigate's chesnut iiiid.			
a remove id.			5
Item diner at Castle, Paternoster Roe		7	0
Item by water from (Lambeth), against wind & tyde	0	0	8
Item a paire of gloves [for] Mistress Anne		1	–
Item Tom going dowe with horses		4	–
Item to Mistress Giner[10] for a quarter ending the 3 of October for Mistress Lettis	5	10	–
Item to my cosen Thickens[11] for consideracon of a 100li. from Midsomer to Mychellmas after viiili.	2	–	–
Item by water from Lambeth to the Temple			6
Item supper at Meeter with Mr Holt[12]		9	8
Item to you xs. with Sir H. Snell.[13] [and] Mr Richard vs.		15	0
Item by water to Detford you, Mr (Holt) & Mr Richard		4	–
Item making Mr Richard's cloake		6	–
Item riben for your hosse iiiyd.		1	–
Item a quarter oz. carnacon silke [for] bease petticoats			9
Item a paire stockings for Tom – carsie			
Item saten list [for] Mr Newdigate, 2 yards			4
Item Mr Holbeach[14] upon his bill versus Swan		11	6
Item 4 doson riben poynts [for] you & Mr Richard		6	6
Item 1 skyne yellow silke [for] Mistress Ane			6
Item 3yd. riben [for] Mr Richard's hose xiid.		1	0
Item 4 doson buttons [for] Mr Newdigate		1	0
Item William Plumley supper, you suping Sir H.S.			8
Item[15] a corrycommb & brush for your hors		3	4

10. Lettice Newdigate's hostess/schoolmistress at Deptford: see i, fn. 251.

11. Ralph Thickens of Thickness or Whitechapel: see i, fn. 84.

12. Edward Holt(e), son of Sir Thomas of Aston, Warws., admitted to the Inner Temple 1618: Cooke, *Students Admitted to the Inner Temple*, 222. A letter from Robert Skinner (Aug. 1620) indicates that John Newdigate had already arranged to share his chamber: WRO, CR 136, B419.

13. ?Sir Henry Snelgrove, kt. 1617: Shaw, *Knights of England*, ii, 165.

14. Of the Inner Temple: see i, fn. 249.

15. The following indented items were bought by William Plumley according to marginal note and bracket.

Item a locke [for] stable x*d*. 2 knots & strings viii*d*.		1	6
Item a paire of showes Tom ii*s*. to him bald (gelding) & sad x*d*.		2	10
Item 3 hors at (Lambeth) 2 nights, 3 half pecks (provander) & ostler		5	3
Item beare & manchet when you alighted there			3
Item geven at Mr Rode's[16] Mr Richard & I lying there 4 nights, a boy wyping boots & maid		1	0
Item carring Mistress An's trunke from Granborow	0	4	9
folium 1	27	17	9
	10	14	

[*fo.1v.*]

Item for Mr Richard his admyssion Grayes Inne[17]	04	00	00
Item he & I bound in x*li*. to the steward for which[18]		1	–
Item carrying things from Oxford to London don	2	0	4
Item to the Temple & 2 men caring them up in the chamber		1	10
Item a doson hooks & eyes for you by Tome	0	–	3
Item to you by Tom from London to Ashteed	1	–	–
Item the half quarter's rent of your chamber att Oxford by Mr Skinner to Mr Sheldon & Mr Newdigate[19]		11	0
Item to Mr Tooke Middlsex rent dew to the king at Mychellmas last 1620[20], acquittance & ingrossing accompt	2	6	–
Item making Mistress Lettis' gowne to Mr Carter, and for things as he found to itt	1	–	–
Item to Mr Holt, your uncles dynig at your chamber	0	10	–
Item to Mr Edward Fytton[21] half yeare consideracon of a hundreth poundes	5	–	–

16. Thomas Rode: see i, fn. 34.

17. The standard payment for the general admission to Gray's Inn: Prest, *Inns of Court*, 38–9. Richard and his brother had been formally admitted in July 1620: see i, fn. 247.

18. i.e. caution money. 'Which' is followed by an obscure figure.

19. ?Remitted to John Newdigate, in the presence of his friend, graduate member Gilbert Sheldon, because he had not remained in residence throughout the summer and autumn.

20. See i, fn. 39.

21. See i, fn. 48.

Item making your cloth gyrdle to Allen		1	4
Item for Mistress Anes physicke to Burges[22]	0	9	0
Item my hors & Peter's i night in Sowthwark		1	6
Item 6yd.[23] 3 quarters dimi. of Spanish cloth at xiiis. for cloake, dublet, hose, boothose, sadle & gloves	4	16	3
Item 4 yd. bayes at iiis. vid.	0	14	0
Item 2yd. blacke cloth – cloake for Mr Newdigate	2	–	–
Item 2 yards <dimi.> blacke cloth – cloake for Mr Richard at xiiis. iiiid.	1	13	4
Item 4yd. (black) bayes at iiis. vid. for Mr Richard		14	–
Item 6yd. stamell shag bayes at 4s. [for] Mistresses Lettis & Anne	1	4	–
Item removing your hors at Cashoulton with you			6
Item Austen dressing your horses that night	0	–	6
Item to Tomme for locks & kyes stable &		1	4
Item when you went from Ashteed to the Temple to Mary for washing		1	–
<December 4>			
Item Lambeth, by water my hors & I to Westminster			3
Item to one walking my hors, going to Mr Richard for kyes			1
Item Peter's supper & myne that night		1	0
Item Dashfeild for your admittance & bond[24]		5	–
Item to the Temple butles[25] for you by Mr Holt		8	–
Item sending downe a lettre by Kidney[26]			2
Item to his porter bring letters & Mr (Gressle's[27]) sadle			3
Item a paire of showes Mistress Lettis		1	10
Item Tolley at the 2 Wrastlers in Watling Street for your bedsteed, which he sayth he will gyve the monie for again[28]		14	–
Item kyrten rodds 2s. 8d. iiii cuppes iis.		4	8

22. ?Of Fleet Street: cf. i, fo. 13v.

23. 'di[mi.]' deleted.

24. John Newdigate was not formally admitted to the Inner Temple until 28 Jan.: see below, fo. 5.

25. Unclear whether 'batles' or 'butlers' intended.

26. London-Coventry carrier: see i, fn. 129. Followed by 'bring Mr G. sad[le]' deleted.

27. Probably Thomas Gresley of Trinity College: see i, fn. 150.

28. 12s. repaid on its return: see below, fo. 18. Inn recorded in C.L. Kingsford ed., *Stow's Survey of London* (2 vols., Oxford, 1971), i, 150, 170.

Item buckerem for teaster & making		5	0
Item a cord & setting it upp		1	4
Item the porter for carying itt			8
Item to Tolleyes man cording & setting up			4
Item William Plumley & my self supper		1	0
Item a paire of broune boots and galoshes for Mr Richard		8	0
< 11 [December] >			
Item Peter's supper & myne		1	–
Item to watter and backe to Detford to Griffen the water man		3	6
< 13th >			
Item William Plumley & myne diners & suppers 2 dayes		4	0
< 14 >			
Item carrying your peece & map up		1	–
	31	8	3
		8	

[*fo.2*]			
Item one *oz.* joyce of licorice for you		0	8
< 15 [December] >			
Item my hors in Holborne 6 nights, hay, provander & ostler		5	0
Item going to Brackenborowes[29], Mr Richard & I breakfast x*d*. chamberlain, I lying there ii*d*.		1	–
Item at Mr Baldwen's[30] lying there, geven to his children & servants for my self & hors		3	–
Item a paire of spurs for your uncle Newdigate[31]		2	–
Item a collered hat & your cap to Mr Beale	1	–	–
< 16 >			
Item William Plumley's supper & myne		1	–
< 17 >			
Item my supper			6
< 18 >			
Item by water to Detford for Mistress Lettis to London & so to Ashteed with your ant		3	4
< By water Mistress Ashton's			4 >
Item to Mr Richard to by him boots		11	0
Item diner in your chamber with your sister		3	3

29. Newdigate's Middlesex estate: see i, fo.2v.
30. Tenant: see *ibid.*
31. Probably Henry Newdigate of Ashtead.

Item a pie for your ant & sister Anne comying		
hongrie to London from Ashteed	1	6
Item a quart claret, your ant's lodging, supper		6
Item a jugg of beare from Pawles[32]		2
< 20 >		
Item a bushell of oysters for breakfast	1	0
Item 2 leges of mutton v*s*. a rabet xvi*d*.	6	4
Item Chester[33] 4 nights at Whitte Hors	2	10
Item bald gelding in London 2 nights then	1	6
Item my supper that night		6
Item a paire of perfumed gloves for you to gyve		
your Ant Newdigate	1	10
Item a paire for Mr Richard to gyve her	1	0
Item a dosen of silke poynts for your sisters to		
gyve your uncle at New Yeares Daye	4	0
Item dying & mending Mistress An's fan	1	0
Item to Mr Coles for the privie seale[34] & for him		
which went with it to get sealed	7	6
< 22 >		
Item my supper that night		6
Item to Mr Granger's dawghter waying the *cli*.		
from Mr Chester, most of it in gold[35]	1	—
Item 2*oz*. of licorice for you	1	4
Item Markham's Booke of Horsmanship[36]	3	10
Item geven Roben the chamber keeper for you	2	—
Item to him for fagotts & candles	1	—
Item to him for dressing Tomes hatt	0	6
Item to my cosen Rode upon his bill[37] 2*yds*. dimi.		
of spottett shag at 3*s*. 8*d*. lyned	9	2
Item 2*yds*. dimi. of Duch bayes at xvi*d*.	3	4
Item 2 ell dimi. of canvas [for] William Plumley		
cassock	3	4
Item i ell canvas for Mr Newdigate's suit at xviii*d*.	1	6
Item dimi. yard poledavis for the same		5
Item 3*yds*. dimi. at xiii*d*. of whit homes	4	1

32. Probably the tavern, brewhouse and bakehouse 'The Paul's Head', near the cathedral: *Stow's Survey*, ii, 12, 14, 17, 359.

33. A horse.

34. Humphrey Colles, feodary of Warws.: Bell, *Court of Wards*, 40, 43.

35. A. Heal comp., *The London Goldsmiths 1200–1800* (Cambridge, 1935), 162, 157, records Thomas Grainger, pawnbroker, 1711–20, but the nearest contemporary entry is Philip Gardiner, goldsmith, c.1624. Chester: see i, fn. 172.

36. A copy had been bought a few months previously: see i, fo. 12.

37. Although not stated in the text, it is clear that this and the succeeding 8 items form part of one bill from Rode.

Item one ell holland at ii*s*. viii*d*. [for] Mr Richard's boot(hose)	2	8
Item for letters brought to my cosen Rode by <porters>		6
Item i yard crimson saye [for the] gentlewomen's petticoats	2	0
Item[38] i ell dimi. of cambricke for Mr Newdigate's ruffe	11	—
Item 2*yds*. cloth for horsclothes at ix*d*.	1	6
Item William Plumley hors & self Lambeth ferry		2
Item a linke from Whithale ii*d*. fagots xii*d*.	1	2
Item candles vi*d*. by water to a play vi*d*.	1	—
Item William Plumley for 3 meales	1	6
Item walnuts by him	0	2

folium 2	6	14	5
	5	13	

[*fo.2v.*]

Item[39] 2 trunks for you & Mr Richard	1	1	—
Item a porter bringing them to the Temple			8
Item carrying Mr Richard's to Grayes Inn filled with thinges			8
Item[40] by William Plumley <to Mr Richard>		5	—
Item by William Plumley 5 meales & Tom one		3	0
Item a paire of spurrs by William Plumley at Poules		1	2
<19[th December]>			
Item Mr Richard, William Plumley & Tom diner		1	6
Item William Plumley & Tom supper		1	0
Item the gonesmyth mending your peece		2	6
Item for mending the bridge of the lute			4
Item scowring the blanquets		2	—
Item i ell holland: handcarchers for Mr Newdigate		4	—
Item ell dimi. cambricke: ruffe for Mr Richard		8	—
Item i yard bayes for a sadlecloth [for] Mr Newdigate		3	4

38. The following indented items were bought by William Plumley, according to marginal note and bracket.

39. This continues from Plumley's bill on the previous side.

40. Followed by 'to Mr' deleted.

Item 1 doson dimi. <lace> for itt and the
    sadle   4   4
Item dimi. *oz.* silke for it   1   2
Item lutte strings & catlings   6   6
Item English catlings   0   10
Item i yard linen cloth to line the sadlecloth   9
Item by Peter[41] the pore at Oxford comming
    thence   4
Item xi doson lace for Mr Newdigate his suit
    xviii*oz.* iii quarter at iii*s.* iii*d. oz.*   2 2   3
Item 3*oz.* dimi. styching & sowing silke   7   7
Item vi*yds.* binding lace [for] gentlewomen's
    bease peticoats   2   6
Item 2 ell of riben to bind them   8
Item dimi. *oz.* silver for Mistress Anne   2   9
Item i ell scarlet bayes for Mr Newdigate's
    dublet   5   0
Item a hatband for Mr Richard of Mr Beale   1   6
Item dimi. ell taffatie for Mr Newdigate's
    dublet   6   8
Item whale bone for it iii*d.* 3 quarter (b. & b.
    the others) 23*d.*   2   3
Item whit thread for Mr Richard's boothosse   6
Item Peter's supper that night at London   6
Item his hors 2 nights at Lambeth   1   4
Item removing his hors Peter   4
Item pastborde ii*d.* Thephilus[42] 8 dayes iiii*s.* 4   2
Item *oz.* licorice viii*d.* a paire of sheares 16*d.* 2 0
Item a paire of pumpes for Tome by Peter   1   6
Item by water from Lambeth to Temple, you
    & Peter   6
Item Peter's diner & supper upon Sondaye   1   0
Item for him self & (Ed. H.) by your apoynt-
    ment   1   0
Item a paire of seasers   4
Item a paire of galloshes of Burges – Peter   2   6
Item a quarter silver [for] Mistress Lettis   1   4
Item 5 yard dimi. of broad cloth for livery
    cloakes [for] Peter & William Plumley at xi*s.*
    iiii*d.* a yard   3 2   4
Item 3 yards of bayes at ii*s.* ii*d.*   6   6

41. The following indented items were bought by Peter, according to marginal note
and bracket.
42. ?A tailor.

	£	s	d
Item silke & lace for them	o	16	6
Item Peter to the ostler, White Hors, for sorell			4
Item Peter diner going from London			6
Item geven to the taberer by your apoyntment <Peter>		1	–
Item to Simons for worke 2 dayes		1	o
Item mending your boots by Peter			3
Item i quarter taunie silke for Mistress Lettis' gowne			6
Item by water to Lambeth for my hors there			9
Item to Tomme going downe to Erdbury	o	2	6
Item for hemmyng Mr Newdigate's ruffe			8
Item sadler of Ewall[43] stuffing & mending 3 sadles, for strapes, & making cheares with web & nales	o	2	6
	12	11	7
	7	19	

[*fo.3*]

	£	s	d
Item to Sir John Tonstal[44] his man setting up hors			6
Item to Francis, your uncle's cooke, by your apoyntment		2	–
Item the sadler covering your cloth sadle		3	–
Item to him for styching silke 7d. stuffing pomell vid.		1	1
Item lether to lyne the sadle 3d. iii webbes xiiiid.		1	6
Item a paire of new panels [for] livery sadle		2	o
Item a paire of sterup lethers for the ould sadle xiid. but bating vid. at all for them, but			6
Item to you for Christmas, Mr Gardner his man		1	–
Item a showe, bald gelding			4
Item 2 queares paper vid. a lettre downe by Kidney			8
Item (black) saten for your dublett	1	12	6
Item holland & cambricke cuffts & stocks for you		4	6
Item sope dimi. firken for Mistress Newdigate[45], your clothes wash		7	6
Item carrying it to my cosen Rode's			3
Item starch for you theare		4	o
Item my hors 2 nights in London iis. iiiid. ostler iid.		2	6

43. Surrey.
44. Friend and protector of the Newdigates: see i, fn. 77.
45. Probably Mary, wife of Henry Newdigate of Ashtead.

Item 4 new showe for him at Hackney	1	5
Item geven cosen Thickens' man lying there 2 nights		6
Item 3*oz.* of lace [for] Mr Richard's cloake 7*s.* 3*d.* silk xix	8	10
Item to my cosen Holme[46] for consideracon of 150*li.* for 6 monthes ending at Christmas last	7 10	0
Item by Peter[47] for one yard quarter (black) cloth for your hose	1 10	0
Item on yard bayes for lynig for them	1	6
Item dimi. ell & nayle taffatie for your dublet	8	–
Item 3 quarter & naile velvet for your cloake cape	6	8
Item 2*yd.* 3 quarter Turkie grogeron at 5*s.* 6*d.*, dublet [for] Mr Richard	15	1
Item deverta to lyne the skyrts	1	3
Item pinking Mr Newdigate's saten suite	4	6
Item drawing the cloake	1	6
Item wax candle for searing	0	4
Item Peter's dyete byuing theise things	1	0
< his hors 2 nights >	1	4
Item crossing water [at] Lambeth him self & hors twyse		4
Item blacke & browne thred	1	3
Item russet silke [for] Mr Newdigate	2	2
Item hooks & eyes for Mistress Lettis' gowne		2
Item Peter going & commyng by water when he went with Mr Richard after Christmas[48]		8
Item setting up horsses Sowthworke then		6
Item a jugge of beare then		2
Item 2 yards of lomeworke [for] Mistress Lettis' ruf	2	4
Item 1 doson hooks & eyes [for] Mr Newdigat's hose (same)		3
Item to Mr Midlemore[49] for half the chambers		

46. Married to a niece of William Whitehall, Ralph Holme or Hulme, clothworker, was a legatee of Whitehall and an executor for Thomas Rode: PRO, PROB 11/165, fo. 18 and 11/173, fo. 23; *Register P.C.C. Scrope*, 28.

47. Subsequent indented items bought by Peter, according to marginal note and bracket.

48. i.e. Back to Gray's Inn from Surrey.

49. Robert Middlemore of King's Norton, Worcs., admitted 1588: *Students Admitted to the Inner Temple*, 120.

	£	s	d
& studies (with Mr Holte) which were Mr Attornies[50]	60	0	0
< this lx*li.* was received backe by Thomas Morton[51] & paid to Mr Newdygate >	75	03	6

Disbursed in this as herby apeareth in the 5 severall leafe sides [of the] Surrey booke from the xiiiith of November 1620 to January xxvith 1620

	£	s	d
Folium 1 Imprimis the first side of the first leaf	27	17	9
item upon the other side	31	8	3
Folium 2 Item	06	14	5
Item one the other side	12	11	7
Folium 3 Item being this lead side	75	3	6
Sum total of this side is	153	15	6

v somes before

Folium 3

[*fos. 3v., 4 and 4v. blank*]

[*fo.5*]

January the xxvith 1620: Mr Newdigate
1   commyng from Ashteed to the Temple

	£	s	d
Imprimis paide to Mr Richard Randle the king's rent of Coton parsonage half yeare ending at Mychellmas last[52]	3	6	8
Item wardship lande half then ending	1	7	9
Item to him for his 2 acquittances	0	1	2
Item a doson hooks & eyes for Mr Richard	0	0	3
Item geven to Mr Richard the 26th	0	5	0
Item a lyne & coler for the byche	0	1	4
Item to Tom setting up my hors ii*d.* drinke i*d.* past bord i*d.*			4
Item for < our parte of > dimi. hundred billetts & fagotts dimi. hundred	0	5	0
Item to Burges for a paire of galosshes	0	2	6
Item my diner 26 of January	0	0	6

50. Probably those of the new Attorney General, Sir Thomas Coventry, who established his seat in Warws. not far from Arbury, and who (1622) employed Gilbert Sheldon as his chaplain. His predecessor, Sir Henry Yelverton, was a member of Gray's Inn. See: *DNB*; *Masters of the Bench of the Inner Temple*, 24.

51. Newdigate steward: see i, fn. 130.

52. See i, fo. 3.

\<Sondaye 27\>			
Item William Plumley & I diner and supper		2	0
\<28\>			
Item his diner & myne upon Mondaye	0	1	0
Item to Mr Chomley[53] for the[54] informacon against Swanes & Rogers	1	2	0
Item to him for an injunction to remove it from common lawe	0	10	0
\<29\>			
Item sending a letter to William Henshawe[55]	0	0	2
Item my diner vi*d.* William Plumley & I supper xii*d.*		1	6
Item to you going to see the king goe to (Parliament)[56]		10	0
Item to Robin for beare & manchet for you		0	6
Item to him for mending the \<fether\> bedd \<& covering\>	0	0	4
Item Mr Chomle his man for the infomacon \<drawing & ingrosing\>	0	10	0
Item Sir James Leay[57] for his hand to it		10	0
Item to his man for getting it		1	0
Item to Picarell the atornie[58] his fee	0	3	4
\<30\>			
Item William's diner & supper & myne	0	2	0
\<31\>			
Item William & my self diner	0	1	0
February			
\<2\>			
Item to Mr Pawle Crowke for Mr Newdigat's speciall admittance[59]	6	13	4
Item my supper	0	0	6

53. Nicholas Chomley of the Inner Temple, barrister 1592 and bencher 1607; *Students Admitted to the Inner Temple*, 109.

54. Followed by 'reply' deleted. Lawsuit see i, fo. 13 and below.

55. Whitehall's nephew, in charge of the day-to-day running of the Arbury estate: WRO, CR 136, B600–25 (account books), B326a (Thomas Henshawe to Whitehall).

56. A session began 30 Jan. 1620/1.

57. Attorney of the Court of Wards: see i, fn. 44.

58. Probably John Pickarell of Norfolk: Bell, *Court of Wards*, 97; *The Records of the Honourable Society of Lincoln's Inn* (2 vols., 1896), i, 161.

59. Paul Ambrose Croke (d. 1631), younger brother of George (see i, fn. 244), obtained in respect of his Reading a special admittance for John Newdigate at a parliament of 28 Jan. 1621: F.A. Inderwick ed., *A Calendar of Inner Temple Records* (3 vols., 1896–1936), ii, 123. See also: *Masters of the Bench of the Inner Temple*, 20; A. Croke, *The Genealogical History of the Croke Family* (1823), 628–9.

Item to Mr Windover[60] drawing an order for an injunction to staye proceedings at common lawe	0	I	0
Item by you[61] a play Blacke Freres	0	I	6
Item at the ordnary	0	3	0
Item for Plumley then	0	0	6
Item a paire of showes	0	3	6
<3>			
Item William Plumley & I supper	0	I	0
<Item to a boy lighting you from the ordinary (Mareman)			3>
Item the attornies hand to the order for staying the suit at common [law]	0	10	0
Item to his man for the same		I	0
<4>			
Item Mistress Giner for <Mistress Lettis> a quarter ending January the 3rd for Mistress Lettis	5	10	0
Item by water from Redriffe[62]	0	0	4
Item William Plumley & I supper	0	I	0
	13	6	11
Suma totallis 22–12–4 above	9	5	5
	22	12	4

[*fo.5v.*]

February the fift 1620

Item to Mr Godsole[63] for the injunction to staye the suit [at] common law	0	4	0
<Mr (Chamberlain)[64] for iiiis. order for it, him & man iiiis.>			
Item my diner at Pawles	0	0	6
Item to Robin for candles 5d. Tom iiid.	0	0	8
Item for ale & manchett to Robin	0	0	5
<7 [February]>			
Item to my cosen Rode which Mr Richard had of him for offisers & other things	0	10	0

60. There is no record of a lawyer of this name at the inns.

61. The following indented items relate to John Newdigate's expenditure, according to marginal note and bracket.

62. ?Redbridge.

63. ?Godsalve: there were several lawyers of this name at the inns.

64. ?Richard Chamberlain of the Inner Temple: *Students Admitted to the Inner Temple*, 133.

Item by Peter[65] of Mr Rode 3 yards <dimi.>			
of black saye at 2s. for your cloth hosse	o	7	6
Item 1yd. of whit homes <Mr Richard>	o	2	2
Item iii quarters of the yard cambrick for your			
cufts	o	3	11
Item iii quarters of [66] canvas [for] Mr Richard		1	0
Item 2 yards dimi. of bustia [for] Mistress Lettis		5	6
Item a copie of Swanes & Rogers answere to Mr			
Wilson[67]	o	1	4
<Mr (Chamberlain) feese not paid iiiis.>			
Item my supper at Paweles	o	o	6
<by me with Mistress Newdigate the vi[th] iis.			
iiiid. shoulder muton & hen		2	6>
Item to Mr Chomley drawing interogatory		11	0
Item to his man for wryting & ingrossing		6	–
<8>			
Item my diner & William's	o	1	0
<9>			
Item my diner & William Plumley's	o	1	0
Item more then <with my brother> xvid. knives			
Mistress (Brearton[68]) iiiis. vid.			
Item iii knives [for] Mistress Brearton	o	4	6
Item for examinig Swaynes & Rogers to Mr			
Parson[69]	o	6	0
Item to Mistress Trussell[70] for a half yeares con-			
sideracon of 80li. dew at Christmas last	4	0	0
Item to Pawle for dressing 2 hens		1	0
Item for a shoulder of mutton, a hen and slyseed			
beeffe, you supping with your uncle Henry[71] at			
his lodging		4	0
<10>			
Item my diner at Pawles	o	o	6
<Peter Walley's dyner then vid.>			
Item my supper that night	o	o	6
<11>			
Item my diner & William Plumley's & supper	o	2	0

---

65. Peter's bill, according to marginal note and bracket.
66. Followed by 'cambricke' deleted.
67. There were several lawyers of this name at the inns.
68. See i, fn. 167.
69. There were several lawyers of this name at the inns.
70. Mary Trussell's loan remained outstanding through the account: see below, fos.
5v. and 10v. Trussell: see *The Visitation of London 1633–5*, ii, 298.
71. Henry Newdigate of Ashtead.

Item Thom Fitton & Ned (Henshawe) xii*d*.
< 12 >

Item by water to Detford & backe with you	o	2	o
Item a paire of vellum leaves for Mistress Lettis & gilding them	o	1	o
Item i*oz*. licorice for you	o	o	8
Item my supper	o	o	6
< barber vi*d*. >	7	19	2
	2	7	

[*fo.6*]
folium 2
< 12 [February] >

Item a copie of Swanes & Rogers' depositions upon the interogatory	o	13	4
< 14 >			
Item at the Mearemaid, Cheapside, you, my self & William diner	o	2	4
Item iii*yd*. red cotten for your hors	o	3	o
Item William Plumley & my supper that night		1	o
Item 2 pippen pyes sent to your ant's lodging, you & Mr Richard supping there		1	o
< 15 >			
Item to Mr Richard	o	11	o
Item to Mr Newdigate at the 2 Angels		5	o
Item paper & waxe	o	o	4
< William Plumley vis. iii*s*. iv*s*. >			
< 18 >			
Item William Plumley's diner & myne	o	1	o
< 19 >			
Item his diner & myne	o	1	o
Item to Batt going to Ashteed	o	1	o
Item by water from Temple to London Bryge		o	4
< 20 >			
Item my diner & Peter's	o	1	o
Item spent at Acten with Mr Lougher[72] vi*d*. by mee		o	–
Item[73] Mr Newdigate & Mr Richard at a playe	o	1	o
Item Mr Newdigate at 2 more	o	2	o
Item i quart whitt wyne, nutmeg & suger	o	1	2

72. John Lowgher, husband of Mary Fitton: see *Introduction* and i.

73. The following indented items were bought by John Newdigate, according to bracket and marginal note.

Item batlings thrice	0	0	6
Item at a taverne fyer	0	0	4
Item at cardes Lodeame	0	1	6
Item at Acton vi*d.* the same night supper ii*s.*		2	6
Item the barber	0	1	0
Item Tower Hill, oysters & wyne Mistress Brerton		1	10
< 20 [February] >			
Item viii*oz.* of mocado < wastcoots > for Mistress Lettis & Mistress An		5	0
Item by water to the Brirge from the Temple with you		0	6
Item a horne to Mr Scott	0	1	0
Item 2 queares of paper	0	0	6
Item to Mr Beale for lynig Mr Richard's hatt		2	0
< xx*s.* William Plumley iii*s.* >			
Item for Mr Newdigate's bever a silver band and for dressing 2 hatts	2	0	0
< 21 >			
Item my diner & William Plumley's	0	1	0
< 22 >			
Item my diner & William Plumleyes	0	1	0
Item your supper & myne with Mr Hoult in your chamber		2	0
< vi*d.* > Item by water with Mistress Lettis to Blacke Freares vi*d.*			
Item a letter from William Henshawe		0	2
< xii*d.* > Renewing my writ against Gilbertt[74]			
< 23 >			
Item William Plumley's diner & myne	0	1	0
Item for his supper before to Pale	0	0	6
Item 2 ornarys for Ned xxii*d.*			
Item a Practis of Pietie[75] [for] Mistress Anne		2	0
Item drawing 2 wastcoots & peesing		3	2
< iiii*d.* . > 2 queyles Mistress Manley[76]	0	–	–
Item supper [in] chamber, you, Mr Richard & my self	0	2	6
Item for mending your lutte	0	5	0
folium 2	6	0	4

---

74. ?Whitehall's private business.
75. L. Bayly, *The practise of pietie: directing a christian how to walke* (1612 etc.), *STC*, 1601.5–1604.
76. ?An attendant on the Newdigate sisters: see below, fo. 13v.

[*fo.6v.*]
< To Mr Newdigate going to Ashteed 1–13 –o[77] >
February xxiiiith 1620

Item for vi yards of lace for cufts [for] Mr New-digate	o	3	o
Item William Plumley's diner & myne	o	1	o
< Ned vi*d.* >			
Item for letters brought up by (Oxford) & (Warrwick) < carriers >		o	9
< 27 [February] >			
Item to him that fetched hors at Lambeth to (Ned)		1	o
Item by water from Lambeth to Temple		o	6
Item a silver penne for Mistress Lettis' tables		o	9
< 28th >			
Item your supper with Mr Holt & Mr Sky-vington[78] < [in] chamber >		1	6
Item your diner & myne that daye with Mr Holt		1	4
Item lettres from Erdbury & Oxforde	o	o	10
< 24 [February] >			
Item to you going to Ashteed xxxiiis., of which you gave me a bill of viiis. vd. laid forth by you as one this side belowe[79], so there remaineth with you but	1	5	7
	1	16	3
		4	

[*Quarter side blank; next entry half-way down*]

March the first 1620

Item your diner & myne with Mr Holt (egs & c)	1	4
Item Batt going with your lettre [to] Ashteed	1	o
Item to Higenson < by you > a paire of gloves [for] Mistress (Miner)	2	o
Item to Pawle 2 ornary for William Plumley	1	o

77. See below, under 24 Feb.
78. Probably Richard Skeffington (c.1590–1647), 2nd son of William, 1st Bt., of Fisherwick, Staffs., and later active in Midlands politics. He was a mutal friend of Holte and Newdigate, and married Anne Newdigate (1626). See: WRO, CR 136, B225 (Holte to Newdigate, 1622), B339 (Richard Newdigate to same); *Staffs. Parl. Hist.*, ii, part ii, 48; *Hist. & Antiquities of Staffs.*, 366.
79. In the middle of the entry under March 1st.

Item that was oweing by Tomme there	2	6
Item my supper	o	6
Item by water with you from Temple to Brig	o	6
Item[80] your supper with Mr Holt in your chamber	1	4
Item a paire of gloves by Mr Newdigate[81]	1	4
Item to Austen by Mr Newdigat	1	o
Item for cutworke by you	o	3	6
<Item to bye showes [for] William Plumley iiis.>		
Item by water	o	1	o
Item setting up hors at Lambeth	o	o	9
Item a gathering at Ashteed	o	o	6
<viiis. vd. Mr Newdigate & me>		
Item a quarter of a pound suger	o	o	4
<2 [March]>		
Item in earnest for the cowtch <William Plumley [for] Downes Race>		
	3	2	o
Item to Robin upon his bill for your breakfasts, tobacco for your uncle & Mr (Fall.), sweet water & other things		8	10
Item xxxviyds. tamett at iis. viid. for my 2 wives[82] to make them gownes & 4 paire of (bodices)	4	13	o
Item for xv yards of stuffe at viis. iiiid. to make Mistress Ane a gowne & for iii quarters of the yard of taffatie	5	17	o
<Peter [? for making] vs.>		
Item to Mr Richard to paye his weeks commons in Lentt		10	o
Item to Robin for half of[83] things which Mr Holt & Mr Newdigate had fetched for them by Robbin, as apeareth by Robinn's bill		6	2
	12	15	7

Total xiiiili. – xis. – 10   Item above   1 16 3

                                                          24 11 10

[fo.7]
<To [faint] for William Plumley vs.>

80. Marginal note: 'for Ned H(?enshawe/olte) illis.' and, deleted, '& in earnest for cowtch William iis. Plumley'.
81. Bought by John Newdigate, according to marginal note and bracket.
82. i.e. Lettice and Anne Newdigate.
83. Followed by 'such', deleted.

March 1620

< 13 >
Item my hors after Mr Bates[84] came home till I went to Brackenborow		o 3 7
< 14 >		
Item spent going thither then		o 4 2
Item by water the Ould Swanne with you[85]		o o 6
Item your diner & myne that daye [in] chamber		o 1 o
< Ned ii*s*. vi*d*. >		
Item to Mr Richard to paye his ordnaryes		o 3 o
< 15 >		
Item for your red sadle		o 12 o
Item for viii ordinaryes, William Plumley		o 4 o
< to you v*s*. received back then xxii*s*. >		
Item the 18th [March] to the landres for washing sythence your commynge uppe		o 10 o
Item to Roben for your breakfasts Tewsday, Wensday, Thorsday & Fryday & a lettre [to] Black Freres		1 o
< 20 >		
Item for fagotts, dyett & things bought by Robin, your half against Mr Hoult		7 o
Item Higenson [for] gloves xx*s*. plaine paire xii*d*. roses for you iiii*s*. received back for a scarfe xii*s*.		o 13 o
Item my hors after I came from Brackenborow till you & Mr Richard went downe being 2 nights		o 1 10
Item my dyete after you went downe, from the xvth to the xxixth a fortnight		8 o
< Robin v*s*. 24 [March] >		
Item to Robin for tending the chamber		5 o
Item carrying a cloake bage into Sowthworke to Sir John Tonstal's cowtch		o o 5
Item soling Mr Richard's bootes at Lether(head)		o o 10
< 28 [March 1621] >		
Item to James, Sir [John] Tonstal's man when you were there, & for bring your cloakbag		o 1 o
< 29 >		
Item a boole silver for the Lady Tonstale		2 17 6
Item geven the cooke & p(antryman), your diner		o 5 o
Item your hors at the Kings Head, Sowthworke		o o 6

84. An associate of Thomas Rode: see below, fo. 14v.

85. The stairs up river from London Bridge, the first indication of a possible visit to Newdigate's future wife's house in Thames Street: see below.

Item geven the prisoners at 4 gaoles[86]		o	4
Item[87] 2 paire of gloves [for] Mr Richard & Mistress Anne		1	4
Item a quarter of yellow taffatie [for] gentlewomen's gownes		3	o
Item powther for Mistress Anne from the apoticary	o	5	o
< Peter vs. >			
Item removing Chester at Ashteed	o	o	4
Item the nursse & mydwife, Lady Tonstall's[88]	o	10	o
Item geven the offysers there then	o	3	o
< Aprill 9 >			
To Gardner bring home Sir John Tonstal's hors	o	o	10
Item to (Stint) fetching hors from Lambeth	o	1	o
Item by water from thence to the Temple		o	6
Item a letter by Kidney	o	o	2
Item carrying Mr Richard's cloakbag [to] Gray's Ine		o	2
Item a paire of cordevant gloves for you		2	6
Item supper you, Mr Richard & my self	o	1	6
< 10 >			
Item diner your self, Peter & I	o	1	9
Item a paire of gloves [of] Higenson	o	1	2
Item to the pore in Ludgate	o	o	2
Item by water from London Brig to (Temple)	o	o	6
Item to Mr Richard Smyth, steward of the Temple, for your commons 5 weeks dimi., one repast	2	3	10
Item supper you, my self & Peter	o	2	o
folium 3	10	17	10
		4	10

[fo.7v.]

Item by Peter[89] to Offill & Chittie for your suite & Mr Richard's	o	4	o
Item Peter when he came up with Mistress Newdigate, for William Plumley & him self diners & suppers	o	2	6

86. *Stow's Survey*, i, 60.

87. Marginal note: 'Mistress New [digate] 76 –7 –o/ 1 –2 –o/ 1 11—'.

88. Sir John and Lady Tonstal's 4th son, John, was born at Edgecombe 15 March 1621: *Surrey Archaeological Collections*, ii, 16. The silver bowl referred to above was probably a christening present.

89. The following indented items are evidently all from Peter's bill.

	£	s	d
Item a paire of bodies [for] Mistress Lettis	0	5	0
Item a lettre to Coventrie by Peter	0	0	2
Item removing the stand hors [at] Casholton	0	0	6
Item crossing water & setting Peter's hors	0	0	6
Item to Jo Lewcocke bring horsses to (Lambeth) when Mr Holt & Mr Greasley[90] came	0	1	0
Item iii quarter blacke & brone thred	0	1	9
Item i quarter of orring thread	0	0	10
Item tinning your sterrups & snafles	0	1	0
Item dimi. pound of whale bone	0	1	0
Item 2 yards buckerom [for] gownes	0	2	0
Item Peter's dyate 2 dayes then	0	2	0
Item his hors then	0	1	6
Item 2 removes bald gelding	0	0	2
Item to Offyll for xi dayes, 3 gownes	0	5	6
Aprill the xith 1621			
Item to Mr Richard to paye his commons	4	10	0
Item Mr Richard, Peter & my self diner	0	1	6
Item to the 2 prisons in Sowthworke		0	5
Item to Peter bring you home with a torch		2	6
<12>			
Item diner your self, Peter & I	0	1	7
Item my supper and Peter's at Pawles		1	0
<13>			
Item to you at Lodeam, Fish Street	0	5	0
Item by water from thence to the Temple		0	6
Item supper in your chamber that night Mr Holt, Mr Skevington, Mr Richard, your self & I	0	3	2
<14>			
Item diner calves Heade & (bar) Mr Holt, your self, Peter & I		3	0
Item by water to Lambeth	0	0	6
Item to Robin upon his bill for candles i*li*. & breakfasts		2	0
Item carrying my cloakebag <from Lambeth to Carr> to meet Batt	0	0	2
<16>			
Item my hors, Whit Hors in Sowthworke	0	0	6
Item my diner that daye at Pawles	0	0	6
<18>			
Item geven at Ashteed, your sisters commyng thence & going to Detforde, to Mary & Nan		2	0

90. Thomas Gresley, formerly of Trinity College: see i, fn. 150.

Item Dicke dressing hors	o	I	o
< Detforde >			
Item to Mistress Giner for Mistress Anne at her (coming)	I	o	o
Item to him that fetched our hors Sowthworke	o	I	o
< Peter vs. >			
Item setting up Watts' hors & haye, Cather-inwheile		o	3
Item Petter & I by water to the Temple		o	4
Item super with your ante Newdigate, your self, Mr Richard & I		4	o
< 19 >			
Item my diner & supper		I	o
< 20 >			
Item supper & wine Mr Holt, Mr Rensford[91], your self, Mr Richard, Peter & I (chamber)	o	4	4
< 21 >			
Item by water from the Ould Swan to Westminster		o	6
Item supper in your chamber you, Mr Richard & my self		I	9
	8	17	11

[fo.8]			
Item[92] a paire of boots for you	o	9	6
Item carrying Mistress Ann's trunke from Ashteed to Sowthworke		2	3
Item a porter & corde to male the trunke		o	3
Item by water to the Temple	o	o	6
< 23 [April] >			
Item my diner & Peter's	o	o	10
< 24 >			
Item your breakefast	o	o	6
Item Peter's diner & myne	o	I	o
Item to Mr Richard by Mr Rawley Newdigate[93]	o	4	o
Item xxi ell holland for your sisters	2	12	6

91. Probably Robert Raynsford of Dallington, Northants., admitted to the Inner Temple 1620: *Students Admitted to the Inner Temple*, 230; *Hist. & Antiquities Northants.*, i, 131.

92. The following indented items were bought by Peter, according to marginal note and bracket. A deleted entry at the top of the page reads: 'Mr Rawley for brother ii*li.*/iiii*s.* Mr Ryc(hard) thereof'. The latter sum is entered below, see 24 April.

93. See i, fn. 253.

	£	s	d
Item i ell quarter hollande [for] sisters' gownes	0	2	11
Item 2 yards dimi. yellow seaye [for] sisters	0	3	5
Item i ell quarter canvas < for them >	0	1	9
Item 2 yards dimi. jaine fustian for the same		2	3ob.
Item half ell canvas [for] Mistress Anne's best gowne		0	10
Item half ell holland for her	0	1	1ob.
Item 3 quarters saye for bordering the gowne		1	5
Item 3 quarters of saye for the sleeves	0	1	5
< 25 >			
Item my diner & Peter's	0	1	0
< 26 >			
Item washing & dying Mistress Lettis' fann		1	0
Item lute strings by him that teacheth		1	0
Item my diner at Pawles	0	0	6
Item super your self, Mr Richard & I in your chamber	0	1	8
Item by water to Detforde & backe Mr Morton, Mr Fytton & 4 more	0	3	6
Item a paire of sesers for Mistress Anne	0	1	0
Item by Peter for 3 doson yards imbrathered lace < [of] Benmon > for your saten suite at xiii*s*.	2	2	3
Item for Mr Richard iii yards blacke riben (breches)		1	3
Item ii*oz*. dimi. of black galonnie for him	0	5	0
Item i*oz*. dimi. quarter Dewey[94] silke & silver lace [for] liverys		3	5
Item 4 doson blacke Paris buttons for Mr Richard	0	1	4
Item 2 *oz*. dimi. quarter blacke galonie & silke	0	5	0
Item v*ozs*. dimi. silver lead lace at iiii*s*. viii*d*. [for] Mistress Anne	1	3	4
Item dimi. *ozs*. tawnie ingraine silke	0	1	6
Item i doson tawnie & silver buttons for her		0	8
Item viii doson bewgle lace for (tamudy) gowns	–		
Item iiii doson yellowe buttons for tham	0	1	4
Item 2*ozs*. yellowe silke to sett on lace		4	4
Item dimi. *oz*. sad russett silke for Mr Richard	0	1	–
< 27 [April] >			
Item by water from Parliament stayers [with] uncle		0	6
Item diner in your chamber your self, 2 uncles & I	0	4	0

94. ?Douai.

Item supper there that night you, Mr Rawley, myself & Peter	o	3	6
<28>			
Item by water with you from the Oulde Swanne	o	o	6
<30. Peter xs.>			
Item Peter & I supper at Pawles	o	1	o
Item to Mr Bosson a gratuitie[95]	o	11	o
Item carrying the monie St Lawrence Lane		o	3
Item my diner that daye	o	o	6
Item for letters <& portage>	o	o	6
	10	08	04

folium 4		5	15
[fo.8v.]			

Maye the first 1621

Imprimis to you at the Temple cundeth going to Westminster	o	10	o
Item by water to the Ould Swan	o	o	6
Item my diner at Pawles	o	o	6
<2 [May]>			
Item by water with Sir John Tonstall with you from Wetminster Dowgate		o	6
Item diner at the Mearemaid, (Cheapside), Sir John, your self, I & 2 men		5	o
Item a paire of gloves by you [of] (Robert Higenson)		1	3
<3>			
Item to Detford to St Mary (Overies)		o	3
Item crossing water at (Redbridge)		o	2
Item to you upper end of Wood (Street)		10	–
Item to Mr Wilson a copie of Swanes answere		3	o
<Mr Chamberlain viiis.>			
<4>			
Item to Sara, the cooke at Mistress (Lulls)[96]		5	o
Item Mr Holbach for tearme fees, drawing information & perusing <books versus Swan>		10	o
Item to Mr Randle the King's rent dew for			

95. The sum suggests a return for considerable services rendered, the name possibly an immigrant from the Lulls circle.

96. Susanna Lulls (c.1597–1654), eldest daughter of Arnold Lulls, merchant and jeweller to James I, who married John Newdigate 27 June 1621: see *Introduction* and Larminie, 'Marriage and the Family', *passim*.

Erdbury & Coton parsonage at our Lady [Day]	4	16	6
Item to Mr James Tooke for Middlesex land liiii*s*. vi*d.ob.* ingrossing half yeares accompt xii*d.* poundage for the exhibition vi*d.* acquitance	2	16	7
Item to Mr Richard in your studie	0	10	0
Item to Mr Chomley perusing answer & interrogatory	0	11	0
Item to Mr Pickerell his fees this tearme	0	3	4
Item with your uncle & ante Lowgher, quart clarett & a pint sacke at supper	0	1	0
<5>			
Item Mr Chomley's man drawing and ingrossing interrogatory verzus Swayne		10	0
Item to Mr Parsons for examynig him	0	3	0
Item to Mr Madoxe[97] for 8 doson bewgle lace	1	1	0
<7>			
Item my supper at Pawles	0	0	6
Item supper in your chamber, you, Mr Holt, Peter & I	0	1	8
Item a paire of cordivant gloves for you		2	6
<Peter xi*s.*>			
Item diner you, Thomas Morton, Peter & I [in] chamber			
Item v yards silk grogron at xx*s.*	5	0	0
Item ii*yd.* quarter Turkie grogron at v*s.* }			
Item ell taffatie at [*blank*] }	1	7	0
Item saten, lace, silke & buttons to Mr (Benion)	2	14	0
<9>			
Item by water from <Westminster to the> Temple	0	0	6
Item by water Ould Swan & backe the xth	0	1	0
<Peter v*s.*>			
Item to Mr Richard at Mistress Lulls	0	5	3
<10th>			
Item diner in your chamber you, (T. Dock.), I & Peter	0	2	0
<11>			
Item to (Kate) at Mistress Lulls ii*s.*[98]		2	0
Item by water the Ould Swan & backe	0	1	0

97. ?William Maddox, merchant tailor, of St Mary at Hill: *Index to Wills Proved in the Prerogative Court of Canterbury 1620–9*, ed. R.H. Ernest Hill (British Records Association xliv, 1912), 182.

98. Followed by 'by water there & back', deleted.

Item lace for your 2 shurts iiii*s*. making xvi*d*.		5	4
<12>			
Item diner in your chamber Mr Holt, your self, William & I	0	1	6
Item to you at 2 severall tymes in your chamber windowe v*s*. and x*s*. the xii of Maye	0	15	0
Item supper Mr Holt, you, Mr Richard, I & William	0	2	0
Item pinking taffatie for your cloake		3	0
<13>			
Item diner & supper William Plumley & I at Pawles	0	2	0
<14>			
Item diner for us 2 at Pawles	0	1	0
	24	05	10
	9	6	

[*fo.9*]

folium 5   May the xiiiith 1621

Item William Plumley his supper	0	0	6
<15>			
Item his diner, William Plumley	0	0	6
Item by water to the Ould Swan & backe		1	0
Item William & I supper at Pawles		1	0
<4*li*. iiii*s*. purs; pocket xx*d*.>			
Item by William Plumley coming to London, his hors & self Lambeth ferry ii*d*. (T. Doc.) mare there, you going to the rac ii*d*. his coming backe by water ii*d*. meting you there ii*d*. bringing over the mare ii*d*. a lettre by Kidney ii*d*.	0	1	0
<16>			
Item William Plumley & I diner & supper Pawles	0	2	0
Item to Mr Stapleton perusing the books[99]	0	11	0
Item by water when you went with Sir John (Tonstal) & his Lady [to] Black Freares & Ould Swan	0	0	10
<17>			
Item by water Swan vi*d*. Fleet vi*d*. back to Swan			

99. Edward Stapleton of Maxstoke, Warws., Bencher of the Inner Temple, the lawyer most closely concerned with John Newdigate's marriage settlement and later accused by him of concealment of evidences: PRO, C 3, 369/41; WRO, CR 136, B345. According to Richard Newdigate's later recollection, the marriage treaty was first drawn up in May 1621: CR 136, B1380.

vi*d*. staying there to Temple steares & backe to White Freares x*d*.	o	2	4
Item to William Plumley for a torche	o	o	10
<18>			
Item 2 doson poynts by Peter Olliff	o	5	o
Item by water from Savoy to the Ould Swan & backe		1	o
Item supper in your chamber your self, Mr Richard, William Plumley & I	o	1	3
<19>			
Item to you commyng from barbing	o	10	o
Item 2 ruffes [for your] sisters xxxvii*s*. box iiii*d*.	1	17	4
Item dyner you, Mr Richard & I with Mr Holt &	o	1	9
Item a quart of sacke by Mr Richard	o	o	8
Item tinning your spurres	o	o	4
<20>			
Item a paire of russet boots for you	o	9	6
Item diner at Pales William Plumley & I		1	o
Item to William Plumley for 5 meales or ordi-naryes laid forth for him self when I was not with him	o	2	6
<21>			
Item to Mr Bolton's man xii*d*. ostler vid. for bring 3 hors when you went [to] Brackenborow		1	6
Item Acton white wyne & suger with Mr Holte		o	6
Item Mr Baldwen's man setting up hors	o	o	6
<22>			
Item William Plumley's diner & myne Pales		1	o
Item to Peter, Mistress Lulls her man	o	1	6
Item by water from the Ould Swan to Temple		o	6
<23>			
Item to Mistress Ane at Mistress Lulls	o	5	o
Item by water to Detford & backe with Mr Holt, Mr Bolton, brother & sisters	o	3	6
Item William's diner & myne at Pawles	o	1	o
Item to Pawle for a rabett for you xiiii*d*. (letter) i*d*.			
<Richard Fych wryting>			
<24>			
Item by water from the Ould Swane you, Mr Richard & I	o	o	6
<25>			
Item my diner at Paules	o	o	6

< 26 >
Item a hat for Mr Richard [?of] Bayle[100]   0   11   0
Item by water the Ould Swan vi*d*. paper 2
(quires) vi*d*.   1   0
Item Mr Richard's supper & myne   0   0   11
< 27 >
Item my supper & William Plumley's at Pawles   0   1   0
Item to Sara at Mistress Lules   0   1   0
< 28 >
Item to Mr Crowke perusing books   1   2   0
Item William Plumley's supper & myne   0   1   0
< 29 >
Item legsberuit for Mr Georg Crowke[101]   4   0
< 30 >
Item to Mr Crowke by you   2   4   0

folium 5th   9   15   6
                                                   5

[*fo.9v.*]
< Before & nowe   Peter   2 17 –0   R. Higenson for W.P.
                                             xiii*s*.
   June 19 taken forth bag   1 19 –0   Item for N. (Hen-
                                             shawe) xxx*s*.
   July 4th to Peter with parcell   1 –2 –0
   Item to Beale   0 10 —
              by H. Thornton   1 –0 –0>
< 28 [May] >
Item tendring your livery continuans[102]   11   0
< 30 >
Item by water the Ould Swanne   0   0   6
Item to Peter, Mistress Luls [her] man, with torch   2   0
Item porter at Ludgate   0   3
< 31 >
Item our diners Peter,William & my self < &
William Plumley supper vi*d*. >   2   0
< 22 [May] >
   Item by William Plumley[103] his diner vi*d*. super
   vi*d*.   1   0

100. The next entry, relating to a silver and silk scarf, has been deleted.
101. ?Authorisation to institute proceedings at law: *cf*. E. Jowitt ed., *The Dictionary of English Law* (2 vols., 1959), ii, 1075.
102. On this, his 21st birthday, John officially passed out of wardship: birth-date, WRO, CR 136, B882; fees for process, Bell, *Court of Wards*, 203–5; background, J. Hurstfield, *The Queen's Wards: Wardship and Marriage under Elizabeth I* (1958), 157–180.
103. The following indented items were bought by William Plumley.

Item 22nd supper vi*d*. 23 supper vi*d*. 25 diner vi*d*.		1	6
Item carying a lettre by Kidney	0	0	2
<26> Item for a linke from Fyshe Street	0	0	6
<27> Item by William for his diner & 30th diner	0	1	0
<29> Item a lettre sent downe, Kidney	0	0	2
<31> Item for his supper, William Plumley	0	0	6
Item to you in the closett with Peter		10	0
Item to Mr Audley[104] for your bond to shew livery		2	0
Item supper with Mr Lowgher [in] your chamber June the first 1621	0	2	0
Item my diner & William Plumley's xii*d*. William Plumley's supper vi*d*.	0	1	6
Item supper in your chamber your self and [*blank*]		2	5
Item to William Plumley for diner & supper	0	1	0
Item the 2nd & 3rd to him, diner & supper	0	2	0
<2>			
Item to Mr Peter Gifforde in part of payment of 210[*li*.] sett downe by Mr Lowgher[105]	40	0	0
Item a cowtch & 4 horsses to Brackenborow	0	18	0
Item diner at Uxbridge	0	18	8
Item horsmeate there then	0	2	8
Item to William Plumley, diner & supper 2nd & 3[rd][106]	0	2	0
<3>			
Item diner in your chamber Mr Holt, Mr Skeyvington, your self & I, 3 at x*d*., you xi*d*. <Porles for 6>[107]	0	1	9
Item supper and breakfast Mr Holt, Mr Skevington, Mr Greysley, Mr Roberte Holt[108] <chamber> <iii*s*.>	0	2	0
<4>			
Item to Mr Stapleton coming [from] Mistress Lulles	1	2	0
Item by water from Temple & backe	0	1	0

104. Clerk of the Court of Wards: see i, fn. 51.

105. In part payment for Coton royalty, conveyed to John Newdigate finally May 1622: WRO, CR 136, B603. See also i, fn. 24.

106. Duplicated above, as was the entry for 1 June.

107. The sum should be 3*s*. 5*d*., but the addition may indicate credit or sharing of the bill.

108. Probably a younger brother of Edward: *cf.* Dugdale, *History & Antiquities*, 873.

<3 [June]>
Item by water the Ould Swan with Mr Skey-
vington   o   6
Item to Robin for i*oz*. tobaco for your unckle
ii*s*. scowring silke (stockings) ii*s*. his bill for
breakefast, bread, beare & suger xii*s*. iiii*d*.   16   4
<5>
Item a lettre by Kidney   o   o   2
Item diner in your chamber your self, Peter,
William & I   o   2   7
<6>
Item Wensdaye <diner>[109] with Mr Lowgher
& Mistress (Lowgher), quart claret, pint sack   1   o
Item supper your self & I [in] chamber   o   1   8
<7>
Item by water with Sir John Tonstal (Swan) & back   1   o
<8>
Item mending windowes your part   o   6   o
Item by water from the Ould Swan [with] Mr
Lulls   o   6
<9>
Item from Westminster [with] Sir John &
Debest[110]   o   6
Item diner [in] chamber [with] Sir John Tonstall o   3   8
Item to Mr Richard in your chamber   o   5   o
Item supper your self, William Plumley & I   o   1   10
<10>
Item diner in your chamber Mr Benet[111], your
self, William Plumley   o   1   10
Item supper in Mr Fallofeild's chamber[112], you &
I   o   2   o
Item by water to the Ould Swan, you & I   o   o   6

                                                  47   14   8
                                                  6   11

109. Addition obscured by deleted entry 'night supper'.
110. Probably Susanna Lulls' 'uncle', Jacques de Beste, a London merchant, who
made himself responsible for paying the greater part of her dowry: WRO, CR 136,
C2719; *Visitation of London*, i, 224. De Beste was at this time a defendant with Arnold
Lulls and others in Star Chamber proceedings relating to the alleged export of bullion:
PRO, STAC 8, 25/19, Pt. 1 25/23, 21/17; *CSPD 1619–1623*, 119; W.C.J. Moens ed.,
Register of the Dutch Church, Austin Friars (1884), *introduction*.
111. Probably either Thomas or Richard Bennett (admitted 1615), sons of Sir
Thomas, alderman, and kin of the Crokes: *Students Admitted to the Inner Temple*, 213.
112. Richard Fallowfield, barrister 1622: *ibid.*, 201.

[*fo.10*]

Monday June the xith 1621

Item diner in your chamber you, William Plumley & I	o	1	9
Item by water to the Ould Swan & backe	o	1	o
Item supper in your chamber you, William Plumley & I	o	1	10
<12>			
Item diner in your chamber you, William Plumley & I		2	o
<13>			
Item to Mr Richard for boots	o	10	o
Item to you in your closett going with Mr Fallowfeild	o	10	o
Item June the 6 William Plumley's[113] diner & supper	o	1	o
<8> Item William Plumley diner & supper	o	1	o
<10> Item supper by him	o	o	6
<11> Item threed i*d*. Withers motto vi*d*.[114]	o	o	7
<12> Item a lettre by Kidney to Erdbury	o	o	2
<13>			
Item to Mr Hurst[115] for drawing the award between you & Mr Giffard	o	8	o
Item by water from Westminster	o	o	6
Item diner your self, Mr Richard, William Plumley & I	o	2	4
<14>			
Item by water to Westminster [with] Mr Lulls [&] Mr Lowgher	o	o	6
Item Mottershed[116] by you in Holborne	o	1	o
Item diner your self, William Plumley & I	o	1	10
Item straberyes then a pint	o	o	3
<15>			
Item diner in your chamber [your] uncles, Mr Haselrig[117], your self & brother Richard	o	4	6
Item by water the Ould Swan	o	o	6
Item to Peter a linke & bring you home		1	6

113. The following indented items are all part of his bill, according to marginal note and bracket.

114. G. Wither, *Wither's motto. Nec habeo, nec caro, nec curo* (1621), *STC*, 25925–25928.7

115. Later described as 'Mr Crowke's man': see below, fo. 18.

116. Servant to the Lowghers: see i, fo. 1v.

117. ?Henry Newdigate's brother-in-law: J. Fetherston ed., *The Visitation of the County of Leicester in the Year 1619* (Harleian Society, II, 1870), 15–16.

Item to Thomas < Mr Rode's man for > receiving Brackenborow rents		1	0
Item to him for lettres boxes	0	0	6
< 16 >			
Item diner Mr Holte, your self, William & I		2	6
Item *oz.* dimi. blacke silke [for] gould dublet & hosse		3	0
Item 5 doson blacke silke & gould buttons		3	4
Item[118] (stuffe) phillip & chaine xiii yards dimi. at iiii*s.* for Mr Richard	2	12	0
Item one ell taffatie for him	0	14	0
Item ix*oz.* quarter of galoone lace at ii*s.* vi*d.*	1	3	2
Item 2*oz.* of silke [at] ii*s.* iiii*d.*	0	4	8
Item dimi. ell cambricke for Mr Richard	0	2	3
Item i ell canvas for his doublett	0	1	4
Item iii*yd.* dimi. white homes	0	3	11
< 16 >			
Item supper your self, Mr Richard, 2 men & I	0	2	0
< 17 >			
Item Sonday diner you, 2 men & I	0	3	2
Item supper you, Francis Hollinshed[119], 2 men		3	0
< 18 >			
Item diner your self, 2 men & I	0	2	3
Item supper < Peter > and my self	0	1	0
< 19 >			
Item for xxv yards broad cloth for liveryes at xi*s.* iiii*d.*	14	3	0
Item to Mr Rawley Newdigat, geven him by my Lady's will[120]	5	0	0
Item by water to the Ould Swan	0	0	6
< 20 >			
Item breakfast for you: rosted beoffe vi*d.* bred & beare ii*d.* dew before ii*d.*		0	10
Item to the Ould Swan by water to mette Sir John		0	6
< 21 >			
Item diner your self, William Plumley & I	0	1	10

118. The following indented items were bought by Richard Newdigate, according to marginal note and bracket.

119. ?Francis Hollingshead of Sandlebridge, Cheshire and of Staffs.: A. Adams ed., *Cheshire Visitation Pedigrees*, Harl. Soc. xciii, 1941, 53. ?Francis Hollenshed of Daventry: Baker, *Hist. & Antiquities Northants.*, 321.

120. Bequest by Dame Anne Newdigate: WRO, CR 136, C1915.

Item by water [to] the Ould Swanne	0	0	6
follium 6	28	01	00
	6	14	

[*fo.10v.*]

Frydaye 22 [June]

Item half an ell more broad clothe for 2 sadles more	0	7	0
Item to William Plumley upon his bill the xii [June]: supper vi*d.* 13th by water to Detford iiii*d.*[121] 14th supper vi*d.* 15 supper vi*d.* 18 a linke iiii*d.* 19th diner vi*d.* 20 diner vi*d.* by water to Detford vi*d.* a linke iiii*d.*	0	4	0
Item diner Mr Salter, Tom, brother Richard	0	5	8
Item to Mr Croke to gyve instructions for drawing the assurance from Mr Giffard	0	11	0
Item a licens	0	14	4
Item supper, Mr Salter with you		3	8
Item to the Ould Swan & backe		1	0
Item to him that teacheth the lute		6	10
<23[122]>			
Item 2 statuts & 2 defezance	1	8	0
Item diner [?with] Sir John Tonstall [?in] chamber	0	3	9
Item by water the Ould Swan 2 botts [?to] Mr Lulls		1	0
Item to Fych[123] for a copie of the order of shewing forth livery	0	1	6
<24>			
Item diner Sondaye in your chamber	0	2	6
<25>			
Item diner in your chamber with Mr Lowgher & his 2 men	0	3	2
Item by water & backe to the Oulde Swan		1	0
<26>			
[Item] diner with Mr Lowgher & your uncle Newdigate	0	6	10

121. Preceded by 'vi*d.*', deleted.

122. The date of major sections of John Newdigate and Susanna Lulls' marriage settlement: WRO, CR 136, C1933, C2719–2721. The witnesses were John Tonstal, Richard Newdigate, William Whitehall, [?] Stapleton and John Bonde.

123. See above, fo. 9.

Item hyer for 2 cowtches to Stepney[124] in earnest   sett after
iiii*s*. to have a peece more

Item a shurtt for you	01	18	0
Item to Mr Coles upon your bill[125]	14	16	0
Item a band & cufts for you	2	3	0
Item a paire of silke stockings for you	1	10	0
Item a girdle	0	15	0
Item in earnest for the cowtch	0	10	0
Item a cale for Mistress Anne <of> Mistress Logg	0	2	0
Item supper you, William Plumley & my self	0	1	8
Item to Mistress Trussell for halfe yeare consideracion for 80*li*. to Mistress Chamber <27>	4	0	0
Item to Mr Chester for vi monthes consideracon of 100*li*. <by Mr Richard> <28>	4	10	0
Item a porter bringing a lettre for Mr Fallofeild to you <30>	0	0	6
Item to you for your lutte bought	2	5	0
Item to Detford for your sisters [by] water <bells vi*s*.[126]>	0	2	6
Item to him that wyned cornet [at] Mr Lulls' <July 5>		1	0
Item to Robin upon his bill for breakfasts, bread and beare from the vth of June	0	12	2
Item a paire of gouldwaights	0	6	0
Item a paire of showes for you by William Plumley		3	6
Item June the 27th to Mr William Chester by Mr Richard dewe then to Sir Anthony by bond, with consideracon as above by Mr Richard also paide	100	0	0
Item to Mistress Trussell for consideracon of xx*li*. from the 28th of November <1620> to the xxxth of June 1621	001	0	0
	139	19	7
	9	7	

124. Where John and Susanna were married 27 June: T, Colyer-Fergusson ed., *Register of St Dunstan's, Stepney* (1898), 127.
125. Probably the mercer rather than the lawyer: *cf.* below, fo. 14v.
126. i.e. Wedding bells?

[*fo.11*]

Disbursed at Ashted
by William Plumley[127]

Item a payre of spurlethers by Will Hill	o	o	6
Item halfe a yard of fustian for Peeter	o	o	8
Item makinge of a canvis cote	o	o	8
Item given to a poore man at the dore	o	o	I
Item for 3 paire of bootes greacinge	o	o	3
Item 3 new shooes for Ball[128]	o	I	o
Item for a locke to John Allium	o	o	6
Item for a chayne for the lime hound	o	o	6
Item caridge of a clokebag from Sothorock to			
Temple	o	o	6
Item to a souldier	o	o	2
Item the first nightes supper for my selfe	o	o	6
for a paire of bandstringes	o	o	3
for a bottle of beare at the chamber	o	o	2
stronge water and sugar for my master	o	o	2
to the porter's wife for 3 letters	o	o	3
for mending of golocias[129]	o	o	2
Munday night supper for my selfe	o	o	6
Tuesday diner	o	o	6
a payre of gloves[130]	o	I	o
to a porter for bringinge me to the (fate m)	o	o	4
for diner and supper on Candlemas day[131]	o	I	o
for a letter brought to the Temple	o	o	I
Sunday dinner, Munday dinner & Tuesday			
supper	o	I	6
Monday dinner and supper	o	I	o
more hott water and suger	o	o	3
Thursday supper	o	o	6
for a linke in Fetter Lane	o	o	3
Saterday dinner and supper	o	I	o
Munday dinner and supper	o	I	o
Tusday supper	o	o	6
for lute stringes	o	o	6

127. Entries on this side are in a different hand, evidently that of Plumley himself.
128. Probably a horse.
129. i.e. Galoshes?
130. Preceded by 'for mending golocias', deleted.
131. 2 Feb.: the bill thus appears considerably out of sequence.

carridge of a letter by Kidne	o o 2
inke for Mistress Lettice	o o 2
Thursday dinner and supper	o 1 o
Friday dinner	o o 6
Saterday dinner and supper	o 1 o
Sunday night supper	o o 6
Munday night supper	o o 6
Tusday dinner and supper	o 1 o
carridge of a letter by Kidney	o o 2
	1 1 2

Item for a bridge for the treble viall	o o 4
for stringes to string it	o o 4
Wensday supper and Thursday supper	o 1 o
Tusday[132] supper & Wensday \<dinner\>		
& supper	o 1 6
Thursday dinner	o o 6
	o 3 8

June the 21th

for a linke at the Bridge foote	o o 4
\<22\> by water to Lambeth with Watt	o o 6
cumming back for Sir John Tunstal by water	o o 2
\<23\> for my dinner and supper	o 1 o
for bringinge my Mistress' trunke by water	o o 8
for virginall wier	o o 3
	o 2 11

July the 6th

for hire of a horse to go to Ashted	o 2 6
\<7\> by water from the bridge to the catt(hedral)	o o 4
for a snafoll at Croydon	o o 4
\<9\> at Epsom for 2 new shooes and 4 removes	o 1 o
payd to him which was dew before	o o 4
\<10\> for a letter by Kidney	o o 2
at Lion Cay for wharfidge	o o 2

132. Preceded by 'For the lute mendinge o −5 −o', deleted.

for caridg of Mistress Lettice's thinges to
   Mr Lulles'   0   0   6

                                 0   5   4

First	−1 −1 −2				
Item	0 −3 −8				
Item	−0 −2 11	Suma xxxiii*s*. ii*d*.			
	0 −5 −4				
	1 13 −2		1	13	2

follium 7   William Plumley

[*fo.11v.*]
    From the xxvith of January 1620 to June
       the xxviith 1621, Mr Newdigate being at
       the Temple, disbursed, and theise folloing
       the severall somes upon every leaf side

		Temple booke		
folium 1	Imprimis the first leaf side	22	12	4
	The other side	7	19	2
folium 2	The second leaf	6	0	4
	The other syde	14	11	10
folium 3	Item	10	17	10
	The other side	8	17	11
folium 4	Item	10	8	4
	The other side	24	5	10
folium 5	Item	9	15	6
	The other side	47	14	8
folium 6	Item	28	1	0
	The other side	139	17	7
folium 7	Item by William Plumley	1	13	2
		332	15	6

Item May the xviiith 1618 my Lady[133] borowed
  of Mr Lowgher c*li*. upon her bonde for consideracon, which monie was retorned up &
  paid the Lady Graye[134], so much being then
  dewe to her with a half yeares consideracon,
  being v*li*.
This c*li*. borowed in March 1618 was paid by me

133. Anne Newdigate.
134. See i, fn. 245.

		£	s	d
to Mr Lowgher iii November 1619, so to him		100	0	0
Item paid him for 3 half yeares consideracon, he having that tyme in his hands xxiii*li.* of my Lady's & myne[135], so to him		12	0	0
Item June the 22th 1620 paid to Mr Edward Fytton which my Lady owed him by bond		50	0	0
		162	0	0

Disbursed:

		£	s	d
As above		332	15	−6
Item this		162	−0	−0
		494	15	−6
Item Surrey booke as in the bottom of the 3 leafe thereof in v severall somes		133	15	−6
		648	11	−0
Suma totall disbursed As above is Received as upon the other side folloinge		648	11	−0
		411	13	−4 [136]
		236	17	−8

[*fo.12*]

November the xiiii 1620 going from Erdbury
to Mr Newdigate in Surrey

Receipts:

	£	s	d
Imprimis your cawsion monie att Oxforde[137]	8	0	0
<28 [November]>			
Item of Mistress Trussell for vi monthes to be paid with consideracon[138]	20	0	0
December the 22th of Sir Anthonie Chester after ix in the c[139]	100	0	0
Item of Mr Baldwin in part of payment of the xl*s.* which he awarded Mistress Hiccocke for faling woode[140]	1	10	0

135. Previous word deleted.
136. The accountant then again totals the disbursements and sets them against receipts, presumably as a double check.
137. Refunded on their departure from Oxford. The college archives suggest a slightly earlier date: Trinity MS, 'Liber Trin. Coll. Oxon.', 1619.
138. See above, fo. 10v.
139. *ibid.*
140. Thomas Baldwen was evidently acting as bailiff at Brackenborough.

Brackenborow rents Mychellmas 1620[141]

Imprimis the Lady Derbie	23	o	o
Item Mr Baldwen	26	5	o
Item Mr Androwe	25	o	o
Item Mistress Winkfeilde	23	6	8
Item William Kelley in part of xxxv*li*.	30	–	–
Item Mr Webb for half the Spring	1	1	8
Item of William Tayler	3	6	8
Item Thomas Mawkins	o	6	8
Item of Mr Baldwen for the meadowe	2	10	o
Item a half yeares exhibition	1	10	–
Item of Kelley for a bull segg and a cowe soulde			
by him 9 10 –	275	06	8

Item for a half yeares rent dewe at Brackenborow
at our Lady Daye 1621 with a half yeares exhibition, as is sett downe particlerly above for
Mychellmas 1620

       136 6 8

       booth which tow
       somes bee

       411 13 4

Suma totall received as above is 411 13 –4 over
& above all I received in that tyme from
William Henshaw[142]

[*fo.12v., blank*]

[*fo.13*]

Received July 1621

Imprimis of you and Mistress Newdigate at your
howse in Temmes Street: received by mee
1000*li*.[143]

Disbursede

141. Sums entered vary slightly from those for Michaelmas 1618: *cf*. i, fo. 2v.

142. As steward at Arbury Henshawe received both Warwickshire rents and income
from sales of farm stock and produce.

143. The house 'commonly called the thee tonnes', situated on the corner of Thames
Street and St Michael's Lane, was conveyed to Newdigate by his future wife 23 June
1621; the money was probably the first instalment of Susanna's dowry, which Jacques
de Beste had promised to pay 'before the marriage': WRO, CR 136, C2719–20.

Imprimis to Mr Maire[144] for the fine, licens of alienacon & recovery with other charges, as apeareth by his bill hereunto anexed[145]	40	6	10

[fo.13v.]

Item to you [in] Temmes Streete	01	0	0
Item at Stepney to Mr Eger[146]	0	10	0
Item to the sextan there then	0	1	0
Item to him for his master, Doctor Goldinge[147]	0	10	0
Item to the pore there & prisoners, Whit Chapell		2	0
Item to Duckett for 2 cowtches & 8 hors	1	6	0
Item to 2 cowtchmen by your apoyntment	0	2	6
Item to Mr Debest's man by your apoyntment telling	0	6	0
Item to Mistress Ginner for (a gratuitie) nothinge[148]	10	0	0
Item a cape of broadcloth for Mr Richard's cloak		1	–
Item dressing his cloak & drawing itt	0	5	6
<4 [July]>			
Item by water from the Ould Swan to the Temple			6
<6>			
Item to you in your chamber going with Mr Fallowfeild to a playe	1	–	–
Item to Mr Cooles for a quarter & nayle of silke for a cape for your cloake	0	8	–
Item to your brother Richard to paye for his commons and other necessaryes	5	10	0
Item 2 paire of boothose worke with white	0	14	–
Item the cowtch hinder harnis, a paire of crewell raynes, lether hedstales, raynes & bitts for 2 horsses	34	15	–
<Item 2 for harnis	3	0	0>

144. ?John Meyer, admitted to the Inner Temple 1600 and 1608: *Students Admitted to the Inner Temple*, 156, 183.

145. No bill annexed to ms., but charges evidently related to the conveyance of the house. The remaining entries on this side have been crossed through, being a repetition of entries on fo. 10v. for 22–30 June 1621; the payment to Maire is recorded again at the foot of the side.

146. Perhaps the curate, although no obvious candidate among the universities' alumni.

147. Probably a mistake for George Gouldman, D.D., (c.1566–1634), Vicar of Stepney and Archdeacon of Essex: J. & J.A. Venn eds., *Alumni Cantabrigienses: Part I to 1751* (4 vols., 1922–7), ii, 230.

148. A gift probably prompted by departure of the Newdigate sisters from Deptford for Thames Street: see below, fo. 14.

Item a paire of long crewell raines xs. lether raines, bitts & spring trees for the forther horsses, with clowtes for the cowtch	I	2	o
Item to Mr Hide for his cowtchman and foure horsses to Erdbury from London	5	10	o
Item geven his man John for his paines by your apoyntment	o	5	o
Item horsmeat in Sowthwarke when you went to Sir John Tonstale's & (Ashteed), 4 cowtche hors & 3 hackneys one night	o	7	8
Item to Francis, your uncle his man, by water from Mr Lulles into Sowthworke & helping with hors	o	o	4
Item 3 raynes & headstales, 2 snaffles & 3 sett of gyrthes	o	7	—
Item 2 paire of spurres for you & your brother	o	4	o
Item geve (Jack), Sir John Tonstall his cowtcheman, by your apoyntment	o	2	o
Item geven at Ashteed to Mary the butler	o	2	6
Item to Dic who had dressed your hors and tended him at Ashteed	o	2	6
Item to Watt by your apoyntment	o	2	—
Item to Mistress Manley getting 6 smoks made	o	2	—
Item to Mistress Ginner for your 2 sisters a quarter	II	o	o
Item to Mr Stapleton for the wrytings	3	o	o
Item July the xi to you going to a playe	I	o	o
Item to Humfrey, Mr Stapleton's man, for wryting the conveance & drawing then	3	10	o
	86	8	6

[*fo.14*]

July the [?12] 1621

Item to Roberte Higenson upon his bill as thereby apeareth for gloves, roses, garters & a doson dimi. of gould & silke poynts	43	00	00
Item pinns & lute strings by William Plumley	o	10	—
Item geven Roberte Higenson by your apoyntment	o	5	o
Item to your uncle & ant Newdigate at divers tymes for your self, brother, sisters, servants & horsses as by her bill apeareth	59	19	9
Item to you	I	o	o

Item to my cosen Holme for a half yeares consideracon of 150*li*.	7	10	0
Item a realme of plaine paper, 2 quere gilt and i*oz*. of hard waxe	0	6	0
Item for your commons to the Steward [of the] Temple	2	5	8
Item a trunke for Mistress Anne	0	10	0
Item a porter carrying it to Temmes Street			3
Item a firken of soope		15	0
Item carrying it from Whitchapel to Temes Street			3
Item a hamper to packe your books in		2	0
Item a porter carrying it to the Temple			3
Item a rodd to put within the canne	0	0	3
Item to Barnerd[149] when he came first to Mr Lulles his howse by your appoyntment	0	1	0
Item the glasse man packing purslanne[150]	0	2	0
Item 2 boxes to packe itt in of the joyner		3	6
Item suger refyned xvii*li*. at xii*d*.*ob*. duble refyned 8*li*. 2*oz*. at xvi*d*. one great loffe duble refyned xii*li*.dimi. at xvi*d*. powther suger 40*li*. at x*d*., all which is 77 [*li*.] iio*z*.	4	7	0
Item olives 2 gallons, capers & 2 barels	0	10	0
Item a keg of sturgeon	0	10	0
Item the porter carrying it to Mr Lulles	0	0	1
Item the smyth for rods & hooks [for] Mistress Newdigat's chamber	0	1	0
Item the first loade carrying to Islington	0	2	0
Item to 2 cowpers heading the dry fatt and casing the clarrett & sacke	0	1	0
Item to Mistress Newdigate by your apoyntment for stockings	2	10	0
Item more to her by Mistress Margare[151] for pinnes	0	11	0
Item the joyner for 2 cases for 2 pictures	0	6	0
Item a hamper to carry downe the juggs	0	1	0
Item an other loade carrying to Islington	0	2	6
Item waying & help those 2 loades at Islington		2	8
Item xx*li*. of starch	0	4	0

149. The new coachman, engaged to drive the coach bought a few days earlier (fo. 13v.), paid with the other servants from Michaelmas 1621: WRO, CR 136, B602–612 (account books).

150. As is evident from wills and inventories, Susanna brought to the marriage much valuable plate and household goods, not to mention coins and jewellery.

151. ?Margaret/Margriet Lulls, Susanna's sister, bap. 1603: *Registers of the Dutch Church*, 47. ?Margaret Henshaw: see i, fn. 37.

Item your uncle's (cowtch) mares at (stable) 7 nightes at xvid. one bushell provander xvid. ostler iiiid.	o	11	o
Item a baskett to put orringes to send (downe)		o	8
Item orringes sent downe in itt		1	8
Item to Mr Carter[152] as by his bill, for vinger, a case for the tearse of claret, a barrell for powther suger, a runlett for the sacke & cowper spoonig them	1	3	o
Item to you more	1	o	o
Item 3 hors which came from Ashteed one night, Bale & my mare 2 nights	o	4	o
Item a loade fromm Temple xviiid. a porter helping packe & load vid.	o	2	o
Item beare by Peter, William Plumley & Robin iiiid. corde then by them iid.			6
folium 2	129	2	o
	9	6	

[fo.14v.]

Item to Mr Coles for 2yd. clothe of silver for a wastcoote for Mistress Newdigate	4	12	o
Item to your landres for a quarter & some more washing and starching	o	17	o
Item to Mr Hill teaching the gentlewomen a weeke in Temmes Street	o	11	o
Item waying the Temple stuf at Islington	o	1	o
Item Towle in Holborne for that loade	o	o	o
Item 2 paire of stockings [for] Mistress Lettis & Mistress Anne	o	14	9
Item to Mr Frauncis Hale[153] for Mr Newdigate's ring sett with diamonds	27	o	o
Item to him in exchang of 3 beare booles waying 37oz. quarter dimi. at vs. viiid.: xli. xis. ixd., the ould plate waying 32oz. dimi. at vs., which came to viiili. iis. vid., as by his bill apeareth	2	9	3
Item to him for a doson of spoones waying xixoz. at vs. viiid.	5	7	8
Item for silver for a tosting forke	o	13	o

152. William and Robert Carter of Walbrooke, both vintners, were recorded in *Visitation of London*, i, 142.

153. Francis Hall of Faringdon Within, goldsmith, was a kinsman of Sir John Tonstal: *ibid.*, i, 341.

Item for a tearse of clarett of Richard Sharman (by Mr Carter, lower end C. Street)	4	0	0
Item one runled canarie of xi gallons at iii*s*. vi*d.* as by his bill	1	15	0
Item of Mr Rode & Mr Bates 30 ell dimi. holland at iii*s*. the ell	4	11	6
Item 27 ell iii quarters at ii*s*. viii*d.*	3	14	0
Item 60 els of sowtish cloth at ii*s*. ii*d.*	6	10	0
Item 3 peeces of tabling contaynig 24 yards at xxi*s*. the peece	3	3	0
Item x ell plaine tabling at ii*s*. iiii*d.*	1	3	4
Item vi doson plaine napkins at ix*s*. the (doson)	2	14	0
Item vi doson of draper napkins at x*s*. vi*d.*	3	3	0
Item 6 elle of canvas to packe in, 2 for this cloth & 4 for the stooles & cheare	0	4	0
Item vi ell quarter holland [for] shirts for Mr Richarde < at iii*s*. >	0	18	9
Item paid for making them & whyting 2 paire of sheets & paire pillobeares sent up by William Henshawe for Mr Richard	0	3	6
Item 4 yards yellow saye by Peter for lynig Mistress Newdigate's petticoote at ii*s*.	0	8	0
Item a paire of silke stockings for Mr Richard	1	10	0
Item garters & roses for him	0	17	0
Item to Mr Benmon for vi doson ashe color & gredelyne buttons for Mr Richard	0	1	8
Item dimi. *oz.* crimson silke ingrame[154] for Mr Richard his dublett	0	1	6
Item 2*oz.* < quarter > of sprig bonding at v*s*. viii*d.* for Mistress Newdigate's petticoote	0	12	9
Item i*yd.* yellowe rybben for itt	0	0	4
Item blacke lace & silke for Mr Newdigate his best hosse & dublett	0	3	0
	78	0	1
		6	

[*fo.15*]

Item 2 paire of bodies [for] Mistress Lettis & Mistress Anne bought at the Goulden Gonne in Booe Lane	0	7	0

Item to my cosen Rode (by Peter) i elle canvas
xvi*d.* dimi. yard poledavis v*d.* 3 yards blacke

154. Reading uncertain.

saye v*s*. vi*d*. i ell canvas i*s*. v*d*. 3 yards dimi.			
homes iiii*s*. i*d*. for your best hosse & dublett	0	12	10
Item xvi yards of Chyna damaske for 2 petticoots			
for 2 petticoots for Mistress Lettis & Mistress			
Anne	4	10	0
Item 7 yards of yellowe saye at ii*s*. the yard to			
lyne them	0	14	0
Item silver binding & silke to sett it one for them	0	15	—
Item to Anthonie for the horsses 3 nights in More-			
feildes	1	4	0
Item at [the] Starr stonde hors, Chester, Bale &			
my mare, hay for them	0	4	—
Item provander for them there	0	2	—
Item to Mr Beale for a whit bever & gould band			
for you	3	—	—
Item for a band & dressing 2 hatts	0	4	0
Item a hat for Mr Richard	0	12	0
Item v showes & i remove upon those hors which			
came from Ashteed	0	1	9
Item washing Mr Newdigate's fanne		1	0
Item 2 sprigges [for] Mistress Lettis & Mistress			
Anne		11	0
Item hors hyered by Roberte Higenson for Mr			
Lulles his man to ride, paid x*s*. received backe			
v*s*., so for it	0	5	0
Item to a man which brought the hors			4
Item by your apoyntment to Peter, Sara &			
(Kate)[155]	1	10	0
Item to Robin Burrig by your apoyntment	0	13	0
Item Peter sending a packe of cloaks to the carryer			
by a porter	0	0	3
Item a locke & kye for the cowtch box	0	1	0
Item setting up horsse at [the] Starr the mornig			
we came forth of London	0	1	0
Item St Albans, Strabers, wyne & suger	—	2	8
Item Dunstable musicke	0	2	6
Item supper 32*s*. breakfast and chamberlaine			
xiii*s*.	2	5	0
Item horsmeate xvi*s*. showing ii*s*. iii*d*.	0	18	3
Item the pore there then	0	0	6
Item Toster baite, sturgion, samon & wyne		9	6
Item supper, breakfast, chamber & cooke (Dain-			
trie)	1	8	6

155. Servants to Mr Lulls: see above.

Item Hesterley for 4630 at 3s. vid. the c[156]	7	15	0
Item Thomas Morton Senior beare & ostlers, Star		0	8
Item beare at Stoni Stratford by him	0	2	2
Item at Mr Hilton's hors xiiis. ostlers is. boots 3d.	0	14	3
Item the boye which Mr Hilton sent to Thrup	0	0	3
Item Granborow 2 boyes walking hors			6
Item i remove & picking Morton's mare's foote			2
Item to Thomas Morton which he gave to a porter at Mr Lulles'	0	0	8
Item to Barnard (by Thomas Morton) that he gave to ostlers in beare	0	0	5
	29	10	2
folium 3		8	

[*fo.15v.*]

To Peter Ollive upon his bill as
followeth upon theise 2 sides

Aprill: Imprimis carrying a lettre to Mistress Lulles from Ashteed, his diner vid. i show & i remove [on] Bale 5d.	0	0	11
Item setting up his hors then	0	—	3
<12>			
Item going to London his supper			6
Item a sallett for you vid. supper vid.		1	0
<13>			
Item Thorsdaye & Frydaye his dyete		2	—
Item 4 doson of buttons for you & dimi. oz. silke		2	4
<19, 20>			
Item his diners & suppers		2	0
Item dimi. oz. silke [for] Mr Richard's cloake cut shorter	0	1	0
<21, 22>			
Item Peter's dyete 2 dayes iis. ioz. nutmegs iiiid.	0	2	4
Item 2 paire of band strings iiiid. threed iiiid.		0	8
<23>			
Item Peter's diner & supper xiid. to the Ould Swan & back xiid.		2	0
<24>			
Item his diner vid. a lettre by Kidney iid.			8
Item supper in your chamber	0	1	10

---

156. ?Oysters.

<25>

Item Peter's dyete v dayes	0	5	0
Item going & coming, the Ould Swanne	0	1	0

<Maye>

Item the 5th and 6 Peter's dyete these 2 dayes	0	2	0

<22>

Item the butler at Harrow Hill	0	1	0
Item a quarter of stiching & a quarter of sowing silke	0	1	0
Item by Peter for his diner			6
Item 2 yards dimi. blacke saye [for] saten dublet & hose		5	0
Item whale bone iiii*d*. past bord 3*d*. threed vii*d*.		1	2
Item dimi. quarter taffatie [for] cape [for] grogron cloake		2	7
Item a doson clasps iii*d*. grynding shears 3*d*.			6
Item when he brought your grogron sute to (London) supper			6
Item diner daye after: diner vi*d*. his hors xvi*d*.		1	10
Item him self & hors being in London 2 dayes		2	10
Item crossing the water Lambeth twyse		0	4
Item an other tyme comming to London: setting up his hors ix*d*. crosing water twyse iiii*d*.		1	1
Item when you went [to] hors race Peter's diner	0	0	6
Item setting up hors at Lambeth	0	–	6
Item geven Mr Newdigate's[157] man Dick by Peter	0	1	0
Item wyne & suger at Stretton	0	0	8
Item to Frauncis carrying backe your horses	0	1	0
Item when you went to Uxbrig (by Peter) for his horsse in London v nights	0	4	9
Item by water to the Ould Swan & backe	0	0	5

<June>

Item at London when you bowght your best suite, his dyete 2 dayes	0	2	0
Item i quarter of buckeron for a cape for your grogeron cloake	0	0	4
Item crossing water ii*d*. a showe & 3 removes vii*d*.			9
Item for your cloth of gould dublett dimi. yard poledavis	0	0	6
Item whale bone iiii*d*. clasps 3*d*. searing candle 4*d*.			10
Item i*yd*. cotton viii*d*. dimi. *yd*. blacke scarg for the sleeves 4*d*.		1	0

157. Probably Henry Newdigate, whose servant Francis appears below.

Item blacke & browne threed & past borde	2	o
Item Peter bring this suite crossing water		2
< 15 [June] >		
Item his supper that night vi		6
Item a tayler wages 3 dayes	1	6
< 19 >		
Item his diner & supper	1	o
Item dimi. *oz.* silke for Mr Richard's dublett	1	o

	3	4	3
		15	

[*fo.16*]

Item i quarter of baies for your hosse	o	1	6
Item claspes for them iii*d*.			3
Item past bord 3*d*. iii quarters more thred xxi*d*.		2	o
Item his hors v nights iiii*s*. i*yd*. buckerom xii*d*.		5	o
< 20 [June] >			
Item his diner vi*d*. dimi. *oz.* carnacon silke [for] Mr Richard		1	8
Item quarter dimi. taffatie [for] dublet sleeves		5	8
Item crossing water twyse 4*d*. setting up hors iii*d*.			7
Item 2 taylors helping to make Mr Richard's hosse, dublet & cloake 4 dayes		5	8
Item 2 doson poynts for Mr Richard		6	6
Item i*yd*. phillip & cheame for him		6	o
Item to Mr Holland for a paper booke for you		1	6
Item dimi. *oz.* silke for [my] Mistress' peticoote		1	2
Item his hors 3 nights		2	4
Item for cords to male things with by Peter		2	8
Item a hat boxe			10
Item covering the pillion, to the sadler of Eueall by Peter		6	4
Temes Streete	2	9	8

Disbursed in this boke in seaven leafe sides going before theise somes:

folium 1	Imprimis the first side	40	−6	10
	The other side	86	−8	−6
folium 2	Item the second	129	−2	−0
	The other side	78	−0	−1
folium 3	Item the theirde	29	10	−2
	The other side	3	−4	−3

folium 4 Item this side as above	2	-9	-8
	369	-1	-6

[*fos.16v., 17, 17v. blank*]
[*fo.18*]

November 1621: Received for the half
yeares rent of Brackenborowes dewe
at Mychellmas last

Imprimis of the Cowtes of Derbie	23	–	–
Item of Mr Baldwen [for] Chamberhiles	24	3	4
Item of Mr Anderowe	25	0	0
Item of Mistress Winkfelde	23	6	8
Item of Tayler	3	6	8
Item of Makins	0	6	8

Item of Mr Baldwen for the meadowe he had
from Kelleyd—nothing of him nor Webber for
the Great Spring because you have taken itt
into your owne hands: the rent was ii*li.* iii*s.*

iiii*d.*	2	10	0
	101	13	4

Also Kelley hath not accompted for this half
yeares rentt.

Nor noe exhibition dewe nowe[158].

Item received of Mr Debeste[159]	500	0	0

    Some received   601 13 -4

< and xii*s.* for the bedsteed which I must geve
you in monie[160] >

Whereof disbursed

Imprimis to Sir Frauncis Englefeilde[161] being the monie which was paid to Mr Bolton at Maye daye last 1621[162]	500	0	0
Item for continuing your livery[163]	00	11	0

158. John Newdigate being out of wardship.
159. An instalment of £1,400 on Susanna Newdigate's dowry was due from de Beste
20 Nov. 1621: WRO, CR 136, C2719. The shortfall here was indicative of things to
come: see Larminie, 'Marriage and the Family', 5–6.
160. Hired from the Two Wrastlers, Watling Street, Dec. 1620 (fo. 1v) for 14*s.*, and
now returned.
161. Of Howlshott, Hants., a relative of Dame Anne Newdigate and a trustee of Sir
John: WRO, CR 136, C371.
162. As part of Mary Newdigate's dowry: see above i, fn. 243.
163. i.e. In the Court of Wards.

Item to Mr George Crowke geving instructions to drawe the booke betweene you & Mr Gifforde	00	11	0
Item a ring for Mr Edward Fytton geven him by <my[164]> Lady's will[165]	00	11	0
Item 3*oz*. Naples silke for Mistress Newdigate	0	6	6
Item dimi. *oz*. whit & dimi. yellowe purle for Mistress Lettis & Mistress Anne	0	1	4
Item dimi. *oz*. soeing gould & dimi. *oz*. silver for them	0	5	6
Item to Mr Hurst, Mr Crowk's man, for drawing the booke	0	9	0
Item a girdle for Mr Richard Newdigate		4	0
Item tinning & rowelling his spurs		0	4
Item dimi. hundreth of neidles [for the] (gentlewomen)		1	0
Item 3 strewes for beare	0	1	0
Item 2 elle holland for Mistress Lettis & Anne	0	7	8
Item to my cosen Holme for half yeares consideracon of 150*li*.	7	10	0
—paid in then thereof fiftie pounds, so nowe but 100*li*. to my cosen Holme, which was retorned downe by (William)			
Item more to Morton & Aston's use by (William Henshawe's) derection xii*li*.[166]			
Item to Henry Thornton, my cosen Rode's man, for portage of letters & other things from the carryers to him	00	0	8
Item 8 paire of gloves for Mistress Newdigate to Roberte Higenson	0	13	4
Item to him which he gave a carryer for carrying downe the bedsteed and (palliases)	1	3	6
Item by Roberte <which he gave a porter> for carrying a bundle from Mr Lules' howse	0	0	3
Item to him sending downe the same	0	2	4
folium 6	5 12	19	5
	4	4	

[*fo.18v*.]

By Mr Richard
Imprimis Ryder's Dictionary for you[167]   00   8   0

---

164. Original word erased.
165. WRO, CR 136, C1915.
166. Probably on Warwickshire estate business.
167. J. Rider, *Bibliotheca scholastica. A double dictionarie* (several edns., 1589–1617),

Item Stephanus Poeticall Dixtionary[168]	o	6	o
Item Baccus his tales in Englishe[169]	o	8	6
Item Senica the philosopher's Works[170]	oo	19	o
Item for Mr Richard Plowdin's Commentary[171]	oo	14	–
Item Molinus Buckler of Faithe[172]		3	–
Item Tellenus Sintugina[173]		4	–
Item for Pirkins[174]			10
Item (by Peter Olife[175]) carrying up Mr Richard his trunke to Hartell		7	6
Item by him for carrying a basket from London to Erdbury (I thinke), sent by Mr (Lulls)	o	1	4
Item 3 yards Turkie grogeron [for] dublet for Mr Richard	o	15	o
Item 22 yards gallonie binding, 2oz. dimi. at iis. iiiid.	o	5	10
Item 1oz. styching & sowing silke	o	2	o
Item dimi. ell taffatie for fasing	o	6	3
Item dimi. yard bayes for sleeves			9
Item dimi. yard canvas to peece the lynig			6
Item past bord for the coller			1
Item 2 yards dimi. for hommes fustian dublet	o	2	6
Item for 4 doson of buttons		1	4
Item[176] to Peter for making dublet & hose		8	o

STC, 21031.5–21034a. The first four items here were bought for John Newdigate, according to marginal note.

168. Duplicating a copy bought earlier: see i, fn. 33.

169. Perhaps an edition of Boccacio: or perhaps King Boccus, *The history of kyng Boccus, & Sydracke*. Tr. by Hugo of Carumpeden, out of frenche (?1537, 1550), STC, 3186–8. J. Boemus, *The description of the contrey of Aphrique* (1554) or *The manners, laws & customs of all nations* (1611), both trans. from French, STC, 3196.5–3198.5.

170. See above i, fn. 188.

171. E. Plowden, *Les comentaries, ou les reportes ... de dyvers cases* (1571 etc.), STC, 20040–20046.7. These second four items were for Richard himself, according to marginal bracket.

172. P. Du Moulin, *The buckler of faith: or, a defence of the confession of faith of the reformed churches in France, against the objections of M. Arnoux the jesuite* (trans. from French, 1620), STC, 7313.

173. Unclear: ? J.I. Tremelius, *Septuagint Bible*, e.g. STC, 2056, would certainly complement the previous purchase.

174. Either John Perkins the lawyer, e.g. ... *A verie profitable booke treating of the lawes of this realme* ... (1555 etc.), STC, 19629–19645, or William Perkins the divine, many possible works, STC, 19646–19764.

175. This and the following indented items were all bought by Peter, according to marginal note and bracket.

176. Followed by 'by' deleted.

My cosen Rod's bill

	£	s	d
Item i ell dimi. Estcontrie cloth [for] hors rubbers	0	0	9
Item carrying the bedsteed from [the] Temple[177]	0	0	6
Item i ell cambricke for Mr Richard	0	8	3
Item i ell holland [for] hancarchers for him	0	3	0
Item paid for carrying 6 yard of cotten from Erdbury & dalivered to Mr Coxe[178]	0	0	7
Item to Hartell carrying a cheese sent to Sir John Tonstall	0	0	10
Item 2 yards webbes cloth for a coote	1	6	0
Item 3 yards of bayes	0	10	0
Item vi yard of rug att xviiid.	0	8	0
Item 2yd. quarter satten at xiiiis. for your dublet	1	11	6
Item vi doson dimi. lace viiioz.	0	16	0
Item xyd. of whit osnebridge at ixd.		7	6
Item to Mr Edward Fytton for consideracon of cli.	5	0	0
Item iyd. dimi. of webbes cloth for your hosse	0	19	6
Item for whiting 2 paire of sheets & 2 paire of pillowbeares sent up by William Henshawe to Mr Richard	0	2	6
Item 4 ell east contrie cloth	0	3	4
Item to Mistress M.[179] for a paire of roses for Mistress Newdigate & a thing to stewe meate in	0	11	0
<November 1621>			
Item to Mistress Mary Trussell, which was borowed of her 28th of November 1620 to be paid with consideracon	20	0	0
Item paid her then for consideracon of 23 weeks beginning the xxviiith of Maye last	0	15	0
Item to Mr Richard to paye in part for [his] chamber[180]	20	0	0
Item left with him to paye for the viall, his commons, fagotts & other necessaryes	7	4	0
	66	2	6

177. See above, fn. 165.
178. Tenant on the Arbury estate: WRO, CR 136, B595–605 (account books).
179. ?Manley: cf. above, fos. 6, 13v.
180. In the Easter term 1622 Richard Newdigate paid another £20 for his chamber: WRO, CR 136, B603. Nov. 1628 he petitioned the Bench that he was in actual possession of a chamber assigned to Mr Thomas Marshe under a lease of two lives held by Sir Thomas Chamberlaine 'and others', and had been 'above seven years': Gray's Inn MS, Book of Orders, i, fo. 374v.

(Memorandum) that I paid Mr Lowgher xx*li.* for
the consideracon of 200*li.* for on yeare, which is
nott set downe. And ix*li.* more I have disbursed
for him which he will come to noe reconig for.
Also be it remembered that there was aboute xv
toddes of Mr Newdigate's woole which had
taken hurtt with lying & being new wounde.
Thomas Shepperd & the woole winder did
mistake & laid it to myne, which I must gyve
account for.[181]

[*fo.19*]

To inqueare for a leasse[182]

Mr C.C. hath a lease of the King's hould for xxi yeares which cost
him 200*li.* & his (lady) nothing, in revertion after 3 yeares, only the
brought him into (fa . . .[183]), & were the procurers of the estating the
land upon him, and sythence caused him to be executor, by which he
shall com to present possession of all after his grand(?father's) death.
(Whose) spheach have bin spoken by gent(lemen) at the table of his
ill carryag, & hurd by dyvers, theat it hath bin laid upon them. The
lady hath bin exceeding angry with them for speake for him, & wished
it were to doe againe, (synce) it was long of them.

< Thomas Smyth of (Over) Haddon knight[184] >

Joyse of licoryse at Whites the apotycary against St Ma(ry)
Jo. Smyth at Mr Porter's without Temple Barr
Doctor Craddocke[185] or Mr Trussell[186]

181. In spite of the contemporary slump in wool exports, sheep, their meat and their
wool, still formed an important part of John Newdigate's income: Larminie, 'Lifestyle
and Attitudes', 48–57.
182. The majority of entries on this page are made vertically, on its upper and lower
halves, and give the appearance of notes made at different times.
183. Reading uncertain.
184. Entry upside down in relation to the rest of the text, and in a similar, but
much smaller, neater hand. This may be a topical reference to Sir Thomas Smith of
Ostenhanger (1568?–1625), who resigned as Treasurer of the East India Company in
1620 on suspicion of corruption: *DNB.*
185. ?John Cradocke, D.C.L.: *Alumni Oxon,* i. ?A medical doctor from the family in
St Dunstan in the West: T.C. Dale ed., *The Inhabitants of London in 1638* (2 vols., 1931),
i, 232, 234.
186. The next and last entry on the upper half of the side is obscured by the binding.
Entries in the lower half duplicate: (1) 9 entries beginning 'Daintrie Ed dressing my
hors' (i, fo. lv.); (2) horizontally) receipts and disbursements from and for Mr Shalcrosse
(i, fo. 15).

V

CAPTAIN HENRY HERBERT'S NARRATIVE OF HIS JOURNEY THROUGH FRANCE WITH HIS REGIMENT, 1671-3

and

ANE ACCOUNT OF OUR REGEMENTS MARCHES FROM THE WINTER QUARTERS TO THER ENTRANCE IN FRANCE

Edited by John Childs

CONTENTS

ACKNOWLEDGEMENT

The transcripts from the Herbert Manuscripts in the National Library of Wales are reproduced with the kind permission of the Librarian and the Trustees of the Powis Castle Estate.

ABBREVIATIONS

Childs, *Army of Charles II*	John Childs, *The Army of Charles II* (London, 1976).
Childs, *Nobles, Gentlemen*	John Childs, *Nobles, Gentlemen and the Profession of Arms in Restoration Britain, 1660–1668* (London, Society for Army Historical Research, 1987)
CSPD	*Calendar of State Papers Domestic*
Dalton	Charles Dalton, *English Army Lists and Commission Registers, 1660–1714* (London, 1892–1904), 6 vols.
DBF	*Dictionnaire de Biographie Française* (Paris, 1933 cont.)
DNB	*Dictionary of National Biography*
DNF	*Dictionnaire de la Noblesse de la France*, ed. A. de la Chenaye-Desbois et Badier (Paris, 1863–73, 3rd edn.), 19 vols.
Herbert Correspondence	*Herbert Correspondence*, ed. W.J. Smith (Cardiff & Dublin, 1968)
HM	Herbert Manuscripts, National Library of Wales
HP	*The House of Commons, 1660–1690*, ed. B.D. Henning (London, 1983), 3 vols.
JSAHR	*Journal of the Society for Army Historical Research*
NLW	National Library of Wales, Aberystwyth
OCD	*The Oxford Classical Dictionary*, eds. N.G.L. Hammond and H.H. Scullard (Oxford, 1973)
OED	*The Oxford English Dictionary*
PRO	Public Record Office, London
S	Flemish shilling
SP	State Papers, Public Record Office

Army Ranks

Gen.	General
Capt.	Captain

Leift. Lieut.	Lieutenant
Corn. Cornt.	Cornet
Quarter. Quart. Qu. Qum.	Quartermaster
Corpll.	Corporal
Sold.	Soldier

INTRODUCTION

Captain Henry Herbert (c. 1643–1691), the author of the 'Narrative', was a troop commander in Sir Henry Jones's Regiment of Light Horse in the French Army between 1671 and 1673. Herbert, who succeeded his brother Edward as fourth Baron Herbert of Cherbury in 1678, pursued a military career for much of his life. His introduction to martial affairs came through his involvement in Sir George Booth's Uprising in 1659. After the Restoration, Herbert entered the Irish Foot Guards as an ensign in which rank he served until 1665, when he transferred into the English establishment as a lieutenant in Lord Carberry's independent company of foot in the garrison of Ludlow Castle. Two years later, on 15 January 1667, he secured a firmer foothold in the English standing army with a captaincy in the Lord High Admiral's Maritime Regiment of Foot, better known as the Duke of York's. He retained this commission until 1680, when he was dismissed from the army because of his support for the cause of Exclusion. Herbert briefly returned to the army in 1689, accepting the colonelcy of a newly-raised regiment of foot for just one month between 8 March and 10 April. A noted duellist and a somewhat raffish young man, Herbert was allowed to keep his commission in the Duke of York's during his secondment to serve as a captain in Sir Henry Jones's Regiment of Light Horse in France from its formation in 1671 until the beginning of 1673. Possibly, Herbert's tour of duty in France was intended to assuage the displeasure of the Duke of York after Herbert had wounded the young John Churchill, the future Duke of Marlborough and then a protégé of York, in a challenge at Landguard Fort in 1671. It may be that Herbert's removal into the French army was a mild form of punishment for this misdemeanour.[1] If so, we have a partial explanation of the vitriolic language sometimes employed by Herbert in his writings. That, however, is speculation and it is equally likely that Herbert volunteered to fight in France in order to acquire experience and further his career. Following his homecoming in 1673, Herbert compiled a narrative of his travels, observations and campaigns in France and the Low Countries between late 1671 and early 1673.[2]

Herbert took a pile of $13\frac{1}{2}$ inch by $8\frac{1}{2}$ inch sheets of gilt-edged paper and folded each in half to form four pages, two on the front and two on the back. He then divided his sheets into two bundles. The Narrative is written on both sides of 29 of these folded sheets, 'blanck's as Herbert

---

1. Childs, *Nobles, Gentlemen*, p. 42; *HP*, ii. 531; A.H. Dodd, *Studies in Stuart Wales* (Cardiff, 1971), p. 83; *Correspondence of the Family of Hatton*, ed. E.M. Thompson (London, Camden society, new series xxiii, 1878), i. 66.

2. NLW, HM 2/14/7a.

calls them on page 16 of the manuscript, making a total of 116 pages. Pages 38 and 39 are empty, as if the author accidentally turned over two sheets at once. The initial pile of sheets contains Part One of the Narrative and consists of 48 pages. Page 49 forms the front cover of the Second Part – '2 Part'. Some material is missing at this point as there is a clear break in the sense between pages 48 and 50. Substantial additions to pages 1, 3, and 28 are included on separate sheets which are wrapped between pages 16 and 17 of the manuscript. Herbert paginated the first part of his Narrative, pages 1 to 48, but did not number the pages of the second part. The final page, 105, of the Narrative is followed by 6 blank pages but on page 112 is a copy of a poem in Herbert's hand. The verses are by Vavasor Powell, the Fifth Monarchist and Puritan divine, and are entitled, 'Of the Late King Charles, of Blessed Memory'. Page 113 is blank but on page 114 is another poem, 'Love from this moment I bid thee defiance'. This is in Herbert's handwriting but whether the author was Herbert or Powell is unclear. Another poem, 'Nine or Ten Easters [?] now are gone and past', has been copied by Herbert on to page 115 and this appears to be his own composition. On the final page, 116, on the back of the second part, is written, 'Journey into France, 1672'. The sheets of the first part are bound together by a bent pin but the second part has been sewn with thread.

The Narrative is part of the second deposit of the Powis Castle Collection which was presented to the National Library of Wales at Aberystwyth by the Earl of Powis in 1959.[3] In the published calendar of the correspondence of the Herbert family, the Narrative was listed but was neither summarised nor described.[4] The editor probably passed it over because of the amount of space that even a paraphrase would have required. Herbert possibly intended the Narrative for publication in some form, either in manuscript or as a printed work, for he consciously addresses an audience and it is too elaborate to have been intended as a mere *aide-memoire*. The manuscript appears to have been checked by the author who has made numerous additions and amendments both between the lines and in the margins. It is likely to have been composed in two sessions. To the conclusion of page 32 in the manuscript, Herbert's story is continuous and without repetition. However, at the opening of page 33, his recollection reverts to 28 April and he retells of his march from Lorraine up to the siege and capture of Wesel. As he has little new to add during this re-tracing, it can only be assumed that the author had put the work aside for a while and then resumed composition without having first checked the point at which he had suspended his account. The

---

3. *Herbert Correspondence*, p. 13.
4. *Ibid*, p. 360 no. 61.

material in these two versions of the campaign from Lorraine to Wesel (pages 28 to 35) is almost identical. This similarity is a clue to the method which Herbert used to construct his Narrative. Either he wrote with the assistance of notes, which have not survived, or, more probably, the Narrative is a fair copy derived from an initial draft. The notes or the draft were probably written whilst Herbert was in France and the Low Countries. The spontaneity of, 'to recount all our adventures to this present, being Valantines day' (page 16), suggests that the Narrative was based on a record of events kept at the time. There are no other breaks in the story and the style of expression and the handwriting give a hint that the Narrative was constructed within a relatively short period.

Also in Parcel 14 of the Herbert Manuscripts are a further 5 folded sheets, on both sides of which is written a Shorter Version of the Narrative. Again, there is no title. This consists of 18 pages. It is in Henry Herbert's hand and was almost certainly composed before he started work on the main Narrative. Most likely, it was an important, intermediate stage in organising the raw material which he had brought back from France into the final and fair copy of the Narrative. It is an attenuated and skeletal version of the Narrative but written hurriedly and with little care or attention to detail and the niceties of syntax.[5]

In this document there is some evidence about the possible motivation for Herbert's literary endeavours. Herbert has nothing good to say of his colonel, Sir Henry Jones. Jones was a fellow-Welshman who had served in Cromwell's army. It is possible that Henry Jones was the son, or a close relative, of Colonel John Jones (1597?–1660) of Maes-y-garnedd, Merionethshire, the regicide who was executed after the Restoration. Herbert's poem on page 115 of the Narrative is devoted to a sarcastic horoscope of Jones's origins.

> Nine or ten Easters [?] now are gone and past,
> Since Mars and Venus in conjunction fast,
> As any Dog and Bitch did signifie,
> The making of our Heroe was hard by.
> Strange prodigies the season of that yeare,
> Made people stare in Wales and every where.
> The father and his neighbour in the spring,
> As tis beleeved, did heare the Cuckow sing.
> The sun was hot in sumer and the Gad,
> Did make the mountaine cattle run like mad.
> The harvest was a late as ere was knowne,
> Corne did not ripen where it was not sowne.

5. NLW, HM 2/14/7b.

Cherries was scarce in winter, twas so cold,
And had a longing seized the pregnant skowld,
As those that knew her humour say it might,
Our theam had been a castling not a Knight.
By those the learned guest as reason 'twas,
That Good or Bad would shortly come to passe.
At Glandowres Birth his father horses stood,
All belly deep, however it came, in Blood.
Soe would Sir Jones his if poor John, his dad,
Had eyther tills or rack or manger had.

Henry Jones was a captain in, or possibly was major of, John Humphrey's regiment of foot in Barbados and Jamaica in 1655 and 1656.
Lucky to survive service in the West Indies, Jones was appointed to
Sir William Lockhart's Brigade which fought alongside the French
army at the siege of Dunkirk and at the Battle of the Dunes on 4/14
June 1658. Jones displayed such gallantry in this action that he was
dubbed a knight bachelor by Cromwell on 17 July 1658 and was
promoted to the lieutenant-colonelcy of John Hewson's infantry regiment. At the Restoration, he found his way into a lieutenant's commission in Lord Hawley's troop in the Royal Horse Guards, probably
through the patronage and influence of George Monck and Sir
William Lockhart. By 1665 he had risen to captain. Two years later,
Jones became the lieutenant of Sir George Hamilton's Troop of
English Gens d'Armes in the French army, the first hint that he had
changed his religion to Catholicism. He retained his troop in the
Royal Horse Guards whilst in France. In 1671 he obtained permission
to expand the Gens d'Armes into a full-sized light cavalry regiment
under his own command. Jones tried to recruit men from his own
troop in the Royal Horse Guards; much to his annoyance, there were
few volunteers.[6] Jones was killed by a bullet through the throat whilst
he was attending the Duke of Monmouth at the siege of Maastricht
in 1673.[7]

Herbert clearly hated Jones. To an aristocrat, Jones was an
unprincipled, ambitious careerist who used any method, good or bad,
to make his own fortunes prosper. Herbert thought him vulgar, a
man not endowed with a gentleman's sense of honour. Some of this
antagonism seems to have stemmed from a clash of personalities as
well as from the difference in social station. Much was sheer hypocrisy
on Herbert's part for he too cheated the muster-master and indulged

6. *Hatton Correspondence*, i. 71; *The Writings and Speeches of Oliver Cromwell*, ed. W.C.
Abbott (Cambridge, Mass., 1947), iv. 854, 952; *The Knights of England*, ed. W.A. Shaw
(London, 1906), ii. 224.
7. SP 78/137, f. 146; Childs, *Nobles, Gentlemen*, pp. 47, 106, 107; C.H. Firth & G.
Davies, *A Regimental History of Cromwell's Army* (Oxford, 1940), ii. 411, 723.

in other sharp practices to the same extent as his commanding officer. Remnants of animosity from the days of the Interregnum—they had been on opposite sides during the rising of Sir George Booth in 1659— may have fuelled their common dislike. The Short Narrative contains broadsides of badly-written invective aimed at Jones. Little of this ferocious material finds its way into the Final Version although some of the allegations and gratuitous abuse creep past the author's self-censorship. In both the Short and the Final Versions, Herbert's style of writing and his literary discipline lose their clarity as soon as he begins a tirade against his colonel. His temper appears to take control of his pen to the extent that his meaning sometimes becomes obscure. Perhaps Herbert intended to publish his Narrative, either in Manuscript or in print, in order to reveal Jones's iniquities to the authorities in England. Herbert probably wanted to establish his interpretation of the regimental history before Jones returned the compliment. There can be little doubt that Herbert was an extremely awkward and quarrelsome young man and Jones probably entertained a jaundiced memory of his conduct whilst under his command. Herbert felt the need to strike first. There is no evidence that the Narrative was ever shown to anyone and Jones's death before Maastricht in June 1673 brought the matter to an end.

Apart from the outbursts against Jones, the Narrative has a pleasant and consistent style well laced with a whimsical and faintly sarcastic sense of humour. It is quite likely that Herbert wrote his Narrative whilst serving at sea with the fleet during the summer of 1673. There would have been little else to do but sit in his cabin on board the *St George* and pour out his vitriol against Sir Henry Jones. The fact that the Narrative stops at the point where Herbert commenced his period of duty as a marine tends to support this notion.

Although Herbert did not go on campaign in the Netherlands and Germany in 1673, Jones's Regiment of Light Horse took the field. This formation remained in the French service until 1678, the Duke of Monmouth assuming the colonelcy after Jones's demise in 1673. Wrapped in Parcel 14 of the Herbert Manuscripts in company with the two versions of the Narrative is 'Ane Account of our Regements marches from the winter quarters to ther Entrance in France', dated 1672.[8] This document is much shorter—$3\frac{1}{2}$ pages on both sides of a single, folded sheet—and is a bare record of the marches made by the regiment enlivened by the occasional, rather bald observation. It is maddeningly brief on the two key episodes of the 1673 campaign, the sieges of Maastricht and Trier, but it does provide a skeletal diary of the movements of Jones's/Monmouth's Horse during this important

8. NLW, HM 2/14/7c. The date was 1673 by the Gregorian Calendar.

year in the Franco-Dutch War. The fact that the manuscript has found its way into the Herbert Collection and has been bundled with the Narratives of the 1672 campaign, suggests that it was written for Herbert by a fellow officer in Jones's regiment. The writer lacks Herbert's style and interest in the countryside and people, but he essays one or two observations away from the strictly military as if attempting to emulate Herbert's work. It is probable that this Account was composed at one sitting after the campaign had ended and the most likely author was Captain Henry Every, later to become Sir Henry Every, third baronet, who was distantly related to Herbert as well as serving as a fellow troop commander in Jones's Horse.[9]

Herbert's Narrative and the Account add considerably to existing knowledge of the part played by the British Brigade in the early years of the Franco-Dutch War which lasted from 1672 until 1678. In so doing, they form a valuable source for the history of British army officers who served abroad during the reign of Charles II. Herbert relates the procedures by which a regiment was raised for service overseas, how it was paid, equipped and supplied, and the arrangements that were made for its accommodation and marches. The reception of Jones's troopers on their arrival in Dieppe was well arranged and, by seventeenth century standards, efficient. This good management continued to guide the regiment across northern France into winter quarters in Lorraine and it was not until the latter stage of the campaign of 1672 that the fallibity of the French commissariat was at last revealed. The Narrative provides further evidence for the continuity of service by British professional officers who moved from one foreign appointment to another. Herbert twice emphasises that the officers who had fought in the British auxiliary brigade in Portugal between 1662 and 1668 formed the backbone of Jones's Light Horse. Many of these gentlemen formed business partnerships, selling their expertise in company and troop command from one employer to another. Records of the activities of Charles II's soldiers in France between 1672 and 1678 are extremely scarce and can only be gleaned piecemeal from collections of correspondence and state papers. To have a substantial manuscript devoted to the affairs of one of the regiments in the British Brigade in France is a notable addition to the source material.

Captain Herbert was gloriously xenophobic. Frenchmen, Dutchmen, Germans, and Lorrainers attracted his censure, and even Welsh-

---

9. Henry Every (c.1653–1709), succeeded as 3rd Baronet of Egginton in 1700. His mother, Vere, was the daughter of Sir Henry Herbert (d.1673), Master of the Revels to both Charles I and Charles II. Sir Henry Herbert was the great-uncle of Captain Henry Herbert (G.E.C., *Complete Baronetage* (Exeter, 1902), ii. 85–6; *Herbert Correspondence*, p. 413).

men whom he found residing in Cologne were not spared his biting pen. Yet he travelled with his eyes and mind relatively open. He commented in considerable detail on the countryside through which he passed and was interested in the local economy, the people and their customs. He seized every opportunity to leave his troop in order to visit major towns, cities, and landmarks near which his regiment happened to pass. On one occasion, his sight-seeing placed him in greater personal danger than he was to experience in action with his regiment. Perhaps he was a trifle gullible in relating some tall stories about the cats of Lorraine or the Virgin of St. Truiden but, generally, he was disbelieving unless he had witnessed with his own eyes. As a younger son, Herbert had not enjoyed the privilege of a Grand Tour. His journey through France, Lorraine, Liège, the Netherlands and the Rhineland was something of a substitute and Herbert certainly conveyed the impression that he intended to make the most of his opportunities to explore foreign culture. For a firm Anglican, Herbert displayed a surprising benevolence towards Catholicism. He took an interest in catholic shrines, cathedrals, churches, and legends although he could not resist a number of waspish remarks. Significantly, when his friend, Dr John Higgins the regimental surgeon, died in Nancy, Herbert retained the certificate, signed by a Huguenot pastor, stating that Higgins had passed from this life professing the faith of Canterbury.[10]

From the point of view of European as opposed to strictly British military history, Herbert's Narrative provides a good deal of information upon the conduct of civil-military relations, particularly during Turenne's march down the Rhine and Moselle in the late autumn and early winter of 1672. On the march to the United Provinces, most of the French Army's needs had been met with magazines which had been established in advance in the lands of the Electorate of Cologne, but as Turenne's corps, with Jones's regiment attached, withdrew from the Dutch Republic, first to Maastricht and then into the valleys of the Rhine and the Moselle, the troops had to live off the land. Herbert recounts the skirmishes and minor battles between the German peasant farmers and the soldiers from the army, many of the latter almost starving. The peasant farmers, or 'boers' as Herbert calls them, appear to have left their villages on the approach of the French army and taken themselves, their possessions, and their livestock into fortified camps in the forests and hills and then waited until the maurading troops had passed through. Regiments acted independently in attacking and raiding these peasant outposts; even small groups and individuals seem to have been encouraged to forage for provisions by themselves. The French supply system was non-

10. NLW, HM 2/14/7c/1.

existent. This state of affairs was partially intentional. By allowing discipline to relax and obliging his soldiers to live off the land, Turenne wasted the countryside and so prevented the Imperial and Brandenburg forces from operating close to the Rhine or the Moselle. In this way, the exposed and advanced position of the French army in the United Provinces was protected from interference towards its flank and rear. From Herbert's evidence, this stage of the Franco-Dutch War resembled the Thirty Years' War, the conflict in which Turenne had learned his trade. Herbert's story of the continual friction between the army and the peasants reveals another aspect of the problem of military supply. By permitting his men to maraud and ravage, Turenne debilitated his army. It lost effectiveness, discipline suffered, and, ironically, the troops failed to find sufficient to eat. It was to solve all these difficulties, but especially those relating to morale and efficiency, that armies in the later seventeenth century began to organise more permanent and embracing supply systems. For Herbert and his comrades, the disturbances between the soldiers and the peasants were as important, if not more so, than the war against the Dutch. In a contest dominated by sieges cavalry had only a limited role to play and saw little direct action—Herbert's and Jones's troopers experienced more fighting against the Rhenish peasants than they did against the Dutch and lost more men in the German forests than in the polders of Guelderland and Utrecht.

Why Herbert left the regiment and returned to England is not clear. There are some hints towards the end of the Narrative that he fully intended to return to France for the 1673 campaign and he left some of his personal equipment and effects behind when he journeyed to London. His great-uncle, Sir Henry Herbert, had written to him on 22 August/1 September 1672 pointing out that should a sitting of parliament be called then Herbert's 'personal appearance will be expected'. In the same letter, he informed his great-nephew that when the regiment went into winter quarters he ought to leave in order 'to do his duty' to the public and 'intend his concerns which need him'.[11] Perhaps this avuncular pressure was decisive, although Herbert writes that it was his long-standing wish to experience marine service on board the fleet which persuaded him to resign his commission in Jones's regiment. After all, Herbert still held his captain's commission in the Duke of York's Maritime Regiment of Foot whose principal *raison d'être* was to undertake the duties of marines. Herbert had a strong desire to witness action at sea and this was fulfilled in the battle off the Texel.[12]

11. *Herbert Correspondence*, no. 354.
12. The *St George*, with Herbert on board, fought at the Battle off the Texel on 11/21 August 1673 (*CSPD 1673*, pp. 522–3).

Despite Herbert's flights of literary fancy, his tendency to embroider good stories, and the hyperbole of his assaults upon the character of Sir Henry Jones, his Narrative is generally reliable. The Account of 1673 is equally sound. The dates in both documents correspond with those in other sources and details can also be corroborated. Both can be accepted as accurate, personal descriptions of the campaigns of 1672 and 1673.

The French invasion of the United Provinces of the Dutch Republic in the summer of 1672 was one of the most spectacular and mobile campaigns in western Europe in the second half of the seventeenth century. The swimming of the Rhine by the forces under the command of the Prince of Condé was its most celebrated episode.[13] Motivated by a desire for *gloire* and to reduce the kingless Dutch to an inferior and dependent political position from which they could not challenge his plans for territorial expansion, Louis XIV overran much of the Seven Provinces within a few weeks. His progress was only checked when the Dutch opened the sluices and created the 'Water Line' to protect the heartlands of Holland and Zealand.[14]

As the Dutch Smyrna Fleet returned into home waters during March 1672, it was attacked off the Isle of Wight by Sir Robert Holmes with a battle squadron of the Royal Navy, an assault contrary to contemporary diplomatic and military protocol. On 17/27 March, forty-eight hours after Holmes's attack, Charles II declared war on the States General. Ten days later, France committed herself to hostilities against the Dutch in fulfilment of the terms of the Secret Treaty of Dover of 1670. The English contribution to the war came principally through her navy, with some assistance from the French, but the Dutch were generally able to hold their own at sea. On land, however, their armies suffered a terrible year and the Dutch state came close to internal collapse. Nominally commanded by the Sun King – although the actual operations were directed by Turenne and

13. On the Franco-Dutch War see, C. Rousset, *Histoire de Louvois* (Paris, 1886), i.; C.J. Ekberg, *The Failure of Louis XIV's Dutch War* (Chapel Hill, 1979); H.A. van Sypestein & J.P. de Bordes, *De Verdediging van Nederland in 1672 en 1673* (The Hague, 1850); M.C. Trevelyan, *William the Third and the Defence of Holland, 1672–1674* (London, 1930); *Het Staatsche Leger, 1568–1795*, ed. F.G.J. Ten Raa & F. De Bas (The Hague & Breda, 1911–59), v.; Robert Fruin, *De Oorlog van 1672* (Groningen, 1972); J.W.M. Shulten, *Het Leger in de 17e Eeuw* (Bussum, 1969); Ferdinand des Robert, *Les Campagnes de Turenne en Allemagne* (Nancy, 1883). Numerous prints and drawings were made of the crossing of the Rhine in 1672, one of which is reproduced in Ragnild Hatton, *Louis XIV and his World* (London, 1972), p. 69.

14. Paul Sonnino, 'Louis XIV and the Dutch War', in, *Louis XIV and Europe*, ed. R. Hatton (London, 1976), pp. 153–60; Paul Sonnino, 'The Origins of Louis XIV's Wars', in, *The Origins of War in Early Modern Europe*, ed. Jeremy Black (Edinburgh, 1987), pp. 112–22; Ekberg, *Failure of Louis XIV's Dutch War*, pp. 3–46; John B. Wolf, *Louis XIV* (London, 1968), pp. 213–46.

Condé with the sieges being managed by Vauban—the French armies amounted to 120,000 men, one of the largest forces then realised in Early Modern Europe. This massive agglomeration of humanity was to be supplied during its march towards the borders of the United Provinces from magazines which had been established in advance in the Electorate of Cologne. Max Heinrich, the Elector, was one of France's allies and he permitted the agents of Louvois to stockpile stores and provisions at four of his fortresses: Neuss, Kaiserwerth, Bonn and Dorsten.

Turenne, with 23,000 men, had assembled near Charleroi, whilst Condé's Army of the Ardennes possessed around 30,000. The remainder of Louis's army was stationed in garrison, mostly in Vauban's new fortresses on the frontier between France and the Spanish Netherlands. Condé's army had assembled and wintered in Lorraine where it had acted as a virtual army of occupation. As Turenne advanced down the River Sambre, Condé left his cantonments around Nancy and marched along the valley of the River Meuse. Turenne, with Louis XIV in attendance, reached Visé, on the Meuse between Maastricht and Liège, on 7/17 May and Condé arrived two days later. Anticipating that the vital fortress of Maastricht, which guarded the line of the Meuse, was the initial target of the French, the Dutch drained their Rhine fortresses of men in order to provide Maastricht with a sufficient garrison. Although Condé advocated besieging and taking Maastricht in order to secure the passage of the Meuse for the advance or retreat of the French armies and to establish a strong post which might deter the Spanish from intervening to support the Dutch, Louis acted on the advice of Turenne. The old marshal saw no prospect of Spain entering the conflict in 1672 and so he argued that valuable time should not be wasted on trying to capture such a powerful fortress. Instead, Maastricht should be masked by French garrisons in Maaseik, Tongeren, Bilsen, St Truiden, Valkenburg and Sittard, to the number of 10,000 men, whilst the main army marched across the Electorate of Cologne to the Rhine and its supply-bases.

The principal defences of the Dutch Republic guarded against an attack from the south through the Spanish Netherlands. Louis's advance on the line of the Sambre-Meuse suggested that the French attack in 1672 would develop from this traditional direction. Dutch soldiers, who garrisoned a number of the Rhine fortresses in the Duchy of Cleves through an agreement with the Elector of Brandenburg, were withdrawn to reinforce Maastricht and the line of the Meuse. Their consternation can only be imagined as they watched the combined French armies march eastwards from Maastricht towards the River Rhine and its denuded defences. By coming at the United

Provinces from the east through Guelderland, the French simply outflanked the Dutch positions and left nearly twenty per cent of the Dutch army isolated and neutralised in Maastricht. Thereafter, resistance was negligible. Although the States General had a total of 54,000 men under arms, most of these were locked up in garrisons and only 14,000 were available for the field army. Even this was discovered to be an optimistic assessment and the real strength of the field army was a good deal lower through the corruption and venality of the officers. The Dutch land forces had been neglected by de Witt, the navy having been given preference in resources. In 1665, the army of the United Provinces had been defeated by the Lilliputian army of Bernard Christopher von Galen, Bishop of Münster, and little had been done in the intervening years to remedy the defects. Condé marched along the right bank of the Rhine with Turenne on the opposite shore and the Rhine fortresses of the Elector of Brandenburg fell in a matter of days – Rheinberg, Wesel, Rees and Emmerich, where the two corps of the French army united on 1/11 June. On the following day, Condé's cavalry and dragoons swam across the Rhine near the Tolhuis at Lobith, a fortified customs post, and occupied the Isle of Betuwe.

This strike rendered untenable the emergency defence line which the Dutch had established along the Oude Ijssel. To add to their troubles, morale was low, equipment and ammunition were in short supply, whilst the whole army was desperately deficient in trained troops. The whole ensemble was only held together by a stiffening of German mercenaries. Such a tiny corps was unable to resist the numerous French and withdrew into Utrecht. On 8/18 June, William of Orange led the Dutch back once more, this time into the maritime province of Holland where they barricaded themselves by opening the main sluices and flooding a strip of polderland between Holland and Utrecht. Two weeks later, the French arrived in force in the city of Utrecht. The 'Water Line' was a provisional and makeshift combination of inundations, fortresses, and temporary earthworks which was only strengthened and expanded into a permanent system of fortifications after the French had withdrawn in 1674.[15] Despite repeated attempts to cross the shallow inundations to attack William III of Orange's handful of men at the five posts of Gorinchem, Schoonhoven, Goede-jan-Verwelle Sluis, Bodegraven, and Muiden, the French advance had been brought to a halt. The Sun King tacitly admitted this unpalatable fact when he left his armies on 22 July/1 August to return to St Germain.

15. J.C.P.M. van Hof, 'Fortifications in the Netherlands, 1500–1940', *Revue Internationale d'Histoire Militaire*, lviii. (1984), pp. 105–9; On the progress of the inundations see, Trevelyan, *William the Third and the Defence of Holland*, pp. 181–206.

To increase the problems of the States General, the forces of the warlike Bishop of Münster, an ally of Louis XIV, attacked Overijssel in early June, obliging that province to submit to the invader. Münster then joined his troops with those of the Elector of Cologne, under the command of the Duke of Luxembourg, and continued his campaign northwards with the object of seizing Friesland. His ambitions were finally frustrated before the walls of Groningen. By the end of the campaigning season of 1672, France and her episcopal allies had occupied two-thirds of the territories of the Dutch Republic. This succession of disasters allowed the House of Orange to be re-established as the national leadership in time of war.[16]

However, the Dutch were not entirely without diplomatic and military help. Elector Frederick William of Brandenburg allied with the Republic in May 1672 after the French had violated the Duchy of Cleves. In the following month, the Great Elector and Emperor Leopold I initialled a defensive agreement aimed at the protection of the Holy Roman Empire from French incursions. This alliance was modest enough, committing the two parties to providing 12,000 men each to guard the territory of the Empire and it was of minimal assistance to the States General in 1672.[17]

Louis XIV had to alter the balance of his plans. The campaign in the Seven Provinces had broken down before the Water Line and there existed a threat of hostile activity along the Rhine from the armies of the Elector of Brandenburg and the Holy Roman Emperor. In addition, there were growing signs of restiveness from the Spanish Netherlands. Condé had been wounded during the crossing of the Rhine and the command of his army was passed to the Duke of Luxembourg. This force faced the Dutch across the inundations while Turenne's corps turned south through the Bishopric of Liège and demonstrated before Maastricht. Convinced, as before, that it was too strong and too well garrisoned to seize without the inconvenience of a lengthy siege, he crossed the Electorate of Cologne to the Rhine and then marched along that river's valley to the confluence with the Moselle, observing the half-hearted manoeuvres of the Imperial forces under Raimondo Montecucoli. Part of Turenne's corps, including the British regiments, then turned south-west and travelled down the Moselle Valley to take up winter quarters in the Duchy of Lorraine. Louis XIV had expelled Duke Charles IV of Lorraine in 1670 forcing him and his handful of soldiers into the Imperial camp. Again, as in the previous year, the French army's winter billets in Lorraine amounted to the duties of an army of occupation. During February

16. See, H.H. Rowen, *The Princes of Orange* (Cambridge, 1988), pp. 112–30; S.B. Baxter, *William III* (London, 1966), pp. 55–85.

17. J.P. Spielman, *Leopold I of Austria* (London, 1977), pp. 58–9.

and March 1673, Turenne conducted an aggressive and devastating winter campaign against the Brandenburg and Imperial forces before assuming his own winter quarters in the Duchy of Cleves.

As Turenne guarded his eastern flank against any German or Imperial intervention in the Low Countries, Louis XIV prepared to make the capture of Maastricht the centrepiece of the campaign of 1673. From its winter quarters, the King's army trudged into the Spanish Netherlands and concentrated around Ghent before passing south of Brussels to invest and besiege Maastricht. The siege lasted from 2/12 June to 20/30 June, Vauban and his 40,000 Frenchmen rapidly overwhelming the Dutch garrison. Some reinforcements were then sent to Condé, who was standing in Utrecht before the inundations, in an effort to encourage him to attempt an advance into southern Holland. At the same time, the English were supposed to mount an amphibious assault on Walcheren and Cadzand. This project remained a technical possibility until the Dutch defeated the English fleet off the Texel on 11/21 August.[18]

Much of Condé's cavalry was then withdrawn. With reinforcements from the King's army, the French cavalry corps, which included Jones's/Monmouth's Horse, marched south through Liège, over the Ardennes, and into the Electorate of Trier. Under the Chevalier de Fourilles, the senior cavalry commander in Louis's army, the French horsemen were cantoned in the countryside of Trier, where they devoured its resources and intercepted traffic on the Moselle. Louis apparently wanted to preserve French influence and strategic interests on the east bank of the Rhine by preventing the Elector of Trier from entering into an alliance with the Holy Roman Emperor. This military occupation, initially designed to threaten the Elector, soon degenerated into a forcible takeover of the Electorate. In August, Fourille's cavalry was augmented by ten battalions of infantry commanded by Lieutenant-General the Duke of Rochefort and Lieutenant-General de Bissy. This corps invested and besieged the city of Trier which fell on 29 August/8 September. In October, the Hague Convention brought both Spain and the Emperor formally into the war against France. Spain had ceded some territory along the southern borders of the Spanish Netherlands to France at the Treaty of Aix-la-Chapelle in 1668. French advances in the United Provinces in 1672 and 1673 threatened to surround the Spanish Netherlands with a ring of hostile lands. In particular, Spain feared for the safety of her port at Antwerp. Towards the end of 1672, Spanish soldiers were serving with the Dutch behind the Water Line, most notably at Schoonhoven, in an effort to hold off the French and protect Antwerp and the free passage

18. Childs, *Army of Charles II*, pp. 183–4.

of the Scheldt. During 1673, the Dutch emerged from their diplomatic isolation and, by the Hague Convention of 20/30 August 1673, joined with Spain, the Holy Roman Empire, and Lorraine. These three states had all been formally neutral towards France and the Dutch Republic during 1672 but they regarded the French successes as sufficient reason to justify their own, direct intervention on the side of the United Provinces. Automatically, this created a state of war between the Spanish Netherlands and Louis XIV. Under the direction of their aggressive governor in Brussels, the Count of Monterey, the Spanish forces threatened the advanced positions of the French around Utrecht and their supply lines along the Rhine and the Meuse. By the end of October, the Duke of Luxembourg had retreated from Utrecht and the French had evacuated the United Provinces by the spring of the following year. At the same time, the Bishop of Münster and the Elector of Cologne were detached from the French camp. The Franco-Dutch War had ended and a European war had begun.[19]

Apart from the naval aspects of the Third Anglo-Dutch War and the 'design' to invade Walcheren in 1673, there was also English involvement in the major land campaigns of the concomitant Franco-Dutch War. Lord George Douglas's Scottish Regiment of Foot was already in the French army, having been in that employ since 1633, and a troop of English Gens d'Armes was formed for the French service in 1667 from amongst the Catholic officers who had been dismissed from the standing army in England. According to the terms of the Secret Treaty of Dover in 1670, Charles II was committed to providing Louis XIV with 6,000 infantry to assist in his land operations against the Dutch. Wentworth Dillon, fourth Earl of Roscommon, travelled to St Germain in July 1671 to make the necessary arrangements for the transfer of these soldiers into French pay. Douglas's Scottish Regiment, consisting of 3,432 men in 33 companies, was the major component of the British Brigade, but Roscommon himself contributed a regiment of 1,664 men, Sir George Hamilton raised 1,500, and the Duke of Monmouth recruited the Royal English Regiment of foot which was also composed of 1,500 soldiers. Later in 1672, the Royal English was reinforced by a second battalion of 824 men under the command of Bevil Skelton. The troop of English Gens d'Armes, whose commander had been Sir George Hamilton, was expanded by its lieutenant, Sir Henry Jones, into a full regiment of light horse consisting of 505 troopers. This regiment was the result of a private contract between the French authorities and its colonel which made it supernumary to the stipulations of the Secret Treaty of Dover, although it enjoyed the private blessing of Charles II. The

19. Wolf, *Louis XIV*, p. 236.

British Brigade remained in the French army until England withdrew from the war by the Treaty of Westminster in 1674. Some of the soldiers then returned to England but the majority stayed in France simply altering their status; instead of serving as auxiliaries of the King of England they became mercenaries.[20]

20. C.T. Atkinson, 'Charles II's Regiments of France, 1672–1678', *JSAHR*, xxiv. (1946), pp. 53–65, 128–36, 161–72; John Childs, 'The British Brigade in France, 1672–1678', *History*, lxix. (1984), pp. 86–7.

EDITORIAL PRACTICE

The Narrative of Henry Herbert has been reproduced in its entirety although certain changes have been made in its layout. In the manuscript, the author wrote a number of additions in the margins and between the lines. These have been incorporated into the transcript.

Herbert gave some dates in the left-hand margin and included others within the text. Unfortunately, he was inconsistent and did not provide precise dates for every major event referred to in the Narrative. When in England, he employed the Julian Calendar but, the moment that he set foot in France, he switched to the Gregorian. He took a little time to adjust and the dating of his first few days in France is slightly inaccurate. To bring some regularity to the Narrative and to assist the reader, the following practice has been adopted in dealing with Herbert's dating. Where he gave a date within the text, this has been retained. The dates which he presented in the left-hand margin have been removed and placed in an annotated chronology which follows the transcript of the Narrative. This chronology has been supplemented by the editor, whose additional dates have been italicised. The chronology gives accurate dating and has been based on the calendars in *English Historical Documents, 1660–1714*, ed. Andrew Browning (London, 1953), pp. 945–8.

Herbert paginated the Narrative up to page 48. He must have written the page numbers on to his folded sheets in advance; there can be no other explanation for the fact that although pages 38 and 39 are blank there is no break in the story between the end of page 37 and the beginning of page 40. The editor has continued Herbert's pagination in this edition from page 49 to the end on page 105, counting page 49 in the sequence even though it is blank. Herbert wrote his page numbers on the top, left-hand corner of each page. In this edition, Herbert's original page numbers appear within pointed brackets in the text < >. The editor's pagination is also placed within pointed brackets but the numerals have been italicised. Neither the Short Version of the Narrative nor the account of 1673 was paginated by its author. Again, the editor has created pagination, which appears in the text between pointed brackets with the numerals in italic.

The Short Version of the Narrative contains notes and the skeleton upon which the longer and final version of the Narrative was based. Where the Short Narrative offers details and observations which Herbert omitted from the Final version, these have been included in the transcript of the Narrative but have been separated from the principal text by double asterisks (**) at the beginning and end of each insertion. Page references to the Shorter Narrative are given within pointed brackets < > and prefixed by '7b'. The invective and the immoderate accusations against Jones found in the Shorter Version have been excised, mainly because of incoherence. The passages in the Final Version are sufficently powerful. The transcript of Herbert's Narrative is thus a complete copy of the Final Version with substantial sections inserted from the Shorter Version.

'Ane Account of our Regements marches from the winter quarters to ther entrance in France' has been reproduced in its entirety. As it is accurately and comprehensively dated within the text there is no need for a separate chronology.

In providing modern renditions of the names of the towns and villages visited by Herbert, the common English form has been adopted. Thus, Ghent rather than Gent or Gand; Louvain not Leuven; Liège not Luik; Tirlemont not Tienen; St Truiden not St Trond; Tongeren not Tongres. Herbert's journeys were traced on Sheets 231, 237 and 241 of the 1:200,000 maps of France produced by Pneu-Michelin (Paris, 1985–8); the 1:350,000 map of Belgium and Luxembourg (Pneu-Michelin, Brussels, 1987); the 1:300,000 map of Belgium, Luxembourg and the Rhineland (Kümmerly and Frey, Bern, 1987); and the 1:300,000 sheet of the Netherlands (John Batholomew, Edinburgh, 1988).

Neither Herbert nor the author of the Account had a sense of punctuation. Herbert's is usually non-existent and, when it does occur, it seems to have been interjected at random. Both the Narrative and the Account have been repunctuated by the editor and Herbert's original marks have been largely ignored. Similarly, Herbert did not write in paragraphs. For the sake of clarity, the editor has created paragraphs. Both Herbert and the author of the Account were sparing in their use of capital letters and the editor has not departed from their usage. All abbreviations in the text, particularly y^e, y^t, and y^m, have been expanded into their modern forms.

Editorial additions and amendments to the text are enclosed within square brackets []. Round brackets () surround items which Herbert himself placed in parentheses.

NOTE ON BIOGRAPHIES

Biographies of the British army officers mentioned in the text of both the Narrative and the Account can be found in John Childs, *Nobles, Gentlemen and the Profession of Arms in Restoration Britain, 1660–1688* (London, Society for Army Historical Research, 1987).

CAPTAIN HENRY HERBERT'S NARRATIVE OF HIS JOURNEY THROUGH FRANCE WITH HIS REGIMENT, 1671 TO 1673

** <7b, 3> July 1671. Honor, that bright Deity, squinted upon our knight[1] and influenced his thoughts that something extraordinary must be done for fame['s] sake. And since Hamilton[2] (to whom he was a fellow lieutenant in the Gens de Arms Anglois[3]) was raising a regiment of foot for the French, why should not he (who had the advantage of him in reputation last yeare for the conduct of his troope, in the others absence) ventour [sic] at a regiment of horse? His mind being thus mounted, he rides post through all the imaginations of this world and att last stumbled and fell upon the resolution of a Col-l[onel's] commission, and had money enough to buy, but haveing never heard of Capitulations,[4] they never troubled his thoughts. Onely the French K[ing's] broad seat run in his mind and superceded all other considerations. And it much perplext him to give birth to this single designe that wanted the midwifry of a good braine and here he was reduced to great extreamity by the ungovernable tide of this ambition. But our Jonah was luckily delivered out of this storme and cast ashore by the feet of Mr Fourile,[5] lieutenant-general of the light horse, who received his proposition at the first word (a promise of some English horses being first made). Fourile offered all the assistance possible. He should have what pay he pleased and for other conditions bid him trouble not himselfe, he would doe all things for him. On this, our glad knight put pen to paper and sent soe promising and subtile a packet for england that the generous and generall consent of the Portugall officers[6] was soon returned him without <7b, 4> without [sic] the least respect of termes for themselves, unwilling by

1. Sir Henry Jones.
2. Sir George Hamilton. See J.C. O'Callaghan, *History of the Irish Brigades in the service of France* (Glasgow 1870, repr. Shannon, 1969), pp. 33–4.
3. The troop of English Gens d'Armes in the French service. Raised by Sir George Hamilton in 1667, it consisted of 100 men, mainly catholic ex-officers from the English establishment (Childs, *Army of Charles II*, p. 26).
4. 'Capitulations' were the terms of contract between the commander of a regiment raised for foreign service and the hiring government (*The First Triple Alliance: the Letters of Christopher Lindenov, Danish Envoy to London, 1668–1672*, ed. Waldemar Westergaard (Copenhagen, 1946), pp. 29, 43–4; John Childs, 'The British Brigade in France, 1672–1678', *History*, lxix. (1984), pp. 386–7).
5. Henri de Chaumejean, Marquis de Fourilles (d. 1720). Fourilles was the principal inspector of the French cavalry (*DBF*, xiv. 782–3; Rousset, *Louvois*, i. 211).
6. The British officers who had served with the British Brigade in Portugal between 1662 and 1668. In the latter year they had returned to England to face unemployment

such a course to question the love or bravery of this soule that was to comand. There satisfaction in serving a man of soe much honor being signified, the news soe transported our heroe that in an exstasie of joy and pride [he] vaunts to Fourile that in England he had lysted for the service the true, legitimate sones of Mars, men borne to conquer, and instances their severall successes in Portugall against the Spanish.

On all heads, articles were neglected, or if they were not, they were such as were not fitt to see day amonge us. For the consequence of a low and bad capitulation was worse then noe articles at all, because articles signed would, for the future, prove a president for such as would undertake the like leavies. Whereas, if none, it rested in the K[ing's][7]? brest how he treated us and that was changeable, better or worse, as we merited and did not engage those that came after into an inconvenience. Putting aside the good articles, all the rest was performed by Fourile. Viz: he [Jones] was alowed 18 pistolls[8] a man, the quarters of assembly, and Loraine to winter in, to which he added the absent officers pay from the date of their comissions to their appearance here, which was six months. To enable him to equip the soldiers, six men out of every troop, there being ten troopes.[9] Instead of 50, being the compleat number of each troop, he gives but 30 cloakes and deducts from the comission [officers] two souce [sous] a day for remount and coat money, and makes the soldiers, out of their owne pay, buy bootes, hatts, lining of their coats and buttons, belt and carbine belts, and other necessaries, which impoverished the soldiers soe they came into the feild without a <7b, 5> a [sic] penny in their pocketts and, much worse then that, in debt to their officers who was forced, in honor, to advance them moneys for the occasion.

After all this, during the campaine he converted their allowance of bread into money, soe starved some and paied himselfe a debt by it

---

or to ride as reformadoes in the English army. They formed a tightly-knit group of veteran, professional officers (P.H. Hardacre, 'The English Contingent in Portugal, 1662–1668', *JSAHR*, xxxviii. (1960), pp. 112–25; *CSPD 1660–85*, p. 461).

7. Louis XIV.

8. The French currency during the 1670s was relatively confused. Its principal denominations were:

12 deniers	=	1 sou
20 sous	=	1 franc or livre tournois
2 livres	=	1 gold pistole
11 livres	=	1 louis d'or

Between 1675 and 1679, the pound sterling was valued at 13 livres tournois. A pistole was therefore worth around 3 shillings sterling (*John Locke's Travels in France, 1675–9*, ed. John Lough (Cambridge, 1953), p. lxvi).

9. Each troop had only 44 men even though its establishment was set at 50. The pay of the six permanent absentees went into the pockets of the colonel and the troop captains, ostensibly to purchase equipment for the soldiers. This echoed the practice in the English army (Childs, *Army of Charles II*, pp. 104–9).

they never owed him and thus putts it out of the power of the officers to reimburse themselves who had laied out for the number of cloakes he gave short, they living of[f] the coats and buttons he gave short and the number of horses he gave short. He made us also beleeve we should be costome [customs] free in England and France, which occasioned many of our equipages to be the greater, but were highly deceived when both the fraight of our very cloathes and liveries, with the costome of our horses, were extorted from us on both sides, English and French shore. And no allowance [was] given us out of the Quarter of Assembly for our extraordinary charges in the march to Loraine, nor any pay till we arrived to our companies.

But to returne and time our relation a little better. Haveing got the comissions, rowtes, and orders of marching, he left France and in September began to colonell [sic] in England where, with some difficultie, he raised 500 men, in his choise refusing the most probable and him that lookt genteely, taking up plow men, Newgatemen, and day labourours. And was at last a pack of the rustiest, ragedst rascalls that ever eye beheld. He divids them into 10 companies, 50 a peice, and officerd them thus:

Sir H.J., Colonel.
First Company: Mr. Warren Lt., Capt Leift;[10] Ned Sheldon, Cornett; Quartermaster Tomson.

2nd.   Leiftenant Colonel;[11] Gwynne Leift.; Cuisse [Cruise] Cornett; Quarter[master] Lawes.

3rd.   Captain Littleton; Leift. Mackartee [Macarty]; Cornett Sheldon < 7b, 6 >.

4th.   Wytherington; Leift. Maine; Cornt. Kirke; Quart. Hutcheson [Hutchinson].

5.   Capt. Slingsby; Leift. Philips; Cornt. Tripe [Trip]; Quarter. Roberts.

6.   Major, Capt. Russell;[12] Leift. Bray; Cornt Sandes; Quart. Sulen [Soulon].

7.   Capt. Pendarris; Leift. Verman; Cornt. Overowne; Qu. Brise [Brice].

8.   Capt. Lanier; Leift. Hill; Cornt.—; Quarter. Gaddise.

9.   Capt. Every; Leift. Osburne [Osborne]; Cornett. Noell; Qu.—.

10.   Capt. Herbert; Leift. Donville; Cornt. Dunbar; Quart. Barnsley.**

---

10. The captain-lieutenant commanded the colonel's company or troop and ranked as the senior lieutenant of the regiment.
11. Lieutenant-Colonel William Littleton.
12. Major Theodore Russell.

< 1 > Upon Saturday 11 of November 1671, I took leave of my brother, the Right Honorable the Lord Herbert of Cherbury,[13] at L'mer Parke[14] neare Montgomery. On Thursday following, we dined with the Earle of Bridgewater at his county house in Buckingham Sheire, called Ashridge, a place neatly scituated between two parkes, the one of red [and] the other of fallow deere. The building, faire and capacious, every waye su[i]table to the great hospitallity of the wise and noble owner. One night we stayed there. Next day we came to London, where we lay onely foure nights.

I kist the King's hands. Osburne was then knighted. The ceremony over, the Duke [of York] took out of his pocket a golden medall, the intended reward of a sea captain who [had] behaved himselfe miraculously well against the Algier pirats.[15] The Duke, discerning a curiosity in me to see the peice, calld for it from another and soe reached it me. After I had lookt well upon it, I waighed it often in my hand, which the Duke observed, told me the waight no[t-with]st[andin]g that [was] not wholy my intent by it. But I cast in my mind the worth of the action by the w[e]ight of the reward. I also affected at this time some other expressions by which to fix me in the memory of this generous prince and persevd [sic] that honor was a glorious possession but a hazardous tinure [sic]. That necessity some times obliges and loads men with honor that nere designed to be troubled with the burthen. But for the gold, I would remember the beauty, neither would I forgett the weight which consisted most in the princes favour that stampt soe much worth upon above the intrinsicke value of the mettle that these bright beames should shine upon my mind to influence, if possible, great actions.

I left the court the next day. Before I took post horses, I went to Sir H[enry] Herbert, at my charge to raise a tombstone over my grandfathers grave[16] to distinguish the ashes of that famous man from ordinary dust. My desires was by him most obligingly fulfilled in my absence, for which favour, and many others from him, I will faithfully account, if God gives me life and oppertunity.

Tuesday the 21, my servants set out for Rye in Sussex by easie

13. Edward Herbert, third Baron Herbert of Cherbury, Henry Herbert's elder brother.

14. Lymore Park, the family seat.

15. This gold medal was probably awarded to Captain John Baddison of the *Swallow* (*CSPD 1671*, pp. 536, 537, 541). Sir Henry Osborne was admitted a knight bachelor on 13 January 1672 (*Le Neve's Pedigree of the Knights*, ed. G.W. Marshall (London, Harleian Society, 1873), pp. 261, 283).

16. Edward Herbert, first Baron Herbert of Cherbury, the philosopher-poet. See *The Life of Edward, First Lord Herbert of Cherbury, written by Himselfe*, ed. J.M. Shuttleworth (Oxford, 1976).

journeys to spare our horses. We saw it upon Friday in the affternoone, where we found Captain [Henry] Slingsby and a great many of our regiment who had laine wind bound there at least a month before. Onely they had once put to sea but were tos[se]d back againe by stormes with great losse and danger for they were forced to sacrifice some of their horses to angry Neptune to save their owne lives. Captain [Henry] Every, and a great many more who came the same day with us, were constrained to stay the sensure of Mr Eolus,[17] that huffing, puffing diety, who was never soe constant as in being crose to us, till Sunday the 3rd of December, during which time we went to see the ruines of the famous towne of Winchelsea, two miles from Rye and on[e] of the Cink [sic] Ports. I doe not remember that ever I saw any towne soe well scituated either for strength or convenience, the[i]r streets many, all in severall crosses. The contrivance <2> appeares very handsome in the sceleton for tis now little better then desolate there being not past 30 houses inhabited and those goe upon crutches too ready to drop into the numerous vaults of their enterred neighbours. The towne being forsaken of the sea as well as her inhabitants, the former dissertion being the cause of the latter and yet I beleeve the haven is, with some small cost, recoverable, for tis said the Jewes offered great sumes for the place to build in, as knowing the advantages of the scituation and the facility of recalling the sea thither. The Jewes would have bui[l]t a synogoge there had not the Dutch warre prevented it. The castle, as I take it built by Henry the 8th, stands, or to speake more properly did stand (for tis now downe), halfe a mile or more from the towne and as far from the sea at this present [time] though formerly it comanded the mouth of the haven. Twas oddly contrived. The fabrick was sexangular as to the outward part of it, with a mighty round towre in the middle and spacious vaults underneath it for the stowage, as I suppose, of necessaries.[18] Her neighbour and sister Rye is ready to follow her in the same fate, for grasse begins to grow in the streets, the haven being much decayed. Tis thinly inhabited or else there is soe little devotion in the inhabitants that for 2 Sundays together we could not number, besides soldiers, twenty auditors to heare divine service and a very good sermon. The people are boorish and have nothing of the English civility in them. The weomen ugly, scarce fit for mareners; <3> a well bread dogge would not eate out of their durty hands. The forknowledge of these beauties

17. Aeolus, the ruler of the winds (*OCD*, p. 15).
18. Camber Castle, built in 1539–40, one of Henry VIII's chain of fortifications constructed along the south-east coast of England during the invasion scare of the late 1530s. The castles consisted of circular, central keeps with hollow, concentric rings serving as primitive bastions. The designs were out-of-date before they were built (Geoffrey Parker, *The Military Revolution, 1500—1800* (Cambridge, 1988), pp. 26–8; B.H. St J. O'Neil, *Castles and Cannon* (Oxford, 1960), p. 51).

was the cause, noe doubt, which made a trooper amongst us carry a Nun of Dog and Bitch Yard[19] along with him hither, in the habit of a canaleer,[20] who prevented some of them from comitting buggery with the beastly townes weomen till she was discovered and sent away. I beleeve she might have proved a good laundresse for she taught 2 or 3 of our gentlemen to starch their linen. They are like to drive a sorry trade of it, for to carry running nagges to France is the same as to bring coles to Newcastle.

About 8 of the clock upon Sunday night, we hois[t]ed sail for Deip [Dieppe], where we arrived with gentle gale upon Tuesday morning by sun rising.

In our passage we had nothing worth the noting, only the seamen were somewhat abashed at the porposes which, in great multitudes, followed and danced about the ships as if they ment to keep their Christmas upon us for they seldome appeared but as the foreruners of great and dangerous stormes, yet we were in a maner becalmed not haveing any gale soe stiffe as to make us seasick, but the mareners and old travellers were only concerned at this omen for we that knew nothing did feare nothing. Perhaps our sins, which use to sinke other men, brought us safe to land for a worse end, but God, I hope, will give us repentance in order to his <4> owne glory and our deliverance.

The charge of exporting horses out of Rye—the costomes and other duties there of one horse:

Statute Costome	5[s]–	0[d]
To the master of the house	2[s]–	6[d]
The townes fee	1[s]–	0[d]
Water Baileife	1[s]–	0[d]
Collector and Controler	1[s]–	7[d]
Slinging	2[s]–	6[d]
Use of the slings	1[s]–	0[d]
Every man by the pol[l or e?]	1[s]–	4[d]
To the sercher of the costomes for a trunk	1[s]–	2[d]
For a portmantle		8[d]
For a cockel[21]	8[s]–	10[d]
To the towne	2[s]–	0[d]
To the mayor	1[s]–	3[d]
To the light h[o]use	2[s]–	0[d]
For anchorage		4[d][22]

19. A London prostitute.
20. A French, female sutler.
21. A small boat to ferry the horse to the anchored ship (*OED*).
22. The total = £1 12s. 2d.

We had pilots to bring us into the haven, which is a very convenient one and capable of vessels of great burthen, where next our heads we had a prospect of 150 weomen, hand in hand, at sh—upon the shore. A lovely sight it was for our first welcome into France. They were no more disturbed with the hooping and holloweing of our men then if they had been gathering roses, but the comon people throughout all France are beastly that way. Here lay the clues into the French diet in an a la mode negligence. Could the nose be unconcerned, the eye had sufficient divertion here. They resembled the naked Indians, haveing no other clothing but what was hudled about their wa[i]st and their back part were of better presence than ther fore. But to all so pagan bad that had not their been of the sex fairer objects, nature had not ordained eyes for the loathsomeness of the object might have else obstructed the necessary design of generation.

The towne is very faire and the streets neat and large, comanded by a well fortified castle and beautified by an exceeding fine church, built by the English, where God is served with much pompe and ceremony.[23] Without the wall is a Hugonett church where you may find the other extreame of affected rudenesse and slovenry. These different dresses—the one of a curtizan, the other of a shitt—made me proud of the grave, matronlike habit of our mother Church of England, who is not soe corrupt as to be suspected of vanity, or so nastie as to appeare meerly carelesse. She doth not paint or weare black patches but she keeps her face clean and is all beauty within.

The towne is rich and well traded, the people industrious and live much upon fishing which they ply very diligently, even in the depth of winter, to the shame of their opposite neighbours in England who love their ease more then their proffit and had rather starve then worke. <5> Tis mighty populous, if we may call them a people who are but slaves who dare not weare good clothes for feare of being suspected to be rich. I have seen there in the streets old weomen yoked two x two drawing of great wheel barrowes, guided behind by one man. And to speake the truth, it is the fittest employment for them. For when they are once forty years old, noe Englishman would suspect them to be of the humane race or that men were ever drawne out of such sinkes. This may serve for the generall character of all French weomen. Indeed, many of them are pretty enough when they are very younge, but when age begins to growe upon them there is noe more signe of beatye left. Then the cowes dung hath of the fine flowers of which it was made.

23. St Jacques, built between the 13th and the 16th centuries. Parts of Dieppe Castle had been refortified by Vauban (Reginald Blomfield, *Sebastien le Prestre de Vauban* (London, 1938), p. 205).

Here we thought to make use of the little broken French we had learnt in England but no body understood us more then we did them, soe we were constrained during the 3 dayes stay there to seek out such as could speake Latine, whose accent and pronounciation made it seem at first to us as strange as their native language. Here we changed our silver to some advantage, a halfe penny in the shilling, and English broad gold went of[f] better, 5s. in the pound.

** <7b, 6> The men were shipt at severall times and in severall places: some at Dover and landed at Cal[a]is, others at Rye and landed at Deipe.** We got ashore by 9 in the morne, where we mett with wonderfull signs of good luck, if the promise holds. Haveing past this shitten or gall, being placed in rank and file and disciplined by the same order of the French army, extending a front above a league and a halfe on the sea shore. ** <7b, 6> Whereat the Mustermaster reviewd us and swore us with the ceremony following, the gouvernour of the towne present. The men [were] drawne up in two rankes faceing in ward. The comissary comanded silence. Our hattes were of[f] and on by his example. Then drew he his sword, soe did the officers likewise. He then askt us whether we would serve the King of France. The generall voice was 'Yea', then, in French, pronounced he the oath to this purpose, 'You are, on the honor of a soldier, to serve the King of France against all his enemies, neither to disert or betray his service, but with obedience and willingnes to submit to all his comands, serving him against all excepting your owne King, the King of Great Brittaine.' And then, by his example, we kist our naked swords and gave a generall acclamation and were dismissed, marching after a small repast of bread and wine to the soldiers, each man to his Quarter of Assembly. The officers only staid in Deipe.** <6> The soldiers marched away imediately, according to their route, unto their Quarters of Assembly. On Friday night we overtooke them quartering in a village called Barqueville[24] where I was and invited to supp with the Markees lady in her castle and was entertained with much civility and treated with as much freedome as a Friday night would permit in that country. She was a lady very well accomplished both for her parts and person and very handsomely attended, and to give this nation but its due, the gentrie are generally as cureteous [sic] and obliging as the boores are rude and churlish.

The next day we removed to a village called St Victor.[25] Our rout, (which is an order subscribed by the Kings owne hand, assigning us the particular places of our quarters every night). In this march we

24. Bacqueville-en-Caux. The regiment followed a route of march which had been laid down by Michel le Tellier on 9 September 1671 (NLW, HM 2/14/7c).
25. St Victor l'Abbaye.

burnt[26] some quarters, preferring moneys before ease, but, to speake truth, our stages were not long, not above 3 or 4 leagues[27] a day, unlesse oure owne covetousnesse made them stretch, and where other men spend moneys by travelling we got by it, yet we had but course [sic] entertainement and the houses so ill furnished that the people did boile us egges in their frying pan.

<7> Our next remove was to Caley[28] and thence to Lion,[29] a towne in one of the Kings forrests, where the cheife ranger then was (a great man) in order to the selling of some of the woods. He sent a person of quality with footmen and torches lighted to envite the officers and their companie to supper with him where we were entertained with great respect. Here we had sejourne, a day of ease, but the conductor put our ease in his pockett and the next day we marched to the famous towne of Gizors, a place often mentioned in our Histories and memorable for many English exploits there.

Here we tooke leave of our old mistresse, the once glorious country of Normandy, and yet the fairest province not onely of France but, I thinke, of the whole world. You may call it whether you will one entire feild or an orchard for tis both, the highways being everywhere planted on both sides with rowes of apple trees that you ride all day in an arbour. Such rowes all a long crossing the plaine feilds affords the loveliest prospect in Nature, noe hedge or ditch in all the country (onely about the villages), not a foot of land but is tilled, and the soile consisting of sand, chalke, and flint is soe dry that they make noe ridges or rean as in England. We found the wayes as faire in December as with us in July. Here is very little hay or pasture. Their cattle is small and runtish, at most as ill favoured as their weomen. I beleeve the people doe begett their owne jaments,[30] only the beasts are the handsomer. The sheep are small, no bigger then our lambes, but they are excellent sweet mutton <8> in my opinion much better then their[31] owne. Their horses are comended and esteemed the best of all France. In their forrests they have wild swine and wolves. Wood for

26. This refers to the practice of allowing householders and innkeepers to avoid having to billet troops provided that they paid for the privilege. In this way, Herbert and his men were able to make a little money during their journey through France. The term 'burning' derives from the habit of an occupying army demanding 'brandtschatzung', or 'burning money', from towns and villages: financial contributions which, if tardily delivered, resulted in buildings being put to the flame (F. Redlich, 'Contributions in the Thirty Years' War', *Economic History Review*, xii (1959–60), pp. 247–54; Geoffrey Parker, *The Army of Flanders and the Spanish Road, 1567–1659* (Cambridge, 1972), pp. 142–3).
27. A league measured three English miles.
28. Cailly.
29. Lyons-la-Fôret.
30. Jument—a beast of burden (*OED*).
31. Herbert has mistakenly written 'their' instead of 'our'.

fuell is noe very scarce comodity in the whole kingdom and yet riding quite from Deip in Normandy to Paris, thence to Shaloon,[32] Verdun and quite to Metz, through the hart of all the Kingdome, I canot say that I sawe one timber tree growing in all this long journey or any tree of oake or beech that would beare a foot square, and yet we past many woods and forests, some of 3 leagues in length.[33]

Next in order to the brutes come in the people to be considered who are the most miserable that ever I sawe. They live like Tantalus, starving in the midst of plenty.[34] A man would distresse himselfe to see the country soe rich and the inhabitants soe poore. I have come into a country church upon a Sunday and I have conceited myselfe to be in England at a dole in a great funerall where they shutt all the beggars up in the church to give them money as they let them out. The whole congregation is patched up of rags; nothing can be more ridiculous, excepting their faces, a dirtier people breathes not. They are much more curious in their feilds then in their houses, for like wormes they delight in dirt. The villages are large and thick sett, in every one a faire manner house or castle, but the other houses are many of them without windows and receive noe light but at the doer which is a great advantage to the weomen for they are <9> best in the darke for the light undoes them.

I have heard it affirmed by persons that thought they understood what they said that the King rayses more moneys yearly from Normandy then the annual rents thereof amounts to, which is strange, if true, but all his subjects are his bees. They gether honey, but not for themselves. He forces the people to buy salt at what rates he pleases and every hous holder is constrained to buy his proportion.

Our next quarter was at Chamen[35] in Picardy. The next day we rode throwe a most pleasant country to the famous towne of Pontois.[36] The villages were so thick that the whole country appeared but one intire towne. Here we found my Lord Hamiltons regiment of English and Irish foot[37] who thronged about us with all signs of joye and their kindnes was to[o] much exprest by drinking and at last almost extinguished by it and quarrelling, a capitall crime in France.

Next day was Christmas day there, when I went post, Higgins and Billingsley[38] with, for Paris and dined that day at St Dennis.[39] We had

32. Châlon-sur-Marne.
33. See, P.W. Bamford, *Forests and French Sea Power, 1660–1789* (Toronto, 1956).
34. See *OCD*, p. 1037.
35. Chaumont-en-Vexin.
36. Pontoise.
37. The Irish infantry regiment of Sir George Hamilton.
38. Dr John Higgins, the regimental surgeon. Probably Lewis Billingsley, who might well have been a young volunteer in Jones's regiment at this time (Dalton, i. 203 et passim).
39. The Abbey of St. Dennis.

noe minced pies yet were as merry as those that had. In this church, the fairest of all France, lye entombed most of the French kings and here they are usually crowned. We had neither faith nor leasure to see the wholy relics of this devout place but haveing said our prayers to God himselfe, that alone can answere them, and walkt a turne or two, away we went to Paris where we arrived at an English Gaulle woman['s] house, Madam Paris by name, in the Fouburge of the St. St. [sic] Germain.[40] < 10 >

Here in Paris we diverted ourselves in seeing the most remarkable things, amongst which the Louv[re]. It stands upon the River Seine, which is no bigger then the Severne. It makes an island in the city which is furnished with most stat[e]ly new buildings. I will not take upon me to tell you the magnificence of this famous pallace. It may suffice that 'tis the royall seate of the King of France and yet he delights more in Vers[a]ille[s], a place of his some few leagues distant from the towne furnished with all the vanities of the universe notwithstanding it is of itselfe a place so barren (as 'tis said) that trees will hardly growe there, soe much doe great spirits please themselves in striveing with nature and seeming to give a law to it. Princes will not have their recreations hold any proportion with vulgar heads. Be it as it will, the fertility of the rest of France may improve a wildernesse and this king will doe what he can in advantage of this place. In this place he was affour being in Paris, soe that we could not satisfie ourselves in seeing our New Master, only we saw at on[e] Monsieur Bennoit the whole court in effigie. There is the King and Queen, the Dolphin, and all the gallants of France, male and female, done to the life in imagery worke and arraid most gorgeously in their full proportions. I must confesse, at first sight, I thought that all these glorious persons were really there. There are, besides, in another roome, all the beauties of Europe, especially those of France and England. Amonge the rest we had the honor to the Countesse of Castlemaine. < 11 > Surely, the whole is a worke of wonderfull art and hath deservedly made the artificer very rich.

In the evening we went to see an Italian play which was as intelligible as a French one. 'Twas a comody, not one jott better then those ridiculous ones of Jack Pudding and Merry Andrews in England, nothing of the poet in it, onely the made [mad] postures of the actors did serve to make the people laugh. The whole contrivance was to the spleen, not to gratify a rationall imagination.

Next day we visited the churches and the most remarkable places

40. Herbert lodged with Madame Paris, à la Croix Blanche, Rue de Maire aux Faubourgs St Germain, Paris (*Herbert Correspondence*, no. 351; B. Rouleau, *Le Tracé des Rues de Paris; formation, typologie, fonctions* (Paris, 1969), p. 71).

of the towne. Upon Sunday, being St Johns Day, we went to Notre Dame, the cathedrall church of Paris, an admirable structure built by the English. Here we heard high masse and sawe a mighty fine pageant of surplices and shaven crownes. The musicke was excellent, in its kind, in my mind to[o] light for a church if not for a taverne. The Archbishop came out just by us and bestowed his blessing (a crosse) upon us. As he past I was afraid that his busines was to examine us what the swans did amonge his geese. After dinner we went to look about us. In the evening we were carried by some English gentlemen to see the opera. 'Tis a play, all sung by the best voices of both sexes in France and danced by the choisest masters in Paris. The musick was all in view in a partition betwixt the pitt and the stage. It consisted of a great number of all maner of violls with other stringed and wind instruments. The scenes sumptuous and all things very ravishing.

I have heard travellers say that Paris was a nest of < 12 > rogues and that it was very unsafe walking the streets after night. That it was soe then I am apt to beleeve, but now 'tis farre otherwise. The severity of this prince hath made the night as secure as the day, not onely in the city but the country even in the midst of the woods and forrests.

Tis not long since an edict of his comanded the citizens to hang out lights as soon as tis darke and, accordingly, from twilight to 12 at night, there hangs acrosse each street betwixt every other house a great glasse sconce or lanthorne, which doe not onely make the streets light but makes a most beautifull shew to those that look upon them from an high place. You would thinke that the stares were descended and transplanted from Heaven to Earth.[41] Duells, that were once so comon in France, are not now heard of. People dare scarce talk of privat fighting such is the stricknes of the King['s] lawes. That whereas there was an edict that noe pages should weare swords, a noble mans son, one of the Courts pages, presumeing upon the nobility of his house and the King['s] favour, made bold to carry a weapon but his presumption cost him his head notwithstanding all the mediation of his great freinds. To challenge the feild is capitall. If two fight, the surviver is executed and the body of him that is killed is drawn naked about the city and dinyed church buriall soe that now you shall see the hottest heads of the male scould it out, not daring to drawe.

The King doubtless is a brave prince. France has not had one[e] so fit for that people since Charlemane. He is true to himselfe and constant to his lawes. There is no trans < 13 > gressing here upon the presumption of favours, but who ever offends, up he goes.

As justice is here severely executed, soe charity is wonderfully

41. Street lighting had been introduced into Paris in 1667 (Leon Bernard, *The Emerging City: Paris in the Age of Louis XIV* (Durham, North Carolina, 1970), pp. 163–6.)

practized. The hospitalls are here great of such liberall endowments
that none are refused. A man canot be attended with more care, and
noe lady, then here. Besides, the abblest phisitians and chyrurgions
are soe diligent in their function that many desperate disseases are
here, every day, cured to the glory of God and the great praise of
them that doe these things meerely for his sake. We bragge much of
faith in England; I would we had such workes as these to condone it.

Tuesday and Wendsday, we rid hard post from Paris to Meaux La
Forte[42] and thence to Chattarery[43] and at Espery[44] we overtook our
route againe. Thursday night we lay at Chalon,[45] a very faire towne
upon the river Marne, as are the former. This last has in it 40 churches
of all maners. From Chalon, we marched to a village called Curtesuc[46]
and nere this village is a faire church and crosse erected in the place
where that great and memorable battle was fought between Attila,
who called himselfe and really was Flagellum et Ira Dei, the scurge
and wrath of God, and the famous Aelius with his Romans and
confederate Gothes on the other side. In which fight, Attila was with
much adoe, overthrowne and Aelius undone for the Consull proconsull
not following the victory, neither indeed intended the utter ruine of
the Hunne because he would have him to ballance his barbarous
confederates or to awe the < 14 > Emperour and consequently, to
make himself nexessary, did let this terrible enemy march away unper-
sued, who, feeling himselfe not e[a]gerly presst, found means to rally
and in his returne wasted Italy and the Roman provinces with fire
and sword.[47] This made the noble Aelius suspected by a jealous
Emperour who presently after destroyed him and the Roman Empire
by the same stroake for they were buried both in the same grave. So
precious a jewell of the crowne is on[e] brave comander, even in
Rome itselfe, where Mars might formerly have gone to schole [sic] to
learne this proffession.

From hence we came to St Monehoe[48] and soe to Verdun, where
the Bishop was prince but the civill part of his jurisdiction is now in
the King of France, where we staid 2 nights and celebrated our
Christmas Day according to the English old Julian accoumpt.

42. Meaux-la-Forte.
43. Château-Thierry.
44. Épernay.
45. Châlon-sur-Marne.
46. Courtisols.
47. The precise location of the Battle of Châlon, or the Battle of the Catalaunian
Plains, A.D. 451, is not known. Aetius Flavius was assassinated in A.D. 454 (J.F.C.
Fuller, *Decisive Battles of the Western World*, ed. John Terraine (London, 1970), i. 207;
OCD, p. 20).
48. St Menehould.

Hence we removed to Marcheville[49] in Loraine, where there is a house of the Augustine fryers who gave an handsome account of that country.

From hence we came to Terre de Goes,[50] our intended winter quarter being called Noveau,[51] upon the River of Mossell nere unto which Julius Caesar built an arch from one mountaine to the other over the river and the valley, about an English mile in breadth, a part of which is yet standing to wittnes the industry of that brave Roman. The country people call it the Divells Bridge, thinking that no body (but nothing or one that can doe nothing) could goe throwe [through] with such a peece of worke. Yet it is to[o] narrowe for to be a bridge, being but 2 yards broad. The truth is, it was intended for an aquaduct to some great place thereabout < 15 > in those days whose very ruines are now destroyed. Onely this of the aquaduct remaines to testifie the greatnes of its mistresses to whome it was but subserviant. Thus we see servants sometimes out live the great families that raised them. The village at the one end of this stupendious ruine avowes it for its Godfather and is still knowne by the name of Julius Arch.[52]

Two leagues from hence is the great City of Metz. We have but one in England that exceed it. It stands upon the Mossell. Tis stronge and rich. Here are Jewes and protestants tollerated. The Bishope was their temporall prince; he is onely now a spirituall one. Here is a great garison of French and the comon randevouz of Swisse, English, and the almost innumerable forces of the French King. All the afforesaid townes, as well as this, swarme with soldiers who onely quarter and passe along with as great silence and moderation as if they were onely people going to church.

In this quarter of Noveau we stayed about nine dayes when there came an order and a rout from marshall Crequi[53] to remove us to Pont a Mauson,[54] a faire town in Loraine. Thence to Toul, another neat towne of the same province, both walled and full of soldiers. Thence we marched to Vaucouleur,[55] soe to Gondrecourt in the Dutchy of Barrois, and here we received billets to quarter in the villages belonging to that provostry. My owne quarters were at Pargny upon the River Meaux,[56] a fruitfull country, the inhabitants rich clownes [sic] finding us not only good wine, beefe, mutton and meat,

49. Marchéville-en-Woëvre.
50. The Forêt de Gorze.
51. Novéant-sur-Moselle.
52. The Roman aqueduct at Jouy-aux-Arches on the Moselle south of Metz.
53. François de Blanchefort, Chevalier de Créquy (1629–87) (*DBF*, ix. 1210–12).
54. Pont-à-Mousson.
55. Vaucouleurs.
56. There are three villages called Pagny, or Pagney, in this region, but only Pagny-la-Blanche-Côte lies on the Meuse.

fish, poultry &c. but also were constrained to pay our men soldiers 6d. per diem for <16> eating it. Hither we came upon the 23 of January, new stile.

<15> While we lived within the Intendancy of Metz, the soldiers pay was 9 s[ous] a day of which in deductions 1 s[ou] for clothes, and 1 s[ou] for remounts, $\frac{1}{2}$ [sou] for hospitall and mules.

To Capt.	£7 – 6[s] – 8[d]
Leift.	[£]4 – 6[s] – 8[d]
Cornt.	[£]3 – 0[s] – 0[d]
Quart.	[£]1 – 13[s] – 4[d]
Corplls.	[£]0 – 9[s] – 0[d][57]

<15> [Herbert's troop was quartered as follows:]

At Pargny,	Capt. [and]	6	[men]
	Quarterm. [and]	2	[men]
	Soldiers	23	[men]
Geroville		4	[men]
Rosier		4	[men]
Ayree		4	[men]
Charee – Cornt. [and]		5	[men] <16>
Espier		$1\frac{1}{2}$	[men]
Uruffe – Leift. [and]		$9\frac{1}{2}$	[men]

Received 4s[ous] a man for the soldiers. For tents, 4 Ells at 15 [sous] a yard.[58]

Here I received horses for my troop. They are generally of a Germaine or Cravat[59] race bought in Straisburg,[60] strong, unruly cattle, providence it seems haveing designed to bring them and their more untenable riders from their remote countries to meet here. Never was match better made, yet I doe not despaire but diligance and care may transforme them into that servisable animall of France called a trooper. For to speak the truth, they have in them that which Cicero desired in his young orators, aliquod quod amputet, something redundant that ought to be loppt off, and I doubt not but shortly I may bragge I have reclaimed more men in 3 months than preaching hath

57. This list of the subsistence pay which the soldiers received whilst they were in winter quarters is given in the margin of p. 15 of the manuscript.
58. This list of the winter quarters appears in the margins of pp. 15 and 16 of the manuscript. The modern names of the villages are: Gérauvilliers, Rosières-en-Blois, Amanty, Cléry-la-Côte, Epiez-sur-Meuse, and Uruffe. On this reckoning, Herbert's troop numbered 59 men and 4 officers.
59. A horse of Croatian origin (*OED*).
60. Strasbourg.

done in so many yeares, or rather may vaunt myselfe to Ulisses, who loosed the charmes of Circes and brought the wild beasts into humane shape againe.[61] To give you an instance of my power, take that of Jack Higgins[62] whose transformation from the bottle and the pipe to temperance and sobriety I doe not a little boast off [sic]. Most of the regiment were under the same enchantment, but now they begin to cast their old haire and put on their new coats. All this is true and may be understood litterally and admitts of not mythologie.

To recount all our adventures to this present, being Valantines day, would be beyond my institucion and a work to[o] big for the blancks here before me. Besides, the learned < 17 > magicians that use to writ romances, doe not use to record the actions of Esquires but Knight Arrants, whom the learned call Esquires, and to give this gracious appelation to Esquires before they can ride will not be permitted by Mr Prician, whom I will not alwaies disoblige though, for my owne part, I have broke his head within this 3 monthes soe often, both in French and Latine, that by this time I beleeve he hath noe more braines than one of us. But now lets returne, if any thing be a digression to a rambler or one that pretends onely to divert himselfe, as I doe here. This observation I made amonge our men—You must know that to be a gentleman is noe more then to be farre from home.

Now our troopers lookt well and particularly my officers, worthy persons. My Leiutenant, being a gentleman of one of the antientest families of all Loraine, and of his grandfather we meet with this sad story.[63]

Loraine, amonge other plagues that haunt this pretty principality scituated between great monarchys, had two mighty families. The head of one was the Count de Sôme[64] and of the others, the Count de Salle,[65] both so potent in their estates and relations that upon a private quarrell, without any respect to their naturall prince, they presumed to breake out into an insolent warre, one against the other. The Duke,[66] in the meantime either not able to make them know their duty or perhaps [un]willing to part the fray till they had spent themselves and become poore enough to be good subjects. This warre, or rather this rout, drew much < 18 > blood on both sides and so consumed both their estates that their ruine was evident to every body but themselves. This being observed by a younger brother of the Count de Salle, a man of sober humour, made an addresse to the

61. Odysseus and Circe (OCD, p. 242).
62. John Higgins.
63. Lieutenant Don Ville.
64. Marquis de Sôme.
65. The Salles family, barons de Rorté.
66. Probably Duke Charles III of Lorraine.

Count and mentioned an accomodation proposing some meanes of reconciliation to prevent the destruction of his house. This wise advice soe enflamed the great man that he told his brother that he was digenerate to thinke of peace with those that had injured him so notoriously and thereupon, consulting with his passion only (which never yet gave good councill) stabbed him to the heart and soe deprived himselfe of the best frend he had. After this foule act he never prospered and nothing remaines now to the family of all the former grandeur but 2 or 300 pistolls p[er] annum and this fatall story. This gentleman goes now by the name of Don Ville, an honest man, noble in despite of his poverty and certainely worthy of better fortune.

My Cornett canot chuse but be very much a gentleman[67] for he was borne in Ireland of Scottish parents. His name is Dunbar. He is soe farre from hypocrisie that he does not soe much as pretend to honesty. He is a younge man, for he sayes he is but 28, yet he recounts heroicall actions of his owne in the warre 30 yeares agoe. He hath served in Portugall and you canot invent a lye or repeat on[e] out of the Knight of the Sunn or Kumant of Romance [sic] but he can either parallell or exceed it. By his owne instances, every thing is a pigmy compared to a Portuguise,[68] and which him that was not in that < 19 > warre knowes nothing, if youle beleeve him (as why should not a gentleman be beleeved that swears). Neither men nor women ever stood before him; he blowes downe all, for you must know his breath is very stronge. To be short, he is a proper fellow and very good company.

My Quartermasters name is Barnsley and deserves as large a description as the Cornett.

Besides these, I have a certaine servant called Forthsith, [a] Scottish corporall, an understanding man you'le say, for he is alwaies of the opinion with his superieur officer. What one of the false loones saye of him, he is as stout a fellow as ever caried a pack, onely sir, a little bash full in the face of his enemy.

Another corporall we had of the same Nation. He is but newly come, therefore can say as yet little of him onely he can speake nonscence in two languages.

Our recreation is hunting, the maner thus. We call out the peasants who bring their fusees[69] into the forest and take their stands. The rest drive the game towards them with shouting and noise. Roebucks, wolves, foxes and wild bores are killd frequently in these chases.

67. Herbert viewed his officers as 'temporary gentlemen'. See his remark on page 17 of the text on p. 457 of this edition.
68. *i.e.* everything pales into insignificance beside the experience of the officers from the British Brigade in Portugal.
69. A flintlock musket.

About this time I went to Nancy, the metropolis of this Noble Dutchy. It was accounted the best fortified towne of Europe; the beautie of it was its strength. The walles, now demolished, and there remaines now noe great miracle, onely tis as a faire towne, the building stone and the inhabitants rich. It stand[s] in a <20> valley, not very broad but fruitfull enough. The Dukes palace is the onely place worth notice which now wants its best ornament, that is its naturall prince. This prince, none of the best, his character is that he never was constant in anything but breaking his word, a perpetuall plague to his subjects and yet beloved of them to admiration. Tis beleeved that he has sold his country to the King of France and that rather because he made noe defence, made the best of his furniture converting all his guns and artillery into pockett pistolls, insomuch that he is thought to have more ready money then any prince in Christendome. Many circumstances there are that would induce a beleefe of this bargane and sale.

In the first place, his title (he being, as the[y] use to say in England, but tenant par curtesie, for he was not right heire to the Dukedome, though he were next heire male). The Salique Lawe not being owned here, he was Duke onely in right of his wife, by whom he had noe children, and to whom, its said, he was not over kind. Her sisters children, who married his brother, are (next to the Dolphin) heires apparent. Who can tell whether this might not perswade him to take money for his terme of life (he being very old) wherewith to provide for his children by the other venture, or, if you please, adventures—pardon the quibble for it concernes the greatest quibbler in [e]xtendere. You may, like wise judges, favour the <21> guesse I am sure. There are historians in the world, I am sure, that would be thought grave and therefore credible, that sometimes talk as improbably. For you must observe that when fam[e]d writters are ignorant of the councells that lead great persons to this or that action, tis their duty to invent and assigne and assigne [*sic*] what causes they please to supply the history out of poetry. Therefore tis that soe many tale-wrights are truely called authors. But least some criticks should suspect them, they need noe more but quote some manuscripts miraculously saved at the burning of some antient place of record and is now to be seen covered with smoaky vellume in one of the libraries of Japan or where you please. Next, he [the Duke of Lorraine] is esteemed as brave and experienced a soldier as any of his time. His subjects are affectionate to him and as perfectly hating the French as he could desire, more indeed than he could deserve. His townes and countrye [are] as defensable as art and nature can make them. Noe other Divell but that of Covetousnesse could tempt him to part with soe rich a province and soe loyall subjects without strikeing one blowe to defend it. And for the towne of Nancy, it might have defended itselfe against anything but such ill fortune or the infidelity of their prince. I shall now leave him to his mirth, which they say is rather increased than diminshed by his losses and infamy, a happy man onely in this; he can turne all his misfortunes into jests, his joking maner having not < 22 > yet forsaken him.

I have visited most parts of Loraine. Tis a countrie that, I suppose, many brave 60 or 70 miles every way, the 4th part of which is, at this present, covered with wood and yet tis strange they almost have no timber but all coppices. You may thinke we did not want fire for the law obliges every bore to cut down and carry away soe many Acres every yeare whether he hath use for it or noe, yet the wood still getts ground upon them. I have told you formerly what live furniture these groves afford. I know but one forrest in all this tract of wood that is defended[70] and that is at Comercy[71] and belongs to a great cleargy man, [the] Cardinal de Ray. The wolves are so numerous that like the French army they are therefore bold, soe bold as to come into villages and carry away children out of their fathers arms. One instance of late there were at De La Ware, nere a monastery of English friars of the Benedictine order.[72] One of the fathers there told me a story and that the last yeare a woman was caried away out of a viniard, whence she wrought, by the said forrest and that there were no more found of her then of Jezebell—the palmes of her hands and the soles of her feet. The same father told me another story. On this occasion, two soldiers of our Regiment in Captain Pendarris his troop fought and one was killed. The survivor, bethinking himselfe of the severitie of the French law, fled into the woods < 23 > where he was assaulted by wolves. He had much difficulty to defend himselfe. He was persued by them and his owne conscience to the very gates of Metz where [he] thought to render himselfe into the hands of justice rather than be devoured alive. Yet he found means to escape from thence to the English convent at Delaware. The good people protected him and beg'd his pardon, that is they solicited so that nobody did prosecute him.

These wild burgesses of the forest are much more modest now then formerly for the country begins to grow populvous agine yet the inhabitants tells [sic] me that one of them will come (at noone day[)] into the feild where the heards man continually waites upon the Cattle of the Village. Hele [sic] take a cowe by the taile, and you must thinke

70. *i.e.* fenced-in and managed for game.
71. Commercy.
72. This probably refers to St Lawrence's Monastery at Dieulouard, Lorraine (*Memoirs of Father Augustine Baker and other documents*, eds. J. McCann & H. Connolly (Catholic Record Society, London, 1933), pp. 269–70).

they must need goe whom the Divills drive, he is soe good a steersman, that by this sterne he will gaile her along into the wood making her to out run her master. When she is there she is his owne and his right is as unquestionable as if he had entered her into the Toll book. He will take a sheep by the eare and whiske him with his taile and soe both off [and] out run the shepherd. I thought myselfe obliged to doe this right to their ingenuity.

And to speake truth, though we are sometimes (a la chasse) the wolves are not much fewer for curbing here and yet the inhabitants confesse that we are lambes in comparison to the French whose insolence, it seemes, exceeds ours and that is very much to wonder.

Here are catts that our men will not shirk to < 24 > sweare are something else. I have seen one of them unlatch a doore and drawe back the iron bolt of a window, goe out, returne, and bolt it agen. At my Cornett[s] quarter there was a light wainscot doer to his chamber. The tricker [sic] was lost, but when it was shut, a cat would come and lye down upon her back, thrust her fore feet under the doer and soe lift it up from the linspe [sic]. I will easily pardon any bodies incredility for I should not have beleeved it myselfe, neither did I untile I saw it.

The face of the soile is the same though not all places alike. It consists of little Hills and narrow valleys, both fruitful. The hills beare corne, and the better thing called wine. The valleys afford hay and the rivers abundance of fish, eales, perch, pickes [sic], roches, chubbs and, in some places, troutes of a great size and goodnes. Pasture they had little and therefore their cattle are small and runtish. They are, for the most part, fed with strawe, winter and sumer, and housed continually for feare of the wolves who are notable freebooters.

The[y] have but smale horses, much like our Welch Tittes,[73] and tis well they are soe for if they were bigger they would spoile the weomen, for they all ride astride. A goodly sight to see the virgins with warre saddles between their legges, verily and indeed [I] saw. But that we are great saints and by the restraints of our imaginations we should be apt to thinke sinfully and wish that we were horses to[o]. The young ladies will make noe scruple to mount a Troopers horse, ride him two or three rings, [and] fire her pistoll at a mark, and that is one of the reasons, in the [opinion?] < 25 > of some phylosophers, that they have not so much haire upon their (comodities) forsooth, as some people report of the English.

The gentry are exceeding curteous and very obliging in their behaviour. Merry they are and wise. The Boores are of the same breed with

73. A little horse (*OED*). See Joan Thirsk, *The Horse in Early Modern England* (Reading, 1978), pp. 25–7.

those about Oxford [and] as ill conditioned. I beleeve they are more crosse then Christians. To eat flesh upon a Friday is a sin against the Holy Ghost. Adultery and Murther are veniall sins in comparison of putting bacon into pease poridge in Lent. You may sooner perswade any woman to make her husband a Cuckold then to lend her spoone to eat flesh poridge on a fish day. They are exceedingly devoted to the blessed Virgin and very good they are unto her for they give her new clothes twice or thrice a yeare to make her very fine. My groome, John Parry, was very much troubled at Noveau to see her dress't up, as he conceived, in poore whores lace. St. Genea (Genesius) is patron of that church. His statue stands over the church door with wooden fiddle in one hand and the fiddle stick in the other. He hath a bunch of ribons of as many colours as any country scraper of them all. The people doe stedfastly beleeve 'tis the very same toole wherewith he got his liveing. That that was his trade, the curate of the place assured me in verbum sacerdotis and I can assure you tis a merry parish to this day.[74] <26> They have a custome there but whereupon it was grounded noe body knowes. Every Goodtide Tuesday[75] all the people that were married that yeare in the seignery, wade through a river that falls into the Mozell nere a place called Novill, so ridiculous a thing is conceited religion.

I once visited Captain Laneers [Lanier] quarters at a place called Champigny [Champougny]. There is a monastery and they have a tradition that a daughter of God knowes which King of Scotland fled thither for religion, her father, forsooth, being an heretick. There she turned shepardesse like an errant Catholick. God save all. Her father heard of her and, in a great rage, brought his army along with him, swearing (by the bread of God) he would kill all her white cattle and her too if she would not come home againe, turne presbiterian, and be a good huswife and look better to her dayry. But she tuch't a little rivulett of water with a white wand that she had in her whiter hand and, behold, the brook did swell up to such a height that she had like to have drowned her daddy and all his ragamuffins. The Devil cursed her well for it. There she lived and there she dyed and there she lyes buried with her arse downe and her c—upward. There the broke is still and anybody may see it for nothing and whosoever doubts of this holy tale is an infidell and an Hugonett, a stubborne hereticke that will not beleeve so faire a demonstration. <27>

Before I part from this fruitfull province, I canot forebeare one notable story of a great lady in the neighbourhood of our winter quarters in the late, cruell warre which soe much destroyed the

74. This refers to the village of Pagny where Herbert was quartered.
75. Shrove Tuesday.

country, that within these ten or twelve yeares they were constrained to draw the plowe with their weomen.[76]

The Baron of Belmount was, in this ware, one of the most potent of the nobles that sided with his naturall prince against the French and Swede. He was a Leift Generall under the Duke of Loraine[77] at the metropolis [of] Nancy. His lady had the kindnes to give him a visit there but was not used by the Duke with that respect she deserved, or at least expected. She being a woman of a fain, masentive [*sic*] spirit, flew away in great disdain to Paris where she obtained comission from the King to raise fines against the Duke which she did soe sudainely and effectually that she much advanced the Kings service in these parts. She fortifies her owne house, which was stronger in her and the courage of her followers than in scituation although tis double moatted and the house itselfe a faire quadrant of stone building. She had alwaies there with her a brave troop of horse which she, in her owne person, alwaies comanded, to the little ease of the Dukes partie. She brought them one day to face Nancy itselfe. Her owne Lord and husband with great force was sent out against her but she charged in the head of her desperadoes [and] made such an impression upon the good man <28> that he and his were quite routed and chased into the towne. After this, none of the partie durst stire further, either by night or day, her intelligence being as great as her Fortune. In the end of this bloody warre, she was at last reconciled to her husband but never to the Duke. She would not dwell long with him neither, but betook herselfe to a monastery where, about 8 yeares agoe, she ended her strange life, her memory being yet and will be still fresh in these parts. Her son is a notable gentleman with whome we had much converse. We entertained one the other with mutuall visits and I have heard him confirme this story with his own mouth.

I had my billet on a gentlewomans, a widow, whose deceased husband gave name to the place. She though, in the depth of winter, had the conscience to treat me in her sumer house in the garden. It was so light a lodging and transparent by reason of the glasse windowes, or the holes therein, that a beleever might observe the Northwinds struggle with our breath and overcome whole sentences by fre[e]zing them in the Aire. These cobweb words hung in the roome so thick that Higgins, with his high crowned hate, destroyed many a delicate speech. Haveing made some sportt with this fancy I put him a work to read some of them, but haveing unadvisedly taken for his mornings draught a doze[n] of Brandy, it thawed the words soe fast that before his eye could wel[l] distinguish, they were resolved into a dewey raine, which wet us somewhat, and soe we lost the benefit of this experiment.

76. The Thirty Years' War.
77. Charles IV, Duke of Lorraine (1604–1675).

Though I have taken the pleasure of telling a tale bordering on the scirts of imposibility, it is not meant soe much to delude the credulous as to entertaine the albeleeving vertuous and to set forth the uncharitablenes of my lodging that time of yeare. This day proved the Eve, or page, of some inhumane saint, for though I was very hungry, his holines alowed me no flesh and little of other belly timber. Here I learnt to boile egges in a frying pan and after the milk in the same. This sup[p]er was soe light that it improved my desire to a vehement longing to see the saint next morning, who I hoped would have kept a better table then his fore run[n]er, his Eve, but I was much deceived. I thought till now that the saints had starved all the Eves in the yeare to make themselves fat but I have learned there are a great many lean saints and not worth the ceremony we alowe them.

Now tis time to take our leave of this country to the great greefe, you must thinke, of the inhabitants and yet few of these hard hearted people shed a teare at our departure, onely some of the tender sex could have wisht us to stay out the 3 quarters of the yeare. We left some of them in a thriveing condition with plenty of matter for their confession next Easter. You see how loath my pen is to part with them as long as the Inke lasts, but the trumpett sounds and we must march.

<16> March 13. I had an order signed by General Vaubrun to assist his gards in taking a Spanish colonel which then quartered privatly at Masey [Maxey-sur Vaise or Maxey-sur-Meuse], but we mist him narrowly, this being the first comand I executed under the French authority.

<28> Came Father John, an English Friar of Delaware, who begged for the life of our soldier who had killed his comarade in [a] duell.

Came the soldiers cloth for coates and 30 cloakes and my comission, signed Louis, bearing date 23 Aug. 1671 of his reigne 29, under written Tillier [Tellier], secr[etary] of state. About this time came our horses, in number 39.

The French pay in the feild, 1672:[78]

	£.	s..	d.
Capt.	3 −	13 −	4
Leift.	2 −	3 −	4
Cornett.	1 −	10 −	0
Quart.	0 −	16 −	0
Corpll.	0 −	16 −	
Soldiers	0 −	5 −	0

78. These figures represent the pay whilst in the field. They need to be compared with the pay received whilst in winter quarters listed on p. 456 above.

Upon the Aprill 28, new stile Aprill [*sic*] we marched to Vaucouleur, a faire towne, famous for the first prankes of Joan the Pucelle [Joan of Arc]. The governour of this place brought her to the desparing Dolphin, whom she so revived that he began to check the fortunes of the English. She, doing wonders in her owne person and the people beleeving all she undertook was assisted by <29> God, was the first to put Brandy in the m[o]uths of that fainting generation. The English tooke, or rather bought her of the Burginians, and burnt her for a witch. The French account her a martyr. Whatever she was, her memory is, and alwaies will be, very precious to this people who could not be freed from the power of the English armes but by miracle.

Thence we marched to Bar le Duc, thence to Clermont,[79] where we overtook our regiment, thence journeing with some French regiments of horse severall removes. We came to encampe nere a great village called Carignion,[80] between Mauson [Mouzon] and Sedan, a fine towne in Luxemburge and of great trade. Hither we came to buy necessaries for the soldiers and the campaigne, which made everything soe deare that it would abate any mans courage to cheapen a comodity. Thus money, the blood of the kingdome, doth circulate. The soldiers in their winter quarters doth spunge the people; the trades man suckes the canaleer dry; the country peasant drawes it againe for provisions; the Court drawes from all and empties itselfe againe by a thousand chanells. Six dayes we stayed here, from whence we travelled through Luxemburge and the famous Forest of Ardon,[81] a vast wilderness of woods yet not unpleasant to such as fancy Malancholy walkes. Here a poeticall sense may find his fine groves, his faunes, his meads, his springs, his rivuletts, his wild beasts, his knight arrants, or any of his <30> implements, but his faire ladyes. The miserable inhabitants flying from their villages into the inaccessable mountaines and woods, from whence they would intercept our straglers, shooting with their fuzees from their covert stands and we, in revenge, burning their townes and houses in such places as we lost many of our soldiers. Otherwise, we took nothing but for the bellies of ourselves and horses. By this time, our army was about 32,000 horse and foot, the Prince of Condy[82] our generall.

About the 13 of May, we encamped nere the City of Leige, famous, or rather infamous, in history for being the most rebellious City in Europe, except Gaunt [Ghent]. 'Twas destroyed to the ground by Charles the Warlike, Duke of Burgundy,[83] but out of the ashes has

79. Clermont-en-Argonne.
80. Carignan, between Mouzon and Sedan. It is now in France.
81. The Ardennes.
82. Louis II de Bourbon, Prince of Condé (1621–86) (*DBF*, ix. 447–52).
83. Better known as Charles the Bold.

sprung up the Phoenix of all these countries. 'Tis scituate upon the River Meux in a most pleasant valley which is filled with buildings along the river that you may ride all the day as if you were in a towne. Here is a colledge of English Jesuits[84] who entertained us with civility. They shewed us the house and gardens, which was a statly fabrick and a wonderful pleasant scituation, the gardens mounted soe aloft it entertained the full prospect of all the towne and country almost. Here is a faire cathedrall church where lye the bones of Sir John Mandevill[85] under a monument of marble built at the charge of the towne. Here he dyed after he had wandered over a great part of the world to belye it.

The King lay about 4 leagues from Mastricke with an army of 12,000 men and hither he came to view our army. <31> He was pleased to say our regiment was much to his liking and soe did old Turene[86] which made our men the willinger to serve for a great day. A faire word from a prince is as good (you know) as moneye, but onely it will not buy Tobacco. He pretended as if he would beseige Mastrick, having surprized Maseick,[87] a neutrall towne belonging to Leige, and clapt a garison into it in so much that the Dutch drew great forces from other places to strengthen this to the number [of] 12,000 but, on a suddain, away we went in several armyes marching day and night through Limburge, Julias [Jülich] and the country belonging to Collon [Cologne]. Eight leagues belowe the City, nere Nuy's,[88] at a little garison of French called Keysserswert,[89] we past the Rheine by a bridge of boats. Thence [we] marched through some part of the Bishoprick of Munster into Cleave where we presently begirt Wesell. The King, Turene, and Luxemburge,[90] at the same time beleaguering Rheinsberge, Orsoy, and Burick [Buderich] all townes upon the same river of Rheine not past 3 or 4 leagues distant on[e] from the other. The garisons were drained, as I said before, to man Mastrick yet there was 26 companies in Wesell. They played upon us with their great gunes very furiously yet we lost few men, which was a miracle, for the bullets came amongst us soe thick that they grew familiar with us. Captain Slingsby[91] had his dog killed just

84. An English Jesuit novitiate was founded in Liège in 1614 (A.C.J. Beales, *Education Under Penalty, 1547–1689* (London, 1963), p. 186).
85. Sir John Mandeville (d.1372). English explorer and traveller. Buried at the Church of Liège (*DNB*).
86. Henri de la Tour d'Auvergne, Vicomte de Turenne, Marshal of France (1611–75).
87. Maaseik, fifteen miles north of Maastricht on the Meuse.
88. Neuss.
89. Kaiserwerth.
90. Francois-Henri de Montmorency-Bouteville, Duke of Luxembourg, Marshal of France (1628–95).
91. Captain Henry Slingsby.

at his head as he lay asleep and the gutts and braines dasht into his face. This seige began the 1st of June. The 3rd after we stormed a fort where they had 130 men, about a musket shot out <32> of towne. This made the burgers paile. Upon the 5th day, being Whitsunday, it was delivered up. The townes men saved their goods. The soldiers were made prisoners for the burgers forced them to yeald. It is one of the neatest townes I ever sawe of the bignesse France, canot shew anything soe cleanly. The same day, all the rest of the townes yeelded soe that we tooke in 4 stronge garisons in one day.

Twas reported and beleeved by such as knew the humour of this King, that he, lying before Rheinsburge with his army and hearing that Wesell had yeelded to us, grew into a great rage that our little army should have the honor to take a towne before his great one [and] sent the defendants a terrible message that if they did not render themselves forthwith he would not spare man, woman or child. And, thereupon, these discreet cowherds, consulting with their wives and children and their owne feares more then with duty or honor, imediately wed their new master thinking it no policy to provoke a man whome they thought so able to be as good as his word, this being a quality inseperable from dastardly people alwaies to make a muster of the enemies power by a multiplying glasse and to view their owne abilities to resist by the diminishing end.

<33> Upon the 28 of Aprill stilo novo, we departed from our winter quarters in Loraine to Voucouleur,[92] where we lay one night upon the hay. Thence to Barleduc and the day following to Clermount in campaine,[93] where we met the rest of our regiment. We had the Tapp.[94]

The order of the Tap:[95]

To the soldiers	3 lbs. of flesh a man
	1 pd. of bread
	3 pints of wine
To their horses	15 pd. of hay
	3 pickettens of oates
	5 pd. of strawe

And the use of fire and kittchen ware.
A Capt. alowed 6 men; a leift. 4; cornt. 3; Quartermaster

92. Vaucouleur. At this point, Herbert repeats his Narrative from p. 28 in the manuscript.

93. Clermont-en-Argonne.

94. The issue of provisions to the soldiers.

95. This list appears in the margin of p. 7 of the manuscript. It has been repositioned here to improve clarity and continuity.

2; and a billet worth between 15 and 30 pence which the
Capt. make benefit of in mainley by false musters.[96]

From thence to our first campe which was pitched in a plaine by a
faire river between Meusen[97] and Sedan, nere a bigge valley called
Carignion,[98] and arrived on the 2nd and 3rd of May. There we staied
6 dayes with 5 or 6 regiments of French horse. In the mean time we
saw Sedan, a very fine towne in Luxemburge, the building faire, full
of horse and foot every man providing himselfe of necessaries for the
feild which made every thing exceeding deare soe that what rapine
gott from the countrie is deposited in the townes to the great impover-
ishing of the one and the enriching of the other. Into this campe came
the Prince of Condy[99] and his son, and Count de Guise,[100] and other
great officers to a review. The 9 of May we mounted againe and
marching through Luxemburge [and] the famous Forest of Arden,[101]
a kind of pleasant wildernes of woods and mountaines, we came nere
unto Namur, where we met the rest of Condees army. In all, we made
about 32000, besides vallets and baggadge-boyes, which were halfe as
many more.[102]

We came from hence to the River Meaxe and followed the stream
to the famous city of Leige which gave so much trouble to the Duke
of Burgundy, Charles the Warlike. We pitched our campe nere the
towne, which was neutrall, yet the King seized upon on[e] of their
<34> townes called Maseick and put therein a stronge garison to
curbe those of Mastricke, which he made shew at distance to beseige
with his great army of 120,000 men, which caused the Dutch to draine
their garisons upon the Rheine to man this place. But the King, after
he had reviewed our army, sent us away, he himselfe staying 2 or 3
dayes behind. We marched night and day through Limburge,
Juliers,[103] and the territories of Collon. 8 leagues below the city we
past the Rheine by a bridge of boats at a place cald Keyserwart,
which he had fortified. On the other side was another army of French,
strongly entrenched. Also, the towne of Nuys,[104] t[w]o leagues higher,
was strongly garisoned with French horse and foot, soe that he has

96. These represent the ration allowances of the officers.
97. Mouzon.
98. Carignan.
99. Prince of Condé.
100. Probaly Bernhard, Comte de la Guiche, lieutenant-general (1642–1696) (*DNF*,
x. 79).
101. The Ardennes.
102. A modern estimate suggests that the size of an army's administrative tail and
its camp-followers was about half that of its fighting strength (Parker, *Military Revolution*,
pp. 77–8).
103. Jülich.
104. Neuss.

the comand of the Rheine so farre, nothing but by his leave being able to pass up and downe those trading waters. Thence we marched, resting but on[e] or two dayes in all this journey, through into the Dukedome of Cleave, belonging to the Duke of Brandenburge but the townes have Dutch garrisons all alonge the Rheine, and upon the first of June we clapt seige to the stronge and faire towne of Wesell, which had therein 24 companies of foot and 2 or 3 troopes of horse. They shot at us with their great guns incessantly, bullets of 40 weight[105] alighting amidst our troopes, yet they noe more amazed our men then if they had been soe many snow-balls. We would not stire from our ground for all this hot worke, and though the English lay more open to their shot then any part of the army, yet we had not much losse but many faire escapes, the balls passing through our rankes and our unconcerned people watching the fall would run and gather them up and lay them in heaps. Captain Slingsby lay asleep upon the ground with his <35> Dog at his head. There comes a canon shot and struck out the Dogs gutts and braines, mixing them in that gentlemans face. The 3rd night our Swisse atackt a stronge fort within musket shot of the towne. It had in it 3 peeces of canon and an 150 men to defend it. It was stormed and taken in a moment with the losse of onely 1 man. This brisk worke soe disheartened the burgers, seeing our men had brought our trenches up close to the walls and were ready to storme them, forced the soldiers to yeeld to hard conditions. They were made prisoners but the towne was saved from pillage and the country defended from plunder, when it was to[o] late. The miserable people, here and ever[y]where, quitting their houses and flying where they could to save themselves from violence, we, and our horses, treading and raking up all their goodly feilds of corne and pasture, soe that they had a timely but very malancholy harvest. The peasants would set upon our straglers in the woods and shoot them from their privy [sic] stands, in revenge of which we would burne their villages and leave nothing undestroyed. The French, and the English too, the Divell a Barrell better herring, loveing mischeife for mischeife sake, would kill cattle and leave them lye to infect the aire haveing noe need of them. They would take a great deale of paines to cleave tables, bedsteeds, and chests for fire when they had other wood enough ready at hand. Noe divell in hell could be more industrious then these caterpillars. They would carry away goods of all sorts till they were a weary, then throw them away. My heart akes to remember <36> their villanye.

But the 5th of June, being Whitsunday, we entred the towne [Wesel] which is rich and neat, as all the Dutch townes are. The same day

105. 40 pounder cannon.

was Rheinberg, Orsoy, and Burick delivered up to the King, the Marshall Tureen, and other armys which had met us here by neerer ways. These four great townes upon the same river were beleaguer'd all at once and taken all in one day, soe that I reckon our campe (and the townes being about 4 leagues distant) to be in circumference 20 English miles, soe that in 5 dayes time we destroyed one of the most fruitfull countries of Europe. Upon Sunday following, we tooke Rees and Emerick. The former made resistance, the latter none for the garrison fled at the noise of us. Griett[106] was also taken by the King. All this was but one weeks worke. These townes are upon the bankes of the river Rheine which gives them wealth and pleasure. This was a faire weeks worke to take 7 goodly garisons soe well fortified in 7 days time from soe warlike a people as the Dutch. The Spaniard never had soe faire a hand over them.

But to begin the next week, we did a feat that will be talkt of as long as the world lasts, in the country of Batavia. The Rheine divides itselfe into two streemes: on[e] goes to Newmegen[107] and to Roterdam and is called the River Wahall;[108] the other goes to Arnhem and Utricht and soe to Amsterdam. In the point of the angle, where the parting of these two mighty streems doe make a < 37 > peninsula, there stands one of the strongest forts of Europe with a garrison of 6,000 men to defend it and impeach our passing the rivers.[109] They had fortified all places where there was possibility of going over. The river was noe where fordable[110] being capable of ships of good burthen; it was nere as broad as [the] Thames at London. The Dutch had fortified a stronge house, which was the costome house,[111] and a faire castle adjoyning, soe nere the water that vessells are fastened to the wall by great rings at high water. Here were great guns that comanded the opposite banck yet all these would not secure them for the Prince [of Condé] past in a boat. His owne regiment of horse and one of Dragoons swam over with the losse of many persons of quality that were overwhelmed by the rapide streames. Our English Regiment swam it in ranke and file to the wonder of all men there. We had onely one man drowned, the honest and brave Captain Pendarris, a person of great courage and experience who, having served with much honor and experience in other countries, especially Portugall, was

106. Grieth.
107. Nijmegen.
108. River Waal.
109. The fortress of Schenckenschans. The peninsula formed by the division of the Rhine is known as the Isle of Betuwe.
110. The water levels in this area were low after a prolonged spell of dry weather. This had been one of the reasons for the Dutch evacuation of the line of the Oude Ijssel (Baxter, *William III*, p. 65).
111. The French refer to this action as the Battle of the Tolhuis.

here cast away by the defect of his horse leaving an excellent memory behind him for his honesty, modesty and natur[e] had made him deare to all those that pretended to either of those qualities.

** <7b, 9> [We] swame over into the Island of Betuw[e]. The Prince of Conde's o[w]n guard lead the way, some guard de corps followed, and our regiment then, by a speciall order which some imputed honorable soe that some <7b, 10> disputes rise from the passage between our Colonel and the Elder Regiments from whence we were comanded. The Germans let fall their arguments and our men, in whole squadrons, the officers in the head of them, swame through and, as the French said, in good rank and fille and lost onely Captain Pendarris. It is true, at first we tooke it as an honourable call to be selected out of many Bodies of Horse to second the Prince now engaged in the Island, but after we found twas onely to be a guard.**

[<38> and <39> are blank in the manuscript.] <40>

Here was a hot dispute. Our men forced their campe. The Dutch threw downe their armes at last and, on their knees, beged quarter, which the generous prince was ready to grant them when in comes the Duke of Longeville,[112] a young hotspurre, nephew to Condy, and cried out, 'Noe, point quartier'. Whereupon, the Dutch reassumed their armes and killed this fiery Duke with at least 100 persons of title and shot the Prince himselfe through the arme. Soe just is Heaven and soe suddaine is God a revenger of evell intentions. This caused the Dutch prisoners to be all put to the sword. The rest fled where they could leaveing their offensive and defensive armes behind them together with their reputation to strawe the wayes withall. It was the opinion of the best experienced comanders in our Regiment that 200 resolute horse might have defended the passe against all the forces of France.

But, wett as we were, we were constrained to be on the guard that night without any tents in the moist, open aire and we were not releeved for 48 hours after. The comon soldiers would have grumbled much at this duty did not the example of their superiors, who were in the same pickle, check their complaints. There were a great number drowned of the best houses of France and indeed, 'tis the glory of this Nation that in all the ill accidents of warre the nobility have alwaies the greatest share, their briske humour exposing them to the greatest dangers.

<41> We have large boats of copper carried upon carts and plankes for the purpose, wherewith they made a bridge over the River to passe the foot and the rest of the horse, baggag, and ordna[n]ce.

112. Charles Paris, Due de Longueville, the nephew of the Prince of Condé (D.NF, xii. 319–20).

In swimeing, the Engligh tyed their pistolls to their hatts soe kept them dry, which the French did not.

This mad pranke was a great advantage to the Kings affaires for the enemy, amazed at our doings, fled befor[e] us not daring to abid[e] the sight of such desperadoes. Here we plundred and destroyed all things. We tooke abundance of brave cattle and many good horses for the peasants were secure not thinking we would be soe mad as to adventure the passe, therefore they did soe expose their goods and all they had to our small mercies. We would sell cowes at 15 sous a peece, such as would give a whole pailefull of milke at one meale. Others that were better husbands would kill them and sell the heds for halfe a crowne. It was ordinary to knock downe an oxe, cut a peice out of his buttock or briskett, and leave the rest to poison the aire.

Hence we marched down the Rheine to Huissen, which yealded at the noise of our comeing. Thence we followed the River and our fortune to the stronge towne of Arnhem, once the dukall seat of Gelderland. This was forced in 3 daies time to yeeld. In taking this towne we lost the Count du Plessis,[113] our leift. generall, who was killd by a great shot.

From hence, part of our army, with the English, returned back to Skenkensconce.[114] We presently set <42> upon it, the horse carry[y]ing faggotts even within carbine shot of the gate and the Swisse breaking ground and running trenches close up to the walls. Upon Munday morning, being the 20 June, this impregnable fort, forsooth, was renderd haveing in it 3,000 foot which might have defended it for ever, but, I beleeve the Spanish pistoll made stronger impressions upon those mercenary knaves then all our great guns would have done had they been planted. Thus you have here a demonstration that gold is better mettle then brasse or iron in the very heat of warre itselfe. Certainely, it was wisely done, for if the traytors had been stubborne we might have ling[e]red about this lousy scons all this sumer and have discovered that secret that we were not irresistable.

June 29. This morning we left this Sckenkensconce and marched down the River Wahall to Newmegen,[115] which was beseiged before by part of our Army. This Kings army at this time lyes before Doesburge, a towne upon the river Issell[116] between Arnhem and Zutphen. 'Tis worth observation that those Nations that huffe and swagger most abroad are many times feeble enough at home. Carthage was once an instance, Italy another. Now the Low Countries and France maybe so too, when the English shall be in humour to attaque

113. Gaston-Jean-Baptiste de Choiseul, Marquis de Plessis-Praslin (*DBF*, viii. 1204).
114. See p. 322 n. 109 above).
115. Nijmegen.
116. The Oude Ijssel.

it and that, I hope, will be the sooner to prevent their vissits to us. Let not England doubt but this great body of France has some seeds of diseases latent in its bowells, some humours that will putrifie and may prove an ague upon any obstructions. It hath the Ricketts, the head is to[o] big, but some of the joynts are crasie. For my part, I am far from thinking this terrible army to be invincible. Its true, its numerous, but take away the Swisse and a regiment or <43> two of Dragoons and the French foot are generally good for little but to serve in steed of fagotts. As for the horse, I confesse they are well mounted and the officers are excellent riders being bread up in that exercise. Although I will alowe them courage enough and a brisknes rather to be admired then imitated, yet those that can receive their first charge are past the worst, Julius Cesars caracter holding still good of them—primus impetus major quam vivorum secundus minor quam terminarus.[117] They are true sparks. They will kindle fire but will not retaine their heat long. The English of old knew better how to fight then how to treat with them and I doubt not but they have the advantage of them still in that particular. This wise prince knowes this well enough. Nor can you urge them to fight without the advantage of 10 to one, or something which might make all sure beforehand. Tis the constant practise of this mighty man to attaque noe place or person but such as he knows can't resist, which is a signe he will noe more trust to the valour of his men then to Fortune. Besides, in any action where there is danger, he is soe kind as to bestowe the honour of it upon strangers rather then on his owne people either holding them more sufficient or more faithfull, which is much in mercenary people. But his conquest, for the most part being over those of his owne nation and the yoake of Soloman being very heavy, he can't chuse but mistrust the fidelity of such as have noe fence to keepe them in but feare. This is to[o] much for our digression, therefore I[']le say noe more but I <44> hope to live to see a young Rehoboam[118] raigne in his stead.

June 23. We had a stronge partie comanded out of our Army lying in campe before Numegen. Our Leift. Colonel[119] went in the head of two battalions of the English and marched downe the river Wahall 6 leagues to the towne of Tiell,[120] which y[i]elded at first sight and soe did 6 or 7 garisons thereabout unto small parties imployed to take them in. Next day we returned to Newmegen, which still holds out.

---

117. *i.e.* they had shot their bolt after their first charge.
118. Rehoboam, son of Solomon, who succeeded his father as king of Judah in 935 B.C. His oppressive rule split Judah into Judea in the south and Israel in the north (C.H. Gordon, *The World of the Old Testament* (London, 1960), pp. 189–91).
119. William Littleton.
120. Tiel.

We batter it incessantly. Doesburge, in the mean time, y[i]elds to the King, soe has Utricht, soe that all Cleave and Gelders, excepting this towne, is wholy become French. This towne was, of old, called Niuiomagum, an Imperiall City.

Tis a shame to thinke of the barbarous behaviour of these most Christian people. These good Catholicks will ravish weomen in the Churches, even before the alter. 24 or more will fall upon one poore girle and never leave her while they feel her pulse beat, scarce then, and yet their civility is admirable for they will invite those that passe by to partake with them in these their dainties. These poore soules goe to heaven through the temple of Mercy, and tis thought there may be weomen in the world, as cold as devotion is now growne, that would willingly undergoe this martyrdoome.

** <7b, 11> The horse had little to doe but cary[r]y faggotts and goe on plundring parties for victuall and forage. Here Cornett Seres,[121] who did the duty of aid major[122] but had noe pay for it, give up his place and comission and rides volunteer and was kil[le]d in a party and the news was the Bores had not given him buriall. He was a gentleman wel[l] beloved and a knot of good fellows resolve to revenge his death. Captain Littleton[123] comands the partie, comes to a Curck [sic] and demands where the body lay. The towne,[124] by this time having gott a safeguard[125] in it, they showed him the place where the poor gentleman lay cram[med] up in a little, pitifull, shallow, short hole. They dug him up and find t[w]o rings on his fingers which the Bores had not discovered in burying him. Verman[126] had them for his paines. While this freindly funerall office was performing to the deseased, an alarm came of some dutch troopes at the townes end. They, on this, mounted hastily and retired without much order to some advantageous ground hard by that over lookt the country and with them fled the safeguard. Haveing here formed themselves into order againe, they sent out comanded men to discover, who brought word from the towne [that] they were a body of French and were pillaging the towne. At which the safeguard bristles and cocks his cap of authority, rides of them and comands them to returne the plunder or be it at their perill. They refused and on the instant marches up Captain Littleton and his party who, upon report of their disobeying the order, demanded what officer comanded them. They replyed,

121. Charles Serres.
122. The regimental adjutant.
123. Ferdinand Littleton.
124. The town where this incident occurred is not named by Herbert.
125. A safeguard was a small party of troops placed in a town or a village by one army to prevent the place from being pillaged by their opponents. In this case, the safeguard was French.
126. Lieutenant Hugh Verman.

'Noe Comission, but one whom they had chosen for that Ensigne.'
On this, Littleton told them he was a Captain and requested obedience
from them. They refused and from words fell to blowes. Littletons
party killed two, routed the rest and took ten prisoner which, on later
<*7b, 12*> consideration he released. To make up the businesse, he
returned all the plunder to the safeguard and marched off.**

We have upon this River a new but useles invention for the passing
to and fro our men and call it a flying bridge. Tis a great boat with
2 keels made in the maner of a fort with great guns in it. It is capable
of 5 or 600 foot and 2 or 3 troopes of horse. Between the keels there
are portcullises to keep little boats from going underneath and soe
secure it from being blowne up.[127]

The town of Newmegen stands upon the Wahall, well <45>
fortified with walls and outworks. On the other side of the River is a
very stronge fort which our men, at their first comeing, forced to
render. From this fort, and a new battery of our owne, our great guns
plaied upon the towne over the river, more out of a designe to afflict
the reched [wretched] people then out of any hopes to prevaile that
way. Our copper bridge boats were then with the King, and soe we
were forced to presse the vivanders boats from Collen [Cologne] and
other places, wherewith, at last, we made a bridge for our carriadges
with all the horse and foot, excepting those that were transported by
the new invention to secure the landing of the rest. Upon Sunday 29,
we past a great part of the Army. Then the seige began to be close.
Our men broak ground at the west side of the towne running the
trenches up through the streeadoes and pallisades of a halfe moon,[128]
which was there well man[n]ed and bravely defended, there being 5
or 6,000 soldiers in towne besides the Burgers, whose interest was a
sufficient whetstone, as some might thinke, to their courage. But I
must tell you, there were many English and Scotts amongst them, one
whole regiment in mood and figure,[129] and those furies kept the Dutch
from doeing here as they had done elsewhere, and were the true
Brandy that made them shew their red noses over the Ramparts.
These honest fellowes gave us liberall entertainment, hot meat all
night and day. The poor Swisse endured all with admirable patience.
They would stand upon a trench with a great deale <46> of

127. Double-hulled ferries were common on the Nieder Rhine during the 17th
century. Some reconstructions can be seen in the Cologne Municipal Museum. Copper
bridging pontoons, 'tin boats', made their campaign debut in 1672 (L. Montross, *War
through the Ages* (New York, 1960), p. 331).

128. A *demi-lune*, or ravelin, was an outwork of two faces and one angle built (to
protect the enceinte between two bastions).

129. Herbert is mistaken here. There were no English regiments in the Dutch army
at this time, although there was a Scottish Brigade of three regiments (Childs, *Army of
Charles II*, pp. 171–3).

unseasonable consideration within pistoll shot of the walles, and consider which was the best way to pitch the stake and place the fagotts as if at home in the country making a hedge. When any of them dropt, as too many did, his fellowes were noe more conserned then if they were really what the Stoicks would seeme to be, viz. without passion. Presently, they stript him and clapt him a brest the trenches to hold up the mold instead of a fagot and this was all the funerall pompe for a deceased Brother.

Here I had six horses killd at one great shot. My Quartermaster shot with a muskett bullet at my Tent doore. Next morning, as I was mounting the guard, my Corporall, Jesses by name, had his horse killed under him by a canon shot that tooke away one of his spurs. It was soe civil to leave him the other to wittnes that he was a trooper. Our bussines was to carry fagots on horse back every night close up to the trenches with danger enough, yet it pleased God we lost but one man of our Regiment and he a Lorainer of the Majors Troop. During this seige the towne did parlee often which made some old soldiers, which had been at the seige of many maidenheads, to conjecture that citties will hold out noe longer then pretty girles when they once come to treat upon conditions. For haveing severall batteries that plaied upon them and some mines ready to spring, and mortar peeces shooting great bumes [bombs] of 100 pd. waight into the <47> towne, soe terrified the inhabitants that upon Friday in the afternoone 8 July, our foot prepared for a storme that night as soone as the mines should make them way, [they] came to a parle[y] which lasted till 4 next day and then was delivered up to the French in whose hands we now leave it and prepare for the next adventure.

** <7b, 13> It is a custome that the officer that looses men or horses at any seige, at the taking of that towne shall have an order for asking to refurnish himselfe with men and horses out of the prisoners equipages, but our bashfull knight[130] would not solicit my case to Tureen,[131] so I lost a dozen horses for want of a words speaking. So ruined my troop, doing with my small number equal duty <7b, 14> with greater troops.**

Upon the 10th July we removed our campe to Graves, a neat towne upon the Meaux, well fortified and furnished both of men and other provisions. Upon report of our armyes looking that way, the [Dutch] soldiers were sent for to Bosleduc[132] but upon second thoughts they were sent back againe. In the interim, our men had possest the towne

130. Sir Henry Jones.
131. Turenne temporarily assumed command of the combined French army after Condé's wound at the Tolhuis (Trevelyan, *William the Third and the Defence of Holland*, p. 163).
132. 's-Hertogenbosch.

and mett these Dutch Gallants in the midway. The Comander in Chiefe drew them into a corne feild and soe, very valiantly, clapt spurs to his horse and left them and the danger behind him. The poore men fought a little but presently threw away ther Armes. About 150 were killed upon the place and in the persuit most of them were taken and stript to their naked skins.

About this time, the Duke [of] Monmouth, [the] Duke [of] Buckingham, and Lord Arlington was with the French King, where the English gallants act upon the French themselves in splendour and equipage.[133]

Our army was gone before to beseige a fort upon the Meax called Creave Court[134] scituate about midway between Bomell[135] and Bossleduc in the out edge of Holland, where I over took them. <48> After some apparatus made, our batteries mounted with canon, and the loosse of a few men, upon the 19th July the fort was yealded. ** <7b, 14> We had no other busines but that of fagotts. We observed that the Germans stoopt and lay flat on their horses and we carried them sitting up right on horse back, which argues a more natural handines in our people.**

Upon the 20th came the King to visite our Army. He ordered a Review to be made that day as we were to passe a bridge of boates that was made to carry us over the Meaux towards Bomell. This was a terrible muster, the oppertunity of cheating being taken from us. In particular, my troop, being much diminished by several losses, my case was somewhat difficult, beyond the supply of witt, yet fortune found out an expedient which made us not onely appeare corpulent but splendid. For that day there came many captaines and officers from the Duke of Monmouths Regiment[136] to see our Army or their acquaintances. Here Captain Richard Savage, my Lord Rivers son, and Mr Downes,[137] another of the Dukes Captaines, ride in my troop over the bridge with us and was willing to gratifie me by thus cheating the Comissary, insomuch we appeared a well timbred troop agen.[138]

133. Arlington and Buckingham had been to seek a peace with the Prince of Orange at his camp at Bodegraven on 25 June/5 July. On the failure of this mission, they proceeded to Louis XIV's headquarters, where, on 29 June/9 July, they concluded the Treaty of Heeswijk which bound the English and the French not to treat separately with the Dutch. At the French camp, Monmouth joined Arlington and Buckingham (Baxter, William III, pp. 86–90; Pieter Geyl, Orange and Stuart (London, 1969), pp. 364–72).

134. Fort Crevecoeur.
135. Now Zaltbommel.
136. The Duke of Monmouth's regiment of Foot, also known as the Royal English Regiment, part of the British Brigade serving with the French army.
137. Richard Savage, Viscount Colchester and later 4th Earl Rivers. Samuel Downes.
138. Herbert clearly expected to be allowed to conduct false musters and regarded cheating the system as a legitimate perquisite.

There are two forts, one called Voorne and the other St Andre,[139] which we had formerly taken in. These were scituated upon a narrow gate of land where the Wahal and the Meaux doe almost meet, but the Meux turnes away to the left and receives the Wahal at Workham[140] 4 or 5 leagues belowe, the greater river here loosing its name to the lesse as if the Rheine had, in a prodigall humour, lent more then the moity of its waterie forces to her sister, the Meaux, to make her entrance into the ocean more pompous[141] <*49*> 2 Part.

** <*7b, 14*> Thence to Bumell, which yealded the next day after we demanded it. Being encamped upon the Rhein, about 6 a clock in the evening came out a small vessell of 8 guns and fired great and small shot at us ashore. The Swise answered them with their musketts for a pretty while, during which a Captain had his head shot of[f] with a canon bullet and had done more mischeife had not an unlucky fire taken in the powder roome and blowne up her steerage, which made her hast home. At midnight, out came such another and forced it was, by us, to sea, and the next morning we were masters of the place and returned.**

<*50*> winter quarters. The abundance of raine at this time made us afraide of inundations which are more dangerous in these Lowe Countries then in France or England, for had the rivers overflowed, as they were very likely, our great armies would have been distressed and, perhaps, been caught in such another trapp as was once a mighty King of France by the over flowing of [the] Nile in a expedition against the Sultan of Egypt.[142] The truth is, we were affraid the Raine [Rhine], the Wahal, and the Meaux, the Ruwer [Roer], and the Domell, with the other auxiliary channells, would prove truer to their countries then the infatuated butter boxes that inhabite there.[143] But, p[er]haps, he that sets bounds to the Ocean had said unto our Army, Hither shalt thou come and no further.

To the wonder of all men, we were ordered to march away, some to one place, some to another.[144] ** <*7b, 14*> Then to Bosleduc agane, where we staid not long ere orders came for us to wait upon the King (who by that time had taken Doesburge[145]) into Flanders in his way for Paris.** The English Regiment was appointed to attend

---

139. St Andries.

140. Werkendam. Fort Loevenstein guarded the confluence.

141. Some material is missing from the manuscript at this point.

142. King Louis IX of France and the Crusade of 1248–50 (Jean de Joinville, *Life of St Louis*, ed. M.R.B. Shaw (Harmondsworth, 1973), pp. 220–64).

143. *i.e.* the rivers would do the work that the Dutch army had failed to achieve.

144. This was the point at which the inundations and the creation of the Water Line brought the French offensive to a halt.

145. Louis XIV's headquarters had been at Doesburg on the Oude Ijssel.

the King with the Kings Houshold, the Gens de Armes, [and] Gua[r]d de Corps, which made a body of 12 or 14 thousand horses, without foot. The 25 of July, we left Bosleduc. It was unholsome, flegmatique meals [sic] for they had drowned all the wayes of approach. This day his Majestie reviewed us and, tis said, was not well pleased with our Colonel because, he s[ai]d, we mustered very thick but marched very thin, soe that some skilfull persons began to read our destiny and to prophesie our Regiment should be broaken. The truth is, our Colonel <51> was a kind of animall by himselfe. I thinke there is no more of his kind, it were a pittie there should—a fellow without soule, sence, or honesty. He hath nothing about him that borders upon vertue, but a kind of brutish courage, the very same and as comendable in a mad dogge as in him. The best quality he has is that he is an open, professed knave and will, many time[s], give caution not to beleeve any thing he says or promises. The utmost of his Bubble [sic] is noe more then this: he has a great dexterity in squeezing, or oppressing, those that are below him to get wherewith to bribe those that are above him. Tis pleasant to observe with what majesty and ridiculous pride he domineers over his inferiours, and with what industry he creeps to and faunes upon and flatters those that fortune had placed above him. See how this Ignis fatuas[146] has led me out of the way, but I returne to the Regiment, whom ill usage, dirt and the comon accidents of warre had made weake. The soldiers, none of the worst, but the meanest of them serving to see themselves made poore slaves to make a base slave rich, they run away to the enemy, or where they could, insomuch that some of our Troopes, from Fifty northern lowtes, as most of them were, they shrunke into 15 and nobody could blame the King of France for <52> he had given this Welch knighthood of ours 100,000[147] to compleat the Regiment but the greatest part of this was converted to his owne use, not a troop receiving its due number of horses, coats, belts, hatts, and these were paid for by the poore soldiers out of their smal pay by dayly deductions soe that there was no privat soldier had more than 4 p[ence] per diem.[148] Good Sir H.J. is at the mercy of anyone that dare tell the King how he has been abused by him.

That night we lay in campe by a village called Boxtell, in Brabant;[149]

146. Possibly a pun on ignis fatuus.

147. Herbert does not indicate in what currency or denomination the '100,000' was given to Jones. It is possible that Herbert has added an extra nought; 10,000 livres would have been a typical sum for equipping a cavalry regiment. See p. 295 n. 8 above.

148. This was about the same as the daily pay received by an infantryman in England. It represents an extremely low wage for a cavalryman who had to maintain his horse as well as his own person (John Childs, *The British Army of William III* (Manchester, 1987), pp. 146–8).

149. Boxtel.

next night at Postell,[150] where there is another village and a monastery of white fryars. After another long dayes march, we exchanged the dry and barren heaths of Brabant and entred the fruitfull territories of Leige. We encamped nere a fine towne called Saint Trudor,[151] or oppidus Trudonense. Here we mett with a civill burger that spoke English. By him I learnt severall things of the place. Being a rigid Romanist he entertained me with this following story of this towne. He told it with much devotion and I listened with civility. They have here a very faire church, and large, and dedicated to the Blessed Virgin in which she had two Images, both adored with great respect, and many miracles were there done but no body know[s] precisly which of the two did them. They thereupon removed the one into another place farther off <53> yet the miracles continued. So, doubtfull that the difficulty remained to which of these holy engines to impute them, they knew that there could be but one right one. The one was nothing like the other in shape or structure. At last, they removed the one which was least favoured into the Bellfry. There it lay for some time in an obscure corner, covered with dust and cobwebbs, without any visits or vowes, till the saint grew angry—as you know it would vex any woman to be soe neglected. She watched, therefore, an opertunity to show her good nature and resentment in on[e] and the same act. On[e] day, when the streets adjoyning were all full of men, weomen, and children, downe she throwes the steeple amongst them, yet none were hurt. But the Image itselfe was either buried in the ruines or else it removed its lodgings to some other quarter where, for all her good turnes, she might at least have some wax lights in her chamber and not be nosed in her owne house by an impudent rivall. This was the last miracle done there and the learned clergy of the place concludes that the true Image is gone and that which remaines is but a Counterfeit because she does not rebuild the steeple which the other threw downe. If you will not beleeve this, doe not beleeve your owne eyes for the steeple is to be seen there, unrepaired, to this day. My advise was <54> they should remove the present Idoll out of the Church and, perhaps, the other would come againe and make them a new steeple, but the good gentleman shaked his head, as if he would have s[ai]d. 'Your councell had been good, had it not come from an Heretick.' Besides, they are affraid that if they should anger the baggage that is in possession, she would little care to throw downe the Church upon their head.

Part of the army rested here two nights but the King and all his numerous guards went away for Paris. Upon the 30 July, we encamped

150. Postel, now in Belgium.
151. St Trond or St. Truiden.

nere another good towne of the same province called Tongresse.[152] Here we would be glad to stay awhile to help the poore people in their harvest which, in this blessed place, is to[o] great for the inhabitants.[153] From Tongresse we removed to Maseick,[154] belonging to the principality of Leige and seized on in the beg[inn]ing of this campain to be a mussle [muzzle] to those of Maistrick, which still stand[s] out. Here we mett with my Lord Duglas's regiment[155] in garisoned [*sic*] and accepted the best Foot in France. It consists of 3,000 men. Nere this towne we past againe over the river Meax and came up close to Maestrick, where we encamped in those rich and fruitfull planes ** <*7b, 14*> within halfe a league of the towne** destroying all the country round us in serch of forage. ** <*7b, 14*> [We] foraged under the very walls, where past some scaramoches.** I reckon our number to be 3,000 horse.[156] The number of horse is greater [by] farre in the towne yet they never would sally out upon us. We keep very <*55*> stronge guards every night and lay ambuscades to cut them off if they should attempt upon us but, to say the truth, it is very difficult to beat up a French quarter, the comanders are soe very vigilent and all passes soe well comanded and secured we are not very subject to a surprise.

** <*7b, 14*> We were constrained to keep stronge guards: viz. a maine guard day and night <*7b, 15*> of a 150 men mounted: a Bywacke[157] of 500 within some few paces of it; and 200 carabines a foot[158] to comand a passe; patroles ever going. A generall word, a by word, and the Alamode do guard.[159] And every second day, 2,000 horse appointed for forage with a stronge guard to protect them. This was hard duty. Every night upon comand. The fortnight expired, came Mr Rochford[160] with 8,000 of the Kings Houshold, who made us drawe yet neerer to the towne and made between him and the

---

152. Tongres or Tongeren.

153. The fertility of the Basse-Meuse region was one of the features that made it attractive to campaigning armies. However, in the decade after 1670, it entered a period of agricultural depression and population decline (M.P. Gutmann, *War and Rural Life in the Early Modern Low Countries* (Princeton, 1980), pp. 23–6, 75–6).

154. Maaseik.

155. Lord George Douglas's Scottish infantry regiment.

156. Jones's regiment was in the cavalry brigade commanded by the Comte de Filiatt, consisting of 3,000 men. In the shorter version of the Narrative (NLW, HM 2/14/7b, p. 14), the brigadier is called 'La Filich'. Possibly, Abraham de la Fite, Marquis de Pelleporc (*DNF*, xi. 251).

157. Bivouac.

158. *i.e.* dismounted cavalrymen serving as dragoons.

159. *i.e.* a system of pass-words—that which is in fashion (*OED*).

160. Lieutenant-General Henri-Louis d'Aloigny, Marquis de Rochefort (d.1676).

towne a Line of Contravalation.[161] We lost men and horses, but not many. A soldier drinking out of an earthen pot (while we were at the guard) at [the] vivanders,[162] who it seemes was more bold than welcome, comes a canon bullet [which] brakes his draught by stricking of his head but did not injure the pot wherein the wine was. Paid the reckoning and the vivandeer packt up his wares and away to a more safe station. Here our Colonel plaid some pranks against the Mastrickers and came of[f] with losse, but his honor, which wanted some of the sences, felt not herselfe t[o]uched all this while.**

Upon the 9th, the greatest part of our men were comanded to leave their sad[d]les, swords, and pistolls behind them and to goe up to the very walls to forage with their sithes, sickles and carbines. We had comanded men in ambuscadoes to favour their retreate should they have been pressed to it by the townes men. Nor could we seriously imagine but the towne, upon this affront, would empty its pispotts upon us, but none would adventure further then protected by their small shot from their outworks, not withstanding we pekeened[163] with them under their very works where their musketts plaied soe hott upon us [that] we withdrew and without losse, and if some of us had had our wills, they would have run in betwixt their out guards and the towne and drawne some away with them like Dutch jugges by their leather eares, but we were comanded to retire.

Upon the 16, there was a stronge party drawne out, 15 out of a troop. This, we imagined, was detached for some extraordinary designe. I followed them. Count de Filiatt, <56> our Brigadeer, comanded in cheife. We marched up the river towards Leige and seized a castle by the way and left a guard in't, and then advanced our party about a league and [a] halfe further and ther discovered a great body of horse which proved to be the K[ing's] Guards and Gens de Arms, in number about 6 to 7,000, comanded by Leift. Generall Rochford. Now we must all acknowledge this man as cheife. At his arrivall we encamped closer to the towne – on the north side of the river side were our post, within lesse than Falkonshot. Thus we lay in the Divells mouth that day and sate on horseback all night. Our videtts[164] discovered that the enemy had made a breach in the wall and were busie all night in raising a battery to welcome us next morning. The French were first aware of it and removed their campe before day further of[f] danger and giveing us English noe notice of it, which made us more then suspect that they had little cared if we

161. A line of contravallation was a series of field fortifications constructed by the besieging army to protect itself against sallies from the surrounded garrison.
162. French sutlers.
163. To skirmish (*OED*).
164. Cavalry outposts, or sentries.

had all been destroyed and, to speake truth, our affections to them were not much more, soe that there was little kindes lost betwixt us. But we kept our post there till far in the day, then orders came to march and we followed and drew up in an adjoyning feild where their great guns did not beare upon us.

In the afternoone [of] the 13 day, they made a sally of 50 or 60 musketteers, the River betwixt our <57> workes and them. They fired orderly and filed off and maintained this sport for an houre at least and were releeved with a fresh party who behaved themselves in the like maner. It moved our laughter but we could not be brought to repartee upon them, it was soe monstrous ridiculous. But on the other side [of] the towne there was brisker worke. Their ordinance, from a little rock that hung over the River, play'd upon the Gens de Armes and the Kings Houshold, for so they call the guards, with their great guns and did them much hurt. Whereupon, a regiment of foot were drawne into a little island under this rock with a purpose to drive them thence, but they were entertained with great and small shott for 4 hours and more till it was night. They did and received some hurts for the dispute was hot. They had the advantage of the place and number, our men haveing nothing but their missive weapons to defend or shelter them. The leiftena[n]t and myselfe had a mind to see the sport, haveing a mind to buy honor at as deare a rate as any, few out bidding us at this coine. This night we were on horseback agen till sunrising, then returned to our tents.

Every day we had pekeening with the enemy. Sir H.J. was soe use haveing the advantage of the wind that [it] blew some attomes of his into their faces <58> [and] he made them returne in despight of their noses. His La[u]ndresse observes that the knights linen have a stronger smell after a fright then at other times when that passion is not on him. This may be worthy the consideration of the Royall Society, at least the nose wise phisician amongst them. In this encounter, the knight lost his pistoll and if his hand had not been fast on, it had been shaked of[f] also, such a violent ague had then seized him. However, God be praised, if it be a thing to thanke God for, he came off well enough but that his heart panted violently, as it had cause for it had much a doe to climbe up from the quicksands in the saddle, all dirt as 'twas, to its ancient seate, his throat, where it still keeps, which is the cause, perhaps, of his stronger breath ever since, cold water, which is a drinke peculiar to him and the Turkes, being not able to wash away the viscuous humour which the poore thing had contracted in the Low Countries. 'Tis said, the generall did chid him for hazarding his person in action, so ill agreeing with his complection. How true that is I canot tell, but 'tis certaine he hath promised his freinds faithfully to doe soe no more and tis observed that this is the first promise that ever he kept. This is the best sport we have and as we use it 'tis a very harmles recreation and no danger at all in it, in so much that wise men themselves need not be ashamed of the exercise. <59> Upon Sunday morning, Leift Colonel, Whetherington[165] and Leift. Verman[166] and myselfe mounted the guard. We were saluted with great guns, two of which took away 2 mens armes and kiled a horse, which was the greater losse for the others were but French men. Here we remained till Thursday morning and if the enemy had knowne how well their guns were planted he had hardly left us horse or man but the guner thought he over shot us and soe gave over, which was not much displeasing to us. This is the 22 August, on which day in the afternoon, a dozen of us left the campe and went to visit Leige, 5 leagues of[f], about our busines, which was to refresh ourselfes. And on the 24 we dined with the English Jesuits who entertained us nobly and communicated their intelligence to us. In the evening, in very dirty weather, we returned to our campe, fording the Meaux at a little garison called the Vessiall.[167] The river was broad and swelled much with the raine, insomuch we wanted but little of swimming. Afterwards, we lost our way in the darke night but I had yet a greater losse then this, for when I came to my tent I found it robbed the night before. The losse was considerable in gold and silver a gold watch and severall rich medall[s] with <60> other curiosities I valued more then my moneys, though, at this time, money was never worth more in the estimation of all people. I made proclamation that if any should convey me my papers, I would forgive them my money and the fact too. Yet, no tidings could be had. I apprehended my corporall, Jesses by name, and 2 or 3 suspicious soldiers. A court-martiall was held for them who adjudged Blunden, one of them, to be burnt in the hand with matches. In this our noble knight was neither kind nor just, because perhaps he thought me to[o] rich to be his slave, for he knew very well that none but indigent people would be brought to comply with his base ends.

Upon the last of August we were ordered to march and leave Mastreckt untaken. We had devoured all the corne and hay in the country round about and that was our businesse. The Governour, whom they call the Rheingrave,[168] was a person of to[o] much honor and courage to be either affrighted or flattered to deliver the place, as others had done, but bravely resolved to endure all extremities rather than admit a blot upon his faire name which in all his very

---

165. Captain Wytherington. The lieutenant-colonel was William Littleton.
166. Hugh Verman.
167. Visé or Wezat, on the Meuse between Maastricht and Liège.
168. The Rheingrave was Jacques Fariaux.

long life he had acquired and preserved.[169] The day before we mounted the guard last the French were on, on[e] of the Monsieurs was at the sutlers and had a pot of wine at his nose, when there comes an unmanerly bullett and carried away his head with it where the poore <61> man could not find it. But providence preserved the pott and the drinke too for better purpose, which made some of our philosphers observe that the Dutch were a frugall people and had rather spill blood than wine.

From hence we marched to the number of 15,000 horse and foot, of which Douglas regiment of Scotts were part, ** <7b, 15> steeling away without beat of drume or sound of trumphet and all his mermidons with him. Onely our Brigade, at this time who lay closest and most undefended from the towne, marched of[f], colours flying, drums beating and trumpetts sounding. And quartered that night before Maseick againe,** and then throw the barren heathes of Brabant till we came to Grave.

Here, upon 5 of September, we past the Meaux in a bridge of boats and the 6 we past Geneperhouse and Genup,[170] a pretty towne upon the river formerly taken by us during the siege of Newmegen. We left also the Ducall towne of Cleave[171] a little on the right hand—tis but weake and untenable and therefore neglected by the French. Nere this place we are now encamped.

On[e] thing remarkable I had almost forgott. In our way from Mastrickt to Grave in Braband, we encamped on[e] night at [a] village called Chamont.[172] I comanded the maine guard with men attacht from every troop in the army. This guard was marched halfe a mile from the campe to a very pretty chappell standing upon a high, barren heath. This chappell was new and about 4 yeares standing. It has our Blessed Lady for its patronesse and her interest in the Count of Flanders hath made it much respected and promised the Curate a faire house adjoyning with liberall endowments. I <62> entered the Chappell to doe my devotions and, behold, it was all hung up with crutches and trusses for here the Blessed Virgin, like a very good huswife, cures all lamenes and ruptures. But there's a little well close to it. I suppose the water to have a minerall tincture of sulphur and allum. Here they wash and drinke and attribute the cure, which is the blessing of God, to the bounty of the Saint. This well was known antiently but was neglected till of late, which gives occasion to these cuning God makers (the priests) to perswade the infatuated people

169. The Dutch garrison numbered 8,400 (Trevelyan, *William the Third and the Defence of Holland*, p. 128).
170. Gennep, on the Meuse.
171. Cleves or Kleve.
172. Chaumont.

that the vertue of the well was lost till the village, about 4 yeares agoe, was forced to turne Roman and by the vowes of some devote [*sic*] weomen our Blessed Lady restored unto the waters the medicinall qualities which they never lost. By which bounty, she got this new church which begins to growe up into a towne and ere long, I doubt not, but 'twill be as famous as our Hollywell. They have bestowed very good cloath upon the Glorious Virgin. She stands above the Altar beckoning with her finger but the devotion of some carried them to[o] nere her. Here I saw and admired at the religion of the French. I sawe some of them, with great reverence, saying their prayers, kneeling to the Image and cringing most humbly, and presently rising up and rifleing the vests and other conceits from the altar as if they had been begging them of her. They said that they <*63*> were poore soldiers and had more need of them then shee. As for her, she might have new ones when she pleased. These rogues cut downe the young trees planted in the church yard and made the priests parlour a house of office, but this is nothing with them. When we lay before Skenkensconce, I saw 6 or 7 of the French foot take a great deal of paines and undergoe much danger to their necks and limbs to pull downe a brick house, that cost 1000^S the building, all for the sake of the irons therein and when they had done they sold all their labour to a Collen Stuller[173] for on[e] shilling, which makes 7 pence.[174] Soe little doe they value their labour when the designe is mischeife.

Upon the 9 September, we passed the Rhein at Wesell over a bridge of boats. Ever since we have marched up the river in the dirtiest ways and weather that our poore rogues were blest withall. Here the armies joyned—the Kings, the Princes,[175] Turens and Filiat['s] 3 brigades. The 12 of this month, we past a large village called Milen[176] on the River Roer[177] which falls into the Rhein a little belowe. Here we were comanded, on paine of death, not to plunder, but the country not performing with us their promises, the next day we were at liberty to all maner of mischeife but the inhabitants had got their best goods away. Now they talk of an Imperiall Army hard by us. If some 500 men either of these two last dayes might easily have ruined us, we were in such confusion.

Upon the 24 we marched through a towne they call Stifft-<*64*>Essen.[178] The inhabitants here have kept their houses by com-

173. A miner from Cologne (*OED*).
174. 20 Flemish shillings to a Flemish pound. 38 Flemish shillings to the pound sterling in the 1690s (D.W. Jones, *War and Economy in the Age of William and Marlborough* (Oxford, 1988), pp. 68–9, 76).
175. Condé.
176. Mülheim, on the River Ruhr.
177. River Ruhr.
178. Essen.

pounding and have a safeguard to protect them.[179] We marched up into the country 2 leagues higher and had quarters assigned us. Here we encountered hunger and thirst. We were faine to thrash up corne and make bread ourselves, beere we could get little, and wine we had at 50 sous the pott, which made many the more familiar with the draw well which afforded us water plentifully.

Sir Harry had laid downe this rule that those that depended upon him were to be as he, Roman Catholicks, i.e. particular, universally and obliged to beleeve impossibilities [and] all that Sir H. sayes, but they will find for any good he intends them they might as well have counterfeited vertue. Such a collection of rascalls he had who, in their winter quarters, were feircer than lions but when they came into the feild were tamer then muttons. Wher[e] as the few that either were borne or bred gentlemen and of honest and liberall education would bestire themselves, worke far harder, lye cold and all these as if they were going to a wedding, when the rest would starve rather than stoop to gather up their food and grumble that meat was not put into their mouthes. These were eaten up alive whilst the other made themselves merry at their toyles and sufferings. The village where we lay was called Killsenkirk[180] and [we] staid there till the last September when orders came, upon a suddane, to march which we did the same day and quartered in a village upon the Roer called Callwiget[181] where there remains the ruine of a stone bridge over the river to Lansburgh,[182] a faire <65> castle on the opposite side belonging to the Duke of Newburgh.[183]

On Sunday morne, being the 2nd October, we marched through our old quarter, Mulheim, where our Brigade passed the River of Roer in a maner by swiming. The rest of the army had a bridge of boates. The truth is, we had few amongst us soe honest to feare drowning. We landed in the Duke of Newburghs country just at the Castle of Brooke.[184] The owner is a gentleman of grave aspect and of good esteem in these parts. Our men were forbidden to plunder but if they had found any that was not too hott nor too heavy, they would have valued the proclamation no more than the Ten Comandements. We rode through woods and deep wayes to Dussedorpe [Dusseldorf]

179. *i.e.* Essen agreed to pay contributions to the French and was accordingly protected by a safeguard. See p. 326 n. 125.

180. Gelsenkirchen.

181. Kettwig.

182. Schloss Landsberg.

183. Philip William, Duke of Palatinate-Neuburg. The Duke had concluded a defensive alliance with the Elector of Brandenburg and the Bishop of Münster in 1671 but in June 1672 he was seriously considering tempting overtures from the French (F.L. Carsten, *Princes and Parliaments in Germany* (Oxford, 1959), pp. 312–19).

184. Schloss Broich.

upon the Rhein, whither I went on[e] day we see the towne but had much difficulty to enter for though the Duke be newter yet he was jealous of the French faith and stood upon his guard. This neat little towne is his ordinary residence. Here is his court, at present in a faire castle. He is a prince of a goodly presence and esteemed wise; he had need to be soe for he lives amongst neighbours to[o] potent for him.

From hence we removed suddainly upon Friday the 7th October and marching through woods and deep ways we came over against Collon.[185] Two nights [we] s[t]aid there and this day removed a league or 2 farther into the country which is a forest where we find nothing but empty houses. The poore people, here and everywhere, flying away with what they have out of our reach, but where <66> they meet with any of the soldiers, they pay them for the old and the new. As its reported, there are entrenched of them upon a little hill in the woods, 3 or 4000. Turen declares he came not here to make war with the Boores and 'tis certaine he countenances them in the defence of their owne without the limitts of our quarter and those that have attaqued them have returned with successe as bad as their designe.

Upon Thursday 14, Mr Biloye,[186] a brigadeer, set on a partie of his men, about 150 men, to plunder and to provoke them, but the Boores, headed by their landlords and masters, beat them off and killed many, notwithstanding there came some 17 English to their assistance of which one was shot through the neck. The French, here as elsewhere, after the first charge never thinke of any thing but flying. The English, in the mean time, must be twenty beaten before they be overcome. Here I canot but take notice that the French will never goe out upon a partie without some English, who are men of purpose for a dead lift [sic] and for whose valour they have more esteem than they have love for their persons. Besides, how it comes I know not, the Germans have much favour for the English. They will not meddle with us or our quarters. By their good wills and when any of us fall into their hands they treat them civily unlesse provoked by much insolence.

Upon the 14th I went to see Collon. I left my horses at a village called Duals,[187] inhabited by Jewes who have their synagoge and free exercise of their religion. I past the Rhein in a paire of oares and upon our coming ashore and admittance within the gate, were recomended unto an Englishman <67> but, upon acquaintance, we found him a Welch man who gave caution, as a generall rule, never in a strange place to trust your country men for they being a people whom ill qualities has driven a broad will be sure to cheat you, and lest this

185. Cologne or Köln.
186. Possibly Jacques Belot (DNF, ii. 886).
187. The suburb of Deutz.

rule should want example, he brought us to his son in laws house where we had ordinary entertainment and an extraodinary reckoning to justifie the old gentlemans observation. This old blade told me that formerly he had been a soldier in Holland. From thence he fled to the Imperiall Army, where he long continued a Corporall of horse untill he was settled in this City where he, for a long time, kept the best taverne in towne till the King of England comeing there[188] during whose residence he was undone by some very eminent persons of the Royall retinue who lived upon him. And, notwithstanding, after the King's restauration he applyed himselfe to them in England yet he could get nothing but assurances of and addition to his ruine by his long and chargeable waiting. This carriadge was the worse to be for that some of those persons were then, and have been since the most eminent blackcoats in this Kingdome.

Collon, or Collonia Agrippina, is a city very ancient, as the sirname imports. Tis large and stronge, finely seated upon the Rheine and makes a great shew of Beauty, but expectation spoils it for the inside is not answerable to the glories which you promised yourselfe at the entrance. However, it is well built. The houses high, the streets not broad, the publick buildings are large yet not very sumptuous. The Cathedrall must be considered not as it is <68> but as it was intended for it is not finished. Upon the top of the steeple hangs a notable crane for the drawing up of stone.[189] The comon people, which are taught here to beleeve anything, will not be perswaded but that it is a pendulous spire hanging here by miracle, I know not how long before the birth of our Saviour, never considering when churches became in fashion or that theirs was dedicated to St Peter or that their towne was of late a Roman Colony.

Here are to be seen the Tombs of the 3 wise men that came to visit our Saviour in the manger—Gasper, Melchor, and Balthasar. The monkes, and other kind people, have made them Kings and are called all over the world the three Kings of Collon.[190] Tis said they dyed in their way homeward, the Westerne Xtians [Christians] purchasing their Tombes of the Easterne, who have made good marchandise of such fictious relickts, and our Hooded marchants gaineing by the bargaine and receive meat, drinke, and clothes from them by retaileing them and their little miracles to the credulous multitude.

188. Charles II stayed in Cologne from October 1654 to the summer of 1656 (M. Ashley, *Charles II* (London, 1973), pp. 81–9).

189. Work on the cathedral church of St Peter and St Mary began in 1248 but came to a halt in 1560. Building did not recommence until 1842, finally to be completed in 1880. The crane, a familiar landmark in Cologne, was atop the stump of the south tower.

190. The Reliquary of the Three Kings, by Michael of Verdun, dates from 1181. It is currently positioned behind the high altar.

I am perswaded that the City is not very rich. Their trading canot chuse but be much decayed since the Rheine is not longer free but in French fetters. Many houses there are uninhabited which is noe good signe of welth. You may walke the streets at this instant without feare of being justled or thronged (they are very narrowe) as if the plague had been there lately.

The Bishope is one of the Electors,[191] but the Dutch, the Emperour, and the French have cast lotts upon his <69> Temporall Vesture and made him a spirituall Ashe of Verdun or as a little piggi in England,[192] and tis worth the observing that the popish princes can feed as heartily upon the bread of the Church as Lutherans and Hugonits.

The place of our aboad is the mighty forest of Bymarweld[193] where we forage and sustaine ourselves by fishing the numerous ponds where we find Carpe, Tench, and Crawfish. The water serves to dresse them and drive them downe. Here are abundance of red deere but we kill but five. Peares and Apples are in great plenty but we can get nothing from the Boores for love nor money but blowes and those, when they find a[d]vantage, they bestow upon us freely and deservedly enough.

October the 20, we made another visit to Collon and returned that night, haveing nothing to doe but progge[194] for forage and other necessaries, our men fighting with the Boores every day somewhere or other, getting sometimes the best, sometimes the worst. But, of late, we are to[o] hard for them, for the poore peasants loose their cattle and their lives too yet they sell both deare enough for they are a stout, or rather a stubborne people and were they nere equall to the French in number or discipline, they would make the monnsieur[s] swime the Rhein once more with a vengeance.

This forest is a goodly tract of Land and belongs cheifly to the Duke of Newburgh, yet there are many other Lords that have their castles and residence here. Here is <70> indeed too much wood, excellent oak and burch, yet in all their worst lands where the soile is not fitt for tillage they take as much care to plant young saplins as if they feared to want fuell after Doomes day, but their woods standes them in good steed to shelter them from the French incursions.

Here our men had surprised some cattle belonging to a Noble man

191. Maximilian Heinrich, Elector and Archbishop of Cologne.
192. Possibly a reference to the acquisition of Verdun by France from the Holy Roman Empire by clause lxxi of the Treaty of Westphalia in 1648, whereby the bishop of Verdun lost his temporal authority (*War, Diplomacy, and Imperialism, 1618–1763*), ed. Geoffrey Symcox (London, 1974), p. 50). It could also be a reference to Nicolas Arnu, a Dominican theologian of Verdun (*Bibliothèque Lorraine ou Histoire des Hommes Illustrés*, ed; R.P. Dom Calmet (Nancy, 1751), pp. 60–1). 'The little piggy' got none.'
193. Probably the Bergischewald.
194. To search for food or forage (*OED*).

nere our Quarters. The Baron complaining to me of it, I assisted him as much as I could in the recovery of them, soe brought him to my Colonel, Sir H.J. The Baron had noe sooner entered his quarter but he was entertained with the sight of his best beefe hanging up by the heeles. This gave him faire hopes that he could have faire redresse when he that should have done him right was the principle theefe. Soe away went the Baron to complaine to Tureen who, I judge, was not at leasure to listen to such small matters. But this is nothing to Sir H.J. who will steal and threaten to hang the poore soldiers for taking lawfull prize when he has taken them from them and sold them for his owne use fourscore at a time. Nay, he has sent out parties to take cattle for the use of the Regiment and, afterwards, he has sold them for his owne use. He hath learnt that much since he began to counterfeit a Roman Catholick, that as the pope is vertually the Church, soe he is vertually the Regiment. Never was match better made, a scabby flock and a mangy sheapheard.

Upon the 26 Oct., we marched all day and part of the night <*71*> to another quarter 9 leagues of[f] up the Rhein towards the 7 burgs,[195] which is a confluence of 7 hills formerly beautified with as many castles, but now fallen belowe their foundations.

We past the strong castle and towne of Seigburge [Siegburg], a garison of the Duke of Newburgs. The castle stands upon a little round hill overlooking the towne and a faire countrie betwixt it and the Rhein. 'Tis scituated upon the river Seige, which is its good mother and hath given it its name. We past the river by ford twice that day and came againe to a quarter in the woods amonge the Boores, who are so bold to keep their guards with [in] 2 musket shot of my house, but they are upon the defensive part onely and doe no harme here but to such as come to assault and robb them. Some of our men went troleing[196] within their liberty and they shot an Irishman through the head just as he was contending with one of his country men who should sweare best extempory and 'tis thought the man that died would have caried it but the unlucky Boore stopt his mouth with an oath in his throat which, had it come out, might, as tis thought, have rechased the bullet. Tis said by those that were present that the shot came three quarters of a mile. Tis not my office to judge any man but tis most certaine that those whom God hath determined for examples to others, he that drawes a bow at randome shall hit them. Our quarter was at an old castle calld Blankenberg, ** <*7b, 16*> our post being the left wing of the Army, extending itselfe in brea[d]th from the River. Our lot was to be thrust up amonge the hills and to be next to the Bores whose guards and barriers would be sometimes within

195. The Siebengebirge.
196. Fishing (*OED*).

30 paces of our quarters which, and hungry stomacks, run our men upon many losses.**[197]

On the first of November I went to see the towne of <72> Bonna [Bonn], antiently called Brennonia, built and named, as the Germans say, by our Brenus and his Gaules.[198] I am willing to beleeve anthing that contributes to the honor of our Country and if any infidell, out of ignorance or envy, misdoubts the story he is now true Welchman and consequently scant a gentleman. It had been called Bonnonia and by Ptolomy, Bonna, and famous for the residence of Helena, the mother of Constantine, the Great.[199] Her house is th[e]re yet to be seen with her chappell adjoyning to it, both of an antient shape. The chappell is stronge and low, of a figure comeing neer round. The house hath nothing to be proud of but of its first inhabitant and is now the habitation of one of the canons of this towne.

In this towne, the Prince Elector of Collon[200] keeps his Court and tis his ordinary residence, Collon itselfe being a more headstrong jade then to be preist ridden.

The Cathedrall here is not very great nor so sumptuous as we expected to have found it being the shop of soe mighty a prelate who does not only make God himselfe every day but here makes as many God makers as he pleases and sends them to worke journey worke [sic] over his whole diocesse. His palace is not finished, and when it is 'twill be a quadrangle spacious enough for his equipage, which comes short of some of our Nobility in England. I saw his stable, the flower of which were some horses <73> sent the Elector by his Majesty of Great Brittaine which, with much ostentation, are shewed to strangers, he being deservedly proud of the favour of soe mighty a prince.

The towne itselfe is newly fortified but 'tis not strong, yet 'tis very pleasant scituated on the French side of the Rheine. It hath a prospect that way larger then the sight of any Argos, though all his eyes would carry as far as a linx. And as it is on the French side, soe I doubt it and beleeve it will be in the French hands ere long. Returning homeward to our quarters from this towne we mett with an adventure which, looking somewhat like those we read in Romances, I will here relate.

About a league from the Towne, in a large plaine, I heard some

197. Turenne's camp occupied a line from the left bank of the Rhine near Königswinter, east through Oberpleis, and into the Siebengebirge around Blankenburg.

198. Brennus, a Gallic king, supposedly captured Rome in 390 B.C. The Roman name for Bonn was Castra Bonnensia (*OCD*, p. 179).

199. Helena, concubine of Constantinius I Chlorus, gave birth to Constantine the Great in A.D. 285. Helena was exiled to Bonn soon after her son's birth (*OCD*, pp. 281–2).

200. The Electors of Cologne had their residence in Bonn from 1238 to 1794. Cologne was an Imperial Free City and thus outside the Elector's direct jurisdiction (Carsten, *Princes and Parliaments in Germany*, pp. 258–60).

feminine shreaks and outcries and, turning my eyes that way, saw three persons in a confused grapple. With that I, who must for this time passe for the Knight Errant, put spurs on my horse and followed by my two Esquires, Dr Higgins and Lindsey,[201] we soon found a French foot man endeavouring to ravish a girle young enough to be a virgin. Notwithstanding the resistance of the sweet Nymph and an old woman, perhaps her mother, but to follow the mode of Romance we for the present will call her her Nurse and suppose the young Frowe [sic] to be some German princesse, though then in the shape and habit of on[e] that carried colly flowers.[202] This soldier had about 30 <74> of his companions about 2 musket shot from the place. These, upon our approach, shouted to him to retire which he did as fast as two legs could carry him. I caused the woman to gather up her garden stuffe and to high then homeward, which they did never staying to see the danger which their cause had cast upon their champion. When they are gone, we persued the ravisher into the midst of his comrades who, by this time, were all with drawne swords divided one against another, some to defend a villaine, others that misliked the device to revenge the insolency, the rogue that caused the brawle fighting very desperately as haveing more courage then honesty. I run headlong amonge the throng of drawne swords and musquetts and fortunately disarmed the cheife of the tumult and then easily qualif[i]ed the rest, they all very gladly submitting to my advance. Thus, with faire words and some blowes, I dispersed them to their sevrall quarters at last. This, without jesting, was an action of more danger then glory but a generous mind canot endure to see wronge although he were sure that the righting of it should want its reward.

But to returne to our story of the Campaigne. The Boores, seeing us soe patient, began to grow insolent. They would drawe up in bodies close to our quarters, beating their drums and faceing us <75> once or twice a day, their gentlemen and officers riding to and fro amonge them as if they were presently to give us battle and as if they could make their partie good against the French powers.

Upon Wednesday 2nd November, some English of Captain Laniers troope went a foraging, perhaps somewhat beyond their limitts. And while they were making their trusses in a barne, the Boores fell fi[e]rcely upon them, killed one man, hurt two and took away with them 6 horses. This affront awakened the English insomuch that Sir H.J. himselfe began to be concerned, not for the Men but for the horses, who were neerer a kind to him to[o] by the fathers side. He imediately made his adresse to a Baron of a Chatteau, whose influence

201. Untraced. Probably a soldier who acted as Herbert's servant.
202. Cauliflowers.

was thought to actuate these country people. He proposed the restauration of these horses as a medium of peace but receiveing an answer
not satisfactory, next morning a stronge party was drawne forth of
the regiment and put into the hands of 3 leiftenants.[203] Leift. Maine[204]
comanded a partie of men on horseback in shoes and stockings with
carbines and swords in the nature of Dragoons, because they were to
engage in woods. Leift. Gwin[205] had the Body, and Leift. Verman had
the reare. As for the Knight himselfe, he stood, as <76> wise men
should, at a distance soe great as to be out of danger and yet soe nere
that he might appropriate the successe, if prosperous to his owne
conduct. The issue was this. Some French, goeing that way a proleing,
were aware of the boores that, waiting our revenge, stood ready to
receive all assaults. These French no sooner saw them at their post
but away they run. This facilitated the victory, for the Boores, encouraged by their flight, left their strength to persue, whereupon Maine
made towards them with his party who received the first fire of the
Boores and then fell upon them a la mode de Anglois who comitted
their saf[e]ty to their swiftnes. But they were so hottly persued by the
English that many of them were slaine, some Irishmen killing them
in cold blood to revenge that of their countrie man Plunckett and to
keep up the costome of their native soile. One Englishman was shot
in the thigh and his wife thereby left to the mercy of the soldiers. They
killed of the Boores, 38 or 40 men, besides burnt all their houses in or
neer their quarter.

[The Shorter Version of the Narrative gives a slightly different
account of this episode.]

** <7b, 16> Haveing lost a man by the bores the night before with
their served guns picking of[f] a man here and there as they pleased
in the viniards—grapes being pleasant to the soldiers, they would
ventur though the contrary was comanded. These affronts we had
often, but next day our men goeing a forageing and car[e]les at their
worke without a centry, the bores came upon them unprovided, slew
some and hurt others and put the rest to the flight and took six of our
Horses. This stured up the roth in the soldiers and officers, especially
in the Colonel who imediately comanded 150 men should be ready
against next day for the battle, thus 100 on horseback and 50 in the
nature of Dragones. Then [he] went to the Comandant of the Country,
Mr Baron, complained of the bores and demanded restitution of the
horses againe, which was promised him and full satisfaction <7b, 16>
by 12 a clock next day. The Colonel was in honor to respect the effect

203. This force amounted to 100 cavalry and 50 dragoons (NLW, HM 2/14/7b.
p. 17).
204. Edmund Maine (Mayne).
205. Richard Gwynn.

of that time but forgetts this engagement in the morning and out rides Don Quixsot with 150 Sancho Panchos, the instruments of his ire, and instantly mett with a party of French foragers that had been repulsed the morning before by the foresaid enemy. He perswades them to face about with them and to looke big and countenance his revenge. Sheldon was clapt in the head of them for decorums sake. He divided his 100 horse into 2 bodies of 50 men. Verman comanded the first and Gwynn the second and Maine the 50 on foot which advanced formost and was upon the bores Barriers before they expected it. The Colonel favoured them with his presence who witnessed to me how much more surprised he was than any man by the distraction of his orders and his faceing about, comonly calld running away. These many successes emboldened the Bores to leave their post and fall on the persuite neer ten score, Now the horse put in, rec[eive]d ther first fire, and soe routed the Bores. Not one got home to their barnes and about 40 were killed of them and onely one of the ours shot in the legge. After this murtherous chase was over, comand was given to give fire to the village and, in a few minutes time, the insolent little village had itselfe in flames and after shrunk to cinders. After the execution over, the Baron returned the taken horses and before the time promised of 12 a clock. Every man exclamed against the cruelty and infiddelity of the Knight who had not patience to stay the time appointed for satisfaction from the Baron but what better could be expected from him who never profest to keep [a] promise in his life.**

But in all this brave action nothing is more remarkable as the admirable providence of Sir H.J. in keeping himself out of Harmes way. For first he considered a bullet was a kind of brute fulmen[206] and knew no difference betwixt the Knight and the Knave. 2ndly, to be killed by a Boor in Germany spoiles anybodies preferment in France <77> for tis observed by the policy of the French Militia [*sic*] whatsoever Collonell is slaine this yeare canot be a Brigadeer the next. 3rdly, he considered he was [still] to chuse his religion. Protestant he was never fixt; the Roman requires faith and workes too and those make him hesitate. Now suppose some more favourable Bullet had spared his beloved life and only lamed him, you know tis noe great satisfaction to halt between two opinions, besides, the most Christian King allowes noe pensions to maimed officers who are supposed to be all wise enough to shift for themselves. 4thly, a scarlett cloake had been to[o] great a Temptacion for a peasant to shot at and to leave it off had been to leave himselfe and the peasant without a distinction. 5thly and lastly, to say the truth, he wanted an head peice now. Though he be hard hearted and hard handed enough, yet his head is

206. Fulmine (*OED*).

as soft as another mans, but now I bear at Block I[']le tell you a story of it.

Tis noe great matter for the day nor yeare, but some time in the memory of man there was a great fight in France when there was no enemy in Europe. His most Christian Majesty, wisely forseeing that his great army would dye of naturall <78> deathes, most of the men growing old Emeriti by neither doeing nor seeing anything but the destruction of garlick and onions, resolved to divide his numerous host into two parts to counterfeit a great battle. There the comanders shewed their skill in choosing their ground, planting their Canon and marshalling the forces, insomuch that the action began to look very terrible to those that had never seen the like, and indeed those that were there, as the Gens de Armes &c., doe talk of it with soe much horror and amazement to this very day that he that has but halfe a Nose may guesse how sencible that they are yet of that days perill. To be short, in the cruell conflict of this mighty mockfight, our Heroe, who is most bold where there is least danger, adventuring to[o] nere a peice of ordinance, had his head shot off with a wadde of strawe that supplyed the place of a Bullet. The King of France, who is very respectfull to strangers and wondring that a brainlesse statue should charge so valiently, he presently sent for a French Chyrurgion, lineally descended by the mother from Talicosius,[207] who had almost lost his trade for want of practice. This skilfull man, with marvelous dexterity, seeing his head was irrecoverable, clapt a Holland Cheese in the place of it, which <79> he hollowed within and made him a Braine of rotten sheeps liver, wormes supplying the room of the old connundrums, that his owne mother, for as she was a dairy woman, would have eaten the one as well as the others. This, you'le say, is a very strange taile and if you call it a lye, or that which is equivalent, say it is impossible. I am too good natured to fall out with good fellows about such triffles but take this along with you for truth that I will stand to—that how impossible or improbable the foregoing story may seem to some of the Royall Scoiety, yet ther is not a man in all Sir H.J. his regiment but will beleeve all the particulars of it as soon as any thing that ever sir Knight said or shall say. Once againe, for it was a fashion in Olivers time, when Sir H. was first knighted, to hold forth one or two reasons more than lastly. The Knight was to[o] great a lover of his native countrie to expose his previous life to the blind mercies of fortune. For, saies he, suppose I should miscarry and ware should be made upon England, what would the King doe for a

<hr/>

207. Gaspare Tagliocozzi (1546–99), of Bologna, one of the earliest plastic-surgeons. He invented the technique of restoring the nose by transplanting tissue from another part of the body (O.H. & S.O. Wangensteen, *The Rise of Surgery* (Folkestone, 1978), p. 531).

Generall [and] a man that knowes how to cosen his soldiers and officers too? Some some [sic] be too younge, others too old. The Duke < 80 of Yorke canot be spared [and] Prince Rupert was never a Gens de Armes and therefore unexperienced. Therefore the King must send into Germany for Count Shonberge[208] or myselfe. If Don Quixot should advance his standard beyond Geography, who but we shall withstand him? Therefore, says he, once more it is written I will stand a farre off and wait the Fortune of my Nativity, yes indeed will I.[209] To conclude. As it is the Duty of Duning men and women to prophesie good things to those that apply themselves unto them, soe it is a duty encumbent upon those that are more concerned in those prophesies not to be wanting to themselves and their propocious stares [stars] in the fullfilling of those predictions. Now if Sanders or Sarah Gunner[210] have cast the Knights nativity water and foretold that he should be great with great men, why should Sir H. flatter and fawne upon all great men and kisse their arses if the fates decree him to be soe? What reason is there that a person of that extraordinary hopes should, like on[e] of the comon people, expose himselfe to more than ordinary hazards? For a lumpe of lead, though heavier, is much like the wind, for as the one bloweth, the other hisseth < 81 > where it hisseth and what have wise men to doe with chance? One thing more and I have done. If Sir H. had exposed his person to danger he might have obliged the regiment by his death and that would have been more then ever he intended in his life. I am now tirred with the barreness of the present subject and shall therefore resume my discourse.

The day of the destruction of the Boores, November 3rd, I was ordered to comand the guard upon Marshal Tureen at the head-quarters whither with 3 men out of every troope in our Brigade. Tureens quarters, which we alwaies call the Kings Quarters in the absence of the King, was upon the Rhein soe was our Guard noe shelter from wind or raine for as it was the Kings quarters soe the guard was in the Kings highway.[211] That which made it most agreeable was a long, cold, frosty winters night which lasted till 12 a clock next day. Then we marched up the Rhein to Lintz,[212] to Hamberstach,[213] an old ruined castle over a village which, with the advantage of its scituation, was able enough to defend that narrow passe against all the world. There we past through a whole country of rocks and

208. Frederick Hermann von Schomberg (1615–90), created Marshal of France in 1675 (DNB).
209. This is a reference to Jones's horoscope.
210. Richard Sanders was an astrologer based in London (Elias Ashmole, ed. C.H. Josten (Oxford, 1966), i. 207, n. 2).
211. Turenne's headquarters were at Erpel on the Rhine.
212. Linz-am-Rhein.
213. Schloss Hammerstein.

viniards up the River to Andernach. There we turned upon the left hand some 7 or 8 leagues < *82* > to seek our regiment who quartered then by a long remove above a castle and towne called Hackenbach and Frebuch,[214] both villages soe obscure that they have no name in the Mappe. Here we are still upon the 9th of November.

On the 17 of November, I went to see Cobletz [Coblenz] which [is] 10 or 12 leagues distant from our present quarters, for we lay at a village called Minnisbach[215] not far from Hakenbach. It proved a long days journey. Towards evening we arrived at [a] castle called Herminsteine,[216] the residence of the Elector of Trier. 'Tis a lovely seat and as stronge as nature or Art could make it. 'Tis scituate upon a high rock which comands the Rhein and the bridge of boates that crosses the river from it to Cobletz. We had some little difficulty to passe but it ended in 3 stivers[217] a horse. We had no sooner entred the towne but we found our expectations had (as they doe everything else) spoiled it. We lookt for beauties and extraordinary rarities, for the towne lookt from the high ground on the opposite side very large and faire but tis not halfe built and is rather a feild then a towne within a wall. Some streets are well enough. Tis scituated strongly upon the confluence of the Rhein and the Mozell and thence it had its name, Confluentia, Cobletz, Coflance and Conflance. Over the latter ther is a faire stone bridge. Who would thinke that this place stands well for trade < *83* > haveing the assistance of these two famous Navigable rivers, besides others that fall into them both above and belowe, but the towne canot be rich for its not full. It fares with Citys as with Bees, the more the richer. I am perswaded it would be a very hard thing to find any towne of very great trade in the Dominion of a petty prince, as they say of the Germans for the most part are, on[e] envying and interrupting the other. Besides, the courts of great princes adde infinitely to the glory and welth of citties, confluence of people contributing more to their greatnesse then the confluence of rivers. The Princes Courts are nothing splendid neither are the people so neat or industrious as the Hollanders who delight in cleanlinesse as much as they doe in homelines.

The Prince, or Bishop Elector, declares himselfe neuter and his country is wasted and foraged by both parties on both sides [of] the

214. Hochstenbach, on the River Wied, or, Hachenburg (Guillaume Del Lisle, *Le Cours du Rhin depuis Worms jusqua Bonne et les Pays adjacé* (Paris, 1704).

215. Possibly Mündersbach which was then spelt, Munersbach (*Ibid.*).

216. Now the fortress of Ehrenbreitstein, on the right bank of the Rhine opposite Coblenz.

217. 20 silver stijvers equalled one Amsterdam guilder in 1680 (J.D. Tracy, *A Financial Revolution in the Habsburg Netherlands* (Los Angeles, 1985), p. 198). The currency in circulation along the Rhine appears to have been the Dutch guilder rather than the Imperial thaler.

river up to the gates of Cobletz. Here were some of the Brandenburgers at the same time with us. A little before they had rob[b]ed 200 or 300 vivandeers of the French returning hom[e]ward for Loraine. If we had mett with them we had gone nere to doe as much for them but they had the good luck to pillage those that pillaged us who pillaged all the world.

The inns here are not as in England or France, for you shall have much adoe to gett your lodging and churlish answers if you aske for anthing they use not themselves <84> but you must be content with what they please to provide and at what rate they please, noe disputing with them, noe more then with us when we have them at our mercies.

Upon the 15, I returned to my quarters late. The horse that Higgins rid tired by the way and within a bowe shott of our quarters, dyed. When we came home we found our men ready to march, and did march all that night through the dismall woods we passed the day before, untill we came to Andernach where, about 2 of the clock in the afternoone, we passed the Rhein upon a bridge of boates ** <7b, 17> into the Country of Treave [Trier]. Some endeavours the enemy made of breaking downe the bridge by great timber[s] they sent downe the stream, but failed their purpose in.**

The 20 and 22 we continued our march up keeping the Mosell on our left hand. We [spent] 2 night[s] in a village called Chiuch,[218] where we surpise[d] the poore people and all their cattle and sheep. We marched after up the river and the 24 November quartered nere Witchley[219] and stay for our foragers which we out marched. The next day after we past the Rhein, Mr Gwin,[220] a Cardigan shire man, lieutenant to the lieutenant-colonel, was declared captain of that troope which was Wytherington['s]; Lieutenant Bray[221] also captain of Pendarris's[222] troope; and Lieutenant Maine[223] captain of the Major Russells[224] if he came not again for he misfortunately broak his legg at St Traday[225] and came no more to us till in winter quarters. These advanced are Portugall officers and very good men and tis certaine our knight would never [have] advanced them but to weaken the Portugall faction in the regiment.

Upon the 26 November, I went to see a house and little towne of

218. Cochem (HM 2/14/7b, p. 18).
219. Wittlich.
220. Richard Gwynn.
221. Arthur Bray.
222. Captain Pendarris had been drowned during the Rhine crossing at the Tolhuis.
223. Edmund Maine (Mayne).
224. Theodore Russell.
225. St Truiden.

the <*85*> Elector of Triers called Witchley, a league from our quarters, which was nere an old ruined castle named Loirburge.[226]

Here we are 27 November and here our men had some scuffles with the boores, who will not be perswaded but that some of the boores are shot free, but they shot some of ours and ours mangled some of them for all their enchantment. We removed somewhat farther into the country to a graveyard belonging to a monastry where we thrashed up the rye and made bread, every man as well as he could, for there was great scarcity of provision. Nothing but what we bought and that deare and nought to[o].

Upon the 3rd December, we marched some 2 leagues crosse the country to a great village, by name Hatham.[227] That night we found nothing but forage and bare walls, the boores haveing carried all things into the woods where they had encamped themselves in too [*sic*] places within halfe a league of the towne. That night there happened a fire in Captain Brayes quarter which burnt downe 3 or 4 houses and one man of his troope in one of them, his name Maxwell, one that had fled out of England for murther (he belonged to my troope and I chopt him for another man with Captain Villars.)[228] The Boores, seeing the fire, came in to quench it, betwixt whom and the industry of our men, the rest of the village was saved. This fire so warmed the spirit of our Colonel that, to the wonder of all men, he was heard to pray, which was much in fashion when Oliver first dubbed <*86*> him, but he had long omitted that the Kings of England and France preferring none for being that way gifted. The fire was, at last, with much labour extinguished and he that will not impute it to the devotion of the knight shall never be thought wise enough for imployment with him. ** <*7b, 18*> From this a league grew betweene us and them and gave them a safeguard but** next morning came a party of French to plunder the Boors 2 campes with whom some English joyned. The Boors made some resistance and killed 4 or 5 of [the] French and lost as many of their owne, but in the end were prevailed upon. The poor wretches left their campe and all they had to the management of the hungry soldiers who brought away much cattle of all sorts and knew not to what use to put them to, the English carrying the greatest part of the booty as being indeed become the greater theeves. In the mean time, the rest of our men, when they had notice, also rifled the campe and came home loaden with sheep, cattle, broad beefe and other provisions, soe that now the poore, starved, sick men began to take courage and comforted their bellies with the hopes of approaching feasts. All hands were busie and

226. Possibly Neuerburg. The castle in Wittlich is known as the Burg Ottenstein.
227. Hosten.
228. Edward Villiers.

the mutton was soon on the coales, some on the spitt, and some in the pott, before the sheep were halfe flayd. To conclud[e] this bloody work, all the regiment was nothing else but a pack of butchers and cooks shufled together. Dureing this plenty came orders to march and as I take it our people in it account themselves not much better than the damned. I dare imagine the Day of Judgement would not have been more terrible to them and the last Trumpett would not have troubled them more then that which <87> sounded Bootes and Saddles. Did you ever see people banished forever, taking leave of all their pleasure? How sad they are at parting, how willing they are to protract the time. Oh, the pitifull lookes of the last farewell, when, unreported, in comes the Kings pardon and finds them in the joyfull embraces of their loves and relations and leaves them to it. If you did or can but conceit [sic] it, you may take an important measure of the Death and ressurection of our hopes for, God be thanked, the order was countermanded and we continued our meale from time to time without intermission till our departure. And now we begin to grow dainty agen—we can scarce eat for want of poynant [sic] sauce. And he that yesterday would have eaten hoafes and hornes now, forsooth, canot endure the smell of Tupp mutton, soe quickly is famine forgotten and as soone doth want blot out the memory of abundance. In the midst of this plenty, luxury began to enter and took place as a bold guest. We were right Englishmen and could not be quiet when things were well. The inhabitants of this village were not greatly sharers in this losse. They had fortified themselves and their neighbours in a wood nere our quarters and our Collonel, Sir H.J., like a very good man, had received their presents and undertook their protection and in order thereunto sent a French volunteer, which he had about him as a Favourite and afterwards made an Aid Major off when I kickt him for some omissions un to me in the cantoning of the <88> quarters. Of him, he made the Boors a guardian angell but gave no orders to the soldiers to forbeare disturbing them. Provision, we had more then enough, yet upon the 9th of December, our people, to keep their hands in use, for good qualities for want of practise are easily forgotten, must needs make a partie to goe rob the poore Boors whom it had been our part to defend. The successe was very su[i]table to the undertaking for these blades, according to their fashion, fell head-long upon the boores, beat them from their workes and then, as if they had nothing to doe, fell a rifling the Barracks, spending all their shot upon the hens and pigs and drinking the wine. Thus the Boors had leasure to rally themselves in the woods and fell furiously upon these secure people. Two of the stoutest fellows of the Regiment, Frizars and Adice, they killed with their fusees. The rest run away with the plunder and shame they had gotten. This was called by the

Boores very false dealing and, to speake Truth, it was soe grosse a
Treachery that Sir H. himselfe seemed to be ashamed of it, but if the
successe had been better he would have thought himselfe very glorious
and have sacrificed to his own wisdom that could soe readily contrive
wayes to deceive those that trusted in him.

Two dayes later I was ordered to comand the maine guard at the
generall quarters, which the French call quartier devoy. It was not
my turne at that time, but the Collonel and Tripp,[229] who was since
killed by the Boores. This gentleman, who serves as aid Major now,
his councell over ruled the Knight as the Knight doth the Regiment,
he being the <89> fittest to regle those of his owne alloy. This duality
in unity would not be satisfied with my reasons, it being the nature
of mean men in office to opposse, if they can, their betters, forced me
to say and sweare I would doe that duty but would doe no other for
the future in that Regiment. This I spoke to the Knights face and the
Knighthood, who knowes me to be bound to my word, I beleeve was
glad of it for if I am able to guesse, Sir H. did not much care to have
a severe Honesty and Honor survey his actions. He could not brook,
perhaps, to be tryed by those rules and therefore was as willing to be
rid of me as a young female siner of her Ghostly father, yet he knew
not well how to part with me lest I should tell truthes in England as
well as in those forraine parts. He therefore setts his witts on worke
and endeavours, by suborning others, to represent unto me the ill
consequences of any desertion from him. But this artifice not taking
effect, he took a more advised way and with fairnes and promises
endeavoured to oblige me, this being by much the most forcible
battery upon a generous spirit, but [I] still persisted in my resolutions
knowing well that the favours of an enemy and the Divells promise
[(]i.e. all these things will I give thee if thou wilt fall downe and
worship me) have the same end and the same charme serves for both,
i.e. avoid Satan.

A regiment is a kind of University. He that lives and means to
continue there must entertaine honorable thoughts as his degrees.
<90> Upon the 14 December, in kindnes to Captain Littleton,[230] a
most worthy officer in our regiment and here sick, I conveyed him to
Treave,[231] accompanied with my Dr.[232] and Lindsey, who both [at]
the same moment fell sick in this towne of the generall and raging
distemper then in the army which had swep[t] away many lives and
di[s]abled far more bodies. In order to their recovery I left them here
and returned to my quarters, which was 10 leagues of[f], with onely

229. George Tripp.
230. Ferdinand Littleton.
231. Trier.
232. Dr John Higgins.

on[e] soldier with me. Yet during my stay in towne, close to the gates of Treave, past by night the Prince of Condee with 7,000 men to recruit Tureen at Witchley,[233] much diminished both in number and force by this sickness and dissertion. This night the Burgers sleep not easily being jealous of a French trick. It wore away with the days approach and now slumber in security.

At my returne to Holhem[234] the quarters of our regiment, orders overtook me on the rode that the English in particular were to march for Metz, there to refresh us for a while after our long campaigne, our regiment being upon its last leggs and nere spent with sicknes and fatigue. Providence, or a careful generall, now fed us with the crumb[b]es of comfort and hopes of rest and health, and on 19, comanded by Monsr Bussie,[235] governor of Nancy, we mounted and march'd to a quarter alotted us with in a halfe league of France. I tooke the oppertunity kindly and in I gott to my sick folkes I left here a few days before where I found Dr Higgins very much indisposed and understanding of our march for Loraine, it made him more willing then I thought able to under goe <91> a journey of that length and trouble, yet I let his inclinations lead him and suffered him, upon much intreaty, to accompany me and so we journeyed together till we overtooke the regiment, advanced then on their way for Metz. But as for Lindsey, I left him for dead, his confessor preparing him also for another journey. Thus both were on the road at [the] same time and Lindsey, in all probability, more likely to be soonest at his journeys end then the Doctor.

20 at Gash.[236]

21 at Tongville.[237]

22nd. we reached Metz, where the Dr['s] sicknes so increased [that] I was faine to leave him and a servant to attend him with able physitians to advise, as any were, while I, with the regiment, continued the march for Nancy. I arrived Christmas Eve, new stile. My Dr lived 7 or 8 dayes then dyed, the servant tells me, a most firme and resolute Protestant according to the Church of England, enduring the curse and sensure of many of the Roman Priests for his obstinacy in religion. He was after buried very decently by a protestant preist and a large attendance of protestants alonge with him to the grave. This particular and his Christian constancy in religion, the Minister certified unto me under his hand and some of his parishoners. There [is] a protestant

233. Wittlich.

234. Hosten.

235. Claude de Thiard de Bissy (d.1701), Governor of Nancy and Commander-in-Chief of Lorraine and the Three Bishoprics of Metz, Toul and Verdun (*Mémoires du Duc de Saint-Simon* (Paris, 1884), iii, 198–9).

236. Canach.

237. Thionville.

church alowed at Metz. At this towne we had a sejourne but our money making officer sold our quiet, our hea[l]th and good will here, for which, I beleeve, he[']le never repurchase for the price he parted with it. We were hardly able to crawle and yet we were forced to march; comanders must have their peniworths <*92*> what ever it inconveniences the soldiers. Never undertaker got more then this Farmer of a Regiment did and justified it as a la mode de France. 'Tis a golden rule and imprinted in his heart, which is hard and for it the fitter touchstone for his plotts and contrivances. He first tryes all his thoughts there and if they prove of the right mettle (let what will come, though the law claimes his horse or the pillory his eares,) he will venture to stampe them into profitt, a coine that may cost him deare ere he dyes if justice be not stark blind and the edge of her sword rebuted against the greatest impieties and wickednes.

Here at Nancy we diverted our selves all we could after our many sufferances in the feild and thought thereby to make our luxuries [luxurious] amends for the long hardships in the Campaine. Our time was pleasant but sometimes ridiculous, and though poor in cash I think we lived the higher for it, and perhaps the rather because in this towne my Lord Roscomans Regiment of Irish foot,[238] which was broaken here, lived at as high a rate and got renowne and good characters amonge them. I beleeve this might be the spur to our follies which made us gallop soe fast after them in the expensive road. It seemes his Lordship had been a little to[o] familiar with the Intendants lady here, by Mr Choisey,[239] which was, as the towne said, the cause of his breaking, but let that passe.

<*93*> All our knots of officers associated very lovingly together and was a caball of eating and drinking as well as of finding fault with our Colonel. We had continuall musick and dancing, diner and supper, and treates were our sports and pastimes. Nor is it unaturall or unpracticall thus outwardly to expresse an inward safisfaction, our present ease and the memory of past hardships and dangers oftimes creates such joyes and such joyes transports men into inumurable irregularities. When Izreall came out of Bondage, their felicities made them erre. That we[']re the Lords o[w]n chosen, I can hardly presume of much of our Tribe. But that which troubled my mirth was, we toasted and did riot while our poore soldiers starved and complaned heavily, the towne being worse for them then the feild being confined

238. Wentworth Dillon, 4th Earl of Roscommon's regiment of Irish foot had been raised in 1671 for the French service. It had been disbanded in Nancy in 1672 and its remaining soldiers had been drafted into Sir George Hamilton's regiment (Childs, *Army of Charles II*, p. 250).

239. Jean-Paul de Choisy, Provincial Intendant of the Three Bishoprics of Metz, Toul and Verdun (D.C. Baxter, *Servants of the Sword: French Intendants of the Army, 1630–70* (Urbana, 1976), p. 177).

to live on their pay which was but 4 pence a day, a narrow livelihood for citizens, as our soldiers were made, since forbid to plunder or steal at the perill of their life. The charge of sho[e]ing himselfe and horse, the repairing his armes, cloathes and sadles, besides filling a hungry stomack twice a day after the toilsome chase after the champaigne lice which stil foraged upon the poor soldiers corps, all this considered out of 4 pence a day looks as severe and as impossible to bee performed as the making brick without strawe, or any other task of that nature. The poore men from the <94> depth of misery, lift up their eyes and complaints and thereby gott some of their officers to stand by and interpose themselves betwixt the Colonels injustice and them otherwise, soe that myselfe and on[e] Captain Lanier, in a rugh [rough] but not disorderly way, demanded a sight of his Capitulations. Which, being denied, we pressed his forfeited promise and faire words which seduced the people hither to bring shame into his face as wheedleing good, honest fellows from good liveings in England, to follow [h]is humour abroad and starve them afterwards here without the least compassion, while he himself grew rich by parsimony and oppression. I could instance much of their pay in his hands, the which he put to the abominable use and extortion of ten in the hundred.[240] Noe, but the Divell would, at this instant, Flee a Flint,[241] when the next angry bullet might have made any man his executer.

The soldiers, now in a kind of mutany, called for Accouns and their arrears and threatened to informe the Intendant of Nancy of his unjust procedure towards them as well in the money which accrued to them by their last winter quarter, and that detained from them for bread in the last campaine. This, with the extremities they now suffered by sicknes and wants and especially in a countrie from whence charity, frightened with the noise of drume and trumpet, had long since took her flight for some more peacefull and plentifull clime. These threats alarmed <95> our Colonel, whose surprise gave us oppertunity to complaine of him in the behalfe of the soldiers to himselfe, and having laid his omissions fairely and impartially before him, it, and the dreaded consequence which might insue (had the Intendant knowledge of all) made the crocadile teares drop before us and promises of amends for the future if we appeased the roaring rabble. We took his word, interchanged promises of great freindship, and then industriously we went about to allay the storme which soe much threatened him from the comon soldiers. Every man went to his charge and preached patience and fare promises of amendment which did the busines for that time. These clouds were no sooner dissipated, but

240. *i.e.* Jones deducted ten per cent of his men's pay and retained it for his own use.

241. Perhaps Jones came from Flintshire.

every moment his ill nature grew more and more visible and especially to those that had a greater influence on the regiment then himselfe, amonge which number, not as ther was much truth in it, but yet his suspicions singled mee and alone, in a long entry, tells me a story. That men of honor should dispute their unkindnes at sword point and not at unkind cariages and repartees, wherefore [he] desired to decide that controversie between us the more noble way. To which I made a short reply. That I knew the danger and severity <*96*> of the French discipline but, notwithstanding, he should not faile of his purpose what ere hazard I run, and therefore told him I was at that instant or at any other time ready to entertaine him with a sword. At this he starts and shit turds extreamly and after some recollection of himselfe, yet in a confused voice and language, he tells me that it was not decent or anithing for the reputation of us officers, as we were English and in a foraine warre, thus to engage in quarrell and, besides, that he conceived matters were not soe irreconsilable on either side. He hop't [hoped] but that we might be freinds againe, adding he should be well contented to beleeve I was not his utter enemy. To which I answered that what I had said he had provoked me to. Besides, if I thought he spoke really his desires, that malice had never yet corrupted my Nature soe far, but I remained master of my civilities and that I could as freely pay him that as formerly till his reformation had created better termes of amity between us. At the end of this, he catches my hand and said, then pray let us be good freinds and cants on that he was extreamly glad that God had put it in our harts to be reconciled and desired that I would not scan all his actions for to[o] many of <*97*> them were governed by passion. To which I accorded and the league lasted all the time I was at Nancy, and made my advantage of it by working Dunbar, that was my Cornett, up to be my Leiftenant, a thing I had long purposed but could not effect till now.

This reconcilement on his part I have reason by the sequell to imagine was onely a pretence, aimeing by my freindship to guild over his character in England, as beleeving I should have spoken great things in comendation, haveing designed my returne home as soone as ever I came to winter quarters, which resolved I performed. His former behaviour had little deserved this kindnes nor could really have laid claime to any true praise besides he had, since our late contract, given me matter enough for comendation and, which was worse, I began to feare his relapps which realy did silence me till I had better proof of him.

Here at Nancy, my servant, Ashley, fell sick of the Army disease,[242]

---

242. Typhoid or Typhus.

soe that I was faine to leave him here with a servant to look after him while I marched away the 19 January, through Pont Mason[243] and reached the provostry of Longwy and Obange,[244] the village alloted them for winter quarters, the 22 <*98*> of January. This Obange is an ugly, durty hole and the most frontier towne of Loraine towards Luxemburge and is within 2 leagues of it and a halfe. I had not staid many dayes in settling my busines as to my company and disposing of my own particular affaire, in case I should not returne, and haveing given a good gelding to my new Leiftenant with 50 pistolls to engage his honesty in the performance of my orders, thenceforth I put my intended journey for England in execution. But first I waited upon my Colonel for my longee [*sic*] which at last, with some difficulty, I prevailed in, yet with it received a severer lecture then I expected from him for kicking his aid major, a fellow boulstered up as his favuret to affront the officers. It was my good luck to pay him in his coine. I tooke the rebuke patiently and, the next day, our Colonel returned me my visit at my quarters at Obange, where I softened his humour with some bottles of muscat wine. He was as pliant to my demands as any weather cock to the insinuations of the wind and afterwards proved as constant to[o] in them. Never was there such a Hocus pocus of complements as he, such a sick pudding of course behaviour as he <*99*> when his interests starts up upon the stage.

After farwell to my knight, who busied me much to entertaine him, my thoughts turned round to their proper point, the fitting me for next dayes journey and after a particular charge to each of my servants, I gave them a pistoll a peice to encourage their care of mine Equipage and the 27 of January parted from Obange betimes in the morne and reached Verdun on my owne horses, Leiftenant Kirck[245] and Barnsley[246] in company with me. Next day, took post, all of us, for Paris and lay there the 30 January at Mrs. Paris, a la croix blanch, dans a rue de Maree Fouburgh St. Germane. Nothing remarkable on the road onely we devided our full in riding post very equally amongst us, being two a piece round.[247] Each man had his OuCue [*sic*]. Barnsley lookt after the post horses, the sadling and diveding the first equally amongst us by turne. Kirke, he was to scold at the rates and bring them downe by arguments and faire means, and my part was [if] words would not take to beat them, which fell often to my turne, and did soe, and I only cropt the 2 horses that threw me and 'twas

243. Pont-à-Mousson.
244. Aubange, now in Belgium.
245. Charles Kirke.
246. Peter Barnsley.
247. This implies that travellers riding post in France were entrusted with the carriage of the mails.

all the mischeife I did this journey. These companions wanted < *100* > it seems, wanted [*sic*] moneys to beare themselves of[f], and rather then leave them in the lurch I bore the charge of their journey to Paris in hopes to meet Bills of Exchange which failed them. After a weeks stay there, haveing seen the vanities of the towne and the procession of St. Michell performed at St. Germains by the French King and Queen and all the Court (by the way, it proved not halfe as glorious and splendid as our St. Georges Day) I took leave of the Duke of Monmouth, my Lord Sunderland, then Embassador, and that night went onward on my way for Calais as far as St. Denis, my kindnes still continuing my charge to my companions on the road.

The 5 February, I parted from St. Denis and was at Calais the 7th. Went abord the Packet boat that day in the afternoone, where I had like to receive prejudice by some stones cast abord us from the key by some French men as they pretended injured by one of Lord Duglasse Captains then abord with us. The stones flew so thick and waity that it grew dangerous. We were faine to call for our pistolls and let fire at them on the shore but did noe mischife, by good luck. This war lasted for all the while we were ha[u]lling out and clearing ourselves of the key.

Upon the 8th we mett the *Julian* out of Dover, being < *101* > now the 29 January Old Stile, and the 30 was at London, in good time against the sitting of parliament which was to be the 4th of February.[248] In our postage from Dover, this Duglas's Captain had another encounter on the road. He and the post boy, riding formost, overtook two gentlemen, well horsed and armed with a servant in livery that was so s[t]ubborne not to give way to his post horse. The captain struck him with his whip. The servant, with a thumping crabtee cudgell, returned him his salutation full upon the pate and down fell our Captain. By this time, I came up and before [he] had got up into his sadle, the gentlemen ride away and [the] servant also. Seeing disorder in his countenance and not knowing what had happened, I asked him the reason for it. He gave me an imperfect account but onely told me he was injured on the road by those men that hast away so fast before. I dared him to gett up and away I rid with him as fast as ever our horses could carry us till we overtook them. I then asket [*sic*] them the meaning of that insolence to offer a gentleman and not give way to the post against the knowne rules of the road? He told me that what was done < *102* > was contrary to his directions and was very sorry for it. I told him that was not satisfaction for blows, to which he said, we'le beat the servant or if that will not doe we['] le give you satisfaction ourselves with our swords. This was very faire and a little

248. Herbert was M.P for Montgomery Boroughs from 1665 to 1678 (*HP*, ii, 531).

surprising from country gentlemen and [I] comended the freenes of their offer but laid hold onely of their first proposition of beating the servant which was done and away we ride and came to Suothwick[249] about 8 at night and was in London halfe an houre after. I had now, according to my desire, just time enough to rest and recover [from] my long journey before the sitting of parliament which began the 4th of February 1672,[250] according to the proclamation. In the time of our sitting, many notable matters did arise in parliament concerning the publick, some great ministers of state arrained, but bribes had taken the edge of envious proceedings away. The papists, who thought themselves secure and above the reach of parliaments, now fell as low as ever they were. There were many more remarkable things which I will not here undertake to enumerate but let them passe to fill the time of a more exact observator then <103> I pretend to, onely we['']le remember this. The parliament subplied [sic] the King very largely for this yeare with an 18 months taxe at 70000 p mensem[251] for the carrying on of this present warre against the Dutch.

Something before the adjourning of the parliament, which was to the 20 October 1673,[252] came our Collonel Sir H.J. to towne and haveing designed myselfe for sea this yeare to save charges, being the last yeare at a greater losse and expence then I could maintaine a second yeare, I deliver'd (by the leave of the Duke of Yorke) my troop in France up againe to him, which had been mighty expensive attending that comand last yeare through France, the greatest part, and Holland and Germany, and now I quitted upon my determination for sea, an employ my curiosity very much invited me to and which I had long since purposed in myselfe but could not bring about till now. But about two nights before the knight came and that I delivered up my troope, I was unwillingly engaged a second in a duall to be between Mr. Felton[253] and Mr. Godfrey.[254] To the first, Captain <104> Withes[255] was second, to the last myselfe was frend. The quarell sprunge from the sex from whence most quarells doe arise but, by great providence, were prevented before fighting being strongly mett upon the Thames by a boatfull of soldiers employed to find us out – such a chance an age may not produce. The officer brought us all before my Lord Harry Howard, High Marshall of

249. Southwark.
250. 1673, if the new year is taken to begin on 1 January and not on 25 March.
251. Passed the Commons on 26 March (*Commons Journals*, ix. 278).
252. The parliamentary session was adjourned on 26 March (*Lords Journals*, xii, 585).
253. Possibly a son of Sir Henry Felton, 2nd Bart., of Playford, near Ipswich, Suffolk (*HP*, ii. 306).
254. Charles Godfrey.
255. Captain Robert With (*CSPD 1673*, p. 529).

England,[256] where the principals, after their story told by us seconds, were made freinds and civilly, without further charge, dismissed. I was in this, as in others of the same nature formerly, drawne in much against my inclinations and many resolves, but when Honor calles all other reasonings within me must be mute. I will admitt noe pleading against this vertue whom I allowe ascendancy and comand over all my other faculties.

Prince Rupert had the Cheife Comand at sea in our Navyes expedition this yeare against the Hollander, the French being to joyne < *105* > with maratime force.

About the 2nd Aprill, the Prince disposed our companions for sea and alloted them their severall stations abord the fleet.[257]

256. Henry, Baron Howard of Castle Rising, succeeded as 6th Duke of Norfolk in 1677 (*DNB*).

257. Herbert resumed his captaincy in the Lord High Admiral's Maritime Regiment of Foot and his company served as marines on board H.M.S. *St George* between 16 April and 20 September 1673 (NLW, HM 2/14/9).

A CHRONOLOGY OF HERBERT'S TRAVELS, 1671–3

1671

July	Jones recruited his Light Horse
11/21 Nov.	Herbert left Lymore Park
16/26 Nov.	Dined at Ashridge
17/27 Nov.	Arrived in London
21 Nov./1 Dec.	Left London for Rye
24 Nov./4 Dec.	Arrived in Rye
3/13 Dec.	Sailed from Rye for Dieppe
5/15 Dec.	Arrived in Dieppe
8/18 Dec.	Left Dieppe for Bacqueville-en-Caux
10/20 Dec.	At St Victor l'Abbaye
11/21 Dec.	At Cailly
12/22 Dec.	At Lyons-la-Fôret
13/23 Dec.	At Chaumont-en-Vexin
14/24 Dec.	At Pontoise
15/25 Dec.	Travelled to Paris
19/29 Dec.	Left Paris for Château-Thierry
20/30 Dec.	*To Châlon-sur-Marne*

1671–1672

22 Dec./1 Jan.	To Courtisols
23 Dec./2 Jan.	To St Menehould
24 Dec./3 Jan.	To Verdun
26 Dec./5 Jan.	To Marchéville-en-Woëvre
27 Dec./6 Jan.	To the Fôret de Gorze

1672

1/11 Jan.	To Novéant-sur-Moselle
7/17 Jan.	Visited Nancy
10/20 Jan.	Left Novéant-sur-Moselle
11/21 Jan.	To Pont-à-Mousson
12/22 Jan.	To Vaucouleurs
13/23 Jan.	To Pagny-la-Blanche-Côte
4/14 Feb.	Still in billets in Pagny
12/22 Apr.	Herbert received his commission
18/28 Apr.	To Vaucouleurs
19/29 Apr.	To Bar-le-Duc
20/30 Apr.	To Clermont-en-Argonne
23 Apr./3 May	Camped at Carignan
29 Apr./9 May	Marched from Carignan

3/13 May	Camped near Liège
22 May/1 June	Opening of siege of Wesel
26 May/5 June	Wesel surrendered
2/12 June	Rhine crossing at the Tolhuis
10/20 June	Fort Schenckenschans surrendered
11/21 June	Marched to Nijmegen
13/23 June	Capture of Tiel
14/24 June	Returned to Nijmegen
19/29 June	Opening of the siege of Nijmegen
29 June/9 July	Nijmegen surrendered
30 June/10 July	Encamped at Grave
9/19 July	Fort Crevecoeur surrendered
10/20 July	Louis XIV reviews the army
12/22 July	To Bomell
13/23 July	To Bois-le-Duc
15/25 July	Left Bois-le-Duc escorting Louis XIV
16/26 July	To Boxtel in Brabant
17/27 July	To Postel
18/28 July	Encamped near St Truiden
20/30 July	Encamped near Tongeren
23 July/2 Aug.	Opening of blockade of Maastricht
30 July/9 Aug.	Forage during blockade
5/15 Aug.	Sally by Maastricht garrison
12/22 Aug.	Visited Liège
14/24 Aug.	Dined with English Jesuits in Liège
21/31 Aug.	Blockade of Maastricht lifted and marched to Maaseik
23 Aug./2 Sept.	To Grave
26 Aug./5 Sept.	Crossed the Meuse
27 Aug./6 Sept.	Passed Gennep
30 Aug./9 Sept.	Crossed the Rhine at Wesel
2/12 Sept.	To Mülheim on River Ruhr
14/24 Sept.	Camped near Essen
20/30 Sept.	Marched from Gelsenkirchen to Kettwig
22 Sept./2 Oct.	To Mülheim
27 Sept./7 Oct.	To Cologne
29 Sept./9 Oct.	Camped near Cologne
4/14 Oct.	Herbert visited Cologne
10/20 Oct.	Second visit to Cologne
16/26 Oct.	To the Siebengebirge
18/28 Oct.	To Siegburg
22 Oct./1 Nov.	Visited Bonn
23 Oct./2 Nov.	Attack by Boers

24 Oct./3 Nov.	Attack by Jones's regiment on the Boer camp. Herbert commands guard at Turenne's H.Q.
25 Oct./4 Nov.	To Linz-am-Rhein
26 Oct./5 Nov.	To Schloss Hammerstein
27 Oct./6 Nov.	To Hostenbach & Minnisbach
30 Oct./9 Nov.	Still at Minnisbach
7/17 Nov.	Visited Coblenz
9/19 Nov.	Marched to Andernach & crossed the Rhine
12/22 Nov.	Marched down the Moselle to Cochem
14/24 Nov.	Encamped near Wittlich
16/26 Nov.	Visited Wittlich
17/27 Nov.	'Scuffles' with the Boers
23 Nov./3 Dec.	To Hosten
29 Nov./9 Dec.	Major attack on Boer camp
1/11 Dec.	Herbert commands the guard at Turenne's H.Q.
4/14 Dec.	Visited Trier
7/17 Dec.	Left Hosten and marched towards France
10/20 Dec.	At Canach
11/21 Dec.	At Thionville
12/22 Dec.	Reached Metz
14/24 Dec.	At Nancy

1673

9/19 Jan.	Left Nancy for Pont-à-Mousson
12/22 Jan.	Winter quarters in Aubange
17/27 Jan.	Left Aubange for Verdun
18/28 Jan.	Left Verdun for Paris
20/30 Jan.	Arrived in Paris
25 Jan./4 Feb.	Left Paris for St Denis
26 Jan./5 Feb.	Left St Denis
28 Jan./7 Feb.	Arrived in Calais
29 Jan./8 Feb.	Left Calais
30 Jan./9 Feb.	Arrived in London
4/14 Feb.	Sitting of Parliament

1672[1]

ANE ACCOUNT OF OUR REGEMENTS MARCHES FROM THE WINTER QUARTERS TO THER ENTRANCE IN FRANCE

< *1* > On the ii of May, the Regement begun there march[2] and marched to Marvill,[3] 5 leagues; the 12 to Steny,[4] 3 league; the 13 to Mosson;[5] the 14 to Maissier, close to Charlevill,[6] the finest and the pleasentest place that ever I saw in my life. The fort is cal[l]ed Mount Ollimpa. Ther is a fine grove—the wood is caled harbor in French. At Cherminy[7] ther is ane Irish Convent which is famous for a library.

From Mazier to Rocroy, 4 leagues, a stronge town. From thence to Phillipvill, 6 leagues, a brave town. From thence we passed near Charleroy and lay that night at Fontain la Vesqu,[8] on[e] league beyond it. From Fontain la Vesqu we marched to Bonisu,[9] in which march we passed Mons, the principall town in [the] Pais de Hainoult, and sejour[e]d ther. From thence we marched to Haut,[10] 7 leagues; from Haut to Oudnar,[11] 7 leagues; from Oudnar to Denis,[12] 3 leagues, wher we arrived the 25 May and encamped that night. From thence we marched with the artillary to a camp near Gante.[13] The 26 we passed over a Cut River[14] near Gante, where Monsier[15] veiwed all that passed, and ther incamped the Kings army.

The 28 our regiment was detached with a squadron of the Regiment d'overn[16] to escorte the artillery to Mastrick, and a Regiment of

1. 1673, if the new year is taken to begin on 1 January rather than on 25 March.
2. The regiment had been wintering in Aubange, near Longwy in Lorraine.
3. Marville.
4. Stenay.
5. Mouzon.
6. Charleville-Mézières.
7. The Cistercian House at Cheminon (A. Schmitt, *Le Barrois Mouvant, 1624–1698* (Bar-le-Duc, 1929), p. 295).
8. Fontaine l'Évêque, four miles west of Charleroi.
9. Probably Boussu, to the west of Mons.
10. Ath.
11. Oudenarde.
12. Deynse.
13. Ghent (Gent or Gand).
14. The Bruges-Ghent Canal (Rousset, *Louvois*, i. 457).
15. 'Monsieur' was the title of Philippe de Bourbon, Duc d'Orléans, (1640–1701), the younger brother of Louis XIV.
16. D'Auvergne.

Fuzilliers.[17] We camped that night near Oudnar. The 29 we marched to Gramon[18] and camped near it, and the 30 of May we incamped near Nenino[19] and had a sejour of 2 days. The second of June, we marched to Noter Dame de Hall[20] <2> wher ther is a fine church famous for miracalls. At that place, the baggadge of the wholl army joyned us wher we had on[e] sejour. The 4th of June wee marched towards Brussells. The 5 wee camped near a litle town called Terlemon[21] wher thos[e] English officers that was so curious to goe see it was well exepted [accepted] by a Spanish major of horse that governed the place and well treated and would suffer no Frenchman to look in. I remember it the better becaus I was ther. The sixt[h] we passed a bridg called Weavre;[22] on[e] sejour. The 9th we joyned the Kings army and pased it [at] a Castell caled Linsmo[23] and camped that night near Sentron,[24] which day, [in] a squadron of our Regiment, the horses break all away to the great damage of the Captains.

On the 11 we marched to Tonger[25] and incampd by the towne side. The 12 of Jun[e], we marched to Mastrick and joyned our brigad and incam[p]ed near the towne in order to a seige wher I was detached to Weezill[26] to bringe more Cannon. On the 24 of June, our Collonell[27] was killed and, the sam[e] night, his grace of Montmoth atackt a demy lune and tooke it.[28] On the 27, the Cont du Lorge[29] atackt the horn work and tooke it. On the 28, Monsier Montall[30] raised a batery of 10 guns very near the wall and, that sam[e] night, made his aproches up to the foss and ther made ther lodgment[31] and the next day the town was surendered. The second of Jully, the wholl army

17. Fusiliers, infantry equipped with bayonets and flintlock muskets rather than matchlocks, guarded the artillery train as they carried no lighted matches to cause a risk of fire or explosion. The French established two regiments of fusiliers in 1672 (Rousset, *Louvois*, i. 238–9).
18. Grammont (Geraardsbergen).
19. Ninove.
20. Hal or Halle. Notre Dame was the principal church.
21. Tirlemont (Tienen).
22. Wavre. In the Narrative, the author has placed Tirlemont and Wavre in the wrong chronological order. His regiment must have stopped in Waure before Tirlemont if it was en route for Maastricht.
23. Possibly Leau (Zoutleeuw) or Linter (Orsmaal).
24. St Truiden (St Trond).
25. Tongres (Tongeren).
26. Wesel.
27. Sir Henry Jones.
28. The Duke of Monmouth served at the siege of Maastricht as a volunteer.
29. Guy-Aldoine de Durfort de Duras, Comte de Lorges (1628–1702), Marshal of France in 1676 (*DNF*, xii. 377).
30. Charles de Montsaulnin, Comte de Montal (1616–96).
31. *i.e.* the French had sapped towards the foot of the glacis and had then launched an assault which had effected a lodgement on the counterscarp.

marched to a camp near Veazy,[32] which is between Mastrick and
Liege, wher in that vally was to be seen a goodly sight of 300 stan-
der[d]s of light hors, <3> besides Guard de Corps, Gan [Gens] de
Arms, and Dragoons.

On the 8th of Jully, wer detached 3 brigades to march into
Holland.[33] That night we camped by Tungere[34] wher the King cam[e]
hence; I also to[o]. So it [was] raised [razed] and blown up. From
hence we marched very hard untill we came to Buxtell,[35] which was
the 12, and ther sejour 2 days as our Brigadeir Sinclar[36] was comanded
out to discourse [with] the Prince of Orange [at] his camp which was
near Breda. On the 14, we marched towards Grave and camped at a
village called Fechill.[37] On the 16 wee arived at Grave and ther mett
us 2 Brigad[e]s of hors[e] and the Prince of Condé. On the 19th we
marched from thence towards Balduke[38] and camped at a place called
Hozik[39] wher wee continued our camp untill the 28th. Then we
marched to a camp called Albeck,[40] wher we lay till the ii of A[u]gust.
Ther we wer detached from the princes army in Sinclares Brigad to
march towards Mastrick.

The first night we incamped at Hezell;[41] from thence to Berno;[42]
now we enter [the] Pais de Liege. From thence to Verver;[43] from
thence to Stoblo,[44] a fin[e] little towne, good walls. Ther we had on[e]
days sejour. From thence to Sinevit;[45] from thence to Sconekré,[46] a
Spanish garison, and camped half a league from it. From thence to a
little burck[47] near Treav.[48] The next day wee passe the Muzell[49] a
little league below Treav at a place caled Pauls,[50] and marched to a
viladge caled Tonge,[51] now in [the] Pais de Treave. From thence to

32. Visé.
33. To reinforce the Prince of Condé in Holland.
34. Tongres (Tongeren).
35. Boxtel, north-west of Eindhoven.
36. Antoine Turgot, Seigneur de St Clair (d.1728) (*DNF*, xix. 263–4).
37. Either Voghel or Volkel, north-east of Eindhoven.
38. Bois-le-Duc ('s-Hertogenbosch).
39. Heeswijk.
40. Aalburg, near Heusden, on the very edge of the inundations.
41. Hasselt.
42. Bearneau, south of Maastricht on the east bank of the Meuse.
43. Verviers.
44. Stavelot.
45. St Vith.
46. Schönecken, south of Prüm in West Germany.
47. Probably a mis-spelling of 'burg'.
48. Trier.
49. River Moselle (Mosel).
50. Pfalzel on the Moselle.
51. Thomm.

a viladge called Ransfeild[52] and sejoured on[e] day. On the 23rd of A[u]gust we marched. Our brigadier had a Cart Blanch [which] did us no good but fatig[u]ed our horses to death to put moni[e]s [in] his purse. From Ransfeild we marched to Neither Manick[53] wher wee cantoned and the next day marched to Over Manick[54] and camped near the viladge.

<4> The next day, being the 24th A[u]gust, wee marched back towards Treave and repassed the Muzell at Palse[55] in the eve[n]ing. Later, by the breake of day, we marched and invested the towne[56] with hors[e] only, wher we continued without firing on[e] at another or corespondance, each upon ther guard. The 30 of A[u]gust, our Infantery and artilery arived and the next night [we] breake ground and continued our aproches and raised 3 baterys, wher of on[e] was upon the edge of the foss, which mad[e] a considerable breach. Severall good oficers kild and many souldiers. Monsieur de Rochfort[57] had ane unhappy shot for it was to[o] high. Had it been a little lower we had been quit of a great enymy.

On the 7th Sep[t]ember, the towne wass surrendered. On the 8th, our Regiment was put in,[58] wher wee ar[e] still, but we expect orders to march every day.

52. Reinsfeld.
53. Nieder Mennick.
54. Ober Mennick.
55. Pfalzel.
56. *i.e.* Trier.
57. Lieutenant-General Henri-Louis d'Aloigny, Marquis de Rochefort (d.1676), Marshal of France in 1676.
58. *i.e.* in garrison in Trier.

VI
LORD CUTTS'S LETTERS, 1695

Edited by John Childs

CONTENTS

ACKNOWLEDGEMENTS

The publication of this edition of Lord Cutts's Letters is by the kind permission of the current owners, Mr. and Mrs. Richard Moore, of 'Hancox', Whatlington, Sussex. The editor is especially mindful of Mrs. Moore's generous hospitality and assistance during the transcription and preparation of these documents. The editor also wishes to thank Dr. Paul Hopkins for drawing his attention to these letters of Lord Cutts.

ABBREVIATIONS

Add. MSS.	Additional Manuscripts
ARA	Algemeen Rijksarchief, The Hague
BL	British Library
Childs, *Nobles, Gentlemen*	John Childs, *Nobles, Gentlemen and the Profession of Arms in Restoration Britain, 1660–1688: a biographical dictionary of British army officers on foreign service* (London, 1987)
CJ	*Journals of the House of Commons*
CSPD	*Calendar of State Papers Domestic*
Dalton	Charles Dalton, *English Army Lists and Commission Registers, 1660–1714* (London, 1892–1904), 6 vols.
DNB	*Dictionary of National Biography*
Ferguson, *Scots Brigade*	*Papers illustrating the history of the Scots Brigade in the service of the United Netherlands, 1572–1782*, ed. James Ferguson (Scottish History Society, Edinburgh, 1899), 3 vols.
HMC	*Reports of the Royal Commission on Historical Manuscripts*
HP	*The House of Commons, 1660–1690*, ed. B.D. Henning (London, 1983), 3 vols.
Luttrell	Narcissus Luttrell, *A Brief Historical Relation of State Affairs from September 1678 to April 1714* (Oxford, 1857), 6 vols.
MSS.	Manuscript
PRO	Public Record Office, London
VCH	*Victoria County History*
WO	War Office Papers, Public Record Office
Army Ranks	
Capt.	Captain
Lt. Col.	
Lt. Colonel	Lieutenant-Colonel

INTRODUCTION

Information about the internal administration of the standing army in late seventeenth century England is far from abundant. Both the War Office Papers in the Public Record Office and the manuscripts of William Blathwayt in the British Library and the Gloucestershire County Record Office are imperfect and often raise as many questions as they answer.[1] In particular, very little material seems to be available to illustrate the processes by which the army in England and Wales was inspected, regulated and controlled by the civilian and military authorities in Whitehall. William III issued numerous orders and proclamations concerning dress, discipline, recruitment, training and mustering but there is a paucity of example as to how these instructions were enforced and given effective teeth. Far more than either Charles II or James II, King William instituted a series of inspections of garrisons, quarters, fortifications and regiments within the British Isles by trusted general officers. This method was introduced in 1689 with the appointment of commissioners to regulate the abuses in the army, their principal charge being to remedy the plague of false musters and to ensure that the army's loyalty had been successfully switched from James II to the new regime.[2] Apart from the semi-ceremonial reviews of individual regiments and brigades executed by the king and some senior officers from time to time, little more was heard of general investigations into the state of the army until early 1695. William was able to keep in close touch with the condition of the British troops serving with the confederate army in Flanders by virtue of his personal command but the regiments in quarters and garrisons in the British Isles, upon which he relied to provide trained replacements for the corps in Flanders and to protect England against the omnipresent danger of French invasion, were frequently beyond his immediate influence. The revelation of the scale of financial corruption in English political and military life which swept through the country during the first half of 1695 indicated that all was not well within the state of Britannia.[3] In partial response to this unsavoury disrobing of public affairs to expose a less than perfect body, William seems to have returned to the notion of instigating general inspections of his army in England.

1. Principally, PRO, WO 4 & WO 5; BL, Add. MSS. 9,719–9, 735 and 38,694–38,707.
2. John Childs, *The British Army of William III* (Manchester, 1987), pp. 26–30, 165–6. The Commissioners for Regulating the Abuses in the Army were appointed on 10 May 1689 (BL, Harleian MSS. 7,018, ff. 251–4).
3. Childs, *British Army of William III*, pp. 46–51, 141–6; Henry Horwitz, *Parliament, Policy and Politics in the Reign of William III* (Manchester, 1977), pp. 146–50.

During the winter and early spring of 1695,[4] John, Lord Cutts, a brigadier-general and Colonel of the Coldstream Guards,[5] was sent to Plymouth and south Hampshire to undertake two tours of inspection. His first series of reviews lasted from 10 January to 8 February 1695 [letters 1–11], and his second dated from 16 to 30 March 1695 [letters 12–22]. In the former excursion, Cutts was entrusted with inspecting the infantry battalions from which a new regiment of foot was to be drafted to accompany the expedition of Captain Robert Wilmot, R.N., and Colonel Luke Lillingstone to reinforce the British garrisons in the West Indies. Cutts was additionally ordered to supervise the embarkation and sailing of this new regiment. Because of the economic consequences of the catastrophic failure of the 1693 harvest, the French navy had been obliged to abandon its attempt to emulate the grand naval strategy of the British and the Dutch and, instead, adopt a policy of interrupting and raiding Anglo-Dutch commerce, the 'guerre de course'. Partly in reply to this strategic retreat and partly to assuage the disaster which had overtaken the Smyrna convoy in 1693, the British and Dutch maritime forces went over to the counter-offensive in 1694. The attack on Brest in June 1694 was the most obvious manifestation of this new policy but considerable efforts were also made to capture French possessions in the West Indies. The authorities in Barbados requested a squadron of five frigates with which to attack French-held Martinique, and Christopher Codrington the Elder, the Governor of the Leeward Islands, asked for a further six warships and some land troops in order to support this assault. Faced with a request for eleven men-of-war, William decided that only six could be spared. Colonel Luke Lillingstone was appointed military commander of this expedition in September 1694, with Robert Wilmot as the naval commander-in-chief. The combined expeditionary force achieved little except the capture of Hispaniola.[6] Having dispatched these troops from Plymouth, Cutts journeyed through Exeter to Salisbury, Basingstoke, Southampton, the Isle of Wight and Portsmouth, inspecting battalions *en route*, before returning to London.

4. Although the volume of letters is headed '1694', this is an Old Style dating with the new year beginning on 25 March. By reckoning the new year to commence on 1 January, the letters fall into 1695.

5. For a general biography of Cutts see *DNB*. Further details of his career will be found in the footnotes to the text, especially numbers 19, 23 and 39, in *HMC, Frankland-Russell-Astley MSS.*, pp. 64–208, and Childs, *Nobles, Gentlemen*, p. 23.

6. Geoffrey Symcox, *The Crisis of French Sea Power, 1688–1697* (The Hague, 1974); W.T. Morgan, 'The British West Indies during King William's War, 1689–97', *Journal of Modern History*, ii. (1930), pp. 398–400; V.T. Harlow, *Christopher Codrington, 1668–1710* (Oxford, 1928), pp. 34, 64–72; John Ehrman, *The Navy in the War of William III, 1689–1697* (Cambridge, 1953), pp. 505–53, 609.

Cutts's second visitation took him back to Portsmouth and the Isle of Wight in order to inspect and regulate the infantry battalions which were to be conveyed to Cadiz, there to join the main battle fleet under Admiral Edward Russell to serve as amphibious forces during operations along the Catalonian coast aimed at halting the French drive from Rosas towards Palamos and Barcelona. In the course of this tour, Cutts was asked to use his political influence as Governor of the Isle of Wight to assist in returning a court supporter at the forthcoming bye-election at Yarmouth [letters 17, 20, 22].

The reports of Cutts's finding during these tours of inspection were sent to William Blathwayt, the Secretary-at-War, in Whitehall and they have now been recovered. They are bound into a single, vellum, foolscap-sized volume entitled, 'Lords Cutts Letters, 1694'.[7] The majority of William Blathwayt's archive was purchased by Sir Thomas Phillipps from Thomas Thorpe in 1836 but when the British Museum bought Blathwayt's papers from the Phillipps Manuscripts on 19 June 1893 at auction, it took only 'the volumes of greatest historical interest'.[8] Lord Cutts's Letters did not fall into this hallowed category, although they now appear as significant as many of the other items included within the British Museum's acquisition. Through a so-far untraced route, the volume came into the possession of Mr. and Mrs. Richard Moore of 'Hancox', Whatlington, Sussex, where its presence was overlooked by the researchers of the Historical Manuscripts Commission.

There are twenty-three holograph letters. Nineteen are reports from Cutts to Blathwayt; one letter is from Blathwayt to Cutts [no. 18]; one is from Captain Edmund Rivett to Cutts [no. 13]; one is from Thomas Cole to Blathwayt [no. 16]; and the final letter is not from this sequence but dates from 1698 and is from Cutts to William Lowndes, Secretary to the Treasury, about a widow's pension [no. 23]. All of the epistles have been bound in chronological order with the exception of no. 22 which unaccountably appears at the beginning of the volume; in this edition, the offending letter has been rearranged into its correct position. Lord Cutts wrote to Blathwayt in his own hand, clearly and legibly, expressing himself in rounded and un-ambiguous prose as befitted a soldier who dabbled in the literary arts. All of Cutts's communications to Blathwayt were endorsed upon their arrival in London but only no. 12 mentions the date and time of receipt. The abstracts of regimental strength and con-

7. For a general biography of William Blathwayt see, G.A. Jacobsen, *William Blathwayt, a late seventeenth century administrator* (New Haven and London, 1932).

8. The volume was MSS. 9,450 in the Phillipps Collection. See, *The Phillipps Manuscripts*, ed. A.N.L. Munby (London, 1968); A.N.L. Munby, *Phillipps Studies* (Cambridge, 1951–60), v. 57–8.

dition which Lord Cutts sent to Whitehall have not been traced; they are not to be found either amongst the Blathwayt Papers in London or Gloucester, or in the War Office Papers in the Public Record Office.

The reports provide very useful illumination of the state of the military in southern England in the middle years of William III's reign when the country had already been at war for six years. Cutts had to deal with the problem of officers who received money with which to pay their men and then refused its legitimate disbursal, as well as with the high level of absenteeism amongst the commissioned ranks [nos. 9, 13, 14, 17, 19]. This, and the general hatred of being dragooned into serving overseas, led to mutinies and threats of mutiny which Cutts appeared to handle in a delicate and tactful manner [nos. 1, 12, 13, 14, 17, 19]. Anxious to build up some personal 'interest' in the army, Cutts concerned himself with supporting suitable candidates for promotion in addition to making sure that he himself was adequately remunerated for the cost and trouble of his tours of inspection [nos. 4, 9, 20]. Above all, Cutts presents a reasonably optimistic impression of the regiments which he inspected. Contrary to the view of the army engendered by the Royston Petition and the revelations of the financial misdealings of agent Tracey Pauncefoot and Colonel Ferdinand Hastings which reached their practical manifestation in the pitiful surrender of the garrisons of Dixmuyde and Deynse to the French later in 1695, Cutts reports the battalions as well up to strength, composed of basically sound men of the right age, decently trained, and commanded by generally attentive officers. There were some very poor officers [no. 20] and a degree of financial maladministration in William Stewart's battalion, but the overall picture which emanates from Cutts's letters must have been encouraging to William and Blathwayt rather than depressing. Cutts succeeded in embarking his two overseas expeditions on time, at full strength, and with battalions of a respectable quality. The only worrying bleak spot was the poor condition of the garrison and fortifications on the Isle of Wight and the uncertain state of civil-military relations on the island [no. 22]. Cutts's attempt to return a court placeman as member of Parliament for Yarmouth foundered in the face of the Whig interest and the local patronage and influence of the Holmes family [nos. 14, 17, 20].

Probably, other tours of inspection had taken place in England between 1689 and 1695. Cutts alludes to two similar imspections [no. 4] and it is more than likely that there had been others in the interim. However, after 1695 the practice became more generally recognised. The Duke of Schomberg and Leinster, the commander-in-chief of the forces in England, undertook a general inspection of all the troops and garrisons in England during July and August 1695,[9] and the same officer reviewed the garrisons and the fixed fortifications in 1699.[10] Major-General William Stewart carried out a full inspection of the Irish Army in March 1696.[11] The system of inspection and review was well established long before George I introduced a regular pattern of regimental inspections in 1716. Four years later, this became an annual ritual for all regiments stationed in England, Scotland, Wales and Ireland.[12]

9. BL, Add. MSS. 9,722, f. 70; Berkshire County Record Office, Reading, Trumbull MSS., Add. MSS. 118.

10. Luttrell, iv. 533, 552, 559, 561.

11. Trumbull MSS., Add. MSS. 118, Sir William Trumbull to Major-General William Stewart, 2/12 March 1697.

12. J.A. Houlding, *Fit for Service: the Training of the British Army, 1715–1795* (Oxford, 1981), p. 297.

EDITORIAL PRACTICE

In the manuscript, the letters are unfoliated. Folio numbers have been added in this edition in order to facilitate any future references. Generally, Cutts's original texts have been left unaltered. Occasionally a comma has been added or subtracted to render a meaning more plainly but the spellings and syntax have been left undisturbed, even in no. 14 where Cutts blamed his 'ill writing' on the fact that he had been woken up in the middle of the night. Cutts was over-fond of employing parentheses instead of commas to isolate a clause in apposition and these are to be found within round brackets in the text. Additions and amplifications by the editor have been placed within square brackets and have been italicised.

A reading of the letters will indicate that Cutts did not expect replies as most of his reports were intended simply to be laid before the King for his information. Where and when replies or additional instructions were sent by Blathwayt, their present locations have been indicated in the footnotes.

LORD CUTTS'S LETTERS, 1695

1 [*ff. 3–4*]

Cutts to Blathwayt, 13 January 1695, Plymouth

Sir,

I send here enclosed an abstract[1] of the state of Colonel Farringdon's[2] regiment,[3] which you'll be pleased to give the king, and acquaint his Majesty, at the same time, that amongst those men I saw there were a great many old men above fifty and boys under nineteen,[4] which the officers do say they will change as soon as they can. I believe if the colonel saw it [*the regiment*] oftener it would be better.

I arrived here last night. I find the garrison extremely sickly, the smallpox and spotted fever[5] being very mortal. This day an officer of Northcote's[6] regiment was buried who died of the spotted fever, and the men die very fast. I have ordered the garrison under arms at seven tomorrow morning, hoping to form the new regiment and embark them by tomorrow night having ordered boats and made all necessary dispositions for it today.[7] I made the detachment out of Colonel Farringdon's regiment at Exeter ordering the officers to march them hither without arms under a guard of men with arms, which happened well for just now I have an account that they mutinied upon the road and if they had been armed it had been dangerous, but they are come within five miles of this place (with the loss of seven men) and will be here early tomorrow. All the companies quartered out of town will be in here tomorrow. By my next, his Majesty shall have an account

1. This abstract is not included amongst the letters and has not been traced.
2. See Appendix.
3. During William III's reign, a battalion of foot possessed a paper strength of 650 privates and NCOs, and 42 commissioned officers (*CJ*, xi. 176–8; Dorset County Record Office, Dorchester, Ilchester MSS., Box 278). In practice, Blathwayt assumed that a battalion contained a maxumum of 600 privates and NCOs (BL, Add. MSS. 9,724, f. 169). The majority of infantry battalions consisted of twelve companies of 50 men each, with one grenadier company.
4. Legal recruiting could only involve unmarried men between the ages of sixteen and forty who were not householders (Childs, *British Army of William III*, pp. 103–19).
5. 'Spotted fever' generally referred to typhus.
6. See Appendix.
7. Lillingstone's battalion had marched into Plymouth ready for embarkation on 27 and 28 December 1694 (*CSPD 1695*, p. 303). On 14 January 1695, Cutts had been instructed to make a draft of 1,200 men from the four regiments in the Plymouth garrison to form a new battalion especially for the expedition to Martinique. Although Lillingstone's regiment was also to sail with this expedition 'entire', its officers were excused service in the West Indies and were promised places in other regiments in England and in Flanders. Only Colonel Lillingstone, three captains, two lieutenants, and one ensign accompanied the expedition (*CSPD 1695*, pp. 305–6).

of the state and condition of the regiments here, of the embarkation and the rest. I did not review any regiments as I came, they being all in motion, but shall do it in my return. As for more particular observations, his Majesty shall have a faithful account of everything when I have the honour to return to his presence. This is what I desire you to acquaint his Majesty with,

I am, most sincerely Sir,
Your most humble and most obedient servant,
Cutts.

Postscript. I hear nothing of Colonel Lillingstone[8]—I desire to know, Sir, what I am to do in case he don't come.

2 [ff. 5–6]

Cutts to Blathwayt, 15 January 1695, Plymouth

Sir,
Yesterday I reviewed the regiments of Lillingstone, Colt,[9] and Northcote; made the detachment (of 1,200 men) and embarked them; and today I have reviewed them on board (man by man) and formed the respective companies according to his Majesty's establishment. Yesterday, in the evening, I disbanded the officers of Colonel Lillingstone's regiment, which was a very great surprise to them all. And, I must confess, I never executed any order with greater trouble and uneasiness. For I really believe the officers had done their utmost to put their companies in a good condition. It seems all the captains of the regiment, as well as the lieutenant-colonel[10] and major,[11] have thought themselves very hardly used by their colonel in many things and this has had the same effect I observed once (in the like case) in Beveridge's[12] regiment. The officers, that their colonel might have no pretence against them, have taken care to make their companies very good. And indeed, I must give this account of the regiment in general, that it was a good regiment, not only strong in numbers but the men (excepting a few) very good men and well-turned. Besides that, the officers, in general, seem pretty men and attached to their business. I could wish most heartily that one of those regiments had been broke

8. See Appendix.
9. See Appendix.
10. Lieutenant-Colonel Theophilus Rabinières.
11. Holcroft Blood. See Appendix.
12. See Appendix.

that more justly deserved it, for I can give but a melancholy account
of the other two regiments. They are not only weak but they have a
great many old men and boys and malingerers, insomuch that, with
difficulty, I made the detachments out of them and was forced to take
several men much against my mind. The officers of Lillingstone's late
regiment received his Majesty's orders very submissively though some
of them were so very touched that they wept. I desire you will lay this
before his Majesty with my humble opinion that he will be pleased
not to dispose of the vacancies in Farringdon's, Northcote's, and Colt's
regiments 'till I have the honour to return to his presence. Tomorrow,
the Jamaica regiment[13] is to be mustered and so soon as the convoy
arrives they'll be ready to sail. You'll please to give his Majesty the
enclosed abstracts.[14] I am sincerely, Sir,

Your most humble and most obedient servant,
Cutts.

Postscript. Colonel Lillingstone arriv'd.

3 [*ff. 7–8*]

Cutts to Blathwayt, 18 January 1695, Plymouth

Sir,
The commissaries[15] have now concluded the muster of the regiment
designed for Jamaica, and I have ordered all the transport ships[16]
designed for that expedition to run out into the Sound with the first
tide tomorrow in order to be in a readiness for their convoy, and to
prevent disorders which may happen whilst they lie so near the shore
and so near one another. This afternoon, 3 or 4 ships that lay near
one another, mutinied; I mean the soldiers in them. They drew their
swords, took off all the sentinels which their officers had placed, and
swore if they [their officers] placed any guards upon them they would
cut their throats. By good fortune I was on board the *Reserve* not far-
off, and so soon as I had notice of the mutiny I rowed immediately
on board the ships where it was (with such officers as were in company
with me) and partly by promises and partly by threats I appeased

13. The 'Jamaica Regiment' was the new regiment being formed at Plymouth to
serve in the West Indies under Lillingstone (see footnote 7).
14. These abstracts are not included amongst the letters and have not been traced.
15. The deputy commissaries of the musters.
16. There were twelve transport ships (Morgan, 'The British West Indies during
King William's War', p. 401).

them quite. But for fear of their repeating their disorder, I commanded 100 armed men from the garrison to keep guard there, with officers proportionable. Their great pretence was money and clothes.[17] I thought the fittest time to punish the leaders would be when they should come out at sea and I shall give orders for it accordingly. If the convoy is here tomorrow (as we expect, supposing him not far-off) I hope they may sail on Sunday. This is what you'll please to acquaint his Majesty with. I hope you have received all my letters and the abstracts of Farringdon's, Lillingstone's, Northcote's, and Colt's regiments. I am, Sir,

Your most humble and most obedient servant,
Cutts.

Postscript. I have purged the detachment over and over again, and now everyone says 'tis as good a one as ever was made.

4 [*ff. 9–10*]

Cutts to Blathwayt, 20 January 1695, Plymouth

Sir,
This afternoon, since which time I have received the honour of yours of the 17th, I had sent you word of the draughts being made by the express that went from here on Monday last about one o'clock in the afternoon, but they were not above half-done nor was Lillingstone's regiment broke 'till about five hours after. I sent you this only to let you know that as soon as anything is actually done, I don't omit the first opportunity to advise you of its being so. Whilst I am writing, Captain Wilmot[18] is come into my chamber. He is just arrived (post) from Falmouth by land. The violent winds hindered his making this port and one or two of his ships have suffered some little matter in their sails and rigging but nothing considerable. He returns to Falmouth tomorrow leaving orders with the *Reserve* to sail out here on Tuesday morning with the ships bound to Jamaica in order to meet him, who designs to sail out of Falmouth at the same time. I have discoursed him about it and he says this will be the best way for the service, wind and weather permitting.

---

17. Service in the West Indies was unpopular amongst both officers and men on account of the high mortality rates. It was rare for an expedition to the Caribbean not to incur 'disorders' during its preparations and embarkation (Childs, *British Army of William III*, p. 126).

18. See Appendix.

You send me word, Sir, the king has granted me three hundred pounds but the warrant is not yet signed &c. You may be sure I should never be dissatisfied with anything that is the king's pleasure but, if this matter be rightly represented to the king, his Majesty will never deny me what he has always allowed to others upon like occasions.[19] I am sure no man ever had less than five hundred pounds upon the like occasion. Colonels and lieutenant-colonels have had as much; Brigadier Luson [sic][20] had as much when he went to Chester, Fairfax[21] had as much, and I'm sure none of them were put to greater expenses than I'm necessarily engaged in, for (besides eating and drinking) in such weather as this one either spoils one's own horses or must ruin one's self in hackneys. It will be very hard for me to have less than everybody else though (I'm sure) no footman or groom earns his wages with more pains. I doubted not an amount of £500 and have taken money upon it, and therefore beg you'll explain it to his Majesty.[22]

I am, with respect, Sir,

Your most humble and most obedient servant,
Cutts.

5 [*ff. 11–12*]

Cutts to Blathwayt, 20 January 1695, Plymouth

Sir,
Since closing my other letter to you of the same date, looking upon my minutes I am forced to add this trouble earnestly to beg of you that the Isle of Wight may not be oppressed with forces.[23] I am sure,

19. This was money to cover Cutts's expenses during his tour of inspection. Cutts was usually short of money and died in debt to the officers of his regiment (*The Marlborough-Godolphin Correspondence*, ed. Henry Snyder (Oxford, 1975), i. 284n.).
20. Identification uncertain. This was probably Brigadier-General Robert, 3rd Baron Lucas, the governor of the Tower of London.
21. See Appendix.
22. The sum of £300 for Cutts's expenses had been suggested by Colonel Joseph Dudley, a client of Blathwayt's and Cutts's lieutenant-governor on the Isle of Wight. See Appendix and the postscript to Letter No. 6.
23. See Letter No. 22. In his role as governor of the Isle of Wight, Cutts suggested that the strategic points of Portsmouth, Spithead, the Solent, and Southampton, were better defended from the mainland than from the Isle of Wight. This strategic appreciation was based more on the need to preserve Cutts's electoral influence on the island than on disinterested military considerations. The Isle of Wight had been greatly 'oppressed' by military billets in 1688 and 1689, and Cutts did not want to jeopardise his own and the government's electoral interest in the forthcoming bye-election at

at this nick of time, it will very much prejudice the service, as I shall easily convince you when I see you, and I assure you it secures the men no more than the main land. For the coasters and little barques that ply up and down there will take them off in the night.[24] I desire you will make the king acquainted with this. I am with respect, Sir,

Your most humble servant,
Cutts.

6 [ff. 13-14]

Cutts to Blathwayt, 22 January 1695, Plymouth

Sir,
I wrote you word in my last that Captain Wilmot was arriv'd. The next day he sent an express to Falmouth to the ships there, with orders to sail out this afternoon to meet the *Reserve* and the transport-ships that were here, resolving to stay here himself to see the transport-ships out. This day, about three in the afternoon, he went on board the *Reserve* (having ordered the signal for unmooring early in the morning). I went on board with him and between four and five I left him under sail, the wind E.N.E., and so rowing amongst the transport-ships, from ship to ship (because they were very backward) 'till I saw them all under sail, I saw at last the Sound clear of them. Captain Wilmot told me, he did not doubt but that the ships out of Falmouth would join him in an hour or two. I sent this morning for all the sick men on shore and gave them well men in their places returning the sick men to the regiments that stay here, so that among the twelve hundred there went away no sick men, and everybody says that never was so good a detachment of that number sent out of England. I have been purging them every day since they have been on board.

I design tomorrow for Exeter and to be Sunday at Salisbury, on Monday at Basingstoke, on Tuesday at Southampton, On Wednesday in the Isle of Wight, and on Thursday or Friday at Portsmouth, where I shall (at any, I mean, of those places) at the times mentioned receive

---

Yarmouth (2 April 1695) by packing the island with unpopular red-coats (Andrew Coleby, 'Military-Civil Relations on the Solent, 1651–1689', *Historical Journal*, xxix. (1986), pp. 959–61; Andrew Coleby, *Central Government and the Localities: Hampshire, 1649–1689* (Cambridge, 1987), pp. 179–91, 231–2; Childs, *British Army of William III*, pp. 10–11; *Returns of Members of Parliament* (London, 1878), pp. 568, 576).

24. A reference to desertion. Cutts thought it as easy, if not easier, for troops to desert from the island as from the mainland.

your commands. All this you will be pleased to lay before his Majesty and believe me sincerely, Sir,

Your most humble and most obedient servant,
Cutts.

Postscript. Dudley is intolerably in the wrong in advising you to draw a warrant for £300 for it, and therefore I beg of you, Sir, not to do it.[25] For if I have not £500 it will be the hardest thing in the world. If I, who make no money but what the king knows of, shall be worse used than others and who sacrifices all considerations on his service, it will be very hard but if you represent it aright I am sure the king will be just to me.

7 [*ff. 15–16*]

Cutts to Blathwayt, 27 January 1695, Salisbury

Sir,
I have this minute received the honour of yours of the 22nd instant, it having come to Plymouth after I had left that place.

I send you here enclosed[26] an abstract of the state of nine companies of Colonel Erle's[27] regiment. His Majesty will see the number and be pleased to consider this is one of those regiments that were ruined at sea the last summer, particularly the grendiers were almost all killed and made prisoner.[28] The men I saw were (excepting a few and those in the nine companies not above ten or eleven in all, I believe) good, seasoned men, and though they are ill in clothes (having a new clothing now in hand[29]) yet they appeared neat and clean. In the whole I really think it a good battalion.

I enquired particularly after their Irish papists but they tell me they are all discharged.[30] The other 4 companies lay too far out of my way. I shall see most parts of Colonel Stewart's[31] regiment tomorrow

25. See Letter No. 4 and footnote 22.
26. This abstract is not included amongst the letters and has not been traced.
27. See Appendix.
28. This refers to the unsuccessful attempt to attack Brest on 8 June 1694 (Childs, *British Army of William III*, pp. 207–39).
29. Regiments received a new set of clothes every two years (Childs, *British Army of William III*, pp. 167–71).
30. Those regiments which served in Ireland between 1689 and 1691 had sometimes recruited native Irish roman catholics into their ranks, contrary to army regulations and the Test Acts. In one or two regiments, English roman catholics continued to serve even though all catholics had been supposedly purged from the army during the first half of 1689 (Childs, *British Army of William III*, pp. 12–13, 114–15).
31. See Appendix.

and then to Portsmouth and so make haste to London. And indeed, I'm glad his Majesty's commands give me an opportunity of passing through the Isle of Wight, it being very much for the service for me to pass a day there upon some private intelligence I have had.

I doubt not but that his Majesty's Jamaica fleet, under Wilmot's command, is in a good way. If the wind continues four or five days more as it has done since they sailed, they'll be in a trade wind and past hazard. I must renew my earnest desire to you that nothing of the £500 be cut off. Indeed, if it be, I shall be used harder than any of my comrades. I am sincerely sir,

Your most humble and most obedient servant,
Cutts.

Postscript. You shall have the next a list of Lillingstone's officers.

8 [*ff. 17–18*]

Cutts to Blathwayt, 31 January 1695, Basingstoke

Sir,
On Monday the 28th instant I reviewed five companies of Colonel Stewart's regiment. On Tuesday 29th I reviewed two more of the same but forebear to give his Majesty an account of them 'till I have seen the rest of the companies of that regiment which will be today and tomorrow, God willing. Only thus much I may hint in passing that what I have seen of them already, for the number, are very good men and in good order.

Yesterday, I reviewed Colonel Venner's[32] regiment (excepting one company which was removed and missed my orders) and of the state of the twelve companies I saw, I send his Majesty an abstract here enclosed.[33] It is neither the best nor the worst regiment I have seen. Colonel Erle's and Colonel Stewart's are a force of men of a better size but, at the same time, Venner has but a few boys and no malingerers. The boys, he says, he will change. Their clothes are new and pretty good and the number his Majesty will see. His Majesty will please to take notice that the 3 corporals (in every company in all the regiments) are included in the number of men under arms for which in computing the complement of every company three men must be deducted out of the number. Which I did because I would not make the abstracts consist of too many heads which would be

32. See Appendix.
33. This abstract is not included amongst the letters and has not been traced.

troublesome to his Majesty, besides that the corporals march in the ranks.

I shall review some of Stewart's companies today at Winchester and lie tonight at Colonel Fleming's[34] (a gentleman very zealously affected to his Majesty, the monarchy, and the church) near Southampton in order to review the remainder of Stewart's regiment at Southampton tomorrow morning. From thence I shall pass into the Isle of Wight, so to Portsmouth, and finish my journey as fast as I can. I omit overall remarks for the service 'till I have the honour to return to his Majesty's presence. I am, Sir, sincerely,

Your most humble servant,
Cutts.

9 [*ff. 19–20*]

Cutts to Blathwayt, 1 February 1695, Stoneham, near Southampton

Sir,
This morning I reviewed the remaining companies of Brigadier Stewart's regiment at Southampton having reviewed two yesterday at Winchester, and I send you here enclosed an abstract of the state of that regiment[35] which you will please to give the king. His Majesty will see the numbers. The men are really very good, well armed and clothed, and, of what I saw, not above fourteen or fifteen in the whole regiment are men that one would desire to change. Besides that they have very much the air of disciplined soldiers (excepting only Captain Vaughan's company,[36] which was part ruined at Brest) and indeed it is one of the best regiments in the service for the numbers. His Majesty will please to remember, 'tis one of those regiments that were ruined at sea last summer. I find a great many officers in this regiment absent from quarters.[37] I believe it would be very much for his Majesty's service if it were ordered that there should be (with every regiment) always one field officer in the quarters; with every company always one commissioned officer (which I have not found everywhere); and that not above a third part of the captains, lieutenants, and ensigns of the same regiment should be absent from the quarters at the same

34. See Appendix.
35. This abstract is not included amongst the letters and has not been traced.
36. See Appendix.
37. Officer absenteeism was a constant problem in the British army at this time (John Childs, *The Army, James II, and the Glorious Revolution* (Manchester, 1980), pp. 37–40).

time. For the want of officers in the quarters is the cause of many disorders and makes a regiment fall away mightily if it is a constant practice. I suppose the absence of Brigadier Stewart's officers is upon some extraordinary occasion for they are, most of them, careful and diligent officers by what I observed in them the last summer [*i.e. during the Brest expedition*].

I send you a list of Lillingstone's disbanded officers[38] with remarks upon such of them as, I humbly presume, ought to be first provided for. There is a company vacant in my late regiment[39] in which Major Massam [*sic*][40] served 'till he was promoted into Lillingstone's. If his Majesty would give Major Massam that company with a clause in his commission to act as major in the absence of the major, it will be a piece of bread for him 'till he can be provided for in his own post of Major Effective and it will be no disadvantage to that regiment. He was very instrumental in bringing Colonel Lillingstone's late regiment to what it was. Colonel Seymour cannot take it ill in this occasion and it may be done as included in his Majesty's general order providing for those disbanded officers in the first vacancies of regiments. Besides that, Massam has been several times wounded in that very regiment. His father is knight of the shire for Essex.

I am now present at Colonel Fleming's. I design to embark tomorrow at Southampton for the Isle of Wight, on Monday or Tuesday for Portsmouth, and so make haste to finish my round. I shall have the honour to write to you again from Portsmouth. You'll please to lay all these matters before his Majesty. I am sincerely, Sir,

Your most humble and most obedient servant,
Cutts.

Postscript. The company vacant in Seymour's regiment is Lewis's[41] which I proposed in Flanders for Colonel Dudley.[42]

38. This list is not included amongst the letters and has not been traced.
39. The colonelcy of Cutts's battalion had been assumed by Colonel William Seymour on 3 Oct. 1694 when Cutts had been promoted to the command of the Coldstream Guards following the death of that regiment's colonel, Thomas Talmash, after the attack on Brest on 8 June 1694 (Dalton, iv. 3, 5).
40. See Appendix.
41. See Appendix.
42. Colonel Joseph Dudley. See Appendix and footnote 22.

10 [*ff. 22–3*]

Cutts to Blathwayt, 3 February 1695, Cowes

Sir,

I have since my arrival here received the honour of yours of 29th January. I am very thankful for what you write me concerning the £500, and I desire you to assure his Majesty that I shall never be unreasonable or troublesome to him in money matters. I always understood that the whole business I was to do should be included in the £500. And you see, by my letters, that I was fully resolved to go through the quarters of those two regiments, Rowe[43] and Coote.[44]

But understanding by yours that they are just upon their march, I sent this to know if his Majesty would have me visit them in their quarters where they are or come up to London (when I have visited the garrison of Portsmouth) and return down to review them so soon as they are removed and to do what else his Majesty shall please to command me. Desiring you to assure his Majesty at the same time that I have no mark of inclination to the one or the other but as it shall be more acceptable to him though their quarters are so very scattered and wide that if their march be near at hand it will be less fatigue to the regiments and less troublesome to the country to review them when they are come together.

I shall wait your answer some time between this and Wednesday night designing to be at Portsmouth at that time, or early on Thursday morning.

Upon examining I find in the Isle of Wight we have but sixty-nine public houses[45] which, at the rate of two beds a house, is a hundred and thirty-eight beds and that, at two men in a bed, will take in but two hundred and seventy-six men, the officers unprovided for. But if the service does necessarily require it (without which it would be my humble opinion not to do it at this time) his Majesty will be pleased to direct an order to me to that purpose, commanding me to quarter such of them in private houses as cannot be contained in public ones which, upon an extraordinary occasion, I suppose, will not produce any ill effect.[46] And I shall do my best to make the thing as easy as it

43. See Appendix.
44. See Appendix.
45. William Blathwayt's survey of all available quarters in England and Wales in 1686—'An Abstract of a Particular Account of all the Inns, Ale Houses, etc. in England, with their Stable-Room and Bedding. In the Year, 1686', (PRO, WO 30/48)—had credited the Isle of Wight with 237 beds and 159 stalls for horses.
46. By the terms of the Disbanding Act of 1679 (31 Charles II, c. 1) and the series of Mutiny Acts after 1689, it was illegal to billet soldiers upon private householders unless the occupier gave his or her consent.

will admit of. Though, just at this time that I am endeavouring to set right the corporations here (in which during my being at sea and in Flanders, the Marquis of Winchester[47] has been doing what mischief he can assisted by Major Holmes[48] and his creatures) I could wish we might be eased quartering in private houses if possible. But what his Majesty commands I shall most readily execute. I am sincerely, Sir,

Your most humble and most obedient servant,
Cutts.

11 [ff. 24–5]

Cutts to Blathwayt, 8 February 1695, Portsmouth

Sir,
Yesterday at my arrival here I received the honours of yours and shall obey his Majesty's commands.

It was about eleven o'clock that I landed here from the Isle of Wight and immediately I reviewed the garrison having sent them notice the day before to be in a readiness.

The forces here are Colonel Gibson's[49] regiment, three companies of Rowe, and two of Coote.

Of Colonel Gibson's regiment I send his Majesty an abstract here enclosed.[50] His Majesty will see the numbers and, as for the rest, there are great allowances to be made for the garrison of Portsmouth and greater for the new-raised regiments. And upon the whole (those two things being considered) I really think Colonel Gibson has not done ill for the time. His officers seem, most of them, pretty men and men of service.

I was to review the soldiers' barracks and do really believe the want of fire is very pernicious to their health and lives. I was also to visit a hospital which Colonel Gibson has formed and supports out of a regimental fund. It is in good order and saves him certainly a great many men. It were much to his Majesty's service if there could be hospitals in all the garrisons as there are in France. But I am of opinion that the same regiment can never possibly support itself always in Portsmouth. Colonel Gibson is willing to try another year but speaks

---

47. See Appendix.
48. See Appendix.
49. See Appendix.
50. This abstract is not included amongst the letters and has not been traced.

doubtingly and says if his regiment be not more fortunate another year than it has been this (as to sickness) he shall be of my mind.[51]

I am just now going into my coach and design to be at London tomorrow night. I forebear to send his Majesty an account of Rowe's and Coote's odd companies 'till I review the whole regiments. You'll please to lay this before his Majesty. I am most sincerely Sir,

Your humble and most obedient servant,
Cutts.

[*Cutts then returned to London. On 12 March 1695, William III ordered him to repair to 'Portsmouth, the Isle of Wight, and elsewhere' to review the regiments of Brigadier William Stewart, Colonel Samuel Venner, Colonel Richard Coote and Colonel Henry Rowe all of which were about to embark on transport ships in order to join Admiral Edward Russell's fleet at Cadiz. These regiments were to act as a force of marines during Russell's drive along the Catalan coast towards Barcelona and Palamos. Cutts was enjoined to supervise the embarkation of these four regiments at Spithead or at St Helens. Finally, Cutts was instructed to order Brigadier Ferdinand Hastings's[52] battalion to march into Portsmouth and there provide drafts to bring the other four regiments upto strength. Any vacancies within the commissioned officers were to be filled from amongst the disbanded officers of Colonel Luke Lillingstone's old regiment. A second letter from Kensington on the following day, 13 March, requested Cutts to ensure that the company officers in the four regiments satisfied their subalterns and private soldiers for any arrears of pay due from service in Ireland or from service with the fleet in 1694.[53]*]

51. Colonel John Gibson's experiment of a regimental hospital, funded by stoppages from the soldiers' pay, appears to have been unique in the British Isles. Not until the establishment of a permanent infirmary for sick soldiers at St Auden's Arch, Dublin, in 1700 was there provision of hospital facilities for the army in the British Isles. Even in Flanders, the British military hospitals were entrusted to private contractors (Robert Steele, *A Bibliography of Royal Proclamations of the Tudor and Stuart Sovereigns, 1485–1714* (Oxford, 1910), ii. 176; BL, Add. MSS. 38,699, f. 23; BL, Add. MSS. 38,700, f. 213).

52. See Appendix.

53. *HMC, Frankland-Russell-Astley MSS.*, pp. 81–2; *HMC, Buccleuch (Montagu) MSS.*, ii. 170–337; *Private and Original Correspondence of Charles Talbot, Duke of Shrewsbury*, ed. William Coxe (London, 1821), pp. 221, 233, 238–42. See Letter No. 2.

12 [*ff. 26–7*]

Cutts to Blathwayt, 16 March 1695, Portsmouth. Endorsed, 'received 17th at noon'.

Sir,
I arrived here this morning at eight o'clock and found things in some confusion. The transport ships (upon examination) fell short of their number about eight hundred,[54] supposing the regiments to be complete (as by the king's instructions they are to be) and the provisions fall short for some five hundred and odd men.

I desire to know if a transport may not be hired and the provisions wanting put on board (not staying for an order) and upon a representation of the thing, the officers being willing to do it, I mean the officers belonging to the transports and victuallers. I don't know how to give them an order but I may desire it of them and, if you like that way, it may be dispatched without delay.

I have reviewed and embarked Coote's regiment of which I shall send an abstract by the next[55] (being now busied in embarking Puisar's[56] regiment, which I have reviewed) and, as yet, we have not had anything like a mutiny, the men going off with a good deal of cheerfulness. But I find some companies in the late Colonel Rowe's[57] regiment are very much out of order as to their money. I desire to know his Majesty's pleasure, whether if an officer refuses to pay his men (having received the money) I am to put another in his place, or confine him, or what I am to do. I mention this because I apprehend some such thing and the wind being like to be fair and the embarkation quick, the thing requires a sudden resolution. This is what I desire you to lay before his Majesty and to give a speedy answer. At my arrival here a mutiny was apprehended but upon my speaking very plainly things were adjusted.
I am sincerely, Sir,

Your most humble and most obedient servant,
Cutts.

54. The carrying capacity of the transports was 800 men less than the estimate given by the Commissioners for Transportation.
55. This abstract is not included amongst the letters and has not been traced.
56. See Appendix.
57. See Appendix. The first three months of 1695 witnessed a series of financial scandals involving regimental commanders and their agents (Childs, *British Army of William III*, pp. 46–51, 141–6).

13 [*ff. 28–9*]

E. Rivett[58] *to Cutts, 19 March 1695, Salisbury. Endorsed, 'Capt. Rivett'.*

My Lord,

According to your lordship's directions I have delivered your letter to Lt. Colonel Hussey[59] and the mayor. I find by Colonel Hussey that the cause of this mutiny was in part occasioned by a discourse that was in the regiment of three of the captains belonging to the companies in quarters, here designed to quit, and that when they had got them to Southampton or on board they would put them off with no money at all. This, I find, was the principal cause and to help them in this affair there was a very great fair here and the country people had made them drunk and it's believed the townspeople and them gave them encouragement.

The Lt. Col. tells me that according to his Majesty's late orders of accounting with and paying the soldiers their sea pay, he had received the brigadier's[60] orders upon the same and had given it out to every captain but they had not done it fully but designed to do it at Southampton and pay them what was due to them, some of them having received fourteen shillings of their sea pay. My time which your lordship allowed me to stay before I sent the express is expired so I will not trouble your lordship with any more only that this night the Lt. Col. sent for a sergeant and a man of each company to him and told them the contents of your letter and told them they should, tomorrow morning, come to their respective captains' quarters and they should be cleared[61] and they seem to be very well satisfied and I hope they will march tomorrow without trouble. The mayor received your lordship's letter very respectfully and was willing to do anything that should be for his Majesty's service, and was mightily concerned that such a thing should happen here. As soon as they are cleared and marched I will make the best of my way to your lordship and give you a fuller account of this affair. I am,

My lord,
Your lordship's most humble and faithful servant,
E. Rivett.

58. See Appendix.
59. See Appendix.
60. William Stewart. See Appendix.
61. 'Clearing' was the issue of the balance of pay due to both officers and men (A. J. Guy, *Oeconomy and Discipline: Officership and Administration in the British Army, 1714–63* (Manchester, 1985), pp. 58–9).

14 [*ff. 30–1*]

Cutts to Blathwayt, 19 March 1695, Stoneham near Southampton

Sir,

Yesterday, about noon, (having embarked half of Brudenell's regiment) I came (in the Isle of Wight yacht) to Southampton, where I received an account from Brigadier Stewart, whom according to appointment I found there, acquainting me that his four companies at Salisbury were guilty of a violent mutiny and positively refused to obey their marching orders, proceeding, at the same time, to very great extravagances. I wrote a letter immediately to the Lt. Col. and another to the mayor of Salisbury signifying to the soldiers thereby the consequences of their folly, but that if they instantly returned to their duty I would not take advantage against them whereas if they persisted in their mutiny I would come forthwith to them and bring such company along with me as should chastise their insolence, and that then it would be too late for them to save themselves, &c. I sent these two letters by Captain Rivett, who is along with me, (a very determinate, bold young fellow, & no fool) with orders to stay 'till he saw them marched and be assisting to the Lt. Col. as also to talk to the soldiers as he saw occasion. He just now sends me the enclosed by an express[62] and I hope all will go well. I thought it my duty to send his Majesty this account forthwith (which, with the enclosed letter, you'll please to lay before him) and as soon as the men arrive and are embarked shall send another account. I never saw a man so concerned as Stewart is; he was ready to tear his hair. He has been very assisting to me in the whole embarkation and I meet with a great deal of civility and respect from him. I shall return (when this is over) to the Isle of Wight and Portsmouth. My being in bed (waked out of my sleep in the night) will pardon the ill writing of, Sir,

Your most humble and most obedient servant,
Cutts.

Postscript. I have engaged my word to the men that they shall have justice.

[*Blathwayt received this letter, with Rivett's enclosed, on 20 March. He replied, 'I am glad things are like to go so well, and particularly for Brigadier Stewart's sake.' Blathwayt also instructed Cutts to exert his electoral influence for Sir*

62. Letter No. 13.

Henry Bellasise[63] *at Yarmouth and requested Cutts to stay in the region of the Isle of Wight until the bye-election had taken place.* (*HMC, Frankland-Russell-Astley MSS.*, p. 83)]

15 [*ff. 32–3*]

Cutts to Blathwayt, 20 March 1695, Cowes

Sir,

Mr. Cole[64] having advanced the last year (upon the head of damages done to the country, &c.) the sum of £252 1s. 10d. and the money given to Mr. Talmash[65] for contingency being some of it spent, and the rest begged of the Queen by Captain Green,[66] I have directed him to apply to you and will myself at my arrival give you a particular account of the same and what I think the proper remedy to be proposed herein or to the method of laying it before the king, Mr. Cole having done it out of zeal for his Majesty's service and it being pretty hard for him to want it. I am with great sincerity, Sir,

Your most humble servant,
Cutts.

From my Lord Cutts about the damages done at the encampment.

63. See Appendix. A bye-election was due at Yarmouth, Isle of Wight, after the sitting member, Sir John Trevor, had been expelled from the House of Commons for taking bribes in return for abusing his office as Speaker to expedite the passage of bills through the House. The election took place on 2 April 1695 and resulted in victory for Henry Holmes; Holmes was also successful at Yarmouth in the general election on 1 November 1695 (Horwitz, *Parliament, Policy, and Politics*, pp. 149–50; *Returns of Members of Parliament* (London, 1878), pp. 568, 576; *The House of Commons, 1715–1754*, ed. Romney Sedgewick (London, 1970), ii. 145–6).
64. See Appendix.
65. See Appendix. The damage referred to occurred when the troops for the expedition to Brest had been encampled around Portsmouth both before and after the abortive assault.
66. See Appendix.

16 [ff. 34–5]

Thomas Cole to Blathwayt, 20 March 1695, Cowes [enclosed with letter no. 15]

Honourable Sir,
I formerly desired my friend, Mr. de Cardonel,[67] to pray your favour in securing me £252 1s. 10d. which I advanced for his Majesty's service to my Lord Cutts in June and August last, when the camp were here and at Portsmouth. The enclosed [*letter no. 15*] is from his lordship thereabout. It's very hard I should be thus long out of my money when my Lord Duke of Shrewsbury[68] (by the Queen's order) wrote my Lord Cutts [*that*] his lordship's bill should be punctually paid.
I beg your pardon for this trouble.

Your most faithful, obedient servant,
Tho. Cole.

17 [ff. 36–7]

Cutts to Blathwayt, 21 March 1695, Portsmouth

Sir,
I have received all your letters and particularly that relating to four companies in Brigadier Stewart's regiment and that concerning the election to be soon in the Isle of Wight.[69]
As to the cause of the mutiny, upon first examination of the matter I find the whole disorder plainly to proceed from a very fault committed by the man, which his Majesty would easily believe when he is informed that Lt. Col. Hussey disobeyed the brigadier's orders and stifled a written order which (by the brigadier's positive command) should have been publicly read at the head of the four companies at Salisbury. The mutiny began in the Lt. Colonel's own company (I suppose not without the greatest provocation though nothing can justify such proceedings) and that company marched into Southampton but twenty-two men strong. I am sorry such a misfortune should fall upon any man but the fault is really such that I dare not conceal it. I have (in obedience to his Majesty's orders) given orders

---

67. See Appendix.
68. Charles Talbot, 1st Duke of Shrewsbury (1660–1718), secretary of state.
69. *HMC, Frankland-Russell-Astley MSS.*, p. 83, Blathwayt to Cutts, 19 & 20 March 1695; BL, Add. MSS. 38,700, ff. 78–9.

for the suspending him, and finding an officer in the regiment who has an act [sic] of Lt. Colonel and a very good character from all hands (besides that I know myself something of his good qualities) I have ordered him to supply the vacancy as a captain. The other nine companies in which the brigadier's orders were obeyed went on board with the greatest cheerfulness in the world and most certainly the others would have done the same had they been treated in the same manner.

Pursuant to his Majesty's pleasure, I have set up Mr. Woosely [sic][70] at Yarmouth. It had been impossible to do it for Sir Henry Bellasise (for some reasons I'll tell you at my return) and if I do it for Mr. Woosely it must be by a very close and diligent application. But (on the other side) a victory in this election will make me master of the island for ever after and make the foundation of his Majesty's interests there much surer. I have sent my cook, wine, and provisions there under the direction of Colonel Hope[71] and design [the remainder of this letter is missing].

18 [f. 38]

Blathwayt to Cutts, 21 March 1695, Whitehall

My Lord,

When I signified to your lordship his Majesty's express pleasure that the sailing of the fleet should in no manner be stopped or delayed on account of land service,[72] 'twas in foresight that the Admiralty would make complaints of the troops not being in a readiness or on board, as they have done this day to his Majesty already in that 150 men were yet wanting of the complement ordered to embark. Hereupon I assured his Majesty that your lordship would, pursuant to directions, that the minute a wind should come fair, supply any defective numbers which might have happened by the mutiny at Salisbury out of Sir John Jacobs's[73] regiment so that the fleet might immediately sail without any obstruction from the forces. As directions are actually sent down by express this afternoon for their sailing accordingly and 'tis not to be doubted, at the same time, but that everything will be in an entire readiness on your lordship's part that there may be no reproaches of our losing the advantage of this fair wind.

70. See Appendix.
71. See Appendix.
72. Blathwayt was anxious that any possible delay in the embarkation and sailing of the four battalions for Cadiz should not be the fault of the army, his own department of state.
73. See Appendix.

Just as I had writ this I received your lordship's letter of this day's date.[74] I am glad, with all my heart, things go on so well and that the forces are in a perfect readiness. Orders are sent for the sailing of the fleet without Dutch ships. I don't answer Brigadier Stewart's letter because I believe him gone but, if otherwise, your lordship will assure him that right will be done.
I am,

Your lordship's most obedient servant,
William Blathwayt.

19 [*ff. 39–40*]

Cutts to Blathwayt, 22 March 1695, Portsmouth

Sir,
This morning, Lt. Colonel Hussey, being arrived from Southampton where he stayed to pick-up scattering men, came to me and endeavoured to excuse himself in this manner. He said, the reason why he did not read the brigadier's orders was because he thought they contradicted the king's orders and he thought it not for the brigadier's service to read them. I told him, I thought he was in fault very much not to read them but I desired he would hear what the brigadier said upon this matter (for I designed to have discoursed the thing with them both together) but he excused himself and desired leave to go to London to clear himself without losing a moment's time, which I did not deny him. Soon after, I spoke with the brigadier and upon discoursing with him cannot but be of opinion that the Lt. Col. has been very much to blame. I send you here enclosed a memorandum[75] given me by the brigadier upon this matter and signed by him, and with it a petition from some of the ringleaders of the mutineers (whom I have caused to be put in prison here) as also the king's orders which, with what the Lt. Colonel will say in his own defence, will enable you to lay the whole matter before the king. Only I must take leave to remark that the brigadier's order is dated some days before the king's order (so that he had ordered the men to be paid before the king's orders came out) and, in the next place, it seems very odd that an inferior officer should take upon him to stifle an order without representing the same, any ways, to his superior.
I must needs say I never saw men go on board with greater

74. See Letter No. 17.
75. This memorandum is not included amongst these letters and has not been traced.

satisfaction and alacrity than the nine companies of the brigadier's regiment that were embarked at Southampton the 18th inst.

You have thus the whole matter before you, with this addition only that there is no commission of a lt. colonel given out but only one appointed to act and that I have directed a company to be kept open 'till the king's pleasure be known (because Lt. Colonel Hussey desired he might be heard) though I believe his Majesty will very much condemn the Lt. Colonel.[76] I am sincerely, Sir,

Your most humble servant,
Cutts.

20 [*ff. 41–4*]

Cutts to Blathwayt, 24 March 1695, Yarmouth, Isle of Wight

Sir,

I have received yours[77] wherein you give me an account of the complaint of the Admiralty that one hundred and fifty men of the land forces were not embarked, which was a very unjust complaint and at that very time that the letter was wrote they were in boats coming on board.

Yesterday, having finished the execution of my orders, I delivered all things in to Brigadier Stewart's hands and (to avoid all sorts of mistakes) I gave him in writing, in the form of a letter, having first read it over and explained it to him, the abstract of my several orders and what measures I had taken thereupon, a copy of which I send you here enclosed and desire you'll please to lay the same before his Majesty.[78] And this is the more necessary that his Majesty may see the great inconvenience of not making the exact calculations which either the Admiralty has not done or the transport-ships did not answer the burthen they were hired for, or they had taken lading in and so straitened the room allowed for the soldiers.

And to explain this matter, you'll please to acquaint his Majesty that after I had embarked all the land forces and given you an account

76. No captain was appointed to command Hussey's company during his period of suspension, temporary command falling to the lieutenant. Hussey's case was not heard by the king until after Cutts had returned to London. The lieutenant-colonel appears to have cleared his name and resumed his duties (*HMC, Frankland-Russell-Astley MSS.,* p. 85, Blathwayt to Cutts, 26 March 1695).

77. Letter No. 18.

78. This copy is not included amongst these letters but the holograph has been printed in, *HMC, Frankland-Russell-Astley MSS.,* pp. 83–5, Cutts to William Stewart, 23 March 1695.

of the same, I went in a pinnace from ship to ship to see how matters went, whether the soldiers had room and if all my orders were rightly executed. And I found, upon a strict enquiry, that though I had embarked upon a computation not exceeding my instructions, at a man and a quarter per ton, yet that upon the whole the soldiers in some ships were very much crowded. Upon which I represented the thing to Captain Warren[79] that, if he could, he might ease some of them upon the men-of-war as far as the South Cape.[80] I likewise ordered the removal of some small number of men from some ships to others.

Things being in this posture, I delivered over all to Brigadier Stewart yesterday in the evening and came by Cowes (where I went on shore and gave some necessary orders) and arrived at this place in my yacht at five this morning.

The corporation have been with me and I have told them what I expect from them.[81] Some words passed between Major Holmes[82] and I but I kept within the bounds of prudence and decency though I put some things very hard upon him (relating to a factious and indirect conduct during my absence) of which he could not clear himself. I design not to stir from this place until the election is over. The success is doubtful but it shall be pushed with all the vigour imaginable.[83] I hope the best but if I should fail, by what I know already I doubt not in the least of another election.[84] And, truly, I have good hopes (though not any assurance) of this. At least my exercising vigorously my interest at this time will most certainly facilitate things for the next occasion.

79. See Appendix.

80. Presumably either Cape St Vincent or Cape Trafalgar. Edward Russell's battle-fleet had wintered at Cadiz and the four battalions joined him there in mid-April 1695 (*Shrewsbury Correspondence*, pp. 231, 233).

81. Cutts clearly expected the corporation to support his candidate at the Yarmouth bye-election. Cutts's predecessor as governor, Sir Robert Holmes, had enjoyed the nomination to one of the two parliamentary seats at Yarmouth. See Letter No. 17. (Colby, *Central Government and the Localities*, p. 229).

82. See footnote 48.

83. Cutts was unsuccessful. His failure to have Robert Wolseley elected may have resulted from the preparations for a general election which the whigs had been making since early 1694, even though parliament was not dissolved until 12 October 1695. Cutts's previous references to the electoral intrigues of the Marquis of Winchester and Henry Holmes (see Letter No. 10 and footnote 47), suggest that the whig interest was well advanced at Yarmouth whereas the court was thoroughly unprepared. Sir Robert Holmes had conceded one of the Yarmouth seats to a whig, Fitton Gerard, son of the Earl of Macclesfield, in the election to the Convention. 'The long run-up to the 1695 election distinguished it from that of 1690' (Horwitz, *Parliament, Policy, and Politics*, pp. 156–7; Coleby, *Central Government and the Localities*, p. 229).

84. Clearly, Cutts hoped that he had accumulated enough evidence of corruption and electoral malpractice to unseat Holmes, should he prove successful, upon a petition.

I have not yet informed you that I put two captains of Colonel Lillingstone's late regiment into Colonel Brudenell's. The one in the room of Captain Edwards,[85] who not only refused or at least neglected to clear with his men after I had positively ordered him to do it within such a time, but tied one neck-and-heels and beat several others for complaining, being then on shipboard with his company and imagining (I suppose) that he should not hear any more of me. I advised with Brigadier Stewart and Colonel Gibson and had the concurrence of their opinion before I came to any resolution in this matter. The other was in room of Captain Burke,[86] who is in Ireland and in treaty (as I was informed) to make over his company to another. If his Majesty thinks fit, he may have a company in Ireland, but it was of absolute necessity for the service to take notice of so great a neglect as being absent when his regiment was going upon service. And I am confident the vigorous and ready execution of his Majesty's orders in matters of this nature will have a very good effect in the discipline of the forces.

I shall give you advice before I leave this place. If therefore you have any commands for me by express, I desire you'll send 'em the nearest way to this place, I am,
Sir,

Your most humble and most obedient servant,
Cutts.

Postscript. I have now an account that at three this morning the fleet was seen off St. Catherine's standing into the middle-Channel-way, with a very fair wind, E and by N. I had not a moment's time (from my necessary attendance on the dispatch of his Majesty's service) yesterday which occasions this express now. I send his Majesty here enclosed the abstracts of the regiments of Stewart, Coote, Brudenell, Puizar, and Jacob, with the abstract of Jacobs's regiment, and an abstract of the whole force embarked in one paper;[87] in all seven papers, all of which you'll please to lay before his Majesty.

Postscript. As to the quality of the regiments, his Majesty has lately had an account from me of all but Coote, Rowe, and Jacob, as to which his Majesty sees the numbers: Jacobs's (late Hastings's) is much mended since last year; Coote and Brudenell's are generally pretty good men; but I found great disorder in Brudenell's (late Rowe's)

85. See Appendix.
86. Probably Captain William Burgh (Dalton, iv. 94).
87. This abstract is not included amongst the letters and has not been traced.

in money matters and discipline.[88] Jacobs's should go speedily into quarters of refreshment.

21 [ff. 45–6]

Cutts to Blathwayt, 25 March 1695, Petersfield, Hants

Sir,
I have sent before to have all things ready at Portsmouth and design to embark the regiments of Coote and Puizar tomorrow, that [*i.e. the battalion*] in the Isle of Wight on Monday, and Colonel Stewart's on Tuesday, having sent orders to that regiment [*Stewart's*] to march to Southampton on Monday. Jacobs's regiment shall have orders to be in Portsmouth on Monday night, or Tuesday, and on Wednesday I hope to finish the execution of my orders which cannot well be done sooner considering the business lies in several places.

His Majesty was pleased to order that Major Massam[89] should have the major's place in the Marquis de Rade's regiment and that the commission was signed, but Colonel Collyer[90] insists upon his promise from his Majesty to keep his company so that Massam's commission must be drawn for major of the regiment and captain of the first company that shall become vacant in the same. I desire you to mention it to the king for me and let Mr. Vernon[91] know his Majesty's orders. Massam is so deserving a young man that he will do everybody justice that is concerned for him. You'll be pleased to do this as soon as may be. I am sincerely, Sir,

Your most humble and most obedient servant,
Cutts.

Postscript. Collyer is willing to quit his company as soon as he can change it for a company in Colonel Mordaunt's[92] regiment in Jersey.

88. See above, p. 542, n. 57, and Appendix.
89. Masham. See Appendix.
90. Probably Brigadier-General Sir David Colyear.
91. See Appendix.
92. See Appendix.

22 [*ff. 1–2*]

Cutts to Blathwayt, 30 March 1695, Yarmouth, Isle of Wight

Sir,

I have received yours of the 26th instant wherein you give me an account of a report as malicious and groundless as 'tis false and scandalous.[93] You may assure his Majesty I shall never make such an indiscreet use of my authority as to give any cause for a just reflection upon his service or my own conduct.

Here is at Yarmouth only the usual number of soldiers; viz: a sergeant, a corporal, and sixteen men, which is very much too little for this place by reason that here is an open bay, unguarded, just by us, and several houses which stand so exposed that ten or twenty men out of a privateer may burn the houses and take the people prisoners. I tell you this that you may see I rather underdo than overdo as to the number of soldiers. Besides that, I have something particular to tell you upon this matter which it is not proper to write.

And now, as to the rest of the island. I must renew my application with earnestness that I may have two companies more of Sir John Jacobs's regiment ordered here (whilst they continue so weak) and, that you may the better comprehend the necessity of this, you may please to consider what necessary guards I have (at the lowest computation), viz: at Carisbrooke Castle, every day, a sergeant or corporal and ten men, without which they [*the local inhabitants*] tear the guard-rooms and pull the castle to pieces, and the castle-major, without such a guard at least, cannot be responsible for anything. Now, Sir, to furnish this guard I cannot have less than a company at Newport considering the accidents of sick and deficient men, and Cowes is so very disorderly a place that there cannot be less than a company there; besides that, without it, a privateer may burn the town. Newport Company and Cowes find the detachments for this place [*Yarmouth*]. I desire you to represent this and that two companies

---

93. This was Cutts's indignant rejoinder to Blathwayt's letter of 26 March 1695 (*HMC, Frankland-Russell-Astley MSS.*, p. 85) in which he mentioned a rumour current in London, 'that your Lordship has ordered two companies from Portsmouth to come and quarter at Yarmouth during the election, where none or no such proportion of men used to be at another time. I hope, my Lord, it is quite otherwise, for that it is a constant rule and his Majesty's express pleasure that all soldiers do ever remove from a place where there is to be an election, as it is absolutely necessary in this case, where the least intimation of such quartering would set the House of Commons in a flame, and make void any election your Lordship should countenance.' See above, p. 385, n. 23.

more of Jacobs's regiment be sent here into the island, two of them amounting to the strength of one.

I am sincerely, Sir,
Your most humble and most obedient servant,
Cutts.

23 [ff. 47–8]

Cutts to William Lownds,[94] *secretary to the Treasury, 18 January 1698, Kensington*

Sir,
The bearer, Mrs. Seaton,[95] having lost her husband in his Majesty's service under my command, and not knowing of the provision made by his Majesty for the widows of officers,[96] hopes, by your favour, [*that*] she may be added to the list. I am,

Sir,
Your humble servant,
Cutts.

94. See Appendix.
95. Mrs Seaton was probably the widow of Captain Patrick Seaton of the Royal Fusiliers (Dalton, iv. 75).
96. Only 99 officers' widows were admitted to pensions payable from the annual military establishment in 1697 (Dalton, iii. 403–4; iv. 289–90; Childs, *British Army of William III*, pp. 156–7).

APPENDIX
BIOGRAPHICAL INDEX OF ARMY
OFFICERS MENTIONED IN THE TEXT

BELLASISE, Sir Henry (d. 1717).
Son of Sir Richard Bellasise of Ludworth, Co. Durham. Lieutenant-colonel of Henry Pearson's foot in the British Brigade in Portugal, 1664, but had returned to England by the end of that year; captain of a foot company in Tangier, 1665; entered the Anglo-Dutch Brigade, 1674, and fought at Maastricht, 1676, Mont Cassel, 1677, and at St Dennis, 1678; colonel in the Anglo-Dutch Brigade, 1678–88; returned to England in the spring of 1688; colonel of foot, 28 Sept. 1689; brigadier-general, 1 Apr. 1689; major-general, Apr. 1692; lieutenant-general, 4 Oct. 1694. Bellasise fought at the Boyne, Limerick, Athlone, Aughrim, and Landen. He was second-in-command of the expedition to Cadiz in 1702 where he participated in the looting of Port St. Maria for which crime he was court-martialled and cashiered. Prince George of Hesse-Darmstadt thought Bellasise to be incompetent and that his propensity for looting dated back to his service in Ireland under William III. 'Bellasise was neither loved nor esteemed, and was considered to combine slight capacity with great avarice.' (CSPD 1664–5, pp. 105, 199, 217; Dalton, i. 51; A.D. Francis, The First Peninsula War (London, 1975), pp. 45, 48–50; S.B. Baxter, William III (London, 1966), p. 387; Het Staatsche Leger, 1568–1795 (The Hague, 1911–59), vi. 255).

BEVERIDGE, William (d. 1692).
Colonel of a newly-raised regiment of foot, 28 Feb. 1689; killed in a duel with Dudley Vanburgh, one of his captains, Nov. 1692 (Dalton, iii. 53). Cutts infers that Beveridge was involved in the financial maladministration of his battalion.

BLOOD, Holcroft (d. 1707).
Son of Colonel Thomas Blood who had attempted to steal the crown jewels in 1671. Studied engineering in the French army; captain of pioneers in James II's train of artillery, 1688; fought with the Williamite army in Ireland, 1689–91; captain in John Foulkes's foot, 1692; major, 30 Oct. 1693; chief British engineer at the siege of Namur, 1695; lieutenant-colonel of Sir Mathew Bridges's foot, 7 July 1702; colonel, 25 Aug. 1705; colonel of the train of artillery at Blenheim, 1704; brigadier-general, 1704; commanded the artillery at Ramillies, 1706; died at Brussels, 30 Aug. 1707 (Dalton, iii. 41; Marlborough-Godolphin Correspondence, ed. Henry Snyder (Oxford, 1975), i. 354n.).

BRUDENELL, Thomas (d. 1707).
Eldest son of Richard Brudenell. Lieutenant in the Anglo-Dutch Brigade, 16 June 1685; captain by 1688; came over to England with William of Orange, Nov. 1688; lieutenant-colonel of John Foulkes's foot, 21 Sept. 1689; lieutenant-colonel of Edward Lloyd's fusiliers, 1 Oct. 1692; colonel of a battalion of foot in succession to Henry Rowe (see below), 13 Mar. 1695; colonel of a marine regiment, 1698; colonel of foot regiment, 1701; major-general, 1 June 1706; died at Gibraltar, 1707 (Dalton, ii. 230; Ferguson, Scots Brigade, i. 513; BL, Add. MSS. 41,812, ff. 5–6; ARA, Raad van State 1928, f. 347).

CARDONNEL, Adam de (d. 1719).
A Huguenot refugee. Clerk in the War Office and personal and military secretary to the 1st Duke of Marlborough, 1692–1712 (*DNB*).

COLE, Thomas (d. c. 1725).
A merchant and resident of Liss Parish, Portsmouth; burgess of Portsmouth, 1689 (*VCH, Hampshire and Isle of Wight*, iv. 85; v. 201; R. East, *Extracts from the Records of the Borough of Portsmouth* (Portsmouth, 1891), p. 370).

COLT, Edward Dutton.
Fifth, and youngest son of George Colt of Colt Hall, Cavendish, Suffolk. Captain in Sir Henry Bellasise's foot in the Anglo-Dutch Brigade until Mar. 1688 when he obeyed James II's recall order and returned to England. Captain in John Hales's battalion in England, 13 Mar. 1688; involved in the army conspiracy which promoted the interests of William of Orange in Nov.–Dec. 1688; major of Hales's, 31 Dec. 1688; lieutenant-colonel, 1692; colonel, 1693; colonel of a regiment of marines, 1698 (Dalton, ii. 151, 228; Ferguson, i. 512; Childs, *Nobles and Gentlemen*, p. 19).

COOTE, Richard (d. 1703).
Lieutenant-colonel of Lord Lisburn's foot, 8 Mar. 1689. Coote had probably seen service in either the French and/or the Dutch armies prior to 1689. Colonel after Lisburn's death at the siege of Limerick, 1691; half-pay, 1697; colonel of a newly-raised battalion, 1702; died at Chester in Mar. 1703 (Dalton, iii. 75).

DUDLEY, Joseph.
President of the Council of New England, 1684–9; president of the Council of New York, 1691–4; brevet colonel, 1694; lieutenant-governor of the Isle of Wight, 1694–1701; governor-general of Massachusetts, 1701–15 (S.S. Webb, *The Governors-General* (Chapel Hill, 1979), pp. 101, 492; *HMC, Frankland-Russell-Astley MSS.*, p. 81).

EDWARDS, Charles.
Reinstated as a captain in Brudenell's battalion, 13 Oct. 1695; captain in John Gibson's foot, 10 Mar. 1702; taken prisoner at Almanza, 1707 (Dalton, iv. 94).

ERLE, Thomas (c. 1650–1720).
Second, but first surviving son of Thomas Erle of Charborough, Dorset. Erle was a militia officer for Dorset until 1688 when he entered the regular army at the time of the Glorious Revolution having been involved in the conspiracy to bring over William of Orange. Colonel of foot, 1689–1709; brigadier-general, 1693; governor of Portsmouth, 1694–1712; major-general, 1696; lieutenant-general, 1703; general, 1711 (*HP*, ii. 268–9).

FAIRFAX, Thomas (d. 1710).
Second son of Sir William Fairfax of Steeton, near Keighley, Yorkshire. Captain of the King's Company in the Irish Foot Guards, 1672; brevet major, 1674; captain in the 1st Foot Guards in England, 1 Nov. 1676; captain of the Guard of Battleaxes in Dublin, 1677; captain in Sir Henry Goodricke's foot in England, 20 Feb. 1678; lieutenant-colonel, 1 Sept. 1678; colonel of a regiment of foot in Ireland, 1684–8; lieutenant-colonel of Lord Castleton's foot, 8 Mar. 1689; brevet colonel, 25 Apr. 1689; colonel of foot, 6 Nov. 1694; brigadier-general, 1697; resigned his colonelcy, 1703; major-general and governor of Limerick at the time of his death in 1710 (Charles Dalton, *Irish Army Lists, 1661–1685* (London, 1907), pp. 79, 113; Dalton, iii. 74).

FARRINGTON, Thomas (c. 1664–1712).
Son of Thomas Farrington of Chislehurst, Kent. Married Theodosia Betenson, daughter of Sir Edward Betenson of Scadbury, Kent. Captain in the Coldstream Guards, 31 Dec. 1688; colonel of a newly-raised battalion of foot, 16 Feb. 1694; regiment disbanded, 1698; commissioner of the Stamp Office, 1698; colonel of a newly-raised battalion of foot, 12 Feb. 1702; brigadier-general, 16 Aug. 1703; major-general, 1 June 1706; lieutenant-general by 1710; died, 7 Oct. 1712 (Luttrell, iv. 417; Dalton, iii. 8, 382; iv. 10, 278; v. 16, 17, 97; vi. 10, 384).

FLEMING, Edward (c. 1653–1700).
Of North Stoneham, near Southampton. J.P. for Hampshire, 1680–Apr. 1688, 1690; deputy-lieutenant for Hampshire, 1682–Apr. 1688; sheriff of Hampshire, 1688–9; M.P. for Southampton, 25 Nov.–31 Dec. 1689, but he was unseated after a petition. His title of 'colonel' emanated from the Hampshire militia (*HP*, ii. 333).

GIBSON, Sir John (1637–1717).
Of Alderston, near Edinburgh. Served in the Anglo-Dutch Brigade from 1675 to 1688 coming to England with William of Orange in Nov. 1688 in the rank of captain. Lieutenant-colonel of Sir Robert Peyton's foot, 28 Feb. 1689; lieutenant-governor of Portsmouth, 28 May 1689; colonel of a newly-raised battalion of foot, 1694; commander of the land forces in the expedition to Newfoundland, 1697; M.P. for Portsmouth, 1701–2; knighted, 1705 (*DNB*; Ferguson, *Scots Brigade*, i. 517; Childs, *Nobles and Gentlemen*, p. 36).

GREEN, Nathaniel.
Aide-de-camp to Thomas Talmash (Tollemache) during the attack on Brest, June 1694. Green had previously been a captain in Lord Lovelace's foot in 1689; captain in Luke Lillingstone's regiment for the West Indies, 24 Dec. 1694. Before the Glorious Revolution, Green may have been a quartermaster in the Queen's Horse, June 1685 to Nov. 1688 (*CSPD 1694–5*, pp. 180–4; Dalton, ii. 5, 121; iii. 76; iv. 33).

HASTINGS, Ferdinando.
A cousin of Theophilus Hastings, 7th Earl of Huntingdon. Lieutenant in the 1st Foot Guards, 1681; captain, 1682; wounded at Sedgemoor, 1685; lieutenant-colonel of the Earl of Huntingdon's foot, 21 Apr. 1686; went over to William of Orange at the Glorious Revolution; colonel of Huntingdon's late battalion, Dec. 1688; fought at Killiecrankie, 1689, and at the Boyne, 1690; cashiered for massive financial irregularities, 1695 (Dalton, i. 170, 281, 294, 315; ii. 19, 72, 143; *CSPD 1687–9*, p. 275; Childs, *The Army, James II, and the Glorious Revolution*, pp. 147, 191; Childs, *The British Army of William III*, pp. 49–51).

HOLMES, Henry (d. 1738).
Son of Henry Holmes of Killmallock, Co. Limerick, and a nephew of Sir Robert Holmes, Cutts's predecessor as governor of the Isle of Wight. Henry Holmes married his uncle's illegitimate daughter, Mary, and thus inherited Sir Robert's properties in the island. Captain of Hurst Castle, Isle of Wight, 1683–1714; lieutenant in Princess Anne of Denmark's foot, 1687; captain, 1687; major, 1692; lieutenant-governor of the Isle of Wight, 1710–14 (*The House of Commons, 1715–1754*, ed. Sedgewick, ii. 145–6; Richard Ollard, *Man of War* (London, 1969), p. 197). See Letter No. 20.

HOPE, John.
Ensign in Lord Albemarle's foot, 1673; fought in Tangier, 1673; ensign in the Coldstream Guards, 1674; brevet major of Sir Lionel Walden's foot, 1678; lieutenant in

the Coldstream Guards, 1680; captain-lieutenant, 17 July 1686; involved in the army conspiracy to bring over William of Orange, 1688; major of the Coldstream Guards, 26 Feb. 1695, a rank which carried the brevet of colonel; out of the army by 23 Apr. 1697 (Dalton, i. 137, 174, 216, 275, 286, 317; ii. 21, 82, 114, 130; iv. 68; Childs, *The Army, James II, and the Glorious Revolution*, p. 159).

HUSSEY, Thomas.
Of Honington, Lincs. Ensign in the Earl of Peterborough's foot, 1673; lieutenant in the Duke of York's foot, 1678–9; adjutant of a foot detachment for Tangier, 1680–3; captain-lieutenant in the Royal Dragoons, 1683; captain in the Queen's Dragoons, Aug. 1685; lieutenant-colonel of William Stewart's foot, 1689; fought in Ireland, 1689–91; brevet colonel, 26 Sept. 1703; commanded Stewart's in Spain and Portugal, 1704; serving in Flanders, 1707 (Dalton, i. 157, 223, 230, 273, 301, 314; ii. 10, 11, 127; iii. 108; vi. 365).

JACOB, Sir John, 3rd Bart. (d. 1739).
Of Bromley, Middx. Ensign in the Earl of Huntingdon's foot, 20 June 1685; captain, 24 May 1686; active army conspirator in William of Orange's interest, Nov. 1688; colonel of Huntingdon's late battalion, 13 Mar. 1689; severely wounded at Killiecrankie, 1689; fought in Ireland, 1690–1; sold his colonelcy to his brother-in-law, James, Earl of Barrymore, for 1,400 guineas in 1702 (Dalton, ii. 34, 76, 143; Childs, *The Army, James II, and the Glorious Revolution*, pp. 38, 147, 191).

LEWIS, Richard.
Lieutenant in John Cutts's foot, 1690; captain in Sir Henry Bellasise's foot, 14 Mar. 1695; captain in Nicholas Sankey's foot in the West Indies, 1706 (Dalton, iii. 166; iv. 91).

LILLINGSTONE, Luke (d. 1713).
Of Ferriby, near Hull, East Yorkshire. Son of Henry Lillingstone, a major in the army in Scotland during the 1650s. Lillingstone was first commissioned as an ensign in Lord Mulgrave's foot in England in 1673, but he joined the Anglo-Dutch Brigade in 1674, rising to captain by 1688; came over to England with William of Orange in 1688; fought in Ireland, 1689–91; lieutenant-colonel of John Foulkes's foot, 1 Oct. 1692; served in the West Indies with this battalion, 1692, and at Martinique, 1693; commander of the land forces for the expedition to the West Indies, 1695; regiment disbanded, 1697; half-pay, 1697–1705; awarded an annual pension of £200 by Queen Anne on 9 Mar. 1702 in recognition of his past services; colonel of a newly-raised battalion, 25 Mar. 1705; brigadier-general, 1708; died in Apr. 1713 and was buried in North Ferriby church (Ferguson, *Scots Brigade*, i. 513; Childs, *Nobles and Gentlemen*, p. 53; Dalton, v. 182; vi. 17).

LOWNDES, William (1652–1724).
Joined the Treasury as a clerk in c. 1675; senior clerk, 1690; Secretary to the Treasury, 1695–1724; M.P. for Sleaford, 1695–1715; St Mawes, 1715–22; East Looe, 1722–4 (*The House of Commons, 1715–1754*, ed. Sedgewick, ii. 225–6).

MASHAM, Henry.
Younger son of Sir Francis Masham, 3rd Bart., and a brother of Samuel Masham, created 1st Baron Masham in 1712, who married Queen Anne's bedchamber woman, Abigail Hill, in 1707. Masham probably served in the Anglo-Dutch Brigade before 1688; captain in John Cutts's foot in 1690; wounded at the siege of Limerick, 23 Aug. 1690; major of Luke Lillingstone's foot, 22 Mar. 1694; major of the Marquis de Rade's

foot, 12 Mar. 1695; this commission renewed in 1702 (Dalton, iii. 166, 370; *DNB;* Horwitz, *Parliament, Policy, and Politics,* p. 350).

MORDAUNT, Henry.
Second son of John, 1st Viscount Mordaunt, and brother of Charles Mordaunt, Earl of Monmouth and 3rd Earl of Peterborough. Served as a captain, probably in his brother's battalion of foot, 1689–94; succeeded his brother as colonel, 25 Apr. 1694; colonel of a regiment of marines, 19 Aug. 1698; commander-in-chief in Guernsey, 1697–8; Treasurer of the Ordnance, 1699; colonel of a newly-raised marine regiment, 1702; major-general, 1 Jan. 1706; lieutenant-general, 1 Jan. 1709 (Dalton, iv. 32).

NORTHCOTE, William.
Fifth son of Sir John Northcote, 1st Bart., M.P. for Ashburton, Devon, and Barnstaple (d. 1676). Captain in Sir John Fenwick's foot, 24 Mar. 1678; major, 1 Jan. 1679; retired to civilian life, resident in Devon, 1679–88; joined William of Orange, Nov. 1688; lieutenant-colonel of Francis Luttrell's foot, 28 Feb. 1689; colonel of a newly-raised regiment of foot, 16 Feb. 1694; retired from the army when his battalion was disbanded in 1697 (*HP,* iii. 156–8; Dalton, i. 231, 257; iii. 63, 384).

PUIZAR, Louis James le Vasseur, Marquis de (d. 1701).
Son of the Marquis de Thouars, a French Huguenot refugee. Succeeded Samuel Venner (see Appendix) as colonel of foot, 13 Mar. 1695. By 1697, Puizar had translated his regiment into a largely Huguenot corps, and he was a beneficiary of the confiscated Jacobite lands in Ireland in 1698 (Dalton, iv. 93; C.E. Lart, 'The Huguenot Regiments', *Proceedings of the Huguenot Society of London,* ix. (1911), p. 479; J.G. Simms, *The Williamite Confiscation in Ireland, 1690–1703* (London, 1956), pp. 88, 97).

RADE, Henri de Caumont, Marquis de (d. 1695).
Son of the Marquis de Montpouillan. Rade was a Huguenot who first sought asylum in the United Netherlands, entering the Anglo-Dutch Brigade as a captain in early 1688; came over to England with William of Orange in Nov. 1688; lieutenant-colonel of John Cutts's foot, 1689; colonel of foot, 1 Feb. 1694; died at Bruges from wounds received in a duel with Colonel Bevil Grenville, summer 1695. Rade seems to have been a somewhat abrasive character (Ferguson, *Scots Brigade,* i. 513; Luttrell, iii. 491; Dalton, ii. 230; Childs, *The Army, James II, and the Glorious Revolution,* p. 134).

REVETT, Edmund (d. 1709).
Ensign in Lord Cutts's foot, 1 Apr. 1692; captain-lieutenant, 1 Aug. 1692; captain, 28 June 1693; captain in the Coldstream Guards, 1 Jan. 1696, a promotion earned by his valour at the siege of Namur in 1695; commission renewed, 1702; distinguished himself at the siege of Gibraltar, 1705; killed at Malplaquet, 1709. In 1697, Revett married the daughter and heiress of Serjeant-at-Law John Thurbane by his second wife Anne Cutts, the sister of Lord Cutts. Revett's death plunged his wife and family into parlous circumstances but Queen Anne awarded them a pension of £200 p.a. (*HMC, Frankland-Russell-Astley MSS.,* pp. xix–xx; A.D. Francis, *The First Peninsula War* (London, 1975), pp. 139, 143, 146; Dalton, iii. 249).

ROWE, Henry.
Captain of a company in the Tangier garrison, 1680–3; captain in the Queen's foot, 1684; lieutenant-colonel, 1689, and described as 'a pretty good officer' during the general inspection of the Dundalk camp; colonel of a battalion of foot, 5 Feb. 1692; cashiered for the financial mismanagement of his regiment, 13 Mar. 1695 (Dalton, i. 272, 302; ii. 25, 132; iii. 7, 107, 242, 274; *CSPD 1695,* p. 316; Luttrell, iii. 450–1).

STEWART, William (d. 1726).
Major of Sir Walter Vane's foot, 13 June 1667; captain in Sir Charles Wheeler's foot, 16 Feb. 1678; major, 17 Oct. 1678; captain in the 1st Foot Guards, 16 Dec. 1685; colonel of a newly-raised battalion of foot, 1 May 1689; brigadier-general by 1694; major-general, 1 June 1696; lieutenant-general, 11 Feb. 1703; general, 31 Jan. 1711; commander-in-chief in Ireland, 4 Feb. 1712. At some time during the War of the Grand Alliance, Stewart was severely wounded in the hand and effectively disabled in that limb (Dalton, i. 83, 211, 246; ii. 63, 114, 129; Luttrell, iv. 721).

TALMASH (TOLLEMACHE), Thomas (1651–94).
Second son of Elizabeth Murray, Countess of Dysart and Duchess of Lauderdale, and her first husband, Sir Lionel Tollemache. Purchased a captaincy in the Coldstream Guards, 1678; lieutenant-colonel of the Royal Fusiliers, 1685–6; resigned his commission in protest at the retention of catholic officers in the army; joined the Anglo-Dutch Brigade as a captain, 1686; came over to England with William of Orange, Nov. 1688; colonel of the Coldstream Guards, May 1689; governor of Portsmouth, 1689; major-general, 1690; lieutenant-general, 1693; fought at Aughrim, Steenkirk, and Landen; commander-in-chief of the expedition to attack Brest, June 1694; mortally wounded, 8 June 1694, and died in Plymouth, 12 June 1694 (*DNB; HP*, iii. 576; E.D.H. Tollemache, *The Tollemaches of Helmingham and Ham* (Ipswich, 1949), pp. 74–5; Childs, *Nobles and Gentlemen*, p. 90; Childs, *British Army of William III*, pp. 222–37).

VAUGHAN, Perkins.
Captain in William Stewart's foot, 1694; had served at the sieges of Athlone and Limerick; captured during the attack on Brest, June 1694, but was exchanged soon afterwards; transferred into Richard Coote's foot, 30 Apr. 1696; half-pay, 1698; captain in Richard Ingoldsby's foot, 31 May 1701 (Dalton, iii. 399).

VENNER, Samuel.
Possibly a son, or close relative, of Samuel Venner, the Fifth Monarchist who led an unsuccessful rising in London in 1661. Venner probably fought in the Anglo-Dutch Brigade or the Dutch army until 1685 when he joined Monmouth's expedition to England and was wounded at Bridport. He subsequently escaped from England and returned to the United Provinces. After the Glorious Revolution, Venner was commissioned lieutenant-colonel of Daniel Dering's foot, 1 Jan. 1690; colonel, 1691; cashiered on 13 Mar. 1695 for the financial maladministration of his battalion (C.T. Atkinson, *The South Wales Borderers, 24th Foot, 1689–1937* (Cambridge, 1937), p. 13; Childs, *Nobles and Gentlemen*, p. 95).

VERNON, James (1646–1727).
Principal secretary of state, 1698–1702 (*DNB; Officials of the Secretaries of State, 1660–1782*, ed. J.C. Sainty (London, 1973), pp. 24, 28).

WARREN, Thomas (d. 1699).
Commander of a fireship, 28 May 1689; captain of the *Grafton*, 1693; captain of the *Windsor*, 1695; commodore of a squadron based on Cadiz in 1697 from whence he was sent to Madagascar in pursuit of pirates; died off Madagascar, 1699 (John Charnock, *Biographia Navalis* (London, 1795), ii. 290).

WILMOT, Robert (d. 1695).
Commander of the *Hopewell* fireship, 19 Aug. 1690; captain of the *Wolfe*, 1692; captain of the *Elizabeth*, 1693; commodore of the expedition to the West Indies, 1695; died off Jamaica, 1695 (John Charnock, *Biographia Navalis*, ii. 375–8).

WINCHESTER, Charles Powlett, Marquis of (1661–1722).
Also styled, Earl of Wiltshire (1675–89); Marquis of Winchester (1689–99); 2nd Duke of Bolton (1699–1722). Winchester was a court whig who had been with William of Orange in the United Provinces prior to 1688 and had returned to England with William's invasion force; M.P. for Southampton, 1681, 1685, 1689–98 (*HP*, iii. 279–80).

WOLSELEY, Robert (c. 1659–1697).
First son of Sir Charles Wolseley, 2nd Bt., the Cromwellian politician. Matriculated from Trinity College, Oxford, 27 July 1666, at the age of seventeen; attended Gray's Inn, 1667; British envoy to Brussels, 1692–6 (Joseph Foster, *Alumni Oxonienses* (Oxford, 1891), iv. 1668; D.B. Horn, *British Diplomatic Representatives, 1689–1789* (London, Camden Society, 1932), p. 6).

VII

GEORGE III AND THE SOUTHERN DEPARTMENT: SOME UNPRINTED ROYAL CORRESPONDENCE

Edited by Ian R. Christie

INTRODUCTION

The following fragment of George III's correspondence once formed part of the archive of Sir Stanier Porten, who served as an under-secretary of state between 1768 and 1782. His papers eventually passed into the possession of the family of Onslow of Ripley Court, Surrey, and were drawn to my attention by a member of that family, Miss Juliana Onslow, later Mackintosh, then a student at University College London. The exact details of how these papers were transmitted to her father, Mr Guy Clevland Onslow, seem to have been lost; but the salient circumstances appear to be, that the Revd. Stanier James Porten, son of the under-secretary, who was rector of Charlwood, Surrey, 1850–1854, was succeeded in that preferment by his son-in-law, the Revd Thomas Burningham, who held it from 1855 till his death in 1883. Burningham was Mr Onslow's maternal grandfather. Of the thirty-five letters of the king in this collection six were addressed to Porten, two to Lord Weymouth, and the remaining twenty-seven to the last of the secretaries of state under whom Porten served, the first Earl of Hillsborough, who was in charge of the southern department from November 1779 till the fall of the North administration in March 1782.[1]

Porten, the son of a London merchant, seems to have begun his career as a merchant trading with southern Europe and thence drifted into the diplomatic service in the capacity of consul, first at Naples during the 1750s and then at Madrid between 1760 and 1766. In July 1766 he was appointed secretary of embassy at Paris to assist the British ambassador extraordinary, the 4th Earl of Rochford, and established a cordial personal connection with him. In July 1768, after Rochford's embassy had come to an end, Porten appears to have been recommended by him to William Petty, 2nd Earl of Shelburne, who was then reorganizing the staff of the southern department and appointed him to the post of under-secretary.

In October 1768 Shelburne resigned and a rearrangement of the secretaryships took place. Rochford was appointed northern secretary and immediately picked Porten as one of his two under-secretaries. Two years later Porten moved with Rochford to the southern department. He remained there after Rochford's retirement in 1775, con-

---

1. I gratefully acknowledge the gracious permission of Her Majesty the Queen to publish the following letters of George III in a private archive, of which she possesses the copyright. I also record my grateful acknowledgement for permission given to make use of and publish these letters, in the first place by the late Mr. G. C. Onslow of Ripley Court, and in the second by his son-in-law, Mr. A. S. Mackintosh. Mr. Onslow's descent from Burningham is recorded in Burke's *Landed Gentry*, and Burningham's marriage to Porten's only daughter in *Gentleman's Magazine*, 1835, ii, 646.

tinuing to serve successively Thomas Thynne, 3rd Viscount Weymouth until his resignation in 1779, and then Wills Hill, first Earl of Hillsborough. When the ministerial changes of 1782 took place the new secretaries of state wished to have their own friends and connections in the under-secretaryships, and there was no room for Porten, for whom provision was made with a commissionership of customs, an office which he held till 1786. An administrator, not a politician, by nature, Porten played the role of man of business in the southern department, and clearly became an efficient and respected government servant. He was honoured with a knighthood in 1772, and in 1774 received the appointment of keeper of state papers – 'one of the only means which the secretaries of state have of rewarding officers for diligence and long service' – a post which he held till his death on 7 June 1789.[2]

Diverse widely unrelated matters of varying degrees of interest are dealt with in these letters. Most material is the correspondence with Hillsborough which – in the Irish context – provides substantial illustration of the close supervision which the king exercised over military affairs.[3] On one or two points these letters materially supplement the royal correspondence printed in the edition by Sir John Fortescue,[4] notably in respect of the attempt to solve the manpower crisis facing the army in the early weeks of 1781. On 8 January the cabinet recommended (and the king agreed) that 8,000 men should be recruited in Ireland, to be placed on the English establishment,[5] and an initial scheme was launched for raising forty independent companies.[6] On 10 February, on hearing a complaint by the commander-in-chief, Lord Amherst, that there were insufficient troops 'for those services that are indispensably necessary', the cabinet recommended the further step of raising in Ireland six regiments for the British establishment.[7] This proposal, accepted by the king, provoked a minor crisis in the administration. Hillsborough, in whose department Irish affairs lay, had not been present at this cabinet meeting, and his disapproval of the scheme was echoed both by Amherst and, more materially, by the man who, under the king, was the king-pin of military administration, Charles Jenkinson, the secretary-at-war. In the end the proposal for the six regiments was shelved;[8] and

---

2. See: *Dictionary of National Biography*; *British Diplomatic Representatives 1689–1789*, ed. D. B. Horn, Royal Historical Society, Camden, 3rd series, XLVI (1932), p.23; J. C. Sainty, *Officials of the Secretaries of State, 1660–1782* (1973), pp.10n., 49, 96.

3. See for example John Brooke, *King George III* (1972), pp.180–2.

4. *The Correspondence of King George III*, ed. by Sir John Fortescue (6 vols., 1927–8).

5. Fortescue, *Correspondence*, V, no. 3236.

6. Letters 20, 21, below.

7. Fortescue, *Correspondence*, V, no. 3266.

8. *Ibid.*, nos. 3292, 3293, 3294, 3297; letters 24, 25 below.

when it was resuscitated in modified form in the autumn, it was recommended by the king that one regiment only should be raised as an experiment.[9] Apart from the additional light thrown on this episode, in which the king seems to have played a significant part in smoothing ruffled ministerial feelings, the correspondence with Hillsborough makes very clear the assiduity with which the king watched over the touchy problem of military promotions and sought to ensure strict adherence to the rules of seniority and purchase.

9. Letter 33 below.

CORRESPONDENCE

I

This letter and the one following allude to a piece of vandalism recorded by the Gentleman's Magazine, June 1771 (p. 284), in its 'Historical Chronicle', under 21 June: 'In the night some villains got into the garden of her Royal Highness the Princess Dowager of Wales at Kew, and destroyed all the green-house plants, which were deemed a very curious collection'. The precautions mentioned in the second paragraph of the first letter were taken because the annual election of the Sheriffs of London and Middlesex was to take place later in the day.

STANIER PORTEN TO GEORGE III

COPY.

Porten presumes to throw himself most humbly at Your Majesty's feet, and to acquaint Your Majesty, that he has been with Sir John Fielding,[10] who is deeply afflicted and affected at what has happened in Her Royal Highness's garden at Kew. As Sir John thinks his presence may be necessary at London this day, he proposes, with His Majesty's permission, to be at Kew between 6 and 7 tomorrow morning, and humbly requests that a gardiner may be ordered to meet him, that he may receive the fullest information, in order afterwards to exert his diligence and activity towards making some discovery.

Sir John has prepared his plan of arrangement, to secure as much as may be possible the public tranquillity, in case there should be a beginning of disturbance this evening. He has recommended to all the justices to be vigilant, and proposes to place a strong body of constables and peace officers between Temple Bar and Southampton Street, and some others to keep in private near Downing Street, and other parts of the town the most likely to be exposed to disturbances. 24 June 1771.

Endorsed: Copy of a note to the King, 24 June 1771.

10. The London magistrate, Sir John Fielding (d. 1780).

2

GEORGE III TO STANIER PORTEN

Queen's House, June 24th, 1771
8 m. pt. 3 P.M.

Mr. Porten punctually meets with my thorough approbation. Sir John
Fielding proposes being at Kew tomorrow morning between six and
seven. I desire he will call on the Green at Haverfield,[11] the Head
Gardiner's house, who as well as his son will be ready to attend him.

3

*For the letters exchanged between the king and Lord North on the subject referred
to in the following letter, see Fortescue, Correspondence, II, nos. 994 and 995.
The king clearly dashed off this note as an afterthought when he had written his
letter to Lord North, for it bears the same time of origin. Porten's papers include
a rough draft of the memorandum which Porten forwarded to the king on the
following day, informing him that there was no fort corresponding with that
mentioned by d'Aiguillon. Porten's first acknowledgement of the king's note is
printed in Fortescue (no. 996), as is also the memorandum, but with no
identification of the sender (no. 997).*

GEORGE III TO STANIER PORTEN

Queen's House, Decr. 29th., 1771
8 m. pt. 9 P.M.

Mr. Porten, I have no idea what the Duke d'Aiguillon[12] alludes to by
talking of a fort erected on the River St. Johns, if it occurs to you, I
wish you would send me an explanation.

4

GEORGE III TO SIR STANIER PORTEN

Sir Stanier Porten, I have given the maturest deliberation to the
papers transmitted by the Lord Lieutenant of Ireland[13] concerning

11. John Haverfield (c.1694–1784) died at Kew aged 90, 21 Nov. 1784 (*Gentleman's
Magazine*, 1784, ii, 799).
12. Armand Vignerot-Duplessis Richelieu, duc d'Aiguillon (1720–1780), French
secretary of state for foreign affairs.
13. Simon Harcourt, Earl Harcourt (1714–1777), was Lord Lieutenant of Ireland
October 1772–January 1777.

the court martial on Lieutenant Broom of the 5th Regiment of Dragoons, and see the conduct of those who composed that court in so very irregular a light, that I think it right to direct these papers to be sent to the Judge Advocate[14] for his opinion, which is losing no time, for he can certainly return them before Lord Rochford's return, and this report will perhaps prevent similar irregularities.

Queen's House.

Oct. 14th. 1773, 25 m. pt. 8 A.M.

5

SIR STANIER PORTEN TO GEORGE III

Draft

Your Majesty having been pleased to authorise the appointment of Lieut. Nicholas Parker to be captain in the 27th Regiment of Foot, Sir Stanier Porten most humbly submits to Your Majesty a commission for Sergeant David Wilson to be Quarter-Master in the said regiment, he being recommended by the Lord Lieutenant in his letter of the 23rd. of August to succeed Lieut. Parker in that office on the latter being appointed a captain, and if Your Majesty is pleased to return the commission with your royal signature for Sergeant David Wilson to be Quarter-Master, notice of the appointment will be given by this night's post to Sir John Blaquiere[15] for the Lord Lieutenant's information.

St. James's, 12 Sept. 1775.

50 m. past 3 P.M.

6

GEORGE III TO SIR STANIER PORTEN

Sir Stanier Porten's diligence has been very commendable in forwarding copies of the draughts to Ireland that the absence of Lord Rochford might not occasion any delay; I have signed the commission for Sergeant Wilson as Quarter-Master of the 27th Regiment.

Kew, Sept. 12th. 1775.

11 m. pt. 5 P.M.

14. Charles Gould (1726–1806), judge-advocate general 1769–1806, knighted 1779.
15. Sir John Blaquiere (1732–1812), chief secretary to Harcourt in Ireland 1772–7.

7

GEORGE III TO SIR STANIER PORTEN

Sir Stanier Porten has conducted with his usual accurateness the contents of Lord Stormont's[16] letter; it is rather mortifying that no intelligence is ever received from abroad till too late to be of the smallest utility. The mode of getting the despatches as proposed by Lord Stormont seems quite impracticable, and I understand from Lord Suffolk[17] that it appears in that light to the Admiral.

56 m. pt. 4 P.M. Queen's House, Oct. 11th. 1777.

8

On 13 March 1778 the French ambassador delivered to Lord Weymouth a written statement to the effect that France had signed a treaty of commerce and amity with the United States of America, in which their status as an independent power was recognized. Weymouth forwarded this to the king immediately. Late that same night he sent the king the recommendation of the cabinet that the British ambassador, Lord Stormont, should be withdrawn from Paris forthwith. This reply of the king to the first of Weymouth's letters gives evidence of the immediate adverse effect upon British military strength in America resulting from the imminent outbreak of hostilities with France.[18]

GEORGE III TO LORD WEYMOUTH

It has been ever understood that the court of France had resolved to leave the declaration of war to us; but I think the strange paper delivered this day by the French ambassador to Lord Weymouth is a manifest declaration of war. He has done perfectly right in summoning the cabinet this evening. The Manchester Regiment must be ordered to Gibraltar instead of St. Augustin, and I have just sent to Lord Barrington[19] that 800 men may be drafted from the additional com-

16. David Murray, 7th Viscount Stormont (1727–96), later 2nd Earl of Mansfield, British ambassador at Paris 1772–8, later secretary of state, northern department Oct. 1779–March 1782.

17. Henry Howard, 12th Earl of Suffolk (1739–79), secretary of state, northern department, 12 June 1771 till his death on 7 Mar. 1779.

18. *Annual Register*, 1778, pp.159–160; Fortescue, *Correspondence*, IV, no. 2907 (undated and misplaced by the editor), and no. 2216.

19. William Wildman Barrington, 2nd Viscount Barrington (1717–93), M.P., secretary-at-war 1765–1778.

panies of the regiments in North America to complete the augmentations of the regiments at Gibraltar. Transport must instantly be prepared for carrying them to that garrison and Col. Greene the chief engineer ordered to propose such of the engineers now at home fit to be employed there.

Queen's House.
March 13 1778, 40 m. pt. 5 P.M.

9

Major General Hector Munro (1726–1805), commander in chief of the East India Company forces at Madras, captured Pondicherry from the French in October 1778, but the news did not reach London till mid-March 1779. George III mentioned his instructions to Weymouth in a letter to North written immediately afterwards and dated sixteen minutes later.[20]

GEORGE III TO LORD WEYMOUTH

Queen's House, March 22nd. 1779
46 m. pt. 5 P.M.

I omitted mentioning this day to Lord Weymouth the propriety of sending an answer to the Nabob of Arcot's letter of congratulation on the taking of Pondicherry; the order for destroying those fortifications gives an opportunity of conveying it.

10

GEORGE III TO LORD HILLSBOROUGH

Queen's House, Dec. 13th. 1779.
25 m. pt. 7 P.M.

The application made by Commissioner Scott[21] of the Excise in favour of an inferior officer of that branch of the Revenue, that the sentence of whipping to be inflicted tomorrow may be respited for a few days, is certainly sufficient grounds for my interposition. Lord Hillsborough will therefore direct the proper steps to be taken for postponing it for a week which is ample time to sift the business to the bottom.

20. Fortescue, *Correspondence*, IV, nos. 2545, 2585.
21. George Lewis Scott (1708–1780), formerly sub-preceptor to the young George III during his 'teens; a commissioner of excise 1758–80.

II

On 12 June 1780 the inhabitants of Southwark voted an address of thanks to the king for his 'seasonable interposition, by sending a military force to their relief', during the height of the Gordon Riots.[22] Arrangements for the presentation of the address were made through Lord Hillsborough.

GEORGE III TO LORD HILLSBOROUGH

For many reasons I think it much better that the Address of the magistrates, gentlemen, and inhabitants of the Borough of Southwark be delivered by Mr. George Onslow[23] and Mr. Polhill[24] to Lord Hillsborough to present it to me, that in the first place will avoid assembling a crowd, and will enable its being inserted in this night's Gazette.

Queen's House, June 10th 1780.
    44 m. pt. 5 P.M.

12

On the 13th Hillsborough wrote informing the king that 'the inhabitants of the Borough have been with difficulty prevented from bringing up the Address',[25] which elicited the following reply.

GEORGE III TO LORD HILLSBOROUGH

It is by no means either advisable or proper at this hour that persons should be encouraged to bring Addresses attended with numbers, it is the number that sign them only that may make them respectable; if the inhabitants of Southwark persist contrary to their first assertion in desiring to bring themselves their Address; I trust not more than three or four persons will be deputed to bring it; this hint will direct Lord Hillsborough on all applications of that kind.

Queen's House, June 13th 1780.
    56 m. pt. 11 A.M.

22. *Gentleman's Magazine*, 1780, p. 295.
23. George Onslow (1731–92), M.P. for Guildford, 1760–84.
24. Nathaniel Polhill (1723–82), M.P. for Southwark, 1774–82.
25. Fortescue, *Correspondence*, V, no. 3070.

13

The following letter replied to one from Lord Hillsborough of the same date, forwarding an application from the Chairman of the East India Company.[26]

GEORGE III TO LORD HILLSBOROUGH

Lord Hillsborough will agreeable to the representation of the Court of Directors of the East India Company signify in the proper form my disallowance of the regulations for the better management of the Town of Calcutta; but at the same time he ought to mention to the Chairman that in future it is expected that more expedition will be used in transmitting any matters that are to be laid from the said Company before me.

Kew, July 3rd. 1780.
25 m. pt. 5 P.M.

14

The occasion of this letter was the birth of Prince Albert, the king's ninth son, who died in infancy, 20 August 1782. Porten's papers include a copy of his reply which is printed from the original by Fortescue (Correspondence, V, no. 3143).

GEORGE III TO SIR STANIER PORTEN

Sir Stanier Porten will order the guns in St. James's Park as well as those of the Tower to be fired on account of the Queen's safe delivery at two minutes past ten of a ninth son. The Queen and child are as well as can be expected. Sir Stanier will give notice that one of the Messengers in Waiting on me shall be here by nine tomorrow morning to carry to Town the account how the Queen has passed the night.

Windsor Castle, Sept. 22nd. 1780.
50 m. pt. 10 A.M.

P.S. The Queen's Page of the Presence will every evening bring to Sir Stanier Porten the list of the enquiries which he will direct the messenger that is to come in the morning the night before to come and receive from him.

26. *Ibid.*, no. 3097.

All the remaining letters in this series were written by George III to Lord Hillsborough.

15

The report of the Commissioners of the Public Accounts was presented to the House of Commons on Monday, November 27th, 1780, and is printed in extenso in the Commons Journals. Sir Guy Carleton was First Commissioner. The king attended Parliament on the 27th, to give the royal assent to a number of Bills.[27]

Windsor Castle, Nov. 25th. 1780.
40 m. pt. 6 P.M.

Lord Hillsborough will acquaint Sir Guy Carleton that I approve of his delivering to me after the levee on Monday previous to my going to Parliament the report of the Commissioners of Accounts, which will enable him to deliver a duplicate that day to the House of Commons.

I always thought the conduct of Sir Henry Cavendish[28] bore strong marks of a flighty imagination, which appears but too well confirmed by his strange letter to the Lord Lieutenant of Ireland; the looking on the non-performance of personal expectations from a man in a representative situation, or in an executive one, [as actionable] is quite unheard of, and Lord Buckinghamshire[29] would be very reprehensible if he could ever admit this as a matter of *personal* litigation.

16

By a letter dated 6.30 A.M., 8 January 1781, Lord Hillsborough, at that moment in conference on the business with Lord Sandwich, the head of the admiralty, and Lord Amherst, the commander-in-chief, forwarded news to the king about a French attack on Jersey: the king's reply follows. Lord Sandwich's proposals for dealing with the situation, to which the king refers, were outlined in a letter written and sent at the same time as Hillsborough's and were confirmed in a cabinet minute dated one hour later that morning.[30] Jeffrey, Lord Amherst (1717–97), commander-in-chief in Britain, 1778–1782, held the post of Governor of Guernsey, 1770–97.

27. *Commons Journals*, XXXVIII, pp. 74–85.

28. Sir Henry Cavendish (1732–1804), at various times a member of both the British and the Irish parliaments.

29. John Hobart, 2nd Earl of Buckinghamshire, Lord Lieutenant of Ireland January 1777–November 1780. The interpolation of the words in square brackets in place of some inadvertent omission on the king's part appears necessary to establish the sense of the passage.

30. Fortescue, *Correspondence*, V, nos. 3234, 3235, and no. 2982 misplaced and misdated by the editor.

Windsor Castle, January 8th, 1781.
20 m. pt. 4 P.M.

I cannot quite agree with Lord Amherst's opinion that the Island of Jersey is not in the possession of the enemy; the Lieutenant Governor of Guernsey[31] is too cautious a man to have expressed himself so strongly if not certain of the intelligence; the proposal Lord Sandwich has sent me seems to be the readiest means of sending succour.

17

Reassuring news of the French repulse at Jersey arrived the next day, but Lord Hillsborough's letter conveying it does not seem to have been preserved among the king's papers.

Windsor Castle, 9th January 1781.
32 m. pt. 4 P.M.

Lord Hillsborough's account from Guernsey of the defeat of the enterprise against Jersey has given me much pleasure; I desire he will communicate to Lord Amherst the strange neglect in the posts being so ill attended so that the enemy passed them unobserved; if the Islands require so large a military force as has been stationed there during the war, it is highly expedient that a diligent officer should have the command of the troops, and that officers should not be absent; the whole command fell to a major of a young regiment. Had the island been conquered I fear with reason great blame would have been thrown on the neglect in letting so many officers be absent.[32]

18

Windsor Castle, 20th January 1781.
Eight o'clock P.M.

Lord Hillsborough has done perfectly right in sending a second commission colonel Reid being an older colonel that [*sic*] Colonel Scott, on this occasion seniority should decide.

---

31. Lieut. Colonel Paulus Æmilius Irving (d. 1796).

32. On the unused inner page is a draft of Hillsborough's letter to Amherst, dated 10 January 1781; the phrasing very closely follows that of the king's letter.

19

Queen's House, February 6th. 1781.
3 m. pt. 7 P.M.

The proceedings of a general court martial held on Lieut. Gregor Farquarson of the 81st Regiment of Foot accompanied by a letter of the 29th December, from Lieut. General Cunninghame, which the Lord Lieutenant[33] of Ireland enclosed in his letter of the 30th December are not of a nature that the communication of them was necessary, for the officer is acquitted by the court of the charge laid against him, therefore it can[not] be proper for the Crown either to dismiss or suspend him; in consequence of this court martial it would have been highly proper for the General Officer commanding the troops in Ireland[34] to have sent an order to the colonel or commanding officer of the 81st Regiment that he should support his authority and inforce due obedience to military discipline through the corps, and that if any neglect shall appear in the corps it will be reported to the Lord Lieutenant, that it may be laid before the King; it will be proper to apprize the Lord Lieutenant of this and to direct him to acquaint Lieut. General Cunninghame that he must issue an order to the colonel or commanding officer of the 81st for that purpose.

As to the application in the Lord Lieutenant's letter of the 10th. past in favour of Captain Bowyer of the 66th Regiment of Foot, who is Deputy Adjutant General of the Army in Ireland that he may be promoted to the rank of major, the request may be granted, a commission therefore for that purpose must be prepared.

As to the Lord Lieutenant's letter of the 20th past on the sentence of a court martial on Lieut. Robinson of the Royal Irish Regiment of Artillery, who is declared guilty of having embezelled a very considerable quantity of gunpowder, which with other artillery stores had been in his charge, and for such offence dismissed the service; it would be highly improper to mitigate any part of the sentence on so glaring an occasion; and whatever favour the Lord Lieutenant may wish to shew to Capt. Robinson as a meritorious officer, must be unconnected with his son the above lieutenant who is certainly undeserving of any attention.

As the letter from the Lord Lieutenant of Ireland of the 22nd past contains several questions relative to the raising the proposed independent companies, it has been communicated to Lord Amherst, whose report is a full answer to them. I therefore enclose it that the answer to the letter may be prepared agreeable to the said report.

33. Frederick Howard, 5th Earl of Carlisle (1748–1825), Lord Lieutenant of Ireland, November 1780–April 1782.
34. Sir John Irwin (c.1728–1788) was commander-in-chief in Ireland, 1775–82.

20

The Lord Lieutenant of Ireland's letter of the 4th. encloses a list of lieutenants willing to raise companies in that kingdom, and a memorial from Captain Thomas Hangerford Townshend of the Battle Axe Guards, the questions relative to the independent companies to be raised have been answered by the directions Lord Hillsborough sent a few days ago by my authority to Ireland, except with regard to the lieutenants of two years standing who have not served as ensigns; such lieutenants are eligible to raise companies, but such as have served as ensigns ought to have the preference if they offer; Captain Townshend is not eligible to raise a company.

The letter of the 31st. of last month encloses a memorial of the principal officers of Ordnance in Ireland in favour of Captain Thomas Jarratt of the Corps of engineers in that Kingdom for the rank of major in the army by brevet, he being a captain of the 22nd. of May 1766.

A commission may be prepared for that purpose but to be dated on the 10th. of November not the 17th. as proposed in the memorial.

Queen's House, February 12th. 1781.

30 m. pt. 3 P.M.

21

Queen's House 18 March 1781.

35 m. pt. 10 A.M.

The forty companies under orders to be raised in Ireland, and of which the Lord Lieutenant has recommended the captains, who have been approved of, now seem to have had sufficient time that it may be now proper to acquaint him with the intention of raising six regiments in Ireland for foreign service; the persons proposed as colonels are Lieut. General Cunninghame whose brother Major General Cunninghame will succeed him in the command of the 14th Regiment of Foot, the Earl of Ross, Colonel Rowley of the late 123rd Foot, Stuart Douglas of the late 108th., Sir John Burgoyne of the 14th Dragoons,[35] and Colonel Maunsell who directs the recruiting service of the regiments abroad in Ireland; the same terms as to the commencement of pay and dates of commissions will be allowed for these regiments as were to the late new-raised regiments in England; the men must be sent to England for inspection before the said regiments can be established.

35. Burgoyne's offer to raise a regiment was shortly afterwards withdrawn (Fortescue, *Correspondence*, V, nos. 3289, 3290).

22

Queen's House 18 March 1781
35 m. pt. 10 A.M.

The Lord Lieutenant of Ireland's letter of the 6th of February encloses several papers respecting the two Guard Ships Britannia and Hibernia which have been fitted as floating batteries for the defence of Dublin Harbour; the representations from Ireland in favour of a cutter carrying from 12 to 18 guns instead of the above batteries seems favourable but it seems best to refer the matter to the Admiralty that a proper decision may be formed.

His letter of the 8th February regarding a proclamation of pardon to such deserters in Ireland as may inlist with any of the officers of the additional companies recruiting there and who are belonging to regiments *serving abroad*; these words have been omitted in the proclamation, they seem essential the proclamation ought to be reprinted and these words added.

In a letter of the same date a further list of lieutenants are proposed for companies; the number now are limited to forty and what exceed that number must provided they are agreeable to the regulations already known to the Lord Lieutenant raise companies for the six regiments now ordered to be raised.

The list of successions in the Lord Lieutenant's letter of the 5th. of February is agreeable to rule the commissions therefore to be prepared agreeable to it.

23

The news contained in the captured French papers referred to in the following letter was in fact correct. In July 1780, Hyder Ali of Mysore had commenced an invasion of the Carnatic, and a detachment of the East India Company's forces under Colonel Baillie was destroyed at Polilur.[36]

Windsor Castle, March 27th. 1781.
15 m. pt. 7 A.M.

The Gazette of the Isle of France which Lord Hillsborough has communicated to me gives an unfavourable account of affairs on the Coromandel Coast; but I own I cannot see why the giving the Ministers notice of it would not as well have been done without giving them the trouble to assemble on the occasion, for no resolution be be formed in consequence of this as yet vague intelligence, indeed if it

36. *Cambridge History of India*, vol. V, p. 283.

was more authenticated, I do not see what could be done from hence, we certainly have neither troops nor ships that can in the present situation be taken either from hence, North America, or the West Indies, and in general a meeting when nothing can be proposed is not a desirable step.

24

This letter and the one following concern the protest of Charles Jenkinson, the secretary-at-war, against the plan for raising six new regiments in Ireland. Jenkinson had a conversation with the king on this matter on 28 March, and later in the day the king wrote to inform the Prime Minister, Lord North, that Jenkinson had put forward 'many very solid reasons' against forming the six regiments; and he desired that North, Hillsborough, and Amherst, the commander-in-chief, should consult Jenkinson on the subject.[37] The next morning he conveyed the same wish to Hillsborough in the following letter.

I wish Lord Hillsborough would see Mr. Jenkinson who I own deserves that civility from the Cabinet that his opinion ought to be asked on augmentations of which as he brings the estimates into Parliament he is much interested. He has I think some very solid objections to the transaction nay some of a constitutional kind, and questions of that nature ought certainly in these days to be avoided as much as possible. Afterwards I trust Lord Hillsborough will also see Lord North; Lieut. G[eneral] Amherst states his brother as not naturally inclined to the measure but adopting it as the sentiment of the Cabinet. I fear there is some job at the bottom of the affair I have not yet been able to discover but considering the shameful one in the loan, it ought to be avoided in other affairs or discredit must be expected.

    Queen's House, March 29th. 1781.
       26 m. pt. 8 A.M.

25

Hillsborough replied immediately, and wrote again later in the day, outlining a proposal for ministerial consultations, and for postponement of the scheme in order to avert the threatened resignation of Jenkinson. The cabinet finally shelved the plan on the 31st.[38] The king wrote the following letter to Hillsborough to inform him that the ground was at last prepared for this step.

    37. Fortescue, *Correspondence*, V, no. 3292; Abergavenny MS. 356. Charles Jenkinson (1727–1808), later Earl of Liverpool, was secretary-at-war 1778–1782.
    38. Fortescue, *Correspondence*, V, nos. 3293, 3294, 3297.

Queen's House, March 31st. 1781.
15 m. pt. 3 P.M.

It is proper Lord Hillsborough should know that Lord North seemed yesterday very willing that the raising the six regiments should for the present be *postponed*, and not taken up again, and that he hoped Lord Hillsborough would mention it at the Cabinet meeting this day; the Lord Lieutenant's letter, the suspicion that each colonel would gain £3,000 and the detriment to the forty companies already ordered which cannot be completed if these new corps are bidding against them, the levy money offered by the companies is said to be six guineas a man, these seem solid reasons without the material one of it being contrary to the opinion of the Secretary at War who must move the estimates in Parliament.

26

Lord Hillsborough may send a respite for the convict whom Lord Guildford has wrote to the judge for an explanation before he intercedes for mercy; the time specified should be Saturday, April 14th. which will prevent any other notice being necessary unless Judge Ashurst should send a satisfactory answer.

Queen's House, April 5th 1781.
5 m. pt. 6 P.M.

27

Undated, but c. April 1781

By the letter of the Lord Lieutenant of Ireland dated March 16th. it is proposed that the independent companies shall be reviewed by General Officers in Ireland; but as they are raised for Britain and [to] be brought over as soon as raised, it is more proper that they should be inspected and reported upon in England and consequently undergo no other review in Ireland than a minute examination of each man by some proper surgeon, who should be very exactly directed to be very particular in examining their fitness for service. This examination will be some security to the officers who have undertaken to raise the men, and may save some money by preventing those who have bodily infirmities being sent over.

The proposals made by Major Generals Maxwell and Gabbett transmitted by the Lord Lieutenant with his letter of the 17th March are less advantageous than what have been offered by others, therefore cannot be taken into consideration.

What the memorial of the Master general of the Ordnance of Ireland sets forth concerning the company of cadets belonging to the Artillery in England does not affect the object, namely a provision for the officers worn out or incapable of further service; but the establishment of invalids might be useful as it would put an end to the plea of the necessity of letting old officers of Artillery in Ireland sell their commissions, but local knowledge is wanting whether part of the service in Ireland could be performed by invalids.

Colonel Preston's memorial for leave to raise a regiment of foot is not admissable, the terms being less favourable to the public than many others that have been presented.

The Lord Lieutenant's letter of the 28th of March enclosed a memorial of the principal officers of the Ordnance in Ireland and of the Field Officers of Artillery and Corps of Engineers in that Kingdom regarding staff pay and forage money; the officers who command the artillery in the different camps in Britain have the same allowances of staff pay, and all the officers of Artillery have forage according to their ranks, in the same manner as officers of the same ranks in the other branches of the Army, the same rule holds good for the Engineers who are on the staff; some officers of the Corps of Engineers receive extra pay when particularly employed in erecting or repairing fortifications.

The lists of successions in the Lord Lieutenant's letters nos. 37 and 39 are regular except a succession to Ensign Geo. Smyth of the 67th. Foot by purchase, he being appointed to a cornetcy on the English establishment, which seems to be a mistake for there is no such cornet on this establishment.

28

Queen's House, May 15th 1781.
30 m. pt. 7 A.M.

On returning to Lord Hillsborough the military papers that have been transmitted and require answers it is proper to observe that the list of promotions that accompanies the Lord Lieutenant of Ireland's letter of the 30th of last month is conformable to rule, the commissions agreeable to it ought therefore to be prepared: his letter of the 3rd instant states the particular circumstances of the loss Lieut. Ryan has sustained of a considerable number of recruits he had raised for an independent company, and proposes a means of saving him from total ruin, both seem in this particular case reasonable and consequently must be complied with.

The letter of the 4th. instant encloses lists of the lieutenants in the

3rd., 19th., and 30th. regiments of foot proposed to be turned over to the 4th., 5th., and 49th. regiments, it is by no means necessary that they should have new commissions, for the officers of the additional companies raised in 1755 were by warrant turned over to the ten regiments raised in that year, and the same mode was followed in 1756 with the additional companies which were turned over to the fifteen new battalions formed in September 1756. A copy may easily be got of the warrants issued on those occasions which I suppose may be easily found at the War Office and should be copied on this occasion.

29

Although this letter bears no year date the one attributed is not in doubt. The only other possible year Hillsborough could have received a letter on this sort of subject in June was 1780, but on 5 and 6 June 1780 George III was in Westminster and dated letters from the Queen's House: he was anxious to keep an eye on the Gordon Riots (Fortescue, Correspondence, V, nos. 3044, 3050).

It is not very likely that any indisputable proof can be brought of the innocence of Vaughan, for if it is not natural it should have been delayed to within so few hours of his execution. Lord Hillsborough will therefore remember that if this is not cleared up before this sevennight that the law must then take its course.

 Windsor, June 6th. [1781].
  35 m. pt. 5 P.M.

30

            Kew, June 16th 1781.
The list of successions which accompanies the Lord Lieutenant's letter of the 26th of May is conformable to regulations the commissions therefore to be prepared therefore agreeable to it; there is no objection to the ensigncy being sold in the 67th regiment of Foot to reimburse in part Capt. Robinson of the Irish Artillery for the purchase of his son's commission.

 The list of successions recommended by the Lord Lieutenant in his letter of the 2nd of the present month is also approved of and the commissions must also be prepared; though Lieut. Col. Tucker of the 2nd. Horse did not purchase, his long and meritorious services give him a claim to sell his commission.

 As to the Lord Lieutenant's recommending Ensign Cowper of the

36th. and Ensign Munro of the 77th. to be Lieutenants in Capt. Featherston's independent company they certainly ought not to have been recommended, being but lately appointed ensigns and consequently not agreeable to the rule observed in the companies raised in this kingdom and transmitted as the rule to be observed in those raised in Ireland; but as the Lord Lieutenant has filled up their ensigncies they will be permitted to be lieutenants on this occasion but they must not serve as a precedent for the other companies raising.

It is proper to observe on the letter of Mr. Eden[39] to Sir Stanier Porten concerning the officers of the Artillery who have purchased being permitted to dispose of their commissions; that those officers who really purchased and are positively unable to do their duty may have leave to dispose of their commissions provided they receive no more than what they expended on their commissions, and that the purchase may be made so easy to the officers who succeed them that they may enter into an engagement never to claim any right in consequence to dispose of their commissions.

31

The Lord Lieutenant proposes in his letter of the 6th. of this month that Ensign Thomas Ahmuty Daniel of the 36th. Regiment of Foot may be appointed lieutenant in Captain Honeyborne's independent company in the room of Lieutenant Roberts who desires to decline; but this ensign having only received his commission on the 30th. of April last cannot be permitted to so rapidly be promoted. As also Ensign Hewetson of the 77th. Regiment who stands in the same predicament.

The two second lieutenants of the Irish Artillery cannot also be appointed lieutenants in Captain Brown's and Captain Pyne's independent companies as it is contrary to rule when officers have entered into the service of the Artillery to promote them in other branches of the army.

Ensign Pyne of Major Dalrymple's Corps cannot also be admitted for by the footing on which that Corps was raised, those officers are not eligible to promotions in other parts of the army.

St. James's, June 21st. 1781.
34 m. pt. one P.M.

---

39. William Eden (1744–1814), the Lord Lieutenant's chief secretary in Ireland.

32

In answer to the Lord Lieutenant's letter of the 29th. ult. assigning his reasons for recommending very young ensigns for lieutenancies in the new independent companies; he has so frequently been told that it cannot be admitted, that he cannot be surprised that it is not acquiesced in; if he cannot find ensigns of sufficient standing for the lieutenancies, ensigns must be named from hence for that purpose, who must pay the money the others had advanced for the new levies, and the vacant ensigncies here by this arrangement shall be recommended to by the Lord Lieutenant.

The officers of artillery cannot be permitted to be placed in the independent companies; the Artillery and the rest of the Army are in the British service considered quite separate, and the same distinction must subsist in Ireland.

St. James's, July 19th. 1781.
7 m. pt. one P.M.

33

Kew, August 1 1781.
30 m. pt. 5 P.M.

I was sorry to find this day from Lord Stormont[40] that Lord Hillsborough was confined by one of his old headaches; I have cursorily looked at the Lord Lieutenant's private letter, and see one evil at the first sight, that Mr. Eden is trying to set the Commander in Chief in Ireland[41] aside the recommendation being apparently without consulting him. I shall in [a] day or two return it to Lord Hillsborough with my opinion that he may in consequence write to the Lord Lieutenant.

34

Windsor, September 6th 1781.

It seemed to me most proper not having returned to Lord Hillsborough the Lord Lieutenant's secret letter of the 23rd of July previous to his departure for Bath, to keep it back till his return from thence. It seems to be matter for serious deliberation whether with the constant

40. Recalled from Paris after the breach with France in 1778 (letter VIII above), Stormont had been appointed secretary of state for the northern department on 27 Oct. 1779.
41. See [note 34] above.

desertion of the troops raised in Ireland it would be wise to raise three new regiments in that Kingdom to enable three others to be drawn from thence for foreign service; at least I am certain if the experiment is to be tried, it should be done with not more than one at first; should that be thought advisable by the Cabinet Lord Hillsborough will acquaint the Lord Lieutenant that one regiment of ten companies of seventy men each may be raised that the command of the regiment must be offered to Colonel Abercrombie of the carabaniers who has offered to raise a regiment, that the eldest major of infantry in Ireland willing to be lieut. col. of this regiment must be recommended and the eldest captain of infantry in Ireland must be recommended for the majority, that he must digest the whole with Sir John Irwine; I do not think the delay that has arisen any inconvenience for it has given room for the independent companies raising in that Kingdom to get forward, every new scheme always hurts the modes already adopted.[42]

35

Headings written by Porten, the rest in the king's hand.

Ireland.
Received 10th September 1781.
It has been found more economical for the public that the officers should dispose of their Batt and Baggage horses in this island every winter and to make the usual allowance for fresh ones in the spring than to forage the whole winter it seems therefore best to adopt the same method in Ireland as probably no service will arise during the winter months.

36

Queen's House, January 19th. 1782.
12 m. pt. 6 P.M.
The Lord Lieutenant of Ireland's letters nos. 124, 126 and 127 require no answers but not having returned them before I think it necessary to say so much on them.
    The list of successions proposed in Ireland and transmitted with the

---

42. This letter relays to Hillsborough objections outlined in a letter written to the king by Charles Jenkinson, which is undated but must belong to the few days prior to 6 September (Fortescue, *Correspondence*, III, no. 1628, misplaced by the editor).

letter no. 141 is perfectly regular the commissions in consequence to be prepared. His letter no. 142 concerning the vacant lieutenancies in the independent companies raised in Ireland for this establishment it is to be remarked that nine of the young gentlemen proposed have already been approved of and Lord Amherst has wrote to Lord Carlisle to acquaint him of such appointment the nine others will as vacancies arise be also appointed for the lieutenancies in those independent companies that have been raised in Ireland that still remain vacant, the Lord Lieutenant is to recommend ensigns who have joined their regiments six months; but it is hoped he will soon send over their names, as if they are called upon for service it is highly inconvenient that these vacancies should subsist. The Lord Lieutenant's letter no. 143 encloses nine ensigns willing to accept of lieutenancies in the independent companies their commissions will be issued as soon as they have made the deposit for aiding the respective captains in the raising the companies to effect which they must being now approved send their applications through the respective captains without which no certainty can be had that they have obtained the assistance on which they depended on raising their companies.

37

When, late in 1781, the British commander-in-chief in America, Sir Henry Clinton, asked to be relieved, Sir Guy Carleton was the king's personal choice for his successor; but owing to personal antipathies his appointment would have precipitated the resignation of the colonial secretary, Lord George Germain, and it did not take place till after Germain's withdrawal from the government early in February.

Carleton had been appointed governor of the fort of Charlemont in February 1778, on his return from Canada, but up till 1782 had never taken any steps to act in this post or claim the salary. He appears to have complied with the king's wish, as he remained governor till his death.[43]

Lord Hillsborough must see my delicacy towards Sir Guy Carleton in not having yet appointed a successor to his Government in Ireland though I have had one in my mind; I wish Lord Hillsborough would write a line to Sir Guy Carleton expressing that I hope his appointment to the chief command in North America will make him recall his wish

43. Ian R. Christie, *The End of North's Ministry, 1780–1782* (1958), pp. 291–8; Fortescue, *Correspondence*, V, nos. 3425, 3468.

of declining the Government I had conferred on him of Charlemount, I should wish as soon as convenient to have his answer.[44]

Queen's House, February 21st. 1781.

13 m. pt. 9 A.M.

38

I return to Lord Hillsborough the papers arrived from Ireland;[45] all seem to combine to humble Great Britain; he is quite right in sending the papers instantly to the Lord Chancellor, and taking the opinion of the Cabinet this day when they of course meet. The Chancellor I do not doubt will be firm on the occasion.

Queen's House, 17th. March 1782.

7 m. pt. 8 A.M.

44. On the unused inner page is a copy in draft of Hillsborough's letter to Carleton, phrased in similar terms.

45. Acknowledging Hillsborough's note of the previous day, Fortescue, *Correspondence*, V, no. 3559.

VIII
JOHN ROBINSON'S 'STATE' OF THE
HOUSE OF COMMONS, JULY 1780

Edited by Ian R. Christie

INTRODUCTION

The 'State' of the House of Commons reproduced here from the original in the Royal Archives at Windsor was prepared during July 1780 by John Robinson, secretary to the treasury under Lord North.[1] Its purpose was to forecast the likely results of an immediate general election. This copy was provided for the information of George III, who had been urging the advisability of a dissolution of parliament for some weeks and who was keenly interested in the possibilities of political advantage to be gained from such a step.[2] There is a presumption that Robinson retained another working copy in his office at the treasury for the use of himself and Lord North; but if this was indeed the case, it was not preserved among his papers, which are therefore much less informative about the general election of 1780 than they are about the run-up to the dissolution of 1784.[3]

Information from this 'State' has been cited both in my own work and in various of the constituency studies and biographies of M.P.s in the *History of Parliament*.[4] Nevertheless, there is some justification for making the document available in print as a whole. The information which it gives about men and places is often different from that noted in the fragmentary 'State' for August 1782 and the complete 'State' for the end of 1783, which have already been published.[5] More important, the 'State' of July 1780 conveys general impressions and overall information of a different nature to that contained in that of 1783, because it relates to a period when politics were in a 'normal' state, that is, there were clear stable alignments between a long-serving administration and an equally long-serving Opposition. This was no longer the case after March 1782. Robinson himself drew attention in a letter of 7 August 1782 to Lord Shelburne to the

1. Ian R. Christie, *The End of North's Ministry, 1780–1782* (1958), pp.34–5. For the general context of events see *ibid.*, pp.3–45. I gratefully acknowledge the gracious permission of Her Majesty the Queen to publish this document.

2. *Ibid.*, pp.20–21.

3. Extensive transcripts of Robinson's papers were made by B.F. Stevens and were edited by W.T. Laprade, as *The Parliamentary Papers of John Robinson, 1774–1784* (Royal Historical Society, Camden 3rd series, vol. xxxiii, 1922). Documents at pp.31–36 relate to the general election of 1780, mainly to specific matters of detail and with no reference to the 'State', and a few others are included in Historical MSS. Commission, *Tenth Report*, Appendix, part VI, at pp.29–37. All these papers were re-examined in 1951 by the present writer on behalf of the History of Parliament.

4. Christie, *op. cit.* Sir Lewis Namier and John Brooke, *The History of Parliament. The House of Commons, 1754–1790* (3 vols., 1964).

5. Laprade, *Parliamentary Papers of John Robinson*, pp.42–8, 65–105. Only the same fragment of the first of these returns exists in fair copy in the Lansdowne MSS. (where Laprade surmised it might be), but with up-dated attributions of political alignments which differ appreciably from those shown in Robinson's own copy.

confused, even bewildering nature of the situation created by the successive collapse of North's and then of Rockingham's ministries:[6]

> Nothing can be more difficult than to form a state of the political sentiments of the House of Commons in the present juncture. In a stable, permanent government to whom gentlemen have professed friendship, with whom they have in general acted, and from whom they have received favours, conjectures may be formed with a tolerable certainty of the opinions which gentlemen will entertain on particular questions, but in a state so rent as this has lately been, torn by intestine divisions, and split into different parties, with an administration to be established, after one has been overturned and another divided, it is the hardest task that can be to class them. The attempt to do it leads into so great a field and requires so large a discussion that it renders the business almost impossible.

Consequently a much greater degree of uncertainty bedevilled Robinson's analyses of the House in 1782 and 1783: they cannot be treated, or made the basis of generalizations, as if they were typical. This is not to say, however, that there ever was much degree of certainty in calculations of this kind. The 'State' of July 1780, when compared with the results of the general election two months later, makes clear the difficulties faced by the treasury secretary, even in a more stable political situation, when trying to forecast what the results of such a leap in the dark would be.[7]

6. Laprade, p.42.
7. Christie, *The End of North's Ministry*, pp.34–8, 157–163. All Members of Parliament and all successful candidates mentioned in the 'State' appear in the *History of Parliament*, and annotation giving information about them has therefore been considered unnecessary.

STATE 1780

	[Present] Hope D'bt					[Future] Hope D'bt		
	Pro.	full	full	Con		Pro.	full	full C
Abingdon								
John Mayor	1				Same, it is hoped—An opposition was threatened but seems withdrawn and a very flattering canvass had been made by Mr. Mayor	1		
Agmondesham								
Wm. Drake Senr.				1	Same			1
Wm. Drake Junr.				1	Mr. Drake Senr. is offner with Govt. than against: in Ministerial Questions he may be against but in great Constitutional points he will always be with, if the Questions are to affect the Govt. or constitution—Mr. Drake Junr. is not of such sound principles.			
St. Albans								
Sir Richard Sutton	1				Mr. Radcliffe, 1 other by Lord Spencer			
Mr. Radcliffe			1					
Aldborough Suffolk								
Richard Combe	1				Mr. Crespigny or a friend	1		
Thos. Fonnereau[8]	1				Mr. Fonnereau again	1		
Aldborough York								
Wm. Baker				1	a friend by the Duke of Newcastle	1		
Hon. Wm. Hanger	1				a friend but not Mr. Hanger The Duke of Newcastle has not arranged his seats, but is gone into the North. Will do it there, he will return in less than a fortnight and I am then to see him immediately.	1		
Andover								
Sir John Griffin Griffin				1	The same most probably. I have put both these gentlemen down as coming in again and against, but I am told that S. John Griffin does not stand well there and is open to attack by a proper man—Inquiries are making.			
B. Lethieullier				1				
Anglesey								
Lord Bulkeley				1	The same unless Sir N. Bayley or Sir John Stanley could be prevailed on to stand; but even then doubtful and should be considered against			
Carried over	5	0	1	6		5	0	1

8. An error; Martin Fonnereau was now M.P., Thomas having died in 1779.

	Pro.	Hope full	D'bt full	Con		Pro.	Hope full	D'bt full	Con
Brought over	5	0	1	6		5	0	1	6
Appleby									
P. Honywood				1	Same, or two others both				
Geo. Johnstone				1	against. One and one by Lord Thanet and Sir James Lowther this time, but here-after Lord Thanet's borough. Mr. Robinson having sold all his property there to Lord Thanet.				2
Arundel									
Thomas Brand				1	With attention friends may				
G.L. Newenham				1	be got in here, unless Lord Surrey should be active, conform and purchase, in that case even perhaps one friend may be got in, however as most cautious only put both doubtful, as I am not clear that Lord Onslow's opinion can be depended upon, that he through Sir John Shelley with Lord Surrey has divided the borough 1 and 1. In that case 1 friend at least.				2
Ashburton									
C. Boone	1				The same again most				
Robert Palk				1	likely—but it is said that some dissatisfaction has arose as to Lord Orford's recommend. Although the electors are inclined to receive a friend from Govt. Accts of this are daily expected	1			1
Aylesbury									
A. Bacon	1				Same again.				
J. Aubrey				1	Capt. Reynolds of the Navy. A canvass for both candidates has been made here, with the greatest success, and Mr. Aubrey beat off the ground.[9]	2			
Banbury									
Lord North	1				The same	1			
Barnstaple									
John Clevland	2				Same—These two gen-tlemen will it is appre-hended come in again without trouble or contest.[10]				
Wm. Devaynes						2			
Carried over	10	0	1	12		11	0	3	9

9. Reynolds did not stand. Thomas Orde and Bacon were the successful ministerial candidates.

10. There was a contest, and Devaynes lost the seat to another government supporter, Francis Basset.

	Pro.	full	full	Con			Pro.	full	full	Co
	Hope D'bt						Hope D'bt			
Brought over	10	0	1	12			11	0	3	

Bath

A. Moysey — 2

Sir J. Sebright — Same with attention; although a contest with Lord Camden's son Mr. Pratt. Mr. Moysey says that he trusts Sir John and he shall carry it, but he wants an assurance of the nomination of a Boy to the Charterhouse and a promise of a living of about the value of £200 p.a. for the son of another voter.[11]   — 2

Beaumaris, Town of

Sir H. Williams — 1 — Same again, or a Friend of Lord Bulkeley

Bedfordshire

Lord Upper Ossory — 1 — Same again. I put Lord Ongley down for, because he generally is so, except in some of the Questions of Economy and Reform and I think he may be mostly depended upon; if attended to and humoured a little for I have generally on trial found him practicable.[12]   — 1

Lord Ongley — 1

Bedford

Sir W. Wake — 1 — Same again. Mr. Whitbread is a very doubtful uncertain man for either side, but if either way I think may be reckoned more hopeful to go in general with Govt., though certain in popular questions. A proposition has been received lately respecting this, to which attention is paying.   — 1

Samuel Whitbread — 1

Bedwin

Paul Methuen — 1 — It is doubtful whether either of these gentlemen may come in again. Methuen has of late always been against. But the borough is Lord Aylesbury's and it is most probable the gentlemen who will come in will be both friends. Lord Cranburn will most likely be a peer very soon, and therefore desires

Lord Cranburn — 1

| Carried over | 14 | 0 | 2 | 16 | | | 14 | 0 | 4 | |

11. Ill health caused Sebright to withdraw, and in the absence of another ministerial candidate, the seat went to the oppositionist, J.J. Pratt.

12. After a canvass Ongley declined and the seat went to Opposition.

	Pro.	Hope full	D'bt full	Con		Pro.	Hope full	D'bt full	Con
Brought over	14	0	2	16		14	0	4	12

Brought over — 14 0 2 16

to have only a temporary seat—perhaps Lord Courtown may be brought in. **2**

Beeralston
Sir F.H. Drake — 1
Hon. G Hobart — 1

Probably neither of these gentlemen for this place but two friends will be brought in, of which I have received the best assurances from the Duke of Northumberland, who has purchased this borough. **2**

Berkshire
John Elwes — Con 1
W.H. Hartley — Con 1

These two Gentlemen will probably come in again unless something particular happens. Mr. Elwes though not against yet mostly is so. An opposition by a friend of Government has been talked of but does not seem in any degree of forwardness. **2**

Berwick
Jac. Wilkinson — Con 1
Hon. Jnᵒ Vaughan — Pro 1

It is expected that General Vaughan will come in again or a person a friend to Govt. to hold the seat in his absence. And it is hoped that Mr. Wilkinson will be thrown out and Sir John Hussey Delaval a good friend be brought in. However as it is contest and a poll to be taken it is at present put doubtful—Lord Lisburne has *now* resolved to offer General Vaughan again.[13] **1   1**

Beverley
Sir Jas Pennyman — Con 1
G.F. Tuffnell — Con 1

It is doubtful whether the same Gentⁿ will come in again. But it equally doubtful whether a friend may be got in for this place. If Sir C. Thompson cᵈ be prevailed on to stand, he would it is hoped carry it. He should be talked to on it. Col. Masters of the East York Regt. would also make a good candidate. But however both against for the present. **2**

| Carried over | 17 | 0 | 2 | 21 | | 19 | 0 | 5 | 16 |

13. Delaval's success without a contest secured both seats for Government.

	Hope	D'bt				Hope	D'bt	
Pro.	full	full	Con		Pro.	full	full	Co
Brought over 17	0	2	21		19	0	5	1
Bewdley								
Lord Westcote 1				Same again clear: Opposition started beat off	1			
Bishops Castle								
Mr. Attorney General 1				Mr. H. Strachey, vice Attny Genl. Same				
Wm. Clive 1					2			
Bletchingley								
Sir Robert Clayton			1	Under circumstances and with attention both these seats may probably be got. One at least seems likely. However for the present only put these doubtful. It is since the above remark *now* settled that Sir Robert Clayton comes in again and a Friend of Govt.— probably Mr. Kenrick now a commissr. of stamps.				
F. Standert			1		2			
Bodmyn								
George Hunt			1	There will be a contest here. it is said Mr. Hunt will be thrown out, & Mr. Wm. Masterman come in, but I fear Sir Jas La Roche may fall. If so, it will remain as before, 1 and 1—which suppose *at present* but if not we shall have two friends.				
Sir Jas. La Roche 1					1			
Boroughbridge								
Anthony Eyre 1				Same again, or the Duke of Newcastle tells me certainly two friends.				
Wm. Phillips 1					2			
Bossiney								
Col. H.L. Luttrell 1				The same again	2			
Hon. Charles stuart 1								
Boston Lincolnshire								
Lord Robert Bertie 1				Supposed will be the same again; Mr. Sibthorpe is mostly with us, but I suppose him only hopeful.	1	1		
H. Sibthorpe	1			Since the above accounts have been received as if it was doubtful whether Mr. Sibthorpe would stand again for this place. Lord Robert Bertie has the strong personal interest there. He is applied to to converse on this business since this account has been received.				
Brackley								
William Egerton 1				Most probably the same again, or whoever the Duke of Bridgwater pleases				
Timothy Caswall 1					2			
Carried over 28	1	2	24		30	1	7	

	Pro.	Hope full	D'bt full	Con		Pro.	Hope full	D'bt full	Con
Brought over	28	1	2	24		30	1	7	17
Bramber									
Thomas Thoroton				1	The same again.	1			1
Sir Henry Gough	1				This borough is divided between the Duke of Rutland and Sir Henry Gough, being burgage tenures.				
Brecon County									
Charles Morgan	1				The same	1			
Brecon Town									
Sir Charles Gould	1				The same, on his brother-in-law, Mr. Morgan's interest.	1			
Bridgenorth									
Thomas Whitmore				1	Most likely the same; but enquiry is making about this borough. Although no light has been yet obtained to give any reasonable ground of expectation to change the Gentlemen.				
Admiral Pigot				1					2
Bridgewater									
Hon. Anne Poulett			1		There will be a strong contest here. Mr. Fox stands on Mr. Allen's interest, but Mr. Poulett thinks that he will carry it with *assistance*. It is however doubtful, and considering Mr. Poulett's conduct, being against us even in some of the most pointed questions against Govt. it may be most prudent to set this down against.				
B. Allen				1					2
Bristol									
Edmund Burke				1	There will be a strong contest between Mr. Coombe, Mr. Brickdale, Mr. Burke, and Mr. Cruger. It is thought Mr. Coombe and Mr. Brickdale may succeed but until they do, set down doubtful and con.				
Henry Cruger				1				1	1
Bridport									
Thos. Coventry				1	Bridport is in a dubious state. Measures have been taken and are pursuing relative to it. Mr. Cary can't come again. It is a chance whether Mr. Coventry may. There is a chance of friends, but it is dubious. Mr. Sturt, son to the member for Dorsetshire proposes to stand. Mr. Townson, Mr. Beckford, and Mr. Joddrell				
Col. Cary	1								
Carried over	32	1	3	31		33	1	8	23

	Pro.	Hope full	D'bt full	Con	Remarks	Pro.	Hope full	D'bt full	Co
Brought over	32	1	3	31		33	1	8	2
					also offer. At present therefore it is thought best to put them down doubtful and con.			1	
Buckinghamshire									
Lord Verney				1	The same again				2
Thomas Grenville				1					
Buckingham Town									
James Grenville				1	It is said to be doubtful whether Lord Temple will bring Mr. Richard Grenville in again. And thought that he may bring in his younger brother. On this account it is canvassed Con. in the abstract, though it was originally set down doubtful, but if Mr. Richd. Grenville comes in, he may be reckoned hopeful, because he never votes against Government.			1	
Jun.			1						
Richard Grenville									
Callington									
Wm. Skrine		1			Mr. Skrine will not come in again, but if he does not two friends almost certainly will, although there is a little question depending at present to arrange it. This is *now* all settled and two friends will certainly come in, 30th July.				2
Govr. Stratton		1							
Calne									
John Dunning				1	This borough stands in rather an extraordinary situation for to have it against Government. It consists of but a small number of voters and the management of the whole is in the power of Mr. Bull who is a *Comms.* of *Taxes* and a *Couns.* of *Appeals* in the Excise. And yet is connected against Government with Lord Shelburne. He is so clearly so that it is a difficult matter to know how to talk to him, but if it is thought right to try him somehow it must be done very cautiously and only at the last moment, for whenever this is done it will sound the alarm.				
Is. Barré				1					
Carried over	34	2	3	36		35	1	10	2

	Pro.	Hope full	D'bt full	Con		Pro.	Hope full	D'bt full	Con
Brought over	34	2	3	36		35	1	10	29
Cambridgeshire									
Sir J.H. Cotton	1				There is a violent contest here. It is thought that Mr. Yorke and Sir Sampson Gideon will come in and therefore it is ventured to put these member down at least hopeful, as it is not thought that Mr. Yorke will not come in inimical to Government and Sir Sampson is a most firm friend.				
Sir Sampson Gideon	1						2		
Cambridge University									
Richard Croftes				1	There will be a strong contest here. Lord Euston, Mr. Pitt, Mr. J. Townshend, Lord Hyde, Mr. Croftes and Mr. Mansfield stand. All speak with confidence but it is generally believed that Mr. Mansfield will succeed. Lord Hyde's success is thought to be very doubtful, therefore best to set them down one Pro one Con; as whichever of the other candidates succeed, such one will most probably be against. Lord Euston will not be of age until after Christmas. Lord Hyde's standing will be of use to Mansfield and interfere much with Mr. J. Townshend.				
James Mansfield	1					1			1
Cambridge, Town of									
S. Jenyns	1				Mr. S. Jenyns intends to quit Parliament. Mr. Keene has taken a line against in almost all the popular questions and indeed does generally go against Admin. in any questions of opposition. He does not stand on very firm ground at Cambridge and may be opposed. Col. Adeane stands for one and Sir Thomas Hatton has been spoken of as another.				
B. Keene				1			1		1
Camelford									
John Amyand			1		Mr. Amyand is dead. Sir R. Payne may come in again if he chooses, but however it is apprehended that we shall				
Sir Ralph Payne	1								
Carried over	39	2	4	38		36	4	10	31

	Pro.	Hope full	D'bt full	Con		Pro.	Hope full	D'bt full	Co
Brought over	39	2	4	38	have two friends brought in for us. Mr. Phillips is sent to to settle it, and expected in Town very soon. It is therefore ventured to put these for Government.	36	4	10	3
						2			
Canterbury									
Richard Milles				1	Mr. Milles declines. Lord Newhaven stands and expects to come in again he is sometimes with, at others against—but he professes great friendship. Mr. Robinson the recorder of Canterbury also stands and Mr. Honywood offered, but may now as he has been nominated for Kent, perhaps withdraw. If Mr. Robinson succeeds he will be an untried and uncertain man and therefore seems most proper to put these gentlemen one doubtful one con.				
Lord Newhaven			1						
									1
Cardiff									
Sir H. Mackworth	1				The same again	1			
Cardiganshire									
Lord Lisburne	1				The same again, though not liked, and if an opposition would certainly be thrown out.				
						1			
Cardigan Town									
Thos. Johnes Junr.	1				Mr. Johnes was lately chosen for Radnor. Mr. J. Campbell was chose for this place in his room—it is expected he will be again chosen without opposition.				
						1			
Carmarthenshire									
John Vaughan	1				The same again, without any opposition.				
						1			
Carmarthen Town									
John Adams	1				Mr. Adams will not come in here again. Two or three candidates are talked on to start for this place. Sir Cornwallis Maude it is thought is most likely to succeed and may not be unfavourable, but being untried it is put down doubtful.[14]				
								1	
Carried over	44	2	5	39		42	4	12	

14. Adam's successor, George Philipps, did in fact support Government.

	Pro.	Hope full	D'bt full	Con		Pro.	Hope full	D'bt full	Con
Brought over	44	2	5	39		42	4	12	32
Carlisle									
Anthony Storer	1				It is reported that Lord Surrey means to stand for this place in opposition to Mr. Storer—that the agreement between Lord Carlisle and Sir Jas. Lowther is not to continue but that the Duke of Portland, Ld. Surrey and Sir Jas. Lowther are all to join against the person Lord Carlisle supports. If so Mr. Storer's success will be very dubious and this is so put.				
Walter Spencer Stanhope				1				1	1
Carnarvonshire									
Thos. Assheton Smith				1	Mr. Smith it is apprehended will not stand again. The candidates are Lord Newborough and Mr. Parry. Lord Newborough ought to have the best interest but he is personally disliked for some slights to the Gentn. and therefore although he thinks he shall succeed yet it is very doubtful. Mr. Parry is connected with Mr. Beard, the Welsh judge, and apprehended to be well inclined and therefore this place is canvassed hopeful whoever succeeds.			1	
Carnarvon Town									
Glynn Wynn				1	The same again and he is much better liked in the county than his elder brother Lord Newborough.				1
Castle Rising									
Robt. Mackreth	1				It is most probable that Mr. Mackreth will be brought in again by Lord Orford. Mr. Talbot will certainly by Miss Howard. 30th July, Lord Orford has fixed upon Mr. Mackreth to come in.	2			
John Chetwynd	1								
Talbot									
Cheshire									
Sir Rob. Sal. Cotton				1	The same again most likely—Sir R.S. Cotton has hitherto gone always against. Mr. Crewe most decidedly so.				2
John Crewe				1					
Chester									
T. Grosvenor	1				The same two gentlemen again.				
Carried over	48	2	5	44		44	5	13	37

	Hope D'bt					Hope D'bt			
	Pro.	full	full	Con		Pro.	full	full	Co
Brought over	48	2	5	44		44	5	13	37
R.W. Bootle				1	Mr. Grosvenor is particularly well inclined to Govt.	1			1
Chichester									
Hon. Wm. Keppel				1	Most likely the same gentlemen again. the duke of				
Rt. Hon. Mr. T. Conolly				1	Richmond would it is apprehended be difficult to attack here—at least no good person is known for it as yet.				2
Chippenham									
Sir E. Bayntun	1				Sir E. Bayntun will come in again, it is thought Mr. Marsh not, but a gentleman Mr. Hudson who is acting Partner in the House, late of S. Sam Fludyer who will be it is said a good friend, but as untried is canvassed hopeful.				
Samuel Marsh		1			30th July. It is now said that there is some doubt whether Sir E. Bayntun will come in.	1	1		
Christchurch									
James Harris	1				Mr. Harris will come in again. Mr. Hyde not—having disobliged the borough. Old Mr. Harris wishes his son to come in but the electors object on account of his absence as he can't while absent support Govt., but on his return they would accept him in room of his father whose health by that time may not permit his attendance. A Friend of Govt. they however wish to have and will take—although Mr. Morant and Mr. Dettany aided by the Duke of Bolton are trying to get ground there from the support of some malecontents.				
Lord Hyde	1								2
Cirencester									
James Whitshed	1				It is not certain that Mr. Whitshed will again come in. Mr. Blackwell it is thought will, but if Mr. Whitshed should not a friend by Lord Bathurst it is hoped may.				
Samuel Blackwell	1								2
Carried over	53	3	5	47		50	6	13	

	Hope D'bt					Hope D'bt		
	Pro.	full	full	Con		Pro.	full	full	Con
Brought over	53	3	5	47		50	6	13	39

Clitheroe

Assheton Curzon	1				The same again although				
Thos. Lister				1	Mr. Lister has been it is said				
					trying the ground against				
					Mr. Assheton Curzon.[15]	1			1

Cockermouth

James Adair				1	If these two gentlemen don't				
Ralph Gowland				1	come in again, yet Sir Jas.				
					Lowther will bring in two				
					Gentlemen against.				2

Colchester

Charles Gray	1				It is apprehended Mr. Gray				
Isaac M. Rebow	1				is too infirm and too old to				
					start again. Mr. Rebow is				
					also in a very ill state of				
					health, but it is uncertain				
					yet who is to stand. There-				
					fore put doubtful, although				
					it is hoped they may be				
					friends if the present gen-				
					tlemen should decline. Mr.				
					Round and Capt. Afflick of				
					the Navy have been spoke				
					of. Mr. Alex. Fordyce has				
					been also mentioned.			2	

Corf Castle

John Bond	1				Most probably Mr. Bond				
John Jenkinson	1				will come in again.[16] Mr.				
					Jenkinson will not but				
					young Mr. Banks who will				
					be a friend, it is appre-				
					hended.	2			

Cornwall

Sir Wm. Lemon				1	The same				2
E. Elliot				1					

Coventry

Col. Holroyd	1				The same				
Ed. Yeo	1					2			

Cricklade

John Dewar	1				Mr. Dewar certainly will				
John Macpherson	1				not come in again—but				
					most likely a friend will—a				
					coalition of interests is				
					talked on between Mr.				
					Herbert and the purchaser				
					of Mr. Nesbitt's estate and				
					then it will be one and one				
					both friends.	2			

Cumberland

Sir Jas. Lowther				1	It is said the same on agree-				
Henry Fletcher				1	ment				2
Carried over	62	3	5	54		57	6	15	46

---

15. Lister's successful machinations deprived Government of one supporter here.

16. Bond's son was elected in Sept. 1780.

	Hope D'bt					Hope D'bt		
	Pro.	full	full	Con		Pro.	full	full	Co
Brought over	62	3	5	54		57	6	15	46

Dartmouth
Lord Howe — 1 — This borough although generally esteemed a Govt. Borough is only canvassed as hopeful because Mr. Holdsworth has not yet been seen, and some reports go as if the present members again look up to it. Further enquiries are making. — 2

Richard Hopkins — 1 — 30th July Mr. Holdsworth is much attached to Lord Howe. His Lordship will therefore have his support. Mr. Hopkins may not. Perhaps Mr. Holdsworth may offer himself; it is now settling.

Denbighshire
Sir W.W. Wynne — 1 — The same — 1

Denbigh Town
Richard — 1 — The same
Myddleton — — — 1

Derbyshire
Ld. Geo. Cavendish — 1 — The same. 30 July. It is now said that Lord George Cavendish will not come into Parliament again and that Lord Richard Cavendish will come in for this county—having given up Lancaster. — 1 — 1

Honble. N. Curzon — 1

Derby Town
Ld. Fredk. Cavendish — 1 — The Devonshire family certainly have this place if they were to exert themselves, but they have hitherto prudently given up one to keep all quiet and probably may do so again. Whether Mr. Coke may again be that person is uncertain. He has often gone with Govt., but oftener against and almost uniformly so in the late questions. It seems most prudent therefore to canvass this place against. 30th July. It is now said that Ld. Fred. Cavendish will not again come into parliament. — 2

Dan Parker Coke — — — 1

Carried over	64	3	6	59		59	8	15	5c

	Hope D'bt					Hope D'bt		
	Pro.	full	full	Con		Pro.	full	full	Con
Brought over	64	3	6	59		59	8	15	50

Devizes

Chas. Garth	1				Mr. Garth will not come in again as he expects to take office, but I apprehend it will be so settled that a friend will succeed him, however as it will be an untried person have only put him hopeful. Mr. Sutton will come in again and has in all the late questions been remarkably firm. 30 July. It is apprehended to be now so fixed that a friend will be brought in.				
Jas. Sutton	1								
						1		1	

Devonshire

John Parker				1	Most probably the same. Mr. Parker never votes with us. Mr. Rolle often does— but is not to be depended upon in any trying question therefore put doubtful. 30 July. A county meeting is called to consider of the persons to be nominated.				
John Rolle			1						
								1	1

Dorsetshire

Humph. Sturt				1	It is not quite certain that Mr. Sturt and Mr. Pitt will come in again both being threatened for their conduct by different parties, but as it is not easy to get Gentn. to stand forwards in a county contest against persons of large property and weight in possession of a County, probably it may remain as at present. Mr. George Pitt is not liked in the county but Lord Rivers is popular.				
Hon. George Pitt	1								
						1			1

Dorchester

Honble. J. Damer				1	Whether Mr. John Damer may come in again is uncertain. He never attends. When he did attend formerly he was constantly against. Since Mr. G. Damer's attachment, Mr. J. Damer has never voted against. It is probable that Mr. G. Damer may come in for this place as his boroughs are disposed of. If so he may be for, but as this				
Wm. Ewer	1								

Carried over	68	3	7	62		61	9	16	52

	Hope D'bt Pro.	full	full	Con		Hope D'bt Pro.	full	full	Co
Brought over	68	3	7	62		61	9	16	52
					is not certain for safety the canvass as yet remains con. It is hoped that Mr. Ewer is sure of coming in again.	1			1
					30 July. Mr. Chapman is talked of to stand but not with much probability of success.				
Dover									
John Henniker	1								
John Trevanion				1	Mr. Trevanion uniformly and constantly votes against and merits an opposition whether it will be right to give him one others must judge and determine but no one ever deserves it more. If an opposition Sir P. Hales would make a good candidate and he can't come in for Downton. Sir Col. E. Smith is a Dover man and has talked of it. He would bustle and fight a hard battle. Mr. Fector must be spoken to on it seriously. He is shy at present and wants to keep peace he says. Mr. Henniker would stand again and can well afford his share of an hearty contest, both from his fortune and the honey he eats from Govt. without much labour.	1			1
Downton									
Sir P. Hales	1				Mr. Shaftoe will certainly come in again and whoever else he chooses.	1	1		
J. Shaftoe	1								
Droitwich									
Hon. A. Foley				1	The same again				
Edward Winnington				1					2
Dunwich									
Sir Gerrard Vanneck				1	The same again unless Mr. R. Jackson who cannot come in again for Romney should come in here instead of Mr. Barne, but in this case the canvass will be the same.	1			1
Barne Barne	1				30 July. Mr. Jackson now says that he has expectations of being again returned for Romney.				
Carried over	72	3	7	66		65	10	16	5?

	Pro.	Hope full	D'bt full	Con		Pro.	Hope full	D'bt full	Con
Brought over	72	3	7	66		65	10	16	57
Durham County									
Sir Thos. Clavering	1								
Sir J. Eden	1				The same	2			
Durham City									
John Lambton				1	The same				
John Tempest				1					2
East Looe									
John Buller	1				The same probably again or				
Wm. Graves	1				another friend of Govt. with Mr. Buller.	2			
S. Edmonsbury									
Sir Chas. Davers				1					
Rt. Hon. H.S. Conway				1	The same again				2
Essex									
John Luther				1	The same again. 30 July. It	1			1
T.B. Bramston	1				is expected that this is to be settled at Chelmsford this ensuing week and it is hoped amicably.				
Evesham									
Sir John Rushout				1	It is said there will be a				
Henry Seymour				1	contest here. Mr. Durand who represented it in the last parlt. it is said will stand again and with success. He was then a good friend of Govt. and therefore one of the members here may be hopeful altho' as most safe is here canvassed doubtful. Neither of the present members are liked in the borough. Sir John Rushout does not attend much, but when he does he is against. Mr. Seymour is living abroad and probably will decline. Further enquiries are making.			1	1
Eye									
Genl. Phillipson	1				Genl. Phillipson will it is				
Honlb. John St. John	1				apprehended come in again. Mr. St. John not, but a relation of the late Lady Cornwallis and a friend to Govt.	2			
Exeter									
Sir Chas. Bampfylde				1	If Sir Chas. Bampfylde				
John Baring				1	should stand there will be a contest. Mr. Cholwich intending to offer himself, he was got excused from being sheriff of Devon for the purpose, and it is hoped will come in and be a friend. Mr.				
Carried over	79	3	7	75		72	10	17	63

	Hope D'bt					Hope D'bt			
	Pro.	full	full	Con		Pro.	full	full	Con
Brought over	79	3	7	75	Baring it is most likely will come in again; the contest was between Mr. Cholwich and Mr. Baring, but as it is probable there will be room for both by Sir C. Bampfylde declining there may be no contest now.[17] Mr. Baring was a friend until Mr. Dunning married his sister. Mr. Cholwich it is very hopeful will be so.	72	10	17	63
							1		1
Flintshire									
Sir Roger Mostyn				1	The same again				1
Flint									
Watkin Williams				1	The same again, as it is believed none of Sir J. Glynn's family will stand. 30 July— It is said that an Opposition might be made there with effect and that A.E. Lloyd would be a good man for it. Inquiries are making.				1
Fowey									
Philip Rashleigh				1	Mr. Rashleigh again and most probably Lord Shuldham or however a friend.				
Lord Shuldham	1					1			1
Gatton									
Wm. Adam	1				Mr. Adam will not come in here again. Mr. Mayne probably may. The other seat will be kept for a double return, least Lord Newhaven should not succeed at Canterbury, and then had on terms. However both are at present canvassed doubtful as the safest way.				
Robt. Mayne	1						2		
St. Germains									
Benjamin Langlois	1				Mr. Elliot has been seen relative to this and his other Boroughs, but he has not been explicit, saying that he must consult his friends in the country and at present it seems very doubtful whether he will bring in the friends of Govt. He is violent against adm. Mr. Peachey certainly does not come in again here standing for Shoreham.				
John Peachey	1						2		
Carried over	84	3	7	78		73	11	21	67

17. Robinson was disappointed here. Cholwich declined and the sitting members were re-elected.

	Pro.	Hope full	D'bt full	Con		Pro.	Hope full	D'bt full	Con
Brought over	84	3	7	78		73	11	21	67
Glamorganshire									
Hon. G.V. Vernon				1	The same again				1
Gloucestershire									
Sir Wm. Guise				1	It is hoped this county may stand as it is now, but an opposition being threatened by Mr. Berkley and if it should be so Mr. Chester's success hazardous. It is prudent to canvass only as one hopeful. Sir W. Guise being always against. 30 July. It is now said that there will be no contest here.		1		1
W.B. Chester	1								
Gloucester City									
Charles Barrow				1	Mr. Barrow will probably come in again. Mr. Selwyn intends to quit this borough and probably a person in opposition will come in, but whether to be let in without an opposition must be considered and determined. It will be a pity it should be given up quietly when it has so long returned one friend, it is however set down both against.				2
G.A. Selwyn	1								
Grampound									
Sir Jos. Yorke	1				Mr. Elliot to be seen again.			2	
R.A. Neville	1								
Grantham									
Lord Geo. Sutton				1	The same again. 30 July. It is now said that Mr. Fr. Cockayn Cust is to come in here instead of Mr. Pere Cust, and he is equally a friend.	1			1
Pere Cust	1								
Great Grimsby									
Jos. Mellish		1			There will be a contest here perhaps, but no effectual one unless Mr. Clayton should join against Mr. Pelham. Mr. Eyre talks of standing but without Mr. Clayton can do but little. It is therefore that Mr. Pelham's brother (Mr. Anderson) and Mr. Jos. Mellish will be again returned, and although Mr. Mellish is not a constant attender yet when he does attend he is generally with, and therefore canvassed hopeful.		1		1
Evelyn Anderson				1					
Carried over	89	4	7	83		74	13	23	73

	Hope D'bt Pro.	full	full	Con		Hope D'bt Pro.	full	full	Con
Brought over	89	4	7	83		74	13	23	73
East Grinstead									
Lord Geo.					The same				
Germaine	1					2			
Sir John Irwin	1								
Guildford									
Sir Fletcher Norton				1	Most probably the same, although Mr. George Onslow threatens the speaker and says that he can turn him out.				
Geo. Onslow	1					1			1
Hampshire									
Jervoise Clarke				1	After the late severe brush it is not likely that anyone will be found to fight this county. The circumstances however have varied much since that contest. The reconciliation of the Duke of Gloucester to the King is one material alteration: many other interests of the good friends of Govt. which were engaged stood neuter: or which were not active last time might be secured and act with Govt. on a plan well formed and above all better management, for that was wretchedly bad the last time. It is though a consideration that men are now heated, have taken decided parts and in these cases often adhere to them until they get cooled even against the conviction of their own minds. This seems to deserve deliberation: Sir H.P. St. John is often with us, but in the late questions was against or shirked. He is therefore only put down hopeful.				
Sir H.P. St. John		1							
						1			1
					Sir Thos. Heathcote or Sir Geo. Rodney have been talked of to be put up.				
Harwich									
John Robinson	1				Probably the same again	2			
Hon. G. A. North	1								
Haslemere									
Sir M. Burrell	1				There is great reason to fear that the Burrells have lost this borough. The persons who had bought up Mr.				
Peter Burrell	1								
Carried over	96	5	7	85		79	14	23	75

	Pro.	Hope full	D'bt full	Con		Pro.	Hope full	D'bt full	Con
Brought over	96	5	7	85		79	14	23	75
					Webb's interest and property have it is said agreed also for the late Mr. Molineux's and by that closed the borough. It has fallen into the hands of persons who purchased on speculation and enquiries are making about them.			2	
					30 July. Sir Jas. Lowther has entered into articles for the purchase of this borough, about 3 days ago—and paid part of the purchase money, though not the whole. It is said that Mr. Norton is to be brought in here.				
Hastings									
Lord Palmerston	1				Two friends if not the same	2			
Mr. Jenkinson	1								
Haverfordwest									
Lord Kensington	1				The same again—a contest started but compromised	1			
Helstone									
Ph. Yorke		1			Not certain whether the same, but two friends.	2			
Fr. C. Cust	1				30 July. Mr. Pere Cust is to come in for this place and Mr. Deane, son of S. Robt. Deane of Ireland, who it is said is a friend.				
Herefordshire									
Rt. Hon. Mr. Harley	1				The same most likely	1			1
Sir Geo. Cornewall				1					
Hereford									
John Scudamore				1	The same most likely	1			1
Sir Richd. Symons	1								
Hertfordshire									
Wm. Plumer				1	The same most likely; as things are at present Lord Cranburn will not think of it or attempt anything, Lord Salisbury being very ill.			2	
Thos. Halsey				1					
Hertford									
John Calvert	1				There is a strong contest at this place. Mr. Calvert, Mr. Baker and Baron Dimsdale standing. Mr. Feilde is incapable. It is hoped that Mr. Calvert and Baron Dimsdale will come in. Mr. Calvert is always a most steady friend. Mr. Dimsdale hopeful, but being untried is here set down doubtful,				
Paule Feilde				1					
Carried over	103	6	7	90		86	14	25	79

	Hope	D'bt				Hope	D'bt	
	Pro.	full	full	Con		Pro.	full	full	Con
Brought over	103	6	7	90		86	14	25	79
					and there being a contest Mr. Calvert only hopeful. Mr. Baker is always most violent against.		1	1	
Heydon									
Beilby Thompson				1	It is hope this borough is so settled as to return two good members. Mr. Thompson it is said declines. Mr. Watson stands for Kent, but as the thing is not yet certain this place is only canvassed hopeful		2		
Honlb. L.T.				1					
Watson									
Higham Ferrers									
Fredk. Montague				1	The same most likely				1
Heytesbury									
Willm. A'Court				1	The Duke of Marlborough it is apprehended is engaged to bring Gen. A'Court in for his life, but it has been suggested to try if the General will not now dispose of that privilege. If not he must come in, the other person will be a friend to Govt.	1			1
Ashe									
Hon. W. Gordon	1								
Hindon									
Henry Dawkins				1	There is a contest here. Mr. Wraxall on the interest of the Calthorpe family Mr. Beckford's nominee until he comes of age, Mr. Kenyon; Mr. Widmore and Mr. Coghlan upon the *old* interest at Hindon. All parties seem secure of success but I should think the chance is in favour of Mr. Wraxall and Mr. Beckford. If so it would probably turn out one and one, but if not, and either of the others succeeded with Mr. Wraxall it will turn out both for—However they are only set as hopeful—now.		2		
Arch. Macdonald	1								
Honiton									
Sir Geo. Yonge				1	The contest here is a strong one. Sir Geo. Yonge and Mr. Coxe the present members and Capt. MacLeod. Capt. Macleod stands here on the canvass by 100 votes, Sir George Yonge next, and Mr. Coxe last, but Sir George is much disliked there and if it should be thought right to				
Law. Coxe	1								
Carried over	106	6	7	96		87	19	26	81

	Pro.	Hope full	D'bt full	Con		Pro.	Hope full	D'bt full	Con
Brought over	106	6	7	96		87	19	26	81
					oppose him and a good active clever man was sent down, it is thought Sir Geo. might be beat. this must be considered and determined.	1			1
Horsham									
Earl of Drogheda	1				It is doubtful whether these Gentn. can come in here again: the seats are at present in suspense, but will be two friends of Government it is hoped.		2		
Jas. Wallace	1								
Huntingdonshire									
Lord Ludlow				1	The same again	1			1
Lord Hinchingbrooke	1								
Huntingdon									
Sir Geo. Wombwell	1				The same again most likely, unless Sir Geo. Wombwell should die or be too ill to come in again, and then a friend would be chosen.		2		
Lord Mulgrave	1								
Hythe									
Sir Chas. Farnaby	1				Mr. Sawbridge has started a contest here, and it is supposed may propose himself and Mr. James—but it is hoped it will be without effect altho' Sir Charles Farnaby is not an active candidate. However as there is a contest he is only put hopeful altho' both Mr. Evelyn and he are good friends.	1	1		
Wm. Evelyn	1								
Ilchester									
Nath. Webb	1				It can't be yet said whether these gentlemen will come in again, not being talked to, or seen, nor Mr. Lockyer having been seen, but he is wrote to, and it is hoped there will be returned two friends. 30 July. The nephew of Mr. Lockyer, who has the commanding interest here it is said is to come in and another friend.		2		
O.S. Brereton	1								
Ipswich									
Thos. Staunton				1	There is a patriotic contest here. What may be the event is yet doubtful, altho' the old members expect				
Wm. Wollaston	1								
Carried over	116	6	8	97		96	20	26	83

	Hope D'bt						Hope D'bt		
	Pro.	full	full	Con		Pro.	full	full	Con
Brought over	116	6	8	97		96	20	26	83

success, however they are only canvassed doubtful.

30 July. Accounts now received say that the old members will come in.

2

St. Ives
Lord Newborough   1
Phil. Dehany

Neither of these gentlemen will come in again. But Mr. Praed, son of Mr. Praed who was formerly in parliament for this borough, and another friend of government.   1 ... 2

Kent
Hon. Ch. Marsham
Thos. Knight Junr.   1

Mr. Knight declines. Mr. Marsham and Mr. Honywood have been nominated at a patriotic meeting. Mr. Watson is proposed to stand, he is not very averse to Govt. and it is hoped he will succeed as he is the most moderate and in time may not be averse.   1   1   1

Kings Lynn
Hon. Thos.
Walpole
C. Molineux   1

Same again

2

Kingston upon Hull
Ld. Robert
Manners   1
D. Hartley   1

Here there will be a contest. Mr. Wilberforce a man of large fortune, the son of the Gentn. who was formerly a merchant of this place, stands and has been well received and it is thought will throw out Mr. Hartley. Mr. Wilberforce professes himself to be an independent man but not hostile to Govt. He is canvassed however doubtful. Ld. R. Manners it is apprehended will be clearly rechosen.   1   1

Knaresborough
Hon. B.
Walsingham   1
Lord G.A.H.
Cavendish   1

Whether Mr. Walsingham will be brought in here is uncertain, but if not it will clearly be two friends of the Duke of Devonshire.   2

Lancashire
Thos. Stanley   1
Sir Thos. Egerton   1

Same again, Mr. Lister having declined the contest as is said.   1   1

Carried over	119	7	8	105		100	20	30	89

	Pro.	Hope full	D'bt full	Con		Pro.	Hope full	D'bt full	Con
Brought over	119	7	8	105		100	20	30	89
Lancaster									
Lord R. Cavendish				1	Neither of these gentlemen may come in again. Perhaps will not offer. There are three gentlemen who at present have entered into the field, and carry on a brisk contest, Mr. Braddyll, Mr. Rawlinson, and Mr. Fenton. All Parties say they are sure, but it is very uncertain who will proceed. Mr. Fenton is the friend of Govt. the other two effect to stand independent; it is therefore canvassed 1 Con. 1 doubtful.				
Sir Geo. Warren				1				1	1
Launceston									
Rt. Hon. Mr. Morrice	1				Neither of these gentlemen will come in again, but two friends brought in by the Duke of Northumberland.				
John Buller	1					2			
Leicestershire									
Sir John Palmer		1			Most probable these two Gentn. will be returned again. Sir John Palmer, although not constantly with, yet is oftener so than otherwise. Mr. Hungerford most generally with except upon very popular questions. They are therefore convassed hopeful.[18]				
John P. Hungerford		1					2		
Leicester									
Hon. B. Grey				1	Most likely the same again. Mr. Grey is always against Govt. Mr. Darker shuffles and is a doubtful man especially on any trying question.				
John Darker			1					1	1
Leominster									
Lord Bateman	1				Lord Bateman it is apprehended will come in again easily. Mr. Cornwall stands for Ludlow, at present a Gentn. not a friend to Govt. it is thought will step forward but it is under consideration to get a friend to start. As yet it must remain doubtful.				
Fredk. Cornwall	1					1			1
Liskeard									
Samuel Salt				1	Mr. Elliot to be seen again				
Edward Gibbon	1							1	1
Carried over	124	9	9	109		103	22	34	92

18. Palmer's successor, William Pochin, proved hostile to Government.

	Pro.	Hope full	D'bt full	Con		Pro.	Hope full	D'bt full	Con
Brought over	124	9	9	109		103	22	34	92
Lostwithiel									
Lord Fairford	1				Whether the same again is				
Thos. Potter	1				not yet fixed, but if not, two friends.	2			
Lewes									
Sir Thos. Miller				1	Sir Thomas Miller and Mr.				
Mr. Hay				1	Hay will not both of them come in here, nor could one of them if properly opposed. Lord Pelham's 2nd son it is apprehended will come in for one—another Candidate is not yet known. As it now stands however it is canvassed doubtful and con. because there may be a contest.			1	1
Lime Regis									
Hon. H. Fane	1				It is hoped the same again.				
Francis Fane	1				Although there will be a contest and a question tried on petition as to the right of voting. The persons who bring forward the contest are friends to Govt. and would act with Govt.—but in this case administration connected and supported by Lord Westmoreland and the members, they cannot be accepted.	2			
Lincolnshire									
Chas. Anderson Pelham				1	Mr. Pelham will most prob-				
Sir John Thorold				1	ably come in again. It is not certain Sir John Thorold will. His conduct in all points opposing Govt. has given offence to many persons of consequence and interest and there is some talk of an opposition, but being uncertain both are canvassed as they now stand against Government.				2
Lincoln									
Lord Lumley				1	The same again probably				
Robt. Vyner	1				although Mr. Scroope threatens an opposition there. it is therefore only canvassed hopeful. Although Mr. Vyner's almost always with Govt. Lord Lumley is always against.		1		1
Carried over	129	9	9	114		107	23	35	96

	Pro.	Hope full	D'bt full	Con		Pro.	Hope full	D'bt full	Con
Brought over	129	9	9	114		107	23	35	96
Litchfield									
Geo. Anson				1	The same most probably	1			1
Thomas Gilbert	1								
Liverpool									
Sir Wm. Meredith				1	There will be a contest. The				
Richd. Pennant				1	question will be whether for				
					one or both. It seems agreed				
					that Sir Wm. Meredith will				
					not come in there again &				
					it is thought Mr. Bamber				
					Gascoyn junr. will succeed				
					him easily. But some are also				
					for attacking Mr. Pennant.				
					Col. Tarleton has been				
					talked of, though absent as				
					yet however nothing is fixed				
					but against Sir William.[19]	1			1
London									
Richd. Oliver				1	At present not more is				
Fredk. Bull				1	settled than for the Associ-				
John Sawbridge				1	ated Livery to take up &				
Geo. Hayley				1	support Mr. Alderman				
					Clark—another good man				
					is wanted			1	3
Ludlow									
Lord Clive	1				There is a contest here, but				
Lord Villiers	1				it is apprehended that Lord				
					Clive & Mr. F. Cornwall				
					will come in here. Lord Vil-				
					liers being abroad declines				
					but a Mr. Beale is set up by				
					the Patriots & discontents of				
					the Town tho' it is thought				
					he can't succeed.	1	1		
Luggershall									
Lord Melbourne	1				Lord Geo. Gordon will cer-				
Lord Geo. Gordon				1	tainly not come in again.				
					Lord Melbourne not yet				
					finally settled. Mr. Geo.				
					Selwyn proposing to quit				
					Gloucester intends to come				
					in here himself.	2			
Lymington									
Edw. Morant				1	Neither of these two Gentn.				
Henry Goodricke				1	will come in again here, but				
					two good friends of Govt.	2			
Maidstone									
Sir H. Mann			1		Most likely the same again.				
Hon. C. Finch	1				Sir Horace Mann is can-				
					vassed against because on				
					the popular questions he has				
					gone against but he is often				
					for, & inclines to support				
					Govt. & the present Con-				
					stitution.	1		1	
Carried over	134	9	10	124		114	25	37	101

19. In September 1780 Pennant also was defeated by a ministerial candidate.

	Pro.	Hope full	D'bt full	Con		Pro.	Hope full	D'bt full	Con
Brought over	134	9	10	124		114	25	37	101
Maldon									
Hon. R.S. Nassau	1				Mr. Harvey came in on the death of Mr. Nassau, & it is expected that he & Mr. Strutt will come in again without opposition.				
John Strutt	1					2			
Malmesbury									
Hon. C.J. Fox				1	Neither of these Gentn. will come in here again, but two good friends of Govt.				
W. Strahan	1					2			
Malton									
Sav. Finch				1	The same again most likely unless Ld. Rockingham may think fit to have Mr. Burke elected here to secure him a seat in case of failure at Bristol.				
Wm. Weddell				1					2
Marlborough									
Sir Jas. Tylney Long	1				Most probably the same	2			
Hon. Jas. Brudenell	1								
Marlow									
Willm. Clayton	1				Mr. Clayton stands very well here. Sir J.B. Warren does not stand well having been near the town but seldom since he was elected. An opposition is expected to arise there, & if a proper person could be found it might be carried for him. At present it stands doubtful. 30 July—favourable accounts have been received of a friend's succeeding.				
Sir J.B. Warren				1		1		1	
St. Mawes									
Lord Nugent	1				Same again	2			
Hugh Boscawen	1								
St. Michaels									
John Stephenson	1				Same again	2			
Fr. Hale	1								
Merionethshire									
E. Lloyd Vaughan				1	The same again				1
Midhurst									
Hon. Hen. S. Conway	1				Neither of these gentn. can come in here again. It is apprehended Mr. Henry Drummond will come in for one. The other is to be arranged for a friend.				
John Ord	1					2			
Middlesex									
John Wilkes				1	Whether anything should be attempted here must be considered & determined. The great difficulty is a good candidate. Such an one with				
Thos. Wood				1					
Carried over	146	9	10	131		127	25	38	104

	Pro.	Hope full	D'bt full	Con		Pro.	Hope full	D'bt full	Con
Brought over	146	9	10	131		127	25	38	104
					a regular systematic plan would certainly & easily carry this county, but then it requires time. Mr. Wood will probably decline & Mr. Byng stand. No other proper candidate has yet been found.				2
Milbourne Port									
Hon. Temple					Neither of these gentlemen will come in here again, but two friends it is hoped.	2			
Luttrell				1					
Chas Wolseley	1								
Minehead									
J.F. Luttrell			1		Young Mr. Luttrell will come in again. Mr. Pownall most probably not, but a friend yet as it is not yet fixed, this borough is canvassed doubtful, although means are taking to fix one.			2	
Thos. Pownall				1					
Monmouthshire									
John Hanbury				1	Most likely the same again	1			1
John Morgan	1								
Monmouth									
Sir John Stepney	1				The same again	1			
Montgomeryshire									
Wm. M. Owen				1	There will be a strong contest. It is said that Ld. Powis and Sir Watkins Williams Wynne have agreed upon Mr. Kynaston. Mr. Mostyn Owen at the head of the independent gentlemen proposes to again stand. He acted as a friend to Govt. for some time, but of late has taken a most hostile part. As a contest it is canvassed doubtful. N.B. Since the above state the affairs of this county have changed their situation. There has been a general meeting of the county within these few days, at which it has been acquiesced that Mr. Owen should stand, & the peace of the county be preserved.			1	
Montgomery									
Whitshed Keene	1				The same again probably	1			
Morpeth									
Peter Delmé	1				Probably the same again	2			
John Wm. Egerton	1								
Carried over	152	9	11	135		134	25	41	107

	Pro.	Hope full	D'bt full	Con		Pro.	Hope full	D'bt full	Co
Brought over	152	9	11	135		134	25	41	10
Newark									
Sir H. Clinton	1								
Geo. Sutton				1	The Duke of Newcastle says he is doubtful whether there will not be a contest here, but if there is it will affect Mr. Sutton's & not his interest. If so a change may be for the better, it can't be for the worse for Mr. Sutton is always against. However it is canvassed con as most safe.	1			1
Newcastle Under Lime									
Lord Chewton	1								
Lord Trentham	1				The same again, unless Lord Chewton or Lord Trentham should be taken to stand for Westminster, but however this is the members returned will be friends to Govt.	2			
Newport Cornwall									
Richd. Bull	1								
John Frederick	1				Neither of these gentln. again, but two friends to Govt. by the Duke of Northumberland.	2			
Newcastle Upon Tyne									
Sir M.W. Ridley				1	A contest is expected here. Sir M.W. Ridley may come in again. Sir Jn. Trevelyan will not. Mr. Bowes it is thought stands foremost & is not adverse. It will be endeavoured by the Duke of Northumberland to bring Sir M. Ridley to an explanation as to his principles before fully supported. At least it is hoped Govt. will get one friend here—although as it is not fixed certainly, it is only canvassed as hopeful.	1			1
Sir John Trevelyan				1					
Newport Isle of Wight									
H. Sloane	1								
Sir R. Worsley	1				It is not yet certain whether Mr. Sloane will come in here again. Sir Rd. Worsley will certainly. And if Mr. Sloane does not another friend to Govt. will come in.	1			1
Newton, Lancashire									
Anty. James Keck			1						
R.A. Gwillym				1	Most likely the same. They are both bad attenders. Mr. Keck often with us when he does attend, but is a doubtful man.			1	1
Carried over	159	9	12	139		140	26	43	11

	Pro.	Hope full	D'bt full	Con		Pro.	Hope full	D'bt full	Con
Brought over	159	9	12	139		140	26	43	110

Newton, Hants

Chas. Ambler	1				Yet uncertain whether Mr. Ambler will come in again here. Mr. Worsley certainly will. 30 July. Information has been rec'd that Mr. John Barrington is to come in here in the room of Mr. Worsley & it is hoped that he will be a friend. And a friend to Govt is to be bro't in vice Mr. Ambler.				
E.M. Worsley	1					1	1		

Norfolk

Sir E. Astley				1	Most likely the same				2
Thos. W. Coke				1					

Northallerton

Dan Lascelles	1				The same. Mr. Dan Lascelles is only put hopeful because in the late popular questions he has gone against, but he is a friend to Govt. & his going so has been more on account of his brother's situation with the county of York than from inclination & he is at least hopeful in another Parlt.				
Henry Peirse				1			1		1

Northampton

Hon. W. Tollemache				1	A contest is talked on here but not yet brought forward. Ld. Compton will not be of age, & it is yet uncertain whether anything can be done, so this place is canvassed as it now stands. 30 July. Lord Althorp will probably come in here for one, & if Ld. Compton was of age he would for the other without a question.[20]				
Sir Geo. Robinson				1					2

Northamptonshire

Lucy Knightley	1								
Thos. Powys				1	Probably the same but it is not yet fixed. Powys's conduct is not approved there are rumours of an opposition to him, but not yet brought forward enough. Sir Wm. Dolben has been talked of, but then there is a prospect of Oxford University for him, altho'				

	Pro.	full	full	Con		Pro.	full	full	Con
Carried over	161	11	12	145		141	28	43	115

20. The election in September 1780 of Admiral Rodney's son on the Compton family interest secured one member for Government.

	Hope	D'bt				Hope	D'bt	
	Pro.	full	full	Con		Pro.	full	full Cc
Brought over	161	11	12	145	this also uncertain. In this situation of things it has been judged best to put them down as they now stand.	141	28	43 11
Northumberland						1		1
Lord A. Percy	1							
Sir Wm. Middleton				1	Lord A Percy will certainly come in again. If a good candidate was got to stand forward, it is thought Sir Wm. Middleton w'd not, & he certainly does not deserve any support from Govt. The last time the voters from the Derwentwater estate carried him his election, & he goes uniformly agt Govt. Now that the Duke of Northumberland & Govt. would act warmly together if Sir Jnᵒ Delaval would stand, it is thought that Sir Wm. Middleton would be thrown out, but Sir J. Delaval is standing for Berwick has canvassed that place & says he is sure of coming in there. However this deserves considn. as Berwick might probably be managed for anʳ friend. It is however canvassed as it now stands.	1		1
Norwich								
Edw. Bacon	1				The same gentlemen again most likely	1		1
Sir H. Harbord				1				
Nottinghamshire								
Lord E.C. Bentinck				1	This county is not yet settled. It is not certainly fixed whether Lord Lincoln is or is not to offer himself. This will be settled by the Duke of Newcastle while in the country & known on his return, which will be in about a week. It is canvassed as it now stands. 30 July. The Duke is returned has been seen & is to fix this next week.			2
Chas. Meadows				1				
Nottingham								
Sir W. Howe				1	Most probably the same			2
Robt. Smith				1				
Carried over	163	11	12	151		143	29	43 12

	Pro.	Hope full	D'bt full	Con		Pro.	Hope full	D'bt full	Con
Brought over	163	11	12	151		143	29	43	122
Oakhampton									
Richd. Vernon	1				Most likely the same	1			1
H. Minchin				1					
Orford									
Lord Beauchamp	1				The same	2			
Honble. R.S.									
Conway	1								
Oxfordshire									
Lord Chas. Spencer	1				The same again	1			1
Lord Visct.									
Wenman				1					
Oxford City									
Lord Robt. Spencer	1				Probably the same again.				
Honble. Pere Bertie				1	Though not certainly known as to Mr. Bertie. He is constantly against & not a good attender.	1			1
Oxford University									
Sir Roger					It has been talked that Sir				
Newdigate			1		R. Newdigate would				
Frs. Page	1				decline & that Sir W. Dolben would come in. Many candidates however have been started Mr. Scott & Mr. Jones of University College & Wenman. But it is now again said that Sir Roger will not quit. And as it is not settled, this place is canvassed one doubtful, especially as Sir Roger has in most of the late questions, tho' not all, gone against. Mr. Page has given a warm support.	1		1	
					July 30. It is said now all be settled & that Sir W. Dolben will come in.				
Pembrokeshire									
Hugh Owen	1				There is a warm contest for this county, Lord Milford having offered himself but it is hoped Mr. Owen will carry it. As a contest however it is only put hopeful.			1	
Pembroke									
Hugh Owen	1				The same it is expected again.	1			
Carried over	171	11	13	154		150	30	44	125

	Hope D'bt					Hope D'bt			
	Pro.	full	full	Con		Pro.	full	full	C
Brought over	171	11	13	154		150	30	44	1
Penryn									
Sir Geo. Osborne	1				Neither of these gentlemen will come in for this place again. Sir Geo. Osborne wishes to come in for a quieter borough, Mr. Chaytor is to fight for Heddon. Sir Fr. Basset is to come in for one member, but he is not content with that & he wants to bring in the other & that Govt. shd. surrender up their interest to him there, desert their friends & put the borough into his hands. It is likely therefore it will end in a contest & perhaps in that case it may be necessary to fight for both members.	1		1	
Wm. Chaytor	1								
Peterborough									
Mattw. Wyldbore	1				Mr. Wyldbore can't come in here again but a Mr. Phipps will on the interest of Mr. Parker of Peterborough & Ld. Fitz-William's acquiescence, Mr. Phipps will be against.				
Richd. Benyon				1					
Petersfield									
Willm. Jolliffe	1				Sir Abr. Hume will not come in again for this borough. Mr. Jolliffe and his brother are to be returned. Mr Jolliffe has very handsomely supported since his being out of the Board of Trade, it is hoped that he will continue to do the like & that his brother will also be a friend. As he has an object, & to him a great one, to attain.[21]	1		1	
Sir Ab. Hume				1					
Plymouth									
Sir Fred. Rogers	1				Sir Fredk. Rogers, it is hoped with Adml. Mann will be returned for this borough at the General Election, altho' there will be a contest & a petition to try the right of election. Mr. Culme who stood and petitioned against Sir Fredk. Rogers will again stand & perhaps with another candidate to join him.	2			
Lord Lewisham	1								
Carried over	177	11	13	156		154	31	45	1

21. Jolliffe's object was a peerage.

	Pro.	Hope full	D'bt full	Con			Pro.	Hope full	D'bt full	Con
Brought over	177	11	13	156			154	31	45	127

Plympton

John Durand	1	It is uncertain whether the		
Wm. Fullarton	1	same gentn. but if not two		
		friends	2	

Pontefract

Rt. Hon. Sir J.	1	Neither of these gentln. will	
Goodricke	1	come in here again. Lord	
Chas. Mellish		Galway will come into his	

own seat. The other is at present in suspence, therefore must only be put down hopeful.   1   1

Poole

Joshua Mauger		1	There will be a contest, Mr.
Sir Eyre Coote	1		Gulston, Mr. Mauger, Mr.

Pitt the son of Mr. John Pitt, Sir Eyre Coote & Ld. Cranburne have all been talked of. Sir Eyre Coote it is said will decline. Lord Cranburne will not think of it in the present state of Lord Salisbury's health. Mr. Mauger has but little chance as an individual & may probably also decline. Mr. Pitt has made professions of friendship to Lord North & it seems likely that the result on the whole will be a return of Mr. Pitt & Mr. Gulston, who is a warm friend.   1   1

Portsmouth

Sir Wm. Gordon	1	The same for this time, but
Genl. Monckton	1	not again without a

compromise wch seems worth considering in this case. The lives now put in they should be good ones, & such as are not likely to vacate for office soon, in order to make a good compromise after the Election, if not can be made now. The pres' members don't quite fall within that line if it is worth attention.   2

Preston

Sir Henry Hoghton	1		
John Burgoyne		1	A contest is talked of but not

yet brought forward & it is probable the same members may be returned.   1   1

	Pro.	full	full	Con			Pro.	full	full	Con
Carried over	185	11	13	158			161	32	47	127

	Hope D'bt					Hope D'bt			
	Pro.	full	full	Con		Pro.	full	full	C
Brought over	185	11	13	158		161	32	47	1
Queensborough									
Sir Chas. Frederick	1				The same perhaps, if not two friends. Query Sir Hugh Palliser or at Saltash, or the 2nd for Scarboro'.	2			
Sir W. Rawlinson	1								
Radnor County									
Thos. Johnes	1				It is hoped the same altho' another contest is threatened.	1			
New Radnor									
Ed. Lewis	1				The same. Altho' there may be a return against him & he be put to a petition again by Mr. John Lewis.	1			
Reading									
John Dodd	1								
Fr. Annesley				1	A contest is much talked of at this place. The Publicans give hopes to all that come, in expectation of getting someone to offer & to have their harvest: But it is hoped that Mr. Dodd is safe against all attack & as to Mr. Annesley it is immaterial no change can be worse. Mr. Temple Luttrell was thought of and tried a little but the conversation seems to have drop't of his standing others have in the like manner been proposed & probably some one will be got to step forward, to make a third man in order to create expences.	1			
New Romney									
Sir Edw. Dering	1				Mr. Rd. Jackson can't come in here again, as Sir Ed. Dering will bring in his son along with himself. 30 July. Mr. Jackson says that Sir Edw. now gives him hopes of coming in again at this place—if so a friend will be gained.[22]	2			
Richd. Jackson	1								
East Retford									
Sir Cecil Wray				1	An attempt will be made here to throw Sir Cecil Wray out by Mr. Amcott's standing with Ld. John Clinton. It will be fixed while the Duke of Newcastle				
Ld. J.P. Clinton	1								
Carried over	193	11	13	160		168	32	47	

22. Robinson was confused at this point and, inconsistently with all the evidence, inserted the figure 2 in the 'Con' column. This error has not been reproduced here.

	Hope D'bt					Hope D'bt		
	Pro.	full	full	Con		Pro.	full	full	Con
Brought over	193	11	13	160		168	32	47	128

	Pro.	full full	Con	text	Pro.	full	full	Con

Brought over — Pro. 193, full 11, full 13, Con 160 | 168, 32, 47, 128

is in the country & known on his return. If it succeeds we shall here gain but at present it is canvassed doubtful — 1 ... 1

Richmond
Chas. Dundas — 1 — Mr. Dundas will come in
Mr. Norton — again but Mr. Norton not:
(William Norton) — 1 — Sir Lawrence on a compromise to secure his son Mr. Thomas Dundas for Stirlingshire is fixed to bring in Lord Graham for Richmond, & it is not certain that Lord Graham will be against Govt. There is no such obligation to Sir Lawrence. — 1 ... 1

Rippon
Wm. Aislabie — 1
Wm. Lawrence — 1 — The same again. They both stand now in the line of hopeful & it is fair to think may do so. Mr. Aislabie can scarce attend. Mr. Lawrence does not often but when he does often with. — 2

Rochester
Geo. F. Hatton — 1
Robt. Gregory — 1 — The interest of Govt. stands so favourably here that it is hoped with management & attention, & a sudden declaration at the moment all being prepared, that Sir Geo. Rodney might be carried with Mr. Hatton. Mr. Gregory is always against. — 2

Rutlandshire
Thos. Noel — 1 — The same again. — 1 ... 1
G.B. Brudenell — 1
Rye
Honble Thos. — 1 — Most likely the same — 2
Onslow
Wm. Dickenson — 1
Reygate
Hble. Jo. Yorke — 1 — The same again. — 1 ... 1
Sir C. Cocks — 1
Salop
C. Baldwyn — 1 — Mr. Baldwyn will not come
N. Hill — 1 — in here again. Mr. Hill will. The other candidate not yet certain, so both are put down doubtful. — 2

| Carried over | 199 | 14 | 14 | 164 | | 173 | 35 | 53 | 130 |

		Hope full	D'bt full	Con			Hope full	D'bt full	C
	Pro.					Pro.			
Brought over	199	14	14	164		173	35	53	1
Saltash									
Sir Grey Cooper	1				Sir Grey Cooper & an^r				
Mr. (Paul)					person in office, not Mr.				
Wentworth	1				Wentworth again probably.	2			
Sandwich									
Phil. Stephens	1				Mr. Stephens it is appre-				
Chas. Brett				1	hended will certainly come in here again. But it is not so certain for Mr. Brett. Sir Richd. Sutton proposing to offer himself & it is hoped will succeed, however not being clearly fixed it is put doubtful.	1			1
New Sarum									
Wm. Hussey				1	The same again probably.				
Hon. Mr. Bouverie				1	But it has been thrown out that Mr. Hussey does not stand well with the electors & some enquiries are making.				
Old Sarum									
Thos. Pitt				1	The same most probably				
Pinckney Wilkinson				1					
Scarborough									
Lord Tyrconnel				1	Lord Tyrconnel has declared and canvassed & unless it should [be thought] proper to start Sir H. Palliser who has a very good personal interest there added to the weight of Govt., His Lordship & Capt. Phipps will come in. If Sir Hugh should be started here, two might be got, or perhaps Capt. Phipps lost; this requires deliberation.				
Honble. Capt.	1								
Phipps						1			
Seaford									
Lord Gage	1				The same gentn. it is hoped	2			
Geo. Medley	1								
Shaftesbury									
Mr. Mortimer				1	There is a contest here, Sir				
Geo. Rous				1	Geo. Collyer & Mr. Mortimer have declared upon Mr. Mortimer's interest. Mr. Sykes upon his own. Mr. Sykes states that he is secure, & if the contest goes on he may probably offer an^r person to stand with him.	1			1
					30th July. Mr. Sykes says that he has a majority for himself and another.				
Carried over	205	14	14	172		180	35	55	

	Hope	D'bt				Hope	D'bt	
	Pro.	full	full	Con		Pro.	full	full	Con
Brought over	205	14	14	172		180	35	55	135

Shoreham

Sir Jn° Shelley — 1
C. Goring — 1 (Con)

Sir John Shelley & Mr. Goring decline. Sir Cecil Bisshopp Sir Godfrey Webster, Mr. Peachey, & Mr. are candidates. The Duke of Richmond supports Sir Godfrey Webster, but it is hoped from the canvass that has been made that Sir Cecil Bisshopp & Mr. Peachey wil come in. — 2

Shrewsbury

Willm. Pulteney — 1 (Con)
John Corbet — 1 (Con)

There is some talk of an opposition here but it has not yet come forward, therefore probably it may be the same persons. — 2

Somersetshire

Richd. H. Coxe — 1 (Con)
Edw. Phelips Esq. — 1 (Con)

Sir John Trevelyan proposes to stand for this county, but he is against Govt. as well as the other gentlemen so that whichever way it turns out nothing will be gained. — 2

Southampton

John Fuller — 1 (Pro)
John Fleming — 1 (Con)

A contest is talked on here against Mr. Fleming. Mr. Fuller is thought safe. Mr. Woodford has talked of offering himself & also Sir Andrew Hammond, who is thought stand most favourably. This town is therefore pro for one & hopeful for the other. — 1 1

Southwark

Henry Thrale — 1 (Pro)
N. Polhill — 1 (Con)

Sir Ab. Hume has sometimes been talked of to stand here, but he is no better for Govt. than Mr. Polhill & has not yet come forward to declare—Mr. Thrale it is hoped is secure. 30th July. Altho' it is now said they mean to push at him.[23] — 1 1

Staffordshire

Sir Wm. Bagot — 1 (Pro)
Sir J. Wrottesley — 1 (Pro)

Same again — 2

| Carried over | 210 | 14 | 14 | 179 | | 184 | 38 | 55 | 140 |

23. An incorrect forecast. Thrale lost his seat to an opponent of Government.

	Pro.	Hope full	D'bt full	Con		Pro.	Hope full	D'bt full	C
Brought over	210	14	14	179		184	38	55	14
Stafford									
Hugo Meynell				1	Mr. Meynell will not come in here again. Mr. Whitworth will, & also it is hoped another friend of Government.[24]				
Richd. Whitworth	1					1	1		
Stamford									
Sir Geo. Howard	1				It is not certain whether these Gentn. come in again, but if not it is hoped 2 friends of Govt. will be brought in by Lord Exeter.				
Henry Cecil	1					2			
Steyning									
Thos. E. Freeman	1				Mr. Freeman will probably come in here again. Mr. Honeywood stands for *Kent* but it is likely may keep this in hand to secure a seat either by being elected himself or having a friend put in. Mr. Freeman is mostly with us, tho' sometimes gives a vote against. 31st July and from further information most certainly has the Borough. Mr. Freeman is a relation of Mr. Honeywood.[25]				
F. Honeywood				1		1			
Stockbridge									
Lord Irnham				1	It is said that this is secured again in the same family it is but however canvassed doubtful altho' Ld. Irnham came round about at once lately & all his family seem doing so too. The borough in fact with attention w'd belong to the Duchy of Lancaster. 31 July. It is now said that Capt. John Luttrell is to come in here in the room of Lord Irnham.				
Honble. James Luttrell				1		2			
Sudbury									
Sir Patrick Blake				1	It is expected that there will be a contest here. Sir Patrick Blake & Mr. Crespigny are expected to come in. If Mr. Crespigny succeeds agt Sir Walden Hanmer he is a friend, & the borough will stand as it does now.				
Sir W. Hanmer	1					1			
Carried over	215	14	14	184		189	39	57	1

24. An incorrect forecast. Both seats went to the Opposition.
25. Both seats went to supporters of Opposition.

	Hope	D'bt				Hope	D'bt	
	Pro.	full	full	Con		Pro.	full	full	Con
Brought over	215	14	14	185		189	39	57	142

Suffolk

Sir C. Bunbury				1	Sir Chas. Bunbury may be				
R. Holt	1				again returned. It is said				
					that Sir John Rous will				
					stand agt Mr. Holt & there-				
					fore this is put down doubt-				
					ful.	1			1
					31st July.				
					Further accounts say that				
					Mr. Holt stands higher in				
					the County than Sir Chas.				
					Bunbury & that probably				
					he will fail. Sir John Rous				
					made a great point to get				
					spared being sheriff this yr.				
					& therefore it is probable he				
					will offer.				

Surrey

Jas. Scawen				1	An opposition is talked of				
Sir Jos. Mawbey				1	here, but nothing arranged.				
					The Gentn. are so divided				
					& jealous of each other that				
					it is very hazardous they will				
					agree even to oppose				
					persons against whom they				
					all exclaim & consequently				
					it is probable these Gentn.				
					may come in again. 31 July.				
					Lord Onslow now says that				
					he has hopes of this county				
					for his son.				2

Sussex

Lord Geo. Lenox				1	Lord Geo. Lenox will it is				
Sir T.S. Wilson				1	apprehended be chosen				
					again—Sir Thos. Wilson				
					not come in, but is said Lord				
					Pelham's eldest son will be				
					chosen. If so we shall *prob-*				
					ably gain one, but as it is not				
					fixed, the old canvass is left				
					from caution, to remain				
					against accidental losses on				
					our side.				2

Tamworth

Thos. de Grey				1	Mr. De Grey will not come				
Anth. Chamier				1	in again here. Who Lord				
					Townshend will elect is not				
					known. Probably his son				
					John, if he does not succeed				
					at Cambridge. If so it will				
					be one against & for this				
					reason it is so canvassed—if				
					not it may be a friend				
					chosen. Mr Chamier will				
					most probably be chose				
					again—if not, a friend.	1			1

Carried over	216	14	14	192		190	39	58	148

	Hope D'bt					Hope D'bt		
	Pro.	full	full	Con		Pro.	full	full	Co
Brought over	216	14	14	192		190	39	58	14
Tavistock									
Rt. Hon. Mr.	1				The same again				
Rigby						1			1
Mr. Fitzpatrick									
junr.			1						
Taunton									
Alex Popham				1	A contest is declared here				
John Halliday	1				against Mr. Popham by				
					Col. Roberts who is a friend				
					of Govt. & it is hoped he &				
					Mr. Halliday will succeed.				
					If so they will be both				
					friends to Govt. But for				
					caution this place is can-				
					vassed as returning one				
					hopeful one doubtful.	1			1
Tewkesbury									
Sir Wm.					The same again most likely				2
Codrington			1						
Jas. Martin			1						
Thetford									
C.F. Scudamore				1	Whether Mr. Fitzroy Scu-				
Hon. C. Fitzroy	1				damore comes in or not is				
					not known, but it is appre-				
					hended Genl. Fitzroy will				
					not, and consequently that				
					the Duke of Grafton will				
					choose a person adverse to				
					Govt. & as such it is can-				
					vassed.				2
Thirske									
Sir Thos. Frank-					Sir Thos. Frankland being				
land				1	disappointed of Greenwich				
Thos. Frankland				1	hospital will not let a friend				
					of Govt. come in for that				
					place, as he once talked of,				
					but the seats are in suspence,				
					& some persons not *adverse*				
					to Govt. are enquiring				
					about this place & may				
					succeed. It is therefore can-				
					vassed only doubtful.				2
Tiverton									
Sir John Duntze	1				Sir John Duntze will come				
J.E. Wilmot				1	in again if his health will				
					permit. Mr. Wilmot is not				
					so clear, but it may be so, &				
					therefore canvassed as the				
					borough now stands.	1			
Totness									
Sir Ph. Jennings					Sir P.J. Clerke, it is thought,				
Clerke				1	will come in again on the				
James Amyatt				1	Bolton interest. But it is				
					thought Mr. Amyatt will				
					not succeed. Mr. Launcelot				
					Browne jnr. stands on the				
Carried over	220	14	14	201		192	40	61	1

	Pro.	Hope full	D'bt full	Con		Pro.	Hope full	D'bt full	Con
Brought over	220	14	14	201		192	40	61	154

interest of Mr. Justice Buller & in concert it is believed with the Bolton interest to throw out Amyatt. It is however canvassed only hopeful, as it is a contest.[26]

Tregony
Hon. Geo. Lane
Parker — 1
Sir Alex Leith — — — 1

It is uncertain yet whether Genl. Parker will come again into Parlt. Sir Alex Leith will certainly not come in for this place. But altho' these two gentlemen do not come in yet it is hoped that two friends to Govt. will.
31 July. It is now settled for 2 friends.

Truro
B. Gascoyne — 1
Geo. Boscawen — — — 1

It is not settled for the Election of these gentn. either, but if they are not chosen it is hoped it will be two friends & not Mr. Geo. Boscawen again, & therefore it is canvassed hopeful. 31 July. A son of the late Adm. Boscawen & heir to Ld. Falmouth is to be brought in for one & Wm. Aug. Spencer Boscawen another son of the late Genl. Boscawen for the other.

Wallingford
John Cator — 1
Sir Robt. Barker — 1

There is an opposition here by Mr. Aubrey who is drove from Aylesbury and Mr. Archdeacon a Jamaica Planter, supported by Lord Abingdon. Sir Robt. Barker will not stand here again, at least if he comes again into parliament, but Mr. Cator stands with another friend of Govt. & says that he is sure of carrying this borough for both. Mr. Cator however is certain— therefore canvassed one for one hopeful.[27]

Values in the right-hand columns for the narrative rows: 1, 1 (interest of Mr. Justice Buller); 2 (Tregony); 1, 1 (Truro); 1, 1 (Wallingford)

	Pro.	Hope full	D'bt full	Con		Pro.	Hope full	D'bt full	Con
Carried over	224	14	14	203		196	43	61	155

---

26. In September 1780 Brown's success brought a gain of one seat to Government.
27. An incorrect forecast. Opposition candidates took both seats.

	Pro.	Hope full	D'bt full	Con		Pro.	Hope full	D'bt full	Co
Brought over	224	14	14	203		196	43	61	15.
Wareham									
Rt. Hon. W.G. Hamilton				1	It is apprehended that Mr. Hamilton will not come in				
Chris. D'Oyley	1				here again, nor is it fixed for Mr. d'Oyley, but it is hoped two friends will be brought in. One only at present fixed, Mr. Farrer from the East Indies.	2			
					31 July. It is now fixed for another friend, Mr. D'Oyley desiring to quit Parliament on acct. of his health.				
Warwickshire									
Sir T.G. Skipwith				1	Most probably the same if Sir Chas. Holte lives or				
Sir Chas. Holte				1	offers again. If not Sir Chas. Mordaunt is talk of who will be friendly.				2
Warwick									
Hon. C.F. Greville	1				It is hoped the same altho' there has been an opposition				
Hon. R.F. Greville	1				started, but it is believed not to be of consequence.[28]				2
Wells									
Clement Tudway			1		Most likely the same		1	1	
Robt. Child		1							
Wendover									
Henry Drummond	1				Not the same again. Lord Verney will bring in two others, but who is not				
Thos. Dummer	1				known. However it is prudent to reckon them against altho' *circumstances* may rise to change this.				2
Wenlock									
Sir H. Bridgman				1	Most likely the same again.				2
George Forrester				1					
Weobley									
Mr. Bayntun	1				Probably the same again. If not two friends to Govern-				
John St. Leger Douglas	1				ment.				2
Westbury									
Hon. T. Wenman	1				Lord Abingdon will scarce bring Mr. Wenman in				
Sam. Estwicke				1	again. Mr. Estwicke he may, but almost probable he will bring both members opponents to Govt.				2
West Looe									
Sir Wm. James	1				Mr. Buller will probably come in here himself & he				
John Rogers	1				will bring in Sir William James both for Govt. & Mr. Rogers must give way.				2
Carried over	234	15	15	209		204	44	62	16

28. An incorrect forecast. The Grevilles lost one seat to an opposition candidate.

	Pro.	Hope full	D'bt full	Con		Pro.	Hope full	D'bt full	Con
Brought over	234	15	15	209		204	44	62	163
Westminster									
Earl Lincoln	1								
Lord Malden	1								

It is not settled who is to stand to combat Mr. Fox. It is said by Persons of consequence & weight that Lord Malden will not do. The business waits for the Duke of Northumberland returning out of the West & the Duke of Newcastle from the north, when it will be immy fixed.   2

Westmoreland									
Sir Mich. le Fleming				1					
Jas. Lowther				1					

Sir Mich. le Fleming may come in again. Mr. Lowther is uncertain, but most likely both will be against, for no opposition to Sir Jas. Lowther is yet declared or formed.   2

Weymouth etc.									
Rt. Hon. Mr. Ellis	1								
W.C. Grove		1							
John Purling	1								
Gabl. Steward	1								

The same again probably except for Mr. Purling, but this is one of the few seats which Govt. have left for high office & convenient change, & therefore it is submitted it ought to be kept as such.   3   1

Whitchurch									
Lord Middleton				1					
Thos. Townshend				1					

The same again.   2

Wigan									
Geo. Byng				1					
John Moreton	1								

Neither of these gentlemen will come in here again unless Mr. Wood sh^d continue Middlesex, & then Mr. Byng will. This borough is canvassed against because the Duke of Portland is supposed to have weight there & may with proper attention probably succeed in bringing in some friends, altho' it has been thrown out that it is open & Sir R. Clayton, the heir who has the most natural interest there has been mentioned as having intentions to stand. If he succeeds he is a friend.   2

31 July. Mr. Moreton is dead & a new election is expected on his death.

Carried over	240	16	15	214		207	45	64	169

	Hope	D'bt				Hope	D'bt		
	Pro.	full	full	Con		Pro.	full	full	Con
Brought over	240	16	15	214		207	45	64	160
Wilton									
Henry Herbert	1				Lord Pembroke will not bring Mr. H. Herbert in again & it is doubtful whether he will bring in Mr. Chas. Herbert. He will perhaps therefore bring in two persons who will be against.				2
Chas. Herbert	1								
Wiltshire									
Ch. Penruddock				1	These two gentn. will probably come in again for this county.				2
Amb. Goddard				1					
Winchelsea									
C.W. Cornwall	1				Mr. Nedham will not come in again for this place. Mr. Cornwall may with Mr. Nesbit who will also be a friend.				2
Wm. Nedham				1					
Winchester									
Henry Penton	1				The same again, & if either of them are changed it is hoped friends will succeed.				2
Lov. Stanhope	1								
Windsor									
Adml. Kepple				1	Mr. Powney has started against Mr. Kepple & it is said will succeed. Mr. Montague will it is thought come in again.			1	1
Hon. John Montague				1					
Woodstock									
Mr. Eden	1				Probably the same again, if not two friends.				2
Lord Visc. Parker	1								
Worcester City									
John Walsh				1	It is said that Mr. Walsh will decline Parliament. Mr. Rous will probably stand again. It is an uncertain place depending much on popularity. If the Gentn. of Worcester & the neighbourhood can agree among themselves they will bring in a person. If not Sir W. Lewes or some such man will get in perhaps. 31 July. It is now said that Mr. Beaufoy is to stand. If he succeeds he will not be unfriendly.			1	1
T.B. Rous				1					
Worcestershire									
Honb. E. Foley				1	The same again most likely.				
Willm. Lygon				1	Mr. Lygon is not violently against, & did not attend in many of the late popular questions.				2
Carried over	247	16	16	222		213	45	66	17

	Pro.	Hope D'bt full	full	Con		Pro.	Hope D'bt full	full	Con
Brought over	247	16	16	222		213	45	66	177
Wootton Basset									
Honbl. H. St. John	1				Mr. Scott will not come in				
Robt. Scott				1	here again. Genl. St. John will it is hoped bring in a friend with him.	2			
Chipping Wycombe									
Robt. Waller			1		Probably the same, tho' as				
Honbl. Thos. Fitz-maurice				1	Mr. Fitzmaurice does not attend it does not answer Ld. Shelburne's wishes, & therefore it may be doubtful whether he will bring Mr. Fitzmaurice in again.		1		1
Yarmouth, Norfolk									
Rt. Hon. Chas. Townshend	1				The same again	1			1
Honble. R. Walpole			1						
Yarmouth, Hants									
Robt. Kingsmill				1	Probably the same again.	1			1
Jas. Worsley	1				31 July. it is now said that Mr. Jas. Worsley does not come into Prlt. again, but that Mr. E.M. Worsley will come in for this place.				
Yorkshire									
Sir Geo. Saville				1	Mr. Lascelles is threatened				
E. Lascelles			1		with an oppos^n for his conduct, which tho' he voted with opposition has been imputed to be with a view to his election not from principle & by his management he has not pleas'd either side. The Patriots despise him, the friends of Govt. in Yorkshire are disgusted with him for his trimming. However no one has yet publicly stood forth, and an opposition for the county of Yorks is so very serious a matter in point of expence for the person attacking as well as the person attacked & would be so also to Sir Geo. Saville the person not meant to be attacked & Mr. Lascelles having ready money to fight with & a fortune not easily hurt, it is probable that weight may deter the party from an attempt against him.				
							1		1
Carried over	250	18	16	227		217	46	67	181

	Hope D'bt					Hope D'bt		
	Pro.	full	full	Con		Pro.	full	full	Con
Brought over	250	18	16	227		217	46	67	181

York City
Lord J. Cavendish — 1 — Probably the same if Lord
Chas. Turner — 1 — John Cavendish will stand for it, but this has been questioned. — 2

SCOTLAND

Aberdeenshire
Alexr. Garden — 1 — The same perhaps, if not a friend Mr. Fergusson or Lord Wm. Gordon — 1

Airshire
Sir Adam Ferguson — 1 — The same — 1

St. Andrews, Forfar, Coupar, Perth & Dundee
Geo. Dempster — 1 — Hopeful to have a friend in col. Fletcher Campbell is trying for these boroughs. The Duke of Athol it is said has also some thoughts of them for his uncle, capt. Murray. If either of these gentlemen succeed they will be friends. — 1

Annan, Sanghar, Lochmaben, Dumfries & Kirkcudbright
Sir Wm. Douglas — 1 — A friend by the Duke of Queensborough if Sir Wm. Douglas does not come in again, but the Duke & he are now reconciled & probably he may be again chosen. — 1

Anstruther Easter etc.
Honble. Geo. Damer — 1 — Not again but Sir John Anstruther, & after a session or two Mr. Anstruther his son. — 1

Argyleshire
Ad. Livingstone — 1 — The same or a friend by the Duke of Argyll. — 1

Bamffshire
Earl of Fife — 1 — The same — 1

Berwickshire
Sir John Paterson — 1 — the same or a friend of Lord Advocate. Candidates. Sir Jnº Paterson, Mr. Scott of Harden. Mr. Renton— whichever of these gentlemen come in will be a friend. — 1

| Carried over | 256 | 18 | 16 | 231 | | 223 | 46 | 68 | 18. |

	Pro.	Hope full	D'bt full	Con		Pro.	Hope full	D'bt full	Con
Brought over	256	18	16	231		223	46	68	184
Brechin, Aberbrothock Aberdeen, etc.									
Ad. Drummond	1				The same, or Sir Dav^d Carnegie both friends.	1			
Bute & Caithnessshire									
Honlbe. Jas. Stuart	1				Mr. Sinclair of Ulbster representing Cathness.	1			
Clackmannan & Kinross									
Ra. Abercrombie	1				Mr. Graham, Lord Newhaven's nephew for Kinross.	1			
Dumbartonshire									
Sir A. Edmonstone	1				The same if dissolved before August. If not there will be a contest & perhaps carried by Lord Graham's interest to Mr. Elphinstone both friends. 31 July. From a conversation Mr. R. had two days ago with Capt. Keith Elphinstone, a compromise seems not unpracticable.	1			
Dumfriesshire									
Sir Robt. Lawrie	1				The same most likely. If not a friend by the Duke of Queensborough	1			
Dunfermline, Culross, Sterling & Queensferry									
Arch. Campbell	1				The same	1			
Dunbar, Lauder, etc.									
Mr. Charteris	1				Mr. Charteris, but if not a friend—Lord Advocate— Mr. Scott.	1			
Edinburghshire									
Heny. Dundas	1				The same	1			
Edinburgh									
Rt. Hon. Sir L. Dundas				1	Apprehended not; with attention & any fair support to the Duke of Buccleugh who will bring in a friend. 31st July. The latest accounts rec'd seem to think that Sir Lawrence can't be hurt for *this time*.				1
Elginshire									
Ld. Wm. Gordon	1				The same or Mr. Fergusson, one of them for this county, & the other for Aberdeenshire, if Garden goes out.	1			
Elgin, Cullen, Kintore, etc.									
Genl. Morris	1				The same—Genl. Grant.	1			
Fifeshire									
J. Henderson	1				Not the same—Genl. Skene	1			
Carried over	266	19	16	232		233	47	68	185

	Hope	D'bt				Hope	D'bt	
	Pro.	full	full	Con		Pro.	full	full	Con
Brought over	266	19	16	233		233	47	68	185
Forfarshire									
Earl Panmure	1				The same	1			
Fortrose, Forres, etc.									
Sir Hector Munro	1				The same. If, in order to preserve the peace of the county of Ross, on Mr. Mackenzie declining, he should not be taken there & then another friend will be brought in here. This is yet in suspence	1			
Haddingtonshire									
Mr. Nisbett Junr.	1				Not the same. Mr. Dalrymple the son of Sir Hugh Dalrymple it is said. 31 July. Mr. Nisbett says he has expectations to carry it—whichever is returned will be a friend.	1			
Invernessshire									
Genl. Frazer	1				The same	1			
Kincardineshire									
Lord Ad. Gordon	1				The same	1			
Kinghorn, Dysart, etc.									
John Johnstone				1	An opposition by Mr. Henderson, the present member for Fifeshire. Doubtful but if Mr. Henderson succeeds will be with us.				1
Kirkcudbright Stewardry									
Willm. Stewart	1				An opposition. Candidates—Mr. Johnstone supported by Lord Galloway. Mr. Alexʳ Stuart a Colonel, Brother to the present member—Mr. Gordon of Kenmure, supported by the Duke of Queensberry—All friends. the same to Govt. whoever succeeds.	1			
Lanarkshire									
Andrew Stuart	1				The same	1			
Linlithgowshire									
Sir Wm. Cunnynghame	1				The same	1			
Nairn & Cromartyshire									
John Campbell	1				Mr. Geo. Ross, or Sir Jnᵒ Gordon. 31st July. Mr. Ross will come in for Cromarty. Sir John Gordon in this case might wish to come in for Ross shire. This however might make a contest, but	1			
Carried over	275	19	16	233		242	47	69	185

| | Hope D'bt | | | | Hope D'bt | | |
	Pro.	full	full	Con		Pro.	full	full	Con
Brought over	275	19	16	233	there will be a meeting soon & then it is to be settled amicably if possible for Rossshire, & Sir Hector Munro's boroughs—Fortrose etc.	242	47	69	185
Orkney & Zetlandshire									
Thos. Dundas Junr.				1	The same, but if an opposition supposed might be defeated—to be considered well.				1
Peeblesshire									
Sir Robt. Murray Keith	1				Not the same. The Solicitor General of Scotland, Mr. Murray.	1			
Peebles, Lanerk, etc									
Sir Jas. Cockburn	1				Not the same, but a friend Mr. Scott, Mr. Colt or Sir G. Elliot as they may or may not succeed in the elections they are at present engaged in.	1			
Perthshire									
Hon. Jas. Murray	1				The same.	1			
Renfrewshire									
John Craufurd Junr.	1				An opposition. Mr. Shaw Stuart of Greenock agreed with Mr. Macdowall to come in to the end of 3 years, in order to throw out Mr. Craufurd. Lord Eglintoune—see on it—Mr. Craufurd would carry it if Lord Eglintowne will join or does not ratify the agreement. Mr. Shaw Stuart is strong against Govt. Query defeat him if no better can be by throwing the election on Mr. Macdowall who is a friend.			1	
Rossshire									
Rt. Hon. J.S. Mackenzie	1				Talks of declining. 2 parties—Ross and Mackenzies—Talk to him on it—whichever way will be a friend. 31st July. Mr. Mackenzie has declared his intention to quit parliament. Ld. McLeod talked of to succeed—Sir Jnᵒ Gordon & Sir Hector Munro—to be settled, vide remarks on Nairn & Cromarty.	1			
Carried over	280	19	16	234		246	47	70	186

	Hope	D'bt				Hope	D'bt	
	Pro.	full	full	Con		Pro.	full	full	Cor
Brought over	280	19	16	234		246	47	70	186
Rothesay, Inverarie, etc.									
Honble. Fredk.					The same most likely	1			
Stuart	1								
Roxburghshire									
Sir Gilbert Elliot	1				A contest, issue uncertain—but which ever way, a friend. Ld. Robt. Kerr stands against Sir Gilbert.	1			
Rutherglin, Dunbarton, etc.									
Ld. Fredk.					The same	1			
Campbell	1								
Selkirkshire									
John Pringle	1				The same	1			
Stirlingshire									
Thos. Dundas				1	The same, having agreed with Lord Graham to bring him in for Richmond, otherwise not.				1
Sutherlandshire									
Honbl. Jas.					The same	1			
Wemyss	1								
Tayne, Wick, Dingwall, etc.									
Genl. Grant	1				A dispute not yet settled, whether Genl. Grant or col. Ross. Either way a friend. 31st July. By the last accounts received it is feared that Genl. Grant will not succeed.	1			
Wigtownshire									
Honbl. K. Stewart	1				The same.	1			
Wigtown, Whitehorn, etc.									
Sir H.W.					If Lord Dalrymple can be nominated a minister abroad, & promoted on that line, a friend may be brought in by Lord Stair for these boroughs.				
Dashwood	1				31 July. This is proposed to be tried, & if it can be, to bring in Mr. Adam.	1			
	288	19	16	235		254	47	70	18⁸

29. As corrected. Owing to arithmetical slips the original document shows these figures thus: THIS P 290 H 19 D 16 C 233, FUTURE P 252 H 47 D 70 C 189.

Abstract and State 31 July 1780
with remarks to this day

	THIS				FUTURE			
	P	H	D	C	P	H	D	C
	288	19	16	235	254	47	70	187
Add the Hopeful as below to the Pros					47			
Add part of the Doubtful as below to the Pros					44[30]			
Add to the Cons the remainder of the Doubtful as below								26[30]
The supposed numbers will therefore be					345			213

30. The correct figures should be 45 and 25, with corresponding changes in the totals. Robinson added incorrectly on the detailed list that follows.

31

		Hopeful may be Pro.	Hopeful yet may be Con.	Doubtful convassed Pro.	Doubtful canvassed Con.
Boston	H. Sibthorpe	1			
Cambridge-shire	Sir S. Gideon & Mr. Yorke	2			
Cambrig. Town	vice S. Jenyns	1			
Carnarvon	Ld. Newborough vice T.A. Smith	1			
Chippenham	vice S. Marsh	1			
2 Dartmouth	31 July 1 pro 1 con				
Devizes	vice C. Garth	1			
Downton	Mr. Shaftoes friend		1		
Exeter	vice Sir C. Bampfylde		1		
Gt. Grimsby	Mr. Mellish	1			
Hampshire	Sir H.P. St. John	1			
Hertford Town	Mr. Calvert	1			
Heydon	2 friends		2		
Hindon	2 friends		2		
Hythe	Sir C. Farnaby	1			
Leicestershire	Pres. Members	2			
Lincoln City	Robt. Vyner	1			
Liverpool	vice Sir W. Meredith	1			
Ludlow	vice Ld. Villiers	1			
Newcastle (Tyne)	vice Sir J. Trevelyan	1			
1 Newton (Hants)	31 July 1 Pro.				
Northallerton	D. Lascelles	1			
Northampton-shire	L. Knightley	1			
Pembrokeshire	H. Owen	1			
Petersfield	vice Sir A. Hume	1			
1 Pontefract					
Rippon	prest members	2			
Ryegate	John Yorke	1			
Shoreham	vice prest members	2			
Southampton	vice J. Fleming	1			
Stafford	vice H. Meynell	1			
Agmondesham	Wm. Drake senr.			1	
Arundel				1	1
Bedford	S. Whitbread			1	
Berwick	Sir J.H. Delaval			1	
Bletchingley	vice Standert			1	1
Bridport	vice Cary			1	
Bristol	vice Burke			1	
Buckingham	vice Rd. Grenville				1
Canterbury	Ld. Newhaven			1	
Carlisle	vice A. Storer				
Carmarthen Town	vice Adams			1	1
Colchester	2 friends			2	
Devonshire	Mr. Rolle			1	
Evesham	One friend			1	
Gatton	Mr. Mayne & a friend			2	
St. Germans				2	
Grampound				1	
Haslemere				2	
Hertford Town	Daron Dimsdale			1	
Ipswich	present members			1	1
Kent	31 July 1 con vice Knight				1
Kingston (Hull)	vice Hartley				1
Lancaster					1
Leicester City	J. Darker			1	
Leskeard				1	
Leominster					1
Lewes	Mr. Pelham			1	
London	vice Oliver			1	
Maidstone	Sir H. Mann			1	
Marlow	vice Sir J.B. Warren			1	
Minehead	J.F. Luttrell & friend			2	
Montgomery-shire	M. Owen				1

31. A column giving page references to the original manuscript has been omitted.

		Hopeful may be Pro.	Hopeful yet may be Con.
Taunton	J. Halliday again	1	
Totness	vice Jas. Amyatt	1	
1 Truro	31st July 1 Pro		
Wells	Robt. Child	1	
Wallingford	vice Aubrey	1	
Weymouth	Mr. Grove	1	
Chip. Wycomb	R. Waller	1	
Clackmannan & Kinross	Mr. Graham	1	
		42³²	
		5	
	Total hopeful	47	

		Doubtful convassed Pro.	Doubtful canvassed Con.
Newport, Isle of Wight		1	
Newton, Lancashire	Keck		1
Oxford Univ^ty	vice Sir R. Newdigate	1	
Penryn	Vice W. Chaytor	1	
Poole	vice Mauger	1	
Preston	vice Burgoyne		1
Retford	Cecil Wray		1
Richmond	Lord Graham		1
Rochester	Hatton & Gregory	1	1
Shropshire		1	1
Sandwich	vice Brett	1	
Shaftesbury	with Sykes		1
Stockbridge	The Luttrells	2	
Suffolk	R. Holt Query 31st July 1 Pro		1
Taunton	vice Popham	1	
Thirsk	Franklands Query		2
Wells	C. Tudway	1	
Westminster		2	
Windsor	vice Keppel	1	
Worcester	Mr. Walsh		1
Yorkshire	Mr. Lascelles	1	
St. Andrews etc.	Col. F. Campbell vice Dempster (if succeeds Pro)		1
Kinghorn etc.	vice Johnstone		1
Renfrewshire	S. Stuart vice Craufurd		1
		44	26³³
		26	
	Total doubtful	70	

32. Incorrectly totalled by Robinson: the figure should be 41. But in this abstract he had omitted one seat for Gloucestershire, which makes up the correct total of 47 Hopeful.

33. See note 30.

INDEXES

I HOSPITALLERS' ACCOUNTS

LATYMER'S CHRONICKILLE

III SCUDAMORE LETTERS

IV NEWDIGATE ACCOUNT BOOK

V HERBERT'S NARRATIVE

VII SOUTHERN DEPARTMENT

VIII ROBINSON'S STATE

Gems & Minerals

All photos, preparation and working of minerals:
Dr. Andreas Landmann, Burghaeldeweg 18, 74889 Sinsheim, Germany
Telephone: 07261/63430; Fax: 07261/155798; *www.mineral-fascination.biz*

Translated from German by Dr. Edward Force, Central Connecticut State University.
Original Copyright © 2004 by SAMMÜLLER KREATIV GmbH titled Edelsteine und Mineralien
Copyright © 2008 by Dr. Andreas Landmann
Library of Congress Control Number: 2008924780

Designed by Mark David Bowyer
Type set in Humanist521 BT / Aldine721 BT

ISBN: 978-0-7643-3066-7
Printed in China

Schiffer Books are available at special discounts for bulk purchases for sales promotions or premiums. Special editions, including personalized covers, corporate imprints, and excerpts can be created in large quantities for special needs. For more information contact the publisher:

Published by Schiffer Publishing Ltd.
4880 Lower Valley Road
Atglen, PA 19310
Phone: (610) 593-1777; Fax: (610) 593-2002
E-mail: Info@schifferbooks.com

Please visit our web site catalog at **www.schifferbooks.com**

We are always looking for people to write books on new and related subjects. If you have an idea for a book, please contact us at the above address.

This book may be purchased from the publisher.
Include $5.00 for shipping.
Please try your bookstore first.
You may write for a free catalog.

In Europe, Schiffer books are distributed by:
Bushwood Books
6 Marksbury Ave.
Kew Gardens
Surrey TW9 4JF
England
Phone: 44 (0)208 392-8585
Fax: 44 (0)208 392-9876
E-mail: Info@bushwoodbooks.co.uk

Website: www.bushwoodbooks.co.uk
Free postage in the UK. Europe: air mail at cost.
Try your bookstore first.

Dr. Andreas Landmann

Gems & Minerals

4880 Lower Valley Road, Atglen, Pennsylvania 19310

CONTENTS

Rose quartz from Brazil

CONTENTS

CONTENTS

CONTENTS

Amethyst rosette from the Palatinate

Gems and Minerals —
a colorful, glittering world

In recent years, minerals and gemstones have enjoyed growing renown and popularity. Rock crystals or amethysts are seen in many homes, and showcases glisten with colorful collections.

At this time, some 3800 different minerals are known, coming from all parts of the world. Thus when one observes a variety of minerals, one can make a world tour and see what treasures are hidden in the interior of our earth. Glittering crystals often show intense colors and varied forms that fascinate the observer and give him pleasure. A look into our planet's history becomes possible, for most minerals are millions of years old and have been created deep in the ground over thousands of years. To this day minerals are developing, unseen by man, all over the world. In every individual crystal, nature creates a small miracle. Again and again, even the expert is fascinated to see that even the smallest crystal shows the exact crystal form that is typical of its species.

Orpiment, China

The great variety of mineral species often makes it difficult for the beginner in the field to get an overview or find a means of orienting oneself. This book is meant to help one acquire an overview of the world of minerals. Here the reader learns to know the most important and best-known groups of minerals. This book is not meant to be a scientific work, but rather a means to the joy and fascination that working with minerals affords. In the descriptions, the reader learns how minerals grow, how they are found, and what significance the precious stones had for mankind in ancient times. For the mineral collector who would like to identify minerals, the most important data for each species are included.

The best-known minerals are those of the quartz group. They are presented in the first part of this book. Then follow the best-known precious stones, such as the sapphire, diamond, and garnet, which everyone has already seen as gemstones. Many other transparent minerals are then portrayed, followed by opaque minerals and gemstones. Next the reader meets several minerals that are created from lava by volcanic activity. The precious metals and ore minerals are also included.

The last section of the book portrays minerals that have been seen only very rarely in mineral books. Thus the reader learns to recognize minerals under the microscope. These pictures are so colorful that they remind one of abstract paintings. Examples of optical effects that occur in many minerals are portrayed. Then comes a look at the world of synthetic minerals, those created by human handiwork. Here the connection is made with our everyday world, which would not be so memorable without the use of minerals.

Peridot, Zebirget Island, Egypt

The Properties of Minerals, and Mineral Identification

The varied colors of minerals: opal, rock crystal with pyrite, barite, and sulfur

Minerals are defined as solid inorganic components of the earth's crust or rocks, uniformly structured internally. Each mineral has a definite chemical composition. If this composition changes, a different mineral with new properties is formed.

To identify minerals, the collector can use properties such as hardness, density, streak colors, and crystal forms. The most important properties will be explained below. They are noted for each mineral in the book.

I. Hardness

Minerals differ in hardness. Their hardness is divided into ten categories on the Mohs Hardness Scale. The hardness of minerals can be compared by attempts to scratch them. If one scratches another, the scratched mineral is softer. The following minerals belong to the Mohs Scale (in ascending order of hardness):

    1. Talc
    2. Gypsum
    3. Calcite
    4. Fluorite
    5. Apatite
    6. Feldspar
    7. Quartz
    8. Topaz
    9. Corundum
    10. Diamond

2. Density

Minerals are heavier than water. A volume of one liter of water weighs one kilogram, but the same volume of a mineral is somewhat heavier, depending on the mineral's chemical composition. The density thus tells how many times heavier than water a mineral is.

A density of 7 thus means that this [p. 16] mineral is seven times heavier than water. The unit of weight is the gram/cubic centimeter (g/cc). Placing the mineral on a scale and reading its weight in grams can test the density.

Then one places the mineral in a measuring cup with milliliter graduations and observes how much the water level increases. This gives the volume of the mineral in cubic centimeters. Thus the density (specific gravity) can be calculated.

Amber from the Baltic Seashore

3. Streak Color

The streak color of a mineral is the color of the bits that the mineral leaves when it is rubbed across an unglazed porcelain plate. The streak color is characteristic of many minerals. Hematite, for example, makes a dark red streak, selenite a white one.

Minerals that are harder than porcelain (hardness >6) make no actual streak, but rub off the porcelain. Such minerals always show a white streak color. For mineral identification, though, it is immaterial whether the white color comes from the mineral or the porcelain plate. In either case, it is used for mineral identification.

4. Cleavage

At first, a mineral is struck carefully with a hammer. Thus many minerals show typical breakage surfaces, which can be perfectly smooth (perfect cleavage, such as diamond or calcite). The surfaces of other minerals are only partly smooth (poor cleavage, such as aquamarine) or completely irregular (fracture, as quartz).

5. Crystal Form

At this time, some 3,800 mineral species are known. The forms of crystals can be described geometrically, giving just seven crystal systems, into which all types of crystals can be organized. Crystals have two-, three-, four- or six-fold symmetries, which apply to the faces of the crystals. The exact description of crystal symmetries is closely linked with mathematical and physical knowledge and is not easy to learn. For such descriptions, mineralogists use computer programs. The seven crystal systems are: cubic, hexagonal, tetragonal, trigonal, orthorhombic, monoclinic, and triclinic.

With all of these possible means of identification, it must be added that the crystals of a single mineral species often occur in nature with many different forms and shapes that can also occur in other minerals. This often makes identification by the properties described above difficult or even impossible.

In case of doubt, only a lot of experience in examining many minerals will help. One only learns to know minerals by holding them in one's hand many times and getting to know them.

For minerals that are very hard to identify, only the chemical analysis of their inner structure helps to make a final decision. This is the domain of the mineralogists who have appropriate machines available at a university.

Amphibolite rock, containing garnet, under the microscope

Rock Crystal —
the best-known type of quartz

Deep inside a mountain in the Alps, in a hollow space thousands of years old, water drips slowly and brings silicic acid.

On the walls of a void, a covering of silicic acid is formed by the evaporation of water, and the first crystals are formed gradually. Crystals of pure silicic acid form as rock crystal.

Rock crystal is the purest form of the quartz group and consists almost exclusively of silicic acid (SiO_2). The crystals are hexagonal, even the smallest ones, which may measure less than one millimeter.

In the Middle Ages it was believed that these crystals consisted of frozen water. The rock crystals took their name from the Greek word for ice, "*krystallos.*"

Nero drank his wine from goblets of rock crystal, to which he ascribed particular thirst-quenching effects. To this day, Native Americans give a newborn child a rock crystal, which is lain on the cradle to protect the baby.

Rock crystals grown on massive quartz, from China

A clear crystal with six surfaces

If one examines the termination of a rock crystal, one will discover a property that makes it different from most other colorless crystals: It has six faces that meet like those of a pyramid.

This can be observed no matter whether the quartz crystal is very small or a meter long. The form of the crystal follows natural laws and always grows in the same shape.

The growth of rock crystal is influenced by the temperature and the pressure that prevail around the developing crystal. Thus many rock crystals have faces in addition to these six basic ones, depending on whether the crystal grew quickly or slowly, whether more silicic acid was stored as a building material on one side of the crystal than on others, etc.

There are typical combinations of faces in quartz crystals, named for the localities where they were found:
• *Dauphiné*/ twins,
• Brazilian twins,
• Usingen types,
• Japanese twins.

In all, several hundred different combinations of crystal faces can be found in quartz, but the six main faces are always present.

Rock crystals from the state of Minas Gerais, Brazil

A Window into Ancient Geological Processes

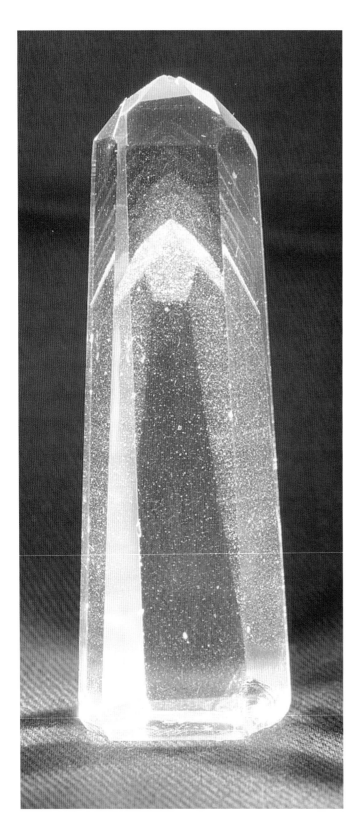

Rock crystal with several
phantom layers inside,
from Minas Gerais, Brazil

A quartz crystal grows deep inside a mountain. After thousands of years a significant clear crystal exists. Now something completely new suddenly occurs in its space in the rock: Water comes dripping down to it, containing not only silicic acid, but also talc. Thus over many years a whitish layer is formed over the crystal.

Other crystals can now no longer grow, but this is not true of quartz. It can go on growing around the grains of talc and enclose them in its crystal body.

Quartz crystals that have enclosed one or more such layers are called phantom quartz. The layers can have any colors, depending on which minerals were deposited on the quartz crystals. Thus the perceptive observer can see which form the quartz crystal had at various states of its development. The "youth forms" of the crystal are clearly visible.

Rock crystal forms unique crystal shapes

A quartz crystal can develop under almost all geological conditions. Thus it is found in many countries of the world.

In Germany quartz has been found in the Black Forest, the Odenwald, the Taunus, and many other localities.

The largest, loveliest, and purest crystals are now found in gem mines in the state of Minas Gerais, Brazil. For some years many crystals with a typical needlelike appearance have also come from China.

An earthquake always involves quartz crystals that develop in the shaking mountain. The crystals may break off their rock base. If water containing silicic acid drips into the aperture again, the broken place of the crystal can heal, forming a second termination, and the crystal is now called doubly terminated.

Devotees of crystal healing use such double-ended crystals as pendants and call them laser crystals, which create rivers of energy and influence them.

Rock Crystal	from "*krystallos*" = frozen ice
Color	**colorless**
Streak/Mohs hardness	**white / 7**
Crystal system	**trigonal**
Cleavage	**conchoidal fracture**
Chemical formula	**SiO_2**

Quartz crystal with second (double) termination, from Brazil

Herkimer Diamonds—
Quartz or Diamond?

Herkimer County in New York State: During excavations, very pure doubly terminated crystals suddenly fall into the diggers' hands. The sparkling reminds the diggers of diamonds, as do the size and great purity of the crystals.

After a closer look, it can be seen that these crystals are especially lovely examples of quartz crystals, only now and then showing small inclusions.

From the name of the county in which they have been found, these quartz crystals are known as Herkimer diamonds.

Their special feature is that they have two terminations. They grew in soft rock and partly in sand, in which they, so to speak, moved while developing and thus could extend freely on both sides. Thus the quartz terminations, which one normally finds on only one end of the crystal, formed at both ends.

Such crystals are up to five centimeters long and show a very strong luster thanks to their great purity. Their uniqueness makes them the most valuable quartz crystals.

Herkimer Diamonds	
Color	**colorless**
Streak/Mohs hardness	**white / 7**
Crystal system	**trigonal**
Cleavage	**none, fracture**
Chemical formula	SiO_2

Herkimer diamonds on agate

Rutilated and Tourmalinated Quartz—
two very special types

A mineral inclusion—what is that? The nicest examples of inclusions of other minerals in quartz are rutilated and tourmalinated quartz. One can see the beautiful interplay of light in the quartz crystal in which the golden rutile or black tourmaline needles have grown.

Quartz crystals develop in a hollow in the rock. At the same time, golden rutile or black tourmaline needles originate from a different part of the hollow. If the crystals are large enough, they contact each other. Now the special properties of quartz come into play: It can grow around other crystals and enclose them. Thus originate quartz crystals with enclosed needles of rutile (rutilated quartz) or, from other localities, enclosed needles of tourmaline (tourmalinated quartz). In rare cases the tourmaline needles that have grown into small channels in the quartz can move back and forth.

In ancient China, tourmalinated quartz was called the Stone of Harmony that was to bring together heaven and earth, Yin and Yang.

Rutile/Tourmaline Quartz	
Color	colorless, with golden or black needles
Streak/Mohs hardness	white / 7
Crystal system	trigonal
Cleavage	none, fracture
Chemical formula	SiO_2

Rutilated and tourmalinated quartz on wood bark, photographed for translucence

Amethyst—
violet quartz crystals from Brazil

Crickets chirp, birds squawk: It is night in the Brazilian jungle. A fire flickers, mineral workers tell each other stories. Nearby, in the thicket, is a narrow entrance to an amethyst mine. Here one hears striking and hammering. In hard underground work, their colleagues remove amethyst druses. Such druses are former hollows in the rock, their rims covered with crystals.

The night ends. The miners go back into the mountain to begin their shift, using their hammers to knock on the new shaft walls created in the night's work. Suddenly one spot in the shaft wall sounds hollow. The amethyst fever grows; a miner with a drill hurries up. For an hour one hears only the grinding of the drill in the rock; then a small hole has been created.

With an endoscope, the miner looks into the hollow and discovers a druse that sparkles with amethyst crystals.

Now hours of hammer-and-chisel work begin to remove the druse from the hard rock around it. The druse now has a long trip before it to the world's mineral collectors.

The most beautiful druses now come from Brazil and Uruguay, but in the Middle Ages such druses were already found in Idar-Oberstein, Germany. Today the German localities are largely exhausted, while large mines are being operated in South America.

Amethyst crystals from Brazil, on fossil sand from the Schwaebische Alb

The amethyst as a violet gemstone

What colors the originally colorless quartz violet to make it into amethyst?

During the growth of amethyst, the water deep in the mountain carries not only pure silicic acid, but also atoms of iron. These are included in the crystals in such small quantities that the eye cannot see an individual iron grain. From now on, the sunlight, which is a mixture of all colors of the rainbow, is absorbed in the amethyst so that only red, green, and violet colors come back out to the observer's eye. Thus the stone looks violet to us.

The ancient Greeks used to wear amethyst, since they hoped for good effects against magic, homesick-ness, drunkenness, and evil thoughts. Hildegard of Bingen ascribed an effect against freckles to amethyst, thus affording a finer complexion.

Today amethyst is still a beloved gemstone. In rare cases it forms rosettes of small crystals, which are suitable for jewelry when cut.

Amethyst	from Greek "amethyein" = against drunkenness
Color	violet
Streak/Mohs hardness	white / 7
Crystal system	trigonal
Cleavage	none, fracture
Chemical formula	SiO_2

Amethyst rosette from a quarry near Idar-Oberstein

Prase—
rare crystalline quartz in an unusual color

Prase: This word means "leek-green quartz." This form of quartz, especially forming nice crystals, is rare. In recent years, such quartz crystals have been found in a quarry in Greece.

The essentially colorless quartz crystal encloses actinolite during its growth. This also means mountain leather, as it is found in felt-like mats deep in the rock of the Swiss Alps.

In its thousands of years of growth, new needles of actinolite grow on the developing quartz crystals again and again, and the quartz grows around them. Thus a green-colored quartz crystal gradually develops. The needles cannot be seen with the naked eye; only under a microscope can they be recognized.

A healing effect was ascribed to prase in antiquity. The Temple of Apollo in Delphi was built largely of prase. This was supposed to assure that the priests always were calm and able to make correct diagnoses.

Prase	from Green "*prason*" = leek-green
Color	**green shining through**
Streak/Mohs hardness	**white / 7**
Crystal system	**trigonal**
Cleavage	**none, fracture**
Chemical formula	**SiO_2 + actinolite:** **$Ca_2Mg_5OH_2Si_8O_{22}$**

Prase crystals, Laurion, Greece

Smoky Quartz—
dark, mysterious quartz crystals

A quartz crystal has grown in its hollow, hundreds of meters below the earth's surface. During its growth it has picked up iron atoms, similarly to amethyst, but the iron content is so meager that the crystal has not yet been turned to violet.

In the rocks of the Alps there are minerals such as zircon that decay over time and thus release natural radioactivity. This occurs in many rocks all over the world and is not harmful to mankind.

If such a zircon mineral decays in the rock that surrounds the quartz crystal, it releases this radioactivity into the surrounding rock. The quartz crystal is also irradiated slowly. Thus it changes internally and becomes smoky brown. Smoky quartz is created.

Smoky quartz, an attractive decorative stone, works mysteriously, since it partially absorbs light. It seems to be glowing from inside. Its main sources are the Swiss Alps, the area around St. Petersburg (black morion crystals come from there), and Brazil.

Since ancient times, people have believed that the rock grows darker in times of danger, for which reasons the Greeks and later the Romans used it to protect their soldiers.

Smoky Quartz	also "morion," from "*moroeis*" = dark
Color	**smoky brown to black**
Streak/Mohs hardness	**white / 7**
Crystal system	**trigonal**
Cleavage	**none, fracture**
Chemical formula	**SiO_2**

Smoky quartz crystals on andesite from a quarry near Idar-Oberstein

Citrine—
the "lemon-colored" quartz crystal

A clap of thunder echoes through the mountain, a gigantic plume of stone dust spreads through the shaft: A meter of the St. Gotthard railroad tunnel has been driven into the mountain again.

In this tunnel, the first Swiss railroad line at the St. Gotthard Pass, many large orifices have been found that were lined with variously colored quartz crystals, including orange to brown-orange citrine crystals. Today the main sources of citrine are Brazil, Argentina, Madagascar, the U.S.A., and Myanmar.

In the Middle Ages all yellow gemstones were called "golden topaz." The use of this old gemstone name causes confusion with the mineral topaz, which has a different chemical composition and likewise occurs in a golden yellow color.

Caesar's legions believed citrine could save their lives and wore it on their chests when they went into battle.

To this day the mineral's sun-yellow color is believed to have a positive effect on the central nervous system and thus improve its wearer's mood.

Citrine	from Latin "*citrus*" = lemon
Color	brown-orange, yellowish
Streak/Mohs hardness	**white / 7**
Crystal system	**trigonal**
Cleavage	**none, fracture**
Chemical formula	SiO_2

Citrine crystals on milky quartz

Rose Quartz—
gently glittering quartz without crystals

Rose quartz is the rose-red variety of quartz. It has had this name since about 1800, on account of its color.

In Governador Valardes, near Rio Doce, Brazil, rare rose quartz that formed small crystals has been found. Normally, though, rose quartz forms masses, translucent at the edges, without crystal surfaces. Important present-day sources are in Brazil and Madagascar.

In Greek mythology it is said that the gods Amor and Eros brought this stone to earth to awaken love through its color.

Its color is caused by inclusions of the finest rutile needles, along with iron atoms, inside the quartz. The rutile needles are actually gold-colored, but exist in rose quartz in microscopically small form, so that their actual color does not show.

Rose quartz is said to influence the magnetic field of television screens. Thus many people put rose quartz in front of their monitors or television screens to decrease the radiation.

Rose Quartz	
Color	**rose red**
Streak/Mohs hardness	**white / 7**
Cleavage	**none, fracture**
Chemical formula	SiO_2

Massive rose quartz from Minas Gerais, Brazil

Agate—
colorful banded quartz

The most colorful variant of the quartz minerals is agate. Just as an amethyst druse is a hollow in the rock, on the rim of which individual crystals have grown, an agate nodule is a hollow that has been filled with thin layers of silicic acid that the water seeping through the rock has brought as its main constituent. The various chemical elements have joined it. The iron content of the water causes the brown, yellow, and red bands of color. Soft blue-green colors are also possible.

Thus one layer of agate covers the last, from outside to inside, until the hollow is filled. Such a filled space is called a nodule.

After being taken from the earth, the nodule is cut into slabs of agate that show cross-sections of the nodule.

For hundreds of years the most varied utensils and decorations have been made of agate. Since the 15th century, Idar-Oberstein and is environs have been a major source of agate. Their world-famous work with gemstones began when the first agates were found there.

Only after the supply of agate decreased there did the importing of agate from Brazil begin, which provides the majority of the supply today.

An agate slice in natural color, from Minas Gerais, Brazil

Agate from native localities

To this day agate can be found in quarries at a few localities in Germany. In the lava rock of the Palatinate an agate with a typical and very beautiful white and red striping is occasionally found.

The agate was named for the Achates river, said to be the same one named Drillo today, in Sicily. The Greek philosopher Theophrastus described the agate around 300 B.C. He ascribed to the agate an effect that helped a person be sensitive to other people.

When one examines the agate layers under a microscope, one sees that these layers consist of small, fine quartz crystals, set vertically to the agate bands. Such finely structured quartz, the individual crystals of which can be seen only from thousandfold magnification upward, is called chalcedony. This is the main constituent of the agate bands.

Agate	
Color	**colorful bands**
Streak/Mohs hardness	**white / 7**
Crystal system	**trigonal**
Cleavage	**none, fracture**
Chemical formula	**SiO_2, microcrystals**

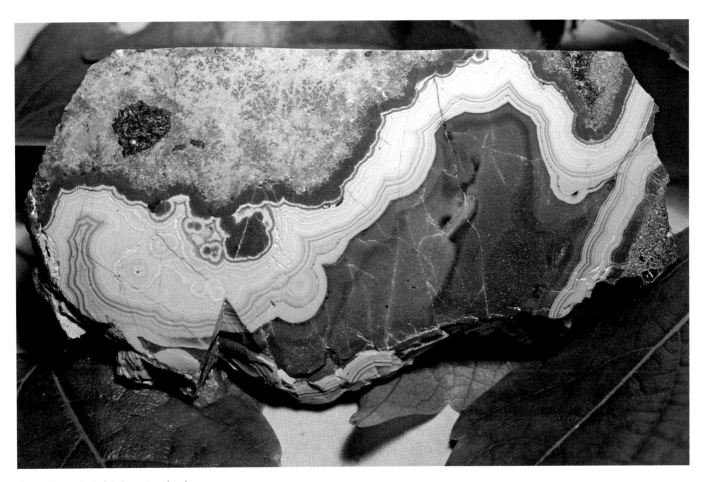

Agate from the Pfalz in natural color

Agate—colorful quartz from the Black Forest

3800

species of minerals—that is the sum of the minerals known worldwide today. And a thousand of these minerals, the clay minerals, form such small crystals that they cannot be seen with the naked eye. We human beings see such crystals only as colorful bands in rock. Only at 20,000-fold magnification can it be seen that the clay layers also consist of individual crystals.

With luck, agate with green layers of clay minerals can still be found in the granite of the Black Forest. These layers are not actual components of the agate, for they are not made of chalcedony.

Thus white to milky bands—veins of water opal—occur again and again in Black Forest agate.

An agate slab from the Black Forest shows a laughing face.

Agate—raw material for cameos

Cameos are regarded as royal jewelry. Particularly beautifully colored pieces were cut from agate so that the individually colored layers lay one atop another.

Then an engraver worked skillfully to carve a relief out of such an object, creating a cameo. Cameo motifs were often women's heads or flowers.

Since antiquity, attempts have been made to color the bands of such a stone more strongly, so as to create more beautiful jewelry.

Thus green, greenish-blue, and blue colors were developed and injected into the interstices of the agate bands. Between the bands of agate there are areas with microscopic pores, which can hold the coloring.

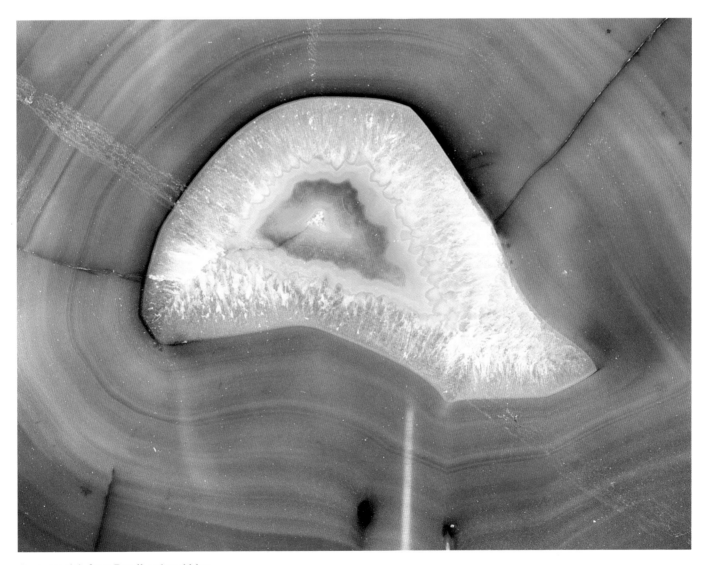

An agate slab from Brazil, colored blue

Agate—natural and colored

Brazil: Finding a new agate locality has brought great joy to the landowners. But mining shows that the newfound agate is almost all gray and shows no bright colors.

Such agates have been colored artificially for many years. The first artificial coloring was done by chance at an evening bonfire of the miners. Agate that lay near the fire suddenly showed stronger coloring of its bands, caused by heat. So it was discovered that heating could enhance colors already present.

Further experiments were not long in coming. Black-and-white banded agates were created by filling the pores of the agate with sugar water, which was then caramelized by dry heating. Thus agates with brown and black bands soon came on the market.

Such colors as ink blue, green, pink, yellow, and violet can also be created by introducing coloring between the agate layers.

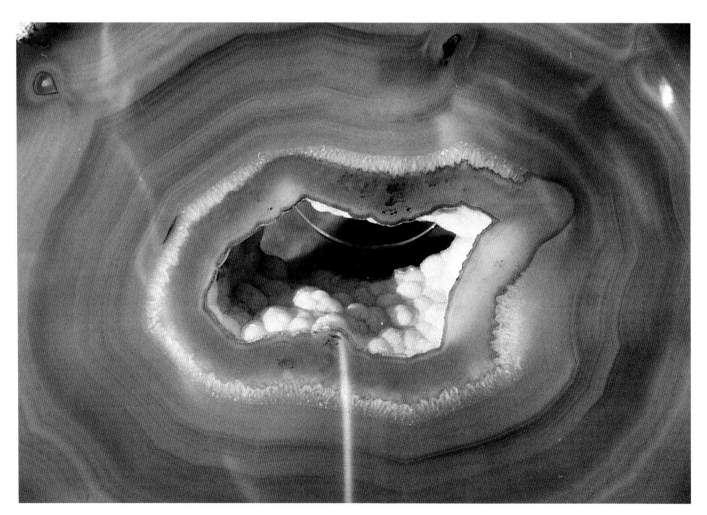

An agate slab from Brazil, colored pink

Moss Agate

A meadow of inclusions in stone? One could imagine moss enclosed in rock when one looks at the inclusions in moss agate. With translucent light in particular, it can be seen that the green color of moss agate comes from small hornblende and chlorite crystals that are scattered irregularly in the stone. The surrounding milk-white mass is chalcedony, which we already know from the light bands of agate.

Individual brownish flecks show that in the development of moss agate there are always traces of iron enclosed in the stone.

The localities with the most beautiful moss agate are found in India. It is also found in numerous American states.

Documentation from Arabic lands tells that the moss agate is the good-luck charm of the gambler, as well as the gardener and farmer.

Indian moss agate

Precious Opal—
the most colorful of all gemstones

We are in Australia, where hill after hill rises by the town of Coober Pedy. Among them are trucks with big drills that cut new shafts. It looks as if moles had dug through the landscape.

Men bore shafts some ten meters deep and dig adits (nearly horizontal mine entrances) through the rock from them to find veins of opal. Two types of opal may be found: those with colorfully flashing fire (black precious opal) and on a white background (white precious opal).

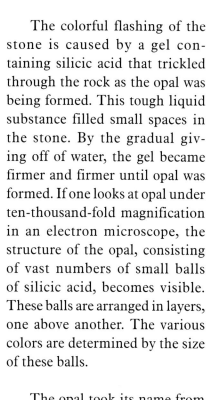

The colorful flashing of the stone is caused by a gel containing silicic acid that trickled through the rock as the opal was being formed. This tough liquid substance filled small spaces in the stone. By the gradual giving off of water, the gel became firmer and firmer until opal was formed. If one looks at opal under ten-thousand-fold magnification in an electron microscope, the structure of the opal, consisting of vast numbers of small balls of silicic acid, becomes visible. These balls are arranged in layers, one above another. The various colors are determined by the size of these balls.

The opal took its name from the old Indian word "*upala*," which meant "precious stone."

Boulder Opal—colorful veins in stone

Veins of precious opal occur most commonly as narrow bands firmly held in the rock. Such a piece of opal has been called boulder opal, from the English word for a chunk of rock.

Pliny described the play of color in an opal in this way: "It has the delicate fire of garnet, the glowing purple of amethyst, the green of emerald and the deep blue of sapphire, so that all the colors glow in a wonderful mixture."

To the Indians, the opal brought good luck. The diggers of Australia would surely agree when they make a unique find.

Opal contains water. Thus it should never be exposed to high temperatures and heat, for it can crack then. It also loses its fine play of colors if it dries out.

The main localities at which opal is found today are Lightning Ridge and Coober Pedy, Australia, and Queretaro, Mexico. There are also a few small localities in Idaho, U.S.A.

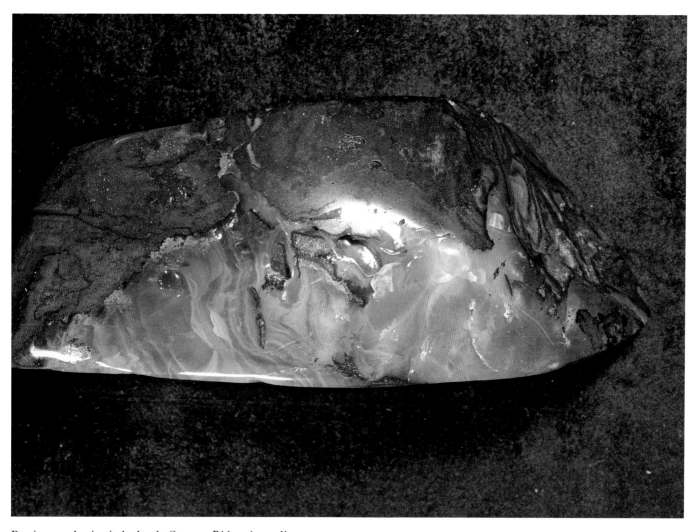

Precious opal veins in bedrock, Country Ridge, Australia

Fire Opal—
examples from Mexican geology

Since about 1780, fire opal localities in Mexico have been known. The renowned natural scientist Alexander von Humboldt brought fire opals to Europe in 1804. He and his contemporaries were fascinated by the intense orange flash of the stones.

Present-day research with fire opal shows that its inner structure, like that of precious opal, consists of layers of many small balls of silicic acid. Fine traces of iron create the orange fire.

The most important localities in Mexico are near Zimapan in Hidalgo province, in Queretaro province, and near Magdalena (the Sadao mines) in the northwestern area.

Other localities are in Brazil, Guatemala, Western Australia, and the U.S.A.

Opal	
Color	**orange to yellow**
Streak/Mohs hardness	**white / 5-6**
Crystal system	**trigonal**
Cleavage	**none, fracture**
Chemical formula	**SiO_2 with silicic gel**

Fire opal in a matrix of pumice

Andes Opal—
gem with a magic blue shimmer

A gentle morning breeze blows. The condor soars in circles high above the Andes.

In the morning stillness, one hears a knocking from somewhere in a valley of the high plains.

On approaching, the mountain climber sees several men working on the rock walls with crowbars, picks, and axes. They obtain light blue stones that have been known for only a few years.

After cutting and polishing, which is done to test pieces on the spot with primitive equipment, the stones begin to glow a light blue from the inside out. It seems as if an inner fire is burning. But no colorful play of colors is to be seen. This is reserved for the precious opals from Australia.

Brown branches are seen in many Andes opals. These are very fine growths of manganese oxides, which form dendrites in cracks in the opal.

Andes Opal	
Color	**light blue to light green**
Streak/Mohs hardness	**white / 5-6**
Crystal system	**trigonal**
Cleavage	**none, fracture**
Chemical formula	**$SiO_2 + nH_2O$**

A drumstick of Andes opal on iron-bearing sand

Tiger-Eye—
raw stones that catch the light

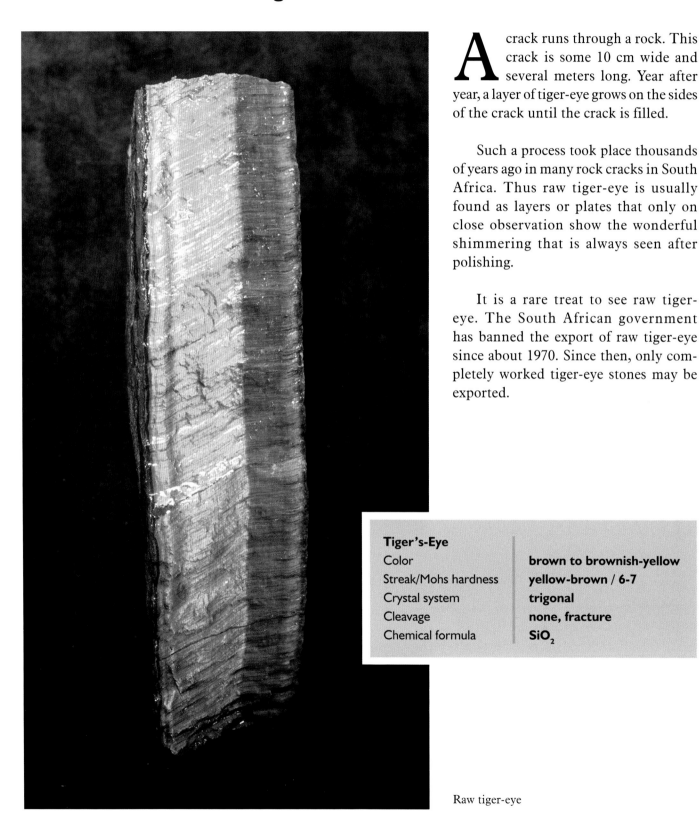

A crack runs through a rock. This crack is some 10 cm wide and several meters long. Year after year, a layer of tiger-eye grows on the sides of the crack until the crack is filled.

Such a process took place thousands of years ago in many rock cracks in South Africa. Thus raw tiger-eye is usually found as layers or plates that only on close observation show the wonderful shimmering that is always seen after polishing.

It is a rare treat to see raw tiger-eye. The South African government has banned the export of raw tiger-eye since about 1970. Since then, only completely worked tiger-eye stones may be exported.

Tiger's-Eye	
Color	**brown to brownish-yellow**
Streak/Mohs hardness	**yellow-brown / 6-7**
Crystal system	**trigonal**
Cleavage	**none, fracture**
Chemical formula	**SiO_2**

Raw tiger-eye

Sparkling golden shimmer

We observe a cut piece of tiger-eye, a fantastic golden shimmering captures us. If one moves the stone back and forth under a light source, lines of light run across the stone like waves.

This shimmer is created by many parallel fibers that run through the tiger-eye. These fibers consist of iron and have grown into the quartz matrix.

In the Middle Ages, tiger-eye stones were thought to protect one against witchcraft and the evil eye, and make one avoid criminal activities.

The most important localities are in South Africa. There the tiger-eye is found near asbestos mines in Griqualand West, some 150 kilometers west of Kimberly, the most famous diamond locality. Tiger-eye is also found in the Ord Range near Mount Goldsworthy in Western Australia, in Myanmar, in the U.S.A., and in southern India.

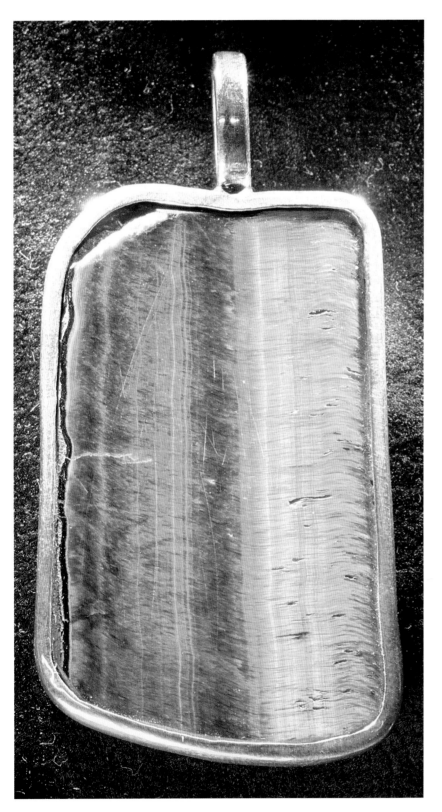

A decorated piece of polished tiger-eye

Hawk-Eye—
mysterious blue in stone

Where tiger-eye occurs, hawk-eye is often found as well. Its splendid blue shimmer is rare and only shows itself in all its splendor when the stone is observed in broad daylight. Its fibers, unlike those of tiger-eye, are not made of iron, but of crocidolite.

If one looks more closely at the stone, one sees that the arrangement of the many parallel crocidolite fibers lie perpendicular to the light line that shimmers back and forth on the stone.

The shimmering effect is strongest when the stone is cut half-round. The shimmer is then reminiscent of the pupil of a falcon's eye. Thus came the belief, probably in the Middle Ages, that an amulet of hawk-eye protected one from the evil eye of witches and magicians. At the time of the Inquisition, women who were suspected of witchcraft had a hawk-eye held in front of them. If they turned their face away when they saw the stone, they were regarded as guilty.

Hawk-Eye	
Color	**dark blue**
Streak/Mohs hardness	**dark blue / 6-7**
Crystal system	**trigonal**
Cleavage	**none, fracture**
Chemical formula	**SiO_2**

Hawk-eye stones from South Africa

Carnelian—
orange as a cornel cherry

Gemstones of the color of a cornel cherry—thus did the Turks of Asia Minor identify this stone because of its color. With its glowing orange color, it ranks among the many quartz gemstones.

It is related to the chalcedony that forms the colorful bands on agate. If one looks at a red agate band under a microscope, one sees that the structure of this agate band is nearly the same as carnelian.

The most important carnelian localities are in Rio Grande do Sul, Brazil, in Uruguay, and India.

Hildegard of Bingen surrounded herself with these quartz stones, colored orange by inclusions of iron, and ascribed a blood-stilling effect to them.

Carnelian	from "*corna*" = cornel cherry
Color	**reddish-orange**
Streak/Mohs hardness	**white / 6-7**
Crystal system	**trigonal**
Cleavage	**none, fracture**
Chemical formula	**SiO_2**

Carnelian stones on moss

Aventurine—
shimmering green quartz

In the 17th century, monks at Murano near Venice developed molten gold, a glass in which "*a ventura*," or "scattered by chance," bits of copper were strewn. Thus the glass takes on a sparkling appearance. From this concept of "*a ventura*" came the name of aventurine quartz. In its green mass, glittering small crystals are scattered by chance, giving the stone its glitter.

The Greeks ascribed to green aventurine, because of its sparkle, the ability to inspire courage, honor, and joy of life.

If one examines aventurine closely under a microscope, one sees that the small inclusions of shiny plates are fuchsite, one of the mica minerals.

Important aventurine localities include Bellary in southern India, Russia, and Tanzania.

Aventurine Quartz	from "*a ventura*," randomly scattered flecks in the stone
Color	**green, white, gray, reddish**
Streak/Mohs hardness	**white / 7**
Crystal system	**trigonal**
Cleavage	**none, fracture**
Chemical formula	**SiO_2**

Brazilian aventurine with iron-bearing sand from the Palatinate

Blood Jasper—
the red type of jasper

Jasper is found all over the world. The lands in which the most beautiful specimens are found include Egypt, Australia, Brazil, India, Canada, the U.S.A., Madagascar, and Uruguay.

A red blood jasper, according to the legend, is said to have decorated Siegfried's sword. The people of India and the Native Americans both regarded jasper as a magic rainstone. The Egyptians engraved scarabs on jasper and used them as amulets.

Very beautiful red-yellow speckled jasper has been found in the Idar-Oberstein region since some 400 years ago. Such discoveries, along with those of agate, led to the founding of the gemstone-cutting industry there, of which some 200 firms still survive.

Blood Jasper	from "*jaspis*" = speckled stone
Color	**red**
Streak/Mohs hardness	**white / 6-7**
Crystal system	**trigonal**
Cleavage	**none, fracture**
Chemical formula	SiO_2

Brazilian blood jasper in rainwater

Multicolored Jasper—
landscapes in stone

The Greek word "*jaspis*" means "sprinkled" or "flamed" stone. And, in fact, jasper is often colorfully sprinkled. Now and then, the many colors even form landscapes or pictures in the stone.

The jaspers are the most colorful opaque members of the quartz group. They have, depending on their appearance, dozens of different trade names and designations. Common to all, though, is the main component of silicic acid. Thus they belong to the quartz group. Many chemical substances get into the silicic acid while jasper develops, causing the colors.

In nature one will not find two jasper specimens that look exactly the same. Thus their recognition is, as so often, aided only by practice and experience in identifying minerals.

The most important trade names include landscape jasper, picture jasper, leopard jasper, blood jasper, and many others.

Jasper	from "*jaspis*" = sprinkled stone
Color	**combinations of natural colors**
Streak/Mohs hardness	**white / 6-7**
Crystal system	**trigonal**
Cleavage	**none, fracture**
Chemical formula	SiO_2

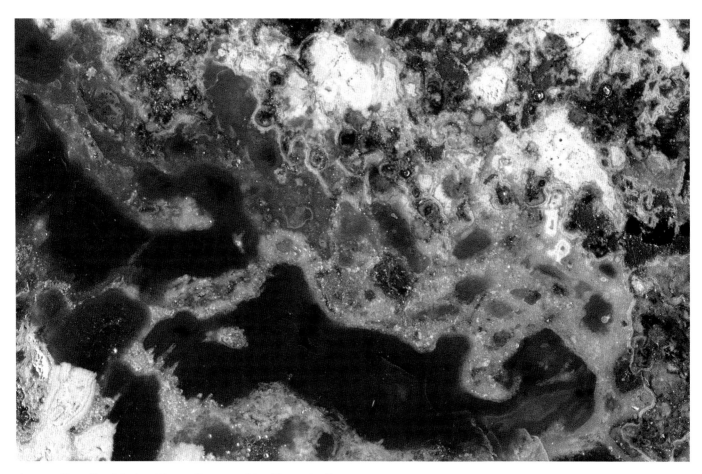

A cut surface of multicolored jasper from near Idar-Oberstein, Germany

Leopard Jasper—circular patterns in stone

A raw stone lies before the saw. Now the saw begins to work, cutting through the raw stone. After the surface is cut, the whole splendor of it suddenly becomes visible: It shows spherical structures in all the colors of nature, colorfully mixed, from light yellow to cream to brown, red, and black.

Such jasper has been found for some years in mines deep in the Brazilian jungle. Because of the many cir-cular patterns, reminiscent of the pattern of a leopard's pelt, the stone got its name of leopard jasper.

Like all kinds of jasper, it belongs to the quartz group. Along with silicic acid, the main ingredient of quartz, there are iron and manganese oxides that provide the colors.

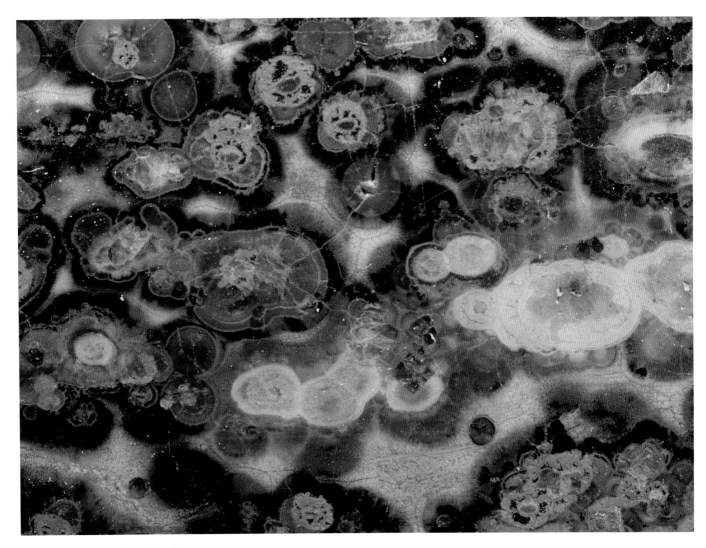

A cut leopard jasper from Brazil

Ocean Jasper—
a new color for jasper

How does the ball get into the stone? If one polishes the green-and-white pieces of ocean jasper, many spherical structures appear, making up almost all of the stone. There are green areas colored by chlorite plus white ones made of chalcedony. These parts of ocean jasper are often spherical, and when cut, they appear as circles.

In the growth of ocean jasper, thin layers of chalcedony form on small crumbs of quartz that lie side by side, covering the bits of quartz layer by layer. This continues until the growing spheres touch each other. Now the crack in the stone in which the jasper grows is filled, and the growth comes to a stop. Colorful ocean jasper with its spherical structures has resulted.

Green-and-white ocean jasper has only been known for a few years, after first being found and extracted in a Brazilian mine.

Ocean Jasper	from "*jaspis*," sprinkled stone
Color	**natural colors, green and white**
Streak/Mohs hardness	**white / 6-7**
Crystal system	**trigonal**
Cleavage	**none, fracture**
Chemical formula	**SiO_2**

Ocean jasper with spherical structure

Petrified Wood—
a representative of quartz minerals

It is night in a swampy area 150 million years ago. The wind comes up; the birds fly from the treetops. The wind grows ever stronger by the hour, becomes a storm. On the next morning the sun rises, and with the dawning daylight the whole extent of the catastrophe becomes visible: Many trees have not survived the stormy night and lie in the shallow water of the swamp.

The long replacement of the wood begins; it will continue for thousands of years, cell by cell. The wooden trunks are covered by shallow water and thus cut off from oxygen. And now a geological oddity takes place: There is enough silicic acid contained in the water to fill the open spaces around the cells of the disintegrating wood. Thus the trunks turn slowly from wood to stone; the trees petrify.

All this has happened in the "petrified forest," which can be found in the presently dry climate around Holbrook, Arizona, U.S.A. The presently petrified wood no longer contain any bits of wood; rather they consist, like the other quartzes, of silicic acid, usually with chalcedony added.

Further localities are in Egypt and in Nevada and Wyoming in the U.S.A.

Petrified wood, with araucaria at the far left, USA

Ancient Tree Trunks—
150 million years old

A tree branch from the desert? But there are no trees there!

Millions of years ago there was no swamp here in the petrified forest (U.S.A.), but rather a blooming swampy landscape with much vegetation. After the trees died off, they were not completely transformed. Little by little, the decaying cells of the wood were filled with silicic acid. Thus they took on the cell structure, to be known today as silicified or petrified wood.

If such branches are cut and polished, flame-like structures can be seen in the petrified wood, making clear to the viewer that there was once life in the wood. With imagination, figures and landscapes can even be seen on the polished surface.

Petrified Wood	
Color	**natural colors, white, gray, reddish, brown**
Streak/Mohs hardness	**white / 7**
Crystal system	**trigonal**
Cleavage	**none, fracture**
Chemical formula	**SiO_2**

Silicified wood from the Petrified Forest, Arizona, USA

Araucaria—
coniferous trees turned to stone

The most colorful silicified woods are petrified araucarias. These coniferous trees can still be found today in the warmer regions of our world. Intense colored bands—red, yellow, orange—alternate with each other and show the viewer a unique variety of structures in the silicified wood.

The great hardness that makes sawing and cutting of petrified araucaria difficult is attributable to the great thickness of the material. The living araucaria had very small pores and thick cell walls. During the petrification, the silicic acid that penetrated into the wood formed very thick, firm layers.

Chemical reactions of the acids in the tree trunks with the penetrating silicic acid created the splendid play of colors by which petrified araucaria can be identified at once.

Araucaria on a conifer branch, USA

Moonstone—
a blue shimmer on a white stone

The tender shimmer of the moon shines on the surface of a rounded polished moonstone. If the stone is moved back and forth in the sunlight, a gentle blue shimmer is caused, following the line over the white stone.

The moonstone comes from the group of feldspar minerals. Feldspar crystals are always a mixture of three minerals: Orthoclase K ($AlSi_3O_8$), Albite Na ($AlSi_3O_8$) and Anorthite Ca ($Al_2Si_2O_8$). In this mineral group there are three well-known decorative stones, first the moonstone, then the sunstone and labradorite or spectrolite.

Since olden times, man has been fascinated by the blue light of moonstone that cannot be seen in the un-polished, rough stone. It occurs only from an arched grinding that lets the sunlight break into the stone.

The most famous occurrence of moonstone is still, as it was centuries ago, in the interior and the south of Sri Lanka. Other lands of origin are Brazil, Madagascar, Australia, Tanzania, and the U.S.A.

Moonstone	
Color	milky white, polished with a blue shimmer
Streak/Mohs hardness	white / 6
Crystal system	monoclinic
Cleavage	good
Chemical formula	$A(AlSi_3O_8) + Na(AlSi_3O_8)$

Moonstones from Sri Lanka on limburgite rock from the Kaiserstuhl, Germany

Labradorite—
the most colorful feldspar

Norwegian labradorite is well suited to be an ornamental stone

It is 1770: It is quiet in the vast landscape of northern Canada. The peninsula of Labrador awakens. Church bells ring, the morning service of the Herrnhuter missionaries has just ended, and the worshippers come out of the building.

The missionary who conducted the service also makes his way homeward. This time he takes a roundabout route and visits a rock face that has long interested him. There it sparkles at him in the morning sunlight: A stone shimmers in blue, golden yellow, and green. He removes the stone from the rock and takes it with him for further cutting.

After the stone is polished, it shows metallically gleaming colors on a greenish-gray background, visible in the light that falls upon it. Labradorite has been discovered.

Labradorite belongs to the feldspar mineral group. It shimmers through numerous parallel layers inside it, which are microscopically finely intergrown. The sunlight that falls on it is broken up into its colorful components by reflection between these layers.

Particularly colorful labradorite is called spectrolite because of its color spectrum.

It is found in Canada and northern Norway.

Labradorite	especially colorful: spectrolite
Color	**metallically shimmering**
Streak/Mohs hardness	**white / 6-7**
Crystal system	**triclinic**
Cleavage	**perfect**
Chemical formula	**$(Ca,Na)(AlSi)2Si_2O_8$**

Amazonite—
a precious stone from the Amazon jungle

The feldspar group had another gemstone to offer: Amazonite. It is opaque and blue-green to dark green. When Alexander von Humboldt returned from one of his voyages, he reported that on the Rio Negro in Brazil jewelry made of amazonite stones was worn. The aborigines had told him that these stones came from the "land of women without men." Thus the name probably does not come from the Amazon River area, but presumably from the land of the Amazon Indians.

The Brazilian natives revere amazonite as a sacred stone.

Mineralogically, amazonite is an orthoclase feldspar, one of the main minerals of the feldspar group. Its green color probably comes from a small amount of copper in the stone.

Today amazonite is found in the U.S.A. (Colorado), Brazil, Kashmir, India, and Madagascar.

Amazonite	
Color	**green, opaque**
Streak/Mohs hardness	**white / 6-6.5**
Crystal system	**triclinic**
Cleavage	**perfect**
Chemical formula	**$KAISi_3O_8$**

Polished amazonite cabochons on dolomite crystals

Aquamarine—
a relative of emerald

What fascinates people more than pure, intensely colored gemstones that glow in the sun?

For centuries, aquamarine has ranked among the most popular and valuable gemstones found in nature's world. Light blue and, in raw stones, light blue-green colors are known to many mineral collectors and indicate aquamarine.

The purest colors come from the Santa Maria mine in Ceara, Brazil. The most intensive colors of aquamarine are named for this mine.

Coming from the mineral group of the beryls, the aquamarine is related to emerald (green), golden beryl (golden yellow), and morganite (rose to red). It has its basic chemistry in common with them; the beryls get their particular colors from traces of other chemical elements. Aquamarine is made light blue by inclusions of iron.

The largest good-quality aquamarine was found in Marambaya, Minas Gerais, Brazil in 1910. It weighed 110 kilograms, was 48.5 cm long, and had a diameter of 41-42 cm.

Gemstones weighing 100,000 carats were carved from this fantastic raw stone.

It is found in many mines all over Brazil, and in Pakistan.

Aquamarine on its matrix rock, marble

Aquamarine—a light blue stone often used in jewelry

Raw aquamarine crystals that are found in mines are often not colored light blue from the start. The natural color, as a rule, is a light blue-green, which does not look like the color shown by cut aquamarine used in jewelry.

The well-known aquamarine blue is attained in most stones by heating to more than 200 degrees Celsius. With this heat, the color changes and the well-known strong blue arises.

This coloring treatment is almost always applied to aquamarine. Yet the intensive blue stones are more valuable than the paler ones, since the color is not always made more intensive automatically by heating. Any stone can only be brought by heating to a maximum color, a color that depends on the quantity of iron atoms in the crystal.

Rarely are aquamarines with a light blue color obtained from the rock. Especially delicate colors come from the Santa Maria mine in Brazil, from which the best-quality aquamarines have also been called "Santa Maria."

Similarly well-colored aquamarines from Africa or Mozambique are called "Santa Maria Africana."

Localities: Minas Gerais, Brazil, and Pakistan

A faceted bright blue aquamarine

Aquamarine	from "aqua" = water and "mare" = sea water
Color	**light blue-green, light blue**
Streak/Mohs hardness	**white / 7-8**
Crystal system	**hexagonal**
Cleavage	**poor**
Chemical formula	$Al_2Be_3Si_6O_{18}$

Emerald—
green beryl with a fantastic shimmer

The Incas worked the mines near Muzo, Colombia in search of emeralds. Forgotten after the fall of the Incas, the old mine shafts were rediscovered in the 17th century and worked again. Emeralds of the very finest quality, with deep green color and almost free of inclusions, come from there.

Emeralds are usually found in gray-black slate or gray limestone.

Fifty years before Christ, Queen Cleopatra operated emerald mines in upper Egypt. They have been forgotten today, and have only historical importance.

The best-known historical emerald locality is the Hapbach Valley in Austria, where small emerald crystals, usually, alas, not of gem quality, are found to this day. The imperial and royal house of Austria had emeralds from there among its crown jewels.

Emerald crystals in natural form

Emerald—a green stone from the jungles of Colombia

The locality of Muzo in the jungles of Colombia: On an outcrop of pegmatite rock, several men, all heavily armed and accompanied by body-guards, meet in the first light of morning. The daily emerald market has opened. Here the most influential mine owners meet and sell their best emeralds that were dug out of the rock the previous day.

Then the stones travel via wholesalers in Bogotá and via importers to us in Europe and America.

Emeralds are very desirable and, in their finest green colors, sell for up to 10,000 Euros per carat when they are nearly free of inclusions.

They are close relatives of aquamarine and belong to the beryl group. The trace element of chromium colors them green.

The main present sources are Columbia and Zimbabwe in Africa.

Emerald	The German name "*Smaragd*" comes from "*smaragdos*" = green stone
Color	green
Streak/Mohs hardness	white / 7-8
Crystal system	hexagonal
Cleavage	poor
Chemical formula	$Al_2Be_3Si_6O_{18}$

A faceted emerald, ready to be set in a fine piece of jewelry

Schorl Tourmaline—
black prisms on light rock crystal

In antique times, tourmaline was already known in the Mediterranean area. But only in 1703 did the first tourmalines from Sri Lanka reach western and central Europe via merchants from Holland. They referred to the tourmaline by a Sinhalese word, "*turamali*," which meant roughly "stone with mixed colors."

When railway tunnels were built in Switzerland in the 19th and 20th centuries, fine black tourmalines were discovered and called "*Schorl*," an old miners' term for "false ore."

These schorl crystals are often found on rock crystal, and form wonderful crystal stages along with them.

Very typical of well-formed crystals is a triangular cross-section with its edges slightly bowed outward. This can be seen best when one looks at the crystal termination from above. Tourmalines often also have longitudinally grooved surfaces. These two properties make it easy to tell tourmaline from other minerals.

Schorl tourmaline crystals on rock crystal

All the colors of nature

It is evening, and the search for tourmalines is over for today. The Brazilian miners sit by the fire and roast meat. Beside them lie the tourmalines that they have found today. While bread is being baked, some flour falls on a tourmaline crystal, and suddenly a miner notices that the flour gathers only at one end of the crystal, while the other end remains free of it. The pyroelectric effect of tourmaline is discovered.

This effect exists because a tourmaline crystal is charged electrostatically when heated. A positive electric charge occurs at one end, a negative charge at the other. This effect is typical of tourmaline and occurs in all crystals, whatever color they have.

Rubellite crystals on fluorite and mica schist, Brazil

Rubellite—
the red color of tourmaline

Tourmaline occurs in all colors. A particularly lovely color, one of the most valuable, is the red or red-violet color of rubellite. In the monarchies of the Middle Ages, rubellite was a popular gemstone found among crown jewels.

In the Kremlin treasures there is a rubellite crystal, cut as a pendant, with a weight of 255 carats and a height of 4 centimeters. It portrays a bunch of grapes. Between 1575 and 1777 it changed owners several times, and has been in Russian ownership for more than 200 years.

Tourmaline	from Sinhalese "*turamali*" = stone with mixed colors
Colors	**black, blue, green, red, pink**
streak/Mohs hardness	**white / 7-7.5**
Crystal system	**trigonal**
Cleavage	**poor**
Chemical formula	**basically $(BO_3)_3Si_6O_{18}(OH)_4$, many trace elements**

A faceted rubellite crystal from Madagascar

Tourmaline—
renowned gemstones from Brazil

The world's greatest occurrence of tourmalines and the best-quality stones come from the Brazilian state of Minas Gerais. Twenty years ago, a rare color of tourmaline, now the most valuable of all, was found near the town of Paraiba: the intensive turquoise blue tourmaline. It was named Paraiba tourmaline after its locality, and can bring prices of several thousand Euros per carat. Other sources are in Afghanistan, Australia, Myanmar, India, and Madagascar.

Tourmalines also occur in Germany, though not of gem quality. Schorl crystals, for example, are found in granite in the Heidelberg area.

Light blue tourmaline in marble, from Brazil

Colorful splendor turned to stone

The tourmaline is undoubtedly the most colorful of all transparent gemstones. It owes this to its special quality of being able to change colors several times within a crystal. This happens longitudinally as well as from the inside out.

Thus it is possible that, in addition to its basic chemical structure (see the table), it can include many different elements that create different colors in the stone. These elements are, among others, natrium, manganese, aluminum, and iron.

Tourmalines also have various names according to their colors: Dravite = yellow to yellow-brown, verdelite = green, indicolite = blue, schorl = black.

A tourmaline with a rose-red core and a green exterior is called "watermelon tourmaline," since its colors resemble those of a watermelon.

The most colorful tourmalines have been found in Madagascar. Here they can be up to 30 centimeters long and show a fantastic play of colors.

Tourmaline crystals with colors varying from blue to reddish-purple.

Ruby —
the jewel of kings

Who does not know the wonderful luster of a beautifully cut ruby? With a deep red color, like a valuable burgundy wine, it glows and shows its fire. Only around 1800 did scientists discover that the ruby is related to the sapphire.

Both stones belong to the same type of mineral, namely corundum. In its pure chemical composition, corundum is colorless, and is colored only by the inclusion of chromium atoms.

A stream splashes, wooden poles stick into the mud. Here miners work in Sri Lanka to loosen the half-dried mud from a streambed and wash it out. After a time, the first raw ruby crystals appear.

The mineralogists call such a gem-bearing mud "gemstone soap." These "soap" localities in Sri Lanka are, after those in Myanmar, the best-known ruby localities in the world. Here too, very valuable rubies are found in certain cases they can be more valuable than a diamond of the same size.

The most desirable color is a deep red with a light violet stripe. Such rubies are found in Myanmar and called "pigeon's-blood red."

Ruby	from "rubens" = red color
Color	rose to intense dark red
Streak/Mohs hardness	white / 9
Crystal system	trigonal
Cleavage	none, fracture
Chemical formula	Al_2O_3

Faceted rubies on Iceland spar

Sapphire —
not just the blue of heaven

Sapphire, like ruby, belongs to the corundum group. Just as the colorless corundum is made red by inclusions of chromium and then called ruby, inclusions of chromium and iron create all the other colors of corundum, which are then called sapphire.

The best-known color of sapphire is a deep blue, from which its name is derived. But sapphires also exist in several other colors, such as green, yellow, pink, and even orange. Only around 1800 was it recognized that the sapphire is related to the ruby and represents its own type of the mineral. Until then, the word "sapphire" often was applied to the present-day lapis lazuli. Green sapphires were erroneously called "Oriental peridot," yellow ones "Oriental topaz."

Large sapphires are very rare and often have their own names, similarly to famous diamonds. The American Museum of Natural History in New York owns probably the largest cut star sapphire, the "Star of India." It has a weight of 536 carats.

In the Bible (the prophet Ezekiel), the heavens are compared with the blue of the sapphire: "Behold, in the firmament that was over the heads of the cherubim there appeared over them as if it were a sapphire stone, as the appearance of the likeness of a throne."

Sapphire	from Greek "saphiros" = blue
Color	all corundum colors but red
Streak/Mohs hardness	white / 9
Crystal system	trigonal
Cleavage	none, fracture
Chemical formula	Al_2O_3

Raw sapphire crystals in various colors

Orange—a color of Indian sapphire

Padparajah—this is the name of the orange-colored sapphire. This name comes from old Indian usage. It means that the stone is as orange as the rising sun. And one is reminded of this tender but radiant light when one observes the Padparajah.

In the Kashmir hills of India there are historical localities over 5000 meters high, where the valuable stones were mined with simple handwork, with shovel or hammer and chisel. Today the best-known localities are in Sri Lanka, where there are more than thirty sapphire mines.

Two famous sapphires, the "St. Edward" and the "Stuart Sapphire," are among the British crown jewels.

Padparajah sapphires

The Diamond —
born of fire under the earth's crust

Forty kilometers under the earth's surface: Three thousand degrees hot, red-glowing magma flows upward from the depths of the earth and strikes the solid rock of the African continent from below. Immense pressure of 20,000 to 30,000 bars prevails here. Heat and pressure compact the carbon in the magma. Diamond crystals are formed.

Many millions of years later: The movement of bedrock creates a deep crack in the African continent, reaching down to the hot magma. The magma rises to the surface, bringing the completed diamond with it. The magma cools and turns to firm kimberlite rock. Such volcanic chimneys filled with kimberlite that contains diamonds are found today in Africa (Zaire, Namibia, Botswana), but also in Australia (the Argyle Mine) and Siberia (Yakutia). The largest known diamond mines are found there.

The diamond is the hardest mineral known to exist on earth. It can be cut only with other diamonds. Its name thus derives from the Greek "*adamas*": the unshakable.

Diamond	from Greek "*adamas*," the unshakable
Color	**colorless to yellowish, seldom in bright colors**
Streak/Mohs hardness	**white / 10**
Crystal system	**cubic**
Cleavage	**perfect**
Chemical formula	**C (carbon)**

A raw diamond crystal

The Diamond—the noblest of all gemstones

In 1871, in Kimberly, South Africa: One of the first European travelers in this—then far-off—land moves across the plains. Suddenly a stone on the ground sparkles at him. At first he does not look at it any more, but then he picks it up and holds the first raw diamond in his hand.

From then on, the region around Kimberly experiences a diamond fever that lasts until 1908. Adventurers from all over the world helped to dig the largest hole ever dug by human hands, the Kimberly Diamond Mine, and to obtain diamonds from it. In the end, the Big Hole is 1070 meters deep and 46 meters wide. In all, 4.5 million carats of diamonds were found here.

Many diamonds are given the brilliant cut, which was invented by Louis Van Berquen in 1456. Only with this cut, which consists of 57 facets, can a genuine diamond be called "brilliant" and develop its own fire, that sparkle that has inspired kings and rulers all over the world since olden times.

In the mysticism of the Middle Ages, this sparkle of the diamond was described as "Divine splendor on earth."

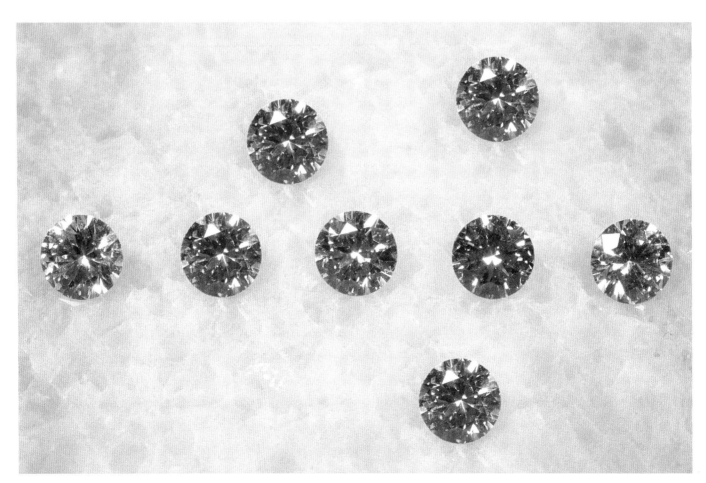

Diamonds with the 57 facets of the brilliant cut are called brilliants

Garnets —
red, yellow, green, colorless

From the Middle Ages to the beginning of the 20th century, all red gemstones were called carbuncle stones. They were often garnets, but could also be rubies or spinel crystals.

Bohemia, 19th and 20th centuries: Many mines and quarries produce the famous Bohemian garnets. From 1900 to 1920, these stones were household words and adorned typical garnet jewelry with countless small, individually hand-faceted crystals.

These stones were minerals from the garnet group, which consists of six basic mineral species. All of these varieties have the same basic chemical composition and are thus related. In part, they can be differentiated by their colors:

Pyrope: dark red crystals (the Bohemian garnets)

Almandine: red tending to violet (Brazil, India, Madagascar)

Spessartine: glowing orange (Myanmar, Brazil, China, Kenya)

Grossular: colorless, yellow, green, brown (Sri Lanka, Brazil, India, Canada)

Andradite: black, brown, yellow-brown (China, Korea, Russia, USA, Zaire)

Uvarovite: dark green (Finland, India, Canada, Poland, Russia)

A faceted almandine crystal

Pyrope —
the Bohemian garnet

The color of pyrope is a strong, pure red, sometimes also brownish-red. In the mica schist of the Oetz and Ziller Valleys, pyrope crystals up to five centimeters are found in their usual crystal form. This form has at most twelve facets and looks like a die with a pyramid on each of its surfaces. The name for this crystal form comes from Greek: Rhombododecahedral (do = 2, deca = 12, hedra = facets).

In a crown among the British crown jewels there are more than 150 carats of heavy red gems that were often regarded as garnets over a century ago. Today it is known that they are spinel, which can be confused with the garnet.

The main localities for pyrope in Bohemia are near Trebnitz (Czech Republic), some 100 kilometers north of Prague.

Garnet	from Latin "*granum*" = grain
Color	**red, yellow, orange, green, colorless**
Streak/Mohs hardness	**white / 6-7**
Cleavage	**poor**
Chemical formula	**$(SiO_4)_3$ + the elements Mg, Al, Fe, Mn in varying amounts**

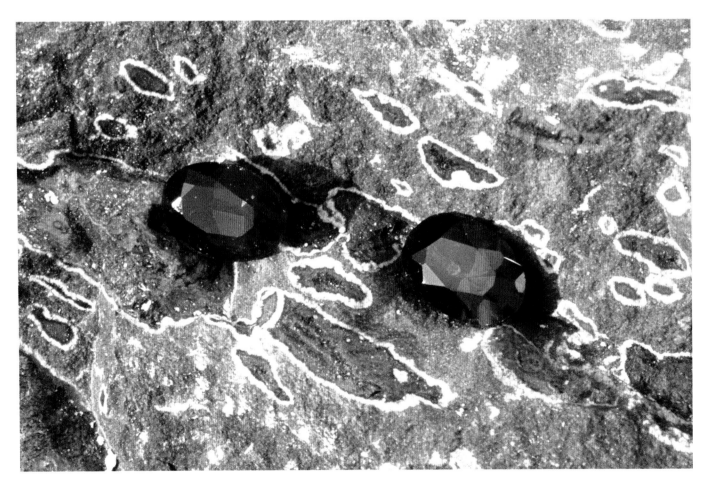

Faceted pyrope crystals on lava rock

Garnet in Mica Schist —
a typical mineral growth in the Alps

Magma pushes out of the earth; the mountain moves. Year after year, the layers of rock move about a centimeter closer to the heavens. This has been happening in the Alps for millions of years.

In a small crack in the rock, small garnets have been exposed to heat and pressure for thousands of years as the rock has moved. For a long time they have had to endure several hundred degrees of temperature and several hundred bars of pressure.

But these are just the conditions that garnets need to grow. Only under heat and high pressure do the chemical elements that build the garnet crystal framework unite in a crystal.

Thus along the chasms that are made ever longer by the movement of the mountains, more and more garnets are formed.

These crystals are now a clearly visible sign to the mineralogist that movement has taken place in rocks over thousands of years. Thus garnet crystals serve the scientist as geological thermometers and barometers, and allow conclusions as to the processes inside the earth that have contributed to building a mountain range like the Alps.

Pyrope crystals in mica schist, Austria

Rhodolite —
glowing red garnet

Rhodolite crystals on Moroccan desert roses

The pyrope, widespread and known in jewelry, is dark red. Lighter and brighter in color is its variety, rhodolite. In these garnets, a light violet color can be observed, especially in bright sunlight.

Since ancient times, legends have been told of sacred garnets that glow from inside. In the Talmud it is written that Noah's ark was lit by a single garnet.

The best-known garnet of the Middle Ages was "the wise one." It decorated the crown of Emperor Otto.

Spessartine —
a glowing orange garnet, colorful as the sun

It happened at the summit of the Rauhenstein, northeast of Aschaffenburg: A hiker discovered orange-colored stones in the rock just as the sun shone on a rock face.

These stones were grown fast in the rock and had to be cut out with a hammer and chisel. When the stones were freed, the sunlight could shine through them and produce an orange-colored sparkle.

Tests showed that this was an orange garnet, which was named Spessartine from then on, after its place of origin, the Spessart.

Spessartine owes its splendidly glowing color to small amounts of manganese that are included in the crystals as a chemical element. It is very rare in gemstone quality, and next to the green demantoid it is the most valuable garnet. It can cost up to 2000 Euros per carat.

Today spessartine is found in Tanzania (the Umba mine), Sri Lanka, Madagascar and Brazil.

Spessartine garnet from the Umba Valley in Tanzania

A Green Garnet?

Only in 1974 was a new, hitherto unknown garnet variety discovered. It had a very unusual color, namely green.

This garnet was found north of the Tsavo National Park in Kenya, Africa, and named for its place of origin. Today the noble green garnet is found in Kenya and Tanzania. It is a color variation of grossular, one of the six main minerals of the garnet group.

The color of tsavoite, also called tsavolite, suggests soft green grass. It is an important export commodity for Kenya, and has been used in many pieces of jewelry since its discovery.

A faceted tsavolite garnet

Spinel —
the gem of kings

A spinel octahedron on marble

"Timur Ruby"—"Black Prince's Ruby": these renowned red gemstones, set in pieces of the British crown jewels, were regarded as rubies for a long time. Today we know that they are spinel. In the British Museum in London there are two spinel crystals that, in an uncut state, weigh 520 carats each and show the desired color, a glowing red.

Thanks to improved scientific equipment, the spinel could be identified as a separate mineral species only 150 years ago. It was always confused with the ruby because it was found at the same localities in Myanmar and Sri Lanka.

The typical crystal form of spinel is the octahedron, which means it has eight facets. If one examines a typical raw spinel crystal, one sees that it consists of two four-sided pyramids.

Spinel	from Latin "*spina*" = pointed
Color	**red, blue, green, black**
Streak/Mohs hardness	**white / 8**
Crystal system	**cubic**
Cleavage	**incomplete**
Chemical formula	**basically $MgAl_2O_4$ + trace elements**

Spinel —
imitation of aquamarine

A Frenchman, M. Verneuil, lived in the 19th century. He invented the first technical process by which large quantities of crystals could be produced artificially.

In this process, magnesium and aluminum oxide powders flow down through a funnel, fall through an oxyhydrogen gas flame, and are melted. The liquid drops fall onto a small plate and form, layer on layer, new synthetic spinel crystals.

These light blue crystals are suitable for use as imitations of aquamarine and are often used in jewelry.

In a red color, such spinels imitate the valuable ruby.

A faceted spinel on limestone

Fluorite? Fluorspar? —
one and the same crystal

"Luck up"—thus do the miners greet each other when they enter a new shaft in a fluorite mine. Again they will spend several hours cutting fluorite out of the shaft walls. Suddenly a miner becomes very happy: Amid colorful fluorite veins that run through the rock merely as colored lines, he has found a pocket that is covered with cubic fluorite crystals.

Such a natural wonder is, of course, not blown up, but carefully loosened from the mountain by hand. Beautiful arrays of many fluorite crystals can still be found today.

The only minc still active in the black Forest, the Clara Pit, is run especially for fluorite.

Fluorite gets its name from the Latin "*fluere*" = to flow. One of its main components, fluorine, is used in fluxes in the chemical industry. Hence its name.

Fluorite (also fluorspar)	from Latin "*fluere*" = to flow
Color	**green, yellow, purple, light blue, colorless**
Streak/Mohs hardness	**white / 4**
Crystal system	**cubic**
Cleavage	**perfect**
Chemical formula	$\mathbf{CaF_2}$

Translucent fluorite cubes from England

Pyramidal form and rare light blue color

The octahedron consists of two four-sided pyramids that have grown together. The apex of the bottom pyramid points downward, that of the upper pyramid upward. The octahedron is a common crystal form of fluorite. If one tries to split fluorite, this form repeats over and over and can be seen in even the smaller pieces.

Today one finds such and similar forms of fluorite in Oelsnitz in Vogtland, Amderma in the Urals of Russia and, especially rich, in China.

Now and then, fluorite is also intergrown with pyrite, which forms a lovely, gleaming golden crust on the fluorite. Such intergrowths are well suited for artistic handicrafts.

Light blue fluorite is rare. The color is caused by a radioactive radiation in the rock that surrounds the fluorite as it grows. Fluorite itself, though, does not radiate and can be placed in the collector's showcase without worries.

Light blue fluorite from the Clara Pit in the Black Forest

Color changes and bands

Weardale in Durham, Alston and Cleator Moor in Cumberland: In these British mines very beautiful fluorite has been found for decades.

The miners who mined these crystals worked with hammers and chisels. Thus they saw every day how fluorite that is hammered does not break apart by chance, but always cleaves with smooth, reflecting surfaces.

This behavior of crystals was already called "spar behavior" by miners in the Middle Ages, giving fluorite its second name, fluorspar.

Also typical of fluorite is a color change in a crystal, which can alternate through lilac, green, colorless, and yellow.

This results in very beautiful bandings, which are advantageous in the use of fluorite in jewelry. Yet fluorite is very seldom set in jewelry, since polished facets wear very quickly on account of their softness.

Fluorite is also used for drum stones, to emphasize their color and sheen especially beautifully. Drum stones are jewels that are worked and polished in a tumbler. Drum stones can be made of all types of stones.

Play of colors in fluorite drum stones, changing from lilac to green and colorless, from China.

Chinese play of colors in chemistry

We are on the Yangtze Kiang, China's great river. A motor ship chugs along the river. There are still a hundred kilometers to Shanghai. Valuable freight is on board. Fluorite taken from a mine was loaded on the ship several days ago and is now on its way to mineral collectors all over the world.

Every day the captain makes his rounds, inspecting the ship to make sure that the beautiful green and purple fluorite reaches its destination safely. From Shanghai, the crystals are then sent further by air.

Chinese fluorites are now the most beautiful crystals to be found in the world. They show intensive green and purple colors, often with zigzag bands in their interiors.

The green color comes from the rare elements ytterbium and yttrium. The purple color probably comes from enclosed iron and manganese atoms as well as the effect of radioactivity in the rock.

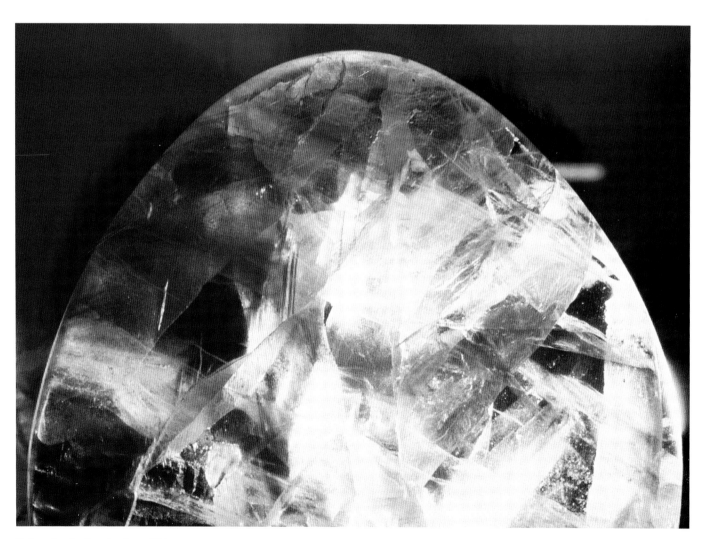

Color play in fluorite from China

Danburite —
a little-known mineral with a bright glow

Danbury, Connecticut, USA: Here Danburite was first found in 1839 and named after its type locality.

When light falls on the crystal, its light, water-clear facets sparkle powerfully. In 1921 the first faceted danburites were used as gemstones. They were stones of a clear transparent and golden yellow color, that came from Madagascar.

Northern Myanmar exported a very large danburite that weighed 138.61 carats. Rose-colored danburite comes from Mexico. Today danburite can be found in Myanmar, Japan, Madagascar, Mexico, Russia, and the USA.

Despite this wealth of localities, one should not forget that it is always a great exception when danburite is found in large crystals or pure gem quality without inclusions.

Danburite	
Color	colorless, wine yellow, brown, rose
Streak/Mohs hardness	white / 7-7.5
Crystal system	orthorhombic
Cleavage	poor
Chemical formula	$CaB_2Si_2O_8$

Danburite from the USA, photographed on a microphotograph of a thin slice of rock

Halite/Rock Salt —
white gold from the homeland

The cooking pot bubbles, the family comes to dinner. Salt is shaken onto the French fries and used to flavor the soup.

Rock salt has been called white gold. In the Middle Ages it was, in fact, as valuable as gold and had to be transported to Germany from Asia. For some 150 years, salt has also been mined in Germany. Whether as shaker salt, a base for fertilizer or a cooking spice, halite finds many uses in our everyday life.

But where does salt actually come from? A drill hammers; bucket chains bring freshly broken salt from the mine tunnels to the nearest loading depot. The mines with the largest shaft diameters today are the salt mines, of which there are many in Germany. One of the most important is the Heilbronn salt mine. Here large areas of salt layers are mined hundreds of meters below the surface. Many shafts have developed into chambers that may be up to 200 meters long and more than ten meters high.

The nice cubic form is noteworthy, for it always forms when the salt crystals have the space and calmness to grow slowly in a hollow in the rock. Then they form their usual crystal shape, in which the surfaces meet at angles of exactly 90 degrees.

A very large rock salt cube from the Heilbronn salt mine, with angles 25 cm long

Rock Salt — white gold in blue

Rock salt and radioactivity: sometimes they can be observed together.

In rare cases, slight radioactivity prevails in the rock in which the rock salt crystallizes. This is usually limited to a few square decimeters of rock where radioactive minerals are present. This natural radiation, which is not dangerous for man, can affect the developing rock salt over thousands of years.

Rock salt consists of the elements sodium and chlorine. In the rare cases in which a salt crystal is exposed to radioactivity, these elements move in the crystal and the crystal structure of the salt is disturbed.

This means that all the colors of the white light that falls on the crystal are absorbed—except the blue rays. Thus our eyes get the impression that the salt crystal is blue.

Such blue salt crystals are rare collectors' items. They are not dangerous, for they themselves do not radiate.

Rock Salt	also Halite
Color	**colorless**
Streak/Mohs hardness	**white / 2**
Crystal system	**cubic**
Cleavage	**perfect**
Chemical formula	**NaCl**

A blue halite crystal from the K+S salt mine in Werra

Sulfur —
out of the steam of the inner earth

We stand in a volcanic crater. All around us the walls are steaming, giving off a yellow smoke. New plumes of smoke form on the ground, others disappear. The scenery is ghostly, and the smell of rotten eggs is everywhere.

Thus we can still experience the formation of sulfur today, for example, in the volcanic crater of Solfatara near Naples, Italy.

Sulfur forms bright yellow crystals that develop in the sulfurous steam of a volcanic channel. If the steam reaches the surface, the water evaporates. The sulfur precipitates on the ground and forms crystals and yellow sulfur crusts.

In our culture, sulfur is an important raw material, such as for the production of sulfuric acid, paint pigments, medicines, and many other uses.

Sulfur	
Color	**yellow**
Streak/Mohs hardness	**yellow / 2**
Crystal system	**orthorhombic**
Cleavage	**scarcely any**
Chemical formula	**S**

A large sulfur crystal from the island of Elba, Italy

Sun-yellow crystals with a history

In the Middle Ages, sulfur was thought to be the smoke from hell. Sulfur vapor was regarded as the smell of it. Alchemists, witches, and magicians used the yellow vapor in their experiments.

Actually, sulfur does not come directly from hell, but arises on our earth in various geological environments. It grows where sulfur steam issues form volcanic craters, but also from the reactions of sulfur-bearing minerals with bacteria. Because of these reactions, lignite and even anthracite coal contain sulfur. Coal-fired power stations need large-scale equipment to remove the sulfur from their combustion gases, catching the sulfur that is freed when the coal is burned. The obtained sulfur now has many uses in medicine and technology.

For the mineral collector, sulfur is an especially beautiful specimen for the showcase, as it glitters powerfully with its sun-yellow color. Beautiful aggregates often contain many dozens of crystals on one piece of rock.

Hundreds of sulfur crystals on limestone, from the island of Elba, Italy

Celestite from Madagascar — crystals as blue as the sky

The Romans already knew celestite, probably from the localities in Agrigento, Sicily.

They called this stone *"Aqua Aura"* because of its water-blue color. The nicest aggregates of crystals now come from Madagascar, but very irregularly because of political unrest. So it may well be that a collector must wait several months before he can obtain a celestite.

Celestite forms aggregates and druses of crystals that can be several centimeters long. Colorless or water-blue crystals whose color can only be seen properly in bright sunlight are typical.

Celestite crystals are often enclosed in dark gray basalt rock. This is especially true of celestite from Madagascar. Other localities include Lenggries, Bavaria, Brandenburg, Carinthia, Austria, and Agrigento, Sicily.

Celestite	
Color	light blue
Streak/Mohs hardness	white / 3-3.5
Crystal system	orthorhombic
Cleavage	one perfect
Chemical formula	$SrSO_4$

Celestite crystals from Madagascar in the noonday sun

Alexandrite —
a green or red gemstone?

The crowd has assembled. High above them on the balcony stand the most important men of the Russian Empire, recognizing the maturity of Tsar Alexander.

This scene took place in 1830. In that year one of the rarest precious stones was discovered and named after the Tsar: Alexandrite. This stone is still one of the least widespread gemstones today, and in good quality it is more valuable than a diamond of the same size.

It has a particular property that scarcely any other gemstone has: Alexandrite can change its color from dark green to red, depending on the source of light. Under artificial light it is red; in daylight it is dark green. This is caused by its particular chemical composition, which encloses small traces of chromium and iron oxides.

Alexandrite belongs to the mineral group of the chrysoberyls, other variations of which are yellow or yellowish milk-white.

Alexandrites that are translucent and show a clear change of colors are big if the crystals measure about one centimeter.

Alexandrite	after Tsar Alexander
Color	**dark green / red**
Streak/Mohs hardness	**white / 8**
Crystal system	**orthorhombic**
Cleavage	**poor**
Chemical formula	**$BeAl_2O_4$**

Alexandrite crystals from Zimbabwe (Rhodesia)

Orpiment —
a remarkable name for a mineral

The German name "*Rauschgelb*" is that of orpiment, half of which is composed of arsenic.

Several hundred years ago, the great painters of the time mixed their paints themselves to be able to begin a new church fresco. At this time, scarcely anything else is daily life was as valuable as oil paint. No factory produced paint in large quantities, so the painters were compelled to prepare their paint themselves. Orpiment was the basis for orange and yellow pigments.

Orpiment	
Color	**yellow-orange**
Streak/Mohs hardness	light yellow / 1-2
Crystal system	**monoclinic**
Cleavage	**perfect**
Chemical formula	**As_2S_3**

Orpiment on quartz from China

Realgar —
crystal needles with an orange-red glow

Arsenic—known for ages as a poison. This chemical element is the main ingredient of realgar. This mineral forms glowing orange-red needles, often as precipitates from hot sources and volcanic gases. Its close relationship with orpiment can be seen in the very similar chemical formluae, and also in the colors, which resemble each other greatly. This relationship does not come about by chance. Natural weather conditions cause the realgar to decay and build a new crystal with its components; orpiment is formed.

In the Solfatara volcanic crater near Naples, realgar occurs along with orpiment. Other localities are Yellowstone Park, USA, Allchar in Macedonia, Bosnia, and Mexico.

Realgar	
Color	**orange to orange-yellow**
Streak/Mohs hardness	**red-orange / 1**
Crystal system	**monoclinic**
Cleavage	**poor**
Chemical formula	**AsS**

Realgar crystals from China

Natrolite —
sprays of white needles

The stillness is complete. Deep in a mountain, a small natrolite crystal stands in a gap in the rock. Water drips slowly onto this crystal over the centuries and brings chemical components that the natrolite needs to grow. Gradually, more and more needles form, radiating outward in various directions from the same point. A fan with a ball-shaped form arises, bearing dozens of crystals after centuries. Thus the typical crystal aggregates of natrolite are formed; they occur in various localities in the world.

Such crystals are also found in Germany, for example, in Maroldsweisach and in quarries in the Vogelsberg near Frankfurt.

As the basis of its growth, the very fragile and sensitive natrolite requires small hollows in the rock, often found in dark gray basalt rock.

Natrolite	
Color	**white**
Streak/Mohs hardness	**white / 5-5.5**
Crystal system	**orthorhombic**
Cleavage	**perfect**
Chemical formula	$Na_2Al_2Si_3O_{18}+2H_2O$

Natrolite sprays on basalt

Cinnabar —
the most important ore of mercury

Somewhere in a goldfield in Canada the machines rattle, a semi-liquid mixture of mercury and powder runs slowly down the sieves and is heated. Mercury vapors rise into the air, bits of rock are sieved out, and pure gold remains in the crucible. With this mercury amalgam method, gold is obtained from rock. But where does the necessary mercury come from?

Here cinnabar shows its importance. It is the most important source of mercury on earth. At first glance one would scarcely suspect that the intensive red mineral is related to the metallic sheen of mercury. Yet if one checks out the chemical composition of the red crystals, it turns out that half of cinnabar consists of the element mercury (Hg) and thus supplies this silvery metal that melts at 25 degrees Celsius after being prepared.

Wherever dying volcanoes release steam into the air at temperatures below 80 degrees Celsius, cinnabar can occur. This process can still be observed today, such as at Monte Amiata in Tuscany. Other localities include Texas, California, Mexico, and Peru.

Cinnabar	also Cinnabarite
Color	**red**
Streak/Mohs hardness	**red / 2-2.5**
Crystal system	**trigonal**
Cleavage	**perfect**
Chemical formula	**HgS**

Cinnabar crystals on calcite

Apophyllite —
a crystal with an inner glow

A pearly luster in a crystal—a rarity among minerals.

Apophyllite shows this effect particularly in the terminations of its crystals. Inside the crystals are reflections of light that remind one of a fish-eye. Thus apophyllite picked up the second name of "Ichthyophthalm": Fish-eye stone.

Apophyllite shows perfect cleavage. That means that, when hit sharply at an angle with a hammer, it breaks into smooth surfaces without having to be polished.

This property occurs in several minerals that are said to have perfect cleavage.

Many localities in Brazil, Indian Mexico, Switzerland, and the USA keep turning up fine individual crystals.

Apophyllite	also Fish-eye Stone
Color	**white, colorless**
Streak/Mohs hardness	**white / 4-5**
Crystal system	**tetragonal**
Cleavage	**perfect**
Chemical formula	$KCa_4F(Si_4O_{10})_2$

Apophyllite crystals from India, photographed on German anthracite

Vanadinite —
the orange-red mineral from the Moroccan highlands

A red vein in the wall of a quarry: Vanadinite, 3000 meters above sea level at a distant site in the Moroccan mountains.

Here the intensively colored crystals are removed by hand; hammers and chisels are the most important tools.

Vanadinite takes its name from its content of the chemical element vanadium (V). This mineral forms splendid aggregates, sometimes with hundreds of crystals on one rock. It is lightly translucent; in strong sunlight the crystals develop a strong glassy luster that makes the crystal form clear to see: hexagonal plates that grow into each other at all angles. The best crystal aggregates come from around Mibladen, Morocco. Vanadinite is also found at the Apache mine in Arizona and Hochobir, Carinthia, Austria.

Vanadinite	
Color	orange, red
Streak/Mohs hardness	yellowish-white / 3
Crystal system	hexagonal
Cleavage	none, fracture
Chemical formula	$Pb_5Cl(VO_4)_3$

Vanadinite sparkles in the morning sun

Olivine —
a witness of gigantic volcanic eruptions

A black island in the Mediterranean. Old volcanic craters are easy to see. Whitewashed houses rise brightly from the black slopes. We are on Lanzarote.

If one goes walking on the beach here, it is not rare to see green flecks of color suddenly in black lava rock: Olivine nodules appear in the burning zone.

What is olivine? It is a green translucent mineral that occurs where volcanism has brought the chemical ingredients that olivine needs from deep inside the earth: Iron, magnesium and silicic acid.

In 1870, the mineralogist Werner named this mineral olivine because of its olive-green color. And in fact, this green is absolutely typical of this stone. Even though in many cases one cannot identify a mineral by its color alone (because it has many colors similar to those of other minerals), olivine is unique in its coloration.

Especially good-quality olivine with few inclusions and intense color are called peridot.

Olivine grains in lava rock from Lanzarote

Green sandy shores

We are in Hawaii. High waves strike against the sand; surfers reach the shore and paddle back out to sea. Whoever is not in the water is sunning him- or herself on the green sand.

Sunning oneself on green sand is possible only in a few places on earth. The most famous of them is the Green Beach in Hawaii. The grains of sand here consist exclusively of the mineral olivine.

For millennia the black lava rock of Hawaii has been subjected to weathering. The lighter black components were washed away, while the heavy green grains of olivine collected on the Green Beach. They are 8.2 times heavier than water.

A one-liter measuring cup filled with these grains thus weighs 8.2 kilograms. The same cup filled with water weighs only one kilogram.

Olivine	also Peridot
Color	**olive green**
Streak/Mohs hardness	**white / 6-7**
Crystal system	**orthorhombic**
Cleavage	**almost none**
Chemical formula	**$(Mg,Fe)_2SiO_4$**

Olivine sand from Green Beach, Hawaii

Peridot—another name for olivine

I ntensive green shimmers at the observer: A peridot reveals all its colorful splendor.

Peridot is the name for gem-quality olivine crystals. Such stones are typified by a very characteristic green such as is not shown by any other mineral. Inclusion-free, intensely colored peridot crystals can weigh up to 50 carats and make splendid gemstones.

The best of such peridots have been found on the island of Zebirget in the Red Sea, 70 kilometers east of the Egyptian coast. Other fine peridots come from Mogok, Myanmar and from Pakistan. Here mining them with tools is not very complicated, since the stones can be removed from the rock walls with pickaxes or hammers and chisels. But only natives do the work, for they are accustomed to the great heights, more than 3000 meters above sea level.

In weeks of walking, the stones are brought, after being mined, to the nearest large city, take roundabout routes to India, and are cut into gemstones there and sent on to Europe. Peridot set in yellow gold is very popular.

Peridot crystal on lava rock, from Zebirget island, Egypt.

Imperial Topaz —
a regal crystal

The name of the mineral topaz, which can occur in the most varied colors, comes from the Sanskrit word *"tapas"* = fire, or from the Greek word *"topazion,"* a name for a light green, transparent gemstone. The Greek *"topazos"* is said to refer to a legendary island in the Red Sea.

Topaz was formerly found in Germany as well. The best-known locality is the Schneckenstein in the Vogt-land of Saxony. The high point of these finds was around 1870. Today topaz in all colors comes almost exclusively from the Brazilian state of Minas Gerais. Here topaz is found in weathered rock, which is washed into valleys and ravines during the rainy season. Such an occurrence with loose bits of rock that contains precious stones is known as gemstone soap.

Colorless topaz crystals are colored light blue by radioactivity, and are then the most common substitute for aquamarine and suitable for fashion jewelry. Naturally blue topaz is very rare and appropriately valuable.

The most famous color of topaz is a powerful brown-orange. Since this color could be worn only by rulers centuries ago, it is called "Imperial Topaz."

Topaz	
Color	**colorless, blue, greenish, brown, orange-brown**
Streak/Mohs hardness	**white / 8**
Crystal system	**orthorhombic**
Cleavage	**perfect**
Chemical formula	$Al_2(F,OH)_2SiO_4$

Imperial topaz on calcite, from Minas Gerais, Brazil

Hauyne —
the rarest gemstone, scarcely known

Sixty thousand years ago: The earth shakes, the animals flee and seek safe hiding places. After days of earthquakes, the catastrophe begins. Volcanic ash rises into the sky, the sun is darkened. For days the volcano spews out incredible amounts of ash and small grains of lava into the sky. The whole landscape is covered with meter-high pumice.

This is what happened in the Volcanic Eifel near Mendig, Germany. And shortly after the lava cooled, many blue crystals appeared, arisen from the molten rock.

This hauyne, as it was named after the French mineralogist R. J. Hauy in 1807, is very rare and occurs only in a single quarry in the Volcanic Eifel mountains.

The crystals that are worth cutting into gemstones measure 5 millimeters at most. Other localities for this splendid blue mineral are scarcely known to date.

Hauyne	
Color	**light to dark blue**
Streak/Mohs hardness	**white / 5-6**
Crystal system	**orthorhombic**
Cleavage	**scarcely visible**
Chemical formula	$\mathbf{(Na,Ca)_{8-4}(SO_4)_{2-1}(AlSiO_4)_6}$

Hauyne crystals on pumice from the Volcanic Eifel.

Ulexite —
the television stone

Ulexite is a white mineral that consists of very fine parallel mineral fibers. The individual fibers can be seen only under a microscope. It was discovered in the mid-19th century and has picked up the name of "television stone" because of its unusual property: A picture that lies under the ulexite appears as if it were on the surface of the stone. The stone "lifts" the picture under it through the effect of its mineral fibers to the upper, polished surface. Thus the picture appears closer to the observer than it actually is.

Ulexite was named after the chemist Ulex in 1849. It is a mineral that occurs mainly in borax lakes and swamps in North and South American desert areas, such as Columbus Marsh, Nevada, Oregon, Peru, and Argentina.

Ulexite is an important source of the chemical element borax, which is widely used in the chemical industry.

Ulexite	
Color	**white**
Streak/Mohs hardness	**white / 1**
Crystal system	**triclinic**
Chemical formula	$\mathbf{NaCaB_5O_6(OH)_6 + 5H_2O}$

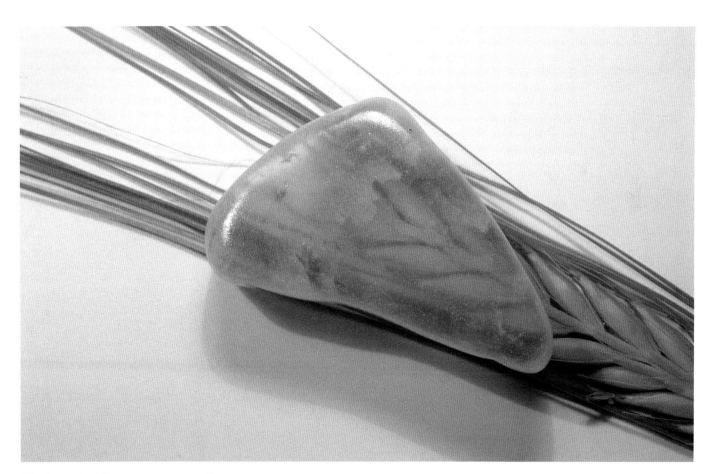

Ulexite as television stone on an ear of grain

Mica —
a familiar mineral family

Probably everybody knows mica. A piece of granite, looked at closely, shows glittering silvery or black surfaces in the stone.

Mica is a whole family of minerals, all of which have the same basic composition and crystal form. A hexagonal form is always seen in large crystals, and is made up of many very thin leaves.

There are various names and colors:

Colorless to silvery: muscovite
shining black: biotite
light violet: lepidolite
greenish or golden: phlogopite

In the everyday world we find mica used as a heat-isolating layer in industrial furnaces, and formerly also in irons.

Very nice crystals are found in Uluguru, Tanzania and the Miami Mica Field of Zimbabwe.

Mica	
Color	**colorless, black, greenish, violet, yellowish**
Streak/Mohs hardness	**none, as crystals are too soft / 2-4**
Crystal system	**hexagonal**
Cleavage	**perfect**
Chemical formula	$\mathbf{AlSi_3O_{10}(OH)_2 + K, Al, Na}$ **in various amounts**

Translucent biotite crystals

96

Muscovite —
the brightest type of mica

The Ural Mountains: In the depths of a Russian winter, the trucks move very slowly, on account of the coldness. The quantity of muscovite taken from the quarry is clearly less than in the summer.

But here in the Urals, enough of the shining silvery crystals are found to make similar ones sought all over the world.

Although muscovite is actually a widespread mineral that occurs in many rocks, it is seldom found in sheets measuring over 15 cm. Muscovite is needed in this form to be used as insulation material later on.

For the collector, muscovite is a charming mineral. As a rule, it forms hexagonal plates or "books" built up of many very thin layers. If the crystals get wet, they can take up some moisture between the sheets and swell up.

When they dry out, the swelling of the layers disappears.

Muscovite crystal aggregates from Russia

Brazilianite —
an apple-green crystal from Brazil

Brazilianite crystal, Paraiba,
Minas Gerais, Brazil

A kilometer beneath the earth's surface: After the last eruption of magma from deep inside the earth, several thousand years have passed. Only the last remnants move through the rock and gradually fill in the cracks. Before the last open spaces disappear, crystals form in them. Out of the remaining magma, sodium (Na), aluminum (Al), and phosphorus (P) separate. A brazilianite crystal is formed at a temperature of several hundred degrees Celsius.

In the same area, millions of years later, miners work their way through the rock and take the loveliest gemstones from these late-filled cracks. One of the rarer gemstones is brazilianite. Only in rare cases does it occur in such purity and color that it is worth being faceted into gemstones.

The main localities are Cons. Pena, Minas Gerais, and Pietras Lavradas, Paraiba, Brazil.

Brazilianite	
Clor	**light green, yellowish**
Streak/Mohs hardness	**white / 5**
Crystal system	**monoclinic**
Cleavage	**perfect**
Chemical formula	$NaAl_3(OH)_2(PO_4)_3$

Epidote —
a little-known intensive green stone

Epidote is really a widespread mineral, but it does not always occur in well-formed crystals.

The mineral takes its name from the Greek concept *"epidosis,"* meaning addition, since it often bears very many crystal facets on its apex. Its other name, pistacite, refers to its pistachio-green color.

A classic epidote locality is the Knappenwand in the lower Sulzbach Valley, Pinzgau, Upper Austria, where it must be taken carefully from thin cracks in the rock by hammer-and-chisel work.

In Finland, too, near the great iron ore deposits near Outokumpo, epidote has been found. Other localities include Brazil, Kenya, Alaska, Mexico, Mozambique, and Norway.

Epidote	also Pistacite
Color	**green, brownish-black**
Streak/Mohs hardness	**gray / 6-7**
Crystal system	**monoclinic**
Cleavage	**perfect**
Chemical formula	**$Ca_2(Fe,Al)_3(SiO_4)OH$**

Epidote from Prince of Wales Island, Alaska, photographed on lava

Calcite —
a widespread mineral, but hard to identify

Calcite can take more forms than any other mineral that exists. Over 2000 combinations of surfaces are known. That makes recognizing calcite and telling it from other minerals difficult in many cases.

In addition, calcite can have many different colors. In pure form, as calcium carbonate, it is white and translucent to opaque.

Through various combinations with iron, manganese, and other elements, its color changes from one locality to another. Orange, yellow, brown, black, and reddish calcites can be found.

The collector who finds calcite in the field and is not sure of its identity can identify it using one simple method: a drop of thinned hydrochloric acid on the crystal makes air bubbles form or the surface bubble as soon as it touches calcite. Thus confusing it with quartz, which often looks very similar, is ruled out.

Calcite	
Color	white, yellowish, brown, etc.
Streak/Mohs hardness	white / 3
Crystal system	trigonal
Cleavage	perfect
Chemical formula	$CaCO_3$

Calcite crystals on limestone, from the Spessart near Aschaffenburg

Calcite, Kalkspat or Kalkstein

Kalkstein (limestone)—this name sounds very much like calcite's second German name, Kalkspat. Limestone is almost identical to calcite in its chemical composition and consists of more than 90% calcite.

Over very long periods, millions of years ago, chalky mud gathered under water, including in the present-day Altmuehl Valley of Bavaria. Millimeter by millimeter, the layers at the bottom of the water grew until they amounted to several dozen meters. The lime of which these layers of rock were formed came from seashells and fish bones that, for the most part, were also made of lime.

After the waters receded some sixty million years ago, dry landscapes, mountains, and valleys of limestone arose. Now rainwater could circulate through the layers of rock. At one place it dissolved some lime; at another it deposited it. Where it precipitated there was now enough concentrated lime to let crystals grow. The beautifully formed calcite crystals with their three-sided terminations arose. A thin skin of iron on the crystals enhanced the yellow-orange color.

Calcite crystals from the Solnhofen lime beds in Bavaria

Iceland Spar —
a crystal with a doubling effect

The German name of "double spar" contains two mysteries. The first, namely the word "spar," is solved if we look back to the Middle Ages, when the miners who worked in deep shafts found that many minerals, when hit with hammers, broke apart with smooth, reflective surfaces. The crystal form was always maintained, no matter how big the crystal was after being hit.

They used the old German word *"spaetig"* to describe this behavior of a crystal when it cleaved. Thus calcite, or lime spar, got its name.

The present-day mineral collector can see this effect easily by breaking a calcite crystal at a quarry and then observing the breakage planes with a magnifying glass. He will always see a smooth, reflective crystal face.

The second mystery revolves around the term "double." But what is double in a calcite crystal? If one places the crystal on a printed paper, a remarkable effect is created. The two images of the letters are slightly displaced. The images even turn around each other when the calcite is moved on the printing. This doubling effect gave clear Iceland spar calcite the German name of "double spar." It occurs because a ray of light that goes into the calcite is always divided into two rays that run parallel through the crystal and return to the viewer's eye as two rays. This effect is called double refraction.

The double refraction of Iceland spar

Crystals fill hollow spaces

Calcite is a mineral that can occur under nearly all of nature's conditions. It grows regardless of whether low temperature and pressure prevail around the forming crystal or the temperature and pressure are both over 100° C deep in the rock of a mountain.

Depending on the temperature and pressure, though, the faces that form on the crystal are changed.

Thus prismatic, acicular, lenticular, thick tabular, reniform or massive calcite can occur.

In the illustration, the chambers inside a petrified ammonite can be seen. In these chambers are long, little calcite needles, formed after the actual petrification of the creature, have grown, almost completely filling the shell.

An ammonite with calcite filling, from Morocco

Aragonite —
a radiating relative of calcite

Aragonite has exactly the same chemical composition as calcite. With other pressure and temperature conditions during crystal growth, aragonite forms crystals with a different form: radiating bundles of acicular crystals.

Aragonite can occur especially near sources of heat, where it forms white crusts and layers around the outflows of hot lime-bearing water. Very beautiful needles can be found near Maria Alm in Austria, as well as at Huettenberg in Carinthia and Erzberg in Styria. There is also a well-known locality in Germany, at Sasbach near the Kaiserstuhl. The name of Aragonite comes from the province of Aragon in Spain, where many of these crystals are found to this day.

Aragonite	
Color	white, yellowish, brown, colorless
Streak/Mohs hardness	white / 3-4
Crystal system	orthorhombic
Cleavage	obscure
Chemical formula	$CaCO_3$

Aragonite from Maria Alm, Austria

Triplets and more

In nature it often occurs that not only one crystal grows from one point, but two or more crystals penetrate each other and form a crystal body.

Without more exact knowledge of the typical mineral form, the observer gets the impression of seeing just one crystal. The surfaces of such a multiple crystal, though, are arranged very differently than those of a single crystal. Thus aragonite forms triplets, which occur mainly in southern Spain, with six outer faces and one flat termination.

Such a crystal form never occurs in a single crystal of aragonite. Thus the illustrated crystal form lets one conclude at once that there are three aragonite crystals here that penetrated each other as they grew.

In pure form, such aragonite triplets are colorless. The brown color comes from the thin skin of iron that covers the crystal.

Aragonite triplet
from southern Spain.

Dolomite —
it gave its name to a mountain range

The Frenchman de Dolomieu hiked through the Alps in the mid-19th century. While taking a close look at the rocks, he discovered white crystals with a somewhat greasy luster. Some of these crystals were slightly curved, and hundreds of them often occurred on one surface of a narrow crack in the rock.

He took some of these minerals with him and examined them later. He had discovered a new mineral, which was named after him: dolomite.

Dolomite is chemically very similar to calcite, but it also contains magnesium in addition to calcium (Ca) and carbonate (CO_3).

Further examination showed that the mountains in which he had found the dolomite crystals consist for the most part of this mineral, although not always in the form of nice crystals. Thus the Dolomites were named after their chief component, the mineral dolomite.

Dolomite	after de Dolomieu
Color	**white, yellowish, brown**
Streak/Mohs hardness	**white / 3-4**
Crystal system	**trigonal**
Cleavage	**perfect**
Chemical formula	**$(Ca,Mg)(CO_3)_2$**

Dolomite crystals on green fluorite, from England

106

Brown crystals

Dolomite on limestone; this growth can be found often in areas with dark gray limestone.

In the Kraichgau near Heidelberg there are many small quarries in which brown dolomite crystals can be found on the limestone, which is quarried as a raw material for the making of cement.

When limestone is burned, the result is burnt lime, which can be made into cement by various means and mixed with other stone products such as plaster.

Here the presence of dolomite in limestone plays a very important role. With its magnesium content, dolomite determines the later properties of the cement, such as firmness and adhesion.

Brown dolomite crystals on limestone, from the Kraichgau near Heidelberg.

Dolomite

Dolomite and calcite are chemically very similar to each other. This also explains why the two minerals are often mistaken for each other.

One can tell dolomite from calcite by the different luster of the crystal faces. Dolomite always has a somewhat greasy luster, while calcite has reflecting surfaces.

Especially lovely dolomite has been found in the Binn Valley of Switzerland, near Leogang in Salzburg, Austria, and near Djefa in Algeria.

Dolomite is a very widespread rock-forming mineral but seldom has well-formed crystals. As a rule, dolomite appears as a whitish band in rock without crystal faces.

Cubic dolomite crystals on calcite, from southern Germany.

Gypsum —
not only useful in construction

Gypsum is known to most people only as a white powder used in home construction. Yet gypsum also occurs in nicely formed crystals.

The crystal forms are varied. In the picture below, clear, transparent gypsum crystals may be seen. They are twinned, in that two gypsum crystals have grown together in each crystal body, penetrating each other. The result was a V-shaped cross-section, which has given the twinned crystals the nickname of swallowtail twins.

When one sees this V-shape in a crystal, one can be sure that it is a twinned gypsum crystal. No other mineral shows this characteristic form.

Gypsum crystals become transparent when they have enough free space available, in the form of a hollow in a rock, while growing. In addition, a short growing time is required, so that the chemical building blocks can orient themselves to each other geometrically. The transparency of gypsum is an exception.

Gypsum	also selenite
Color	**white, colorless**
Streak/Mohs hardness	**white / 1-2**
Crystal system	**monoclinic**
Cleavage	**perfect**
Chemical formula	$CaSO_4 + _2H_2O$

Gypsum crystals on limestone, southern Germany

Gypsum or selenite — two names for the same mineral

The motor roars, the wings glisten in the sunlight. The pilot flies his airplane slowly over the Ries near Noerdlingen. He flies over Noerdlingen and then farther to the southwest. From up there he admires the circular shape of the Ries. It is the largest meteorite crater in Germany. Here a meteorite some two kilometers long struck and formed the depression in Bavaria's landscape, several kilometers in diameter. At the edge of the Ries, the aviator now flies over a quarry. In the quarry, several dark gray veins of clay can be seen, even from an airplane.

In the quarry itself, several geologists are examining the clay. What have they found? The clay contains clear, transparent, twinned crystals of gypsum up to ten centimeters long. They had not expected such things in the Ries. In the moist clay, long after the meteorite struck, gypsum crystals had formed, and in their growth they had included bits of the surrounding clay.

In addition to the twinning, hourglass-shaped structures are also found in the crystals, and are very nice to see in the light that shines through.

Gypsum crystals with hourglass structures, from the Ries, Noerdlingen, Germany

Selenite needles

We are in the mountains of Romania. From behind the next mountain slope, knocking and hammering are heard. Mineral collectors are collecting aggregates of fine acicular crystals. In some places the needles are green, in others white. Still other sites have orange-brown needles.

With all the colors, they are all the same mineral, which is actually colorless: they are selenite needles. The various colors come from coatings of other minerals that formed layers while the selenite crystals were growing and now pretend to be a strange color of selenite.

Selenite needles from Romania

Fibrous gypsum — a natural conductor of light

Another visual form of selenite has many thin parallel crystal needles. This is fibrous gypsum. If one looks at the front of the needles, a ray of light can pass through the needles, even if the piece of fibrous gypsum is 25 centimeters long.

Light that enters at one side of the gypsum is carried along by a light ladder of glass fibers. So it seems to the observer as if the crystal is glowing outward from the inside.

Such unusual fibrous gypsum has been found on the Moroccan highlands as a layer in the rock, some 50 cm thick, and removed by muscle power.

Opposed to this shimmering fibrous gypsum are the crystals known as Marienglas. They are transparent plates of gypsum through which the observer can look. Such crystals are found in Bohemia, the Czech Republic, and Foerste in the Harz Mountains.

Fibrous gypsum crystals from the mountains of Morocco

Desert Rose —
artistic formation from the desert

The air trembles in fifty-degree heat. In the middle of the Tunisian desert, several camels plod slowly through the sand. A small snake crawls through the sand and waits, half buried, for its prey.

Fifty centimeters to a meter below the snake are wonderful works of art created by nature only in desert sand: gypsum desert roses.

It rains very rarely in the desert. But when it happens, the water very quickly trickles down into the ground. If it brings some gypsum with it below the surface sand, then grains of sand stick together and form desert roses.

Such gypsum roses consist of many ribs that penetrate each other. The effect of heat colors the edges of the ribs white. The result is a picture that shows the artistic creativity of nature.

Gypsum	and sand = quartz grains
Color	**yellowish**
Chemical formula	$CaSO_4 + 2\,H_2O + SiO_2$

Desert roses from the desert of Tunisia

113

Sand Rose —
a natural wonder from desert sand

One or two meters under the desert sand surface: fans, ribs, leaves of sand sleep until they are discovered. They have formed over the centuries. During each rare rainfall, some lime cement reached the depths and glued some more grains of sand to a rib. Thus sand roses are formed, artistic structures that can be up to a meter long.

They consist of glued grains of sand, thus of quartz.

Gypsum	and sand = quartz grains
Color	**yellowish**
Chemical formula	$CaSO_4 + 2H_2O + SiO_2$

Sand roses from Egypt

Barite —
a widespread white mineral

Barite is a white mineral that can be found in many parts of the world. It is white and opaque, and often forms crystals that look like ribs. These ribs can penetrate each other irregularly or be arranged in almost parallel lines, as can be seen in the picture.

When openings and cracks are present in rock, hot water can circulate through the rock, which the mineralogist calls "hydrothermal". If barium (Ba) and sulfur (S) are dissolved in it and the hot water evaporates on contact with the rock, these ingredients remain and are deposited on the rock. Small barite crystals are formed. They go on growing if hot water brings new material to them.

After centuries, beautiful arrays of crystals, consisting of many barite ribs, have often been formed.

Barite	also Heavy Spar
Color	**white, yellowish, brownish**
Streak/Mohs hardness	**white / 3-3.5**
Crystal system	**orthorhombic**
Cleavage	**perfect**
Chemical formula	$\textbf{BaSO}_4$

Barite crystals in the sunshine

Barite—an important mineral in Sauerland mining

Meggen and Dreislar: two places where mining has been carried on for many years. Here there are tunnels several hundred meters below the surface, in which barite is mined. It occurs here as both beds in the rock and impressive crystal aggregates.

Barite is an important material for many things in our daily lives. The chemical element barium (Ba) is obtained from barite. Barium is a part of many chemical substances used in medicine and chemistry.

Barite in a ground condition is also used as a filler for high-priced art-printing paper, and as a pigment for oil paint. Dispersion paint for walls can also be made, showing an intense white from the barium powder they contain.

The typical barite crystals from the mine in Dreislar have a yellowish color. This is created by a thin coating of iron on the surface of the crystals. Inside, the crystals are rosy white.

Barite crystals with iron coverings from Dreislar

Barite or Heavy Spar

Barite received its second name, "heavy spar," from one of its properties, namely its specific gravity.

The specific gravity of a mineral tells how heavy it is in comparison with water.

Water weighs one kilogram per cubic decimeter, or per liter of volume. Because of its chemical composition, barite has a much higher weight. A volume of one liter, filled with ground barite, weighs 4.5 kilograms. Thus barite is 4.5 times heavier than water.

In rare cases, barite can be found in a particular crystal form, called *Meisselspat* (chisel spar) in German. Here the crystals are particularly thick and have a point that looks like a chisel. Such crystals are often translucent, which is a rarity for this mineral. The nicest chisel spars from southern Germany are presently found in the Clara Pit, the only still-active quarry in the Black Forest.

Chisel spar barite, Clara Pit, Black Forest

Rhodochrosite —
a rare gemstone from the depths of the earth

In the 13th century, the Incas gave up their silver mining in Argentina. Since that time, rose-colored stalagmites have grown on the floors of the shafts. Manganese, carbon, and oxygen united, drop-by-drop, to form rhodochrosite crystals. These crystals are now the most beautiful rhodochrosites found anywhere in the world.

Rose and white banded crystal aggregates, which have been made into jewelry since 1950, are found most often. If the rose and white bands are circular, the stone is called Inca rose. Particularly rare and costly collectors' pieces are transparent, intensive red rhodochrosite crystals.

Rhodochrosites, some of which are 10,000 years old, were found in Germany in the highest rock layers of various iron and manganese mines: Nassau, Bockenrod in the Hessian Odenwald, Schaebenholz near Elbingerode in the Harz, and the Wold Pit near Herdorf in the Siegerland. Other important localities are in North America and southern Spain.

Inca rose with circular bands, shown in snow, from North America.

The name comes from the Greek *"rhodochrosis,"* meaning "rose-colored." The Indians gave the stone as a symbol of love and revered it as sacred. They also believed it would cure headaches and attributed the power to improve one's mood to it.

The making of decorative silver chains with rhodochrosite panels has long been very popular. The light shines softly through the stone, and along with the polished silver, the jewelry looks very harmonious and reinforces its wearer's smile.

The largest transparent, strongly red rhodochroste, which was even cut with facets, weighs 59.65 carats and comes from South Africa.

Rhodochrosite with its rose and white bands can easily be told from rhodonite, which is banded in rose and black.

Rhodochrosite	also "Mangan Spar" or "Inca Rose"
Color	**rose to red, translucent**
Streak/Mohs hardness	**white / 3-4**
Crystal system	**trigonal**
Cleavage	**perfect**
Chemical formula	**McCO$_3$, manganese carbonate**

Rhodochrosite panels set in polished silver

Rhodonite —
named after the rose

Rhodonite was already known in ancient times. The Greeks named it rhodonite (stone of the rose) after its color. Its typical appearance makes it unmistakable. No other mineral shows this rose color with black bands.

Fifty-degree heat by day, ten-degree coolness at night. These are the conditions under which rhodonite crystals are mined in Australia. One of the most important deposits of rhodonite is at Broken Hill, New South Wales. Other localities have been found in Tanzania, about 120 kilometers from Kilimanjaro. In the Urals too, 25 kilometers from Sevrdlovsk, rhodonite is being mined again after a pause in the seventies.

Rhodonite is widely used in jewelry. The ancient Greeks attributed to this mineral the effect of warning against danger. It is apparently thought to increase the heartbeat as soon as danger threatens.

Rhodonite	from Greek "*rhodon*" = rose
Color	**rose with black bands**
Streak/Mohs hardness	**white / 5-6**
Crystal system	**triclinic**
Cleavage	**perfect**
Chemical formula	**$CaMn_4Si_5O_{15}$**

Polished rhodonite from Australia

Malachite —
a green mineral, best known when banded

Power shovels roll through the kilometer-long quarry. Trucks loaded with rock drive to the nearest preparation facility. We are in the Urals, in one of the world's largest copper deposits.

Fine-ground stone rolls along the conveyor belts, copper-colored stones gradually become visible, and some green pieces can be seen. They are malachite, that shine from the rock with their intense green color.

Malachite is green and opaque. This mineral often forms small balls that, when seen through a microscope, are composed of many thin acicular crystals. These needles all grow out in a fan-shape from one point. Thus the ball shape is formed.

Malachite	from Greek "*malache*" = mallow
Color	**green, partly banded**
Streak/Mohs hardness	**green / 4**
Crystal system	**monoclinic**
Cleavage	**good, but scarcely visible**
Chemical formula	$\mathbf{Cu_2CO_3(OH)_2}$

Malachite balls on milestone, along with yellowish calcite crystals.

Malachite

Schaba, in southern Zaire, now supplies the loveliest malachite crystals, which every mineral fan has in his showcase.

Splendidly banded specimens of malachite are found in the Urals. If this malachite is polished, the whole splendor of the alternating dark and light green bands appears, glowing strongly. These colors make malachite a desirable decorative stone.

Since malachite is not very hard, it can easily be reduced to powder. This powder was used in the Middle Ages as a paint pigment for fresco painting, and also as eye shadow.

The ancient Egyptians obtained malachite from the Sinai Peninsula and carried it as an amulet. In the Egyptian Book of the Dead it is written that the goddess of heaven lets "stars fall as green stones."

Malachite is closely related to azurite, which is a deep blue. The chemical formluae of these two minerals are almost identical. Azurite can turn to malachite by absorbing water.

Polished malachite with bands, from the Urals, Russia

Azurite —
a mineral as blue as the heavens

Azure blue—a familiar concept for the intense blue of the summer sky. And azurite is similarly colored. This mineral has the intense blue coloring of all opaque stones.

Like malachite, it can also be banded, alternating between light and dark blue.

Particularly lovely single crystals, which are also translucent, have been found in Tsumeb, Namibia. Such translucent azurite crystals are very rare. As a rule, azurite is found as a colored layer in rock. To the great painters of the Middle Ages, ground azurite was a popular and very valuable paint pigment.

Such discoveries were already made in many forms in the Middle Ages. Neubulach in the Black Forest has a mine from this period, in which the loveliest arrays of azurite were found for hundreds of years. Today these crystals can be admired in the display mine and the museum there.

Azurite	
Color	**blue, sometimes banded**
Streak/Mohs hardness	**blue / 3-4**
Crystal system	**monoclinic**
Cleavage	**perfect**
Chemical formula	$Cu_3(CO_3)_2(OH)_2$

Azurite crystals on calcite, with malachite, from Tsumeb, Africa

Chrysocolla —
already known to Greek goldsmiths

Gravel copper, gravel malachite, copper green: These old names refer to chrysocolla, a blue-green massive mineral found in rock without crystalline form.

We are visiting a goldsmith in ancient Greece and looking over his shoulder. He is just working on a complicated yellow-gold bracelet. The richest lady in town has ordered it. The bracelet is almost finished; only the setting for the stone that will adorn the bracelet is lacking. It is already night. In the flickering light of his candle, the goldsmith heats the bracelet and the setting, strews some blue-green powder on the place where the setting is to be attached, and begins to solder. And in a few minutes he attaches the setting to the bracelet.

What helped him? It is the blue-green powder, ground chrysocolla. In ancient times this mineral was used as gold solder. With its help, beautiful jewelry found in archaeological excavations was made. Chrysocolla can still be found today, usually in copper deposits such as Bisbee, Arizona, the Lizard in Cornwall, England, and Bogoslovsk in the Urals.

Chrysocolla	from Greek *"chrysocolla,"* gold solder
Color	**blue-green**
Streak/Mohs hardness	**greenish-white / 2-4**
Crystal system	**amorphous**
Cleavage	**none**
Chemical formula	**$CuSiO_3 + H_2O$**

Blue-green chrysocolla grown in pieces of limestone

Sugilite —
a modern gemstone with a short history

V ery rare and only known as a gemstone for a short time: this is sugilite. It was first described by the Japanese Dr. K. Sugi in 1944, and has been named after him. In all the world there is only one sugilite locality, in an aegirine-stenite rock on the island of Iwagi, Japan.

Sugilite is expensive. A stone weighing just a few grams, but with good color, can cost several hundred Euros.

Sugilite was formerly offered falsely as Sogdianite, until more precise test methods made it possible to place this stone correctly in the system of minerals.

Sugilite	
Color	**violet**
Streak/Mohs hardness	**white / 7**
Crystal system	**hexagonal**
Cleavage	**obscure**
Chemical formula	$\mathbf{(K,Na)_2(Ti,Fe)_2(Li,Al)_3Si_{12}O_{30}}$

A sugilite ornament from Japan

Jadeite —
a traditional gem from China

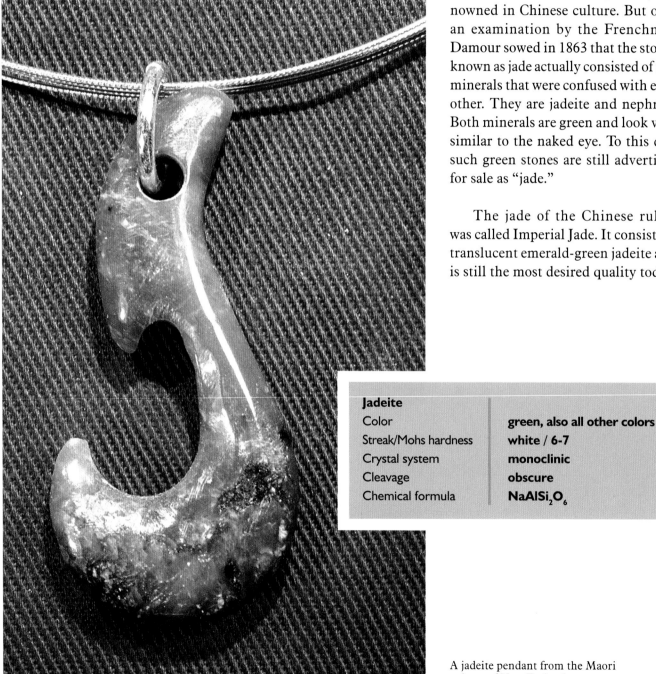

The name of jade comes from the times of the Spanish conquest of Central and South America, and was named *"piedra da ijada,"* meaning something like "hip stone," as it was thought to heal hip disorders.

For 7000 years, the green stones called jade have been especially renowned in Chinese culture. But only an examination by the Frenchman Damour sowed in 1863 that the stones known as jade actually consisted of two minerals that were confused with each other. They are jadeite and nephrite. Both minerals are green and look very similar to the naked eye. To this day, such green stones are still advertised for sale as "jade."

The jade of the Chinese rulers was called Imperial Jade. It consists of translucent emerald-green jadeite and is still the most desired quality today.

Jadeite	
Color	**green, also all other colors**
Streak/Mohs hardness	**white / 6-7**
Crystal system	**monoclinic**
Cleavage	**obscure**
Chemical formula	**$NaAlSi_2O_6$**

A jadeite pendant from the Maori culture of New Zealand

Nephrite —
used for millennia as a decorative stone

Over two thousand years ago, jade was used in China for cult activities and to pray to the gods, and worked into mystic figures and carved pictures. In pre-Columbian America jade was valued more highly than gold. The Spanish conquest abruptly ended the art of jade cutting in America, but this branch of art still blossoms in China.

If one travels to China today, green stones, often artistically worked, are offered in many stores. Most of these stones, though, are not pure jadeite, but nephrite. Nephrite occurs more commonly in nature and can be confused with jadeite.

From the region of Lake Baikal in Russia comes nephrite that is sold under the name of Russian Jade.

Nephrite	
Color	green, also all other colors
Streak/Mohs hardness	white / 6-6.5
Crystal system	monoclinic
Cleavage	obscure
Chemical formula	$Ca_2(Mg,Fe)_5(OH,F)(Si_4O_{11})_2$

Nephrite animal figures carved in China

Sodalite —
related to soda water

Sodalite and soda water got their names from their high content of sodium, the English name for German Natrium.

If one looks at the chemical formula of sodalite, it can be seen that it is largely composed of sodium.

Dark blue sodalite with fine white banding is very popular for jewelry. This stone can also be worked easily to make bowls and other decorative objects.

It occurs at many localities, but seldom in a strong blue color. For example, it occurs in Bahia, Brazil, in Greenland, India, and Ontario, Canada. Transparent sodalite crystals are even found in Namibia, and are very rare collectors' pieces.

Sodalite	from English "sodium"
Color	blue, with white bands
Streak/Mohs hardness	white / 5-6
Cleavage	not visible
Chemical formula	$Na_8Cl_2(AlSiO_4)_6$

Raw sodalite in its typical form

Kyanite —
two hardnesses in one mineral

To identify a mineral, it always helps to test its hardness. To do this, one uses the ten minerals of the Mohs Scale, which represent hardnesses from 1 o 10. Hardness 1 is the softest, represented by talc; hardness 10 is the hardest, the diamond. To test the hardness, one takes the minerals in order of hardness and tries to scratch the mineral to be tested. If there is no scratch, the unknown mineral is harder than the test stone from the scale. If there is a scratch, then it is softer than the test stone.

Kyanite has gained its second name of disthene from the Greek term "*di stenos,*" meaning two hardnesses. If one scratches kyanite longitudinally, its hardness is 4 to 5; if one scratches it transversely, its hardness is 6 to 7.

Kyanite often occurs as fine blue crystals that grow in marble. Especially lovely crystals are found in Tessin and Tyrol.

Kyanite	also called Disthene
Color	**blue**
Streak/Mohs hardness	**white / 4-5, 6-7**
	crosswise
Crystal system	**triclinic**
Cleavage	**perfect**
Chemical formula	Al_2SiO_5

Kyanite crystals that grew on marble

Larimar —
a new gem from the Caribbean

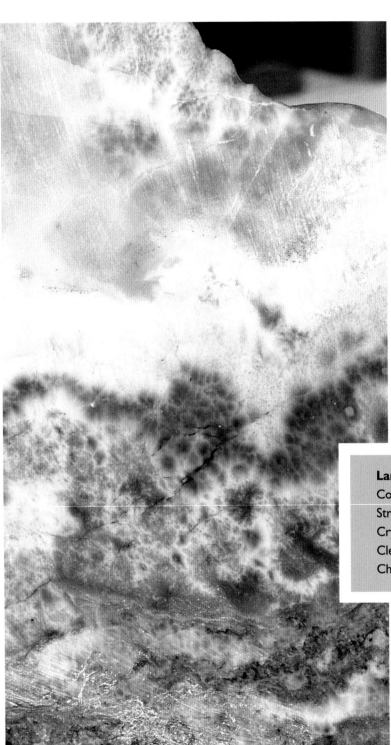

The Dominican Republic is the home of the newest of modern gemstones, larimar.

Only about three years ago did this stone come on the market. It already enjoys great popularity among many women.

Its light blue color is reminiscent of the vastness of the sky. Usually without crystal form, it is found as light blue bands in lime-bearing rock.

Its light blue glowing power has inspired the Native Americans of the Caribbean to regard larimar as a good luck charm and healing stone.

Larimar	
Color	**mottled light blue**
Streak/Mohs hardness	**white / 6**
Crystal system	**triclinic**
Cleavage	**obscure**
Chemical formula	**$NaCa_2Si_3O_8OH$**

Raw larimar, a cut piece from the Dominican Republic

Lapis Lazuli

L apis lazuli has been found in the Hindu Kush region of Afghanistan for more than 6000 years, and is still dug with muscle power and the simplest tools in trackless areas. In prehistoric times, lapis lazuli was already used for decorative purposes. In the Middle Ages, this mineral was the pigment of ultramarine, the color of kings.

Lapis lazuli is a mixture of various minerals with the main constituent of lazurite. Augite, calcite, diopside, enstatite, mica, hauyne, hornblende, nosean and pyrite may also be present. Thus lapis lazuli can almost be called a rock, though a rare and valuable one. The intense blue colors are most desired.

Pyrite often gives lapis lazuli the look of a starry sky.

Lapis Lazuli	from Arabic-Latin "blue stone"
Color	**blue**
Streak/Mohs hardness	**light blue / 5-6**
Crystal system	**cubic**
Cleavage	**obscure**
Chemical formula	$\mathbf{(Na,Ca)_8(Al,Si)_{12}(O,S)_{24}}$ $\mathbf{(SO_4),Cl_2(OH)_2}$

Lapis lazuli

Lapis lazuli, cut as a decorative stone

Lapis Lazuli

The legends of lapis lazuli go back to 5000 B.C. To the Assyrians, lapis lazuli was the sacred stone Uknu, which brought the blue of the sky and thus the light of the gods to earth.

All over the world there are churches and temples decorated with this stone in fresco or intarsia work.

Its deep blue color comes from enclosures of sulfur, but only in rare cases is it divided evenly throughout the stone. Thus there is often a play of color, with alternating lighter and darker areas.

Turquoise —
gem of the Native Americans

Turquoise got its name from the Crusaders who found this stone in Turkey and named it after that country.

Long before the Crusaders first saw this stone, it was known to the Native Americans. In the American Indian reservations are the mines from which the best quality of turquoise is taken.

Turquoise can have shadings from light to dark blue and be crossed by veins from the rock. This mineral often occurs as an aggregate, a light blue mass in which countless light blue crystals have grown together. This mass is often very soft and not optimal for jewelry. In such cases it is stabilized, saturated with artificial resin.

This increases its sturdiness in jewelry and, above all, prevents bits of dirt from getting into the surface of the turquoise and discoloring it dark green, which often happens after long wearing. It is then no longer possible to clean the turquoise. Thus turquoise should never be worn directly on the skin.

Turquoise	
Color	**light blue to dark green**
Streak/Mohs hardness	**white / 5-6**
Crystal system	**triclinic**
Cleavage	**none**
Chemical formula	$CuAl_6(PO_4)_4(OH)_8 + 4H_2O$

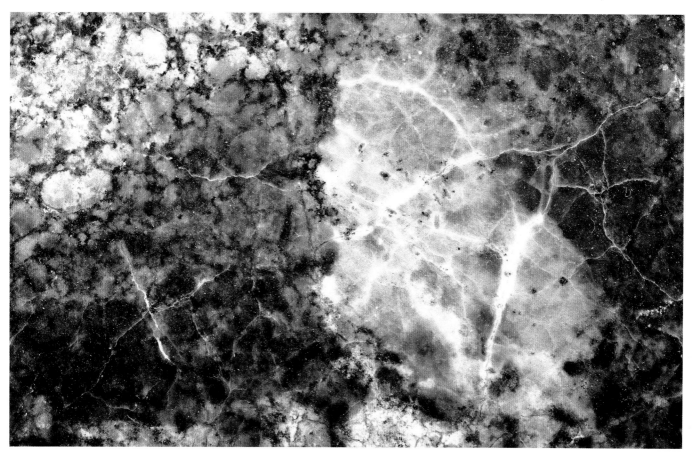

Light blue and dark green turquoise in rock

Moldavite —
stone witness of a meteorite's impact

It happened millions of years ago: A meteorite flew toward the Noerdlingen Ries. With its tremendous speed of some 70,000 kilometers per hour, the glowing meteorite struck the earth's crust and melted the rock around the impact site. 900-degree drops of melted rock flew into the air, glowing red. There the high winds cooled them in a few minutes; still in flight, they turned into solid stone. Moldavite stones had formed. Winds blew them hundreds of kilometers to the Moldau region of the Czech Republic, where they are now found in quarries in Ceske Budejovice, Bohemia and Terbic, Moravia.

Through fast cooling within a few minutes, a glassy structure was formed in moldavite instead of crystals.

Only around 1970 did scientists find that moldavite consists of melted rock from the Noerdlingen Ries.

Moldavite was already used in jewelry in the Stone Age. It was probably worn as an amulet to represent fruitfulness.

Moldavite	also Bouteillenstone
Color	bottle green to brownish-green
Streak/Mohs hardness	white / 5
Crystal system	amorphic
Cleavahe	not definite
Chemical formula	$SiO_2 + Al_2O_3$

Moldavite from the Czech Republic on black lava from Stromboli

Tectite —
witnesses of mighty geological processes

Rock glass—thus tectites can be described. One of the best-known tectites is green moldavite.

In many places on our earth, impact craters of meteorites are found. Every meteorite impact caused tremendous heat and very high pressure, to which the rock around the crater was exposed. Parts of the rock melted and were flung into the air as molten drops. They cooled in flight and fell to earth as tectites. The wind formed their often oval shapes.

According to where they are found, tectites have been given various names: Australite, billitonite, muong-gong-glass and moldavite are just a few trade names of tectite.

Tectite	from Greek "*tektos*" = melted
Color	**all natural colors are possible**
Streak/Mohs hardness	**various**
Crystal system	**amorphous, glassy structure**
Cleavage	**none**
Chemical formula	**varies by locality**

Black tektites from the USA

Pele's Hair —
crystal needles sent from heaven

Clouds pass over the crater's rim in the morning mist. It is cool, the sun is just coming over the horizon. Distant drums are heard, then silence. Suddenly the monotonous chant of the priests is heard; the wind has changed.

We are in Hawaii. The priests pray to Pele, their goddess of fire and volcanoes. They find her hair on the ground and call it Pele's hair. They take this as proof that Pele was there during the night.

To mineralogists, Pele's hair is rock that lies around the crater's rim in thin needles as fine as hair. It originated from lava that was blown into millimeter-thin needles when gas broke out in the last volcanic eruption. After a short flight through the air, it fell to the ground, soft and glistening.

The fine needles consist of rock glass and are best found at the volcanoes of Hawaii.

Pele's Hair	after the Hawaiian goddess Pele
Color	**brownish-green**
Crystal system	**amorphic, glassy structure**
Composition	**varies by locality**

Pele's hair from Hawaii

Rock Spray —
born of heat and gas

A volcano erupts; gas and ash fly into the air, along with small drops of molten rock (lava), more than 1000 degrees C hot.

The gas that is in the lava drops escapes abruptly during the flight of the drops through the air. The lava foams and is solidified in minutes by the cold wind. Rock spray is formed and slowly trickles to earth.

Such processes can be observed in volcanic eruptions, especially where the volcano has flung much gas into the air along with lava.

Rock Spray	
Color	**brownish-green**
Crystal system	**amorphic, glassy structure**
Composition	**varies by locality**

Rock spray, Hawaii

Obsidian —
magma turned to glass

W e are in Ethiopia 2000 years ago. A Roman runs across the plains and stumbles over black stones. They look very different from the lighter rocks that form the ground and cliffs here.

He takes the stone in his hand and notices a glowing sheen where the stone has broken. In his tent he examines it further and discovers that the stone shows fibrous lines where it has broken. After examining other stones of this type, he sees that the broken surfaces always show these structures.

The Roman's name is *Obsius*. The stones were named Obsidian after him.

Today we know that obsidian is a rock glass. Thus it is lava that slowly flowed down the slopes of a volcano and solidified within days or weeks. This is a very short time for a geological process, so that no time remained for crystals to form inside the hardening mass. Thus an amorphous, unstructured rock glass was formed.

Obsidian	
Color	**black, gray, brown**
Streak/Mohs hardness	**white / 5-7**
Crystal system	**amorphous, glassy structure**
Composition	**varies by locality**

Obsidian from Berg
Ararat, Turkey

Shimmering surfaces

Particularly liquid lava, flowing quickly down the slope of a volcano, can form fine layers of rock glass that are baked together instantly. This happened in Mexico millions of years ago.

Today obsidian is found there that, after cutting and polishing, shows a wonderful play of colors. Turned the right way in the light, all the colors of the rainbow suddenly appear on a uniformly black stone and shimmer metallically on the surface.

The play of colors is caused by the light being broken into its spectral colors. This occurs only perpendicularly to the thin obsidian layers inside the stone.

Rainbow obsidian from Mexico

Snowflake obsidian

I f a piece of obsidian lies buried deep in the rock for thousands of years, small crystals will sometimes form in it that had no time to form during its rapid hardening during the volcanic eruption. Such white crystals, called spherolites, grow from grains of sand or other small particles that were enclosed in the obsidian since its formation. These white crystals give snowflake obsidian its name.

Especially lovely snowflake obsidian is found in Utah and is used to make jewelry and decorative objects.

Snowflake obsidian, Utah, USA

Native Copper —
gleaming metal

Only a few minerals consist of a single chemical element. One of these is native copper, with the chemical symbol Cu. A metal is called "native" when it occurs in a pure form.

Our everyday life would be impossible without copper. In the form of drainpipes, roofing, cooking pots, and jewelry, copper finds widespread use. There are almost always other copper minerals, such as cuprite, azurite or malachite, found where native copper occurs.

When copper reacts with the moisture in the air, it turns green, creating verdigris.

The largest open-pit mine in the world is a quarry in Chile that descends a kilometer down into the earth. Chile produces up to 800,000 tons of copper per year here.

Copper	
Color	**copper-colored**
Streak/Mohs hardness	**copper / 2-3**
Crystal system	**cubic**
Cleavage	**none**
Chemical formula	**Cu**

Copper from Chile

Silver —
metal of kings

W ho does not know the fine shimmer of silver? Since ancient times it has been one of our most important cultural possessions. Vases, tableware, and jewelry of all kinds have been signs of the silversmith's art and the king's wealth for ages.

Freiberg in the Joachim Valley and St. Andreasberg are renowned localities at which native silver has been found in the Harz and Erzgebirge.

In the Odenwald near Heidelberg too, silver was found in the Middle Ages, such as at the Anna-Elizabeth Mine in Schriesheim.

The monks of Witiken monastery near Alpirsbach in the Black Forest knew in the Middle Ages of the silver in the rocks of their area. Thus silver was mined centuries ago in the Black Forest.

Silver, like gold, has a particular property that makes it so valuable for making jewelry: It can be beaten and worked into fine sheets without tearing.

Thus the loveliest jewelry is made of this precious metal to this day.

Silver	
Color	**silvery**
Streak/Mohs hardness	**silver / 2-3**
Crystal system	**cubic**
Cleavage	**none**
Chemical formula	**Ag**

Native silver on rock crystal

Gold —
noblest of all metals

Native gold on rock crystal, Switzerland

Alaska in 1820, during the gold rush: Every day new gold seekers arrive in the Yukon area after months of exhausting travel through snow, ice, and coldness. They are impatient and have a gleam in their eye. They want to stake a claim and begin to seek gold. The gold claims are in an area of about 100 by 100 meters, and belong to the registered gold hunters. But not every claim contains gold. Most prospectors have made the long trip here from the ends of the earth in vain.

Only a few prospectors, the first who could claim the areas with rich gold veins along the Yukon, actually became rich.

Gold is brought to the surface from the depths of the earth by magma and is then found in gold deposits. Very rarely is it found in the form of nuggets, as it is on the Yukon River. Usually it is scattered in rock as very fine grains, and must be separated from the rock with much technical effort.

Gold	
Color	**golden**
Streak/Mohs hardness	**gold / 2-3**
Crystal system	**cubic**
Cleavage	**none**
Chemical formula	**Au**

Antimonite —
structures of silvery needles

Stibnite, antimonite, antimony gleam: three names for a mineral composed of a framework of silvery needles. It is the most important ore of the chemical element antimony, which has much chemical importance. Stibnite is always found where native gold occurs, such as in Wolfsberg in the Harz or the Casparizeche in Arnsberg, Westphalia.

Today the mineral collector gets the best specimens from China, South Africa or Bolivia, where there are great deposits of this mineral.

In Baia Sprie, Romania, large rod-like crystals of stibnite have been found.

Stibnite	also antimonite
Color	**gleaming silvery**
Streak/Mohs hardness	**dark gray / 2**
Crystal system	**orthorhombic**
Cleavage	**perfect**
Chemical formula	**Sb2S3**

Stibnite crystals from China

Sphalerite —
silvery-yellow bands from deep in the mountain

The German name of sphalerite. Schalenblende refers to the cuplike structure of aggregates of this mineral. It has a metallic luster and is opaque. But the sulfur content is always higher in one of the mineral bands, and that band is colored yellow. Thus arises the charming play of colors in sphalerite, which comes into its own after the surface is polished.

Sphalerite is the most important ore of zinc, which as had many uses in our everyday lives, especially in the 1940s and 1950s. Zink bathtubs, buckets, and bowls are good examples of the use of this metal.

Sphalerites that interest the mineral collector occur mainly in Peru today, where they are cut and polished on the spot.

Sphalerite	also zinc blende
Color	**gleaming silver plus yellow**
Streak/Mohs hardness	**white / 3-4**
Crystal structure	**cubic**
Cleavage	**perfect**
Chemical formula	**ZnS**

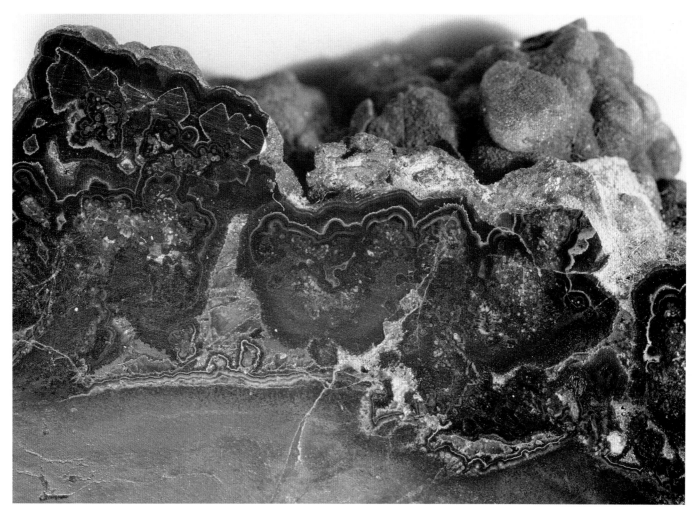

Sphalerite from Peru

Sphalerite—ore mined even before the Romans

The water drips. The shaft deep underground is damp; the miners work with hammers and chisels, cutting into the mountain two centimeters per day. They are seeking sphalerite veins, which are hard to recognize in the rock. The Roman miners had only lamps with small flames, giving about as much light as a single candle. They worked twelve hours a day, always searching for the next ore vein.

Fine-banded structures, yellow-brown and silvery, sometimes also translucent brown, always light up the shaft wall when lamplight flickers. Only in daylight do these minerals, the Wiesloch sphalerites, give off their whole colorful splendor.

For 2000 years. here in Wiesloch near Heidelberg, sphalerite has been mined and smelted. The Celts found the first pieces; the Romans introduced the right means of working large quantities and made the Wiesloch area an important center of ore minerals.

Sphalerite from Wiesloch, near Heidelberg

Honey Sphalerite —
an orange ore

Honey sphalerite, the most beautiful color of this mineral. If it grows very slowly and evenly deep in the rock, then its components, zinc and sulfur, can blend peacefully. The pure crystal structure of sphalerite results, without inclusions, cracks or other faults.

Such sphalerite has an orange color and is translucent. This is a great rarity among ore minerals. Since the color is reminiscent of honey, this pure sphalerite was called Honigblende in German. For a mineral collector, such a piece is a rarity requiring a long search.

Localities include Trepca, Yugoslavia and Bleiberg in Carinthia.

Honey sphalerite, the orange variety of that mineral.

Hematite —
widespread iron ore with many crystal forms

Where does the iron that we use come from? It is smelted from a mineral that exists in great quantities but rarely in beautiful crystals: hematite.

Hematite consists almost completely of iron and occurs at many localities in the world. In the Middle Ages it was already mined in several South German mines, in the Black Forest, around Pforzheim, and in the Odenwald. Hematite is still the most important iron ore and the basis of almost all the metals that we use commonly. Without iron mining, steel production would be impossible.

Hematite has also been called bloodstone. This name comes from the fact that the mineral leaves a red-brown streak of mineral powder when it is drawn over an unglazed porcelain plate. With its high iron content, hematite colors the cooling water of the cutting machine blood-red when being worked.

Hematite	also red iron ore, iron gleam
Color	**gray, red, black**
Streak/Mohs hardness	**red-brown / 6**
Crystal system	**trigonal**
Cleavage	**none**
Chemical formula	**Fe_2O_3**

Hematite on sandstone, Neuenbuerg near Pforzheim

Glass-headed Hematite

If one looks closely at hematite, one can see that ball-shaped or grapelike forms occur on the hematite veins. Such balls are called glass-heads. This term may well come from the older word "*Glatzkopf*," which was softened.

The ball-shaped form of the hematite glass-heads results from a particular manner of growth: Starting from one point, very many extremely thin crystal needles grow simultaneously in all directions. Circulating water in the rock always covers the entire surface of the growing glass-head. Thus the individual crystal needles in the glass-head can grow equally fast. The result is the form of a ball.

If one looks at a glass-head from the side through a loupe, the fibrous structure of the individual acicular crystals is easy to see.

Glass-headed hematite, seen from the side.

Hematite as Iron Mica

From a crack in the rock, gas streams steadily out of the ground and forms a cloud of vapor, meters high. A metallic smell hangs in the air.

We are on the isle of Elba. There are many such clouds rising from the ground here. The mineralogist calls them fumaroles. The vapor contains iron; it transports released iron out of the ground to the surface. Around every smoking hole, fine, glittering crystals have formed for many years; they shimmer like silver. They are platy hematite. Irregularly joined to each other, they inter-grow and form mineral aggregates that unite hundreds of crystals in small areas.

Now and then, single plates are colored greenish, bluish or reddish. This is a very thin coating of iron oxide that forms through the reaction of the iron with the moisture in the fumarole smoke.

Such crystals of hematite have been called *Eisenglimmer* in German for their similarity to mica.

Hematite plates, grown together as crystal aggregates.

Pisolitic Limonite —
iron ore from the depths of the mines

Bean ore—since antiquity, a particular form of iron ore, mined in the Saarland for centuries, has been so called by this alternate name.

Millennia before the beginning of mining, small brooks flowed and ground water found its way through the rock. Small bits of iron floated in these waters, smoothed to rounded stones gradually by constant motion.

Chemically, these rounded, beanlike pieces of ore consist of iron and some moisture. Minerals with this composition are called limonite and are closely related to hematite.

In the last few centuries, limonite has become an important iron ore in the Saarland and has been put to many uses in everyday human life. Smelters and rolling mills turn great quantities of this mineral to steel. Remains of these industrial landscapes can still be seen in the Saarland.

Limonite	
Color	**brown, brownish-black**
Streak/Mohs hardness	**brown / 5-5.5**
Crystal system	**orthorhombic**
Cleavage	**not recognizable**
Chemical formula	**FeO(OH)**

Pisolitic limonite from the Saarland

Magnetite —
mineral with drawing power

Magnetite is an iron ore with very strong magnetic power. Chemically closely related to hematite, this mineral also consists mainly of iron. Magnetite has the highest formative temperature of the iron ores.

Millions of years ago, in a kilometer-long underground bubble in magma, some two kilometers underground, the temperature was more than 1000 degrees C, and red-hot molten rock rolled upward from below, from left to right. Out of great depths, new magma kept rising and seeking space in the bubble.

Centuries later, the magma had cooled to a few hundred degrees Celsius and slowly solidified. This is the moment at which the first chemical materials coalesced in the rock soup. Then individual crystals of magnetite swam in the semi-liquid magma. With every year, more iron was deposited around these crystals, which grew

steadily. At the same time, the magma cooled more, until temperatures of 150 degrees C were reached. Then the formerly molten rock was solid, and the magnetite crystals were enclosed in it. A magnetite-bearing diabase rock had formed underground over thousands of years.

Such rocks now hold the deposits of magnetite, which is mined as one of the most important ores of iron.

Magnetite	
Color	**black**
Streak/Mohs hardness	**gray / 5**
Crystal system	**cubic**
Cleavage	**incomplete**
Chemical formula	**Fe_3O_4**

Magnetite crystals grown on the rock

Tiger Iron —
mineral with stripes

Like the striped pelt of a tiger, bands form on an aggregate of iron ore and tiger-eye, which is thus called tiger iron.

All ore minerals already noted in this book can occur as bands in tiger iron. One finds components of hematite, limonite, and magnetite. By reacting with the dampness in the air, some bands of the tiger iron have turned rust-red. In between, the interested observer finds shimmering golden bands of tiger-eye (see above, in the quartz minerals) that show their wavy shimmer when the stone is moved back and forth.

All the colored bands unite to form a very beautiful decorative stone. Because of its great iron content, though, it is relatively heavy and weighs some 5.5 grams per cubic centimeter, about twice the weight of granite.

Tiger-iron localities include some of the great iron deposits in the USA and Namibia.

Tiger Iron	
Color	**red-brown and gray with golden bands**
Streak/Mohs hardness	**red-brown / 5-6**
Chemical composition	**iron oxide plus tiger-eye**

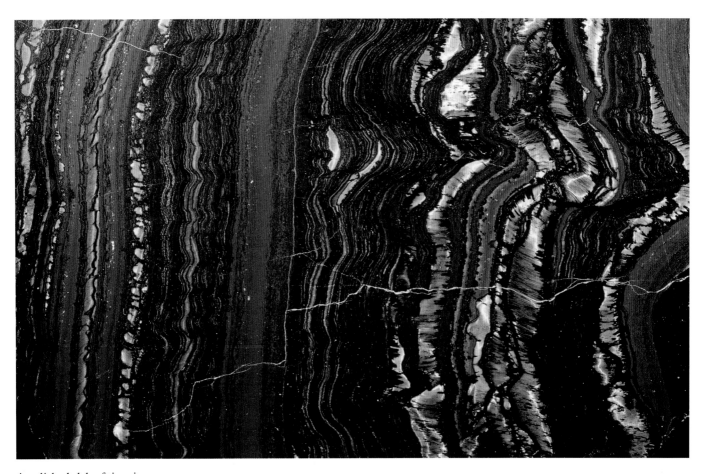

A polished slab of tiger iron

Fool's Gold —
a familiar name for golden pyrite

This mineral gets its name, pyrite, from the Greek word "*pyros*," meaning fire. In the Stone Age, this mineral was used to make fire, since it gives off sparks when struck.

The medieval alchemists were searching for the Philosopher's Stone, with which they wanted to create gold. With pyrite, they thought they were very close to their goal. This is probably the source of the German name "cat gold," though the origin of the name is not clear to this day.

Pyrite consists of iron and sulfur. Minerals that contain sulfur have been called "Kiese" by miners, giving pyrite another German name: *Eisenkies*.

Pyrite is a common mineral that forms under the most varied geological conditions and is found in a great variety of rocks. It is an important iron ore and a popular collectors' mineral that gives its glow to every showcase. The main localities are in Peru, Bolivia, Mexico, and the USA.

Pyrite	also *Katzengold, Eisenkies, Fool's Gold*
Color	**golden**
Streak/Mohs hardness	**greenish-black / 6-6.5**
Crystal system	**cubic**
Cleavage	**none**
Chemical formula	**FeS_2**

Pyrite crystals grown together into a large crystal, USA

154

When growing, pyrite takes various crystal forms depending on the temperature and pressure. There are cubic crystals and those with apparently pentagonal faces. Octahedral crystals are also found, looking like two pyramids that grew side by side.

Such octahedra are shown in the picture. Hundreds of crystals, showing the same crystal form regardless of their size, have combined to form a glittering aggregate.

Such collectors' pieces are found chiefly in the pyrite mines of Peru.

If one holds such a piece in one's hand, one notices the great weight. With a density of five grams per cubic centimeter, pyrite is five times as heavy as water.

Gleaming pyrite crystals have combined to form an aggregate from Peru

Pyrite —
golden cubes from Spain

In the quarries of southern Spain, a soft limestone is quarried as a building stone. In this limestone, gleaming golden cubes are found again and again. The mineral pyrite has grown into the rock.

In soft limestone, the crystals can form their true shape, the cube. Pyrite belongs to the cubic crystal system, one of the seven systems that describe the crystal geometry of all minerals. A small pyrite crystal grows larger as, atom by atom, the ingredients of iron and sulfur accumulate. Here in the limestone of Spain this could occur, because the pyrite crystals can push the soft rock around them aside and continue to grow.

If one measures the angle between two faces of such a pyrite cube, one finds an exact 90-degree right angle. The faces glow without being polished. Since pyrite thus takes the ideal cubic crystal form, there is no tension inside the crystal and the natural glow occurs.

Pyrite cubes in limestone, found in Spain

Marcasite —
a relative of pyrite

Marcasite—this mineral has the same constituents and chemical formula as pyrite, but differs in its crystal structure. If the ingredients of marcasite, iron and sulfur, join at low temperatures of 5 to 30 degrees C, and pressures of only a few bar, the crystal structure of marcasite results.

Marcasite occurs in many rocks. But only in one locality on earth, in Illinois, USA, are discs of marcasite found that look like suns and are only a few millimeters thick. Such marcasite suns are popular collectors' pieces.

The sulfur that is present as a constituent of marcasite does not come from a rock, but from animals and plants that once lived in the ocean. The dead animals decay on the sea floor and release sulfur. Along with the iron in the sea water, they form marcasite, which settles in ever-thicker layers of mud. After many thousands of years, this mud is so thick that it solidifies as slate clay. Today we find it in quarries.

Marcasite	
Color	**golden, often tarnished**
Streak/Mohs hardness	**greenish-black / 6-6.5**
Crystal system	**orthorhombic**
Cleavage	**scarcely present**
Chemical formula	**FeS_2**

Marcasite sun, Illinois, USA

Abstract Art in Stone

Ordinary rocks can show an unexpected colorful splendor when they are examined with the right techniques. All the colors in this picture are original colors that the rock shows under a microscope.

Thus does this picture originate: With a diamond saw, thin slabs, one millimeter thick, are cut. Stuck to a glass plate, they are ground to a thickness of 0.2 mm and then polished. Now light can shine through them. Under a special type of microscope, the individual mineral grains of which the rock is made can be seen in color.

With special lenses and lighting techniques in the microscope, mineral grains that appear gray or white in nature appear in typical colors. The color that shows is an important clue when the mineralogist wants to determine which minerals compose a rock. Along with the scientific observation, fantastic plays of color appear, looking like intensely colored abstract art. Yet it is unadulterated nature that appears here.

Mica schist	
Color	**as a piece of rock, light gray to greenish**

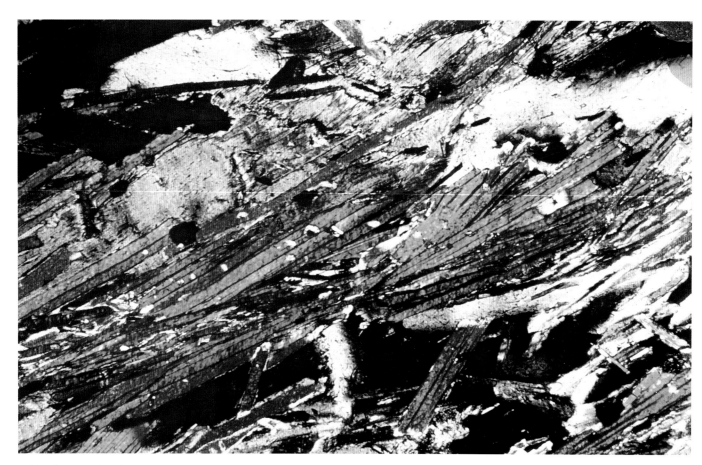

Schist from Scotland. Width of the section: 3 mm

Under the Microscope

Garnet amphibolite is a very dark, almost black rock with individual garnet crystals enclosed. If one grinds this rock very thin, the individual crystals can be seen in various colors under the microscope:

Hornblende: mottled dark green
Garnet: large orange and light blue flecks
Feldspar: dark gray and black
Epidote: dark red and dark green

These colors are not comparable with the colors that the crystals show when one looks at the piece of rock with the naked eye. The colors are created through the meager thickness and various means of illumination in the microscope. Yet they are typical of every mineral and allow the mineralogist to identify the rock without having to make chemical analyses of the mineral grains.

Garnet Amphibolite	
Color	as a piece of rock, dark gray to almost black

Garnet-bearing amphibolite rock from Tessin, Switzerland. Width of the section: 3 mm

Granite —
a rock from the depths

Granite, like all rock, is a mixture of various minerals. In a thin slab under the microscope, the crystals of the following minerals can be seen:

Biotite mica: fibrous green areas
Feldspar minerals: orange-red grains
Quartz: rusty red areas
Garnet: pink or light blue grains

Granite exists in nature in many colors. In the Black Forest there is light, whitish granite, as well as rose-colored and brownish types.

All of these colors are caused by the various minerals in the rock and the varying proportions of the individual minerals. Seen under a microscope, the mineral grains appear in different colors.

Well-known granites from the Black Forest are called Forbach granite and Seebach granite according to their localities. They are widely used as building stone, such as in garden walls and stairs.

Granite	
Color	**as a piece of rock, light gray, whitish, cream, reddish**

Granite from Novate, Italian Alps. Width of the section: 3 mm

Gneiss —
melted and recooled rock

A mountain moves. With a pressure of several thousand bars inside, layers of rock are slowly pushed upward—as the Alps have for 60 million years. To this day the Alpine peaks rise about one centimeter per year. Individual layers of rock are thus moved, and move against each other.

Such geological movements create enormous heat from friction. At the borders of two layers, the rocks almost melt, the minerals in them rearranged in a semiliquid rock soup and form patterns with light and dark layers. Thus gneiss is formed.

Gneiss also shows its constituents under the microscope:

Garnet: colorful, somewhat oval areas
Feldspar: dark gray and black grains
Rutile: long, slim surfaces

Gneiss	
Color	**as a piece of rock, light gray, white, and black stripes**

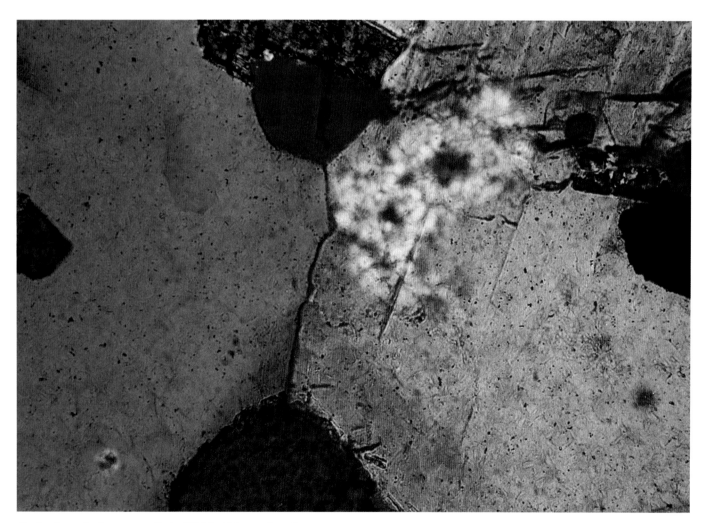

Gneiss from the Ivrea zone, Italy. Width of the section: 3 mm.

Amber —
orange gold from the Polish coast

The German name "Bernstein" comes from the Greek "*bernen*," to burn. Amber can be ignited with a candle flame and will then burn. Amber is fossilized tree resin that solidified in the course of several thousand years.

A mineral is an inorganic solid substance in the earth's crust with uniformly combined elements. Thus in a strict sense Amber is not a mineral, since it consists of carbon and hydrogen, two chemical elements from organic chemistry. Yet amber should not be missing from a mineral book, for like gemstones, it is often used in jewelry and is worked with the same machines and processes.

The major localities for amber are on the Baltic Sea coast from Poland to Latvia and the narrows of Courland. The world's largest amber mine is in Palmnicken, Poland. Almost all the amber worked in Poland and sold all over Europe comes from here.

The amber room in St. Petersburg, which was rebuilt in the most recent years, has gained great renown. All its walls are covered with amber in artistic shapes.

Amber	also Succinite
Color	**golden yellow, orange, brown, greenish**
Streak/Mohs hardness	**orange-yellow / approx. 2**
Crystal system	**amorphous**
Cleavage	**none**
Chemical composition	**approximately $C_{10}H_{16}O$**

Amber from the Baltic coast of Poland

Amber is fossil tree resin, in most cases from the *Pinus succinifera* variety of pine. This species of pine no longer exists.

Forty million years ago, pine forests grew in the Tertiary era.

The sun shone, insects buzzed through the air, swarms of gnats danced. It was a restful summer day. Again and again, mammals rubbed their antlers on the pine trunks; the pine bark was brittle.

In some places resin oozed out, shimmering yellow and sticky. Some ants ran up the tree trunk, but sud-denly they could not go forward. The ant pathway was broken by a big drop of resin. An incautious ant went on and stuck fast to the resin. Days later, another drop of resin ran down the trunk and enclosed the ant.

The resin hardened, fell off the trunk and was moved several times to puddles, streams, and finally into the sea. Amber had been created.

Today amber is an important witness to the flora and fauna of those times, and gives information on the types of plants and animals that lived then.

Amber from Poland, with two ants enclosed

Plants and animals of many types are enclosed in amber. There is pollen from various trees, plus needles from evergreen trees, leaves, butterflies, flies, ants, fleas, and even small frogs enclosed in amber.

Amber with such uncommon enclosures is rare and very expensive. Such examples give scientists an excellent opportunity to study the biological conditions of the late Tertiary era.

Often one finds colorless bubbles in amber, as in the picture on this page. These bubbles consist of water and a turpentine-bearing oil. They are regarded as remains of the cell liquid of the pine trees. Slow warming in rape oil can make the amber clearly transparent.

Amber from the Baltic
Sea coast of Poland

Optical Effects —
Iris and Labrador Effects

"Irisizing" was already mentioned by Agricola in 1546. He used this term to describe a lighting effect on the surfaces of minerals, caused by sunlight striking them. The light falls on a crystal and is mirrored by many very thin parallel layers in the crystal, then reflected to the viewer's eye.

Thus a play of color is caused that shows all the colors of the rainbow on the surface of a polished crystal.

Irisizing can be observed in moonlight, which shows a blue shimmer of light on a white background.

Labradorizing with strong, partly metallic glittering reflections is shown by labradorite as well as rainbow obsidian.

The effect of labradorizing on a piece of labradorite

The Cat's-Eye Effect

Many minerals are built up of countless thin fibers. If light falls on such a mineral from a small source of light, such as a bulb, the light is reflected in a special way. A line of light is formed, perpendicular to the direction of the fibers; it wanders back and forth over the stone when one moves the stone under this light.

This effect is best seen when the mineral is cut and polished with a spherical surface.

This cat's-eye effect was first examined in the mineral chrysoberyl, a yellowish transparent gemstone. It can also be seen (very rarely) in rose quartz, as well as in sapphires and rubies. In this book, the cat's-eye effect can be seen in tiger-eye, hawk-eye, and selenite.

If several groups of parallel fibers occur in a mineral and are oriented in different directions, then (rarely) several light lines occur on the stone, and can then form a six-pointed star (rose quartz, ruby, sapphire).

The cat's-eye effect is seen on a selenite crystal cut in a rounded form.

Light Refraction in Crystals

Light refraction means that a ray of light that enters a crystal is mirrored on the internal crystal structure, redirected, and broken up. In the process, it can change its direction before it comes back out of the crystal. Light refraction occurs mainly in transparent minerals.

The pictures on this page show two faceted spheres of quartz. The left one is illuminated by a bulb with a strong beam of light. The sphere looks almost equally bright and shows no special light effects.

The sphere at the right is illuminated from below by a point of violet light. Although only one point of

light (about 2 mm in diameter) is under the sphere, more than ten violet points of light appear on the whole surface of the sphere. This shows that the light of the single bright point is reflected numerous times in the sphere, broken up, and redirected. A single beam of light that enters the quartz sphere comes out of the sphere simultaneously in many places and passes from there to the viewer's eye.

This effect is enhanced by the smooth surfaces (facets) that were cut on the quartz sphere. Thus a sparkling and glowing of the crystal is caused. It is also known as "fire" in precious jewels.

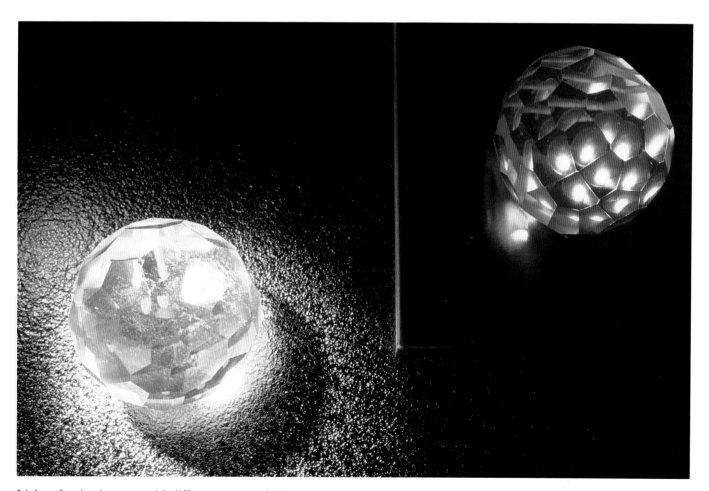

Light refraction in quartz with different sources of light.

Synthetic Crystals —
Zirconia — widespread imitation of diamonds

In 1976 the first synthetic zirconia was made by man. For some 150 years, attempts have been made to imitate the formative conditions of natural minerals (temperature, pressure, chemistry) to create the chemical combinations that are present in them. The goal of these crystal-growing methods has been to create rare and desirable minerals, particularly precious stones. This was meant to meet their demand for jewelry and technical purposes.

There are also synthetic crystals that do not exist at all in this form in nature. Among them are the zirconia crystals, which consist of the chemical elements zircon (Zr) and oxygen (O). More and more of them have been used in jewelry since 1976, and they are now the most commonly used imitation of the diamond. The fire of a well-cut zirconia is even somewhat more powerful than that of a real diamond.

By adding small traces of other chemical elements, any desired colors can be created.

When zirconia are made, they form an interior crystal structure, just as natural minerals do. Thus zirconia rank among the minerals, but they simply do not come from nature, but from a machine.

Zirconia	not to be confused with zircon (the mineral)
Color	**all colors**
Streak/Mohs hardness	**white / 8**
Crystal system	**cubic**
Cleavage	**good**
Chemical formula	$\mathbf{ZrO_2}$

Zirconia stones in various colors and cuts

Synthetic Rubies — suitable for jewelry

Ruby is one of the most valuable natural gemstones. In top quality, with powerful color and free of inclusions, it is very rare and more valuable than an equally large diamond.

At the beginning of the 19th century, many people had a desire to wear jewelry with faceted rubies, but they could not afford these stones as natural gems.

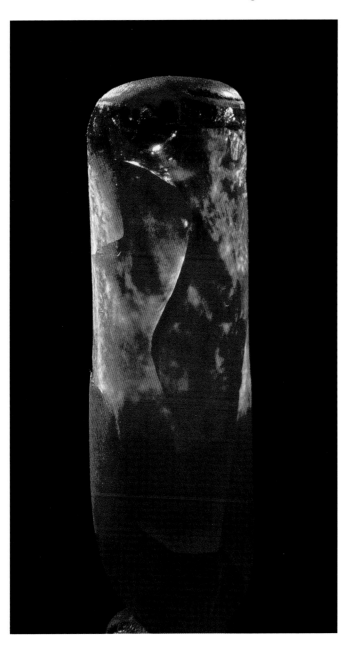

Thus the chemist A. Verneuil invented a process in 1888 by which artificial rubies could be made. The synthetic rubies then became available on the market.

The Verneuil process functions in this way: Al_2O_3 (aluminum oxide) powder is poured into a funnel. A small hammer beats on the funnel, the powder flows slowly through it and falls out the bottom of it. At the lower end of the funnel, an oxyhydrogen gas flame burns. This is made of hydrogen and oxygen gases, which meet and react to water in a 2000-degree Celsius flame.

The powder from the funnel is melted and, drop by drop, falls some 50 centimeters down to a metal plate. Here a synthetic ruby crystal builds up, layer on layer.

By adding Cr_2O_3 (chromium oxide) powder to the powder in the funnel, the resulting crystal becomes red (ruby); by adding Fe_2O_3 (iron oxide), the crystal becomes blue (sapphire). The shape of the thus created crystal is called the Verneuil pear.

Ruby and Sapphire	
Color	**rose to intense dark red, blue**
Streak/Mohs hardness	**white / 9**
Crystal system	**trigonal**
Cleavage	**none**
Chemical formula	**Al_2O_3**

A Verneuil pear, synthetic ruby

Rubies — also used as bearings in watches

Ten jewels, fifteen jewels—such inscriptions are found again and again on the dials of expensive watches.

This means that the pinions and wheels in the clockwork are mounted in stone bearings. This allows the clockwork to run more regularly and last longer. Even after decades, such clockworks still function without problems.

A high hardness of these stone bearings is required so that they do not wear out. Synthetic rubies, with their hardness of 9, are ideally suited for this use. They are worked into microscopically small discs and rings that can be set into the clockwork.

Ruby	
Color	**rose to intense dark red**
Streak/Mohs hardness	**white / 9**
Crystal system	**trigonal**
Cleavage	**none**
Chemical formula	**Al_2O_3**

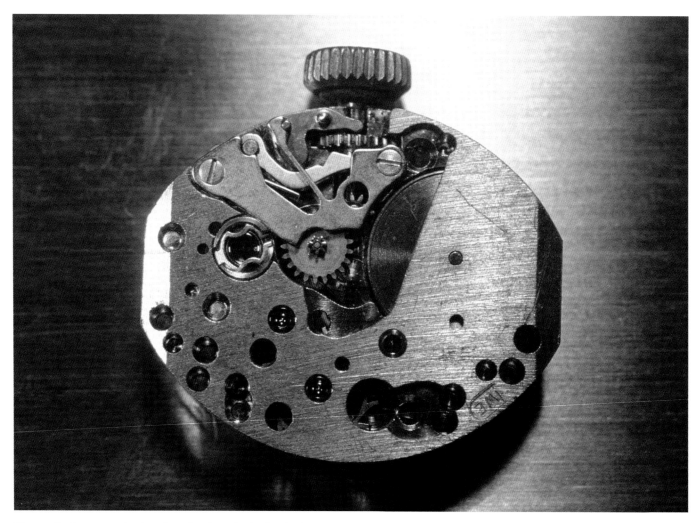

Pieces of ruby are used as bearings for the axles in the clockwork.

Quartz Crystals — important raw materials for technology

Oscillating quartzes: these electronic components are built into many everyday products today. They regulate sending and receiving frequencies in radios, cell phones and wristwatches. They are also found in many electronic controls, like the ABS and the motor regulators of cars.

The oscillating quartzes consist of a small plate of quartz that is held in a metal bracket between two springs. On both sides of the quartz, silver plates have been fastened to serve as electrodes. Now an electric switch, which has been built around the oscillating quartz, moves the quartz to make it oscillate. The quartz returns the swinging motion to the electronics and stabilizes the frequency that is now sent out by the switch.

Thus the quartz in a wristwatch oscillates 32,768 times before the second hand moves one second further. In other devices such as mobile radio transmitters, the quartzes oscillate up to 210 million times per second.

Here the piezoelectric effect that the quartz possesses as one of its properties is utilized: By applying electric tension to two faces of the quartz plate, the quartz expands. Reversing the polarity of the tension makes the quartz contract. Thus the oscillation of the quartz is created.

So that the piezoelectric effect in the crystal occurs at optimal strength and thus can be used technically, very pure quartz crystals are required. They occur very rarely in nature. Therefore such quartz crystals are made artificially in Chinese and Russian factories. Synthetic rock crystals are created.

A synthetic quartz crystal from a Chinese factory, original growth form

Quartz	
Color	**colorless**
Streak/Mohs hardness	**white / 7**
Crystal system	**trigonal**
Cleavage	**none**
Chemical formula	**SiO_2**

Bismuth Crystals — glittering collectors' items

For several years, brightly shining metallic crystals with curved edges have been seen. They are made of bismuth (Bi), which is crystallized synthetically in this form.

Similarly to casting tin, pure bismuth is melted in a crucible, but then cooled slowly and controlled. At a precisely determined temperature, small grains of bismuth arise in the molten material. When these grains are present, the rest of the growth proceeds in just a few hours. Additional bismuth atoms join the first grains. This process easily continues to the edges and rims of the crystals. A curved growth takes place, since the edges grow much more quickly than the middles of the surfaces.

In this process, the bismuth also reacts with the moisture in the air around it. Thus the thin coatings of color are formed on the bismuth crystals.

Bismuth	
Color	silver, often blending into colors
Streak/Mohs hardness	gray / 2-2.5
Crystal system	cubic
Cleavage	none
Chemical formula	Bi

Synthetic bismuth, a product of melting

Silicon Carbide — an important grinding material in many tools

Silicon carbide (SiC) is the second hardest material that man can make, second only to synthetic diamonds. On the hardness scale of minerals from 1 to 10, SiC is at 9, which makes it useful as a grinding material. The grains on many emery papers consist of this crystal, which is ground after being produced at the desired grain size.

Loose grains of SiC are used to grind precious stones and minerals.

They are produced by heating silicon powder and carbon together to over 1000 degrees C in large ovens. The two materials unite and form shining gray crystals. After the oven cools, the crystals are removed and ground into grinding powder.

The colors of the rainbow can be seen on many of these crystals. These colors result from reactions of the still-ho crystals with the moisture in the air.

Silicon Carbide	
Color	**gray-black, blending into many colors**
Streak/Mohs hardness	**gray-black / 9**
Crystal system	**hexagonal**
Cleavage	**good**
Chemical formula	**SiC**

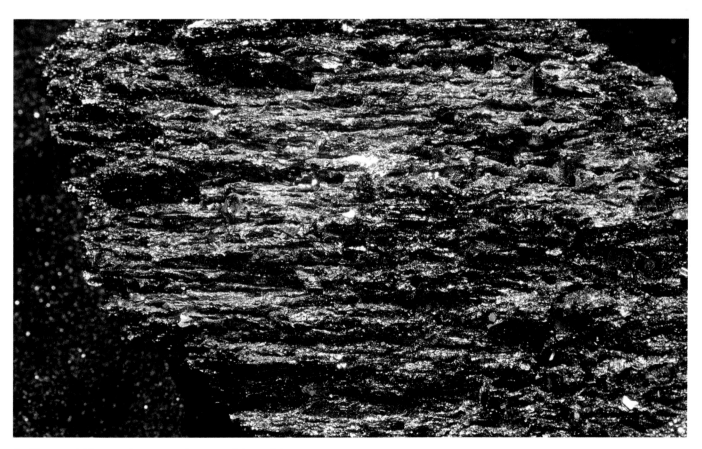

A silicon carbide crystal aggregate just out of the melting oven.

Glossary

Aggregate: A piece of rock on which many crystals of one or more minerals have grown together.

Carat: Unit of weight of precious stones. One carat = 0.2 gram.

Crystal: Form of a mineral that grows in a hollow or crack in rock. Individual surfaces take shape, meeting each other at definite angles (see "Mineral").

Druse: A hollow space in rock, the outside of which is grown with bands or crystals. In the inside there is still a hollow space.

Inclusions: Cracks, liquids or bits of other minerals that have grown into a crystal. They often allow differentiation between genuine and artificially produced crystals of a mineral type (such as natural or synthetic rubies).

Lava: Molten rock on the surface of the earth, up to 1000 degrees C, which comes out in volcanic eruptions.

Light Refraction: bending of a light ray that enters a crystal. Refraction is a measure for the strength of the bending of the light ray. The higher the refraction, the more strongly the light ray is bent and reflected back and forth in the crystal. Thus the sparkling of a crystal occurs.

Magma: Liquid rock inside the earth, a temperatures up to 2000 degrees Celsius.

Mineral: An inorganically formed solid component of the earth's crust, uniformly built from inside. A mineral can be merely a band of color in a rock or, with enough space, can form its own surfaces (see "Crystal").

Mineral Group: A combination of different-looking minerals that have the same chemical ingredients and are thus related: ruby and sapphire, quartzes, aquamarine and emerald.

Nodule: a formerly open space in a rock, which is completely filled with mineral bands and crystals. There is no empty space left (for example, agate).

Silicic Acid: The main constituent of many minerals, the silicates. Formula: SiO_2 (silicon dioxide).

Trace elements: A different chemical element added in small quantities to the essential chemical composition of a mineral crystal, often causing color variations.

Index

Note: mineral formulas that differ from those in the German
edition were taken from the *Glossary of Mineral Species.*